ECONOMIC RIGHTS

This edited volume offers new scholarship on economic rights by leading scholars in the fields of economics, law, and political science. It analyzes the central features of economic rights: their conceptual, measurement, and policy dimensions. In its introduction, the book provides a new conceptualization of economic rights based on a three-pronged definition: the right to a decent standard of living, the right to work, and the right to basic income support for people who cannot work. Subsequent chapters correct existing conceptual mistakes in the literature, provide new measurement techniques with country rankings, and analyze policy implementation at the international, regional, national, and local levels. Although it forms a cohesive whole, the book is nevertheless rich in contending perspectives.

Shareen Hertel is an Assistant Professor of Political Science at the University of Connecticut and holds a joint appointment with the University of Connecticut Human Rights Institute. She specializes in comparative politics, human rights, and international development. Dr. Hertel also has served as a consultant to foundations, nongovernmental organizations (NGOs), and United Nations agencies in the United States, Latin America, and South Asia. She has written professionally on the United Nations' role in economic and social development and helped develop a standard for labor rights monitoring in global manufacturing (SA8000). She is author of *Unexpected Power: Conflict and Change among Transnational Activists* (2006), as well as numerous scholarly articles.

Lanse Minkler is an Associate Professor of Economics at the University of Connecticut and Director of Socioeconomic Rights at the University of Connecticut Human Rights Institute. Much of his research has concerned worker knowledge contributions and worker motivations. Most recently, he has been interested in the intersection between ethics and economics, resulting in the book *Integrity and Agreement: Economics When Principles Also Matter* (forthcoming). His current research interests center on economic rights, most particularly on the right to work. He has served on the Editorial Board of the *Review of Social Economy* and recently finished a term as Associate Editor for that journal.

Economic Rights

CONCEPTUAL, MEASUREMENT, AND POLICY ISSUES

Edited by

Shareen Hertel
University of Connecticut

Lanse Minkler
University of Connecticut

CAMBRIDGE
UNIVERSITY PRESS

32 Avenue of the Americas, New York NY 10013-2473, USA

Cambridge University Press is part of the University of Cambridge.

It furthers the University's mission by disseminating knowledge in the pursuit of education, learning and research at the highest international levels of excellence.

www.cambridge.org
Information on this title: www.cambridge.org/9780521690829

© Cambridge University Press 2007

First published 2007, 2011
Second Edition 2012
Reprinted 2013

A catalogue record for this publication is available from the British Library

Library of Congress Cataloguing in Publication data

Economic rights : conceptual, measurement, and policy issues / edited by Shareen Hertel, Lanse Minkler.
    p.   cm.
Includes bibliographical references and index.
ISBN 978-0-521-87055-9 (hardcover)
1. Distributive justice.   2. Human rights.   3. Basic needs.   4. Economic policy.
5. Social policy.   I. Hertel, Shareen.   II. Minkler, Lanse.   III. Title.
HB523.E363   2007
330 – dc22   2007020993

ISBN 978-0-521-87055-9 Hardback
ISBN 978-0-521-69082-9 Paperback

For Jo and Fé

Contents

Contents

Contributors

Clair Apodaca is an Assistant Professor of International Relations at Florida International University and has served on the Executive Committee on Human Rights of the American Political Science Association as Section Secretary. Her areas of research include United States foreign policy, the international protection of human rights, and women's human rights. Her work has appeared in *International Studies Quarterly, Human Rights Quarterly, Journal of Refugee Studies*, and *Asian Survey*.

Albino Barrera is Professor of Economics and Humanities at Providence College, where he teaches economics and theology. He has published in the *Journal of Development Economics, History of Political Economy, Review of Social Economy, Journal of Business Ethics, Journal of Religious Ethics, Downside Review, Journal of Peace and Justice Studies, Labor Law Journal*, and *Forum for Social Economics*. His recent books are *Modern Catholic Social Documents and Political Economy* (Georgetown University Press, 2001), *Economic Compulsion and Christian Ethics* (Cambridge University Press, 2005), and *God and the Evil of Scarcity: Moral Foundations of Economic Agency* (University of Notre Dame Press, 2005).

Kaushik Basu is Professor of Economics and the C. Marks Professor of International Studies in the Department of Economics, Cornell University, and the Director of the Program on Comparative Economic Development at Cornell. He has held visiting positions at Princeton University, Harvard University, and the Massachusetts Institute of Technology, as well as the London School of Economics, among others. Dr. Basu is Editor of *Social Choice and Welfare* and has served on the editorial boards of the *Journal of Economic Perspectives, Journal of Development Economics, World Bank Economic Review*, and other journals. A Fellow of the Econometric Society and a recipient of the Mahalanobis Memorial Award for contributions to economics, Kaushik Basu has published widely in the areas of development economics, industrial organization, game theory, and welfare economics. He is also a contributor of articles to magazines and newspapers, including the *New York Times, Scientific American, India Today*, and *Business Standard*.

Audrey R. Chapman is the Joseph M. Healey Chair in Medical Humanities and Bioethics at the University of Connecticut's Health Center. A specialist on economic, social, and cultural rights particularly the right to health, and bioethics, she has served on several UN expert committees to develop indicators for monitoring human rights, and as a consultant to international foundations, governments, and religious and nongovernmental institutions. She is the author, coauthor, or editor of sixteen books and numerous articles and monographs related to human rights, health, and genetics, including *Core Obligations: Developing a Framework for Economic, Social and Cultural Rights* (Intersentia, 2002). Dr. Chapman has served on the faculty of Barnard College, the University of Ghana, and the University of Nairobi, among other institutions.

David L. Cingranelli is Professor of Political Science at Binghamton University of the State University of New York. He studies the human rights practices of governments from a scientific, cross-national comparative perspective – as reflected in his work on the Cingranelli and Richards (CIRI) Human Rights Project (http://www.humanrightsdata.org). The project, which has received funding from the National Science Foundation and the World Bank, offers easily accessible, high-quality, annual information on government respect for a broad array of human rights in every country in the world. Covering twenty-six years (i.e., 1981–present), 13 separate human rights practices, and 193 countries, the CIRI Human Rights Project is the largest human rights data set in the world. Dr. Cingranelli is also coauthoring a book on the human rights consequences of structural adjustment programs.

Susan Dicklitch is an Associate Professor of Government at Franklin & Marshall College in Lancaster, Pennsylvania, and the author of *The Elusive Promise of NGOs in Africa: Lessons from Uganda* (Palgrave, 1998) as well as articles published in *Human Rights Quarterly, Development in Practice, Journal of Contemporary African Studies, International Politics*, and the *Christian Science Monitor*. She has served as an expert witness on Cameroon and Uganda in several political asylum cases in U.S. Immigration Court.

Jack Donnelly is Andrew Mellon Professor of International Studies at the University of Denver and has held academic posts at universities throughout the United States and in Costa Rica, Uruguay, and Israel. Widely published, his books include *Universal Human Rights in Theory and Practice* (Cornell, 2003, 2nd edition) and *International Human Rights* (Westview, 1998, 2nd edition) along with numerous book chapters as well as articles in journals ranging from the *American Political Science Review* to the *Journal of Human Rights, Human Rights Quarterly, International Affairs*, and *Ethics and International Affairs*. He is on the editorial board of major publications in the human rights field and is an internationally active lecturer.

Peter Dorman is on the faculty of The Evergreen State College in Olympia, Washington, where he teaches political economy. He has researched and written on labor standards in national and international contexts for more than twenty years and is author of *Markets and Mortality: Economics, Dangerous Work and the Value of Human Life* (Cambridge University Press, 1996) and many articles and reports on working conditions, child labor, international trade, and other topics. He has also served as a consultant to the U.S. Department of Labor and the International Labour Organization.

David P. Forsythe is University Professor and Charles J. Mach Professor of Political Science at the University of Nebraska-Lincoln. He has taught and done research on human rights and humanitarian affairs for almost four decades. In 2003, the Midwest Section of the International Studies Association presented him with the Quincy Wright Award for distinguished career achievements in international education. His most recent books are *The Humanitarians: The International Committee of the Red Cross* (Cambridge University Press, 2005) and his coedited volume *American Foreign Policy in a Globalized World* (Routledge, 2006).

Sakiko Fukuda-Parr is a professor in the Graduate Program in International Affairs at The New School (New York) where she teaches human development and works on global policy issues for development. From 1995 to 2004, she was the Director and lead author of the UN Development Programme's *Human Development Reports*, including the 2000 report *Human Rights and Human Development*. She also has had a diverse career within UNDP and the World Bank, working in dozens of countries in Africa, the Middle East, and Asia. She is the founding editor of the *Journal of Human Development: Alternative Economics in Action*.

Mark Gibney is the Belk Distinguished Professor at the University of North Carolina-Asheville. His published work includes articles in *Human Rights Quarterly, Harvard Human Rights Journal, Fletcher Forum of World Affairs, Peace Review, International Studies Journal,* and the *Boston University Journal of International Law,* among others. In addition to his most recent authored book, *Five Uneasy Pieces: American Ethics in a Globalized World* (Rowman & Littlefield, 2005), Dr. Gibney also has edited several volumes including *World Justice? U.S. Courts and International Human Rights* (Westview, 1991) and *Judicial Protection of Human Rights: Myth or Reality?* (Praeger, 1999), as well as the forthcoming volume, *The Age of Apology: The West Faces Its Own Past.*

Michael Goodhart is an Assistant Professor in the Department of Political Science at the University of Pittsburgh, where he also holds a secondary appointment in Women's Studies. His research focuses on democratic theory and human rights, especially in the context of globalization. He has published in journals such as *Democratization, Human Rights Quarterly, Polity,* and the *Journal of Human Rights.* His book *Democracy as Human Rights: Freedom and Equality in the Age of Globalization* was published by Routledge in 2005. He is a past president of the American Political Science Association's organized section on Human Rights (2004–05) and is the Review Editor for *Polity,* the journal of the Northeastern Political Science Association.

Philip Harvey is a Professor of Law and Economics at Rutgers School of Law–Camden. He is the author of *Securing the Right to Employment* (Princeton University Press, 1989) and coauthor, with Theodore Marmor and Jerry Mashaw, of *America's Misunderstood Welfare State* (Basic Books, 1990). His research focuses on policy responses to the problem of unemployment, and he has published widely on that subject in both law reviews and economics journals. He currently is working on a coauthored book assessing the development of American social welfare law from a human rights perspective.

Shareen Hertel is an Assistant Professor of Political Science at the University of Connecticut and holds a joint appointment with the University of Connecticut Human Rights Institute. She specializes in comparative politics, human rights, and international development. Dr. Hertel also has served as a consultant to foundations, nongovernmental organizations (NGOs), and United Nations agencies in the United States, Latin America, and South Asia. She has written professionally on the United Nations' role in economic and social development and helped develop a standard for labor rights monitoring in global manufacturing (SA8000). She is the author of *Unexpected Power: Conflict and Change among Transnational Activists* (Cornell, 2006), as well as numerous scholarly articles.

Rhoda E. Howard-Hassmann is Canada Research Chair in International Human Rights at Wilfrid Laurier University in Waterloo, Ontario, and a Fellow of the Royal Society of Canada. Among her more recent publications are *Human Rights and the Search for Community* (Westview, 1995) and *Compassionate Canadians: Civic Leaders Discuss Human Rights* (University of Toronto, 2003). She is also coeditor of *Economic Rights in Canada and the United States* (University of Pennsylvania Press, 2006) and *The Age of Apology: The West Confronts Its Past* (University of Pennsylvania Press, forthcoming). In 2006, Dr. Howard-Hassmann was named the first Distinguished Scholar of Human Rights by the Human Rights Section of the American Political Science Association.

Mwangi S. Kimenyi is an Associate Professor of Economics at the University of Connecticut and has published widely in areas of poverty and income distribution, public finance, and public choice and economic development. He is also author or editor of seven books and the founding Executive Director (1999–2004) of the Kenya Institute for Public Policy (KIPPRA), which was recognized as the premier policy institute in Africa by 2004. Kimenyi is recipient of many awards and honors including the Georgescu–Roegen Prize in Economics (1991) Outstanding Research Award, Global Development Network (GDN) of the World Bank (2001), and he has been nominated for *Who Is Who Amongst American Teachers* (2004). His current research focuses on governance and institutional reforms in developing countries.

Lanse Minkler is an Associate Professor of Economics at the University of Connecticut and Director of Socioeconomic Rights at the University of Connecticut Human Rights Institute. Much of his research has concerned worker knowledge contributions and worker motivations. Most recently, he has been interested in the intersection between ethics and economics, resulting in the book *Integrity and Agreement: Economics When Principles Also Matter* (University of Michigan Press, forthcoming). His current research interests center on economic rights, most particularly on the right to work. He has served on the Editorial Board of the

Review of Social Economy and recently finished a term as Associate Editor for that journal.

Wiktor Osiatyński is a University Professor at the Central European University in Budapest. He taught at Stanford University, Columbia University, the University of Chicago Law School, and other universities in the United States and Europe. His main field of interest has been comparative constitutionalism and human rights, and he has published more than twenty books. In the 1990s, Dr. Osiatyński codirected a center for the Study of Constitutionalism in Eastern Europe at the University of Chicago Law School and served as an advisor to the Constitutional Committee in his native Poland. He was responsible for proposing the constitutional formulation of social and economic rights.

David L. Richards is Assistant Professor of Political Science at the University of Memphis and Co-Director of the CIRI Human Rights Data Project (http://www.humanrightsdata.org). He has published research studying the associates of government respect for human rights through a variety of lenses, including economic globalization, democratic institutions such as national elections and political parties, the end of the Cold War, and information globalization. This work has been supported by organizations such as the National Science Foundation and the World Bank, and has appeared in journals such as *International Studies Quarterly*, the *Journal of Peace Research*, the *Canadian Journal of Political Science*, and *Social Science Quarterly*, as well as in several edited books by scholarly presses. His current work addresses the impact of economic globalization on women's status and the formation of U.S. citizens' attitudes about torture.

Sigrun I. Skogly is Reader in Human Rights Law at Lancaster University. She has published extensively on issues related to international human rights obligations, in particular on economic, social, and cultural rights. Her publications include *The Human Rights Obligations of the World Bank and the IMF* (2001), *Beyond National Borders: States' Human Rights Obligations in Their International Cooperation* (2006), and articles in a number of journals, including *Human Rights Law Review* and *Human Rights Quarterly*. In addition to her academic career, Dr. Skogly has been actively involved with a number of human rights organizations and is currently President of FoodFirst Information & Action Network (FIAN) International.

Shawna E. Sweeney is a Visiting Assistant Professor in the University of Massachusetts Dartmouth Policy Studies Department and Senior Research Associate at the UMass Dartmouth Center for Policy Analysis. She completed her doctoral dissertation at the State University of New York at Binghamton, where she served as a Research Assistant for the Cingranelli and Richards (CIRI) Human Rights Data Project. Her dissertation explains cross-national variations in government protections of women's economic, social, and political rights and was supported by a grant from the National Science Foundation. Her main areas of interest are comparative politics, women's studies, economic globalization, and international political economy.

Acknowledgments

The ideas in this edited volume stem from a number of intellectual sources, and our thanks are widespread as well. First and foremost, we are grateful to the University of Connecticut Human Rights Institute – in particular, Director Richard Ashby Wilson – for his vision and support of a research program on economic rights that has evolved steadily over the past several years. We have benefited from the lively scholarly community interested in economic rights research at our home institution – specifically, faculty members involved in our Economic Rights Reading Group. Together with Richard Wilson and Tom Wilsted, Director of the Thomas J. Dodd Research Center, we were fortunate to organize an international conference on economic rights, hosted in Storrs in October 2005 in conjunction with the tenth anniversary of the Dodd Center. The papers in this volume initially were presented at that meeting. We are grateful to Rachel Jackson and Jean Nelson for their administrative support on the conference itself, to the authors for their steady work on revising the papers thereafter as the volume took shape, and to Joshua Jackson for excellent copyediting. Finally, we thank John Berger of Cambridge University Press for his advice and commitment to this book and the series of which it is part.

1 Economic Rights: The Terrain

SHAREEN HERTEL AND LANSE MINKLER[1]

If morality is centrally concerned with harm and the intent to prevent or minimize harm, then world poverty is the great moral issue of our time. Yet with all of the attention on security and political freedoms it would not seem that way. Consider some telling comparisons. From 1998 to 2005, terrorism killed twenty thousand people globally (UNDP 2005, 151). In contrast, in one year (2001), twenty-two million people died preventable deaths due to deprivation – that is, from poverty (Commission on Human Security 2003, 6).[2] In that same year, almost 1.1 billion people lived on a dollar-a-day or less, and over 2.7 billion (i.e., slightly under half of the earth's population) lived on $2 a day or less (Chen & Ravallion 2004).[3] Despite this evidence of unfathomable suffering experienced by much of the world's population, military security and political freedoms capture the most attention.[4] Moreover, despite recent pioneering intellectual work, economic rights remain less well articulated conceptually than civil and political rights, less accurately measured, and less consistently implemented in public policy (Steiner & Alston 1996; Kunnemann 1995). But a different kind of freedom and a new kind of security need to share center stage. For billions of people, freedom from deprivation and the kind of human security arising from that freedom are crucially important. Economic rights are perhaps the best way to secure that freedom, and new scholarship needs to emerge to lead the way.

Because economic rights are human rights, they are rights belonging to all human beings by virtue of our humanity. That means that *all* humans have an inherent

---

[1] We thank Audrey Chapman, Serena Parekh, and Richard Ashby Wilson for insightful comments that improved this chapter.

[2] As another comparison, Thomas Pogge (2005) estimates that the death toll from all wars, civil wars, genocides, and other government repression was two hundred million in all of the twentieth century. By his count, it took only eleven years at the end of the century for approximately the same number of deaths to result from poverty.

[3] This is the authoritative source on global poverty headcounts. It is true that there has been some progress; the 1.1 billion number represents a four hundred million decrease from twenty years earlier, whereas China itself saw a four hundred million decrease over that period.

[4] As Scott Leckie (1998, 83) laments: "[M]ost would recoil in horror at the deprivation of freedom of life when active violence is involved, but display considerably more tolerance when human suffering or death stem from preventable denials of the basic necessities of life such as food, health care or a secure place to live. Ambivalence towards violations of economic, social, and cultural rights – whether by those entrusted with their implementation or those mandated to monitor compliance with them – remains commonplace."

right to the resources necessary for a minimally decent life. Economic rights may mean more than that, but they surely mean at least that.[5] Anyone anywhere who suffers from severe poverty not of their own choosing is having their economic rights violated. If we were to actually enforce economic rights, there would be no involuntary poverty anywhere in the world.

Of course, such a claim needs extensive scrutiny; that is what this book aims to achieve. But, if true, this claim carries tremendous implications for governments, private citizens, international actors, and corporations. Typically, when considering world poverty, scholars and policy makers alike focus on poverty's elimination as a desirable social goal, not as any individual's inherent entitlement. For instance, economists have historically recommended income growth strategies as the primary means to reduce poverty. The focus has been mostly on accumulating physical and human capital and enhancing macroeconomic stability, but the "Washington Consensus" that emerged in the 1980s also included an emphasis on securing property rights and the privatization of state owned enterprises. More recently, economists have acknowledged the role of income redistribution as a way of reducing poverty, mostly by focusing on careful institutional design.[6] Newer policy recommendations include not only investment in social infrastructure in order to improve government accountability, openness and the business climate (i.e., legal institutions that promote investment by securing exchanges and contracts), but also credit institutions to funnel capital to the poor. Although not denying a role for international aid, most economists seem to place the responsibility for installing these institutions squarely on domestic governments.[7]

Some policy makers and even economists are arguing that although these approaches are important, they are insufficient to eradicate world poverty. As a result, member states of the United Nations unanimously adopted the Millennium Declaration in September 2000. After consultation with many international organizations (the World Bank and International Monetary Fund (IMF) chief among them), a roadmap emerged that includes eight important goals, accompanied by associated targets and indicators. The first goal is to eradicate extreme poverty and hunger. It sets a target of reducing by half the percentage of the world's population living under $1 a day by the year 2015 (from the base year of 1990). The second target does the same for those who suffer from hunger. The last goal – Goal 8, to "develop a global partnership for development" – includes target 12, which entails "a commitment to good governance, development, and poverty reduction both nationally and internationally."[8] Indictor 32 of Goal 8 calls on OECD counties to donate 0.7%, and "lower developed countries" to donate 0.15% of their GNPs in order to achieve poverty reduction. As Sakiko Fukuda-Parr argues in this volume,

---

[5] Among the many who view economic rights primarily as assuring a minimum floor are Shue (1996), Copp (1992), and Beetham (1995).

[6] For a good discussion of the intellectual history and evidence of poverty reduction strategies in the economics profession, see Besley and Burgess (2003). Also, see Kimenyi's contribution in this volume.

[7] In addition to Besley and Burgess (2003), see Easterly (2003).

[8] To see the complete list of goals, targets and indicators, go to http://www.developmentgoals.org. Also see the 2003 Human Development Report, which is explicitly devoted to the Millennium Development Goals.

Goal 8 is fundamentally important because it explicitly recognizes the shared duties and responsibilities that all states have to end world poverty. More generally, by moving to a human rights framework the elimination of poverty becomes more than just a desirable, charitable, or even moral policy goal. It becomes an international duty of states.

That is not to say that sound domestic economic policies and institutions that promote income growth and job creation are not crucial. Indeed, they are. For one thing, there is a clear inverse statistical relationship between the numbers of people in poverty and growth (see Besley & Burgess 2003). Moreover, those who are employed at minimally decent jobs can provide for themselves and their families, so job creation and promotion policies can play an important role in any poverty reduction agenda. But, by themselves, such policies do not go far enough to meet the obligations associated with economic rights. Economic rights require that each and every person secures the resources necessary for a minimally decent life.

To ground this notion more fully, we should clarify what we mean by "economic rights." The principal human rights documents are the *Universal Declaration of Human Rights* (UDHR) adopted by the United Nations General Assembly in December 1948, and the associated covenants: the *International Covenant on Economic, Social, and Cultural Rights* (ICESCR) and the *International Covenant on Civil and Political Rights* (ICCPR), both of which were passed in December 1966 and entered into force in March 1976. Combined, the three documents are often referred to as the *International Bill of Human Rights*. The human rights enumerated in these documents are usually conceptually founded on notions such as autonomy, purposive agency, human need, or human dignity – the concept explicitly employed in the documents (these justifications will be discussed further in the next section).

Although there can be problems with this simplifying distinction, we may say that the first twenty-one articles of the UDHR refer primarily to civil and political human rights, whereas articles 22–30 refer to economic, social, and cultural rights.[9] For us, although not necessarily all the other authors in this volume, articles 23, 25, and 26 enumerate three fundamental economic rights.[10] First comes the most basic economic right – the right to an adequate standard of living – or as explicitly spelled

---

[9] Article 16 refers to marriage and family, and is probably best thought of referring to social rights. Article 17 refers to property rights, which may be thought of as both a political and economic right (Libertarians strongly support property rights, but not economic rights). The origin and history of such distinctions is the topic of Jack Donnelly's chapter in this volume. No matter how one distinguishes among different human rights, Donnelly is in the camp that argues that all of the human rights recognized in the UDHR are indivisible and interdependent. Nevertheless, indivisibility and interdependence do not eliminate the necessity for conceptual distinctions. To illustrate, consider the metaphor of a game such as golf. That game requires both the conceptually distinct objects of golf clubs and golf balls. Although they are mutually reliant on each other for the task at hand, both kinds of equipment require different types of engineering. Similarly, all human rights are mutually reliant on one another, but each distinct right requires different policies and institutions so that all can best serve people in the game of life.

[10] We started to develop this conceptualization in Hertel (2006). As we will see in section 4, this definition corresponds to how at least some activists conceive of economic rights in their grassroots efforts. Harvey (2003) also highlights articles 23 and 25 as he distinguishes between the right to work and a conditional right to a Basic Income Guarantee. Article 22 refers to social security, which we see as mutually reinforcing of paragraph 1 of article 25. The much maligned article 24 deals with the

out in the first clause of the first paragraph of article 25: "Everyone has the right to a standard of living adequate for the health and well-being of himself and of his family, including food, clothing, housing, and medical care and necessary social services...."[11] But because an adequate standard of living also requires a basic education, we include it as well, as specified in article 26.[12] The second economic right is the right to employment without any discrimination, and at "favourable remuneration ensuring for himself and his family an existence worthy of human dignity," as articulated in the third paragraph of article 23. This right is protected in part by the right to join trade unions, as specified in paragraph four of article 23. The third economic right is to what is sometimes called a Basic Income Guarantee (BIG), and is referred to in the second clause of the first paragraph of Article 25: " . . . [everyone has] the right to security to in the event of unemployment, sickness, disability, widowhood, old age, or other lack of livelihood in circumstances beyond his control."

Those three basic economic rights are also included in and expanded on in the ICESCR.[13] Article 11 of the ICESCR covers the right to an adequate standard of living, whereas articles 12 and 13 cover rights to health and education, which are all bundled in our earlier characterization of the most basic economic right. The ICECSR refers to the second economic right in articles 6, 7, and 8, which all elaborate specific elements of employment rights (including protections for free choice of work; provisions for equal access to training, fair wages and promotion; and protection of trade union rights). And article 9 includes income protection in the form of social security and social insurance, which corresponds to BIG, the third economic right mentioned earlier.

There are several things to note about our three-part conceptualization of economic rights. First, the basic right to an adequate standard of living is quite clear as to what it implies. It explicitly refers to the level of nutrition, shelter, and medical care necessary for adequate health and well-being. It establishes a minimum floor of well-being to which each human has a right. Of course, there will be individual differences; a grown man needs significantly more calories and clean water than an infant in order to sustain an adequate level of well-being, but the requisite amount of calories and water needed is reasonably determinant in each case. Adequate shelter refers to whatever modest housing will protect one from the local elements. Adequate medical care can be more difficult to define because some individuals require a great amount of medical services in order to achieve the same well-being as someone who is otherwise fit and healthy. However, when interpreted as a minimum, the right to adequate medical care

---

right to rest and leisure "including periodic holidays with pay." We see this primarily as a further requirement of the right to work – particularly as it relates to forced overtime.

[11] We interpret food to include water. *No* sustenance is possible without clean water.

[12] The right to education is sometimes referred to as a social right, possibly because the act of educating requires language, which is a social institution. We include it as a basic economic right because it would be virtually impossible to provide for one's own adequate standard of living without some minimal level of education. Still, as with property rights, it is best to not just think of the right to education as one "type" of right.

[13] Notably, and unlike the UDHR, the ICESCR is a treaty that establishes monitoring by a specific body, the Committee on Economic, Social, and Cultural Rights.

means that everyone has the right to access to routine health care such as basic immunizations.[14]

How these criteria should be met is a question best answered by public discussion between technical experts, policy makers, and citizens so that technical, social, and cultural considerations could all get a fair hearing.[15] Although there may seem to be some arbitrary line drawing when *applying* the fundamental economic right to an adequate standard of living, this is not peculiar to such a right or its foundations. As indicated by just one example from ethics, the acceptability of "white lies" or lying to prevent great harm does not conceptually undermine the moral precept "lying is wrong" espoused by virtually all great moral traditions and religions. It just means that blurry lines can give rise to reasoned disagreement in some applications (see Bok 1978).[16]

Now consider the reasons for why and how we differentiate among the three economic rights. The first thing to note is that virtually all conceptual justifications for human rights apply to the basic economic right to an adequate standard of living. Suppose that any individual was not entitled to an adequate standard of living. She would not be entitled to be free from malnutrition, would not be entitled to be free from exposure to the elements, and would not be entitled to be free from crippling illness. Such an individual would not be assured of the minimal conditions necessary to be autonomous (self-legislating), or a purposeful agent because she could not fulfill her own plans or objectives, or be free from deprivation.[17] The claim becomes most obvious in the case of people who die from malnutrition, exposure, or sickness.

It might seem that the same could not be said for either of the other two economic rights. That is, any individual who does not have the right to employment could still be autonomous, a purposeful agent, or free from deprivation so long as they possess the other economic right, in this case to BIG, because it could secure an adequate standard of living. The same is true for those who could work for wages even if they did not have a right to BIG, but they did have a right to employment. However, it is hard to see how either just a right to employment or just a right to BIG could individually fulfill the basic right to an adequate standard of living. The right to employment provides no relief to those unable to participate in the labor

---

[14] Copp (1992) and Beetham (1995) are among the many authors that address this issue, and both recognize that meeting adequate health care needs is problematic. Copp (1992, 245) addresses the resource/obligations issue, one that we will discuss further in the next section, by proposing a "stop-loss provision" that "would specify that a state is not obligated to exceed a defined relative cost in order to enable any given person to enjoy an adequate standard of living."

[15] We will discuss this political process more in sections 3 and 4.

[16] For instance, Kant saw *any* lie as violating the moral law, whereas (act) Utilitarians would endorse any lie so long as it prevented a greater harm. Sissela Bok (1978) argues that the best way to handle difficult cases of when it is or is not permissible to lie would be to appeal to a jury of reasonable persons.

[17] Similarly, Copp (1992) emphasizes the centrality of the right to an adequate standard of living as a way to meet basic needs, and also notes that basic needs fulfillment is consistent with a variety of moral theories. Unlike us, he does not consider the other economic rights – to employment or to BIG – or their relation to an adequate standard of living (or "The Right" as he calls it). Moreover, in his framework The Right is a conditional right against the state, with no role for international obligations.

market (young, elderly, severely disabled); some kind of social security will also be required to fulfill those individuals' basic economic right to an adequate standard of living. For such people, the right to BIG instantiates that right.

But the right to BIG *by itself* also suffers from some fairly significant problems. First is the cost. One (1999) estimate for the U.S. places the cost of BIG in that country at $1.7 trillion per year, effectively doubling federal spending (Harvey 2003). Next is the fact that even if that obstacle could be overcome for all countries of the world, BIG would still do nothing to guarantee jobs for those who want them, thereby doing nothing to remedy violations against the right to work.[18] Finally, a conceptual problem arises if a universal right to BIG means that there is also a right *not* to work.[19] The basic idea behind BIG is that everyone should get sufficient income for an adequate standard of living quite apart from wage labor. That would seem to indicate that a right to BIG is a right not to work. But if everyone enjoyed such a right, the right to an adequate standard of living would be meaningless because there would be no economic resources to distribute in the first place. Perhaps this conceptual challenge could be overcome, but it does appear problematic.

For all of these reasons, both the right to employment and the right to BIG must be used in some combination with each other in order to realize the basic economic right to an adequate standard of living. Combined, the right to employment and BIG are instrumental to that end, but taken all together the three rights are mutually constitutive. The right to an adequate standard of living defines the necessary conditions that the other economic rights must fulfill. Note, moreover, that this conceptualization allows for cultural, social, and historical differences. So long as the right to an adequate standard of living is honored, whatever combination of the other economic rights society employs is up to that society, provided the combination is nondiscriminatory.[20]

In the rest of this chapter, we will discuss some of the important issues surrounding economic rights in more detail. We consider conceptual, measurement, and policy issues, in turn, first by discussing some of the key points and then by briefly describing the unique contributions from the authors included in this volume. Those contributions emerged from a conference held at the University of Connecticut in October 2005 with the same title as this book. All of the scholars and invited guests at the conference had the single aim of thinking critically about

---

[18] See Harvey's chapter in this volume.

[19] Michael Goodhart recognizes this issue in his contribution to this volume.

[20] For example, most proponents of BIG do not subscribe to the kind of conditional version offered in article 25 of the UDHR. By limiting it to those who are otherwise unemployable (or limiting it in any way), a conditional vision tends to, among other things, exclude those who do valuable work in the household. Michael Goodhart offers such a critique in his chapter in this volume. It seems to us that a still conditional version of BIG could accommodate that objection for the reasons given. One virtue of the right to employment is that it creates economic resources by definition, while also enabling the rights-holder to actively participate in fulfilling their own well-being. For more on the right to employment, see Harvey Philip's chapter in this volume. Relatedly, Wiktor Osiatyński argues, in his chapter in this volume, that economic rights should be severely circumscribed because most people meet their own needs by participating in the market. In contrast, only government can provide civil and political "services," and that is why civil and political rights are enshrined as rights more readily than economic and social rights.

the following issues. Nevertheless, the final section of this chapter addresses one important omission from both the conference and this volume, namely, the role of social movement activism in the actualization of economic rights.

1. CONCEPTUAL ISSUES

Philosophers, lawyers, political scientists, and others have wrestled with a wide range of conceptual human rights issues. In this section, we touch on a few of the most important with respect to economic rights, including their foundations/justifications, and obligations.

a. Foundations

The UDHR intertwines dignity and rights in its earliest provisions. The fifth paragraph of the Preamble reads:

> Whereas the peoples of the United Nations have in the Charter reaffirmed their faith in fundamental human rights, in the dignity and worth of the human person and in the equal rights of men and women and have determined to promote social progress and better standards of life in larger freedom.

The very first article reads in full:

> All human beings are born free and equal in dignity and rights. They are endowed with reason and conscience and should act toward one another in a spirit of brotherhood.

The Covenants are even more explicit about the relationship between dignity and human rights. The second paragraph in the Preamble of each reads: "Recognizing that these rights derive from the inherent dignity of the human person . . ." When it means inherent worth, dignity can be used to justify human rights in general because those rights assure and protect the intrinsic value of all human beings. However, like virtually all groundings for human rights, dignity as a foundation is contentious. For instance, Wiktor Osiatyński suggests in this volume that dignity is too vague a concept to provide a tight grounding for human rights.[21] In stark contrast, in Alan Gewirth's conception of human rights (discussed later), human dignity is universal and the result of purposeful action. For Gewirth, that all human beings possess dignity is literally true in the sense of moral realism, and dignity is sufficiently precise that human rights are needed to assure and protect purposeful human action.

It is worth noting that any current contentiousness about the foundations of human rights does not derive from the absence of careful thought and consideration before the drafting of the UDHR.[22] The drafting body, the Commission on

---

[21] Moreover, he references Hollenbach (1982), who further suggests that this vagueness leaves the concept almost vacuous. To overcome this problem, dignity would have to be linked to particular freedoms, needs and relationships.

[22] That is not to say that there are not any current, valid conceptual controversies. But the bigger problem involves mustering the political will necessary to commit to the binding agreements on resources needed to fulfill human rights in general, and economic rights in particular.

Human Rights, included international governmental representatives of considerable intellectual heft. For instance, China appointed a diplomat with a doctorate and a strong background in Confucianism. Lebanon chose a former professor of philosophy, whereas France picked a professor of international law. The commission had access to and advice from expert staff, as well as a variety of international organizations. In order to help reconcile the inevitable differences and to answer philosophical questions that arose during the its deliberations, the commission invited written comments from 150 people, including the diverse voices of Kabir and Ghandi from India, the anthropologist A. P. Elkin from Australia, and the philosopher F. S. C. Norththrop of Yale University, among others. Moreover, UNESCO convened a special Committee on the Philosophical Principles on the Rights of Man in 1947. Throughout, the goal was not to achieve consensus among the multitude of doctrines represented but, rather, common ground on which to base the UDHR.[23] Dignity as a concept was an important component of their choice.

More recently, scholars have sought to investigate the roles of claiming, needs, agency, autonomy, and freedoms in conceptualizations of human rights in general, and economic rights in particular. All of these conceptualizations ultimately refer to the necessity of fulfilling human needs as necessary conditions for what it is to be uniquely human. For instance, in a highly influential article, Joel Fienberg suggests that claiming is what gives rights their special moral significance and what necessitates correlative obligations from others (Feinberg 1970). Significantly, basic human needs constitute at least *prima facie* claims. Feinberg sympathizes with the view that those needs do not have to correspond to duties for anyone in particular. For him, "Natural needs are real claims if only upon hypothetical future beings not yet in existence. I accept the moral principle that to have an unfulfilled need is to have a kind of claim against the world, even if against no one in particular" (Feinberg 1970, 72). Moreover, he suggests that to think of someone as having human dignity is to think of them as a potential claims-maker.

Consider some other important foundations for human rights. Henry Shue (1996) focuses on basic rights, or the minimum reasonable demands that everyone can place on the rest of humanity. No self-respecting person would consent to lesser demands. What is distinctive about basic rights is that their enjoyment is necessary for the enjoyment of all other rights. There are two kinds of basic rights: security rights and subsistence rights. The first refers to the right to be free from murder, torture, rape, and assault; the second refers to rights to unpolluted air and water, adequate food, clothing, shelter, and health care. Security can be associated with civil and political rights, subsistence with economic rights. But for Shue, they are both basic. "Deficiencies in the means of subsistence can be just as fatal, incapacitating, or painful as violations of physical security. The resulting damage or death can at least as decisively prevent the enjoyment of any right as can the effects of security violations" (Shue 1996, 24). For Shue, then, all rights are founded on basic rights and basic rights are founded on the reasonable, minimal demands required for self-respect.

Purposeful human action provides another kind of foundation (Gewirth 1992, 1996). All agents or prospective agents freely deliberate on their ends, and those ends chosen are deemed worthy by the agents. An individual agent deems her

---

[23] This brief history comes from the excellent account offered by Lauren (1998, 219–25).

purposes worthy because she deems herself worthy, in part because of her own purposiveness. But purposeful action requires freedom and well-being. Thus, the purposive agent is entitled to the rights to those things by virtue of her necessity to actualize her own worth. Moreover, because this attribution of worth is attributable to purposiveness, the rational agent must also attribute the same worth to other active or prospective agents. Therefore, these rights, human rights, are universal. To deny the necessity of human rights is to deny the conditions necessary for purposeful action and hence one's own worth, which is a logical contradiction. As noted earlier, for Alan Gewirth, humans possess dignity because they engage in purposeful action.

Some argue that the fulfillment of basic needs is a necessary condition for human autonomy. For instance, David Copp defines basic needs as those things a person requires regardless of other goals or desires. Copp (1992) includes nutritious food and clean water, the ability to otherwise preserve the body, rest and relaxation, companionship, education, social acceptance, and self-respect. Autonomy refers to the ability to form one's own values and to live one's life accordingly. So if one is deprived of basic needs, they are deprived of both the physical and psychological integrity required for autonomy. Because the right to an adequate standard of living as described in article 25 of the UDHR and article 11 of the ICESCR goes a long way to meeting these basic needs, its ultimate justification resides in the interest each person has in assuring his or her autonomy.

A more expansive notion of freedom provides another kind of foundation. In his contemporary classic *Development as Freedom* (2001), Amartya Sen argues that the development should not focus solely on economic growth with its utilitarian foundations but, rather, on the kind of development that would promote various kinds of freedoms. Because we all have reason to value good and long lives, we should all value not only political and civil freedoms but also freedom from undernutrition, poor health, illiteracy, and economic insecurity. Recently, he more explicitly extended the idea in relation to human rights (Sen 2004). Human rights can be justified because of the freedoms they confer, and that goes for economic as well as civil and political rights. Always, which freedoms a society chooses should be the result of public discourse and deliberation.

b. Positive versus Negative Rights and Obligations

Negative rights refer to the entitlement to be free *from* interference. Civil and political rights are often given as examples; we have the right to be free from restrictions on our speech, movements, associations, political choices, and so on. Positive rights refer to entitlements *to* something, like the provision of welfare goods. When considering human rights, sometimes civil and political rights have been referred to as negative rights, economic and social rights as positive rights.[24] Hopefully, the previous section will have demonstrated that such a distinction cannot rest on the justifications for any human right because any justification used applies to all human rights equally.

---

[24] Similarly, civil and political rights have been called "first-generation" rights, economic and social rights "second-generation" rights. We do not continue that terminology here because it perpetuates a false distinction.

Obligations provide another candidate for distinguishing between different human rights. Historically, it was thought that negative rights entail negative correlative obligations, whereas positive rights entail positive correlative obligations.[25] Negative rights merely require governments and others to refrain from interfering with an individual's plans, but positive rights obligate government and others to actually provide something to an individual. Based on this kind of a distinction, Maurice Cranston (1967) famously derided economic and social rights as debasing real human rights (civil and political) because the former depends on a government's ability to pay. A universal right cannot depend on a particular government's economic circumstances, the argument goes, because "ought implies can." Moreover, the identities of those holding negative obligations are precise: the government and everyone else has the obligation not to interfere in another's plans. The same cannot be said for positive obligations; who exactly is obligated to provide the aid required to fulfill economic rights? Furthermore, even well-off governments would have difficulty meeting the obligations associated with positive economic rights because those rights could refer to boundless aspirations (e.g., perfect health). We have already offered a definition of economic rights that emphasizes a minimum floor; although such a conceptualization addresses boundless aspirations, the objection about negative versus positive obligation warrants serious consideration.

The most compelling response first notes that *all* human rights require governments to take costly actions. In the first instance, the civil human right to be free from slavery obligates the government to not engage in slavery. However, the government is also obligated to stop others from engaging in slavery. That *does* require resources in the form of the provision of police protection, labor inspections, and so on. The right to a fair public hearing (trial) requires a costly legal system. The same goes for private property rights. The right to freely choose our political representatives is also anything but free. Therefore, it simply is not true that some human rights entail costly obligations while others do not, so that can not be a basis for distinguishing between different human rights.

Henry Shue takes the argument further by redefining the obligations associated with any basic right (1980, 52). He suggests that all basic human rights entail duties (a) to *avoid* depriving, (b) to *protect* from deprivation, and (c) to *aid* the deprived. With respect to security rights, such as the right to be free from torture, his formulation means that there are duties not to eliminate a person's security (avoid), to protect people against the deprivation of security by other people (protect), and to provide security for those unable to provide it for themselves (aid). But exactly the same taxonomy applies to subsistence rights, which are integral to economic rights. In that case, there are duties to not eliminate a person's only available means to subsistence, to protect their only means of subsistence from deprivation by other people, and to provide subsistence for those unable to provide it for themselves. Shue's formulation simultaneously blurs the purported distinction

---

[25] Philosophers are quick to point out that although rights do necessitate correlative obligations, the reverse is not true; that is, obligations do not necessitate correlative rights. For instance, deontological ethics, such as that of Immanuel Kant, specify duties without any necessary appeal to rights.

between negative and positive obligations, while providing a coherent account of obligations inherent to all human rights, at least basic ones.[26]

Nevertheless, the question about the exact identity of duty bearers is an important one, and constitutes one of the most fertile areas of research on the conceptual foundations of economic rights. Typically, the primary duty bearer is assumed to be an individual's own government, just as it is in civil and political rights. That interpretation derives partly because historically it is governments that have been the primary human rights violators, and partly for practical reasons. One's own government is best situated to uphold any given individual's human rights. But that interpretation has been broadened to account for the interrelated notions of wider responsibility and also the resource constraints experienced by poorer countries. For instance, James Nickel (2005, 396) argues that human rights really require a division of labor of duties along the following lines: (1) governments are the primary duty-holders with respect to their own citizens; (2) governments have the duty to respect the rights of other citizens; (3) each individual has the negative duty to respect all other individuals rights; (4) citizens have the responsibility to promote human rights in their own country; and (5) "governments, international organizations and individuals have back-up responsibilities for the fulfillment of human rights around the world."

In a somewhat controversial thesis, Thomas Pogge (2002a; 2005) argues that richer nations are obligated to provide assistance to poorer nations because the particular history and institutionalization of the current global international order – built on the foundations of slavery and colonization – have caused benefits to the rich and harm to the poor.[27] Because alternative, feasible global orders are available, the well off are responsible for the massive suffering of the poor, and therein lies the source of their obligation. In any case, as a practical matter, the notion of wider responsibility is recognized in international agreements such as the ICESCR and the Millennium Development Goals, both of which call for international assistance. In fact, according to Skogly and Gibney in this volume, those international human rights agreements justify the obligations for international

---

[26] Another possible distinction, one coming from Kant (1956 [1788]), concerns perfect versus imperfect obligations. Perfect obligations refer to inviolate obligations, which for Kant, were the negative injunctions comprising the moral law. The obligation not to torture is an example. In contrast, imperfect obligations refer to desirable acts we should do, but are under no compulsion to do. Improving one's own knowledge and character are examples. It turns out, as Sen (2004) notes, that all human rights entail both kinds of obligations. Sen uses the example of those witnessing a killing. There is the imperfect obligation to try to stop it, but not the perfect obligation. If one can help, the obligation is to consider doing so. To use Shue's framework, governments (and others) have the perfect obligation not to eliminate either a person's security or only means to subsistence. But when it comes to costly actions by government (or others), the obligations may be imperfect in both cases. Just as a government should shepherd the resources to aid those in need of subsistence, so, too, is it under the imperfect obligation to shepherd the resources to provide the police, legal, and political systems necessary to protect its citizen's security. All basic rights entail both perfect and imperfect obligations. That is not to say that particular rights might not entail a different bundle of perfect and imperfect obligations; it is simply to say that the distinction is not peculiar to any particular human right.

[27] In the same spirit, Elizabeth Ashford (2006) carefully argues that international obligations seem masked because the pertinent relationship is between a large group of indirectly responsible agents and a large group of victims.

assistance. Such a legal foundation hinges on justiciability, a topic to be discussed shortly in the policy section of this chapter.

This brief tour has highlighted not only the various justifications of economic rights but also the joint nature of those justifications. *All* human rights are similarly justified, even if there exist conceptual differences around the edges. Such a claim might then lead some to question the validity of *any* human right. Because that kind of objection is about the nature of human rights in general, it is beyond our scope here. But the objection that human rights are on shaky ground always seems to reduce to a normative claim about whether one person should have reason to take into account the welfare of another. Those arguing against human rights base their objection on positive and normative assertions about human self-interest. Those arguing for human rights counter that the existence of human empathy, the ability to identify with others, the ability to consciously reflect about truth and duty, and evolutionary mechanisms that select for those who cooperate with others all provide motivations beyond self-interest.[28] Without wading into those waters, we merely point out that human beings at least have the capacity to consider the welfare of others, as innumerable acts of helping, decency and cooperation among people (both known and unknown) suggest. That simple observation settles the debate on whether or not human rights are possible – indeed, they are.

c. Contributions to this Volume

In the first contribution, Jack Donnelly attacks the myth that Western industrial democracies as a whole were, and are, opposed to economic rights. We already touched on the misconception that human rights emerged solely as a western construct. Through careful historical research, Donnelly debunks the notion that the West supported civil and political rights and only reluctantly acquiesced to economic rights in order to secure passage of the UDHR. One purported reason for that false bifurcation is that the West recognized that economic rights are nonjusticiable. Donnelly's lucid treatment of the justiciability issue exposes yet another false distinction between different kinds of human rights. Both his historical account and his fresh treatment of the justiciability issue will likely provoke much debate.

Three of the authors in this volume offer new justifications for economic rights. Wiktor Osiatyński takes a different tack, one that *does* preserve the distinction between civil and political and social and economic rights, but on a novel basis. To do so, Osiatyński differentiates between kinds of needs. All humans need the ability to express ourselves and also fairness in our interactions with others, just as we need nutrition, health, and education. All such needs are important; the distinction lies in how these needs should be fulfilled. In Osiatyński's account, only government can provide the services to meet some needs. Only government can

---

[28] For instance, on empathy (and identification), see Jenks (1990); on identification see Nagel (1978); on conscious reflection, see Korsgaard (1986 and 1994); and on evolutionary mechanisms, see Frank (1988). If a person holds a proposition such as "harming others is wrong" or "minimizing harm is right" to be true, she has reason (though not necessarily overriding reason) to support human rights (Minkler forthcoming, ch. 8). That kind of analysis appeals to what philosophers call internalist reasons: the truth or perceived truth of a proposition provides the motivation for acting in accordance with that proposition.

provide political and civil services such as police protection, fair trials, protection of free speech, and so on. In contrast, most people acquire the services to meet their other needs in the market, primarily through their own efforts. We buy our own food, shelter, education, and medical care, although the last two may be provided by government if they are otherwise deemed social goals. But Osiatyński's point is that because political and civil services can only be provided by the state, human rights are required to assure that provision. In contrast, because most people can fulfill their other needs on their own in the market, social and economic rights should be circumscribed to cover only those that can not meet those needs through no fault of their own (e.g., severe disability, young or old age, etc.). Although one could argue about a further requirement for an *a priori* classification of needs before describing what government should provide versus what it does provide, Osiatyński's conceptualization has certainly influenced our own thinking about economic rights. His emphasis on the responsibility for each to try to provide for his or her own subsistence needs not only limits society's obligations but also provides a strong justification for the right to work.

In a following chapter, Albino Barrera provides a new kind of justification for economic rights. Barrera argues that if one supports the notion of an efficient economy (i.e., one that uses the least amount of resources to produce a given output bundle), as most economists do, then one should also support economic rights. To achieve this conclusion, Barrera first notes that the nature of the economy has changed to emphasize knowledge, its production and use, and that implies the importance of human capital formation. But human capital formation hinges on basic needs being fulfilled, needs that the market itself cannot always fulfill. Hence economic rights are required to meet basic needs, basic needs fulfillment is required for human capital formation, and human capital formation is required for the efficient operation of the knowledge economy.

Michael Goodhart uses a similar kind of reasoning, focusing on human emancipation instead of an efficient economy. Goodhart shows that a commitment to an emancipatory version of democracy also implies a commitment to economic rights. Working in the tradition of emancipatory democrats such as Paine and Wollstonecraft, Goodhart uses emancipation to mean political freedom, equality, independence, and freedom from domination. And like Franklin D. Roosevelt's admonition that "a necessitous man is not a free man," a person in need is subject to domination – the control of another who has resources one needs. Thus, the function of economic rights is to assure emancipation and also to secure other fundamental rights (à la Shue). Goodhart emphasizes subsistence rights more than economic rights, particularly as embodied in BIG, because only BIG can assure that subsistence needs are met for all.

The section concludes with Philip Harvey's contribution that explicitly focuses on the right to work. Harvey offers a conceptual clarification about the right with the hopes of nudging advocates to better recognize all of its varied elements. To do so, he distinguishes between four dimensions of the right: the quantitative, the qualitative, the distributive, and the scope. For instance, recent International Labour Organization efforts have focused on the qualitative, or "decent work," aspect of the right, whereas BIG proponents have focused on the scope, or what kind of work "counts." Harvey suggests that advocates are missing a central component of the right, namely, the quantitative dimension, because they have abandoned the goal of full employment (whereby everyone who wants paid employment should be entitled to it). In addition to spelling out why he thinks that is mistaken, Harvey also provides a definition and measure of full employment that is consistent with the right to work.

2. MEASUREMENT

Given some of the debates over the conceptual status of economic rights reviewed earlier, it is not surprising that this type of human right poses particular measurement challenges. In this section, we first distinguish economic rights indicators from earlier data on economic development and more recent human development indicators. By tracing the historical emergence of economic rights indicators, we aim to eliminate at the outset some of the (considerable) confusion over the basic nature of these indicators. Next, we explore attempts at measuring government "effort" to fulfill economic rights – particularly in light of notions of "maximum-available resources" and "progressive realization," which qualify related state obligations under international law. Third, we explore the challenge of obtaining data on economic rights that is disaggregated by gender and other characteristics. Disaggregated data is essential to determining how equitably (or not) resources are distributed – which, in turn, is central to analyzing the realization of economic rights.

a. Economic Rights Indicators – A Brief Historical Perspective

The modern conception of human rights and corresponding institutional structures for implementation are relatively new – less than a century old. When drafted in 1948, the UDHR placed all rights on an equal footing in theoretical terms. But the institution-building that took place in the human rights regime *after* the promulgation of the UDHR had the practical effect of hampering the measurement of economic rights – and, with it, their monitoring and implementation. A treaty monitoring body was created for the ICCPR and began work immediately on the treaty's entry into force (in 1976), whereas it took nearly a decade for the ICESCR's treaty-monitoring body to be created (in 1985). This meant that expertise on developing indicators for monitoring and assessing economic rights performance lagged behind that on civil and political rights from the outset (Alston 1992). The following section traces the evolution of economic indicators in general; it focuses first on base indicators of economic growth and human development, then on rights-based approaches to development, all as predecessors to contemporary efforts at measuring economic rights.

Because for most of the twentieth century the dominant economic paradigm was growth-oriented, one common problem that emerged in relation to economic rights measurement was the overly facile equation of economic growth with economic rights. Economic development is a necessary but not sufficient condition for the attainment of economic rights. From a measurement perspective, Malhotra and Fasel (2005, 17) point out that socioeconomic development data has generally failed to convey information on mechanisms for redress and/or accountability that are vital to understanding the processes by which economic rights are protected.

For instance, poor people may be granted temporary work by the state – but how evenly is the work distributed? Are there equitable rules of access for obtaining particularly desirable jobs? Are there special considerations given to vulnerable groups (for example, female-headed households) in access to state-provided work relief? Are there means by which unemployed people can hold the state accountable for inequities or inefficiencies in delivery of such work? Simply counting the state revenues spent on "work relief" would not account for these types of concerns.

Todd Landman (2005, 39) distinguishes between three general types of human rights measures: measures of *de jure* protection of human rights, as expressed through legal commitments; measures of *de facto* enjoyment of human rights on the ground; and what he terms measures of "various components of public policy, such as inputs, processes, outputs, and outcomes." Measures of *de facto* enjoyment of rights can be further distinguished, Landman explains (2005, 44–45), among events-based measures, standards-based measures, and survey-based measures.[29] The measurement of economic rights for much of the past half-century has fallen short because the *de facto* enjoyment of economic development (or lack thereof) was often equated with economic rights – instead of measuring the more nuanced components of access, redress, and accountability, highlighted earlier, by Malhotra and Fasel.

The launching of the UN Development Programme's annual "Human Development Index" (HDI) in 1991 ushered in a focus on human development, which inched the academic and policy communities closer to developing robust measures of economic rights. The HDI integrates GDP, education, and longevity data for all UN member states and ranks them in terms of human development. Its creation presaged the shift toward an explicitly rights-oriented approach to development defined in the mid-1990s by the UN Office of the High Commissioner for Human Rights as a process that expressly links development to rights. It also emphasizes accountability, empowerment, participation in decision making by people at all levels of society, as well as nondiscrimination and attention to vulnerable groups (Marks 2003, 6). The rights-based approach to development applies to all categories of rights, but is particularly relevant to discussion of economic rights, because it takes people's participation centrally into consideration.

Participation is integral to achieving economic rights. Significantly, the UN *Convention on the Rights of the Child* of 1989, which came into force in 1990 and quickly became most widely ratified convention in UN history, includes explicit language on children's right to participate in decision making concerning their well-being (article 12). Such explicit references to participation were new in human rights treaty law, and the CRC was thus an important forerunner to later policy documents that would refine the notion of participation as central to rights-based

---

[29] As per Landman (2005, 44): "Events-based measures . . . count specific occurrences of human rights violations, be they against individuals or groups. Standards-based measures use the legal ideal established by the international law of human rights and then code country performances on limited ordinal scales that reward and punish countries for their human rights records. Survey-based scales use survey data on individual level perceptions of human rights on the ground."

development. This shift coincided with scholarly interest in the consolidation of democracy and economic development in postauthoritarian settings in the 1990s – including proposals for land and resource redistribution in the pacted transitions to democracy that followed civil wars and regime change in Central America and elsewhere (de Soto & del Castillo 1994). In part, the shift was also related to the broader integration of the concept of governance into discussions of development – fueled by increasing concern in the 1990s over the detrimental impact that corruption can have on the development process.

Even the World Bank – an institution with an officially nonpolitical mandate, according to its Articles of Agreement – began to explore rights-based development approaches in earnest in the 1990s (Ackerman 2005) along with the UN Office of the High Commissioner for Human Rights (2004) and numerous NGOs.[30] Scholarship on grassroots movements for environmental justice (Fox & Brown 1998; Khagram 2004) and against contemporary forms of economic globalization (Bandy & Smith 2005) also has grappled – albeit often indirectly – with the concept of economic rights as it relates to popular participation in economic policy making.

But the rights-based notion of development – for all its attention to accountability, empowerment, and participation – remains more of a slogan than a concrete framework for measuring human rights, particularly economic rights. As Landman observes (2005, 49):

> [T]here remains a lack of clarity concerning the precise scope of state obligation and the core content of individual economic, social, and cultural rights, which in turn makes it difficult to identify events and practices that clearly amount to violations... [and] there continues to be a debate over how economic, social, and cultural rights are to be realized progressively through the use of the maximum available resources. Such a view of progressive realization implies that the protection of such rights is still relative.... It has been impossible so far to provide meaningful and comparative measures of these rights for global comparative analysis.

The following sections address Landman's observations in detail.

b. Measuring "Effort"

International law requires all states that have signed and ratified binding treaty law – such as the ICESCR – to make an effort toward fulfilling all economic rights to the maximum extent possible.[31] Maximal, not minimal effort is the baseline. Economic rights, however, do not have to be realized immediately – but, instead, can be realized "progressively" (i.e., over time) in light of differences in the amount of resources available to countries at varying stages of development. Article 2,

---

[30] A comprehensive bibliography on a rights-based approach to development is available from Inter-Action (a U.S.-based policy and advocacy organization that counts 160 development and humanitarian NGOs as members): http://www.interaction.org/rba/documents.html#intro.

[31] International treaty law – or "hard law" – places more binding obligations upon states than does "soft law" (i.e., declarations or conference documents). The UDHR, however, has assumed the force of customary law over time, both because it has informed constitutional drafting in scores of countries and because its principles are widely incorporated into domestic statutes (Henkin, Neuman, Orentlicher, & Leebron 1999, 295–98).

paragraph 1 of the treaty articulates the nature of this obligation for rich and poor states alike as follows:

> Each State Party to the present Covenant undertakes to take steps, individually and through international assistance and co-operation, especially economic and technical, to the *maximum of its available resources*, with a view to *achieving progressively the full realization* of the rights recognized in the present Covenant by all appropriate means, including particularly the adoption of legislative measures. [emphasis added]

Progressive realization is not an excuse for inaction, however, and mainstream legal interpretations of the ICESCR reinforce this explicitly. The Limburg Principles on the Implementation of the *International Covenant on Economic, Social and Cultural Rights* (drafted by a group of international legal experts, 2–6 June 1986, Maastricht, The Netherlands) state in Part B, paragraphs 21–24:

> The obligation 'to achieve progressively the full realization of the rights' requires States parties to move as expeditiously as possible toward the realization of the rights. Under no circumstances shall this be interpreted as implying for States the right to defer indefinitely to take steps to fulfill their obligations under the Covenant. Some steps . . . require immediate implementation . . . such as the prohibition of discrimination. . . . The obligation of progressive achievement exists independently of the increase in resources; it requires effective use of resources available. Progressive implementation can be effected not only by increasing resources, but also by the development of societal resources necessary for the realization of the rights recognized in the Covenant.

However, the processes for state reporting on the ICCPR and ICESCR assume the distinction between immediately binding and "progressively realized rights," and the data collected to fulfill reporting requirements also mirrors this distinction. The very existence of the distinction has rendered it relatively easier to establish a baseline for reporting related to the ICCPR than the ICESCR. Setting baselines for measuring violations of economic rights as well as fulfillment – even of the fundamental economic rights to an adequate standard of living, to work, and to basic income guarantees – has been hobbled by conflicting notions of "how much is enough" or "what is appropriate" for fulfillment, particularly fulfillment over time.

Debates over a "living wage" provide a good example. Both the UDHR and the ICESCR include related provisions: Article 23 of the UDHR stipulates the "right to just and favourable remuneration ensuring for [a worker] himself and his family an existence worthy of human dignity," whereas article 7, paragraphs a, (i) and (ii) of the ICESCR refer to "remuneration which provides all workers, as a minimum, with fair wages" and "a decent living for themselves and their families." If the legally established minimum wage is not enough to enable a worker to meet this wage threshold, then how much above that minimum wage is necessary to ensure a "decent living?" How do cross-cultural factors affect the calculation of a living wage? What role should the state versus private sector employers play in fulfilling such a wage? What type of phase-in is permissible in moving from an existing substandard minimum wage to a living wage?

Rosenbaum (2000; 2004) and a team of colleagues in the nongovernmental sector have calculated living wage standards for a number of countries using a participatory methodology involving workers themselves in gathering data. And American economists have taken a renewed interest in the issue with the passage of living wage ordinances in municipalities throughout the United States.[32] But there are not yet agreed-upon international standards for calculating living wage globally.

Moreover, some authors, including Donnelly in this volume, have argued that the distinction between immediately actionable versus progressively realized rights is itself overstretched. They point to empirical evidence of the difficulty people face in exercising the civil and political rights to which they are supposedly immediately entitled – particularly in poor countries. For example, although the state's obligation to fulfill the right to a fair trial may be immediately actionable, citizens of democratic but developing countries such as Costa Rica are nevertheless incarcerated for lengthy periods of time while awaiting trial. In that country, one in four inmates is in this position. The rates are even higher in neighboring Central American countries – for example, in Honduras, three in four inmates are awaiting trial (O'Donnell, Vargas-Cullell, & Iazzetta 2004, 132).

There is also debate over how to evaluate a given state's efforts not only to use its own resources to fulfill economic rights but also to effectively use the resources available to it through international development assistance for this purpose. As noted earlier, in the Limburg Principles the obligation of states under the ICESCR is to use resources as effectively as possible. And monetary increases in aid are not the only resource necessary to achieve the fulfillment of economic rights; the Limburg Principles clearly state that society's resources also can play a key role.

And there is debate over how to measure the effort of wealthier states to do their part in enabling poorer ones to realize economic rights. The literature on cosmopolitanism has grappled extensively with the nature of this type of obligation (Pogge 2002a; Brooks, Miller, & Pogge 2002) as do several authors in this volume, discussed later. In practical terms, UNDP first vetted the idea of a "20/20 initiative" in 1992 – a plan whereby poor countries would dedicate 20% of their budgets to provision of basic social services, and donors would channel 20% of their aid to this end. The 20/20 formula was endorsed at the UN World Summit for Social Development in 1995, and has since recirculated in the context of discussions over the UN Millennium Development Goals (Vandemoortele & Tostensen 2003). The challenge, however, is to reframe related discussions in terms of economic rights – rather than charity – and to measure accurately government "efforts" to this end.

c. The Importance of Disaggregation

Data on economic development, access, and participation, which are integral to building accurate measures of de facto economic rights enjoyment, tend to be

---

[32] For detail on the efforts to promote adoption of living wage ordinances in U.S. cities, see Stephanie Luce (2004). See also Robert Pollin (2005, 3–24).

reflected in aggregate measures (e.g., GDP/capita, mortality rates, etc.). This, in turn, has hampered the development of economic rights measures. National statistical offices worldwide have only begun to compile gender-disaggregated data since the mid-1970s. And these data are still not routinely or comprehensively gathered, nor disaggregated across other categories such as race, ethnicity, or disability, which would help determine the level of discrimination (or lack thereof) in a given population. Nor are data regularly compiled on distribution of economic resources at the local, national, regional, or international level.[33]

Past *Human Development Reports* have disaggregated data for some states by gender and race to illustrate the powerful impact that inequality can have on overall development outcomes in a given state – although this is not standard practice with respect to race, the results are revealing. The 1993 Human Development Report (UNDP 1993, 18) reported that white citizens in the United States ranked number 1 in the world in terms of human development, whereas African Americans ranked number 31 (next to Trinidad and Tobago in the country rankings) and Latinos ranked number 35 (next to Estonia).

As a compliment to the HDI, the UN Development Programme has developed a "Gender-related Development Index" (GDI) reflecting differential achievement by gender, along with a "Gender Empowerment Measure" (GEM) to rank countries according to the level of women's participation in political decision making, their access to professional opportunities, and their earning power (UNDP 1995). Yet as useful as these measures are, they do not capture the processes by which gender equality (or inequality) is institutionalized over time, nor the means available to women for redress – both key components of economic rights.

d. Contributions to this Volume

Despite all of these measurement challenges, several chapters in this volume break new ground by offering actual indices for ranking country performance on economic rights and by developing new conceptual tools for measurement. But, first, Audrey Chapman revisits the "violations approach" developed in her seminal 1996 article, analyzing its utility and limitations along with those of three additional approaches: one focused on core obligations, another on individual country budget analysis, and the third on various indicators and benchmarks. Then, in the next chapter, Clair Apodaca focuses in particular on a specific set of variables for measuring "progressive violations." She appeals directly to the ICESR for her list of basic subsistence rights, and then offers a pyramid of measures, from quantitative to qualitative. For instance, with respect to the right to work, Apodaca suggests

---

[33] National level statistical bodies, particularly in developing countries, often lack trained staff and adequate budgets for maintaining annual surveys, which can create significant "missing data" problems for researchers. Moreover, collecting gender disaggregated data at the field level would require surveys designed to identify the role gender plays in shaping household income accumulation and consumption patterns. But international and national bodies charged with setting the standards for data collection have not always issued clear guidelines. Indeed, states are often reluctant to recognize or address the longstanding inequalities and abuses that give rise to gender-based and other forms of inequality. Poor economic rights measures are thus in part a reflection not only of technical shortfalls but also of a lack of political will (Beetham 1995; Hertel 2006).

using the quantitative measure of unemployment rates, along with looking at government funding for training and work programs, as well as in-depth qualitative studies on a state's economic conditions affecting employment. Both Chapman and Apodaca highlight the ongoing challenge of capturing distributional inequities and standardizing that information across countries.

Mwangi Samson Kimenyi develops a "pro-poor index" of economic growth that ranks government effort to implement macroeconomic policies that benefit the poor at the domestic level. Kimenyi defines pro-poor growth as economic expansion associated with reductions in relevant measures of poverty; in such a scenario, income growth by the poorest group exceeds the average income growth rate. Kimenyi acknowledges that preexisting high levels of inequality can reduce the impact of even the best intentioned policies, and argues that growth with redistribution is the key to achieve poverty reduction and overall human development. His chapter explores a range of institutional factors that affect related policy development and poverty reduction effectiveness.

Next, David Cingranelli and David Richards develop a general index for ranking country "willingness" to fulfill economic rights. The index draws on data from a sample of 191 countries from the years 1980 to 2000 (i.e., the Cingranelli and Richards Data Set, available at http://www.humanrightsdata.com). The authors argue that countries with more resources gain an unfair advantage if rankings simply reflect the overall rate of growth irrespective of how it is channeled. Hence, Cingranelli and Richards score countries based on how much they raise the living standards of their poorest residents, given what would be expected in light of the state's existing resources. If a country raises the standard of living of the poor more than would be expected given resource constraints, its ranking is higher than a comparably wealthy country that does only as much or less than what would be expected, given its resources.

Shawna Sweeney, in turn, draws on the Cingranelli and Richards Data Set to develop a highly detailed, cross-country analysis of respect for women's economic rights in 160 countries from 1981 to 2003. Sweeney's innovative approach provides evidence that political secularism, democracy, trade globalization, and economic development all positively impact women's economic rights attainment.

3. POLICY

Three of the principal policy challenges related to economic rights are: specifying the nature of obligations; demonstrating the justiciability of these rights; and determining the appropriate institutional framework and/or mechanisms for implementing such rights. This section takes up all three in turn.

a. Obligations

In human rights law, the state has traditionally been considered the obligated party because states are parties to the treaties central to the human rights regime. Legal scholars (particularly in the liberal tradition) have been careful to delineate a zone of privacy around individuals that the state must respect and protect in relation to civil and political rights.

Eide's (1989) classic respect-protect-fulfill framework, however, captures the scope of responsibility more fully. States must not only refrain from causing harm themselves and endeavor to protect their citizens and residents from harm, they must also set in place an enabling environment for the realization of human rights. The state has a vital role to play in crafting a policy and regulatory framework within which economic growth and distribution with equity can take place, just as it must set in place the enabling environment for the realization of civil and political rights through the creation of a functional judicial system, for example.

The obligation for respecting, protecting and fulfilling economic rights also can be extended to another important sector of nonstate actors – namely, corporate actors. The extension of obligations to private corporations reflects the reality that although such corporations do not set public policy per se, they can exercise indirect influence over elected or appointed officials who do, both through political contributions and through the threat of exit (Hirschman 1970). Moreover, corporate activities can affect significantly the quality of life for people in those states where corporations source production inputs, produce goods and services, and market them (Hertel 2003). The idea is that corporations have the power to compromise the enabling environment in which rights are realized; corporate responsibility and obligation derives from that power.

Yet, as Craig Scott (2001a; 2001b) explains, efforts to hold corporations responsible for even the most classic human rights violations – "such as detention and torture of environmental activists, union leaders, or political opponents of government policy regarding the company" – are in their "very embryonic" stage at best (2001b, 568). Legal experts such as Beth Stephens (2001; 2002) have traced efforts to use the U.S. court systems to this end. But, as Scott points out, there remains considerable debate over what the "appropriate juridical forms of regulation and site of institutional scrutiny" should be (2001b, 568).

The only instruments in international law that explicitly include corporations as obligated parties are either nonbinding declarations of principle – such as the International Labour Organization's 1977 *Tripartite Declaration of Principles Concerning Multinational Enterprises (MNEs) and Social Policy*[34] – or voluntary codes of conduct or auditing standards adopted by companies themselves. The latter may reference binding treaty law (such as the ICESCR, CRC, or key ILO conventions), but they do so only to set a normative baseline for action by companies because states, not corporations, are the entities directly bound by such treaties.

Moser and Norton (2001, vii–viii) have developed several key concepts useful for interpreting the economic rights obligations of state as well as nonstate actors. They argue that the responsibility to fulfill rights obliges the state "to *facilitate, provide and promote*" the conditions necessary to do so (emphasis added). For example, the state has the obligation not only to protect property rights but also to ensure equal access to economic opportunity both through effective enforcement of

---

[34] Additional examples include the Organization for Economic Cooperation and Development (OECD) Guidelines for Multitnational Enterprises (2000) and the United Nations "Norms on the Responsibilities of Transnational Corporations and Other Business Enterprises with regard to Human Rights" (2003). For an extensive review, see the UN Economic and Social Council, Commission on Human Rights (2005).

nondiscrimination laws and through legislation aimed at promoting the well-being of vulnerable groups.[35] This, in turn, has led Moser and Norton to develop a "*how-does-who-claim-what-from-whom*" framework for "applying rights to sustainable livelihoods." The framework undergirds a "channels of contestation matrix" used to map the institutional channels through which claims can be made, the nature of claims, the methods of staking claims, and the nature of obligation. The matrix helps illustrate the manner by which economic rights are fulfilled through a process of social struggle involving civil society actors as claimants and the state as well as corporate actors as obligated parties.[36]

b. Justiciability

The ability to settle something in a court of law – the justiciability of an issue – has been considered a major stumbling block for the implementation of economic rights for much of the past half century. We first draw insights from Donnelly's chapter in this volume to suggest that nonjusticiability lacks strong theoretical grounds and is more an artifact of institutional design than a reflection of the inherent nature of economic rights themselves. We then present concrete evidence of how economic rights can be dealt with through the legal system.

At present, economic rights are not as well institutionalized as their civil or political rights counterparts. There are countries with constitutional guarantees and/or legislation on the books related to economic rights; however, there are many countries without them. The nonjusticiability of economic rights is an artifact of the historically constrained choices made concerning how to construct the institutions of the human rights regime in the 1940s to 1960s, as well as subsequent decisions at the national level concerning how to instantiate such rights in law.[37] It is not a reflection of the inherent character of these rights, although this argument is often made.

The official treaty monitoring bodies of the UN system, as well as the many non-governmental organizations that fill the human rights sector, have tended to focus their efforts around monitoring negative rights abuse – disproportionately in the civil and political realm – which has only contributed to the entrenchment of the view that economic rights are nonjusticiable. When economic rights are litigated on at all, the groups that have brought suits or lodged complaints with intergovernmental treaty bodies have focused on arbitrary and discriminatory treatment rather than distributive justice. In so doing, they have employed a "violations approach" (Chapman 1996) to monitoring economic rights that is aimed at shifting the paradigm away from progressive realization of economic rights toward a focus on immediately realizable rights, such as the right to nondiscrimination in access and treatment. Such an approach has been attractive to advocates because it could be mapped onto existing legal strategies; the perpetrator–victim–remedy

---

[35] See also Green (2001, 1071–72).

[36] Foweraker and Landman (1997) trace a similar process of contestation in relation to civil and political rights in their work on citizenship rights and social movements.

[37] These "contingent political decisions" are richly detailed in Donnelly's contribution to this volume.

line of argument is easier to adjudicate in court than progressive violation (Roth 2004).[38]

Indeed, those who argue against the justiciability of economic rights claim that the perpetrator and victim are easier to judge in the case of civil and political rights than economic ones. Judging abuse of so-called negative rights is more straightforward, they claim, than judging nonfulfillment of "positive" rights. Tracing "who-has-harmed-whom-and-how" is easier, this argument runs, when the nature of harm is immediately evident (as is the case with negative rights) and can be linked to a readily identifiable source of harm, than when there are questions over the extent to which harm has been done or who the agent of harm is (Roth 2004).

But the argument against the justiciability of economic rights is problematic on a number of levels. First, the negative/positive rights dichotomy itself is a false one, as we have already noted. Most rights have both a positive and a negative dimension. The right to a fair trial entails not only protection against the denial of the trial itself but also provision of the legal infrastructure to make the trial possible.

Second, Beetham and others (including Chapman in this volume) argue it is possible to specify a minimal floor for economic rights, which means that "such rights can increasingly be justiciable, and amenable to individual petition and complaint" (Beetham 1995, 48).[39] Chapman, both in this volume and in other work, has detailed efforts by the Committee on Economic, Social, and Cultural Rights to define such "core" obligations in relation to the right to health.[40]

Sometimes it is thought that the nature of economic and social rights claims do differ from civil and political rights because economic rights claims are treated less as individual claims than as statements of public policy goals. But there are elements of economic rights – such as labor rights – that are already readily justiciable, as will be discussed later. And there are public policy goals with distinctly civil or political rights character (such as military defense) that are also not framed in terms of individual rights claims yet are not denigrated as simply wishful thinking in the manner that economic rights often are.[41]

Virginia Leary (1996) has demonstrated the justiciability of labor rights, and their central relationship to human rights, more generally. As she explains, several core labor rights standards should be considered part of international customary law – law to which states are bound regardless of whether or not they have actually signed a treaty. Because prohibitions on slavery and on torture are already considered part

---

[38] This view contrasts with that of Pogge (2002, 2005) and Ashford (2006). Those authors argue that by implementing and supporting an international economic system that harms the poor, the economic rights of the poor are violated precisely because rich nations are violating the (negative) obligation not to harm.

[39] Beetham cites 1992 reporting by the UN Committee on Economic, Social and Cultural Rights that explored creating an individual complaint mechanism under the ICESCR. See Annex IV of the Seventh Session of the Committee, UN Doc E/C 12/1992/2, pp. 87–108, cited in Beetham (1995, 48).

[40] Defining core rights is not an unproblematic exercise. As Chapman points out, a minimum "floor" could eventually become a "ceiling" (Chapman, in this volume). Moreover, this type of "thinking small" in the course of setting priorities for core rights goes against the grain of what most human rights advocates are accustomed to doing (Chapman & Russell 2002, 195–97).

[41] See Donnelly's chapter in this volume.

of customary international law, analogous practices in the workplace such as forced or bonded labor (prohibited under ILO Conventions 29, 105, and 182) also should be prohibited under customary law. Leary argues that the international community is moving toward the inclusion of freedom of association (protected under ILO Conventions 87 and 98, among others) in the category of customary law as well.

Human rights advocates have also used the Alien Tort Statute (also known as the Alien Tort Claims Act of 1789) available under U.S. law to file suit on behalf of foreign plaintiffs harmed by the actions of multinational corporations acting alone or in concert with a foreign state.[42] The types of crimes central to modern suits have included summary execution, torture, and slavery – all occurring in the context of the workplace or work-related settings. These suits demonstrate starkly the manner in which civil, political, economic, and social rights violations overlap. They also demonstrate new attempts at enforcing the accountability of nonstate actors extra-territorially. As will be discussed later in section 4, such innovations in legal advocacy are the hallmark of creative activists committed to expanding the legal purview of economic rights.

c. Implementing Economic Rights

One of the frustrations for scholars and policy makers interested in economic rights application is that the intensity of debate over conceptual and measurement issues seems to overshadow practical discussion of how to implement such rights. In this section, we explore questions related to the types of legal, institutional, and normative frameworks necessary for realizing economic rights on the ground. We also include some cautionary notes by veteran human rights scholars included in this volume.

The most conventionally "familiar" mechanisms for economic rights implementation are at the international level, namely, UN treaties on various aspects of economic rights and their respective monitoring bodies (either created under the language of the treaty itself or afterwards, as in the case of the Committee on Economic, Social, and Cultural Rights). The following overview provides only the most basic facts and highlights several key debates.[43]

The monitoring bodies specific to each convention – one for the ICESCR, another for the CEDAW, another for the CRC, others for the various ILO conventions or regional human rights conventions, and so on – have all developed significant bodies of knowledge on key aspects of their respective treaties. Work by Sepulveda

---

[42] For a critique of activists' use of the Alien Tort Claims Act, see Gary Clyde Hufbauer and Nicholas K. Mitrokostas (2003). For a proponent's view, see Terry Collingsworth, "The Alien Tort Claims Act – A Vital Tool for Preventing Corporations from Violating Fundamental Human Rights."

[43] Alston (1992), Hunt (1996), Eide, Krause, and Rosas (2001), Sepulveda (2003), and Chapman and Russell (2002) all offer fine-grained accounts of important institutions in the human rights regime that address economic rights, along with analyses of the difficulty of enforcing rights of this nature through international law. Sepulveda (2003) and Alston (1999; 2005), in particular, also highlight the role of regional courts and human rights implementation mechanisms (such as the European Court of Human Rights and the Inter-American Court of Human Rights).

(2003), Chapman and Russell (2002), and Eide et al. (2001) details the evolution of core concepts and reporting approaches developed in relation to specific aspects of the ICESCR, such as the right to access to health care. In particular, they explore the shift from a "violations" approach to an "obligations" approach to reporting, which Chapman further refines in her contribution to this volume. The challenge to monitoring and implementing rights from an "obligations" approach is specifying a core set of obligations (i.e., what Chapman terms in this volume "minimum core content"). Work on the rights to food, education, and health has advanced in this regard, with Hunt (1996) developing key concepts in relation to the minimum essential levels of the right to access to health services, in particular.

Moving from the international to the national level is natural in a discussion of economic rights implementation because states parties to treaties are responsible for fulfilling the obligations of the treaty at the national level, and have obligations to support other states in doing so through international assistance and cooperation, as discussed earlier. Action on implementing economic rights varies at the national level. In the discussion of national-level approaches that follows, we draw heavily on work by Wiktor Osiatyński (included in this volume), Sunstein (2004), and Sachs (2005).

The first sphere in which to institutionalize economic rights within the state itself is through constitutionalization. Constitutions may either include directive principles regarding economic rights (framed similarly to policy goals) or an actual listing of enforceable rights. Sunstein (2004, 140) characterizes constitutions accordingly as either expressive or pragmatic constitutions. The rights expressed in concrete terms in a constitution are rendered enforceable through a constitutional court or through the decisions of the comparable highest court of the land, in the absence of a constitutional court.

South African jurist Albie Sachs (along with Osiatyński in this volume) offers concrete examples of how differing countries have dealt with economic rights constitutionally. For instance, the South African Constitution includes provisions on housing (section 26) and health care, food, water, and social security (section 27). As Sachs explains, whereas the Indian Constituent Assembly adopted a postindependence constitution, "which included socio-economic rights simply as directives of state policy, making it clear that they were not in themselves to be enforceable by courts" (2005, 84), the South African constitution includes an "equality clause" in its Constitution that prohibits "negative discriminatory conduct" and includes language obliging the state to facilitate "ameliorative action to redress patterns of disadvantage" (2005, 84–85). The cases that Sachs and others on the South African Constitutional Court have decided show how creatively activists can use the existing provisions to demonstrate the state's culpability for failing to put in place programs and policies to address basic human needs.

A second sphere in which to institutionalize economic rights is through the legislature. Economic rights may be included in the regulatory framework of a country, as originally determined through legislative action. Labor regulations, for example, are enshrined in labor law and enforced through monitoring carried out under the auspices of regulatory agencies (such as the Department of Labor, in the case of the United States), which may, in turn, include specific divisions to monitor particular types of rights (such as the Wage and Hour Divisions of the U.S. Department of Labor, which monitors compliance with regulations on working hours and minimum wage/overtime pay).

The legislature also may exercise its power in carrying out a provisioning role in relation to economic rights. Lawmakers at the national level negotiate annual federal budgets; those at the state and local level carry out parallel processes at these lower levels. Together, they approve the allocation of the funds necessary to provide goods and services directly to people otherwise unable to satisfy their needs independently (i.e., to people who are exercising their rights-based claims to state support, through traditional social welfare programs, for example). Legislatures approve other forms of subsidies as well – such as funds for public universities, or for veterans benefits – along with laws that create incentives (such as tax write-offs) for individuals who will subsidize charitable activity carried out in the nongovernmental realm, which also enables people to fulfill their rights to subsistence, and so on.

There is considerable debate over what the "correct" role of government is in relation to economic rights – debate considerably more complex than the traditional arguments over "big" or "small" government. Choices over institutional design are influenced by debates over how to insulate key policy priorities from politicized attack, and how to create safeguards for the weakest while at the same time building in flexibility to ensure that newly vulnerable populations, as well as new priorities and problems, can be addressed in the future (Sachs 2005). This volume includes contributions by scholars who are optimistic about the implementation of economic rights, as well as contributions by scholars who argue that we should proceed with caution.

d. Contributions to this Volume

The chapters in this section of the book are diverse in their approaches to the issues. Some challenge conventional wisdom on the "impracticality" of implementing economic rights, whereas others raise new cautions. In the first group, Sigrun Skogly and Mark Gibney insist on the responsibility of wealthier states for providing multilateral development assistance to those states not able to fulfill the basic economic rights of their own citizens. They argue that such an obligation is well instantiated in international law, and binding. Rather than charity, international development assistance is an obligation of states in the international system. Sakiko Fukuda-Parr's contribution in this volume, which analyzes Goal 8 of the UN Millennium Development Goals from an economic rights perspective, illustrates the practical challenges of working through this particular framework for implementation.

David Forsythe, in stark contrast to Skogly and Gibney and Fukuda-Parr, argues there are neither international rights to assistance nor corresponding state oblifations. Moreover, he argues that using an economic rights framework to address the domestic obligations of countries such as the United States can be counterproductive. American citizens, in particular, are not accustomed to thinking of social welfare in terms of rights. Instead, there are core rights (such as the right to education) around which American society has developed "constitutive commitments"

(Sunstein 2004).[44] For the sake of political expediency, Forsythe argues, it makes sense to focus on these rather than to push for the acceptance of economic rights as an overarching normative framework.[45]

Susan Dicklitch and Rhoda Howard-Hassmann analyze the political economy of policy choice through a comparative analysis of development policy in Ghana and Uganda. Counter to much of the prevailing human rights literature, they argue that structural adjustment policies can play a critical role as a catalyst for domestic political and institutional reforms that ultimately enable states to fulfill the basic economic rights of their citizens. Economic growth is a necessary but not sufficient condition for the fulfillment of economic rights, Dicklitch and Howard-Hassmann argue. Distribution with equity is apt to be far better achieved in a comparatively stable economy than one vulnerable to erratic macroeconomic or sectoral policy shifts, or to endemic corruption.

The last two papers make their points by considering the same important topics, worker protection rights and child labor. Kaushik Basu, in a chapter based on his keynote address at the conference, asks if we should be allowed to trade away our rights. For instance, should a miner be allowed to give up his safety rights and work in an unsafe mine, but at a wage that would allow him to feed his family? To answer that kind of question, Basu offers a new framework that includes "maintainable" and "inviolable" preferences. Maintainable preferences are those we do not normally consider ethically wrong, while inviolable preferences are those maintainable preferences that we should furthermore not have to pay a price for. We should not have to pay a price (in the form of a lower wage) for wanting to be free from sexual harassment in the workplace, for instance. For Basu, preferences that are inviolable should determine which rights are nontradable. Unfortunately, the story is not so simple because sometimes nontradable rights conflict, as in the case in which a parent should have the nontradable rights to both food and also not to send her child to work. Basu urges caution; in our zeal for economic justice we should not unwittingly implement rights in an imperfect world without carefully considering the real life consequences. In this way, he is similar to other seasoned human rights scholars in this volume, in particular Wiktor Osiatyński, David Forsythe, and Susan Dicklitch and Rhoda Howard-Hassmann, who urge us to use extreme care in how we would invoke economic rights as against other policies and institutional options.

In the final chapter, Peter Dorman challenges the "developmentalist" school, which holds that implementing occupational safety and health regulations or eliminating child labor are policy choices too costly for developing countries to undertake given their financial limitations. In contrast, Dorman argues that both worker safety issues and child labor are not in and of themselves impediments

---

[44] In his contribution to this volume, Osiatyński cites Louis Henkin (1981, 230), who makes a similar point – namely, that the "social contract is a continuing conception" and develops with time to embrace the needs of people.

[45] Forsythe quotes at length Harold Honju Koh (former U.S. Assistant Secretary of State for Democracy, Human Rights and Labor, and now Dean of Yale Law School), who articulates a political rationale for why *not* to press for U.S. ratification of the *Convention on the Rights of the Child*. According to Koh, it is in the best interests of American children to channel the political and economic resources that otherwise would be spent on a protracted battle for ratification toward concrete programs that serve the same ends.

to economic growth. To the contrary, in the case of worker safety conditions, he argues that unsafe working conditions are a bigger problem for the developing than the developed world, and that the extra burden is hampering economic growth. Similarly, Dorman shows how child labor results from more than just poverty, with cultural factors and gender biases also playing key roles. Moreover, based on some of his previous work, Dorman calculates the net economic benefits of eliminating of child labor, and finds them to be positive and significant for virtually all regions of the world. Contrary to the received wisdom, a lack of development is not a reason to delay action on child labor; rather, it is a reason to accelerate such efforts.

4. SOCIAL MOVEMENT ACTIVISM ON ECONOMIC RIGHTS

In the United States more so than in Europe or in developing or transitional countries, there has been a particular reluctance to embrace economic rights *qua rights* for much of the past half century – in large part, a legacy of the Cold War rights divide (Ford Foundation 2004, 8; Sunstein 2004). Yet renewed challenges to the marginalization of economic rights are coming from the "bottom up" within the United States itself. A wide range of traditional social justice organizations and grassroots activists have increasingly embraced the language of human rights in order to justify their work in defense of poor and socially vulnerable groups (Ford Foundation 2004). Not all of these groups frame their work in terms of economic rights; however, those that do have pushed the "traditional" human rights movement and the scholarly community to address economic rights more directly than in the past. For example, the grassroots Kensington Welfare Rights Union has mobilized poor people in defense of their own economic rights, using the UDHR as the central framework for a national Poor People's Economic Human Rights Campaign. As one organizer explained, by using the very same notion of economic rights introduced earlier in this chapter (Ford Foundation 2004, 53):

> [W]e were concerned that the poor would turn against one another over crumbs that trickled down. Our human rights concept helped workers see that none of them are getting what they deserve, and our particular focus on Articles 23, 25, and 26 of the Universal Declaration allowed for a common vision of opportunity and economic well being for all people.

Indeed, poor people themselves have been among the most active in bringing economic rights to the fore in the 1990s through creative social protest, worldwide. There are numerous examples. Indigenous people in Mexico coalesced as a rebel army – the Zapatistas – and launched a nationwide guerilla rebellion to protest corporate-led globalization and long-standing grievances against the state on the day the North American Free Trade Agreement (NAFTA) took effect (1 January 2004). Protests have taken place throughout the Andean region against government privatization of essential services, particularly water. People living with HIV/AIDS, together with their advocates throughout the global South, have protested the World Trade Organization's (WTO) rules on intellectual property, demanding that cheaper, generic alternatives to AIDS drugs be manufactured and distributed without penalty. The richness and complexity of social movement activism on economic rights is obvious from just these few examples.

Although this book does not include a chapter dedicated to the topic, social movements organized by poor people themselves, together with their allies, have played a critical role in pushing economic rights to the fore of contemporary human rights activism. These movements are vital to understanding not only the conceptual evolution of economic rights but also their application in policy.

Social movements are collective challenges to power (Tarrow 1998).[46] They are part of the broader phenomenon of contentious politics. Actors involved in social movements carry out education, organizing, policy advocacy, legal, and scholarly work (Ford Foundation 2004, 7). They protest grievances and make claims on resources by invoking the language of rights, even in the absence of constitutional or statutory protection for particular rights. For example, when protesters demand that governments or international drug companies fulfill the *right* to HIV/AIDS treatment access, they are using one of the key strategies of social movement activism. They are framing expansive claims in "rights" terms – even if those rights are not guaranteed constitutionally or statutorily yet in their country – in order to enlarge the bargaining arena.

Kaushik Basu argues in this volume that "the mere assertion of a law or a right or a rule at times creates pressures that lead to partial enforcement, even though there may be no formal mechanism for enforcement." Social movement-based actors strategically invoke the language of rights in order to "create pressures for ... enforcement." By invoking the normative force of human rights in defense of their own needs, such grassroots protesters can change the nature of their interaction with powerful government or private sector representatives. Instead of offering petitions for help, they can demand that rights be fulfilled – explicitly referencing documents such as the UDHR, the ICESCR, or the *Convention on the Rights of the Child*, all of which codify key economic rights. In so doing, they transform their status from that of supplicants to claimants. As Philip Alston explains (cited in Green 2001, 1095):

> Needs can be deferred until those in power think it might be timely to address them. Needs can be defined and formulated by experts; they are usually seen to be eminently flexible and relative.... Rights, on the other hand, belong to individuals, who can and will assert them and strive to give them meaning and substance. They can be neither expropriated, nor defined, nor arbitrarily put on the back burner, by officials.

Empirically, activism on economic rights is as varied as the problems of marginalized people themselves. Francis Fox Piven and Richard Cloward's (1977) seminal work three decades ago highlighted the dynamics of "poor people's movements" in the United States, where activists have often married public protest with skilled use of the courts. In countries with a strong tradition of public interest law, such as the United States, nongovernmental organizations have helped poor or other marginalized people bring individual as well as class-action suits before courts in

---

[46] The full definition of social movement: "collective challenges, based on common purposes and social solidarities, in sustained interaction with elites, opponents and authorities" (Tarrow 1998, 4).

various jurisdictions for decades. But litigation is time-consuming, expensive, and limited by the scope and interpretation of law itself – including in the United States, where activists are increasingly resorting to international human rights standards to push domestic courts to reinterpret economic rights, in particular.[47]

In countries with a legacy of corruption or inefficiency in the legal system, including many developing and transitional countries, activists have had to opt for strategies other than legally based ones. Often, they have employed traditional street protest coupled with new forms of contentious action, such as cyberactivism (Arquilla & Ronfeld 2001) to convey their demands, leveraging information and mobilizing supporters in the process. For example, the Johannesburg-based network CIVICUS (which electronically links some one thousand people in over one hundred countries through its Web page and regular email newsletters) has mobilized people in civil society, worldwide, to press for policy change and social awareness of critical issues related to the protection of civil society and the promotion of issues such as economic rights awareness. This network is explicitly global in its focus, whereas other networks are more local in theirs. The Philippines-based group PhilRights, for example, aims to establish an NGO-based monitoring system for economic, social rights, and cultural rights in that country. Staff of PhilRights have skillfully used the internet to make people outside the country aware of their work and to share their innovative approach to economic rights monitoring and analysis.[48]

Tactically, activists involved in advocacy on economic rights employ a variety of approaches. Some use narrow labor rights issues (such as working conditions, wages, or freedom of association) as a wedge into negotiations over broader economic rights issues (such as the right to an adequate standard of living). By putting clear-cut labor rights grievances on the table, they aim to expose the deeper structural forces underlying these problems, which are often rooted in nonfulfillment of economic rights. Others, however, work in the opposite direction – making broad claims around social justice rather than pointed economic rights-specific demands. Actors involved in the anticorporate globalization "movement,"[49] for example, have made a wide range of claims for global economic justice. They have demanded everything from living wages to changes in global trade rules to write-off of multilateral debt in the context of broader challenges to what they term corporate-led globalization. Although some actors have invoked the term "economic rights" explicitly when making such demands, many have only inferred it. The broad focus on global justice has complicated the response to the movement, not only on the part of governments or private sector actors but also on the part of actors involved in the traditional "human rights" movement, which has been cautionary about claiming as its own such a heterogeneous set of actors (Hertel

---

[47] Cindy Soohoo, a human rights attorney interviewed for the Ford Foundation's seminal report on grassroots human rights advocacy within the United States, observes: "When you're talking to traditional civil rights lawyers, they are saying our traditional standards aren't working, we need something else." The report notes that the "inadequacy of existing [United States] laws with respect to economic rights such as the right to health and fair wages" has "sounded the alarm for US attorneys" (Ford Foundation 2004, 39).

[48] See Human Rights Network on the Web, http://www.hrnow.org/about/a000218_au_prights.htm.

[49] Amory Starr (2000) discusses the breadth of actors involved in anti-corporate-globalization protests. For additional background, see Hertel (2005).

2005). Yet as Kumi Naidoo (Director of CIVICUS) and his research collaborator, Indira Ravindran, have written (2002):

> From a substantive perspective, both sets of agenda need each other . . . to explain many of the inconsistencies in international and national politics. Human rights activists have, over the course of four decades, made governments accountable to citizens – inventing and perfecting several advocacy and campaign tactics which benefit other global movements. Anti-globalization activists have thus demonstrated that the focus on governments as the sole violators of human rights and dignity is no longer relevant. . . . If it is possible to cast human rights activists and social/economic rights activists into two separate camps, then clearly they have much to offer each other. . . . At a very minimum, it is now becoming obvious that in troubled times, civil and political rights are as likely to violated as social and economic rights.

5. CONCLUSION

The purpose of this introductory chapter was twofold. First, we sought to evaluate the scholarly and policy work on economic rights in an organized, comprehensive fashion. Second, we sought to place the novel contributions of this volume within that framework.

To see all humans as possessing economic rights may prove to be the most effective way yet of addressing world poverty. Of course, that would require that we know what economic rights are, so this chapter has provided a coherent definition that focused on the right to an adequate standard of living, the right to work, and basic income guarantees. Yet some would still question the validity of economic rights as not having the same conceptual support as their more familiar human rights counterparts, civil and political rights. We invoked the literature to show that this view is mistaken: the same foundations that justify civil and political human rights also justify economic rights.

What does remain, however, are significant controversies about the features of the obligations associated with economic rights, and their policy implications. For instance, significant disagreement exists about whether or not economic rights should be constitutionalized, and also about who the obligatory parties should be. Measurement problems arise not only because of the way economic rights fulfillment has been treated in international law but also because of some inherent difficulties in acquiring adequate data to do the job. We closed this chapter with a discussion of social movement activism, focusing on the role nongovernmental organizations and grassroots activists have played in pushing economic rights to the fore of academic and policy discussions – and the ongoing pressure "from below" to translate these concepts meaningfully into action.

The authors in this volume contribute to these debates in novel ways. Some address lingering misconceptions about economic rights. Others offer new justifications. Still others offer new ways of classifying, implementing, and measuring economic rights. In fact, because there have been so few attempts to systematically measure government efforts to implement economic rights, the chapters in that section in particular stand out as crucial new additions to the literature. Taken together, the chapters in this book not only deepen the inquiry into economic rights but also help to define the terrain for the future.

REFERENCES

Ackerman, John M. 2005. Human Rights and Social Accountability. Working Paper 86, Social Development Papers: Participation and Civic Engagement. Washington, DC: The World Bank.

Alston, Philip. 1992. *The United Nations and Human Rights: A Critical Appraisal.* Oxford: Clarendon Press.

Alston, Philip. 1999. *The European Union and Human Rights.* Oxford: Oxford University Press.

Alston, Philip, and Olivier de Schutter, eds. 2005. *Monitoring Fundamental Rights in the EU: The Contribution of the Fundamental Rights Agency.* Oxford: Oxford University Press.

Arquilla, John, and David Ronfeldt, eds. 2001. *Networks and Netwars: The Future of Terror, Crime, and Militancy.* Santa Monica, CA: Rand Corp.

Ashford, Elizabeth. Forthcoming. The Duties Imposed by the Human Right to Basic Necessities. In *UNESCO Volume VII: Freedom from Poverty as a Human Right,* ed. Thomas Pogge. Oxford: Oxford University Press.

Bandy, Joe, and Jackie Smith. 2005. *Coalitions across Borders: Transnational Protest and the Neoliberal Order.* Lanham, MD: Rowman and Littlefield.

Beetham, David. 1995. What Future for Economic and Social Rights? *Political Studies* 43: 41–60.

Besley, Timothy, and Robin Burgess. 2003. Halving Global Poverty. *Journal of Economic Perspectives* 17 (3): 3–22.

Bok, Sissela. 1978. *Lying: Moral Choice in Public and Private Life.* New York: Pantheon.

Brooks, Thom. 2002. Cosmopolitan and Distributing Responsibilities. *Critical Review of International Social and Political Philosophy* 5 (3): 92–97.

Chapman, Audrey. 1996. A Violations Approach for Monitoring the International Covenant on Economic, Social and Cultural Rights. *Human Rights Quarterly* 18 (3): 23–66.

Chapman, Audrey, and Sage Russell. 2002. Introduction. In *Core Obligations: Building a Framework for Economic, Social and Cultural Rights,* ed. A. Chapman and S. Russell. Oxford, New York: Intersentia.

Chen, Shaohua, and Martin Ravallion. 2004. How Have the World's Poorest Fared since the Early 1980s? World Bank Policy Research Working Paper 3341.

Collingsworth, Terry. n.d. The Alien Tort Claims Act – A Vital Tool for Preventing Corporations from Violating Fundamental Human Rights. International Labor Rights Fund (Washington, DC), available at: http://www.laborrights.org/publications/ATCA.pdf.

Commission on Human Security. 2003. *Human Security Now.* New York: Commission on Human Security.

Copp, David. 1992. The Right to an Adequate Standard of Living: Justice, Autonomy, and the Basic Needs. *Social Philosophy and Society* 9: 231–61.

Cranston, Maurice. 1967. Human Rights, Real and Supposed. In *Political Theory and the Rights of Man,* ed. D. Raphael, 43–53. Bloomington: Indiana University Press.

de Soto, Alvaro, and Graciana del Castillo. 1994. Obstacles to Peacebuilding. *Foreign Policy* 94: 69–83.

Donnelly, Jack. 2003. *Universal Human Rights in Theory and Practice.* 2nd ed. Ithaca, NY: Cornell University Press.

Easterly, William. 2003. Can Foreign Aid Buy Growth? *Journal of Economic Perspectives* 17 (3): 23–48.

Eide, Asbjørn. 1989. Realization of Social and Economic Rights: The Minimum Threshold Approach. *International Commission of Jurists Review* 43: 40–52.

Eide, Asbjørn, Catarina Krause, and Allan Rosas. 2001. *Economic, Social and Cultural Rights: A Textbook.* 2nd ed. Dordrecht, Netherlands: Martinus Nijhoff.

Feinberg, Joel. 1989. The Nature and Value of Rights. In *The Philosophy of Human Rights*, ed. M. Winston, 61–74. Belmont, CA: Wadsworth.

Ford Foundation. 2004. *Close to Home: Case Studies of Human Rights Work in the United States*. New York: Ford Foundation.

Foweraker, Joe, and Todd Landman. 1997. *Citizenship Rights and Social Movements: A Comparative and Statistical Analysis*. Oxford: Oxford University Press.

Fox, Jonathan, and L. David Brown, eds. 1998. *The Struggle for Accountability: The World Bank, NGOs, and Grassroots Movements*. Cambridge, MA: MIT Press.

Frank, Robert. 1988. *Passions Within Reason*. NY: Norton.

Freeman, Michael. 2002. *Human Rights: An Interdisciplinary Approach*. Cambridge, UK, and Malden, MA: Blackwell.

Gewirth, Alan. 1992. Human Dignity as the Basis of Rights. In *The Constitution of Rights*, ed. M. Meyer and W. Parent, 10–28. Chicago: University of Chicago Press.

Gewirth, Alan. 1996. *The Community of Rights*. Chicago: University of Chicago Press.

Green, Maria. 2001. What We Talk About When We Talk About Indicators: Current Approaches to Human Rights Measurement. *Human Rights Quarterly* 23 (4): 1062–97.

Harvey, Philip. 2003. The Right to Work and Basic Income Guarantees: A Comparative Assessment. Paper presented at the 2nd Congress of the US Basic Income Guarantee Network, Eastern Economics Association Meetings, New York City, Feb. 21–23.

Henkin, Louis. 1981. Economic-Social Rights as "Rights": A United States Perspective. *Human Rights Law Journal* 2 (3)–(4): 223–36.

Henkin, Louis, Gerald L. Neuman, Diane F. Orentlicher, and David W. Leebron. 1999. *Human Rights*. New York: Foundation Press.

Hertel, Shareen. 2003. The Private Side of Global Governance. *Journal of International Affairs* 57 (1): 41–50.

Hertel, Shareen. 2005. What Was All the Shouting About? Strategic Bargaining and Protest at the WTO Third Ministerial. *Human Rights Review* 6 (3): 102–18.

Hertel, Shareen. 2006. Why Bother? Measuring Economic Rights – The Research Agenda. *International Studies Perspectives* 7 (3): 215–30.

Hirschman, Albert O. 1970. *Exit, Voice, and Loyalty: Responses to Decline in Firms, Organizations, and States*. Cambridge, MA: Harvard University Press.

Hollenbach, David. 1982. Global Human Rights: An Interpretation of the Contemporary Catholic Understanding. In *Human Rights in the Americas: The Struggle for Consensus*, ed. Alfred Hennelly and John Langan, 9–24. Washington, DC: Georgetown University Press.

Hufbauer, Gary Clyde, and Nicholas K. Mitrokostas. 2003. *Awakening Monster: The Alien Tort Statue of 1789*. Policy Analyses in International Economics 70. Washington, DC: Institute for International Economics.

Hunt, Paul, Siddiq Osmani, and Manfred Nowak. 2004. Summary of the Draft Guidelines on a Human Rights Approach to Poverty Reduction. Prepared for the United Nations Office of the High Commissioner for Human Rights, New York. Available at: http://www.ohchr.org/english/issues/poverty/docs/SwissSummary1.doc.

Hunt, Paul. 1996. *Reclaiming Social Rights: International and Comparative Perspectives*. Aldershot, UK, and Brookfield, VT: Dartmouth Publishing.

Jencks, Christopher. 1990. Varieties of Altruism. In *Beyond Self-Interest*, ed. J. Mansbridge. Chicago: University of Chicago Press.

Kant, Immanuel. 1956. *Critique of Pure Reason*. Trans. L. W. Beck. New York: Bobbs-Merrill. (Orig. pub. 1788.)

Khagram, Sanjeev. 2004. *Dams and Development: Transnational Struggles for Water and Power*. Ithaca, NY: Cornell University Press.

Korsgaard, Christine. 1986. Skepticism about Practical Reason. *Journal of Philosophy* 83: 5–26.

Korsgaard, Christine. 1994. The Sources of Normativity. In *The Tanner Lectures on Human Values*, vol. 15, ed. G. Peterson. Salt Lake City: University of Utah Press.

Kunnemann, Ralph. 1995. A Coherent Approach to Human Rights. *Human Rights Quarterly* 17: 323–42.

Landman, Todd. 2005. *Protecting Human Rights.* Washington, DC: Georgetown University Press.

Lauren, Paul Gordon. 1998. *The Evolution of International Human Rights.* Philadelphia: University of Pennsylvania Press.

Leckie, Scott, 1998. Another Step Towards Indivisibility: Identifying the Key Features of Violations of Economic, Social and Cultural Rights. *Human Rights Quarterly* 20 (1): 81–124.

Luce, Stephanie. 2004. *Fighting for a Living Wage.* Ithaca, NY: Cornell University Press.

Malhotra, Rajeev, and Nicolas Fasel. 2005. Quantitative Human Rights Indicators: A Survey of Major Initiatives. Paper prepared for the Turku Expert Meeting on Human Rights Indicators, Turku/Abo, Finland, 1–13 March.

Marks, Stephen P. 2003. The Human Rights Framework for Development: Seven Approaches. Working Paper Series No. 18, Francois-Xavier Bagnoud Center for Health and Human Rights, Harvard School of Public Health.

Miller, David. 2002. Cosmopolitanism: A Critique. *Critical Review of International Social and Political Philosophy* 5 (3): 80–85.

Minkler, Lanse. Forthcoming. *Integrity and Agreement: Economics When Principles Matter.* Ann Arbor: University of Michigan Press.

Moser, Caroline, and Andy Norton. 2001. *To Claim Our Rights: Livelihood Security, Human Rights and Sustainable Development.* London: Overseas Development Institute.

Nagel, Thomas. 1978. *The Possibility of Altruism.* Princeton: Princeton University Press.

Naidoo, Kumi, and Indira Ravindran. 2002. The Consequences of a Rights-Based Understanding of the Anti-Globalisation Movement for Global Civil Society. *e-Civicus* 190 (7–13 Dec.), http://www.civicus.org/new/media/E-CIV%20190.pdf.

Nickel, James. 2005. Poverty and Rights. *The Philosophical Quarterly* 55 (220): 385–402.

O'Donnell, Guillermo, Jorge Vargas Cullell, and Osvaldo M. Iazzetta. 2004. *The Quality of Democracy: Theory & Applications.* Notre Dame, IN: Notre Dame University Press.

Office of the UN High Commissioner for Human Rights (OHCHR). 2004. *Human Rights and Poverty Reduction: A Conceptual Framework.* New York: United Nations.

Organization for Economic Cooperation and Development (OECD). "The OECD Guidelines for Multinational Enterprises," 8 September 2000.

Piven, Frances Fox, and Richard A. Cloward. 1977. *Poor People's Movements: Why They Succeed, How They Fail.* New York: Pantheon Books.

Pogge, Thomas. 2002a. *World Poverty and Human Rights.* Cambridge: Polity Press.

Pogge, Thomas. 2002b. Cosmopolitanism: A Defense. *Critical Review of International Social and Political Philosophy* 5 (3): 92–97.

Pogge, Thomas. 2005. Real World Justice. *Journal of Ethics* 9 (1): 29–53.

Pollin, Robert. 2005. Evaluating Living Wage Laws in the United States: Good Intentions and Economic Reality in Conflict? *Economic Development Quarterly* 19 (1): 3–24.

Rosenbaum, Ruth. 2004. *El Salvador Sustain-ability.* Hartford, CT: Center for Reflection, Education and Action.

Rosenbaum, Ruth. 2000. *Making the Invisible Visible: A Study of Purchasing Power of Maquila Workers in Mexico 2000.* Hartford, CT: Center for Reflection, Education and Action.

Roth, Kenneth. 2004. Defending Economic, Social and Cultural Rights: Practical Issues Faced by an International Human Rights Organization. *Human Rights Quarterly* 26 (1): 63–73.

Sachs, Albie. 2005. The Judicial Enforcement of Socio-Economic Rights: The Grootboom Case. In *The Constitution in Private Relations: Expanding Constitutionalism*, ed. Andras Sajó and Renate Uitz, 79–97. Utrecht: Eleven International.

Scott, Craig. 2001a. Toward the Institutional Integration of the Core Human Rights Treaties. In *Giving Meaning to Economic, Social and Cultural Rights*, ed. Isfahan Merali and Valerie Oosterveld, 7–38. Philadelpia: University of Pennsylvania Press.

Scott, Craig. 2001b. Multinational Enterprises and Emergent Jurisprudence on Violations of Economic, Social and Cultural Rights. In *Economic, Social and Cultural Rights: A Textbook*, 2nd ed., ed. Asbjorn Eide, Catarina Krause and Allan Rosas, 563–95. Dordrecht, Netherlands: Martinus Nijhoff.

Sen, Amartya. 2001. *Development as Freedom*. New York: Alfred A. Knopf.

Sen, Amartya. 2004. Elements of a Theory of Human Rights. *Philosophy and Public Affairs* 32: 315–56.

Sepulveda, M. Magdalena. 2003. *The Nature of the Obligations under the International Covenant on Economic, Social and Cultural Rights*. Antwerpen, Belgium: Intersentia.

Shue, Henry. 1996. *Basic Rights: Subsistence, Affluence, and U.S. Foreign Policy*. 2nd ed. Princeton: Princeton University Press.

Starr, Amory. 2000. *Naming the Enemy: Anti-Corporate Movements Confront Globalization*. Annandale, NSW, Australia: Pluto Press.

Steiner, Henry J., and Philip Alston. 1996. *International Human Rights in Context: Law, Politics, Morals*. Oxford: Clarendon Press.

Stephens, Beth. 2001. Corporate Liability: Enforcing Human Rights through Domestic Litigation. *Hastings International and Comparative Law Review* 24 (3): 401–13.

Stephens, Beth. 2002. The Amorality of Profit: Transnational Corporations and Human Rights. *Berkeley Journal of International Law* 20 (101): 101–47.

Sunstein, Cass. 2004. *The Second Bill of Rights: FDR's Unfinished Revolution and Why We Need It More than Ever*. New York: Basic Books.

Tarrow, Sidney. 1998. *Power in Movement*. 2nd ed. Cambridge: Cambridge University Press.

United Nations, Economic and Social Council, Commission on Human Rights (Sixty-first session). 2005. Report of the Sub-Commission on the Promotion and Protection of Human Rights: Report of the UN High Commissioner on Human Rights on the Responsibilities of Transnational Corporations and Related Business Enterprises with Regard to Human Rights. UN Doc. E/CN.4/2005/91 (Feb. 15, 2005).

United Nations Development Programme (UNDP). 1993. *Human Development Report 1993*. New York: Oxford University Press.

United Nations Development Programme (UNDP). 1995. *Human Development Report 1995*. New York: Oxford University Press.

United Nations Development Programme (UNDP). 2003. *Human Development Report 2003*. New York: Oxford University Press.

United Nations Development Programme (UNDP). 2005. *Human Development Report 2005*. New York: Oxford University Press.

United Nations Sub-Commission on the Promotion and Protection of Human Rights. "Norms on the Responsibilities of Transnational Corporations and Other Business Enterprises with Regard to Human Rights," U.N. Doc. E/ CN. 4/ Sub. 2/2003/12/Rev. 2 (2003).

Vandemoortele, Jan, and Arne Tostensen. 2003. Progress on Doha, Monterrey and HIPC: A Review. Paper prepared for a UNDP/CMI high-level seminar on "Achieving the MDGs: Strengthening Mutual Accountability," Bergen, Norway, May 7–8.

2   The West and Economic Rights

JACK DONNELLY

The West is regularly presented as indifferent, even hostile, to economic, social, and cultural rights. Economic and social rights "are largely dismissed in the West." "Philosophically the Western doctrine of human rights excludes economic and social rights." "The dominant Western conception of human rights . . . emphasizes only civil and political rights" (Chomsky 1998, 32; Pollis 1996, 318–19; Muzaffar 1999, 29; compare Pollis & Schwab 1979, xiii; Wright 1979, 19; Henry 1996, xix; Felice 2003, 7; Senarclens 2003, 141). This story often takes a "three generations, three worlds" form: successive generations of civil and political, economic, social, and cultural, and peoples' rights being championed by the West, the socialist countries, and the Third World, respectively (Vasak 1984; Vasak 1991; Marks 1981; Berting 1990, 197–201; Flinterman 1990; Mbaye 2002, 47–48; Smith 2003, 46–47; Tomuschat 2003, ch. 3; Ishay 2004, 10–11, ch. 2–4; compare Galtung 1994, 109, 151–54).[1] In this telling, economic and social rights were largely forced on a resistant West, which not only continues to pursue a one-sided emphasis on civil and political rights but has intensified this narrowness in recent years (Evans 2001, 57, 60–61; Otto 2001, 55; Puta-Chekwe & Flood 2001, 41; Felice 2003, 7).

This standard story, which I label the myth of Western opposition, has virtually no basis in fact. The first three sections of this chapter demonstrate this by examining the Western role in the development of international human rights norms. The remaining sections critically examine the (sometimes related but equally indefensible) claim that there is a categorical difference between justiciable civil and political rights and nonjusticiable economic and social rights. These two parts of the chapter are linked in their defense of the principle of the interdependence and indivisibility of all internationally recognized human rights, which I will argue has

---

[1] For an extended general critique of idea of (three) generations of human rights, see (Donnelly 1993, 125–31).

I thank Daniel Whelan both for sharing his ongoing research and writing on economic and social rights and for several interesting conversations on topics related to this paper. I also thank Dave Forsythe and Lanse Minkler for their comments on an earlier draft, and Jaewon Lee for research assistance.

been given more serious attention and greater practical effect in the West than in any other regional or ideological grouping of states.

THE UNIVERSAL DECLARATION OF HUMAN RIGHTS

Adherents of the Western opposition thesis typically argue that Universal Declaration of Human Rights, the foundational document of the global human rights regime, undervalues economic, social, and cultural rights, which were included only in the face of Western opposition. Neither of these claims bears scrutiny.

"The UDHR contains primarily civil and political rights (those favored by Western nations) as well as a few economic, social, and cultural rights (those championed by the Third World and the Soviet bloc)" (Renteln 1990, 30). "The priority given to civil and political rights over economic, social, and cultural rights" is the result of the fact that the Declaration "was drafted without the participation of the majority of the peoples of the world" and thus largely reflects Western priorities (de Sousa Santos 2002, 45). "The primacy of political rights in the Declaration is clear: of the thirty articles only three, one of them dealing with property rights, can be considered as dealing with economic rights" (Pollis & Schwab 1979, 5; compare Evans 1996, 92; Evans 2001, 104; Puta-Chekwe & Flood 2001, 39).

Although counting articles is a pretty silly way to determine whether a class of rights has been properly enumerated, even a "scorecard" approach fails to support the Western opposition thesis. Of the twenty-seven articles in the Universal Declaration that enumerate rights, seventeen (articles 3–15, 18–21) deal (primarily or exclusively) with civil and political rights, whereas eight (articles 16, 17, 22–27) address economic, social, and cultural rights. (Articles 2 and 28 are best categorized as both/neither). But these articles vary systematically in their level of specificity. Article 25 includes rights to food, housing, medical care, and social insurance, under a general right to an adequate standard of living. Article 23 combines the rights to work (including rights to equal pay and just remuneration) and to form and join trade unions. Conversely, freedoms of thought and religion and of opinion and expression get separate articles (18 and 19) as do rights to a fair trial and the presumption of innocence (10 and 11). Adjusting the scorecard so that we count rights at a comparable level of aggregation yields a tally more like fifteen to twelve. Counting words produces a similar picture: 616 to 526. Given the crudeness of such measures, it seems fair to say that the Universal Declaration gives roughly comparable attention to civil and political and economic, social, and cultural rights.

How, though, did this result come about? "The insistence on including SE [social and economic] rights as rights of equal status in the UDHR was the result of the demand of the USSR and its bloc of nations" (Gavison 2003, 54 n. 46). "Western states originally resisted including economic and social rights in the Universal Declaration" (Henkin 1995, 191). "The West proposed proclaiming at the world level *only the civil and political rights.* . . . It was only in a second stage, given the hostility of the Socialist countries and under strong pressure from the Latin Americans . . . that the West agreed to incorporate into the Universal Declaration a number of economic and social rights as well" (Cassesse 1990, 35).

As Bard-Anders Andreassen (1992, 333) delicately puts it, "this theory is not verified . . . by the records of the meetings of the Commission. Right from the beginning of the Commission's work the drafts included rights to social and economic goods and benefits" (compare Morsink 1999, 222–30, Eide & Rosas 1995, 528). None of the three passages quoted in the previous paragraph advances even a single supporting source, because the record, which is clear and unambiguous, points in almost exactly the opposite direction.[2]

The Atlantic Charter of August 14, 1941, committed Britain and the United States to "securing, for all, improved labor standards, economic advancement and social security" and the goal "that all the men in all lands may live out their lives in freedom from fear and want." This language, initially proposed by Britain (Palley 1991, 27), draws directly on Roosevelt's famous "Four Freedoms" speech. This Atlantic Charter had nothing to do with the Soviet Union or its concerns. The Soviets and other allies did endorse it in the January 1942 Declaration of the United Nations. From there we can trace a fairly direct path to the inclusion of human rights in the Charter, and from there to the Universal Declaration. But economic and social rights were central to the Anglo-American, and broader Western, vision of human rights from the very outset of the process of international norm creation.

Economic and social rights were included in the initial draft of an international declaration of human rights prepared in the U.S. State Department in the fall of 1942, including "the right to enjoy such minimum standards of economic, social and cultural well-being as the resources of the county, effectively used, are capable of sustaining" (quoted in Whelan 2005, 24). As Secretary of State Cordell Hull put it in a radio address in July 1942, "Liberty is more than a matter of political rights, indispensable as those rights are. In our own country we have learned from bitter experience that to be truly free, men must have, as well, economic freedom and economic security" (quoted in Whelan 2005, 24).

At the United Nations, "the inclusion of social and economic rights was an uncontroversial decision, tacitly agreed to beforehand. . . . From the very beginning of the drafting process, it was agreed to include these rights in the Declaration" (Samnoy 1999, 11; compare Eide 1995, 28–29; Eide & Eide 1999, 528). A draft human rights declaration developed by the American Law Institute (1946) was submitted by Panama to the San Francisco conference and again at the first session of the General Assembly. "In line with the predominant thinking at the time, both in the United States and elsewhere, the draft contained a number of economic and social rights" (Eide & Eide 1999, 527).[3] This ALI draft was one of the principal sources used by John Humphrey, a Canadian, in drawing up the original Secretariat draft of the Universal Declaration (Humphrey 1984, 32), which included rights to health care, education, work, good working conditions, "an equitable share of national income," public assistance for families, social security, food, housing,

---

[2] I have not ransacked the literature for obscure passages by lightweight scholars. All three are internationally known professors at major universities, with Henkin and Cassese ranking at or near the top of any list of postwar American and Italian international legal scholars. See also Mbaye 2002, 45: "[I]t was due to the socialist countries, particularly the U.S.S.R., that the Universal Declaration of Human Rights included economic, social, and cultural rights" [my translation].

[3] Articles 1–9 and 16 deal with civil and political rights, whereas articles 10–15 deal with economic and social rights. Not only is the proportion similar to that of the Universal Declaration, there is also greater specificity in the case of civil and political rights, with separate articles for religion, opinion, and speech and for assembly and association.

"healthy surroundings," rest and leisure, and participation in the cultural life of the community (see Morsink 1999, 132).

In opening the first meeting of the Commission on Human Rights – which, we should recall, was created as a subsidiary body of the Economic and Social Council – the Assistant Secretary-General for Social Affairs, Henri Laugier, a Belgian, charged the delegates with "showing . . . that today . . . the declaration of the rights of man must be extended to the economic and social fields" (E/HR/6, p. 2). Economic and social rights remained central when Humphrey's draft was revised by René Cassin, of France, who had a long interest in and involvement with economic and social rights (Agi 1998, 255–62, 358–65). And the American delegate and Chair of the Commission, Eleanor Roosevelt, supported economic and social rights throughout the drafting process.

"The United States, the United Kingdom, Australia, India, and Lebanon were more or less ambivalent about a detailed enumeration of these rights, and preferred to include them in general terms" (Samnoy 1999, 11–12; compare Andreassen 1992, 335; Tomuschat 2003, 28–29). But this had nothing to do with either principled or practical opposition to economic and social rights. For example, Australia also strongly supported Cassin's initial draft of the general statement that in the final version of Article 22 asserted: "Everyone . . . is entitled to realization . . . of the economic, social and cultural rights indispensable for his dignity and the free development of his personality" (Andreassen 1992, 339 (citing E/CN.4/SR.65); compare Morsink 1999, 230).[4]

The Western opposition thesis becomes patently ludicrous if we look at what Western states were doing at home while drafting the Declaration. Consider Britain, where economic and social rights had been making steady (if sporadic and incremental) progress for several decades, especially following the 1911 National Insurance Act. The 1942 Beveridge Report established a framework for the postwar welfare state that was widely endorsed pretty much across the political spectrum. Additional momentum was provided by the 1944 White Papers on Social Insurance and Employment Policy, along with the creation of a new Ministry of National Insurance. And a flurry of major legislation immediately after the war – the Family Allowance Act in 1945, the National Insurance, National Insurance (Industrial Injuries), and National Health Service Acts in 1946, and the Children Act and National Assistance Act in 1948 – created a system of universal national welfare rights. A similar story can be told about the United States in the 1930s and 1940s (Sunstein 2004, ch. 3, 4), as well as Canada, Australia, and most continental European states.

It simply is not true that several Western delegates "had some difficult accepting these new rights as human rights" (Mbaye 2002, 41 [my translation]). Not a single Western state pressed for a Declaration without economic and social rights. Quite the contrary, almost all insisted that economic and social rights were an essential element of the Declaration. The Universal Declaration was drafted precisely at the time of the flowering of the Western welfare state and was seen by most Western states as part of the process of consolidating an understanding of human rights

---

[4] More generally, see Andreassen 1992, 321, 337–45, 351–52; Morsink 1999, 222–30, 334.

that prominently features economic and social rights. Even Tony Evans, who argues powerfully against the hegemonic Western bias of the global human rights regime, allows that "western states did not reject the idea that economic, social and cultural rights had a proper and appropriate place in any twentieth century declaration" (1996, 77).

Western opposition to and Soviet responsibility for including economic and social rights in the Universal Declaration is, as Ashild Samnoy puts it, "a myth" largely attributable to "later political developments" (1999, 11; compare Craven 1995, 8–9, 16). After the 1940s, economic rights did get caught up in Cold War controversy.[5] This political controversy was then projected backwards, in a perverse exercise in revisionist history. More generally, the three worlds, three generations story is a creation of the late 1970s and 1980s. Even for the 1980s it is hard to take seriously, requiring us to accept that the extensive and effective welfare states of Western Europe were somehow a reflection of indifference or hostility to economic and social rights. For the late 1940s, it is not merely false, but almost exactly the opposite of the truth.

THE INTERNATIONAL HUMAN RIGHTS COVENANTS

On first sight, the International Human Rights Covenants appear to support the view that "Western states viewed economic, social, and cultural rights with suspicion" (Puta-Chekwe & Flood 2001, 41). The initially envisioned single treaty was divided – largely through Western influence – in order to define less stringent obligations with respect to economic, social, and cultural rights. But this simply is not a reflection of the fact that "socialist and capitalist cultures pursued human rights attributes of their political ideologies, one by emphasizing social and economic rights, the other by giving priority to political and civil rights" (Stacy 2004, 164).

The crucial passages appear in article 2 of the International Covenant on Civil and Political Rights (ICCPR) and the International Covenant on Economic, Social and Cultural Rights (ICESCR), respectively:

> Each State Party to the present Covenant undertakes to respect and to ensure to all individuals within its territory and subject to its jurisdiction the rights recognized in the present Covenant . . . to adopt such laws or other measures as may be necessary to give effect to the rights recognized in the present Covenant . . . [t]o ensure that any person whose rights or freedoms as herein recognized are violated shall have an effective remedy . . . [and] to develop the possibilities of judicial remedy.

> Each State Party to the present Covenant undertakes to take steps, individually and through international assistance and co-operation . . . to the maximum of its available resources, with a view to achieving progressively the full realization of the rights recognized in the present Covenant by all appropriate means, including particularly the adoption of legislative measures.

---

[5] The Soviet bloc states did abstain on the final document, for reasons including an allegedly insufficient emphasis on economic and social rights. Even if we take this Stalinist rhetoric seriously, though, it shows at most that the socialist states wanted to go even further than their Western counterparts. It says nothing about the depth, range, or sincerity of the Western commitment – which was powerful, deep, and of immense practical significance.

The clear implication is that civil and political rights can and should be made justiciable in national law. Economic, social, and cultural rights, however, are treated less as individual legal claims than solemn statements of important public policy goals. For economic and social rights, states are obliged (only) to do what resources allow toward progressive realization.

Although these are important differences, nothing in either Covenant questions the paramount substantive importance of economic, social, and cultural rights.[6] The implicit logic, instead, is that most states have the immediate capability to create subjective civil and political rights (Hohfeldian claim rights) in national law for all individuals. Few states, however, have the resources to provide comparable legal guarantees for most economic and social rights.

Differences in article 2 were also supported by the argument that "economic and social 'rights' could not be effectively enforced by mandate or injunction of a court" (Henkin 1995, 191); that they "cannot be made immediately effective by legislative and judicial action" (Green 1956, 45). Section 5 critically addresses this claim. Here, two points need to be made.

First, the differences in article 2 are rooted in a particular conception of the nature of individual rights in national and international law. They involve no denigration of economic and social rights. In 1949, as the drafting work began, the U.S.S.R. and Australia jointly proposed including economic and social rights (Morphet 1992, 78). Only a tiny minority of commentators, and not a single Western state, seriously resisted international legal recognition of economic and social rights – so long as they were formulated in the "proper" terms of progressive realization. No Western state voted against the ICESCR in either the Third Committee or the General Assembly. All Western states, except the United States, have ratified both covenants.

Second, the understanding of economic and social rights as goals of state policy, rather than justiciable individual rights, is *not* distinctively Western. Quite the contrary, it was shared by virtually all states. *No* state, Western or non-Western, seriously proposed – in the sense of being willing to adopt as a matter of enforceable national law – treating economic, social, and cultural rights as matters of immediate rather than progressive realization.

Consider the actual treatment of economic and social rights in communist states:

> Certain social welfare services were indeed provided to a very great number of citizens . . . although they were not provided in terms of rights, i.e. the respective claims were not enforceable in an independent court. These services were administered on a more or less reliable and egalitarian basis as in-kind additional compensation to one's salary. The state had no duties in this respect; it provided

---

[6] It is also worth noting that the Covenants do not appeal to a substantive distinction between positive and negative rights. Even granting that there is a moral distinction between positive and negative right, rooted in a categorical moral difference between acts of commission and acts of omission – Lichtenberg (1994) presents a strong argument to the contrary – this distinction does not match up with that between civil and political and economic and social rights. Many civil and political rights are "positive," not simply in the thin sense that all rights have costs associated with their effective guarantee (Holmes & Sunstein 1999), but in imposing very substantial financial and political burdens. Legal rights are particularly notable in this regard. Consider also the costs of electoral and penal systems.

its services on a discretionary basis and in exchange for loyalty in everyday life. (Sajó 1996, 141–42)

In comparison with the complete and utter lack of civil and political rights and freedoms, the situation in the field of socio-economic rights . . . perhaps was more or less satisfactory. . . . But even here the peasant's position was wretched . . . and our free medical care became utterly notorious. And naturally, one also need not speak about socio-economic rights for the millions of innocent victims of the Gulag. . . . Although massive repressions in our country were discontinued after the death of Stalin, the idea of the individual's complete subordination to the collective, and most of all to the state, continued to dominate in all spheres of our society's life. . . . In conditions of a totalitarian state, the presence of any sort of rights or freedoms is in general not possible, even theoretically. (Myullerson 1991, 13–14, 16)

The Soviets, for all their talk about economic and social rights, treated them exactly as the Covenant does; namely, as important goals of social policy rather than individual rights enforceable in national courts. This is how most economic and social rights have been treated in most of the Third World as well. Ironically (at least from the perspective of the Western opposition thesis), only in the West has substantial general progress been achieved in making a wide range of economic and social rights justiciable.

One other feature of the Covenants might seem to support the Western opposition thesis. The Civil and Political Covenant both created a Human Rights Committee to review periodic state reports on compliance, and included an Optional Protocol authorizing the Committee to consider individual communications alleging violations. The Economic and Social Covenant, by contrast, did not create a committee of experts, and even today still lacks an individual complaint mechanism.

The absence of a complaint mechanism, however, does not reflect a lower status for economic and social rights (see also section 4). Rather, it flows directly from the differences in the obligations in the two covenants. Without nationally justiciable obligations to respect and assure economic, social, and cultural rights for all individuals, a quasi-judicial supranational complaint procedure makes little sense (compare Tomuschat 2003, 92).

The initial absence of a Committee on Economic, Social, and Cultural Rights, by contrast, certainly was unjustifiable.[7] Reviewing state reports is a valuable monitoring and promotion activity suitable for all internationally recognized human rights – as the Committee has, in fact, demonstrated in its practice. But this defect cannot be blamed on the West. There is no evidence that it seriously bothered the Soviet bloc and Third World, let alone that their sustained efforts to create a Committee were blocked by the West.[8] And this error was corrected when the Committee was created, with substantial Western support, in 1985.

---

[7] Even more problematic is the name "Human Rights Committee" for a body that deals only with civil and political rights. This is indeed an affront to economic, social, and cultural rights. But, again, it is hard to put the blame on the West.

[8] In fact, Alston (1992, 478 [citing A/C.3/L.1360]) notes that in the final stages of negotiating the details of the Covenant, the United States proposed creating a committee of experts, but this proposal drew little support. (I thank Daniel Whelan for drawing this passage to my attention.)

THE EUROPEAN REGIONAL REGIME

The European regional regime presents a similar picture. This story is especially revealing because it shows the states of Western Europe – the historical and numerical core of the West – acting largely independently of the rest of the world.

As with the covenants, civil and political and economic and social rights have a different legal status and are subject to different implementation practices. The 1950 European Convention of Fundamental Rights and Freedoms is restricted to civil and political rights, which are treated as justiciable individual rights subject to regional judicial enforcement. Economic and social rights are treated in the 1961 European Social Charter (revised in 1996), which imposes less stringent obligations that are not enforced by a regional court.

These differences, however, have nothing to do with any reticence toward economic and social rights. Rather, they reflect a particular conception of the appropriate nature of international/regional legal obligations. As the Parliamentary Assembly put it in Recommendation 838 (1978), "in order to be incorporated in the Convention, any right must be fundamental and enjoy general recognition, and be capable of sufficiently precise definition to lay legal obligations on a State, rather than simply constitute a general rule" (quoted in Berenstein 1982, 265). Thus, the list of civil and political rights in the European Convention is significantly narrower than in the Universal Declaration, lacking rights to recognition as a person before the law, nationality, freedom of movement, asylum, to take part in government, and to periodic genuine elections. As the Committee of Experts explained in its 1984 report introducing Protocol No. 7, it included "only such rights as could be stated in sufficiently specific terms to be guaranteed within the framework of the system of control instituted by the Convention" (quoted in van Dijk & van Hoof 1998, 681).

Consider also Protocol No. 1, adopted in 1952. It adds the right to political participation, one of the more glaring gaps in the Convention's list of civil and political rights. But it also adds the right to property – an economic right – and the right to education – a social or cultural right. These rights are fundamental, generally recognized, and justiciable. The fact that they are economic, social, and cultural rights did not preclude their inclusion.[9]

Furthermore, we should disparage neither the substance nor the implementation procedures of the Social Charter. Part I goes well beyond the ICESCR, listing nineteen rights and principles (expanded to thirty-one in the 1996 revised Social Charter) that must be accepted by parties "as a declaration of the aims which it will pursue by all appropriate means." Part II then adds more detailed obligations: states were initially required to adopt five of seven core articles and a total of no less than forty-five numbered paragraphs (increased to six of nine core articles and sixty-three of ninety-eight numbered paragraphs in the 1996 revision). And these rights typically are defined in more detailed and demanding terms. For example, article 9 of the ICESCR reads, in its entirety: "The States Parties to the present

---

[9] The European Convention also includes the right to marry and found a family (article 12). Although this right appears in the Civil and Political Covenant, it is probably least awkwardly classified as a social right.

Covenant recognize the right of everyone to social security, including social insurance." Article 12 of the Social Charter requires parties not only to "establish or maintain a system of social security" but to assure that this system meets, in the 1961 Charter, the requirements of International Labour Convention (No. 102) Concerning Minimum Standards of Social Security; or, in the revised Social Charter,[10] to satisfy the European Code of Social Security, which includes several pages of detailed standards for benefits for medical care, sickness, unemployment, old age, work accident and disease, family, maternity, disability, and survivors.

Although the Social Charter is not subject to judicial enforcement, the European Committee of Social Rights subjects periodic state reports to fairly rigorous scrutiny, with explicit, paragraph by paragraph, judgments of conformity or nonconformity. For example, the Committee's Conclusions for Norway in the two year cycle 2004–2005 cover over eighty pages. And conclusions of noncompliance are further reviewed by the governmental committee. This is far more rigorous review than under either covenant. In addition, selected regional and national employers and workers organizations and NGOs have since 1998 been authorized to file complaints. These partner groups are also involved in the work of the governmental committee.

Could more be done for economic, social, and cultural rights in the European regional regime? Of course. Does the European regional regime give too much emphasis to a legal positivist conception of rights that exaggerates the importance of courts? Perhaps – a point to which we will return in a moment. Does the European regional regime disparage economic and social rights? Not at all. Quite the contrary, the European Social Charter provides a substantively more demanding list of rights and a significantly stronger review process than the ICESCR or any other regional system. This is the best evidence available of the attitude of Western states – acting alone, without any Soviet or Third World pressure – toward economic and social rights. Once more, then, the Western opposition thesis is not merely wrong, but almost exactly the opposite of the truth.

JUSTICIABLE AND DIRECTIVE RIGHTS

The remainder of this chapter examines in greater detail the issues of justiciability and progressive realization. I will argue that all internationally recognized human rights, both civil and political, and economic, social and cultural, are justiciable; that is, can be made subject to judicial enforcement through the mechanism of individual legal claims.[11] In other words, the nonjusticiability of economic and social rights is as mythic as Western opposition, although Western legal positivists are principally responsible for this myth. I will also argue that the dichotomous presentation of rights as either justiciable or subject to progressive realization is mistaken. All human rights have what I will call a directive dimension, and even those human rights that are immediately justiciable are also subject to progressive realization.

[10] Available at: http://conventions.coe.int/Treaty/en/Treaties/Html/139.htm.
[11] For a broader critique of other grounds on which some theorists have argued against recognizing economic and social human rights, see Donnelly 2003, § 2.3, which draws heavily on Shue 1980. Here I focus solely on the issue of justiciability.

Elsewhere, I have argued at length for the virtues of legalization (Donnelly 2005). Authoritative international human rights norms are a creation of international law. National law has been the principal mechanism by which those rights have been implemented. National courts have been a vital locus of the day-to-day struggle for human rights. The central point of much human rights advocacy is to assure effective legal guarantees. Here, however, I focus on the tendency, especially among positivist lawyers, to give excessive and overly doctrinaire attention to justiciability.

Nonjusticiability is regularly presented as a defect of rights in general and of economic and social rights in particular. For example, Alexandre Berenstein claims that including economic and social rights in the European Convention would give them "a higher value than that attaching to them at present, because they would be raised to the rank of fundamental rights and given special protection identical to that now given to the rights and freedoms set forth in that Convention" (1982, 261). Matthew Craven describes the ICESCR as "a poor relation to the Covenant on Civil and Political Rights, suffering in particular from a weaker implementation procedure" (1995, 352). Similar complaints were common about the Convention on the Elimination of Discrimination Against Women until the Optional Protocol was added.

The argument that all human rights should be implemented through identical judicial procedures everywhere merits careful critical examination, although below I will suggest that it is misguided. The assumption that justiciability gives a right, or is evidence of, higher value is ludicrous. Access to courts is a poor, even perverse, measure of social (recognition of) value.

National defense is one of the highest obligations of the state. No country, however, permits individuals to take the government to court if it fails to meet these obligations. Conversely, the fact that the right to education is included in the European Convention simply does not mean that European states or publics see it as a "higher" value than, say, rights to food, medical care, or social insurance. Certainly if we look at government budgets in Europe, and most other countries as well, it is civil and political rights that are, literally, the poor relation.

The obsession with justiciability is exemplified by the legal positivist maxim "no right without a remedy." This is a fairly uncontroversial conceptual claim if we understand "remedy" broadly. Serious problems, however, arise from the unstated assumption, common to many positivist lawyers, that there is no (real) remedy without a court. It is certainly true, and well worth emphasizing, that judicial remedies usually enhance the value of a right to a right-holder. Justiciability, however, does not exhaust the essential functions of rights, and justiciable rights are not the only kind of rights.

Even legal rights may be nonjusticiable. Consider the American practice of "unfunded mandates," in which Congress recognizes a right (entitlement) but does not provide the necessary supporting funding. The No Child Left Behind Act is a currently prominent example. The legal rights in question are not justiciable, but neither are they just ordinary public policy goals. Right-holders (and their advocates) are empowered to make claims on the state that would not otherwise be available, even if they cannot make those claims to a court.

More generally, constitutional rights in many countries are more directive statements of principles than a source of justiciable legal claims. Cass Sunstein's distinction between "pragmatic" and "expressive" constitutionalism (2004, ch. 8) may not be the ideal language to capture these differences. "Expressive" provisions may, as Sunstein himself emphasizes, have important practical effects. We need to be wary of implying a sneering "merely" before expressive, and we must not confuse the distinction itself with Sunstein's own opposition to constitutional recognition of most economic and social rights (1996; 2004, 175). I prefer the labels "remedial" or "justiciable" (which identifies a particular pragmatic process) and "directive" (which more precisely identifies the positive function of "expressive" provisions).[12] The crucial point, though, is to appreciate these different functions of rights.

JUSTICIABILITY AND PROGRESSIVE REALIZATION

Returning to human rights in particular, I will argue that all internationally recognized human rights should be constructed to have both directive and remedial functions. Even justiciable rights have important directive functions: they prohibit, require, permit, constrain, enable, empower, and otherwise channel and direct action and resources. And without in any way denigrating the importance of justiciability, we must be careful not to obscure other important social, political, and even legal functions of (human) rights.

Furthermore, justiciability is not an inherent feature of any particular right or set of rights, specified in relatively broad, abstract terms. "The right to x is – or is not – justiciable" is an after the fact description of the consequences of a series of contingent political decisions. It tells us something important about the social, legal, and political systems of the country in question but nothing about the inherent character of the right.

Many internationally recognized economic and social human rights are justiciable in numerous states. Consider articles 6–8 of the ICESCR, which recognize an extensive set of worker's rights. "Reasonable limitation of working hours" (Article 7(d)), for example, has been the subject of state regulation in Britain for over two centuries, and is neither more vague nor less justiciable than, say, the right "to trial within a reasonable time" recognized in article 9 of the ICCPR.

Why, then, the repeated claim that economic, social, and cultural rights are not justiciable? I want to suggest that it is significant measure an artifact of the historical moment when the global and European human rights regimes took shape. The contingent historical fact that most economic and social rights were not widely justiciable in national law in the late 1940s and early 1950s was mistakenly generalized into a false juridical doctrine.[13]

In the years following World War II, the implications of making most civil and political rights justiciable was relatively clear. For example, in most legal systems "cruel, inhuman or degrading treatment or punishment" already had, or could readily be given, a fairly concrete meaning. Given the strong substantive

---

[12] "Nonjusticiable," however, would be a poor choice. It is a residual – rather than a defined – category, and it draws our attention to an absence (of justiciability) rather than what is positively done by such rights.

[13] In seeking a more complete account, we would probably need to turn next to the fact that legal positivism occupied a commanding place in British jurisprudence and considerable power in the United States and on the continent as well. It is also probably not a coincidence that most of the strongest proponents of the claim that economic and social were not justiciable were from common law countries. More generally, "the decisive difference between the two categories of rights might in the end depend on the depth of the legal tradition" (Viljanen 1994, 63).

commitment to these rights of not only almost all Western state but also a number of Third World states as well, it is relatively easy to understand how these rights were given a justiciable form in the ICCPR. But this was a decision to *make* these rights justiciable, rather than a recognition of their inherent character.

The jurisprudence of most economic and social rights, by contrast, was limited or nonexistent, except in certain areas of workers rights (making it no coincidence that articles 6–8 of the ICESCR are formulated in much more readily justiciable terms). Furthermore, international and regional human rights norms were being established precisely as welfare states were dramatically expanding. Western states thus were profoundly unsure about the practical implications of justiciability – and thus unwilling, especially given the general economic fears and uncertainties of the immediate postwar era, to accept what appeared as potentially open-ended obligations. The diversity of national practices was also greater in the case of economic and social rights. Even in Europe, where most states had a half century or more of experience with social insurance systems, the threats covered and the mechanisms of provision varied considerably. This made negotiating detailed justiciable obligations extremely difficult. Add dramatic differences in resource bases, especially across regions, and it was almost impossible to imagine global recognition of anything more than a severely truncated list of seriously justiciable economic and social rights. Directive rights thus made legal and political sense.

The differences in the covenants also reflected the fact that the Soviet bloc and many Third World states were "less concerned with the legal niceties of drafting than with the inclusion of the widest possible range of rights" (Green 1956, 38). Whatever the text said, they intended to treat even civil and political rights as directive rather than justiciable. Therefore, because the differences in article 2 did not greatly concern them, but were of great significance to most Western (and some Third World) states, the issue provoked relatively little serious controversy.

When we look beyond the contingent features of this particular drafting process, it becomes clear that *every* right in *both* Covenants could easily and plausibly be formulated as justiciable. Conversely, every right in both covenants has vital expressive, directive, or progressive dimensions. Consider article 14 of the Civil and Political Covenant, which recognizes the right to "a fair and public hearing by a competent, independent and impartial tribunal established by law." This right is further specified to include the presumption of innocence and certain "minimum guarantees," including prompt and detailed information on the charge, time and facilities to prepare a defense, trial without undue delay, choice of counsel, free legal counsel, the opportunity to examine witnesses, the free services of an interpreter, and protection against testifying against oneself. This specification of justiciable individual rights, however, is a purely contingent drafting decision. Article 14 might just as easily have read "everyone has a right to a fair trial," much like the general directive statement of the right to social security in the ICESCR quoted earlier.

CONCEPTS, CONCEPTIONS, INSTITUTIONALIZATIONS

Asbjørn Eide distinguishes phases of idealization, positivization, and realization in the development of any particular human right (1999, 602–04; 1995, 37–38). Here I will use Krzysztof Drzewicki's four-step variant: rights pass through the stages of idealization, conceptualization, and positivization, on the way to full realization (1995, 172). Drzewicki's first three phases parallel a distinction I have drawn in a different context between concepts, conceptions, and institutionalizations of rights (2003, § 6.4). Schematically, we can imagine rights moving through a process of more precise specification, starting with a broad, fairly abstract concept or ideal – for example, fair trial or social insurance – moving to more detailed conceptions, and finally acquiring precise institutional form (including, but not necessarily limited to, "positivization" understood as justiciability).[14] *All* human rights are subject to this logic.

These "stages," however, should be seen not as successive phases in a linear progression but as recurrent moments in a recursive process of continuous development. Positivization can be immensely valuable. Nonetheless, we miss much of the impact of human rights if we focus too heavily on justiciability. All internationally recognized human rights – in all countries, at all times – are subject to "progressive realization." Institutionalization, even positivization, ought to be, and often is, not an end but an occasion for further reflection on the adequacy of the conceptualization or institutionalization of a particular concept/ideal – perhaps even reflection on the adequacy of the overall structure of rights concepts/ideals.

American jurisprudence speaks of a living constitution. The European Court of Human Rights practices "evolutive interpretation." Even where there is a constant commitment to the concept of a particular right, the detailed substance of that right – at the level of conceptions and institutionalizations – changes, in response to social learning and new decisions, circumstances, and values. The particular demands of any internationally recognized human right appropriately vary with time and place (within limits set by overarching rights concepts and conceptions).

Consider Niger, which as I write (in the summer of 2005) is teetering on the edge of famine. Does it really make sense to say, following article 14 of the ICCPR, that every Nigerian charged with any criminal offense ought to enjoy an effective justiciable right to free assistance of counsel and, if needed, free access to an interpreter? That seems to me a gross offense against any plausible conception of social justice. Although the ICCPR clearly and explicitly demands a particular positivization of the right to a fair trial, *in these circumstances* these obligations clearly ought to be seen as directive principles to which Niger (and other similarly situated states) should strive – in the future.

Compare the right to food. Article 11 of the ICESCR recognizes "the fundamental right of everyone to be free from hunger." Institutionalizing this as a justiciable individual right to food in the face of famine is a very real possibility. It would, of course, require international cooperation, as envisioned in article 2 of the Covenant. International assistance in the face of famines, however, has in fact been generally forthcoming, in a halting ad hoc way, for the past two decades. Pressing for a justiciable right to famine aid thus may make sense within the broad project of progressive realization. A justiciable right to assistance in the face of malnutrition, however, is politically utopian. But this does not make freedom from hunger an

---

[14] In practice, the process is likely to move in both directions with reactions against particular institutional abuses provoking broader reflection on the nature of the values at stake and the kinds of rights necessary to check these particular abuses.

empty ideal, any more than the absence of free legal counsel makes the right to a fair trial an empty ideal.

In every country, for each human right, a similar dynamic is (in principle at least) at play, differing in details depending on historically contingent social, political, legal, and economic conditions. The purpose of human rights is to secure certain requisites of a life of dignity. It is dangerous to focus too obsessively on the single mechanism of individual legal remedies. Whether justiciable or not, all human rights have powerful directive effects that we should not denigrate. One might even see justiciability as a particularly robust kind of directive effect: it legally requires particular social allocations of resources and effort. And the interplay between directive and remedial functions is an essential feature of all human rights.

MINIMUM GUARANTEES, MAXIMUM GOALS, MULTIPLE PATHWAYS

Another cut on these issues is provided by the idea of a "minimum core content," an idea first brought to prominence by the Committee on Economic, Social, and Cultural Rights (CESCR) in paragraph 10 of its General Comment No. 3 (1990).[15] The underlying idea is that every state party is obliged "to ensure the satisfaction of, at the very least, minimum essential levels of each of the rights" in the Covenant. The Committee, however, goes on to claim that "any assessment as to whether a State has discharged its minimum core obligation must also take account of resource constraints applying within the country concerned."

We can resolve the tension between minimum and resource-dependent obligations by returning to the idea of a recursive process of progressive realization. Given the current diversity of states, universal minima have very limited utility. Immediate realization in the form of universal justiciability is possible only for a lowest common denominator conceptualization or institutionalization. Global minimum obligations thus will require too little of most states. We need (at least) several tiers of increasingly demanding "minimum" standards. And in most countries, most of the actual work of human rights is performed not by the universal floor set by a minimum core content but by higher "minimum" obligations tailored to particular countries (or groups of countries) and by directive demands for further progressive realization.

The general obligation to maximum effort – "to the maximum of its available resources, with a view to achieving progressively the full realization of the rights recognized" – has different implications in different places and at different times. And this obligation is not diminished, let alone satisfied, by meeting universal or even contingent minimum obligations. There is always more to be done; the directive force of internationally recognized human rights, whether civil and political or economic, social, and cultural rights, is never exhausted. The overarching concept of the right needs to be seen as imposing increasingly broad, deep, and stringent demands depending on both past achievements and available resources. The European regional regime presents a striking example of continually escalating regionally variable minimum obligations that, over time, transform aspirational

---

[15] Available at: http://www.unhchr.ch/tbs/doc.nsf/(symbol)/CESCR+General+comment+3.En?Open Document.

directive goals into new minimum obligations that then set a baseline for further progressive realization.

None of this is meant to criticize the idea of minimum content or the often associated "violations approach" (Chapman 1996). My point instead is that a universal minimum core content, especially when seen in largely justiciable terms, only begins to address the demands of internationally recognized human rights. It certainly does not specify the appropriate standard to which to hold most states. Minimum immediately justiciable obligations should be our principal focus only in cases of severe resource shortages. In general, they should be seen as important, but limited concrete steps toward the progressive realization of *maximum* obligations.

Finally, let me repeat that this argument applies equally to all internationally recognized human rights. Although most of the recent work on core or minimum obligations has been in the context of economic and social rights (see, e.g., Chapman and Russell 2002), this reflects differing political and jurisprudential histories rather than inherent features of civil and political or economic, social, and cultural rights. The interplay of minimum and maximum standards, justiciable and directive claims, and immediate and progressive realization is no less important for civil and political rights than for economic, social, and cultural rights.

CONCLUSION: INDIVISIBILITY AND THE WEST

This brings us back, in a fairly novel way, to the interdependence and indivisibility of all internationally recognized human rights. Not only are there no systematic qualitative differences between civil and political and economic, social, and cultural rights, there also is much that we can learn about the nature of even well established civil and political rights by looking at them through the lens of themes more commonly associated with economic and social rights.

More generally, interdependence and indivisibility has been a theme running through this entire chapter. The West strongly supported – in fact, insisted on – including economic and social rights as a central element of the Universal Declaration. They did so precisely at the time that most Western countries were consolidating a comprehensive welfare state system of guaranteeing these rights. And the resulting liberal democratic and social democratic welfare states have had a generally enviable record on economic and social rights, without in any way sacrificing civil and political rights. If we are looking for a region that has taken interdependence and indivisibility seriously – not just in word but in practice – we can do no better than the West.

The West did support two separate covenants, but this had nothing to do with opposition to economic and social rights. Rather, it involved reluctance to accept justiciable individual rights across the broad range of internationally recognized economic and social rights. General theoretical claims that economic and social rights are not (cannot be) justiciable, which were advanced by many Western (and a number of non-Western) governments, certainly are mistaken – as the ensuing experience of most Western states, which have made many economic and social rights subject to judicial and quasi-judicial remedy, clearly indicates. But the fact remains that *no* group of countries wanted to treat economic and social rights as justiciable. Furthermore, during the period covered in this chapter, not only did

most Soviet bloc and Third World countries in practice fail to treat even civil and
political rights as justiciable, they made less progress than most Western countries
in giving justiciable legal effect to individual claims of economic and social rights.

The centrality of economic, social, and cultural rights to international human
rights norms reflects the fact that core human rights values such as dignity, autonomy, security, and equality have essential economic, social, and cultural – as well as
civil and political – dimensions. The interdependence and indivisibility of human
rights is an expression of the multidimensional nature of a life of dignity worthy
of a human being. Over the past half century, the West has a record of theoretical
and practical support for interdependence and indivisibility, including economic
and social rights, second to none, and better than most.

REFERENCES

Agi, Marc. 1998. *René Cassin, Prix Nobel de la Paix (1887–1976): Père de la Déclaration
universelle des droits de l'homme*. Paris: Librairie Académique Perrin.
Alston, Philip. 1991. No Right to Complain About Being Poor: The Need for an Optional
Protocol to the Economic Rights Covenant. In *The Future of Human Rights in a Changing
World: Fifty Years since the Four Freedoms Address. Essays in Honour of Torkel Opsahl*, ed.
A. Eide and J. Helgesen. Oslo: Norwegian University Press.
American Law Institute. 1946. Statement of Essential Human Rights. *Annals of the American
Academy of Political and Social Science* 243: 18–26.
Andreassen, Bard-Anders. 1992. Article 22. In *The Universal Declaration of Human Rights:
A Commentary*, ed. A. Eide, G. Alfredsson, G. Melander, L. A. Rehof, A. Rosas, and T.
Swinehart. Oslo: Scandinavian University Press.
Berenstein, Alexandre. 1982. Economic and Social Rights: Their Inclusion in the European
Convention on Human Rights. Problems of Formulation and Interpretation. *Human
Rights Law Journal* 2 (3–4): 257–80.
Berting, Jan. 1990. Social Change, Human Rights and the Welfare State in Europe. In *Human
Rights in a Pluralist World: Individuals and Collectivities*, ed. J. Berting et al. Westport, CT:
Meckler.
Cassesse, Antonio. 1990. *Human Rights in a Changing World*. Philadelphia: Temple Univer-
sity Press.
Chapman, Audrey R. 1996. A "Violations Approach" for Monitoring the International
Covenant on Economic, Social and Cultural Rights. *Human Rights Quarterly* 18 (1):
23–66.
Chapman, Audrey R., and Sage Russell, eds. 2002. *Core Obligations: Building a Framework
for Economic, Social and Cultural Rights*. Antwerp: Intersentia.
Chomsky, Noam. 1998. The United States and the Challenge of Relativity. In *Human Rights
Fifty Years On: A Reappraisal*, ed. T. Evans. Manchester: Manchester University Press.
Craven, Matthew C. R. 1995. *The International Covenant on Economic, Social, and Cultural
Rights: A Perspective on its Development*. Oxford: Clarendon Press.
de Sousa Santos, Bonaventura. 2002. Toward a Multicultural Conception of Human Rights.
In *Moral Imperialism: A Critical Anthology*, ed. B. E. Hernández-Truyol. New York: New
York University Press.
Donnelly, Jack. 1993. Third Generation Rights. In *Peoples and Minorities in International
Law*, ed. C. Brolmann, R. Lefeber and M. Zieck. The Hague: Kluwer.
Donnelly, Jack. 2003. *Universal Human Rights in Theory and Practice*, 2nd ed. Ithaca, NY:
Cornell University Press.

Donnelly, Jack. 2005. The Virtues of Legalization. In *Legalization and Human Rights*, ed. B. Cali and S. Meckled-Garcia. London: Routledge.

Drzewicki, Krzysztof. 1995. The Right to Work and Rights in Work. In *Economic, Social and Cultural Rights: A Textbook*, ed. A. Eide, C. Krause, and A. Rosas. Dordrecht: Martinus Nijhoff.

Eide, Asbjørn. 1995. Economic, Social and Cultural Rights as Human Rights. In *Economic, Social and Cultural Rights: A Textbook*, ed. A. Eide, C. Krause, and A. Rosas. Dordrecht: Martinus Nijhoff.

Eide, Asbjørn. 1999. Article 28. In *The Universal Declaration of Human Rights: A Common Standard of Achievement*, ed. G. Alfredsson and A. Eide. The Hague: Martinus Nijhoff.

Eide, Asbjørn, and Allan Rosas. 1995. Economic, Social and Cultural Rights: A Universal Challenge. In *Economic, Social and Cultural Rights: A Textbook*, ed. A. Eide, C. Krause, and A. Rosas. Dordrecht: Martinus Nijhoff.

Eide, Asbjørn, and Wenche Barth Eide. 1999. Article 25. In *The Universal Declaration of Human Rights:A Common Standard of Achievement*, edited by G. Alfredsson and A. Eide. The Hague: Martinus Nijhoff.

Evans, Tony. 1996. *U.S. Hegemony and the Project of Universal Human Rights*. Houndmills, UK: Macmillan Press.

Evans, Tony. 2001. *The Politics of Human Rights: A Global Perspective*. London: Pluto Press.

Felice, William. 2003. *The Global New Deal: Economic and Social Human Rights in World Politics*. Lanham, MD: Rowman & Littlefield.

Flinterman, Cees. 1990. Three Generations of Human Rights. In *Human Rights in a Pluralist World: Individuals and Collectivities*, ed. J. Berting et al. Westport, CT: Meckler.

Galtung, Johan. 1994. *Human Rights in Another Key*. Cambridge: Polity Press.

Gavison, Ruth. 2003. On the Relationship between Civil and Political Rights, and Social and Economic Rights. In *The Globalization of Human Rights*, ed. J.-M. Coicaud, M. W. Doyle, and A.-M. Gardner. Tokyo: United Nations University Press.

Green, James Frederick. 1956. *The United Nations and Human Rights*. Washington, DC: The Brookings Institution.

Hehir, J. Bryan. 1980. Human Rights from a Theological and Ethical Perspective. In *The Moral Imperatives of Human Rights: A World Survey*, ed. K. W. Thompson. Lanham, MD: University Press of America.

Henkin, Louis. 1982. Economic-Social Rights as "Rights": A United States Persepctive. *Human Rights Law Journal* 2 (3–4): 223–36.

Henkin, Louis. 1995. *International Law: Politics and Values*. Dordrecht: Martinus Nijhoff.

Henry, Charles P. 1996. Introduction: On Building a Human Rights Culture. In *International Rights and Responsibilities for the Future*, ed. K. W. Hunter and T. C. Mack. Westport, CT: Praeger.

Holmes, Stephen, and Cass R. Sunstein. 1999. *The Costs of Rights: Why Liberty Depends on Taxes*. New York: W. W. Norton & Company.

Humphrey, John P. 1984. *Human Rights and the United Nations: A Great Adventure*. Dobbs Ferry: Transnational.

Ishay, Micheline. 2004. *The History of Human Rights: From Ancient Times to the Globalization Era*. Berkeley: University of California Press.

Lichtenberg, Judith. 1994. The Moral Equivalence of Action and Omission. In *Killing and Letting Die*, ed. B. Steinbock and A. Norcross. New York: Fordham University Press.

Marks, Stephen P. 1981. Emerging Human Rights: A New Generation for the 1980s? *Rutgers Law Review* 33 (2): 435–53.

Mbaye, Keba. 2002. *Les Droits de l'homme en Afrique*, 2nd ed. Paris: Editions A. Pedone.

Morphet, Sally. 1992. Economic, Social and Cultural Rights: The Development of Governments' Views, 1941–88. In *Economic, Social and Cultural Rights: Progress and Achievement*, ed. R. Beddard and D. M. Hill. New York: St. Martin's Press.

Morsink, Johannes. 1999. *The Universal Declaration of Human Rights: Origins, Drafting, and Intent.* Philadelphia: University of Pennsylvania Press.

Muzaffar, Chandra. 1999. From Human Rights to Human Dignity. In *Debating Human Rights: Critical Essays from the United States and Asia*, ed. P. Van Ness. London: Routledge.

Myullerson, Rein A. 1991. Socialism and Human Rights. In *The Future of Human Rights in a Changing World: Fifty Years since the Four Freedoms Address. Essays in Honour of Torkel Opsahl*, ed. A. Eide and J. Helgesen. Oslo: Norwegian University Press.

Otto, Dianne. 2001. Defending Women's Economic and Social Rights: Some Thoughts on Indivisibility and a New Standard of Equality. In *Giving Meaning to Economic, Social, and Cultural Rights*, ed. I. Merali and V. Oosterveld. Philadelphia: University of Pennsylvania Press.

Palley, Claire. 1991. *The United Kingdom and Human Rights.* London: Stevens & Sons/Sweet & Maxwell.

Pollis, Adamantia. 1996. Cultural Relativism Revisited: Through a State Prism. *Human Rights Quarterly* 18 (2): 316–44.

Pollis, Adamantia, and Peter Schwab. 1979. Human Rights: A Western Construct with Limited Applicability. In *Human Rights: Cultural and Ideological Perspective*, ed. A. Pollis and P. Schwab. New York: Praeger.

Pollis, Adamantia, and Peter Schwab. 1979. Introduction. In *Human Rights: Cultural and Ideological Perspective*, ed. A. Pollis and P. Schwab. New York: Praeger.

Puta-Chekwe, Chisanga, and Nora Flood. 2001. From Division to Integration: Economic, Social, and Cultural Rights as Basic Human Needs. In *Giving Meaning to Economic, Social, and Cultural Rights*, ed. I. Merali and V. Oosterveld. Philadelphia: University of Pennsylvania Press.

Renteln, Alison Dundes. 1990. *International Human Rights: Universalism versus Relativism.* Newbury Park, CA: Sage.

Sajó, András. 1996. Rights in Post-Communism. In *Western Rights? Post-Communist Application*, ed. A. Sajó. The Hague: Kluwer Law International.

Samnoy, Ashlid. 1999. The Origins of the Universal Declaration of Human Rights. In *The Universal Declaration of Human Rights: A Common Standard of Achievement*, ed. G. Alfredsson and A. Eide. The Hague: Martinus Nijhoff.

Senarclens, Pierre de. 2003. The Politics of Human Rights. In *The Globalization of Human Rights*, ed. J.-M. Coicaud, M. W. Doyle, and A.-M. Gardner. Tokyo: United Nations Univ. Press.

Shue, Henry. 1980. *Basic Rights: Subsistence, Affluence, and U.S. Foreign Policy.* Princeton: Princeton University Press.

Smith, Rhona K. M. 2003. *Textbook on International Human Rights.* Oxford: Oxford University Press.

Stacy, Helen. 2004. International Human Rights in a Fragmenting World. In *Human Rights with Modesty: The Problem of Universalism*, ed. A. Sajó. Leiden: Martinus Nijhoff.

Sunstein, Cass R. 1996. Against Positive Rights. In *Western Rights? Post-Communist Application*, ed. A. Sajó. The Hague: Kluwer Law International.

Sunstein, Cass R. 2004. *The Second Bill of Rights: FDR's Unfinished Revolution and Why We Need It More Than Ever.* New York: Basic Books.

Tomuschat, Christian. 2003. *Human Rights: Between Idealism and Realism.* Oxford: Oxford University Press.

van Dijk, P., and G. J. H. van Hoof, eds. 1998. *Theory and Practice of the European Convention on Human Rights.* The Hague: Kluwer Law International.

Vasak, Karel. 1984. Pour une troisième génération des droits de l'homme. In *Studies and Essays on International Humanitarian Law and Red Cross Principles in Honour of Jean Pictet,* ed. C. Swinarski. The Hague: Martinus Nijhoff.

Vasak, Karel. 1991. Les différentes catégories des droits de l'homme. In *Les Dimensions universelles des droits de l'homme,* ed. A. Lapeyre, F. de Tinguy and K. Vasak. Bruxelles: Émile Bruylant.

Viljanen, Veli-Pekka. 1994. Abstention or Involvement? The Nature of State Obligations under Different Categories of Rights. In *Social Rights as Human Rights: A European Challenge,* ed. K. Drzewicki, C. Krause and A. Rosas. Turku/Abo: Institute for Human Rights, Abo Akademi University.

Whelan, Daniel J. 2005. Antecedents of the Universal Declaration (unpublished manuscript).

Wright, John T. 1979. Human Rights in the West: Political Liberties and the Rule of Law. In *Human Rights: Cultural and Ideological Perspective,* ed. A. Pollis and P. Schwab. New York: Praeger.

3 Needs-Based Approach to Social and Economic Rights

WIKTOR OSIATYŃSKI

Social and economic rights are one of the most controversial issues in the theory and practice of rights. They are often referred to as the "rights of the second-generation" distinct from the "first-generation rights" that include civil liberties and political rights.[1] However, the very category of social and economic rights is unclear and somewhat confused. Rights to own property and the freedom of enterprise are, in fact, basic freedoms rather than social rights: they empower an individual and limit the government's intrusion rather than suggest the government's benefits or regulation.[2] Also a number of other social and economic rights resemble personal freedoms or political rights.[3] It seems as if they were inserted into the category of "social and economic rights" primarily because there was no agreement on the immediate judicial enforcement of these rights.

However, even when we deal with social rights in a more narrow sense, we discover that they assume a very broad range of roles for the state. Free choice of employment and protection against unemployment (UDHR art. 23(1)) imply a protective role of the state. Many social rights call for a regulatory role of the state.[4] Very few social rights demand direct provision of goods and services by the state.[5]

---

[1] This distinction has historical character. It is true that civil liberties emerged long before the concept of social rights was formulated. Martin P. Golding (1978) points to theoretical difference between option-rights discussed by William Ockham in the fourteenth century and the claim-rights formulated, according to Golding, by Rudolf von Ihering in the second half of the nineteenth century.

[2] For Maurice Cranston (1973, 50) the right to private property is a civil right "inseparable from liberty." In fact, it is, for Cranston, the foundation of all other liberties (ibid.).

[3] For example, the right to form unions – article 23(4) of the Universal Declaration of Human Rights (hereinafter "UDHR") – is a form of freedom of association applied to industrial relations. Other "social and economic freedoms" are the equality before law for all children (UDHR art. 25(2)); the rights of parents to choose children's education (UDHR art. 26(3)); or the right to free participation in cultural life (UDHR art. 27(1)). The right to intellectual property (UDHR art. 27(2)) resembles a property right, whereas creative and academic freedoms – mentioned in article 15(3) of the International Covenant on Economic, Social and Cultural Rights (hereinafter "ICESCR") – are very close to the freedom of expression. Finally, the right to education – especially in the context of UDHR article 26(2) – resembles a political right.

[4] For example, just and favorable conditions of work (UDHR art. 23(1)); equal pay for equal work (UDHR art. 23(2)); just and favorable remuneration (UDHR art. 23(3)); the right to rest and leisure (UDHR art. 24).

[5] Social security in the event of unemployment, sickness, disability, widowhood, old age, or other lack of livelihood beyond one's control (UDHR art. 25), but even here the provision of benefits in cases

Finally, some social and economic rights deal with values and directives that can at best be the goal for social policy but they are to be implemented by nonstate actors or through international measures.[6] There is much less confusion with the other categories of rights. Civil liberties protect individuals and civil society from undue intrusion by the state while a number of political rights assume direct action of the state to ensure citizens' participation in government. Very rarely, civil and political rights directly regulate the behavior of nonstate actors who are to provide benefits to other people.[7] In what follows, I will deal primarily with social rights in a narrow sense, related to social security needs of individuals.[8]

The second controversy concerns the very status of social rights as human rights. Maurice Cranston dismissed the concept as "lofty ideas" and presented a number of arguments against social rights. His main thesis was that economic and social rights cannot be transformed easily into positive rights and secured by legislation. They also are not universal moral rights, for a great number of them concern only one particular group of people (e.g., employees). Moreover, universal moral rights have to be of paramount moral importance; this can hardly be said about a right to holidays with pay. "It is a paramount duty to relieve great distress, as it is not a paramount duty to give pleasure," wrote Cranston (1973, 67). Finally, economic and social rights – as distinct from other categories of rights – do not impose any universal duty (ibid., 65–71). Other critics point to the difficulty of assigning anyone the responsibility of meeting – or failing to meet – positive rights, as well for the interdeterminacy of social rights, which may mean different things for different people in different situations.[9]

Some arguments against social rights are related to the effectiveness of direct provision of services by a state, of implied arbitrariness and possible corruption as well as the incentive for state welfare agencies to perpetuate the problem rather than to solve it. Richard Epstein emphasized economic arguments claiming that welfare decreases the level of production, which then could be redistributed. "Robin Hood was a bad man with good motives. By analogy, government welfare programs are bad institutions with good motives" (Epstein 1987, 34).

Still other controversies focus on moral aspects of social rights, particularly in relation to individual incentive and responsibility for one's own life. Although the opponents of social rights emphasize their demoralizing effects, the defense of social rights focuses on dignity that cannot exists without basic social security.

---

of sickness and old age are regulatory duties of the state through medical insurances and pension funds.

[6] For example, social security (UDHR art. 22); remuneration ensuring existence worthy of human dignity (UDHR art. 23(3)); adequate standards of living (UDHR art. 25(1)); protection of motherhood and childhood (UDHR art. 25(2)); the participation and sharing in culture, arts and scientific advancement (UDHR art. 27(1)).

[7] There exists, however, a theory of indirect regulation – the so-called horizontal application of civil liberties among individual citizens. "Precisely on the account of the fundamental character of these rights it is difficult to appreciate why they should deserve protection in relation to public authorities, but not in relation to private individuals," write authors of a comprehensive study on the European Convention on Human Rights (van Dijk and van Hoof 1990, 17).

[8] Whenever my discussion refers to rights dealing with protections other than basic security, the term "social and economic rights" will be used.

[9] For a short review of liberal individualistic objections to welfare rights, see Barry 1990, 79–82.

Similarly, without security people cannot protect and claim their civil liberties to participate freely in political life.

Louis Henkin argues that social and economic rights are fundamental even if they are not constitutional, as is the case in the United States. Henkin's moral argument is that all society benefits from all members, even if they are called "useless" (for example, the economy, market and competition can "benefit" from unemployment, thus making the unemployed as "useful" as the ones who have jobs). His historical argument says that the "social contract is a continuing conception," which develops with time to embrace the needs of people. Therefore, some rights that were not acknowledged at the end of the eighteenth century are becoming essential two hundred years later (Henkin 1981, 230).

Even when social and economic rights are recognized as human rights, there is no doubt about their character as aspirations as distinct from the clear and present enforceability of civil and political rights. Although some international documents speak about the indivisibility and interdependence of all kinds of rights,[10] that formulation does not satisfy either the proponents of the priority of civil and political rights, nor their opponents who put more weight on social and economic rights than on civil liberties. In fact, it has always been the status of social and economic rights that separates various concepts of human rights: this was a crucial dividing line between the liberal concept of rights, on the one hand, and the socialist concept, on the other.[11]

Some authors attempt to transcend the differences between liberal and socialist concepts.[12] Interconnectedness finds a particularly elaborated dignity-based justification in the Catholic concept of rights. According to David Hollenbach (1982, 17), the fundamental value that underlies the Catholic concept of rights is:

> neither simply the liberty of the individual person stressed in the liberal democracies nor simply the social participation and economic well-being stressed in various ways by Marxism and socialism. Rather the theory maintains that respect for freedom, the meeting of basic needs and participation in community and social relationships are all essential aspects of the human dignity which is the foundation of all rights.... Any political, economic, or social system which is to be morally legitimate must provide respect for these spheres of freedom, need, and relationship.

Today the attachment to social and economic rights is one of main differences between the South and the North.[13]

---

[10] Article 5 of the "Vienna Declaration and Programme of Action," adopted by the World Conference on Human Rights on 25 June 1993, states: "All human rights are universal, indivisible and interdependent and interrelated. The international community must treat human rights globally in a fair and equal manner, on the same footing and with the same emphasis." (See Ishay 1997, 482.)

[11] For a description of the socialist concept of rights, see Wieruszewski 1988.

[12] "Freedom from fear is inextricably linked to freedom from want. Liberty and citizenship are rooted in opportunity and security," concludes Cass R. Sunstein's book (2004, 234) on social and economic rights.

[13] Adamantia Pollis (2000, 19–20) presents an outstanding explanation of the crucial role of social rights for the difference in the very understanding of rights in Western and non-Western societies: "In both traditional and Western societies there is a concept of equality, but its meaning is substantively

An ongoing controversy concerns differences between social rights and two other categories of rights, namely civil liberties and political rights. One set of arguments holds that social rights are realized through the state, while civil and political rights entail protecting people from the state. It has been claimed that civil and political rights are "rights from," whereas social and economic rights are "rights to." Isaiah Berlin (1969) has made an elaborate distinction between two concepts of freedom – negative and positive freedom. An additional argument along these lines is that social rights, as distinct from civil liberties, cost money.

These arguments are misleading and do not hold up under scrutiny. The only valid distinction along these lines is between rights and freedoms.[14] All rights are positive and require action on the part of the state. This includes also political rights that place obligations on the state to organize elections and to establish and uphold other mechanisms for citizens' participation in the political process. All rights cost money – the right to participate is costly to ensure, as is the right to access to courts. Although freedoms imply the inaction of the state and seemingly do not cost money, freedoms make very limited sense without any mechanism for protection of freedom. Freedoms need to be enforced and individuals should have a right to a remedy. Even the seemingly most inactive freedom – that is, freedom of contracts – makes no sense without state-run mechanisms for the enforcement of contracts between individual persons. Once again, we talk about positive rights that imply action of the state and cost money.[15]

Another suggested difference between the second and the first generations of rights is that civil liberties and political rights limit the state, whereas social and economic rights increase its power. Most civil liberties directly limit the governments' intrusion into spheres restricted for individuals and for an independent civil society. Social and economic rights, by contrast, place on the state numerous obligations that justify the intrusion into civil society and the ever-growing control of individuals. It is true that social rights and social welfare were often used by authoritarian regimes as justifications for violations of civil liberties and political rights.[16] However, the protection of civil liberties, the defense of internal peace, fighting crime and, more recently, the war against terrorism have also been used to justify the limitations of other civil liberties and the increase in the use of coercive powers of states. Even without authoritarian abuse, police and security powers – indispensable for the protection of civil liberties – also empower the state.

One of the elements of the empowerment of a state is the increase in its regulatory powers. It is often said that although civil liberties and political rights apply to the

different. In traditional societies entitlements in terms of power, authority, and privileges are differential, dependent on one's status in the communal group, but economic and social rights are equal entitlements for all members. Conversely, in Western liberal societies individual civil and political rights are equal entitlements, but economic and social rights are differential."

[14] "The conceptual linkage between personal rights and claiming has long been noticed by legal writers and is reflected in the standard usage in which 'claim-rights' are distinguished from other mere liberties, immunities, and powers, also sometimes called 'rights,' with which they are easily confused," writes Feinberg (1989, 67).

[15] For an extensive discussion of the costs of rights and freedoms, see Holmes and Sunstein 1999.

[16] "It should be noted that authoritarian regimes, whether Marxist or not, invariably defend the priority of socioeconomic rights" (Tesón 2001, 394).

relations between an individual and the state, social and economic rights call for an extensive regulation of relations between individuals. Trade relations, conditions of work, insurance and pensions regimes are examples of such regulations. Although this thesis is true at first glance, it becomes more problematic when we take into considerations the protection of values underlying particular rights. We will then see that values protected against the state by civil liberties – such as life, personal inviolability, privacy, property, freedom of religion and many others – are also protected from the intrusion or violation by other individuals. The protection is offered by the penal code, civil code and other laws issued and enforced by the state. Thus, the state is actively regulating interpersonal relations also in the sphere of civil liberties.

A more profound difference concerns the providing (rather than regulatory) function of the state. Every state provides goods and services to its citizens. In the case of civil and political rights, the provision of services by far outnumbers the delivery of goods (or money that could be used to buy goods). Courts, police, and criminal justice systems render services rather than provide goods.[17] In the case of protection of civil liberties and implementation of political rights, however, the state has monopoly on the provision of necessary services and goods. Social rights, by contrast, imply the delivery to some people of the very same goods and services that others, often a majority, earn through their own efforts or buy on market. Most people earn their living, buy medical insurance or at least contribute to it, save part of their earnings for future pensions and insure themselves from other risks. Some people are unable to do so. When this inability is not their own fault, they are entitled to claim such services or goods as a matter of rights. The state plays a subsidiary role making up for the shortcomings of markets or for individual handicaps. No one buys court services or voting rights on the market. Whenever someone tries to do so, it is punished as corruption. This difference quite often tends to justify the skepticism toward social rights on the part of those people who earn or buy their welfare, particularly among those who are not eligible for social services because they have just barely passed the dividing line separating those eligible for benefits from the ones who must take their own responsibility for the quality of their lives.[18]

In conclusion, the differences between social rights and other categories of rights are not as clear-cut as it is usually assumed. Undoubtedly, in the case of social rights the regulatory and providing roles of the state are more emphasized than its merely protective functions. This means that the implementation of social and economic rights directly depends on and influences the public policy of a state. Although the limitations of the state should be clearly defined in a constitution, the implementation of positive tasks of the state, as well as setting public policy

---

[17] The notable exceptions are goods provided directly to inmates within the prison system and to military personnel, as well as disaster relief considered by Holmes and Sunstein (1999, 234–236) as a form of protection of property rights.

[18] This difference, however, pre-assumes the existence of markets as well as health and pension insurance systems. It has been less relevant in subsistence economies, in conditions of slavery and servitude, in a feudal village, in the communist – and to great degree in postcommunist – economies. As noted by Adamantia Pollis (2000, 19–20), "In traditional societies . . . economic and social rights are equal entitlements for all members."

goals and priorities, belong primarily to the political process. Statutes rather than constitutions should reflect such choices and decisions.[19]

This leads us to the controversy about legal status of social rights. International documents do not provide for effective international enforcement of social and economic standards. The reporting procedure provided in Part IV of the ICSECR is not binding on the states. International covenants suggest that such rights are incorporated into the internal legal framework of states. This implementation can be on the level of statutes. Nevertheless, numerous constitutions include detailed chapters on social and economic rights.

One reason for the attempt to incorporate social rights into constitutions is historical in character. At the end of the nineteenth and the beginning of the twentieth century, the U.S. Supreme Court consistently invalidated welfare regulations by the states as violating constitutional property rights and freedom of contracts. From then on, social reformers in Europe sought to enshrine social rights in constitutions or, at least, insert into a constitution a general provision that could counterbalance property rights on a constitutional level.

Another reason for the attempts to put social rights into constitutions has political character. The poor, discriminated against, and most needy people – even when they are a numeric majority – usually do not have sufficient say about laws and budgets. People who care about their interests and needs want to formulate them as constitutional rights and thus put them above the political process.

In some constitutions the formulations of social rights do not differ from civil and political rights; this implies identical enforcement, or lack thereof (e.g., a number of post-Soviet constitutions). The Constitution of South Africa makes social and economic rights as justiciable as civil liberties and political rights. Other constitutions offer different enforcement to at least some social and economic rights than to civil liberties (e.g., Czech Republic, Slovak Republic, Poland). There exist constitutions that contain chapters on social and economic goals of a state (e.g., Spain, Portugal) or directive principles guiding public policy (e.g., India). Still others have just one general clause that is used by the governments to introduce social and welfare policies on a statutory level (e.g., Germany). At times, the reference to social goals is made only in a preamble to the constitution (e.g., France, Sweden). Finally, some constitutions do not make any room for social and economic rights (e.g., the text of the U.S. Constitution).[20] This short review indicates that even an extensive welfare state does not require having many social rights written in the constitution, as the cases of Sweden, Germany, England and France show. Political will and the availability of resources seem sufficient.[21]

This diversified picture of the regimes of social rights becomes even more complex when we take into consideration the adjudication of constitutional courts. In some cases, courts have limited the justiciability of social rights included in

---

[19] For detailed analysis of the dynamics between rights and political process, see Glendon 1991; Osiatyński 2000.

[20] For detailed discussion of social and economic rights in various constitutional systems, see Osiatyński 1996, 241–50.

[21] "It is true that many democratic states do include welfare claims and entitlements within their structures of positive law, but these derive from normal political processes and may very well be arbitrary" (Barry 1990, 80).

a constitution (e.g., some decisions of the Constitutional Court of Hungary). In other instances, constitutional courts have used provisions on rights to invalidate public policy of the government (e.g., the Constitutional Court of South Africa) (see Sunstein 2004, 209–229; Sachs 2006). The Supreme Court of India provided enforceability to social and economic rights on the basis of a constitutional concept of dignity and the right to life. Even in the United States, the adjudication of the Supreme Court after the New Deal gave life to some social and economic rights.

This, however, does not solve all related theoretical and empirical questions. Some of them relate to the separation of powers and the interference by the courts in the allocation of resources and formulation of state budgets; these functions are usually restricted to the executive and the legislature. Already discussed differences between the legal protection of rights and the political process are particularly relevant here. Other questions are related to the effectiveness of the direct provision of services by a state, to the implied arbitrariness and possible corruption in service delivery as well as the incentive for state welfare agencies to perpetuate the problem rather than to solve it.

Still other questions focus on the allegedly demoralizing moral aspect of social and economic rights that are said to decrease the recipients' motivation for their own effort. As noted, other people earn or buy benefits provided by social rights. They may feel uncomfortable when some people receive the same good and services without effort and contribution to society.

Finally, there is a problem of the applicability of the very concept of rights and right enforcement mechanisms to the aspirations that are to be "achieved progressively" "to the maximum of the available resources" (see ICESCR art. 2). Purely legalistic language of rights may turn out to be inadequate for meeting such public goals. Although the language of rights was appealing to the drafters of the Universal Declaration of Human Rights in 1948, the differences in enforcement led to the separation of social, economic, and cultural rights into a separate covenant. Today, the language of rights as applied to all values protected by international covenants only increases confusion and, in fact, prevents the usage of rights enforcement mechanisms when they may be applicable to human rights. For example, it seems impossible to enforce (by legal means) the right to work, proposed in article 6 of the ICSECR,[22] or the "continuous improvement of living conditions" (article 11), or the right to "the highest attainable standard of physical and mental health" (article 12), or the right "to enjoy the benefits of scientific progress and its applications" (article 15). By contrast, it seems possible to assure the right to form trade unions (article 8) or the right to social security (article 9).

The traditional approach to social and economic rights is unable to provide an answer to these questions or to clarify confusion. It seems that more clarity and far better implementation prospects can result from *shifting the emphasis from*

---

[22] Phillip Harvey challenged the conventional wisdom of today, according to which the right to work is only declaratory and means primarily the choice to work or compensation in the case of unemployment. Harvey shows how the right to work is subordinated to other policy choices, primarily the need to counter inflation. He claims that "the right to work is entitled to far more deference that it normally receives" (2002, 469). Harvey argues that a functional equivalent of full employment can be achieved by the direct job creation by government.

social and economic rights to social needs and treating rights as one of a number of instruments that help to satisfy such needs.

Thinking about social and economic rights, we often tend to treat as a matter of rights everything that is involved in a particular realm of social interactions. For example, when we talk about the right to health, we may think that every aspect of health care should be covered as a matter of rights. When we think about the right to education, we often claim that every kind and every level of education should be a matter of right. This attitude changes when we think about needs. There can be no doubt that every person has health-related needs. It does not mean that every aspect of that need should be granted to every person as a matter of rights and entitlements. A great majority of health-related needs are and will always remain the responsibility of a person. Our life-style, diet, use of substances and exercise regimes define our health to a greater extent than health services. Many health-related needs are covered by private contracts, by insurances and other instruments that do not necessarily imply universal rights that impose obligations on the state. Only some health-related needs should be fulfilled as a matter of rights. Every society should define these needs, and such a definition is dependant on a society's situation, needs, available resources, customs, and mode of health services.

In short, a needs-based approach to social and economic rights assumes that all people have valid social and economic needs that should not be dismissed. However, there is a very broad range of instruments to fulfill such needs. Human rights and rights-related claims are just one of such instruments, and subsidiary at that. It means that we should have recourse to rights when, and only when, a given need cannot be satisfied in another way.

This leads us to a discussion about the essential content of social rights. What are the values that such rights serve? Undoubtedly, social rights serve human dignity. "The dignity principle requires that people not be denied the means to satisfy their basic needs" (Christiansen 1982, 260). Dignity, however, is a rather vague concept; its openness was one of the main reasons it was selected as the common ground on which various philosophies of rights could be reconciled.[23] To look for the content of social rights, we need to go beyond dignity itself.

Social rights are often linked with equality and social justice.[24] Although all rights assume equality in treatment of individuals without discrimination, social rights were to assure economic equality. Equality of living conditions, however, cannot be a matter of rights. Economic equality depends on social choices and can become a guiding principle of social policy. But no one can claim equality of conditions regardless of his or her effort. The American concept of equal opportunity is closer to the idea of liberty and is served sufficiently by civil liberties and political

---

[23] "[T]he notion of human dignity is nearly empty of meaning. Unless it is further specified, the notion of human dignity lacks all references to particular freedom, needs, and relationships. It is for this reason that most ideological systems can appeal to human dignity for moral legitimacy. Therefore, unless the relationship between the transcendental worth of persons and particular human freedoms, needs and relationships can be specified, the notion of dignity will become an empty notion" (Hollenbach 1982, 18).

[24] In socialist concept of rights, social rights were clearly to serve equality. Social justice served the role of ideological justification of the communist revolution (see Wieruszewski 1988).

rights.[25] Social rights are sometimes identified with well-being or welfare. This is also misleading because well-being should primarily be a result of personal efforts rather than a claim protected by rights.[26] Finally, social rights are also not identical with justice even without the adjective "social."[27]

It seems to this author that the closest and most convincing links exist between social rights and basic needs. As mentioned earlier, social rights do not and cannot serve all needs. They serve just some needs. The rights that serve needs are related to security of the person. Here again, the distinction between categories of rights becomes elusive. For civil liberties also protect the need for security, whenever such security may be threatened by the state (or other people). Social rights protect physical security whenever the very survival of a person is threatened, regardless of the cause of such a threat. It can be excessive exploitation by the others, it can be state oppression or politically or economically induced hunger. It also can be the amendable shortage of resources or threats posed by the elements. In such cases, the concept of social rights may justifiably apply.

The content of social rights usually goes beyond mere physical security. Physical security can be assured by eight hundred calories and shelter, as was the case in concentration camps. Very few people would claim that this is enough for a life with dignity. For a dignified life, basic needs should be satisfied. Thus, the concept of basic needs becomes crucial for understanding social rights and for the very capacity to make use of all other rights. "Opportunity for education, for religious observance, for companionship, and for political participation, any or all of these can be effectively denied by manipulation of vital services. For when we are forced to a choice between these genuine goods and basic needs, we will usually choose the needs as more urgent" (Christiansen 1982, 262).

The definition of what are basic needs is not an easy task. Physical survival is a necessary but insufficient condition for having basic needs met. Physical survival of a slave or a serf is assured, but their dignity is violated in that they cannot give their lives meaning and worth or act as autonomous persons. For Drew Christiansen, the satisfaction of basic needs results from dignity understood as one of "two corollary principles which seem to be entailed in a notion of a moral minimum" (1982, 260).[28] "The kind of dignity envisioned in the moral minimum pertains to an individual's control over goods vital to him and entails respect on the part of the authorities for that prerogative." The authorities should accordingly protect people from actions that exploit "an individual's basic vulnerabilities" (ibid.,

---

[25] This is one of the reasons why mainstream American thought has tended to limit the concept of human rights to civil liberties and political rights and reject social and economic rights.

[26] Here again, social policy can be oriented toward assuring everyone a relatively high level of well-being (provided the availability of resources) as was the case in Sweden and other welfare states. Of course, welfare policies, when legislated, create rights. Such rights, however, cannot be considered human rights for they do not meet the test of universality. They are also not absolute, in a sense that they can be limited if the resources are no longer adequate or social priorities change.

[27] There are many conceptions of justice that emphasize various bases for what we consider just. Merit or desert-based conceptions of justice cannot be reconciled with claiming social benefits or services. For a more in-depth discussion of the relationship among principles of justice, need, equality, and desert, see Christiansen 1982, 266–79.

[28] The other principle is decency that "requires that no one be forced to endure degrading living conditions because of a correctable mal-distribution of resources" (Christiansen 1982, 260).

261). But dignity, for Christiansen, "is not linked simply to independent control of resources, but to choice of activities and the potential to enjoy other values" (ibid., 286).

This connects basic needs with the concept of autonomy that is crucial for individual dignity and freedom. David Copp claims that "people must have the ability to meet their basic needs in order to be fully autonomous." It is because without the fulfillment of basic needs a person cannot set goals and make choices about one's own life. In turn, "the inability to form values, or to evaluate one's life in terms of one's values, or to choose how to live one's life, or to implement such a choice seems to mark a degradation of one's autonomy or rationality" (Copp 1992, 234, 254).

Copp suggests a list of goods and services that are "either basic needs or forms of provision for a basic need." It includes the following:

> the need for nutritious food and clean water, the need to excrete, the need otherwise to preserve the body intact, the need for periodic rest and relaxation (which I presume to include periodic sleep and some form of recreation), the need for companionship, the need for education, the need for social acceptance and recognition, the need for self-respect and self-esteem, the need to be free from harassment. (Copp 1992, 252)[29]

This is a high order of needs. Providing everyone with the entitlement to such goods and services as a matter of right would require large resources. Copp realizes this and qualifies the right to adequate standard of living, which is based on his concept of basic needs, by the availability of resources. "It is the right of every person to an adequate standard of living *if* his society is wealthy enough to provide an adequate standard to every member" (ibid., 236).

The right to adequate standard of living combined with the concept of basic needs would, then, serve as a guideline for economic and social policy of the state. Whenever a society has sufficient resources, assuring basic needs for everyone should take priority over the increase in general welfare, economic growth or other considerations. This is because "the goal of respecting the autonomy of the citizen ought to have priority over the goal of promoting the general welfare or economic efficiency" (ibid., 258).[30]

Even though Copp writes about The Right (to adequate standard of living), many of the things in his list of basic needs cannot be met through right-based instruments. Rights and corresponding duties cannot create and sustain companionship, cannot assure acceptance and recognition or self-respect. These are the values that an individual needs to take care by one's own efforts. No state action can substitute for individual responsibility for the fulfillment of such needs.

---

[29] Copp's list was adapted from David Braybrooke (1987). A. C. Pigou (1952) proposed a less inclusive list of what is needed for minimum standard. Pigou's minimum included "some defined quantity and quality of house accommodation, of medical care, of education, of food, of leisure, of apparatus of sanitary convenience and safety where work is carried, and so on" (Copp 1992, 249). As we see, Copp added the needs for relationships, recognition, and self-worth that did not exist in earlier formulation of Pigou.

[30] Similarly, Christiansen shows the failure of economic growth strategy for meeting basic needs of the poor worldwide. He claims that development strategies should focus on the betterment of conditions of the poor rather than on general economic growth (1982, 246–50).

The same is with other basic needs; even when the goods or services necessary for their fulfillment can be provided by outside persons, the primary responsibility rests with an individual. As mentioned earlier, social rights consist of the provision to some people of such goods and services that others earn by their own effort or exchange on the market for the fruits of their labors. Therefore, the others should not carry the burden of one's irresponsibility or culpable neglect of one's own needs. Even the proponents of welfare rights agree that such rights should not be granted automatically.[31] One of them is Alan Gewirth, who nevertheless suggests that no one can "rationally demand of other persons that they help him to have basic well-being unless his own efforts to have it are unavailing" (Barry 1990, 81). Drew Christiansen dismisses as false the assumption "that a need-based conception of justice excluded the duty of self help . . . it is mistaken to view a basic needs policy as abetting indolence, because self-reliance is an intrinsic part of the dignity which needs policies try to promote" (Christiansen 1982, 279).

David Copp discusses an example of a person that consciously gambled away resources provided for his family's well-being. Such a person can make pledges based on egalitarian arguments or ask for charity. But he does not have a claim on extra resources.[32] In fact, individual responsibility is at the very essence of Copp's right to adequate standard of living. For his right does not entitle a person to have his or her needs secured or satisfied. It is the right "to be *enabled* to meet their basic needs; I am not proposing a right to be *provided* with what one needs" (Copp 1992, 252). Alan Gewirth seems to share this attitude.[33]

Other proponents of welfare rights are more generous than Copp. Henry Shue believes that there are duties not just to enable everyone to meet their basic needs but "to provide for the subsistence of those unable to provide for their own" (1980, 53). A great majority of the advocates of constitutionalization of social rights believe in something more than just "enabling" people to meet their basic needs. Similarly, many welfare programs are providing goods and services that directly satisfy the needs of destitute people. Such goods and services are often considered a matter of rights.

Such rights, however, differ from civil liberties and political rights in two respects. First, we can make a claim contingent on some effort of a person to fulfill the need by oneself. We demand that those on unemployment benefits actively look for job. We do not, by contrast, make police protection of one's personal integrity contingent on his proof of self-defense against an assault. We do not expect a person exercising the right to court to try to solve the dispute by taking justice into her own hands. Second, I believe that we may make the provision of needs contingent upon the contribution to society.

This is a controversial point. Civil liberties and political rights are absolute. They are not contingent on the performance of duties to state or society. In fact,

---

[31] For discussion of the relationship between positive action and personal responsibility, see Barry 1990, 80–81.

[32] Moreover, "he could hardly justifiably complain of being treated unjustly simply on the ground that the situation resulting from his gambling is one in which he cannot achieve an adequate standard of living" (Copp 1992, 242).

[33] "We have duties to help persons to fulfill their generic rights of agency when they cannot do so by their own efforts" (Gewirth 1996, 61).

the most elaborate constitutional provisions in the sphere of civil liberties concern the protection of people who violated their duties toward community: convicted criminals in prisons and people suspect of crime during investigations and trials. The reason is that they are exposed to a naked coercive power of the state and need special protection. Why should we treat social rights differently?

I suggest that this is where two differences between the two generations of rights matter. First is the already discussed fact that social rights provide some people with goods and services that others earn with their own effort. Moreover, those who are able to provide for themselves contribute an extra effort – through taxes and other mechanisms – to cover costs of meeting the needs of the recipients. Entitlements to benefits without some form of contribution to others may violate the sense of fairness and justice.

The second difference is historical in character. Civil liberties and political rights emerged as rights and the obligations on the part of state followed. English nobles demanded freedoms and the king granted them the Magna Carta, assuming obligations not to violate the liberties acknowledged. The nobles, in fact, claimed that they had had these freedoms before 1215. So did the colonists in America before the Declaration of Independence. In the nineteenth century, the advocates of democratization claimed that people have a right to participate in government and the authorities were made to comply. Obligations and limitations followed.

In the case of social rights there was a different sequencing. They emerged from original obligations. Initially, these were obligations between individuals within a society. A member of a rural community should not pass by a needy person without showing him or her mercy or charity. A needy person also had an obligation to help the more needy or to do something for the community. Such obligations were very strongly emphasized by religion (e.g., the story of the Good Samaritan in the Gospel) and other moral authorities in the society, as well as in the upbringing of children. They were enforced by parish rules and by customs of a society. In a medieval city, the care of the needy was taken over by the patricians and by the authorities of a city; one can find traces of this system in the Spanish medieval *hospedales* in Spain and Italian cities which initially took care of all needy people, not just sick ones. The inhabitants of the *hospedales* had some obligations to work if they were able to do so; the guests could be asked for some services as well. During the period of absolutism, these social obligations of the society were taken over – along with other institutions of the society – by absolutist kings and states. With the language of rights becoming more potent, the original obligations were transformed into rights.[34] The original bonds of mutual obligations were lost in the process. Nevertheless, even during and after the Great Depression the needy were helped within a broad – and extremely successful – program of public works. Today, the sense of unconditional entitlement and the break of the link between help and obligations has caused perverse results.[35]

---

[34] The revolutionaries of the nineteenth century did not use the language of rights, perhaps because they did not have access to courts or other mechanisms of enforcement of social rights; thus, they had no choice but to use the language of revolution.

[35] Many highways and dams in the United States and Germany were built, since the 1930s, by unemployed people on relief. Some of those highways are still in use. In today's Poland, close to 20% unemployment coexists with an almost complete lack of highways and with the inability to find

I postulate, therefore, that the right to an adequate standard of living, or, to having basic needs met, should not be unconditional. It can be made contingent on a proven effort to have one's own needs met and on an obligation to contribute in some way to society.[36] Guaranteed income would be morally acceptable only if it was pay for some work or service rather than a handout. The requirement of contribution would also address the issue of dignity and self-worth that are neglected by benefits without contribution to others.[37] The organization of the ways in which such contributions could take place without coercion should be one of main tasks of public authorities, particularly on the local level.[38]

* * *

The needs-based approach to social rights calls for a limited and diversified role of the state in enabling an individual to meet one's needs. Most often, social and economic needs of individuals are met by individual and community efforts; people satisfy them directly within the family, or earn means necessary to buy needed goods and services on the market. Many social, economic, and cultural needs are satisfied collectively, within extended family, local community, or professional and other associations. The role of the state should be subsidiary although, at times, it becomes crucial. The state can play a number of distinct functions in this realm. Not all functions of the state imply the existence and enforcement of rights.

1. REGULATORY FUNCTION

Proper fulfillment of social and economic needs may call for the regulation by the state of markets, conditions of work, environmental protection as well as the criminalization of certain behavior threatening social, economic, and cultural needs of others. Taxation needed for social programs and plans for redistribution are also forms of regulation.

Market relations, based on private contracts, create rights between persons involved. The state enforces such contract in the same way as all other contracts. Some contracts, however, are forced and guaranteed by the state. This is the case with social security insurance, health insurance, and pension plans in which the

---

anyone who would do simple menial jobs with pay just slightly higher than unemployment benefits.

[36] Such contribution would not have to be a formal full-time job. Half-time jobs or other forms of part-time work, including services to the community in times of emergency, could be acceptable. The main factor would be community needs and the recipient's abilities. For example, Christopher Jencks suggests that for single mothers of young children, half-time work would be "far more reasonable goal than full-time work," provided that "all school districts offered year-round, half-day pre-kindergarten programs" (2005, 86).

[37] Such a solution would require a new way of thinking about what kind of activities merit respect and self-worth. I believe that there are vast possibilities of using unemployed and needy people in the realm of personal services and the betterment of quality of life. The problem is that such services like reading to children and to aged people are not considered "work."

[38] In 1996, before the Temporary Assistance for Needy Families bill that replaced Aid to Families with Dependent Children program was adopted, President Clinton's welfare team unsuccessfully "had hoped to guarantee jobs for able-bodied welfare recipients who would not find work and child care for those who could. The Republicans wanted to save money, so they rejected these guarantees" (Jencks 2005, 76).

contracts among an employer, the employee, and the insuring agency are made compulsory by the state. The state often also assumes responsibility in the case of insolvency of the insuring agency. In such cases, an insured person has a secondary claim against the state for the fulfillment of the contract.

The state also can support or enhance charity – through tax deductions, private charitable lotteries using public space, and state resources for this purpose and through other incentives. Such activities do not create formal obligations on the part of the donor, nor rights on the part of beneficiary, except for fairness in the events of risk of corruption or favoritism.

One of regulatory functions of the state is protecting a weaker party in private contracts. Labor laws and consumer regulations are good examples. In such cases, the state creates rights that can be used by private persons against other private persons and that are enforced through state courts. The concept of basic needs leads some authors to conclusions that may increase such protective function of the state.[39] Others recognize the society's obligations toward individuals even though such obligation can be moral and not necessarily create rights.[40] It seems that such long-term goals can be fulfilled, for and in the name of a society, by the state. This leads us to the second function of the state in the fulfillment of economic needs.

2. SETTING PUBLIC POLICY GOALS

The state can introduce policies aimed at maximum possible employment, at facilitation of housing needs, and at the protection of the environment, public health, etc. The implementation of such public policy goals requires the allocation of resources in the state budget. In a majority of modern democracies there is an unwritten consensus that public policy also should take into consideration the needs of the poorest, the most helpless, and the most vulnerable groups. This is particularly important for the basic needs concept because many basic needs cannot be served without proper public policy. In fact, some needs can be served better by public policy than through rights-based instruments.

Some basic needs have collective character and can be met only by public action, as in the case of water supply, sanitation, and schooling. Even though people construct and buy houses individually, housing for the needy usually requires public policy. The fulfillment of basic needs also calls for specific government programs and policies to stimulate employment or to assist in the case of unemployment (for example, through subsidization of basic commodities or through public work employment).[41] Copp suggests that even though the state does not have a duty

---

[39] For example, Henry Shue suggests that the right to subsistence creates a duty of the state "to protect people against deprivation of the only available means of subsistence by other peoples" (1980, 53).

[40] David Copp claims that a poor society has a duty "to strive for the capacity of providing something as close as possible to an adequate standard of living for all it members as soon as it can" (1992, 244). It also "ought to enable as many as it can to come as close as possible to an adequate standard of living while treating each of its members fairly" (ibid.). Copp does not explain, however, how society could fulfill this duty.

[41] Christiansen claims that "employment is rightly conceived of as a primary goal of needs policy, not only because it is the surest way to make men and women self-supporting, but also because it is an important element in upholding self-esteem and a sense of purpose in people's lives" (1982, 263).

to feed every person, it "must ensure the availability of food supply sufficient to enable everyone to have a nutritious diet" (1992, 242). This definitely requires the adoption of public policy.

Beyond mere public policy, the state should design institutions that help people meet their basic social and psychological needs. It is particularly relevant, too, with regard to basic needs that cannot be satisfied by the state, like self-respect or social acceptance. Copp gives an example of national medical insurance scheme "that would provide a person with an entitlement to psychological counseling."[42] Gewirth suggests that the state should introduce "appropriate and justified macro-economic policies and institutions" by virtue of which "even the poorest can gradually surmount their economic and related afflictions and move closer to equality" (1996, 99).

Generally, the policies resulting from the concept of basic needs should serve the worst-off segments of population. They include redistributive policies. Basic needs, however, are not identical with equality.[43] In fact, the satisfaction of basic needs creates clear-cut limits to redistributive policies. Such policies cannot worsen the situation of the better-off below their basic needs and should stop when the needy have an opportunity to enjoy an adequate standard of living (see Copp 1992, 247).[44]

Does public policy of the state create rights? There is no simple answer to this question. Some specific rights are postulated within the basic needs concept. One of them is the right to subsistence. This right implies duties of the state that should be fulfilled through appropriate policies and services. Henry Shue claims that the right to subsistence implies a duty of the state "to provide for the subsistence of those unable to provide for their own" (1980, 53). Another derivative of the same right is the duty on the part of the state to avoid depriving a person of his or her only available means of subsistence. If Shue's ideas are accepted, the duty and correlative right he proposes would increase, in fact, the very concept of personal liberty. It means that the state could not intrude – through otherwise legitimate taxation or justifiable confiscation resulting from liability or punishment – into properties necessary for one's subsistence. Inviolability protected by personal freedom would extend into the means necessary for subsistence. Such a postulate has radical consequences.

2.1. Enforcing Public Policy Goals

In practice, the most difficult problem with social rights is the *enforcement of public policy goals*. Such goals are usually enforced by political means. However,

---

[42] "But a state clearly could not ensure that people are able to meet needs of these kinds" (Copp 1992, 252).

[43] Joel Feinberg considers the principle of need "not an independent principle at all, but only a way of mediating the application of the principle of equality" (1973, 111). David Miller claims that concepts of needs and equality are almost identical. W. G. Runciman considers need a subordinate norm to equality which is, for him, the key principle of justice. For discussion of their ideas, see Christiansen (1982, 268–69), who disagrees with them and treats needs and equality as separate principles.

[44] In another place the same author writes, "Perhaps it is true that the government is not entitled to enforce transfers from the rich to the poor once the point is achieved that the worst off are enabled to meet their basic needs." Copp claims that "the better off have a duty to pay their share *until* the point is reached that the worst off are enabled to meet their basic needs" (1992, 260).

there exists a danger that a democratic political process may neglect the needs of the most vulnerable and needy groups of citizens.[45] Therefore, some special mechanisms to support needs-based policies can be designed. Such mechanisms can grant social policies special position as compared to other political choices. This can be done either through constitutional provisions about social policies (or about social rights) or through decisions of a constitutional court. In both cases, a general norm in a constitution is indispensable without necessarily making particular social rights directly enforceable by courts.[46]

One example of special treatment of social tasks by the state was Poland's draft Bill of Rights and Freedoms (1992, later aborted). It contained a section on the goals of the state in social, economic and cultural matters. Such goals did not create directly enforceable rights but obligated the state to take care of the enumerated goals in its policies (and, accordingly, in the budget). To give constitutional tasks more weight in a political process, the draft bill suggested that the government, with a yearly motion for the approval of the government's spending (the absolutorium), would be obligated to submit a detailed report on what it did in the realm of social and economic goals of the state. Such a report was to include not only state expenditures, but also independent assessments of the effectiveness of steps taken by the government. Another form of the reinforcement of needs-based political process could be a supermajority needed during the voting on the motion for the absolutorium. Although all other parts of the budget could require a simple majority of votes for approval, the report on the social and economic tasks of a state might need 61%, or a two-thirds, majority. Without such large support, the government would face the same consequences as in the rejection of the absolutorium – that is, the dismissal.[47]

Experience proves that vulnerable populations and the weakest groups of a society cannot always rely on political process even if their needs and social goals are included in a constitution. In such cases, the courts can intervene by using constitutional provisions to demand from the executive and legislature the development of public policy in the spheres of social welfare. They also can make a

---

[45] "It is understandable that welfare philosophers should demand the constitutional protection of welfare rights, since it is almost certainly the lax political rules of majoritarian democracies, and the discretion granted to officials, that have caused the failure of post-war welfare policies aimed at both equality and the relief of deprivation: coalitions of group interests have submerged the widespread desire for some form of welfare for the needy that exists in a community" (Barry 1990, 80).

[46] Of course, social rights in a constitution play the same role of assuring priority to certain goals in political decision-making about the allocation of resources. It seems that protection of the weakest is an important motivating force behind Philip Harvey's defense of the right to work. According to him, it deserves a place in economic policy debates "precisely because they are likely to conflict with public preferences. In political democracies, majoritarian interests tend to be self-enforcing, but minority interests often need the special protection that rights-based claims provide." Harvey argues that "unemployed workers constitute just such a minority in need of special protection, particularly in periods of relative prosperity when their interests are likely to conflict with the policy preferences of a majority of the population" (2002, 470).

[47] Another solution was suggested by David Trubeck at the very beginning of the postcommunist transition in Poland. While discussing an argument about the lack of available resources for welfare in bankrupt economies, Trubeck noted that by the time resources would be generated, a new power structure would emerge opposed to increased welfare spending. Trubeck proposed that a constitution precommits a certain percentage of the future growth in the GDP to social expenditures. (Suggested by Trubeck in a discussion about new constitutions in postcommunist countries that took place in Kazimierz, Poland, in early 1990.)

judgment as to whether or not a given public policy protects constitutional values and principles.[48] To respect the principle of separation of powers, the courts should refrain from issuing executive orders designing a particular welfare policy. This task should be left to the executive and legislature that may be reviewed, once again, by a constitutional court.

In general, public policy, by itself, does not create enforceable rights. It seems implausible that employment policies create an automatic right to get a job, or that a housing policy automatically creates an enforceable right to housing. However, when a given public policy is implemented and introduces the mechanisms for provision of goods or services, those eligible acquire a right to receive benefits. Such rights usually have statutory character and can be terminated when the policy changes.

3. DIRECT PROVISION OF GOODS AND SERVICES

Public authorities may also directly provide goods or services to members of vulnerable groups that cannot provide for themselves, that do not have sufficient means to buy needed goods and services on the market, and/or that are victims of past discrimination.

As mentioned, it may be necessary for the state to provide for the poor such basic services as water supply, health clinics, schools, and, when needed, food distribution. Some goods and services can be provided as a *matter of rights*. Such rights can be based on a statute or on a specific constitutional provision. As noted, statutory rights are protected against the executive's discretion, but only within the limits of a statute; the majority can grant such benefits as well as take them away. Constitutional rights are protected also against the majority by the judiciary and constitutional courts.

It seems that a *majority of social rights can have statutory character.* They imply the redistribution of resources and choices between competing values; such choices belong to the political process rather than to judicial competence. The statutory character of social rights also would render them less "absolute" and open the possibility of making the exercise of such rights contingent on the two conditions discussed earlier – the recipient's prior effort to satisfy the need, and the requirement of a contribution to society.

Some social and economic rights, however, should have *constitutional protection* and be granted unconditionally. It seems that the design of directly enforceable constitutional social rights could be ruled by the following principles:

1. Basic needs should be satisfied unconditionally for all people kept under coercive power of the state.
2. Although social rights may be made contingent on the requirement of a recipient's prior effort and his or her contribution to the welfare of a society, constitutional rights should be granted unconditionally to vulnerable

---

[48] This precisely happened in South Africa, where the Constitutional Court rendered unconstitutional the government's housing policy on the grounds that it did not respond properly to the needs of the most vulnerable groups in the society (see Sachs 2005).

populations, including the disabled, whose potential for contributing to the society is usually neglected by market and politics.

3. Constitutional rights should not exceed the minimum necessary for enabling a person to meet his or her basic needs. Rights in excess of this threshold can be granted by a statute and limited later if a democratic society decides to change its priorities. Such rights also could be enforced, on the basis of individual claims, by the court but only within the limits set in a statute.

4. Every individual should have a constitutional claim to courts in every case of discrimination in the enjoyment of rights, regardless of their constitutional or statutory character. Such a claim would be based, however, primarily on the general antidiscrimination clause in a constitution rather than on provisions about particular rights.

It is important to remember, though, that many important social and economic needs cannot be satisfied even with the use of rights. Making social rights constitutional does not necessarily help the situation of the rights holders. Rights are not easily translated into the improvement of social conditions or the increase of an individual's control over his or her life. To change the conditions and give people a dose of control over their lives, the access of vulnerable populations to vital resources should be increased.[49]

CONCLUSIONS

I believe that the needs-based approach may be helpful to limit some confusion implied in the notion of social and economic rights as rights. It clarifies the distinction between social policies and rights. It also helps illustrate the difference between various remedies attached to particular rights. The main postulates of the needs-based approach to social and economic rights can be summarized as follows:

1. The state should play a subsidiary role in the fulfillment of social and economic needs of the people. In some cases, however, this role is crucial for the very possibility of living a dignified life.

2. The most important mechanism of state intervention in the social sphere is regulation, adoption and implementation of general policies, creation of mechanisms and institutions that enable the satisfaction of collective needs, and, exceptionally, direct provision of goods and services to the needy. For these roles, statutory regulations and statute-based policies and rights are the norm.

---

[49] A promising approach to this problem is merging the concept of rights with the idea of capabilities developed by Amartya Sen and Martha C. Nussbaum. According to Nussbaum, the capabilities approach is not limited to formal rights, but is interested in what a right-holder is "actually able to do and to be ... it is concerned with what is actually going on in the life in question: not how many resources are sitting around, but how they are actually going to work in enabling people to function in a fully human way" (2001, 222). The development of capabilities should be the goal of public policy. It seems that this approach can form a new resource for the fulfillment of basic needs. (For the discussion of the concept of capabilities, see also Sen 2000, 74–76, 87–110.)

3. Constitutional principles should assure that the needs of vulnerable populations and that the worst-off are not neglected by the political process. Constitutional courts may demand the formulation of proper public policy and review its constitutionality.
4. Constitutional rights should protect a minimum based on basic needs, particularly for vulnerable populations.
5. All remaining social and economic needs can be left for social policy of the state, as defined by statutes and state budgets.

It is important, however, to always keep in mind that state-enforceable rights and state action in general cannot replace individual and social responsibility for meeting a great majority of basic human needs.

REFERENCES

Barry, Norman. 1990. *Welfare*. Minneapolis: University of Minnesota Press.

Braybrooke, David. 1987. *Meeting Needs*. Princeton: Princeton University Press.

Berlin, Isaiah. 1969. Two Concepts of Liberty. In *Four Essays on Liberty*, 118–172. London: Oxford University Press.

Christiansen, Drew. 1982. Basic Needs: Criterion for the Legitimacy of Development. In *Human Rights in the Americas: The Struggle for Consensus*, ed. Alfred Hennelly and John Langan, 245–88. Washington, DC: Georgetown University Press.

Copp, David. 1992. The Right to an Adequate Standard of Living: Justice, Autonomy, and the Basic Needs. In *Economic Rights*, ed. Ellen Frankel Paul, Fred D. Miller Jr., and Jeffrey Paul, 231–61. Cambridge: Cambridge University Press.

Cranston, Maurice. 1973. *What are Human Rights?* New York: Taplinger.

Epstein, Richard A. 1987. The Uncertain Quest for Welfare Rights. In *Constitutionalism and Rights*, ed. Gary C. Bryner and Noel B. Reynolds, 33–62. Provo: Brigham Young University.

Feinberg, Joel. 1973. *Social Philosophy*. Englewood Cliffs, NJ: Prentice Hall.

Feinberg, Joel. 1989. On the Nature and Value of Rights. In *Philosophy of Human Rights*, ed. Morton E. Winston. Belmont, CA: Wadsworth.

Gewirth, Alan. 1996. *The Community of Rights*. Chicago: University of Chicago Press.

Glendon, Mary Ann. 1991. *Rights Talk: The Impoverishment of Political Discourse*. New York: Free Press.

Golding, Martin P. 1978. The Concept of Rights: A Historical Sketch. In *Bioethics and Human Rights*, ed. Elsie L. Bandman and Bertram Bandman, 44–50. Boston: Little, Brown and Company.

Harvey, Philip. 2002. Human Rights and Economic Policy Discourse: Taking Economic and Social Rights Seriously. *Columbia Human Rights Law Review* 33 (2): 363–471.

Hayden, Patrick. 2001. *The Philosophy of Human Rights*. St. Paul, MN: Paragon House.

Hennelly, Alfred, S. J. and Johan Langan, S. J., eds. 1982. *Human Rights in the Americas: The Struggle for Consensus*. Washington, DC: Georgetown University Press.

Henkin, Louis. 1981. Economic-Social Rights as "Rights": A United States Perspective. *Human Rights Law Journal* 2 (3–4).

Hollenbach, David. 1982. Global Human Rights: An Interpretation of the Contemporary Catholic Understanding. In *Human Rights in the Americas: The Struggle for Consensus*, ed. Alfred Hennelly and John Langan, 9–24. Washington, DC: Georgetown University Press.

Holmes, Stephen, and Cass R. Sunstein. 1999. *The Costs of Rights: Why Liberty Depends on Taxes*. New York: W. W. Norton.

International Covenant on Economic, Social, and Cultural Rights, *opened for signature* Dec. 16, 1966, G.A. Res. 2200A (XXI), 21 U.N. GAOR Supp. No. 16 at 49, U.N. Doc. A/6316 (1966), 993 U.N.T.S. 3.

Ishay, Micheline R. 1997. *The Human Rights Reader*. New York: Routledge.

Jencks, Chrisopher. 2005. What Happened to Welfare? *The New York Review of Books* 52, no. 20 (December 15): 76–86.

Nussbaum, Martha C. 2001. Capabilities and Human Rights. In *The Philosophy of Human Rights*, ed. Patrick Hayden, 212–40. St. Paul, MN: Paragon House.

Osiatyński, Wiktor. 1996. Social and Economic Rights in a New Constitution for Poland. In *Western Rights? A Post-Communist Application*, ed. Andraś Sajó, 233–69. Boston: Kluwer.

Osiatyński, Wiktor. 2000. Constitutionalism, Democracy, Constitutional Culture. In *Constitutional Cultures*, ed. Miroslaw Wyrzykowski, 151–8. Warsaw: Institute of Public Affairs.

Pigou, A. C. 1952. *The Economics of Welfare*. London: Macmillan.

Pollis, Adamantia. 2000. A New Universalism. In *Human Rights: New Perspectives, New Realities*, ed. Adamantia Pollis and Peter Schwab, 9–30. Bolder, CO: Lynne Rienner Publishers.

Sachs, Albie. 2005. The Judicial Enforcement of Socio-Economic Rights: The Grootboom Case. In *The Constitution in Private Relations: Expanding Constitutionalism*, ed. Andras Sajó and Renate Uitz, 79–97. Utrecht: Eleven.

Sen, Amartya Kumar. 2000. *Development as Freedom*. New York: Anchor Books.

Shue, Henry. 1980. *Basic Rights: Subsistence, Affluence, and U.S. Foreign Policy*. Princeton: Princeton University Press.

Sunstein, Cass R. 2004. *The Second Bill of Rights: FDR's Unfinished Revolution and Why We Need It More Than Ever*. New York: Basic Books.

Tesón, Fernando R. 2001. International Human Rights and Cultural Relativism. In *The Philosophy of Human Rights*, Patrick Hayden, 379–396. St. Paul, MN: Paragon House.

van Dijk, Pieter, and Godefridus J. H. van Hoof. 1990. *Theory and Practice of the European Convention on Human Rights*. Boston: Kluwer Law and Taxation.

Wieruszewski, Roman. 1998. The Evolution of the Socialist Concept of Human Rights. *SIM Newsletter* 1: 27–37.

4 Economic Rights in the Knowledge Economy: An Instrumental Justification

ALBINO BARRERA

I. JUSTIFYING ECONOMIC RIGHTS

This chapter argues that if one supports efficiency in the knowledge economy, one would also have to support economic rights. There is no consensus among scholars, philosophers, and policy makers on the justification, content, and strength of human rights. Even more intractable is the issue of whether or not economic rights exist at all. Trimiew (1997, 103–68) summarizes three strands of arguments against economic rights. First are the contentions that see an irreconcilable incompatibility between civil-political rights and economic rights. Economic rights give rise to positive obligations that may in fact infringe on the civil-political rights of others. After all, the satisfaction of economic rights entails rival consumption, because they require interpersonal transfers of real resources across economic agents. The second set of objections view the claims of economic rights as incomprehensible. For example, Cranston (1967) argues against economic rights because (a) they are culturally conditioned and therefore not truly universal, (b) they are not always of paramount ultimate value (as in the case of the oft-cited right to a paid vacation [article 24, UN Universal Declaration of Human Rights]), and (c) they are not practicable (as in the case of the right to full and gainful employment for all peoples). Finally, there are those who argue that economic rights only serve to worsen the condition they are meant to ameliorate because they may breed dependency and free-ridership.

Economic rights have been justified on the basis of both their intrinsic worth and their instrumental utility. Two examples of intrinsic-worth justifications are the natural-law approach to rights and religious traditions' call for respect for human dignity. John XXIII (1963) uses natural-law reasoning to argue for the existence of economic rights. Because human beings are corporeal, they require the use and consumption of material goods for their survival, basic health, and flourishing. Human nature itself requires that people have access to the fruits of the earth for their growth and development. There is an unavoidable economic dimension to human life, however one may define its purpose, because the use of material goods is integral to its continued existence. Economic rights, per se, come with human nature. An even stronger and more direct intrinsic justification of the existence of economic rights come from religious traditions. Take Christianity, for example. Central to its anthropology is the belief that the human person is created in the image and likeness of God and that the earth has been given by God, as Creator, to humans in order to satisfy their needs (Genesis 1:26–31). Human beings enjoy a dignity intrinsic to their personhood, and this dignity includes the right to access the fruits of the earth, a divine bequest that humans are to share among themselves with no one excluded. This has been called the principle of the universal destination of the goods of the earth (Pontifical Council for Justice and Peace 2004, 96–104).

Economic rights also can be justified on the basis of their utility. Three examples are Henry Shue's (1980) interdependence argument, Alan Gewirth's (1982) principle of generic consistency, and A. K. Sen's (1984) capabilities approach. Henry Shue (1980) notes that political and civil rights are widely accepted as intrinsic and central to human liberty. Shue argues that economic rights are necessary conditions if political and civil rights are to be actualized at all. Take the case of the poor. The freedoms of speech, movement, and religion are hollow and meaningless to them if they have to scrounge constantly for the basic necessities to keep body and soul alive. Civil and political liberties mean little to people who are constantly shadowed by death and disease. In fact, most would even be willing to forego such freedoms for the chance to stay alive. Thus, political and civil rights need economic entitlements if such liberties are to be actualized to begin with. For Shue, economic and political-civil rights, although distinct from each other, are inseparable. The latter claims work only if their concomitant economic requirements are satisfied. Economic rights are justified by "piggy-backing" them off political and civil rights' widespread appeal and acceptance (Trimiew 1997, 169–230). Shue's justification of economic rights is aptly called instrumental because he bases it on the interdependence of economic and political/civil rights. As Raz (1982, 112) notes, autonomy is genuine only to the extent that choices are not "dictated by personal needs." The more pressing these unmet needs, the less room there is for freedom.

Gewirth justifies economic rights on the basis of Kant's categorical imperative of acting in such a manner that the principle of one's action can be generalized for everyone else in the community without exception. Gewirth (1982, 40) argues (1) that people act for ends that they perceive as good and (2) that freedom and well-being are necessary conditions that enable people to act on their chosen ends. Since purposive human agency is possible only with freedom and well-being, (3) people will claim for themselves a right to freedom and well-being, and in so doing, (4) also grant the same right to other prospective purposive agents. Gewirth calls this the principle of generic consistency. If people want to have access to the necessary resources that enable them to act, then they must be willing to accord to others the same access that they want and need for themselves. Economic rights are instrumental for purposive action.

A. K. Sen (1984) is critical of utilitarianism, welfarism in particular, as a framework for normative economics. Human welfare should not be based on the satisfaction of individual preferences but should be based instead on the ability of people to act on their chosen goals in life. In other words, economic agents' "functionings and capabilities" are central to their capacity for action and, by extension, their enjoyment of freedom. Such capacity for a real freedom of action can only be acquired over time with the use and consumption of material resources. The necessary means to develop and enable such "functionings and capabilities" must be protected by rights.

Note that Shue's interdependency argument, Gewirth's principle of generic consistency, and Sen's capabilities approach to rights are all instrumental justifications of economic rights, based on the utility of these claims for achieving larger ends. In this chapter, I argue that another instrumental justification for economic rights can be made, this one based on the nature and requirements of the knowledge economy, and using neoclassical economic arguments to boot.

I make such an instrumental justification in two steps. First, I make the case for the importance of human needs satisfaction in the knowledge economy. Because human capital is at the heart of a "learning" economy, long-term productive efficiency is dependent on how well the community develops its human resources in the earlier rounds of economic activity. Human capital formation in the earlier periods of market activity will shape the degree to which the fullness of efficiency is attained down the road. Such human capital development, however, is dependent on the satisfaction of basic human needs. Second, I argue that because of market failures, such needs will not always be met. After all, unfettered market operations are better suited for allocating scarce resources to their most valued uses rather than distributing these according to human needs. Thus, extra-market mechanisms, such as economic rights, are needed to ensure that economic agents procure a minimum basket of goods and services that develop their skills and capacity to participate in the subsequent rounds of a knowledge economy that is ever more exacting in its human capital requirements.

II. WHY PRODUCTIVE EFFICIENCY MATTERS

Shue's (1980) web of civil and political rights, Gewirth's (1982) purposeful action, and Sen's (1984) "functionings and capabilities" provide strong foundational bases for an instrumental justification of economic rights, because these are goals that are valued by any reasonable person. I propose that the same can be said of productive efficiency as a goal, that is, being on the nation's production possibilities frontier and maximizing its full potential given its available resources. Despite their differences on a whole host of issues, both neoclassical and heterodox economists would agree that productive efficiency is a necessary condition for sustained long-term economic growth. Regardless of nations' preferences for their political systems, no economy can long endure the wasteful disposition of its resources, as it will bump up against the physical constraints of a finite earth. Thus, reasonable people value the proper stewardship of scarce personal and communal resources, even if only out of their self-interest and concern over their future provisioning.[1] If this is an accurate characterization of human concerns, then, I argue that any reasonable person in this new era inaugurated by the knowledge economy should also value economic rights, because they are foundational for productive efficiency.

The efficient use of a nation's scarce resources matters because (1) this maximizes the collective welfare and (2) is a necessary condition for the long-term viability of the community. Economic history provides abundant empirical evidence to support this claim. The implosion of the Soviet-style economies in 1989, in

---

[1] Thus note the universal appeal, among mainstream economists, of Robbins's (1932/1952) definition of economic activity as the allocation of scarce resources to their most valued uses.

contrast to the vibrancy of Western-style capitalism, is in large part a result of the productive efficiency of the latter. The breathtaking economic performance of China in the last twenty-five years, unparalleled in modern history, can be attributed to the reforms it adopted from 1979 onward – specifically more market-oriented, efficiency-enhancing polices. The move by many other nations toward a more market-friendly political economy, in the last half of the last century, reflects an appreciation for the central importance of economic efficiency (Yergin & Stanislaw 1998). The stark difference between nations that reaped the full benefits of liberalization (e.g., the newly industrialized nations such as the Asian Tigers) compared to the failed states in sub-Saharan Africa, which have even regressed in the last thirty years, is due largely to these nations' divergent abilities to use their natural and human resources productively (Dollar & Kraay 2001). Productive efficiency matters, not only in the textbook model of the perfectly competitive market, but in practice as well. Economic history and empirical evidence suggest that nations can ignore productive efficiency only at their own peril. The judicious and productive use of scarce resources, especially in the face of rival consumption of finite resources, is a pragmatic goal that reasonable people would want to have in their community.

III. INSTRUMENTAL JUSTIFICATION, PART 1: THE CASE FOR HUMAN NEEDS SATISFACTION

There are at least three reasons for why needs satisfaction should be the starting point for building productive efficiency, to wit:

1. Needs satisfaction is essential for human capital formation, the well-spring of value creation in the knowledge economy.
2. Needs satisfaction safeguards against permanent marginalization, due to the increasingly frequent and more severe adverse pecuniary externalities in the knowledge economy.
3. Needs satisfaction is an ex-ante, preemptive measure that is much cheaper than ex-post corrective action.

Note that I am using human needs satisfaction in a very broad sense to include not only the commonly acknowledged basic needs of food, clothing, shelter, and medical care but also an education that is broad enough to inculcate civic virtues. After all, there are moral preconditions for the smooth functioning of the market (Schultz 2001).[2] Each of the aforesaid three reasons is discussed in the following sections.[3]

---

[2] Let us take trust as an illustration of this moral precondition if the market is to function at all. The time of payment and the time of delivery are rarely coincident in most economic transactions. Thus, parties in an exchange will simply have to trust that others will keep their word and live up to their contractual obligations. The same thing can be said of employer-employee relationships. Employers cannot supervise their workers all the time in order to ensure that they are giving a full day's work for their pay. Beyond a certain point, market participants simply have to accept each other's commitments at face value.

[3] This instrumental justification of economic rights, based on their utility in attaining long-term productive efficiency in the knowledge economy, can be easily formalized using familiar neoclassical

A. Needs Satisfaction Is Necessary for Efficiency Because Human Capital Is the Source of Value Creation

Uncertainty is the bane of economic agents. Insufficient, incomplete, and erroneous information complicate market participants' optimizing exercise in finding the most favorable disposition of their resources. Thus, one would think that the better and relatively more complete information afforded by information-communication technologies (ICT) is a welcome boon. Unfortunately, this is not an unadulterated blessing. The technological breakthroughs in microelectronics have been wildly successful to the point of producing a literal flood of data. And herein lies the problem within such a promising opportunity.

The deluge of data provided by ICT encumbers market participants with the new, additional, threefold task of sifting, analyzing, and then using relevant data.[4] This entails having to go through an enormous amount of materials, separating relevant from irrelevant data, recognizing their varying degrees of importance and urgency for decision making, turning them into relevant and coherent information, and then analyzing and making sense of them for use in the next rounds of economic activity.

And as if this were not enough as a challenge, one must remember that this entire exercise will have to be done in a timely and competent fashion in view of the accelerated pace of economic life that has drastically reduced the window for decision making. Shapiro and Varian (1999, 8–9) note that the distinctive feature of the Information Economy is not the total volume of information available, but the revolutionary improvement in our ability to manipulate such information. This changes the nature of competition to one of making sense of information

---

tools. In particular, Becker's (1965) and Lancaster's (1966) household production model can be easily modified to incorporate the key role played by human capital.

$$Q = K f(x, t)$$

where:

Q = Beckerian-Lancasterian commodities (such as nutrition, learning, rest, fellowship, etc.)
K = human capital (reflected in skills, talents, aptitudes, etc.)
x = goods and services (such as food, clothing, books, etc.)
t = time expended in producing Beckerian-Lancasterian commodities

The higher the human capital (K), the more efficient is the household production function. Moreover, this human capital is endogenous, as it is a function of previous periods' consumption of Q. In other words, human capital is path dependent and needs to be developed. By extension, this model could easily be used to describe the national production function, in which case K stands for the social and collective human capital.

[4] Shapiro and Varian (1999, 8–9) dispute the claim that the Information Economy has led to an increase in the total amount of information available. Instead, it is immediate access to such information and the ability to work on them that are truly distinctive. I agree with Shapiro and Varian on the latter but not on the former claim. After all, one must remember that in our better ability to manipulate information for our own ends, we are in effect producing new information. Thus, an improvement in our ability to handle and analyze information brings in its wake an increase in the volume of new information, as we are constantly adding the fruits of our analysis to the existing body of knowledge. Thus, there is a self-feeding dynamic in which more data and better information-handling technologies lead to even more analysis and even more information produced for the next rounds of economic activity.

and acting on it before anybody else. Competitors have access to the same kind of data, and it is the agile and competent market participants, who are able to turn data quickly into usable information and knowledge and act on them, that will profit handsomely from the enormous rewards that the knowledge economy has made possible. The knowledge economy has essentially turned economic agency into a race against competitors in transforming data into usable information and actionable knowledge for the purpose of reaping rents.

As the Information Age seeps into ever more areas of the marketplace, and society for that matter, there will be an increased reliance on codifiable knowledge, as even more market participants become adept at using them and as more decisions are based on them. Thus, even the dynamics of market operations make information increasingly more significant as a source of wealth creation compared to earlier periods of economic history. However, even more important than codifiable knowledge is tacit knowledge.[5] Codifiable knowledge is useless if it cannot be employed to good effect. In fact, it even turns into an obstacle if it ends up unnecessarily using up scarce time and resources. It is tacit knowledge that holds the key to sifting through codifiable knowledge and recognizing what is relevant and what is not. It is tacit knowledge that assigns an order of importance in going through the deluge of data and information coming out of a wired, globalized economy. It is tacit knowledge that makes the necessary connections between various pieces of information and recognizes the profit opportunities they present. And, most important, it is tacit knowledge that provides the know-how in marshaling the necessary resources to act on such information and to reap gains for oneself or at least protect one's interests from impending harms.[6] Thus, Lundvall (2001, 276) notes a paradoxical turn of events in the Information Age. Even as the price of information has dropped sharply and even as microelectronics has greatly expanded our capacity to deal with information, contemporary market participants are confronted with more, not less, demanding requirements in the ICT-driven economy because of the increased complexity of the knowledge base and the much faster speed with which such knowledge has to be internalized. More than ever, tacit knowledge is getting to be even more important. Far from reducing the realm of tacit knowledge because of the greater ease and the lower cost of

---

[5] There are two types of knowledge: explicit (codified knowledge) and implicit (tacit knowledge). Lam (2000, 490) notes that these two types of knowledge can be distinguished from each other in terms of their codifiability, acquisition, and potential for aggregation. First, codifiable knowledge is that which can be completely recorded in written format; it can be readily reduced to a binary code and be easily stored, replicated, and transmitted in whatever media desired. Tacit knowledge, by contrast, pertains to all other kinds of learning that cannot be fully documented, as they are internal to the person. Examples of such kind of knowledge include competence in skills and technical proficiency that come with experience. Second, codified knowledge lends itself to complete appropriation via book learning, as it can be completely abstracted, documented, and then transmitted separate from a "knowing subject." Tacit knowledge, by contrast, can only be acquired through actual experience ("learning by doing") or through extensive interaction with the author-source of such knowledge.

[6] Cowan, David, and Foray (2000, 224–25, 227) note that codified and tacit knowledge are complementary. On the one hand, tacit knowledge is needed to make sense of and use codified knowledge. On the other hand, codified knowledge facilitates the acquisition of tacit knowledge by speeding up the process of learning. One can build on others' experience and avoid their mistakes to the extent that these have been recorded and analyzed as part of codified knowledge.

codifying knowledge, information and communication technologies have ended up expanding both the scope and role of implicit knowledge even further.

In addition to the contemporary dilemma of having to sift through and use a superfluity of data in a timely fashion while racing against the competition, there is yet another feature of economic life that highlights the pivotal importance of augmenting tacit knowledge. Market activity is by its nature a repeating "game" of endless rounds of economic exchange. Such endless iteration raises the challenge for tacit knowledge in two ways: successive rounds of economic activity will keep on raising the bar, and the ability to learn and adapt becomes an even more important element of tacit knowledge.

What makes the knowledge economy even more daunting is that not only does it use and require an enormous amount of codifiable and tacit knowledge for the current economic cycle, it also produces ever increasing amounts of new codifiable and tacit knowledge that will have to be incorporated in subsequent rounds of economic activity. In other words, later economic rounds will demand even more from market participants because of (1) the larger volume of data/information to sift through and analyze, (2) the ever shortening response time to entrepreneurial opportunities or threats given the accelerating pace of economic life, and (3) most important, the emergence of new or better competition that may now come equipped with improved tacit knowledge acquired from the earlier rounds of economic activity. In other words, besides facility in processing and using data, the knowledge economy also requires agility in learning. What makes tacit knowledge even more central in the knowledge economy is its ability to learn from mistakes (both its own and its competitors') and improve on its decision-making ability. Tacit knowledge is auto-correlated; it iterates and quickly learns from what worked or did not work in the earlier rounds of economic exchange. Tacit knowledge is essential in the extremely fluid and dynamic setting of what has sometimes been called the "learning" economy (Lundvall 1998). It is called a "learning" economy instead of the knowledge economy in order to stress unambiguously that what is critical in our postindustrial era is not so much the higher level of know-how required, as is the capacity to learn, adapt, and improve on the discoveries already revealed by earlier rounds of market activity. The insight advanced by T. W. Shultz (1975) over three decades ago captures the essence of what is at stake here: there is an enormous premium attached to the economic agent's ability to deal with sudden changes and disruptions to established routines.

The central and increasing importance of tacit knowledge in the knowledge or learning economy necessarily points to the pivotal role of its mirror image: human capital. It is human capital that animates tacit knowledge; the latter is embedded in the former. Consequently, a knowledge or learning economy that highlights the centrality of tacit knowledge ultimately points to the importance of human capital development. And the latter is possible only if market participants have the necessary material means to meet their needs. Information is power, but only if economic agents know how to use it in a timely and appropriate manner. Moreover, market participants should also be adept at learning and adapting. Tacit knowledge is essential for both tasks, and beyond tacit knowledge, well-developed human capital. Tacit knowledge is agent-specific. What the subject brings with him/her determines the scope and depth of the resulting tacit knowledge. For this reason, needs satisfaction that builds human capital is a constitutive element of productive efficiency in the knowledge economy.[7]

B. Needs Satisfaction Is Both a Direct and an Indirect Safeguard Against Adverse Pecuniary Externalities

Globalization is essentially a process of greater "marketization" in which ever more segments of society are driven by market rules. Moreover, it is primarily an economic phenomenon in which nations are increasingly tied together in cross-border exchanges of goods, services, and factors of production (such as labor and capital). However, there is a downside to such greater interdependence and heavier reliance on the market. It renders economic agents more vulnerable to unintended consequences.

Pecuniary externalities are intrinsic to market operations, and some of them can occasion particularly severe consequences. Workers who have lost their livelihoods overnight because of cheaper imports, offshore outsourcing, downsizing, or the transfer of manufacturing plants overseas are well aware of the havoc that international trade can wreak on personal lives. Market deepening and widening, ever stiffening competition, and the accelerating pace of economic life all compound this vexing problem of unpleasant spillover effects within the marketplace; these ripple effects come with ever increasing frequency, often occur so suddenly as to provide little time to prepare for a transition, and can be so severe in altering lifestyles and livelihoods.

The hyperdynamism of change in the knowledge economy may be outpacing our ability to adapt to and digest its pecuniary externalities. There is the danger of creating a new underclass of marginalized members of the community who are not able to adjust and adapt fast enough to keep up with the changes imposed by a rapidly evolving "learning" economy. The human person is at ever greater risk of getting left behind by the ever-ratcheting demands of the knowledge economy coupled with its unexpected, frequent, and often damaging changes wrought by the marketplace. This, I submit, is a second reason for why needs satisfaction is a constitutive element of long-term productive efficiency in the knowledge economy. If tacit knowledge is indeed the key to creating value and sustaining the knowledge economy, then needs satisfaction must include safeguards to ensure that market participants are not irreversibly marginalized by adverse pecuniary externalities and permanently unable to participate and contribute to economic life in a meaningful and productive manner. It is in the self-interest of the knowledge economy to husband its pool of human resources. After all, human capital is the source of wealth creation. Lundvall (1994, 34) describes the dangers well when he notes that, "[t]here is a growing risk that IT becomes an acronym for Intellectual Tribalism."

---

[7] One pattern that is readily observable in the literature on technological change is the importance of both social and human capital across all facets of technological innovation, from development to use to further development. Thus, as it is technical change that provides the knowledge economy with its potency and vibrancy, human capital is essentially the building block of this learning economy.

Adverse pecuniary externalities are an unavoidable part of market operations, and it remains for the knowledge economy to mitigate the damage that these inflict on its own foundations: human and social capital. It makes rational economic sense to ensure that needs satisfaction as a criterion of distributive justice includes the necessary provisions for market participants to recover from the unavoidable chance and contingencies of market operations and, in such recuperation, to be in a new position to continue putting in their share of sustaining the common economic life. It is in the self-interest of the economy to get valuable human resources back on stream in the economy as quickly as possible after they have been set back by negative pecuniary externalities. After all, the collective tacit knowledge is dependent on the quality of the pool of human capital from which it is drawn. The larger and the better the quality of such a pool, the larger is the synergy produced because knowledge creation is both auto-correlated and interdependent. People build not only on their own knowledge and experience but also on others' observable knowledge and experience.

C. Needs Satisfaction Is Prudent Ex-Ante Action Compared with More Expensive Ex-Post Correction

It is in the self-interest of market participants in the knowledge economy to be ahead of the curve in heading off damage to its human resources. Ex-ante planning and preemptive action are often much cheaper than ex-post correction and damage control. This is particularly true when speaking of human capital. Take the case of child labor and child malnutrition. In foregoing an education because of the need to supplement meager household incomes, children are condemned to a lifetime of illiteracy and poverty. Malnutrition at an early age often results in irreversible physical and mental disabilities. In both of these cases, the drain on society and its opportunity losses are enormous in view of the large foregone human capital that will not be available in future rounds of economic activity. These opportunity losses will be sizable in a knowledge economy characterized by increasing returns, a quicker tempo of economic life, and a path dependence in which those who have more will have even more in later rounds. All this is not even to mention that it is much better for people to be productive than to be dependent on the rest of the community for their needs.[8]

Child labor and child malnutrition are merely two cases that clearly emphasize the superiority and cost savings of ex-ante planning and action compared to ex-post correction and damage control in a knowledge economy. The same arguments can be made with regards to fighting tropical diseases, such as malaria and river blindness. In addition to the intrinsic value of good health, there is an additional instrumental argument that can be made for aggressively preventing tropical diseases in order to avoid the large economic losses from subsequent debility, morbidity, and mortality.

Lundvall (1998, 45–46) argues that the conventional response to social exclusion has been ex-post in which governments provide social safety nets, such as

---

[8] Of course, the strongest argument against child labor and child malnutrition is the intrinsic dignity of the human person.

unemployment insurance and other forms of transfers. He argues that such an approach will become increasingly difficult in the years ahead because of the greater numbers of people requiring assistance, the stiffening resistance of taxpayers to further fiscal impositions, and the chronic, rather than temporary, nature of the problem of social exclusion. Sizable income transfers will be untenable given the stricter monetary and fiscal regimes required by globalization (Lundvall 1998, 283). The push for a more market-oriented European Union (EU), away from its traditional social economy, is reflective of these competitive pressures (Blair 2005). There is much sense in what Lundvall and his colleague note in a later article:

> *Social and distributional policies* need to focus more strongly on the distribution and redistribution of learning capabilities. It becomes increasingly costly and difficult to redistribute welfare, *ex-post*, in a society with an uneven distribution of competence. (Lundvall & Archibugi 2001, 150; emphasis in original)

Besides the increasing difficulty and expense of "repair" policies to deal with the costs and negative effects of rapid change, Lundvall (2001, 283) also argues that a "market-led speed up of innovation" goes only so far in being effective in the short term, but not when it comes to laying the groundwork for the next techno-economic revolution. This requires deliberate effort and preparation, such as a national innovation policy. I am more optimistic than Lundvall in viewing the market as an incubator of the technological breakthrough of the next Kondratieff cycle. After all, one must remember that all the carrier inputs of the long-wave cycles we have had so far (textiles, coal, steam power, steel, electricity, oil) emerged spontaneously from within the market economy and not through a deliberate government policy of discovery. Having said this, I also believe that there is nothing wrong with a national policy of making the market even more effective in nurturing technological discovery and change by improving the key factors in invention and innovation: social and human capital. Of course, beyond a certain point, extra-market interventions can prove to be deleterious to the efficient functioning of the market and consequently hurt its innate capacity for discovery, as the Austrian school of economic thought holds (Kizner 1997). To my mind, a market-led technological discovery and intelligent extra-market innovation policies are not mutually exclusive. Within limits, the latter is nothing but the improvement of the preconditions underlying market operations.

In a knowledge economy, it becomes imperative to ensure a more even distribution of competence. In the first place, there is a self-reinforcing path dependence by the nature of the market. Such a dynamic is strengthened even further in the knowledge economy because of the auto-correlated nature of tacit knowledge and the roundabout manner by which it is accumulated. Those who have poor human capital to begin with will find it increasingly difficult to catch up with the fast rising cost of participating meaningfully in the marketplace; they will find themselves rapidly marginalized. Moreover, it is also very likely that relative inequality will worsen. Second, market deepening and widening in the postindustrial economy have produced enormous gains and much faster rounds of economic exchange. This means that the opportunity losses from having human resources marginalized from mainstream economic life will be much more substantial relative to a nonknowledge economy. It is much better to ensure people's continued participation in the market, according to their skills and potential contribution, instead of pursuing posterior damage control. The opportunity losses themselves represent resources that could have been used in ex-ante action to develop human capital. Ex-ante intervention pays for itself by avoiding even larger ex-post opportunity losses, in addition to the direct cost of ameliorative measures. In summary, it is in the self-interest of participants in the knowledge economy to ensure that human needs are satisfied as these are the building blocks for a vibrant pool of human capital that will effect productive efficiency in the long term. As will be argued in the next section, economic rights ensure the satisfaction of these human needs.

IV. INSTRUMENTAL JUSTIFICATION, PART 2: THE CASE FOR ECONOMIC RIGHTS

Should needs satisfaction be even considered as a separate distributive criterion in a knowledge economy, considering that it has become a necessary condition for productive efficiency? Should we not simply subsume needs satisfaction as a constitutive part of efficiency – as a criterion of distributive justice? After all, *homo oeconomicus* is rational; left on its own, the market will internalize the importance of human capital formation and consequently pursue a strategy of needs satisfaction in its optimizing calculations. If knowledge has indeed become the source of value creation, such a shift will be immediately reflected in the market's price signals, and economic actors will find it in their own self-interest to change their decisions accordingly. The market, after all, has a proven track record of agility and responsiveness to rapidly changing conditions. Despite the market's proven ability to compel economic agents to incorporate significant exogenous events in their decisions, I claim that needs satisfaction and its proximate goal of human capital formation will not necessarily be internalized by the market in its pursuit of productive efficiency, and will in fact require extra-market intervention.

There are at least three reasons for why needs satisfaction as a criterion of distributive justice, or as an economic goal, can be accomplished only with the assistance of extra-market intervention. In the first place, the market is driven by the formal and informal rules of a bounded rationality that has slowly emerged over time. *Homo oeconomicus* uses rules of thumb in making economic decisions. The superfluity of choices available is simply too overwhelming and beyond human computational capabilities (Simon 1976). This is not even to mention the time it would take to calculate the optimum set of means for every economic end pursued. These formal and informal rules of thumb are strengthened and develop further over time as economic agents observe them; moreover, they are embedded within market institutions themselves. Consequently, there is a self-reinforcing path dependence in market operations.

Even while these formal and informal rules of thumb evolve and are augmented or amended, the requisite change called for under the knowledge economy (needs satisfaction as a prerequisite of productive efficiency) is not marginal at all, but drastic, controversial, and even disruptive for certain market participants. One must not underestimate the enormity of the shift that must take place in subsuming needs satisfaction and its goal of human capital formation as a constitutive part of productive efficiency. This fifth Kondratieff cycle (ICT – information and communication technologies) is no ordinary techno-economic paradigm shift, because, unlike the first four long-wave cycles, our current Information Revolution transforms the very core of market operations. As a consequence, relative to the earlier four Kondratieff cycles, the techno-economic paradigm shift occasioned by ICT demands even more substantial changes in the human capital that economic agents bring with them to the marketplace.

Even as the market is a very responsive institution to changed conditions, incorporating human capital formation as a proximate means to attaining productive efficiency is nevertheless a major discontinuity from how the modern marketplace has been operating all along. The market is simply not configured to conflate the distributive and allocative dimensions of price. But the biggest hurdle is the lack of any natural or easy way of combining these two facets of the price mechanism in actual practice. The market is geared toward allocating scarce resources to their most valued uses through the price mechanism. *The modern economy, both in theory and in practice, operates purely on the basis of the allocative dimension of price in which the value of goods, services, and factors of production are set according to their last opportunity cost.* This dynamic has both beneficial and adverse ramifications. However, these pecuniary externalities are simply accepted as necessary, unavoidable, collateral effects of the market's primary task of putting resources to their best uses. Thus, both in theory and in practice, the unfettered market is not designed to ensure the satisfaction of everyone's needs, much less the development of their human capital. Incorporating the distributive dimension into the allocative function of price requires changes down at the level of every individual economic actor in the economy. This not a marginal change, and it will come about only if the market provides compelling incentives for economic agents to realize that paying attention to everybody's needs satisfaction and human capital formation in a knowledge economy eventually redounds to their own self-interest. What specific form these incentives ought to be, how they can spontaneously arise in a marketplace, and how to incorporate them in price signals – these are the key questions that must be answered if the requirements of the knowledge economy are to be internalized in a market that has traditionally operated exclusively with an allocative goal. And even if these incentives can indeed be provided in a concrete way to market participants (thereby avoiding the need for extra-market intervention altogether), there are still nonetheless two market failures – discussed later – that must be overcome.

A second reason for why the market will most likely not spontaneously include needs satisfaction in its allocative task is the problem of an intertemporal externality. Even if economic agents appreciated the central importance of human capital as a source of value creation in the knowledge economy, the market may still fail to provide for human capital formation or needs satisfaction as a regular part of its unfettered operations. The first part of this chapter argued that needs satisfaction is a necessary condition for long-term productive efficiency in the learning economy. Such a strategy of needs satisfaction will require both interpersonal transfers of resources and short- and medium-term welfare losses for those who will have to curtail their consumption or forego income in favor of economic agents who require further human capital formation, in order for the latter to be able to contribute productively in the knowledge economy. Unfortunately, there is a substantial time lag before such investments pay off. Economic agents who will be required to make such sacrificial interpersonal economic transfers may have a very high time preference, that is, a high discount rate. If their time horizon is indeed short, it is a rational decision on the part of economic agents not to effect such transfers, whether directly through gifts and grants or indirectly through taxes. Long-term productive efficiency will not be of interest or of concern to such economic actors. This is an intertemporal market failure in which the knowledge economy will be unable to reach its optimum point of productive efficiency in the long run, given the short time horizons of earlier market participants. Earlier generations may not be interested in intergenerational transfers. Extra-market intervention is needed to override the high discount rates set by economic agents in their calculations.

A third reason for why we ought not to expect the market to develop human capital on its own, as part of its normal operations, is the problem of the commons and the prisoners' dilemma. Even if we were to assume, for the sake of argument, that economic agents have a low discount rate, it may still not be in their self-interest to effect such interpersonal economic transfers. We still have to deal with yet another market failure. Even if rational economic agents were fully aware of the importance of developing the human capital of their fellow market participants for the sake of a bigger pie down the road in the next rounds of economic activities, there is nothing to prevent these economic agents from simply free-riding on the voluntary compliance of others. Such free-riders may simply leave it to their fellow market participants to effect, at the latter's own expense, such requisite transfers as they (the freeloaders) will still be able to reap the long-term benefits without having to make any sacrifices. After all, a knowledge economy that is productively efficient in the long term benefits everyone in the economy. This is akin to the prisoners' dilemma, in which the optimum solution is achieved only with a cooperative strategy that eschews self-interested behavior and that trusts there will be no cheating or free-riding on the part of anyone. These are unrealistic standards to expect of economic agents, especially in a complex, globalized economy of impersonal and anonymous economic transactions. Consequently, extra-market interventions may be required to override such collective-action problems and to ensure enforcement of requisite interpersonal transfers.

In summary, even under the most heroic assumption of rational economic agents, there is no guarantee that the knowledge-based market will spontaneously incorporate needs satisfaction as a constitutive element of productive efficiency in response to the distinctive requirements of a learning economy. There are formidable practical and conceptual problems, to wit: how to make price signals reflect the importance of human capital formation for long-term efficiency, how to broaden the short-term horizon of market participants, and how to get around the problem of free-ridership.[9] Unless we are able to resolve these problems, we have to rely on extra-market interventions to effect the human capital formation and its requisite strategy of needs satisfaction that are necessary for attaining

[9] Other possible hurdles to needs satisfaction include racism, sexism, corruption, extremely low initial levels of personal and social capital, market rules that are skewed in favor of the rich and the powerful, and the adverse effects of capital mobility. My thanks to the editors for this observation.

long-term productive efficiency in the knowledge economy. It is highly unlikely that the market will be able to do this on its own without some gentle nudging.

V. ECONOMIC RIGHTS AS A VENUE FOR NEEDS SATISFACTION

The market does not arise in a vacuum; institutional preconditions play a hugely important role in the smooth and proper functioning of the market. Moreover, the market has a self-reinforcing path dependence, and radical changes can only be effected via extra-market interventions. This paper has argued that part of the preconditions of the knowledge economy is the satisfaction of needs that are critical for human capital formation. Such needs satisfaction as a proximate goal (distributive dimension of price), however, is a radical departure from the usual end with which markets operate (allocative function of price).[10] Consequently, extra-market interventions are required to ensure the proper development of human capital as part of the knowledge economy. The market will not spontaneously adopt a dynamic of needs satisfaction on its own. Such extra-market intervention can be through private voluntary action, governmental policy, or a combination of both. Nongovernmental economic action is a very broad topic in itself, and in what follows, I will only examine some public measures that can be adopted in pursuit of a strategy of needs satisfaction. In particular, I examine an instrumental justification for economic rights.

Despite their attendant controversies and conceptual problems, economic rights hold the key to implementing a strategy of needs satisfaction. *One can say, in a very restricted sense, that as property rights are to the industrial economy, so are economic rights to the knowledge economy.* Property rights are an essential precondition if the market economy is to work at all. No exchange is possible if people do not have the right to give away what they are exchanging, nor is there an incentive to exchange if one cannot be assured that one can keep what one gets in return from that exchange. The importance of the existence and proper enforcement of property rights is clearly seen in the wide disparity in the vibrancy of the Western capitalist economies compared to the centralized, Soviet-style economies of the twentieth century. We are just at the dawn of the knowledge economy, and it is too early to be able to present empirical evidence of a like function and central role for economic rights.[11] However, the importance of human capital in the rise of the Asian Tigers and cubs, in the rapid industrialization of China, and in the emergence of Bangalore as a high-tech provider is well documented. Based on these preliminary results, one can infer the importance of a strategy of needs satisfaction

---

[10] Market price has a twofold dimension. In the first place, price signals alert economic agents to the requisite adjustments they must make in their decisions, in the face of changes in the marketplace. This is the allocative dimension of price; that is, the ability of price to put scarce resources to their most valued uses. Second, price also has a distributive dimension to it because it determines the incomes people get from their market activity. For example, factor input prices, such as wages and returns to capital, determine how the economic pie will be divided up between workers and owners of capital.

[11] The emergence of the personal computer in the 1980s and the rise of the Internet in the 1990s mark the age of information and communication technologies and, therefore, the dawn of the knowledge economy.

in building local human capital. Economic rights are one way of locking in such a strategy of needs satisfaction and human capital development.[12]

Critics are skeptical of economic rights because of their indeterminacies regarding their justification, content, and addressees. They point to the lack of clarity on why the needs of some translate into positive obligations that must be fulfilled by others (Trimiew 1997, 115–26). Moreover, even if we were to assume that there is a legitimate justification for the existence of economic rights, it is unclear what such rights entail, much less how their scope is to be determined. In addition, who are the addressees of these economic obligations?

This chapter's instrumental justification of needs satisfaction as a criterion of distributive justice in the knowledge economy partially dispels some of these uncertainties. Take the question of justification. Economic rights can be justified on the basis of (1) the pivotal contribution of needs satisfaction to long-term productive efficiency, and (2) the inability of the market to internalize such a necessary dynamic. Economic rights serve as a form of extra-market intervention to facilitate the community's internalization of needs satisfaction and human capital formation in its economic life. Moreover, as has already been observed, the content of the needs that must be satisfied becomes much easier to identify because of the instrumental justification we are using. Because we are justifying needs satisfaction on the basis of its utility in promoting long-term efficiency, goods and services that are essential for human capital formation become prime candidates for inclusion as economic rights. Finally, one also can easily identify addressees of such an instrumental justification of economic rights. Beneficiaries of the resulting efficiency (or at least the increment in the efficiency due to human capital formation) have an obligation to shoulder the cost of effecting such gains. One advantage of an instrumental justification of economic rights, compared to arguing from their intrinsic worth, is that it is relatively easier to be more concrete and particular in making claims since the focal point becomes the outcomes and utility afforded by these rights. Dispelling some of the indeterminacies of economic rights is a collateral benefit of this study.

Another collateral benefit of this study is in carrying A. K. Sen's position on "functionings and capabilities" a step further. To what end is it worth expending resources developing people's capabilities? Besides the "intrinsic" justification of such an exercise based on the inherent dignity of the human person, one can add an instrumental, proximate goal for A. K. Sen's approach. "Functionings and capabilities" take on added value because they are instrumental for ensuring the long-term viability and health of the knowledge economy.

VI. SUMMARY AND CONCLUSIONS

This chapter has articulated an instrumental justification for needs satisfaction as a criterion of distributive justice. Over and above its intrinsic value of preserving

---

[12] As I had mentioned, this is a very restricted analogy because property rights are essential for market operations. In contrast, a knowledge economy can still operate without economic rights, albeit below its full potential. Property rights are a must, while economic rights are critical only for ensuring the optimal performance of the knowledge economy.

human life and basic health, needs satisfaction has an instrumental utility in the manner by which it facilitates the attainment of long-term productive efficiency in the knowledge economy. Needs satisfaction has functional value for the following reasons: it builds the human capital that is critical for the acquisition of tacit knowledge; it provides safeguards against the greater and more frequent negative pecuniary externalities of globalization; and it preempts more costly ex-post ameliorative action. Knowledge has become the well-spring of value creation in the learning economy. Thus, the vibrancy of future growth in the knowledge economy is dependent on the quality of human capital, which in turn requires needs satisfaction in the earlier periods of economic activity. Needs satisfaction in the earlier rounds of economic life become building blocks in reaching efficiency in the later rounds.[13]

The aforementioned strategy of needs satisfaction requires extra-market intervention, such as economic rights, in order to get around the high discount rates of market participants and the free-ridership that stems from the problem of the commons and the prisoners' dilemma. Unfortunately, there has been much debate about whether or not economic rights exist.[14] Part of these disagreements revolves around the conceptual basis for economic rights. Economic rights have been justified based on their intrinsic value and on their instrumental utility. This chapter adds to the instrumental justification of economic rights, and it accomplishes this with the use of neoclassical economic arguments to make the case for the existence of such extra-market economic claims. Economic rights have practical value as means to the formation of human capital, which is essential to the long-term vibrancy of the knowledge economy. A truly efficient knowledge economy requires conflating the distributive and allocative roles of price together. The market will not do this on its own because of a variety of market failures: a self-reinforcing path dependence that is used to operating only on the basis of the allocative dimension of price, an inter-temporal externality in which economic actors have a short time horizon, and the problem of the commons and the prisoners' dilemma in which free-ridership is a superior strategy for individual market participants. Economic rights can be effective at rectifying these market failures; they provide de facto shadow prices for those goods and services in the basket of needs that are essential for human capital formation. Shue (1980) has provided an instrumental justification of economic rights in terms of their role in actualizing political and civil rights. This chapter, by contrast, presents an instrumental justification of economic rights from a different angle: a justification based on the utility of economic rights in laying the foundations for productive efficiency in the learning economy.

REFERENCES

Arora, Ashish, Andrea Fosfuri, and Alfonso Gambardella. 2002. *Markets for Technology: The Economics of Innovation and Corporate Strategy.* Cambridge, MA: MIT Press.
Becker, Gary. 1965. A Theory of the Allocation of Time. *Economic Journal* 75: 493–515.

---

[13] It is like an intertemporal smoothing of consumption for the entire community.
[14] This is in addition to the even more fundamental debate on whether or not human rights exist at all.

Blair, Tony. 2005. Speech to the European Parliament, June 23, 2005. http://www.fco.gov.uk/Files/kfile/UKEUPresidency2005_Sp_PM_EuropeanParliament_230605,0.pdf.

Cohendet, Patrick, and Pierre-Benoit Joly. 2001. The Production of Technological Knowledge: New Issues in a Learning Economy. In *The Globalizing Learning Economy*, ed. Danielle Archibugi and Bengt-Ake Lundval. New York: Oxford University Press.

Cowan, Robin, Paul David, and Dominique Foray. 2000. The Explicit Economics of Knowledge Codification and Tacitness. *Industrial and Corporate Change*, 9 (2): 211–53.

Cranston, Maurice. 1967. Human Rights, Real and Supposed. In *Political Theory and the Rights of Man*, ed. D. D. Raphael. London: Macmillan.

Dollar, David, and Awart Kraay. 2001. *Trade, Growth, and Poverty*. World Bank Globalization Policy Research Working Paper No. 2615. Washington DC: World Bank.

Dosi, Giovanni, Keith Pavitt, and Luc Soete. 1990. *The Economics of Technical Change and International Trade*. New York: New York University Press.

Gewirth, Alan. 1982. *Human Rights: Essays on Justification and Application*. Chicago: University of Chicago Press.

John XXIII. 1963. *Pacem in Terris*. Boston: Daughters of St. Paul.

Johnson, Bjorn, Edward Lorenz, and Bengt-Åke Lundvall. 2002. Why All This Fuss about Codified and Tacit Knowledge? *Industrial and Corporate Change* 11 (2): 245–62.

Kirzner, Israel. 1997. Entrepreneurial Discovery and the Competitive Market Process: An Austrian Approach. *Journal of Economic Literature* 35: 60–85.

Kuttner, Robert. 1997. *Everything for Sale: The Virtues and Limits of Markets*. New York: Alfred A. Knopf.

Lam, Alice. 2000. Tacit Knowledge, Organizational Learning and Societal Institutions: An Integrated Framework. *Organization Studies* 21 (3): 487–513.

Lancaster, Kelvin. 1966. A New Approach to Consumer Theory. *Journal of Political Economy* 74: 132–57.

Lundvall, Bengt-Åke. 1998. The Learning Economy: Challenges to Economic Theory and Policy. In *Institutions and Economic Change: New Perspectives on Markets, Firms and Technology*, ed. Klaus Nielsen and Bjorn Johnson. Cheltenham, UK, and Northampton, MA: Edward Elgar.

Lundvall, Bengt-Åke. 2001. Innovation Policy in the Globalizing Learning Economy. In *The Globalizing Learning Economy*, ed. Danielle Archibugi and Bengt-Åke Lundvall. New York: Oxford University Press.

Lundval, Bengt-Åke, and Daniele Archibugi. 2001. Introduction: Europe and the Learning Economy. In *The Globalizing Learning Economy*, ed. Danielle Archibugi and Bengt-Åke Lundvall. New York: Oxford University Press.

Pontifical Council for Peace and Justice. 2004. *Compendium of the Social Doctrine of the Church*. Vatican City: Libreria Editrice Vaticana.

Rawls, John. 1971. *A Theory of Justice*. Cambridge, MA: Belknap Press.

Raz, Joseph. 1982. Liberalism, Autonomy, and the Politics of Neutral Concern. In *Social and Political Philosophy*, ed. Peter French, Theodore Uehling, Jr. and Howard Wettstein. Minneapolis: University of Minnesota Press.

Roberts, Joanne. 2000. From Know-how to Show-how? Questioning the Role of Information and Communication Technologies in Knowledge Transfer. *Technology Analysis and Strategic Management* 12: 429–43.

Robbins, Lionel. 1932/1952. *An Essay on the Nature and Significance of Economic Science*. London: Macmillan.

Schultz, Theodore W. 1975. The Value of the Ability to Deal with Disequilibria. *Journal of Economic Literature* 13: 827–46.

Schultz, Walter. 2001. *The Moral Conditions of Economic Efficiency*. Cambridge: Cambridge University Press.

Schumpeter, Joseph. 1942. *Capitalism, Socialism and Democracy.* New York: Harper.

Sen, Amartya. 1984. Rights and Capabilities. In *Resources, Values and Development.* Cambridge, MA: Harvard University Press.

Shapiro, Carl, and Hal Varian. 1999. *Information Rules: A Strategic Guide to the Network Economy.* Boston: Harvard Business School Press.

Shue, Henry. 1980. *Basic Rights: Subsistence, Affluence, and U.S. Foreign Policy.* Princeton, NJ: Princeton University Press.

Simon, Herbert. 1976. From Substantive to Procedural Rationality. In *Method and Appraisal in Economics*, ed. S. Latsis. Cambridge: Cambridge University Press.

Solow, Robert. 1987. We'd Better Watch Out (Book Review). *New York Times*, July 12.

Trimiew, Darryl. 1997. *God Bless the Child That Got Its Own: The Economic Rights Debate.* Atlanta, GA: Scholars Press.

Triplett, Jack. 1999. The Solow Productivity Paradox: What Do Computers Do to Productivity? *Canadian Journal of Economics* 32: 309–34.

Von Hippel, Eric. 1994. "Sticky Information" and the Locus of Problem Solving: Implications for Innovation. *Management Science* 40: 429–39.

Yergin, Daniel, and Joseph Stanislaw, 1998. *The Commanding Heights: The Battle Between Government and the Marketplace That is Remaking the Modern World.* New York: Simon and Schuster.

5   "None So Poor That He Is Compelled to Sell Himself": Democracy, Subsistence, and Basic Income

MICHAEL GOODHART

Critics have long denigrated economic rights, viewing them as less coherent, less important, and less defensible than traditional civil and political rights. Despite their inclusion in the Universal Declaration of Human Rights (UDHR) and their articulation in the International Covenant on Economic, Social, and Cultural Rights (ICESCR), the critics insist that the content of economic rights, their nature, and their relationship with other rights remain inadequately theorized. Moreover, persistent philosophical doubts – including objections to the alleged "positive" character of economic rights, questions about the purported interdependence and indivisibility of human rights, worries about the specificity of the obligations arising in connection with economic rights, and fears about the illimitable character of those obligations – render economic rights conceptually wobbly and politically precarious. It is true that theorists of social justice generally eschew rights-based approaches, though activists and advocates increasingly adopt the language of human rights in making their demands. And whether we attribute skepticism toward economic rights as primarily ideological or sincerely conceptual, there is no debating that economic rights remain "in question" in a way civil and political rights do not. In an era of rapid and profound social and economic transformation, and in a political context in which human rights are emerging as the dominant transnational normative discourse, it is urgent that we revisit the conceptual foundations of economic rights: the lack of theoretically sound and politically persuasive arguments for economic rights jeopardizes efforts to build momentum for humane, sustainable, and democratic economic priorities.

Building on this intuition, this chapter provides a broad, democratic justification for human rights and fleshes out its implications for theorizing and implementing economic rights. The idea is to articulate and defend a justification for these rights that all those committed to democracy should have reason to find appealing and persuasive. The chapter begins with a brief survey of a way of thinking about democracy that emphasizes achieving freedom, equality, and independence for all. In this emancipatory tradition of democracy, human rights provide the vocabulary of democratization – the language of democratic empowerment. The second and third sections offer a contemporary reformulation of this idea, one I call *democracy as human rights* (DHR); I emphasize how economic rights figure in guaranteeing emancipation, focusing on the right to guaranteed subsistence. The next section shows how this account addresses the conceptual weaknesses and philosophical worries about economic rights surveyed earlier, stressing the interdependence and indivisibility of human rights and the obligations to which economic rights give rise. Section 5 advocates unconditional subsistence ("basic") income paid to all members of society as the most effective way to realize the right to guaranteed subsistence. Basic income, unlike the welfare state or right to work proposals, guarantees subsistence in a way consistent with emancipation and with other democratic human rights. The last section considers two common objections to basic income – its cost and political feasibility – arguing that neither compels abandoning support for basic income.

Throughout the chapter, I shall focus on the right to guaranteed subsistence rather than on a wider range of related social and economic rights. I want to clarify from the outset that the subsistence right achieved through basic income provides only one part, albeit an important one, of an effective social guarantee for all of the democratic human rights. Indeed, part of my purpose is to demonstrate the interdependence and indivisibility of human rights on the democratic account offered here. As subsistence rights have been the most contentious, the most uncertain theoretically, and the most difficult to implement, focusing on their justification, conceptualization, and implementation seems appropriate in light of my broader aims.

I

Modern democratic theory finds its distinctive form and principles in the theory of John Locke: "Men being ... by Nature, all free, equal and independent," Locke wrote, "no one can be put out of this Estate, and subjected to the Political Power of another, without his own *Consent*" (Locke 1960, II § 95). The simple premise of natural freedom and equality undermines justifications for natural authority and subjection: "the doctrine of natural individual freedom and equality was revolutionary precisely because it swept away, in one fell swoop, all the grounds through which the subordination of some individuals, groups or categories of people to others had been justified" (Pateman 1988, 39–40).

Curiously, Locke's theory ended up justifying the exclusion of many individuals, groups, and categories of people nonetheless; *independence* plays the central role in explaining this exclusion. By independence, Locke (1960, §§ 4, 54) apparently meant a state or condition in which one need not ask leave of any other in disposing of one's property – property crucially comprising, as always for Locke, all of one's rights. Everyone is naturally independent in this sense, but independence can be surrendered through consensual submission to the will of another – whether through marriage contracts ("to ... obey"), through contractually based condition of servitude (including traditional servant status and wage employment), through conquest (which establishes slavery on the basis of a default consent), or through a social contract.[1] Why would individuals possessing equal rights consent to subordination of this kind? According to Locke (1960, § 54), the answer lies in their natural inferiority: "though I have said ... *That all Men by Nature are*

---

[1] Political philosophers have been accustomed to focus only on the last of these four mechanisms, thereby losing sight of independence as a necessary requirement of citizenship in Locke's theory.

equal, I cannot be supposed to understand all sorts of *Equality*"; factors such as age, virtue, birth, alliance, benefit, and "excellency of parts and merit" create distinctions among individuals, along with sex and race. Natural "inferiors" consent to their own subjection because of these relative disadvantages, and their resulting dependence disqualifies them from membership of civil society, which comprises only free, equal, independent individuals.

Thus, Locke managed to have it both ways; everyone is naturally free, equal, and self-governing with respect to rights in the state of nature, but some individuals nonetheless contract into subordination because of their "natural" inferiorities. Independence, for Locke, is a status ultimately determined by natural distinctions; freedom and equality of rights for Locke only guarantee that subjection is consensual, not that it is eliminated (Goodhart 2005, ch. 3; Pateman 1988). It did not take long, however, for the excluded to seize on the universal promise of freedom and equality in rejecting the arguments from natural inferiority to political subjection. Theorists such as Paine and Wollstonecraft conceived democratization as the universalization of freedom, equality, and independence for all. In this view, independence became a critical concept with an *emancipatory* thrust, one aiming at an egalitarian state of independence for all.

A defining characteristic of emancipatory democracy is its adoption of natural or human rights as the language of democratic empowerment.[2] Thinkers in this tradition sought emancipation *through* rights, including rights to suffrage and to economic independence. From the seventeenth century, when Rainsborough (Sharp 1998, 103) insisted that "even the poorest he that is in England has a life to live as the greatest he," until the nineteenth, when feminists such as Elizabeth Cady Stanton and John Stuart Mill insisted on economic independence and the democratization of home life (Stanton 1875; Mill 1989), emancipatory theorists argued for democratization through extending human rights *to more people and to a wider set of social relations and institutions.* This emphasis on rights is distinctive in two respects: first, as theorists such as Paine and Wollstonecraft make abundantly clear, an egalitarian conception of rights has a dramatic leveling effect. Rights can exclude or empower; in the emancipatory tradition rights have an inclusive, and thus radical and empowering, thrust. Victims and opponents of exclusion recognized early on that the formal universality of rights could be used to attack the privileged conceptions of citizenship and independence established by contract theorists (Goodin, Pateman, & Pateman 1997). Thinkers in this tradition also realized that economic independence was a necessary condition of political emancipation, a connection clear in Paine's scheme for basic income and in Wollstonecraft's analysis of the corrupting effects of dependence on liberty. Indeed, feminists – for obvious reasons – understood with acuity that without an independent means of subsistence, moral and political freedom were impossible. Susan B. Anthony (1871, 139–40) quotes, improbably, Alexander Hamilton in this connection: "take away my right over my subsistence and you possess absolute power over my moral being."

---

[2] Calling these rights *human* rights might seem controversial, but calling them anything else misses what is distinctive about this tradition: namely, its emphasis on the universality of a broad range of rights, including social and economic rights. Just as we talk of liberals and liberalism in the seventeenth and eighteenth centuries, before the term was coined, it seems appropriate to talk of human rights in this instance.

Some have argued that thinkers such as Paine and Wollstonecraft should be considered radical liberals. On this view, Locke provides all of the necessary theoretical resources for achieving democracy: rights, freedom, equality, and independence (Ashcraft 1993; cf. Donnelly 1989, ch. 4). There is no question that these concepts figure centrally in liberalism, but liberalism's emphasis on property rights and privacy, and its general inattention to domination, mean that it captures only part of what the emancipatory theorists mean by freedom and independence; classical liberal theory has also historically had little sympathy for economic rights.[3] Others maintain that these thinkers should be understood within the republican tradition, which staunchly opposed domination. Such an understanding is anachronistic, however; even contemporary defenders of republicanism acknowledge that the classical republican conception of freedom could not be universalized, anchored as it was in notions of virtue, wealth and virility that made citizenship for servants or women inconceivable (e.g., Pettit 1997). It also was skeptical of rights, instead stressing a notion of public virtue that potentially licenses extensive state interference in individuals' lives in the name of the common good. Moreover, both liberals and classical republicans always regarded independence as a marker of citizenship rather than a political objective.[4]

To reiterate, the emancipatory tradition of theorizing about democratization emphasizes economic and political independence as inextricably intertwined and as central to an egalitarian notion of emancipation achieved through extending human rights to more people and more spheres of life. It thus combines theoretical elements often associated with liberalism and republicanism; in this emancipatory tradition – which comprises the Levellers, Rousseau, Paine, Wollstonecraft, Condorcet, the Chartists, Mill, and Stanton, among others – human rights enable democracy and emancipation for all.[5] Rather than shoehorn these theorists into the liberal or republican molds, I call them emancipatory democrats; doing so reminds us that "democracy is as much about opposition to the arbitrary exercise of power as it is about collective self-government," even though this oppositional aspect of democracy is not frequently mentioned in the academic literature (Shapiro 1999, 30). Calling these thinkers democrats also underscores their *egalitarian* understanding of emancipation; as Walzer (1983, xii) argues, "the experience of subordination – of personal subordination, above all – lies behind the vision of equality. . . . The aim of political egalitarianism is a society free from domination." In the following section, I outline a reinterpretation of democratic theory that aims to recapture and reformulate this emancipatory spirit.

II

The conception of democracy I call *democracy as human rights* (DHR) articulates a view of democratic human rights grounded in freedom, equality, and

---

[3] Liberal property rights are *political* rather than *economic* rights. Locke, for instance, articulates not a right to *own* property but, rather, a right *to use and dispose of* property without interference by government or concern for social claims.

[4] I stress *classical* republicans, as many contemporary proponents do see nondomination as a universal political ideal and recalibrate their theories accordingly.

[5] For a more extensive treatment of this tradition, see Goodhart (2005, ch. 6). Several of these thinkers advocated basic income schemes, a fact relevant and suggestive for the argument I shall offer later. For a history of such schemes, see Van Parijs (2004).

independence. DHR is a *political commitment to universal emancipation through securing the equal enjoyment of fundamental human rights for everyone.* By emancipation, I simply mean what the emancipatory democrats meant: a state of freedom, equality, and independence, of being subject neither to domination nor to unwarranted interference.[6] Understanding democracy substantively in these terms – as a project of emancipation – clarifies and specifies the democratic ideal. In calling DHR a political commitment, I acknowledge its account of emancipation through human rights to be a moral and social aim or aspiration (Donnelly 2003, 16ff.), and specifically, a democratic one. There is good reason to be optimistic about the persuasive power of such an account: around the world, no ideas have proven more attractive or more useful than democracy and human rights. Moreover, both ideas are universal in the sense identified by Sen (1999a) and Beitz (2001); namely, that they are ideas everyone might have reason to value. Recovering this emphasis on human rights as the language and instrument of emancipation revivifies democracy itself, which in its atrophied electoral and procedural forms can seem like a fairly moribund and uninspiring ideal.[7]

I have defended DHR at length elsewhere (Goodhart 2005); here I want to emphasize two aspects of the argument particularly relevant for understanding the justification it provides for economic rights. Before doing so, however, I should clarify that although the ensuing discussion does not emphasize responsive and representative politics, these remain crucial to DHR as a general conception of democracy. Its focus on fundamental rights *supplements* representative government; it is not meant to supplant it. Furthermore, DHR provides a different and more coherent justification for popular government than those typically offered, a point to which I return later.

The first point I want to make concerns what it means to secure a right. In brief, securing a right means providing social guarantees for its enjoyment. Shue argues that a social guarantee implies correlative duties associated with rights; as he puts it, "a right is ordinarily a justified demand that some other people make some arrangements so that one will still be able to enjoy the substance of the right even if – actually *especially* if – it is not within one's own power to arrange on one's own to enjoy the substance of the right" (Shue 1996, 16; cf. Vincent 1986). Some duties and obligations attach to specific individuals (or to people generally) while others are shared or collective responsibilities to be met through the design of proper social institutions. For a right to be secured, its actual enjoyment must be socially guaranteed against standard threats (Shue 1996, 13; Pogge 1992). This requirement entails that the rights in question must be generally recognized and understood, that standard threats to the rights must be identified and means of addressing them devised, and that those means must be incorporated into legal and social institutions that are adequately empowered actually to check the threats (they must be fully funded, must have the appropriate

---

[6] I shall use emancipation and nonsubjection interchangeably. Subordination establishes subjection when it entails restrictions on freedom or equality.

[7] Some version of this more robust ideal of democracy and human rights seems implicit in the work of many activists who view democracy and human rights as sides of a coin (see, e.g., Aung San Suu Kyi 1995).

jurisdiction, and so on). It is not enough that as it happens rights are not being violated at the moment (Shue 1996, 16). This institutional requirement for securing rights figures below in the comparison of basic income schemes with alternative programs.

The second aspect of DHR I want to address concerns *fundamental* rights. In DHR, fundamental rights are defined as all those rights necessary for emancipation. This is admittedly an act of definitional fiat. The definition is not *merely* stipulative, however, because it is possible to work out what emancipation requires. Doing so involves both analytic and experiential reasoning. Analytically, one can develop an account of which rights must be secure to prevent domination and unwarranted interference, to eliminate subjection (I sketch such an account later). This analytic description of fundamental rights must, however, be viewed as provisional and open-ended, because the political commitment animating DHR is a commitment to *achieving* emancipation for everyone. With respect to achievement, any analytic account of fundamental rights will be incomplete in at least two ways. First, it will almost certainly leave open the possibility that differently situated others – whose material, physical, emotional, or positional experience diverges from societal norms – will remain vulnerable to forms of subjection that the analytic accounts miss (see Young 1990a, 1990b). Second, analytic accounts are also likely to be incomplete in their comprehension of what is actually required to secure rights; again, situational differences will shape individuals' experiences and condition their capabilities, impacting the guarantees needed to secure enjoyment of their rights.[8] For these two reasons, analytic accounts of fundamental rights must be supplemented with experiential accounts, accounts articulating real instances in which subjection persists despite the enjoyment of fundamental rights as specified so far. New rights might be necessary, or new understandings of what counts as a standard threat and what is needed to counter such threats effectively. Indeed, changing social circumstances mean that what is necessary for emancipation will always be in flux. In this light it is clear that *any* account of rights will be necessarily provisional and open-ended; stipulating that fundamental rights are those that, together, constitute emancipation thus establishes a critical standard and creates a check against the exclusionary operation of biased accounts of rights.

A second respect in which rights in DHR are *fundamental* concerns what we might call, following Shue, their "basicness." A basic right is one whose secure enjoyment is a condition of the secure enjoyment of the other basic rights (Shue 1996, 16). When one such right is threatened, none is secure. To see this, consider how fundamental rights constitute emancipation: by protecting individuals from subjection, that is, from domination and unwarranted interference. When any of the fundamental rights is denied, the rights-holder is potentially subject to the arbitrary will or actions of another person, of the state, of a corporation, or of some other actor. "Potentially" is an important modifier here: the credible threat of interference coupled with the means (the lack of institutional impediments) to carry it out is, like the sword of Damocles, a form of domination. Thus, when

---

[8] Nussbaum (1997) and Sen (2001) show how a capabilities focus can clarify what elements of a right need to be secured.

one fundamental right is insecure, all are insecure. Some critics accuse Shue of circularity, alleging that unless there is at least one right whose "basicness" is known independently such an account cannot get off the ground. For Shue, the right to security is so widely recognized as fundamental that it provides an unproblematic, practical starting point. Whatever one makes of Shue's position, my account of fundamental rights is not vulnerable to this critique because in DHR fundamental rights are defined in relation to emancipation. That they are basic in Shue's sense is characteristic of fundamental rights in the way just described, but not definitive of them. Critics might object that the political commitment to emancipation is an inadequate grounding for an account of rights, but this is a very different charge from circularity – one that I address later.

A fully specified analytic account of fundamental rights would require lengthy exposition. For simplicity, I shall flesh out the idea of fundamental rights by outlining four broad "clusters" of rights that give the notion some substance.[9] Rights relating to *liberty and security* concern the physical safety and integrity of individuals, their freedom of activity, choice, and movement, and their right to noninterference in matters of personal or intimate concern. Rights concerning *fairness* entitle people to equal treatment before the law and in politics and society. These rights include guarantees concerning legal and criminal procedure (due process, adequate representation) and equal access to public benefits, services, and opportunities. *Civil and political* rights encompass rights and guarantees concerning one's social and political activities. These include freedoms of assembly, conscience, and expression, a right to choose one's own lifestyle, and rights to political participation. That the rights in each of these clusters should be fundamental in each of the above senses is clear. Each is necessary to prevent subjection, and the secure enjoyment of each is a necessary condition of secure enjoyment of all the others. If one's physical security is not guaranteed, intimidation, physical violence and involuntary restraint (including detention), and other means can be used to undermine rights like free expression and association. Without guarantees of fair legal procedures and equal access to public benefits, one's physical security and political rights can be similarly challenged. Political rights, including especially the rights to expression and suffrage, provide the means through which people can safeguard their rights and well-being; without such rights, there would be no institutionalized mechanism for ending abuse, corruption, and destructive policy pursued by the government (see Howard 1983).

The final cluster of rights is *social and economic* rights; because economic rights, and subsistence rights in particular, are my primary concern here, the remainder of the chapter focuses on them.[10]

---

[9] I borrow the term "clusters" from Held (1995), who uses it to denote bundles of rights associated with his seven sites of power in modern societies; for a classification similar to mine, see Beitz (2001). Nothing in the theory rides on the classification of any particular right or on the names assigned to the categories.

[10] I have elsewhere described these rights as rights to an *adequate standard of living*, including things such as "food, shelter, affordable access to health care, a living wage, a decent education, choice in family and relationship status, and rights to enjoy and participate in one's culture" (Goodhart 2005, 143). These rights were enumerated as exemplary; the analysis that follows is intended to revise, deepen, and extend this earlier treatment.

III

Which social and economic rights are fundamental in the dual sense described above? Two relatively uncontroversial ones are education and health care. The right to education is clearly fundamental in both of the senses invoked here. It is key to emancipation in that without it one can be easily deceived and manipulated by others, leaving one open to domination and unwarranted interference in fairly straightforward ways. Education is also basic, if for no other reason than that without an adequate education it is difficult to understand one's rights and to navigate the system of social and legal institutions available to protect and promote them. The right to health care is fundamental for emancipation in that its denial or removal endangers one's life and well-being. To limit (or threaten) a person's access to or quality of health care would be to subject that person to a particularly cruel and callous form of dependence. Without a social guarantee, those who control access to health care would enjoy dominance over applicants for it, and could easily oppress them. The right to health care is also basic. Ill health constitutes a direct mental or physical threat, much like a beating. The right to health care ensures that no one is left without recourse in the face of such threats. Although health cannot always be guaranteed, what can and must be ensured is that all members of society are enabled to maintain their health or address health problems through access to health care.[11] Preventative care, both individually through the medical system and generally through public health measures, can be an effective and efficient approach to this right. Without a guaranteed right to health care, ill health or its associated costs can quickly swamp the exercise of one's other rights.

Other social or economic rights that would qualify as fundamental include rights to join unions and to bargain collectively, to safe and dignified working conditions, to equal opportunity in employment and to equal pay for equivalent work. Whether such rights should be classified as social and economic rights, rights to fairness, or political rights is unclear, but it is also unimportant. The clusters are merely a shorthand for discussing fundamental rights; they do no conceptual work. Indeed, as these examples show, many rights function in a variety of ways to guarantee emancipation and secure other rights.

There is one further economic right that, although much more controversial, I shall argue qualifies as fundamental: the right to a guaranteed subsistence. The epigraph from Rousseau in the chapter's title makes clear why guaranteed subsistence should count as fundamental. In explicating that freedom and equality constitute the greatest good and the object of all systems of legislation, Rousseau argues that equality "must not be understood to mean that degrees of power and wealth should be absolutely the same, but that, as for power, it stop short of all violence and never be exercised except by virtue of rank and the laws, and that *as for wealth, no citizen be so very rich that he can buy another, and none so poor that he is compelled to sell himself*" (Rousseau 1997, 78 [my emphasis]). Rousseau's intuition here is frequently taken to be against too wide an inequality of wealth in society,

---

[11] For this reason, I emphasize a right to health *care* and not to *health*. The ICESCR's "highest attainable standard" of health criterion seems problematic for numerous reasons that I cannot elaborate on here.

and no doubt Rousseau sees vast disparities as problematic. Yet he also objects to extreme poverty on the grounds that it effectively obliges the poor individual to "sell himself," to enter into a dependent relationship with a wealthy one. Rousseau felt that such dependence undermined the social contract, because as a moral form of association establishing genuine freedom, the social contract can only comprise equals. It cannot include anyone dependent on another, for such unequal individuals cannot be truly free.[12] Hamilton recognizes something similar – as does Anthony – when he declares that a person who depends on another for his subsistence is subject to the latter's absolute power over his moral being.

Each of these thinkers negatively demonstrates how the right to subsistence facilitates emancipation: an individual lacking a guaranteed subsistence is dependent upon those who control her subsistence. As Wollstonecraft (1995, 67ff) saw, this lack of independence not only undercuts the dependent's rights but also inhibits the development of liberty and its associated virtues, rendering dependent persons servile and vicious. The discussion also suggests why a right to guaranteed subsistence is basic: when one depends on another for subsistence, the provider becomes a master. The dependent person dare not protest any abuse or mistreatment, because in doing so she jeopardizes her survival by risking the master's displeasure and the loss of subsistence. This dependency obtains whether the "master" is a lord, employer, husband, government, or social service agency. Thus, the *right* to guaranteed subsistence qualifies as a fundamental right in the senses described here. This general right comprises several component rights, including guarantees of adequate food, clothing, shelter, and an income sufficient to meet other basic needs.[13] I shall consider the right to guaranteed subsistence in detail below. Before doing so, however, I want to show how DHR's general account of economic rights addresses the concerns canvassed at the outset.

IV

Conceptually, DHR offers a clear and cogent account of the nature and content of economic rights. These rights are justified by their centrality to emancipation. In this respect they are identical to all of the other fundamental rights conceived by DHR: their content is determined by what is required to secure emancipation. This way of conceiving human rights has the distinct advantage of providing a single justification for a wide variety of rights, one based in the social and moral aims underpinning democracy's emancipatory commitment. One might, of course, reject this democratic commitment, but one might equally reject any of the other moral, social, or metaphysical justifications advanced for rights; human rights have no strong foundations in this sense (Donnelly 2003, 18ff). The standard of deductive proof is inapposite in discussions of moral concepts and should be abandoned; there is simply no need to "get beneath" human rights in this sense (Rorty 1993, 115–16). My aim is to provide better arguments for economic rights, arguments that appeal to the obvious attractions of human rights and that place them on firmer political ground.

---

[12] This explains why Rousseau excludes women from the social contract (see Goodhart 2005, ch. 3).

[13] Articles 6, 7, 9, and 11 of the ICESCR all contain provisions related to a guaranteed subsistence.

This is perhaps an appropriate place to address the common objection that democracy and human rights are, if not incompatible (indeed, the empirical evidence suggests otherwise), at least often in tension with one another (e.g., Donnelly 2003, 191ff; Freeman 2000; Zakaria 2003, 1997). Two responses are necessary to address this objection fully. The first concerns how we conceive democracy. On what Leader (1996) has in another context called an "oligarchic" conception of democracy, the majority possesses an inherent right to rule. On this conception, illiberal democracy is certainly a real danger, as the majority might exercise its oligarchic right tyrannically in violating the rights of minorities (whether ethnic, religious, or political). Yet this oligarchic conception of democracy, which follows from a certain simplistic and problematic notion of popular sovereignty, is indefensible if we take the freedom, equality, and independence of the person seriously. On the emancipatory view, the right to democratic representative government is among the fundamental rights. Seen this way, the supposed tension between democracy as a political method and human rights as a set of substantive guarantees is resolved through the recognition that the political method itself is only justified insofar as it conduces to the secure enjoyment of the other fundamental rights. Majority tyranny achieved through electoral mechanisms contradicts the premises that justify representative government in the first place.

A critic might reply that such theoretical demonstrations do nothing to prevent majority tyranny and illiberal democracy in practice, asserting that liberal constitutionalism is an essential check on democracy. Yet constitutions also get violated with regularity; no theory, no document, can guarantee adherence. What is required, whether one prefers the label "constitutionalism" to democracy or the other way round, are institutions to secure rights against standard social threats. Among such institutions must be a participatory and democratic political system, because, as Mill (1972, 275) put it, "the rights and interests of every or any person are only secure from being disregarded when the person interested is himself able, and habitually disposed, to stand up for them." Only a democratic political system provides the institutional guarantee for this ability to stand up for one's rights: "we have no reason to believe that it is possible to design non-participatory procedures that will guarantee that even basic rights are in substance respected" (Shue 1996, 84). These views are echoed by theorists in the emancipatory tradition who recognized the close connection between the right to suffrage and the protection of other rights. As described earlier, a democratic political system is a fundamental right in the senses that DHR requires – necessary for emancipation and for the secure enjoyment of other rights. It is hard to see why we should favor the democratic political method at all unless it is explained this way: it is neither more efficient nor more likely to result in wise or enlightened policy than other methods (Schumpeter 1942), and the modicum of control it affords to particular citizens cannot be seriously regarded, at least within modern nation-states, as relevant to individual autonomy (Dunn 1998; Pateman 1970).

DHR also addresses philosophical concerns about the "positive" character of economic rights, about the interdependence and indivisibility of human rights, and about the obligations associated with economic rights. It has been shown repeatedly that many rights have both positive and negative dimensions; scholars have so consistently disproven the notion that rights can be classified as strictly negative or positive (as requiring only restraint by government or individuals as opposed to requiring "positive" action or resource expenditures on the part of government or individuals) that extended consideration of this point barely seems worthwhile (Donnelly 2003, 30–31; Okin 1981, 238ff; Shue 1996, 35–64). Perhaps the positive/negative distinction only seemed significant historically because liberal justifications for rights rested on arguments for noninterference. "Positive" rights do require interference, but it is not *unwarranted* interference; proponents of nondomination, both republican and democratic, have long recognized some forms of interference as necessary and appropriate for securing freedom. That preventing domination often requires interference demonstrates why both liberal and republican accounts, taken alone, are insufficient to secure emancipation.

The interdependence and indivisibility of human rights is widely accepted among scholars and practitioners today, mainly as a shorthand refutation of the now-discredited "generations of rights" thesis (Nowak 2005, 37ff). Enshrined in the 1993 Vienna Declaration, interdependence and indivisibility recognize the equal standing and importance of all human rights. This view improves on the ill-conceived and ideologically tainted attempts to separate rights into artificial categories or generations. Only a few scholars, however, have explored the analytic bases of this claim (e.g., Howard 1983; Sen 2001; Shue 1996). DHR provides grounds for an understanding of human rights as genuinely indivisible and interdependent normatively and conceptually. The argument for emancipation demonstrates the *normative* indivisibility of fundamental rights: all are necessary for emancipation. The argument for fundamental rights as basic in Shue's sense demonstrates the *conceptual* interdependence of fundamental rights: unless all are secure, none is. DHR thus provides moral and analytic grounds to substantiate claims that human rights are indivisible and interdependent.

The final philosophical concern about economic rights has to do with the nature of the obligations they entail. It is sometimes claimed that who has the duties or obligations associated with economic rights is unclear (the specificity objection); it is also sometimes claimed that economic rights create never-ending redistributive duties or require too much from individuals (the illimitability objection). On a traditional interactional approach, general duties relating to human rights remain ambiguous (see Sen 2004). On the institutional approach embraced here, however, there is no such problem. Providing guarantees for economic rights is a collective obligation that falls on society at large and requires the careful design of institutions enabled effectively to guarantee those rights. Any modern welfare state demonstrates what it means to institutionalize a society's economic obligations. The specificity objection, then, can be dismissed.

The illimitability objection introduces problems concerning both the scope of the economic rights and duties (what they are and on whom they fall) and their magnitude (what and how much must be done) (Shue 1983, 602). DHR prescribes a clear and coherent account of what economic rights there are; as a universal conception, it conceives these rights as applying equally to everyone. DHR also clarifies the nature of the duties associated with these rights through its requirement of institutionalized social guarantees of rights. On whom the duties fall is a complex question whose answer lies beyond the scope of this essay. I will only state, without elaboration, that the universality of the democratic commitment entails that *ultimate* responsibility for guaranteeing all fundamental rights is universal, and thus global, even if states are assigned *primary* responsibility (see Goodin 1988; cf. Copp 1992, 241).

Specific questions regarding the magnitude of the duties corresponding with DHR's economic rights cannot be answered before working out the specific policy implications of those rights, a task I undertake in the next section of this chapter. More generally, however, DHR is immune to the most common criticism leveled against economic rights – namely, that they create endless or illimitable obligations in the quixotic pursuit of economic equality. DHR differs from many accounts of social justice in that its aim is not to reduce material inequality generally; rather, DHR envisions fundamental rights – including economic rights – as a floor, the minimum necessary to secure rights and emancipation (cf. Copp 1992). A democratic society might, as a matter of policy, institute rights and benefits beyond this floor, but such decisions are the stuff of politics. Here I want to stress that the three main economic rights indentified in DHR – education, health care, and the composite right to subsistence – can all be met without unending transfers. Most developed countries, and many developing ones, already provide their citizens with education and health care. Moreover, because DHR calls for guaranteed subsistence, not reduction or elimination of inequality, it does not introduce an unending burden of ongoing redistribution. Of course, many societies might lack the resources to meet these economic obligations; unlike Copp (1992), I do not see this inability as a sign that these rights are conditional, but rather as a trigger for wider (global) social obligations. I do not want to suggest that the obligations and expenditures entailed in meeting DHR's requirements are inconsequential; my point is only to show that, although substantial, these requirements do not involve the kind of ongoing, illimitable transfers that opponents of economic rights frequently invoke in decrying them.

Before turning to questions about how best to secure the right to subsistence, it might be valuable briefly to contrast DHR's emancipatory justification of fundamental rights with justifications that appeal to agency or autonomy (e.g., Gewirth 1982; Copp 1992). The rights generated by these different accounts are quite similar; the main differences lie in the nature of the justifications themselves. One important difference concerns the common objection that justifications based in agency and autonomy invite problems with respect to rights for those who lack full agency or full autonomy. Like any capability-based approach, agency- and autonomy-centered accounts seem to exclude those unable to act or choose in the specified manner. Also, such accounts historically have been susceptible to abuse whenever dominant groups *deny* the rationality or capacities of some categories of persons whose rights they violate. DHR avoids such exclusions, because it is grounded in a commitment to emancipation for all. On this view, an individual's rights are not conditioned upon ability. Similarly, agency- and autonomy-based accounts carry a good deal of metaphysical baggage; those who reject the underlying ontological claims will not be able to endorse the rights generated by these accounts. DHR's emancipation-related justification of rights appeals to an egalitarian political commitment, making it much more susceptible of the kind of overlapping consensus (substantive agreement based in diverse and multiple reasons) that seems crucial for any global account of human rights (Taylor 1999). This type of justification is more persuasive, more compelling, and more inclusive in a diverse and pluralistic world.

In the remainder of the chapter I shall focus on how best to realize the right to guaranteed subsistence. I do so for two reasons. First, proper specification is crucial in ensuring that the fundamental rights function as they are conceived – as interdependent and indivisible rights mutually constitutive of emancipation. Second, the lack of specificity of economic rights has contributed to their misunderstanding and misrepresentation; spelling out what the right to guaranteed subsistence requires should help to remedy this problem.

V

In this section, I shall argue that the fundamental right to guaranteed subsistence requires the social provision of a basic income. I shall make this argument by explaining in outline what a basic income scheme meeting the requirements of DHR would look like, and by showing why key features of this scheme – its unconditionality, its generality, and its security – are necessary features of any program adequately fulfilling the *fundamental* right to guaranteed subsistence justified above. Basic income is compatible with both a broader regime of social provision and with a guaranteed right to decent employment for all who seek it, but neither of these programs (nor both together) adequately secures the right to guaranteed subsistence; both leave individuals open to domination and unwarranted interference.

There are many basic income schemes circulating today, schemes that vary considerably in their justification and operation (Wispelaere & Stirton 2004). I understand basic income as a social transfer paid to all citizens on a regular (monthly) basis. Payments should be set at a level ensuring that all members of society can meet their subsistence needs (for food, clothing, shelter, and other basic needs).[14] The details of this scheme need not detain us here; various measures of subsistence exist, and we need only accept that it is in principle possible to set the value of the payments accurately enough so that they do in fact guarantee subsistence income for all.[15] Basic income is paid to all individuals regardless of their economic means, family or employment status, willingness to seek paid work or accept jobs, or any other status or requirement (Purdy 1994, 33; cf. van Parijs 1995). It is, however, consistent with "clawback" mechanisms, the use of tax structures to recapture the full amount of the payment from many individuals; how many is a question of how the tax scheme is designed in light of broader policy objectives and economic incentives. This caveat is important, because without such mechanisms basic income becomes extremely expensive; with clawbacks, however, the cost drops dramatically (van Parijs 2001, 22; Harvey 2004a, 18ff, 26).

---

[14] I have in mind something like the "decent minimum" proposed by Barry (1997) and Pateman (2003).

[15] Rights to education and health care cover many of the contingencies that might impact any individual's ability to satisfy subsistence needs through the basic income (this is especially true if we treat disability payments as part of the health care regime). Also recall that DHR provides a standard for assessing the adequacy of basic income: it must effectively guarantee the secure enjoyment of all fundamental rights.

Proposals for basic income schemes have a long intellectual history (see van Parijs 2004; also Dowling, Wispelaere & White 2003; Rothschild 2001). They have attracted attention recently amid heightened concerns about the viability of the welfare state and the feasibility of full employment in an age of resurgent economic neoliberalism (Offe 1992; Standing 1992; although on the full employment question, see Harvey 2004a, 2004b; Mitchell & Watts 2004; Noguera 2004). I depart from much of the literature on basic income in treating it primarily as a *democratic* program rather than one concerned with poverty reduction, with reconfiguring the right to work, or with other, principally economic, goals (cf. Pateman 2004, 2003). Calling basic income a *democratic* program emphasizes that its primary justification is its role in achieving and securing emancipation for all members of society. This justification figures centrally in the response to arguments, recently presented by several scholars, that basic income provides only a poor or partial substitute for the right to work (Harvey 2004a, 2004b; Mitchell & Watts 2004). It is hardly surprising that basic income does less well than a right to work in satisfying the right to work. The goal of basic income, however, is not to guarantee the right to work; it is to guarantee the right to *subsistence*. Indeed, if we consider the rationale behind the right to work articulated in the ICESCR, it is clearly to provide an adequate standard of living for all.[16] For reasons clarified in the ensuing discussions, the right to work manifestly fails to provide a secure guarantee of an adequate standard of living (or what I am calling subsistence) and to the extent that it is successful that success comes at the expense of other aspects of emancipation.

Three aspects of basic income programs prove crucial in satisfying the requirements of a fundamental right. The first is their *unconditionality*. Because basic income is not contingent on willingness to work or on conformity with any behavioral or lifestyle constraints, it provides three important freedoms that other social welfare programs, including traditional welfare states and the right to work, cannot. The first is the freedom *from* employment. Given the long and problematic association between employment, masculinity, and citizenship and between marriage and the subjection of women, breaking this association is important for ensuring women's equal emancipation (Pateman 2004; Alstott 2001; cf. Mill 1989). Moreover, the economic sector itself is highly undemocratic, both in its ethos and in its organization. Domination is commonplace – for instance, through threats of termination or layoffs. Basic income "allows individuals more easily to refuse to enter or to leave relationships that violate individual self-government, or that involve unsafe, unhealthy, or demeaning conditions" (Pateman 2004, 96), whether those relationships are personal or in the paid economic sector. A right to subsistence

---

[16] Critics might object that because the right to work is enshrined in the UDHR and the ICESCR, neglecting it undermines any claim to have provided a complete or satisfying account of economic rights. While recognizing the importance of these documents and the consensus they represent, I would note that they provide little justification of the rights they enumerate and little insight into how best to conceptualize human rights. This statement is not a criticism: the UDHR and the covenants were not intended as philosophical treatments of rights. Because the question at issue here is precisely to address the persistent *problems* with economic rights as presently conceived, it would be counterproductive to treat these formulations as sacrosanct. The guaranteed right to subsistence, I maintain, captures the spirit of the right to work enumerated in these documents, but improves upon its formulation and implementation.

tied to employment obviously cannot provide many of these important freedoms, as it only amplifies the worker's dependence on paid employment. Indeed, unless the right to work included unconditional unemployment benefits for those unable or unwilling to work in the jobs available, it would not guarantee subsistence at all; separate income support schemes would be required (Harvey 2004b, 10). Traditional welfare states, insofar as they include "workfare" requirements, similarly fail to break the coercive link between employment and full enjoyment of one's rights.[17]

A second fundamental characteristic of basic income is its *generality*. It is paid to everyone, helping to eliminate the stigma currently associated with receipt of social welfare benefits, most importantly by breaking the relationship between work and freedom (cf. Dore 2001, 83). Basic income would liberate everyone – not only those in paid employment – from dependence, a radical departure in a wage-based society too inclined to confuse freedom with consumption and employment with independence and moral rectitude. Eliminating the stigma that attaches to receipt of welfare payments – whether in the form of the dole or of government make-work – is the only way to secure for all individuals the equal public standing that democracy requires. In conjunction with the unconditionality of benefits, basic income's generality would also greatly reduce the coercion and domination exercised *through* the provision of social benefits (Handler 2004, 79–86, 199–208). Among the antidemocratic effects of existing social welfare regimes are that the behavior of "clients" is tightly monitored and controlled, and that the receipt of benefits often entails significant burdens in the way of reporting, appearances before caseworkers or administrative judges, and the like. These requirements often demean recipients, subjecting them to domination by agents of the state on whom they depend for their subsistence (Fitzpatrick 2000, 166). Such requirements also make the provision of benefits more costly and less effective (in terms of successfully targeting those who need assistance) (Goodin 1992). Similarly, right to work programs would not free individuals from dependence on their employers and would leave them open to domination by bureaucrats administering whatever backup schemes might be in place for those who cannot find (or who reject) work on the terms made available by the state.

Finally, because basic income is paid serially and stretches across an individual's entire lifetime, it provides *security* that other schemes for guaranteeing subsistence lack.[18] Basic income cannot be squandered or forfeited; there is no risk of exhausting one's eligibility, or of losing one's job, or of failing to meet the changing requirements prescribed by bureaucracies or politicians. Basic income thus satisfies the fundamental right to guaranteed subsistence in a way that no program with work or other eligibility criteria can – institutionalizing an effective, dependable guarantee of economic independence for everyone. This security provides a

---

[17] Harvey (2004a, 28ff) notes that much of the conflict surrounding program eligibility takes place against the backdrop of a world where full-employment has not been realized; the unavailability of work for all who want it makes such debates particularly sharp. But presumably the implication of Harvey's argument in a full-employment world would be consensus on the *ineligibility* for benefits of those who refused work for whatever reason. This demonstrates the importance, from a democratic perspective, of an unconditional guarantee of subsistence.

[18] It compares favorably on this score with proposals for citizens' grants (cf. Ackerman & Alstott 1999).

considerable measure of freedom to individuals reckoning their life paths in light of opportunities and threats that might arise in connection with a range of social, economic, or political risks encountered in the course of a lifetime. Consider several instances in which the security of basic income might enhance someone's freedom considerably: in a decision to leave an abusive relationship; to leave unsatisfying or undignified work to launch an independent business, pursue further education, or devote oneself to poetry; or, to run for political office. In each case, basic income enables freedom in ways that other programs cannot. Moreover, it does so in a way that is compatible with and facilitates the secure guarantee of the other basic rights. The unconditionality, generality, and security of basic income rules out opportunities for domination and oppression in its implementation. As these examples make clear, those who understand human rights as rights of agency and autonomy should find basic income schemes attractive as well.

As Harvey has argued, there is no need for advocates of basic income and the right to work to be antagonists; both argue, on parallel tracks, for programs that would enhance the dignity and well-being of all members of society (Harvey 2004b). There is also no need for advocates of basic income to deny the considerable benefits of employment or the importance of a fair opportunity for everyone to work (cf. Harvey 2004b, 38, 26).[19] Indeed, the availability of decent work for everyone who wants it is a goal shared by many advocates of basic income (e.g., van Parijs 1995; Standing 1992). Advocates of basic income and the right to work often differ on the *feasibility* of creating decent work for everyone. The former tend to believe that only by reducing the number of job-seekers, a goal they claim basic income facilitates, can full employment be achieved.[20] Proponents of the right to work, by contrast, see no practical difficulty (as opposed to political ones) in providing jobs for all and maintain that reducing the number of job-seekers will not translate into jobs for all who want them. I shall not address the difficult economic questions involved in adjudicating this debate, mainly because it is clear on the democratic justification advanced here that *even if* decent work were available for all who wanted it, basic income would still be required to satisfy the fundamental right to guaranteed subsistence. Advocating basic income does not entail denying the utility and desirability of right to work schemes or of other forms of social provision, such as job training or disability benefits. It does entail insisting, however, that only basic income satisfies the fundamental economic right to a guaranteed subsistence that democracy demands.

VI

In lieu of a formal conclusion, I want to address two common objections to basic income schemes (and to ambitious social schemes generally): cost and political

---

[19] We must be wary, however, in treating claims about links between unemployment and ill health or crime as claims against BI, for two reasons. First, these claims usually refer to *involuntary* unemployment; second, poverty is often an intervening variable in cases of involuntary unemployment, one that would be eliminated if a basic income scheme were in place.

[20] It does so, they maintain, in two ways: by enticing some individuals to leave the paid workforce, freeing jobs for others, and by creating possibilities for low-wage but otherwise attractive work (see Van Parijs 1995).

feasibility. It is frequently objected that basic income would impose massive costs on the economy, costs that would destroy competitiveness and undermine productivity. It is true that financing basic income would require a significant *reallocation* of social resources, yet it is far from clear that such a shift would have the devastating impact many suppose. It is worth recalling in this connection that the negative income tax – the program most resembling basic income tax in its design and cost (see van Parijs 2001, 10ff, 1995; Barry 1996) – was advocated by Milton Friedman and endorsed by Richard Nixon – figures hardly known as fiscally reckless. It should be emphasized that financing basic income would require the *reallocation* of social resources. Given the amounts spent in rich and developing countries alike on warfare and the armaments of warfare, it is hard to argue that societies lack the resources to finance spending programs deemed necessary for security; that the type of security delivered by basic income is economic rather than military is a political, not an economic, distinction, one to which I shall return shortly. The macroeconomic effects of basic income will also vary depending on how it is financed; although increased income and estate taxes are often mentioned, consideration should also be given to the taxation of social bads – pollution, the production of solid waste, the consumption of carbon-based fuels – as mechanisms for generating socially-responsible welfare (cf. Barry 1998, 155).[21] Globally, mechanisms such as a Tobin tax or Global Resource Dividend should be considered as an additional source of potential revenue (see Round 2000; Mendez 1997; Overseas Development Institute 1996; Pogge 2001).[22]

Much ink has been spilled debating the effects of basic income on labor force participation, on the lowest-wage jobs, and on overall social productivity as well as in weighing the possible savings in reduced administrative costs, elimination of redundant programs, and so forth. Rather than engage these arguments directly, however, I want instead to raise an objection to cost *as an objection* to basic income or other schemes for guaranteeing economic rights. Such objections give too easy a pass to the existing economic order. The social costs of systemic failures such as high levels of poverty, structural unemployment, and an ecologically unsustainable mode of production, combined with incentives for economic enterprises to inflict the negative externalities of poverty, unemployment, and environmental degradation on society at large, mean that the current system is a great deal more expensive than is typically recognized. To object to basic income because of its costs, in light of such facts and of present expenditures on war and on corporate welfare, is like the pot calling the kettle black. In addition, the democratic costs of economic dependence are rarely considered. Basic income would surely be expensive, but the relevant question is how the magnitude of those expenses and the benefits associated with them would compare with the costs and benefits of the current order. Among basic income's benefits must be counted the secure guarantee of subsistence for all in a way compatible with the enjoyment of other fundamental human rights – a goal current systems, European- as well as American-style, have failed

---

[21] As Alstott (2001) notes, although such taxes might normally appear regressive, this problem would be mitigated if revenues were dedicated to a progressively redistributive program such as BI.

[22] Because I have not addressed the question of which social units should be responsible for delivering basic income, I shall avoid specific recommendations.

to meet (see Handler 2004). If we are truly committed to freedom, equality, and independence for all, basic income looks like a smart – indeed, an unavoidable – investment.

The postwar consensus on social security in the Western world has been showing fissiparous tendencies, as pressures brought on by global economic competition, populist tax revolt, and changing patterns of migration have challenged the solidarity on which such schemes are predicated. In the developing world, neoliberal programs for structural adjustment have all too often meant that public-sector spending directed toward satisfying economic rights has been sacrificed at the altar of fiscal discipline. That is not to say that there is no support for social security in the West, or that structural reform is either unnecessary or uniformly unsuccessful; it is rather to point out that the main challenges to realizing economic rights are, as they have always been, political rather than economic. It is instructive in this light to review Paine's (1999) calculations on the cost of his proposed income supplements.

The political challenges are, however, quite daunting. Skeptics will quickly point to the numerous obstacles confronting basic incomes schemes (or any other ambitious social schemes), among which we must count a widespread aversion to taxation, and a neoliberal economic orthodoxy hostile to social spending and adept at exploiting economic insecurity as a disciplinary tool. How, they might reasonably ask, can it even be worth talking about basic income in such a political context? The answer is that although basic income seems utopian in *this* political context, political contexts do change – sometimes quite dramatically. They do so in part because political arguments help to change them; advocates of economic rights thus have a responsibility to develop and refine arguments that resolve the long-standing conceptual and philosophical worries about economic rights and to provide simple, coherent, and appealing visions of their benefits and attractions. I have tried in this chapter to show that there is a way of thinking about democracy and human rights – one dating back centuries – that envisions them as two sides of the coin of emancipation. In reformulating this tradition in contemporary terms, I have suggested that a coherent justification for and account of fundamental human rights can give substance to our intuitions about and commitments to freedom, equality, and independence for all. I have argued that a guaranteed subsistence – institutionalized in the form of a basic income – is an integral part of that democratic commitment.

Philippe van Parijs (2001, 124) insists that "even in the seemingly most hopeless situations, it is part of some people's job to keep exploring and advocating the politically impossible." In politics, he might add, the impossible becomes possible with surprising frequency and startling quickness. So we advocates of a right to a guaranteed subsistence have a job to do: to prepare for and bring about the day when this impossibility becomes real.

REFERENCES

Ackerman, Bruce, and Anne Alstott. 1999. *The Stakeholder Society*. New Haven, CT: Yale University Press.

Alstott, Anne. 2001. Good for Women. In *What's Wrong with a Free Lunch?*, ed. J. Cohen and J. Rogers. Boston: Beacon Press.

Anthony, Susan B. 1992. Suffrage and the Working Woman. Home Life. In *The Elizabeth Cady Stanton – Susan B. Anthony Reader: Correspondence, Writings, Speeches*, ed. E. C. DuBois. Boston: Northeastern University Press.

Ashcraft, Richard. 1993. Liberal Political Theory and Working-Class Radicalism in Nineteenth-Century England. *Political Theory* 21 (2): 249–72.

Aung San Suu Kyi. 1995. *Freedom from Fear and Other Writings*, revised ed. Ed. M. Aris. New York: Penguin Books.

Barry, Brian. 1996. Real Freedom and Basic Income. *Journal of Political Philosophy* 4 (3): 242–76.

Barry, Brian. 1997. The Attractions of Basic Income. In *Equality*, ed. J. Franklin. London: Institute for Public Policy Research.

Barry, Brian. 1998. International Society from a Cosmopolitan Perspective. In *International Society: Diverse Ethical Perspectives*, ed. D. R. Mapel and T. Nardin. Princeton: Princeton University Press.

Beitz, Charles R. 2001. Human Rights as a Common Concern. *American Political Science Review* 95 (2): 269–82.

Copp, David. 1992. The Right to an Adequate Standard of Living: Justice, Autonomy, and the Basic Needs. In *Economic Rights*, ed. E. F. Paul, F. D. Miller Jr., and J. Paul. Cambridge: Cambridge University Press.

Donnelly, Jack. 1989. *Universal Human Rights in Theory and Practice*. Ithaca, NY: Cornell Univ. Press.

Donnelly, Jack. 2003. *Universal Human Rights in Theory and Practice*, 2nd ed. Ithaca, NY: Cornell University Press.

Dore, Ronald. 2001. Dignity and Deprivation. In *What's Wrong with a Free Lunch?*, ed. J. Cohen and J. Rogers. Boston: Beacon Press.

Dowling, Keith, Jurgen de Wispelaere, and Stuart White. 2003. Stakeholding – a New Paradigm in Social Policy. In *The Ethics of Stakeholding*, ed. K. Dowling, J. de Wispelaere, and S. White. New York: Palgrave.

Dunn, John. 1998. Democracy, Globalization, and Human Interests. In *International Conference Democracy, Community, and Social Justice in an Era of Globalization*. University of Denver. [copy on file with author]

Fitzpatrick, Tony. 2000. *Freedom and Security*. New York: Palgrave.

Freeman, Michael. 2000. The Perils of Democratization: Nationalism, Markets, and Human Rights. *Human Rights Review* 2 (1): 33–51.

Gewirth, Alan. 1982. *Human Rights: Essays on Justification and Applications*. Chicago: University of Chicago Press.

Goodhart, Michael. 2005. *Democracy as Human Rights: Freedom and Equality in the Age of Globalization*. New York: Routledge.

Goodin, Robert E. 1988. What is So Special about Our Fellow Countrymen? *Ethics* 98 (4): 663–86.

Goodin, Robert E. 1992. Towards a Minimally Presumptuous Social Welfare Policy. In *Arguing for Basic Income: Ethical Foundations for a Radical Reform*, ed. P. van Parijs. London: Verso.

Goodin, Robert E., Carole Pateman, and Roy Pateman. 1997. Simian Sovereignty. *Political Theory* 25 (6): 821–49.

Handler, Joel F. 2004. *Social Citizenship and Workfare in the United States and Western Europe: the Paradox of Inclusion*. Cambridge: Cambridge University Press.

Harvey, Philip L. 2004a. *Income, Work and Freedom*. Berkeley Electronic Press Legal Repository. Available at: http://law.bepress.com/expresso/eps/413/.

Harvey, Philip L. 2004b. The Right to Work and Basic Income Guarantees: Competing or Complementary Goals? *Rutgers Journal of Law and Urban Policy* 2 (1): 1–48.

Held, David. 1995. *Democracy and the Global Order: From the Modern State to Cosmopolitan Governance*. Stanford: Stanford University Press.

Howard, Rhoda E. 1983. The Full-Belly Thesis: Should Economic Rights Take Priority Over Civil and Political Rights? Evidence from Sub-Saharan Africa. *Human Rights Quarterly* 5 (4): 467–90.

Leader, Sheldon. 1996. Three Faces of Toleration in a Democracy. *The Journal of Political Philosophy* 4 (1): 45–67.

Locke, John. 1960. *Two Treatises of Government*. Ed. P. Laslett. Cambridge: Cambridge University Press.

Mendez, Ruben P. 1997. Financing the United Nations and the International Public Sector: Problems and Reform. *Global Governance* 3 (3): 283–310.

Mill, John Stuart. 1972. Considerations on Representative Government. In *Utilitarianism, On Liberty, and Considerations on Representative Government*, ed. H. B. Acton. Cambridge: Cambridge University Press.

Mill, John Stuart. 1989. The Subjection of Women. In *On Liberty and Other Writings*, ed. S. Collini. Cambridge: Cambridge University Press.

Mitchell, William, and Martin Watts. 2004. A Comparison of the Macroeconomic Consequences of Basic Income and Job Guarantee Schemes. *Rutgers Journal of Law & Urban Policy* 2 (1): 64–90.

Noguera, José Antonio. 2004. Citizens or Workers? Basic Income vs. Welfare-to-Work Policies. In *10th Conference of the Basic Income European Network*. 19–20 September, Barcelona.

Nowak, Manfred. 2005. Indivisibility. In *The Essentials of Human Rights*, ed. R. K. M. Smith and C. van den Anker. London: Hodder Arnold.

Nussbaum, Martha C. 1997. Capabilities and Human Rights. *Fordham Law Review* 66 (2): 273–300.

Offe, Claus. 1992. A Non-Productive Design for Social Policies. In *Arguing for Basic Income: Ethical Foundations for a Radical Reform*, ed. P. van Parijs. London: Verso.

Okin, Susan Moller. 1981. Liberty and Welfare: Some Issues in Human Rights Theory. In *Human Rights: Nomos XXIII*, ed. J. R. Pennock and J. W. Chapman. New York: New York University Press.

Overseas Development Institute. 2000. *New Sources of Finance for Development* [Briefing Paper]. Overseas Development Institute, 1996 [cited 2000]. Available at: www.oneworld.org/odi/odi_briefing196.html.

Paine, Thomas. 1999. *The Rights of Man*. Mineola, NY: Dover.

Pateman, Carole. 1970. *Participation and Democratic Theory*. Cambridge: Cambridge University Press.

Pateman, Carole. 1988. *The Sexual Contract*. Stanford: Stanford University Press.

Pateman, Carole. 2003. Freedom and Democratization: Why Basic Income is to be Preferred to Basic Capital. In *The Ethics of Stakeholding*, ed. K. Dowling, J. de Wispelaere, and S. White. New York: Palgrave.

Pateman, Carole. 2004. Democratizing Citizenship: Some Advantages of a Basic Income. *Politics and Society* 32 (1): 89–105.

Pettit, Philip. 1997. *Republicanism: A Theory of Freedom and Government*. Oxford: Oxford University Press.

Pogge, Thomas W. 1992. Cosmopolitanism and Sovereignty. *Ethics* 103 (1): 48–75.

Pogge, Thomas W. 2001. Eradicating Systemic Poverty: Brief for a Global Resources Dividend. *Journal of Human Development* 2 (1): 59–77.

Purdy, David. 1994. Citizenship, Basic Income, and the State. *New Left Review* 208: 30–48.

Rorty, Richard. 1993. Human Rights, Rationality, and Sentimentality. In *On Human Rights: The Oxford Amnesty Lectures 1993*, ed. S. Shute and S. Hurley. New York: Basic Books.

Rothschild, Emma. 2001. Security and Laissez-Faire. In *What's Wrong with a Free Lunch?*, ed. J. Cohen and J. Rogers. Boston: Beacon Press.

Round, Robin. 2000. Time for Tobin. *The New Internationalist* 320: 19–20.

Rousseau, Jean-Jacques. 1997. *The Social Contract and Other Later Political Writings.* Trans. J. C. Bondanella. Ed. V. Gourevitch. Cambridge: Cambridge University Press.

Schumpeter, Joseph A. 1942. *Capitalism, Socialism, and Democracy.* New York: Harper and Row.

Sen, Amartya. 1999a. Democracy as a Universal Value. *Journal of Democracy* 10 (3): 3–17.

Sen, Amartya. 2001. *Development as Freedom.* New York: Alfred A. Knopf.

Sen, Amartya. 2004. Elements of a Theory of Human Rights. *Philosophy and Public Affairs* 32 (4): 315–56.

Shapiro, Ian. 1999. *Democratic Justice.* New Haven, CT: Yale University Press.

Sharp, Andrew, ed. 1998. *The English Levellers.* Cambridge: Cambridge University Press.

Shue, Henry. 1983. The Burdens of Justice. *The Journal of Philosophy* 80 (10): 600–08.

Shue, Henry. 1996. *Basic Rights: Subsistence, Affluence, and U.S. Foreign Policy.* Princeton: Princeton University Press.

Standing, Guy. 1992. The Need for a New Social Consensus. In *Arguing for Basic Income: Ethical Foundations for a Radical Reform*, ed. P. van Parijs. London: Verso.

Taylor, Charles. 1999. Conditions of an Unforced Consensus on Human Rights. In *The East Asian Challenge for Human Rights*, ed. J. R. Bauer and D. A. Bell. Cambridge: Cambridge University Press.

Van Parijs, Philippe. 1995. *Real Freedom for All: What (If Anything) Can Justify Capitalism?* Oxford: Oxford University Press.

Van Parijs, Philippe. 2001. A Basic Income for All. In *What's Wrong with a Free Lunch?*, ed. P. Van Parijs, J. Cohen and J. Rogers. Boston: Beacon Press.

Van Parijs, Philippe. 2004. *A Short History of Basic Income.* Available at: http://www.etes.ucl.ac.be/BIEN/BI/HistoryBI.htm.

Vincent, R. J. 1986. *Human Rights and International Relations.* Cambridge: Cambridge University Press.

Walzer, Michael. 1983. *Spheres of Justice: A Defense of Pluralism and Equality.* New York: Basic Books.

Wispelaere, Jurgen de, and Lindsay Stirton. 2004. The Many Faces of Universal Basic Income. *Political Quarterly* 75 (3): 266–74.

Wollstonecraft, Mary. 1995. *A Vindication of the Rights of Men and a Vindication of the Rights of Woman.* Ed. S. Tomaselli. Cambridge: Cambridge University Press.

Young, Iris Marion. 1990a. *Justice and the Politics of Difference.* Princeton: Princeton Univ. Press.

Young, Iris Marion. 1990b. Polity and Group Difference: A Critique of the Ideal of Universal Citizenship. In *Feminism and Political Theory*, ed. C. R. Sunstein. Chicago: University of Chicago Press.

Zakaria, Fareed. 1997. The Rise of Illiberal Democracy. *Foreign Affairs* 76 (6): 22–43.

Zakaria, Fareed. 2003. *The Future of Freedom: Illiberal Democracy at Home and Abroad.* New York: W.W. Norton and Co.

6 Benchmarking the Right to Work

PHILIP HARVEY

INTRODUCTION

The prevailing view among both progressive and conservative economists in the United States today is that unemployment cannot be driven much below the 4 to 6 percent range – well above the 2% level that progressive economists in the 1940s considered achievable (Clark et al. 1949, 14).

This is an uncomfortable reminder that in an earlier era progressives had higher hopes concerning the possibilities for eliminating involuntary unemployment than they do today. In the 1940s, progressives thought they could guarantee the availability of enough good jobs to provide decent work for all job-seekers, thereby moving from a world of perennial job shortages to one of sustained "full employment" in which the "right to work" would be secured. Today, few progressive economists (and fewer still of those who have the ear of progressive policy makers) think that goal is achievable. Instead, they implicitly or explicitly accept the view that job shortages are either inevitable in a market economy or cannot be eliminated except by making unacceptable sacrifices in job quality, and that public policy accordingly should aim to ameliorate the bad effects of those shortages rather than eliminate them.

Why does this matter? It matters because the achievement of full, and decent, employment occupies a foundational role in the vision of a good society – that has guided progressive reform efforts ever since the end of World War II – was built in the 1940s, and for which no satisfactory substitute has yet to been found.[1] Believing it possible to provide decent work for all job-seekers, 1940s progressives envisioned a society that not only guaranteed its members the traditional freedoms of classical liberalism but also the positive rights necessary to turn formal freedom into real freedom, formal equality into real equality, and formal democracy into real democracy.

---

[1] The most ambitious attempt to find a replacement for full employment as a foundation for the progressive reform agenda consists of proposals to provide all members of society with an unconditional basic income guarantee as a way of eliminating poverty and promoting individual freedom (Van Parijs 1995; Standing 2002). Unfortunately, I do not believe that such a guarantee would provide a satisfactory substitute for securing the right to work, as that right is conventionally defined (Harvey 2003; 2005).

Nowhere was this vision more clearly expressed than in Franklin D. Roosevelt's 1944 State of the Union Message, in which he expressly noted the inadequacy of the political rights guaranteed by the U.S. Constitution to secure all of the human rights proclaimed in the U.S. Declaration of Independence (Roosevelt 1944).

> This Republic had its beginning, and grew to its present strength, under the protection of certain inalienable political rights – among them the right of free speech, free press, free worship, trial by jury, freedom from unreasonable searches and seizures. They were our rights to life and liberty.
>
> As our nation has grown in size and stature, however – as our industrial economy expanded – these political rights proved inadequate to assure us equality in the pursuit of happiness.
>
> We have come to a clear realization of the fact that true individual freedom cannot exist without economic security and independence. "Necessitous men are not free men." People who are hungry and out of a job are the stuff of which dictatorships are made.
>
> In our day these economic truths have become accepted as self-evident. We have accepted, so to speak, a second Bill of Rights under which a new basis of security and prosperity can be established for all – regardless of station, race, or creed.

The first item in Roosevelt's proposed second economic bill of rights was "[t]he right to a useful and remunerative job in the industries or shops or farms or mines of the nation."

Nor can Roosevelt's speech be dismissed as a rhetorical nod to concededly unachievable goals. New Deal economic and social planners had been busy since the earliest days of the Roosevelt administration developing and, when they could, implementing strategies for securing all of the rights Roosevelt enumerated – including, in particular, the right to a decent job. For them, the president's "Second Bill of Rights" was not pie in the sky. It was the New Deal reform agenda expressed in the rights-based language of human rights that increasingly was being used at the time to describe its aims (Harvey 1989; Forbath 1999).

Four years later, the progressive vision Roosevelt articulated was given more authoritative expression in the economic and social provisions of the Universal Declaration of Human Rights.[2] Once again, the right to work was listed first among the economic and social rights enumerated in the text, and for the next three decades progressive reform agendas in developed market societies were informed by the hopeful presumption that full employment was achievable.

---

[2] Nothing could be further from the truth than to think of the Universal Declaration – G.A. Res. 217A, U.N. GAOR, 3d Sess., U.N. Doc. A/810 (1948) – as a foreign document alien to American values. It is more properly viewed as an international affirmation of the New Deal's guiding philosophy, which was first articulated very clearly in the social welfare planning documents that presaged Roosevelt's 1944 State of the Union Message (Committee on Economic Security 1935; National Resources Planning Board 1943), was refined in the influential 1945 Statement of Essential Human Rights authored by a drafting committee working under the auspices of the American Law Institute (American Law Institute 1945), and finally embodied in language drafted by a United Nations committee chaired by Eleanor Roosevelt, the American President's widow and tribune of New Deal values within his administration (Glendon 2001).

Then something happened to shake the confidence of progressives in the achievability of this vision. At the risk of oversimplifying a complicated historical turning point, I will suggest that it was the stagflation crises of the 1970s that effected this change by causing progressives to lose confidence in their own ability to achieve full employment. In the mid-1970s, the full employment foundation of the progressive reform agenda seemed to crack under the weight it was carrying, and progressives found themselves not only on the defensive – not only scrambling to protect the social welfare programs and institutions they had devoted their lives to building but also without a clear vision of how to move forward in achieving their long term policy objectives.

In this chapter, I assess the fate of the 1940s era full-employment/right-to-work policy goal in the wake of the stagflation crises of the 1970s. I argue that progressives have responded to their loss of faith in full employment by concentrating instead on securing those aspects of the right to work that appear not to require the achievement of full employment, while modifying their view of full employment itself to reflect their new, more modest expectations.

Believing that this abandonment of the full-employment/right-to-work policy goal is both unnecessary and pernicious in its effects on efforts to secure economic and social rights in general, I propose a conceptual clarification of the right to work that distinguishes its different dimensions. Having distinguished the separate dimensions of the right to work, I underscore the importance of securing all aspects of the right and assess how progress in securing each aspect can be measured. In that regard, I applaud recent efforts by the International Labour Organization to define and promote the realization of the qualitative and distributive aspects of the right to work, and I also applaud the growing attention progressives have paid to expanding what I term the scope of the right. I am critical, though, of the trend to discount or ignore the importance of securing the quantitative aspect of the right to work – the dimension traditionally associated with the achievement of full employment. To provide a conceptual counterweight to that trend, I conclude the chapter with a technical definition of full employment that is consistent with the goal of securing the quantitative aspect of the right to work. This definition is suitable for gauging the effectiveness of United Nations' efforts to "promote . . . full employment" (UN Charter, art. 55), and for monitoring the performance of compliance with the obligations of governments, international organizations and nongovernmental actors to secure "universal and effective recognition and observance" of the right to work.[3] It is my hope that this definition will encourage progressives to think more carefully about what is needed to secure all aspects of the right to work and to devote more attention to the task of monitoring and assessing the performance of public policies in achieving that goal.

---

[3] Because the Universal Declaration is not a treaty, most (but not all) international lawyers take the view that it does not impose legally binding obligations on nation states. A less frequently noted consequence of its nontreaty status, though, is that it was intended to describe the rights-based obligations not only of nation-states but also of individuals and nonstate institutional actors in society. The Declaration's preamble, quoted later, makes this clear. Hence, it is just as appropriate to query whether the actions of nonstate actors honor the rights recognized in the Universal Declaration as it is to address the same query to the actions of nation-states.

THE FULL-EMPLOYMENT/RIGHT-TO-WORK POLITICAL AGENDA

The Universal Declaration of Human Rights occupies a special place in international law. Adopted by the General Assembly of the United Nations in December 1948 by a vote of 48 to 0,[4] the document was intended to establish

> a common standard of achievement for all peoples and all nations, to the end that every individual and every organ of society, keeping this Declaration constantly in mind, shall strive by teaching and education to promote respect for these rights and freedoms and by progressive measures, national and international, to secure their universal and effective recognition and observance, both among the peoples of Member States themselves and among the peoples of territories under their jurisdiction (Universal Declaration of Human Rights, Preamble).

As noted earlier, the "common standard of achievement" recognized in the Universal Declaration encompasses not only the so-called negative rights associated with classical liberal political theory but also a set of positive rights associated with social democratic theory. Among the latter, the right to work occupies a particularly important position because of the role it plays in supporting efforts to secure other economic and social rights. This contributory function stems in part from the breadth of the right to work itself,[5] and in part from its effect on both the level of unmet social needs in a society and the level of resources available to meet those needs. Because of this dual effect (reducing unmet needs while simultaneously increasing societal resources), a society that is successful in securing the right to work is likely to have a relatively easy time securing other economic and social rights recognized in the Universal Declaration (e.g., the right to adequate food, decent housing, adequate health care, a good education, income security for persons who are unable to be self-supporting, and so forth). By contrast, a society that fails to secure the right to work (as most do) is likely to find it very difficult to secure other economic and social rights as well. In this respect, the right to work occupies a position among economic and social rights that is analogous to that occupied by freedom of speech among civil and political rights.

That being the case, one would expect advocates of economic and social rights in general to attach special importance to securing the right to work. Indeed, one would expect it to be at the top of virtually all progressive reform agendas; however,

---

[4] Eight countries abstained on the final vote. They were Byelorussia, Czechoslovakia, Poland, Saudi Arabia, South Africa, the Soviet Union, Ukraine, and Yugoslavia.

[5] As it is defined in the Universal Declaration, the right to work itself encompasses a broad set of entitlements constitutive of economic and social rights in general. First, it is a right actually to be employed in a paying job, not just to compete on terms of equality for scarce jobs. Second, the jobs made available to secure the right must provide "just and favorable conditions of work" and pay wages sufficient to support "an existence worthy of human dignity." Third, the jobs also must be freely chosen rather than assigned. In other words, job-seekers must be afforded a reasonable selection of employment opportunities and the right to refuse employment. Fourth, the right includes an entitlement to "equal pay for equal work," which implies a lack of invidious discrimination among different population groups, and also as between persons doing similar work in different occupations or for different employers in the same occupation. Finally, the right includes the right of workers to "form and join trade unions for the protection of [their] interests," thereby ensuring that workers will have the opportunity to share in the governance of their workplaces (Universal Declaration of Human Rights, Article 23). For a more extended discussion of the right, see Harvey 2002.

this is decidedly not the case today. Although politicians of all stripes promote a myriad of policy proposals by citing their putatively positive effect on job growth, there is virtually no organized political support, and very little public advocacy, for the claim that governments have a duty to adopt policies guaranteeing all job-seekers access to decent jobs. That claim, so succinctly expressed in the Universal Declaration, has virtually disappeared from public discourse.

What accounts for the sparse attention given to the right to work in progressive reform proposals today, a status that is strikingly different from its centrality to the progressive reform agenda in the 1940s? I believe the key to understanding this change lies in the changing attitudes of progressive economists toward full employment as an economic policy goal.

Although the achievement of full employment is not identical to the goal of securing the right to work (Harvey 1999), the two objectives were viewed as virtually synonymous in the 1940s. As explained earlier, the idea that access to work should be viewed as a fundamental right had been percolating within the Roosevelt administration for some time before it found expression in the president's 1944 State of the Union Message. At the same time, progressive economists were embracing the Keynesian notion that full employment could be achieved by macroeconomic manipulation of the aggregate level of demand in market societies. Popularly understood as the elimination of involuntary unemployment, the achievement of "full employment" was generally understood to be the economist's answer to the question of how the right to work could be secured.

This understanding of full employment's meaning was less clear in the economics literature itself. The term "full employment" had been used by economists since the early 1920s to describe the policy goal of providing work on a continuous basis to a country's entire labor force (Hobson 1922, 6–7, 40; Commons 1923, 642, 644), but it was not until the 1940s that this usage became widespread and the term assumed something approaching iconic status in public policy discourse. For economists, though, the term's meaning was never that clearly defined or understood, and a certain fuzziness surrounded its use by professional economists regardless of (or perhaps because of) its popularity and positive connotations (Rees 1957). Despite this endemic vagueness in the precise meaning of the term, progressive economists continued to conceive of full employment as a macroeconomic condition in which involuntary unemployment was eliminated by the achievement of high enough levels of aggregate demand to provide paid employment for everyone who wanted it; and as long as a substantial group of economists thought that goal was achievable, advocacy of the right to work continued to be associated with the full employment policies promoted by these economists. We see that association in the Employment Policy Convention adopted by the International Labour Organization (ILO) in 1964 (International Labour Organization 1964, art. 1, ¶¶ 1–2), and in the right to work provision of the International Covenant on Economic, Social and Cultural Rights, adopted by the General Assembly of the United Nations in 1966 (United Nations 1966, art. 6). Thus, to the extent the goal of securing the right to work was still being promoted in the 1960s,[6] the achievability of that objective was perceived to

---

[6] In the United States, the commitment of human rights advocates to economic and social human rights was so attenuated during the 1950s that right-wing opponents of the right to work were able to appropriate the term for their own use, adopting it as the rallying cry of an employer-funded

depend on the viability of the full employment strategies Keynesian economists had been advocating since the 1940s.

Given this history, it is hardly surprising that when both popular and expert faith in Keynesian economics collapsed in the stagflation debacle of the 1970s, advocacy of the full employment/right to work policy goal was profoundly affected. The prevailing view among both progressive and conservative economists since then has been that unemployment rates cannot be driven much below the 4 to 6% range without triggering an unacceptable increase in the rate of inflation – well above the 2% level that progressive economists in the 1940s equated with full employment (Clark et al. 1949, 14). The result of this loss of faith in the achievability of full employment (in the 1940s sense of the term) has been that progressives, and particularly progressive economists, have become hesitant to advocate either full employment or the goal of securing the right to work as public policy goals.

Full employment has largely disappeared from the progressive political agenda, while the term itself is increasingly used by progressives in the same way it is used by conservatives. That is, the "full employment" designation is used to refer to the lowest level of unemployment considered prudent for the government of a market society to try to maintain. In a murky nod to the more robust conception of full employment that an earlier generation of progressive economists embraced, progressive economists today prefer to say that the economy is "close to" full employment rather than "at" full employment when they believe unemployment rates have fallen about as low as it is possible; but, other than that, the only difference between conservatives and progressives in their usage of the term is that progressives tend to believe the sustainable level of unemployment is somewhat lower than conservatives think it is. In the United States, for example, conservative economists seem to feel comfortable using the term when unemployment rates fall to the 5–6% range, whereas progressive economists don't start using the term until unemployment rates fall to the 4% level (and even then typically with the "close to" qualifier noted above) (see, e.g., Bernstein & Baker 2003).

As regards the right to work, progressives have either stopped talking about it or have sought to redefine the right in ways that deemphasize the importance of full employment as a means of securing it. For most progressives, this has involved an increased emphasis on what I will define later as the distributive and qualitative aspects of the right to work (a strong commitment to equal employment opportunity and the achievement of decent wages, benefits and working conditions for all workers) and a decreased emphasis on what I shall define later as the quantitative aspect of the right to work (ensuring the availability of enough jobs to provide paid employment for everyone who wants it). These progressives seem to hope that the achievement of equal employment opportunity will ensure that no one need wait too long for a job, thereby obviating the need to provide enough jobs to employ all job-seekers simultaneously.

For a smaller number of progressives, the advocacy of decent work and equal employment opportunity has been combined with a commitment to providing

antiunion campaign that is still active today. Since then, several generations of American progressives have grown up thinking that the right to work is a right-wing, antiunion slogan (see National Right to Work Committee, available at http://www.nrtwc.org).

increased societal support for nonmarket work in the form of an unconditional income guarantee. For these "Basic Income" advocates, the traditional conception of the right to work is dismissed as improperly focusing on paid employment, rather than the full range of creative activities in which people can and do engage both inside and outside the market. Viewed from this perspective, a better way to guarantee the right to work would be to guarantee people a livelihood free of the obligation to seek and accept paid employment (Standing 2002).

Because of these tendencies, progressives are no longer identified – either in their own eyes or the eyes of the public – as advocates of the right to work proclaimed in the Universal Declaration. And given the cornerstone role that right plays in the Universal Declaration, progressives may feel constrained in their embrace of the entire document.

This tendency has been most noticeable in the advocacy work of organizations like the ILO, whose support for the 1940s conception of full employment and the right to work was particularly pronounced in the pre-1970s period. The enduring attraction of the right to work goal can be seen in the ILO's current promotion of "decent work for all" (Somavia 2000), but it is significant that a new term has been adopted to replace the right to work as a policy goal. More significantly, the organization's efforts to define decent work and formulate policy recommendations for securing it illustrate how profoundly progressive economists have been affected by their loss of faith in the achievability of full employment.

When the ILO undertook to formulate an employment strategy capable of achieving "decent work for all," the strategy it embraced virtually ignored the quantitative aspect of the decent work vision (the "for all" part of the "decent work for all" goal) in favor of a forceful advocacy of a wide range of rights *at* work (the "decent work" part of the goal) (International Labour Organization 2002). In truth, the employment strategy promoted in the ILO's *Global Employment Agenda* does not aim to achieve full employment – at least not in the 1940s sense of the term – nor to secure the right to work.[7] Fairly stated, the goal promoted in the document is merely to ensure that all paid employment is "decent" and to reduce involuntary unemployment to the minimum level consistent with price stability, while promoting increases in labor productivity to create "more room for growth oriented demand policies" (ibid., 4).

The same tendency can be seen in subsequent efforts by the ILO to define benchmarks for measuring progress in achieving the organization's "decent work" policy goal. A recent issue of the *International Labour Review* was devoted to this subject (International Labour Organization 2003). The articles published in the issue – most of them authored by members of the ILO's technical staff – propose a panoply

---

[7] The *right* to work is never mentioned in the document (International Labour Organization 2002) – a startling omission given its prominence in the Universal Declaration of Human Rights, the International Covenant on Economic, Social, and Cultrual Rights, and the ILO's own Employment Policy Convention No. 122. "Full employment" is mentioned only five times in the document (ibid., 4, 45, 85 & 89), and only once in a context that suggests its original connotation (ibid., 45). Significantly, that reference notes that the World Summit for Social Development endorsed the full employment goal articulated in Convention 122, but it does not make clear whether the ILO itself still views the goal as achievable. Based on the evidence of this document, it would be reasonable to conclude that it does not.

of indicators, but what is most striking about these indicators is their focus on the quality of paid employment and the degree to which equal employment opportunity has been achieved, as opposed to the task of assessing how close an economy has come to achieving full employment and/or securing the right to work.

If even the ILO has lost faith in the full employment/right to work policy vision, maybe it is time to accept the vision's demise. Maybe the *sub silentio* amendment of the Universal Declaration to which progressives have acceded – striking out its recognition of the right to work in the 1940s sense of the term – should be acknowledged. Maybe it is time to admit that the only right to work progressives think is achievable is one that strives to guarantees decent work for all wage laborers, equal employment opportunity for all job-seekers, and 4% unemployment – whether or not that qualifies as full employment in the original sense of the term.

Before countenancing such a step, though, it is important to note just how much the loss of faith in the goal of securing the right to work, as it was conceived in the 1940s, depends on a loss of faith in just one strategy for achieving that goal – the simple Keynesian strategy of boosting aggregate demand until the labor market clears. Perhaps the problem lies not in the goal but in the too easy acceptance by progressives of this strategy, and in their failure to commit themselves to the task of fashioning an alternative strategy for securing all aspects of the right to work. The lack of scholarly literature addressing the topic of how to secure the right to work – the policy goal that comprised the *raison d'etre* for progressive interest in full employment in the first place – speaks volumes in this regard.

Before conceding that the right to work as it is defined in the Universal Declaration is beyond our reach, I believe progressives should feel a duty to explore – systematically and thoroughly – whether alternative strategies exist that could secure the right. After all, claims that access to work should be viewed as a human right were asserted long before the publication of Keynes' *General Theory*, and other strategies for achieving full employment or its functional equivalent have been advocated both before and since progressive economists embraced the Keynesian prescription for achieving that goal. Indeed, within the New Deal administration of Franklin Roosevelt, where the policy goal of securing the right to work reached its fullest development in the 1930s and early 1940s, the strategy originally advocated for achieving that goal was decidedly un-Keynesian. It assumed that private sector demand could never be relied upon to provide paid employment for everyone who needed it, even at the top of the business cycle, and that direct government job creation was therefore essential to provide "employment assurance" for all job-seekers (Committee on Economic Security 1935, 23–30; National Resources Planning Board 1943, pt. 3, 226–88). Before writing off the right to work recognized in the Universal Declaration, this and other possible strategies for securing that right deserve a focused and complete assessment.

It is not the purpose of this chapter to undertake such an assessment, though I have contributed elsewhere to that task (Harvey 1989; 1995a; 1995b; 1999; 2000a; 2000b; 2002). The more limited goal of this chapter is to address the question of how full employment and the right to work should be defined for benchmarking purposes. In other words, the question I hope to help answer is how full employment and the various entitlements comprising the right to work should be measured for purposes of assessing the relative capacity of different strategies to achieve full employment (or its functional equivalent) and to secure the right to work.

THE FOUR DIMENSIONS OF THE RIGHT TO WORK

As noted earlier, the right to work recognized in the Universal Declaration is a multidimensional entitlement. For purposes of assessing alternative strategies for securing the right, I believe it is useful to group those dimensions under four headings. The first three refer to what I call the quantitative, qualitative, and distributive aspects of the right, while the fourth refers to its scope.

The quantitative aspect of the right to work. The quantitative aspect of the right to work is intended to protect the right of job-seekers actually to be employed in freely chosen jobs, not simply to compete on terms of equality for scarce employment opportunities. Securing the right accordingly requires that the number of jobs available in an economy exceed the number of persons wanting paid employment,[8] that those jobs be of a type suited to the skills of the labor force, and that no barriers exist that would prevent job-seekers from filling those jobs. This condition is what the term full employment was understood to mean when it first gained popular currency in the 1940s.[9]

The qualitative aspect of the right to work. The qualitative aspect of the right to work includes those factors that determine whether a particular job qualifies as "decent work" in the sense in which the ILO uses the term. These factors define the terms and conditions of a particular job – including such things as pay, fringe benefits, hours of work, working conditions, workplace governance, employment security, and so forth. For the right to work to be secured, it is not enough that the number of jobs available in an economy exceed the number of job-seekers; instead, those jobs also must provide "decent work." This means that a particular job must satisfy certain minimum standards to be counted as securing a particular individual's right to work. Moreover, because securing the right to work is itself instrumental to the broader goal of ensuring all members of society the opportunity to freely develop their personhood,[10] the employment

---

[8] It might be theoretically possible to secure the right to work in an economy with fewer jobs than job-seekers, but it would require the achievement of a set of conditions that probably would be harder to achieve than full employment. For a more extended discussion of this point, see Harvey (2002, 437–67).

[9] The clearest statement of this conception of full employment is the one popularized by William Beveridge (1944, 18):

> It means having always more vacant jobs than unemployed men, not slightly fewer jobs. It means that the jobs are at fair wages, of such a kind, and so located that the unemployed men can reasonably be expected to take them; it means, by consequence, that the normal lag between losing one job and finding another will be very short.

[10] The economic and social provisions of the Universal Declaration are contained in Articles 22–28. All of these rights are designed to promote the "full development of the human personality," a phrase that appears in slightly different form in three of the Declaration's articles (articles 22, 26 and 29), and whose spirit pervades the entire document. As one commentator has noted, "the right to 'the full development of the human personality' was seen by most delegates to the committee that

opportunities a society provides to secure the right to work also must be of sufficient variety and type to fulfill that role. Accordingly, the qualitative features employment opportunities must possess to satisfy the right to work depend on the developmental needs of a population as well certain absolute quality requirements.

The distributive aspect of the right to work. Just as the operational content of the right to work reflects the Universal Declaration's overarching commitment to the free development of the human personality, so, too, does it reflect the Declaration's similarly strong commitment to the equal worth and equal rights of all persons.[11] This means that the achievement of equal employment opportunity and equal conditions of employment for all persons – regardless of such differentiating characteristics as their race, gender, religion, national origin, political opinion, social class, or other analogous status – is also essential to secure the right to work. This, in my view, is the proper object of policies designed to overcome or eliminate what I shall refer to later as *structural* barriers to employment.

The scope of the right to work. When the Universal Declaration was drafted, it is safe to assume that the principles embodied in the right to work were generally viewed as applying only to wage employment. In other words, the right to work was originally conceived as a right to a paying job. Nevertheless, the language defining the right to work in the Declaration does not limit its scope to wage employment, and because a large proportion of the world's population works in capacities other than that of a wage laborer, the question naturally arises as to whether and how the right applies to nonwage employment – whether of a hunter/gatherer, a subsistence farmer, an independent producer of agricultural or other commodities, or one of the many categories of unpaid family care or volunteer community service workers on which even fully developed market economies depend for their survival.

It is not the purpose of this chapter to try to answer these questions, but I have argued elsewhere that the boundaries of the right to work and the mechanisms appropriate for securing the right for nonwage workers should be considered in conjunction with other economic and social rights recognized in the Universal Declaration (Harvey 2003, 23–27).

The Universal Declaration adopts what can be described as a two-legged strategy for ensuring that all persons enjoy an adequate standard of living. One leg of this strategy consists of the right to work. The other leg consists of the right to income support for persons who are not able to be self-supporting. The two legs of the strategy are intended to provide income security for all persons, but the entitlements comprising the two legs do not apply to separate people so much as

---

drafted the Universal Declaration as a way of summarizing all the social, economic, and cultural right in the Declaration" (Morsink 1999, 212). The role played by the economic and social provisions of the document in achieving this overarching goal is to ensure that all members of society are guaranteed access to the resources, opportunities and services they need to fully develop and express their own personhood within communities that accept the collective burdens of mutual support and respect.

[11] This commitment is most clearly expressed in articles 1 and 2 of the Declaration.

they do to separate circumstances that may apply serially or simultaneously to the same individuals (Harvey 1989; 2003; 2005).

Because the Universal Declaration recognizes that all members of society are entitled to a decent standard of living, deciding whether the right to work should be viewed as applying to particular categories of nonmarket or nonwaged work involves not so much an inquiry into whether the activity is worthy of societal support but how that support should be provided, the level of support to which persons engaged in the activity should be deemed entitled, and the nature and extent to which all of the corollary entitlements associated with the right to work should apply to persons engaged in the activity. Justice may dictate that persons engaged in a particular activity be compensated but not necessarily in the form of a wage. The level of compensation to which they are entitled may vary widely, just as it does for people engaged in different types of wage labor. Concerns over working conditions may need to be addressed but not necessarily by means of the same mechanisms used to regulate the working conditions of wage laborers. As the right to work is extended to categories of work other than wage labor, the mechanisms for securing the right will also extend beyond those associated with wage labor. There is no simple formula for addressing these issues. It is *terra nova* for human rights advocates, and substantial theoretical and empirical work is needed before the landscape is adequately mapped. The task should be welcomed, though, as an important undertaking in the continued development of human rights standards.

One contribution to this effort that I think is helpful, but flawed, consists of proposals to guarantee all members of society an unconditional basic income (BI) irrespective of the their participation in the labor force. Advocates of the BI idea argue that if such a guarantee were pegged at a sufficiently high level, it would eliminate poverty in one fell swoop – thereby guaranteeing the right to a decent standard of living recognized in the Universal Declaration. They also argue that it would secure an adequate or possibly superior form of the right to work by subsidizing everyone's ability to engage in personally fulfilling, self-directed activities outside the labor market (van Parijs 1995; Standing 2002; Rey 2004; Noguera & Raventos 2005).

I have argued elsewhere that a BI guarantee in the form favored by most advocates of the idea – a universal grant paid individually and without conditions to all members of society – should be thought of as an expensive but otherwise desirable means of partially securing the right to income support, but that it would fail to provide an adequate substitute for the right to work. This is true, I maintain, whether the right to work is thought of as including only wage labor or as including various forms of nonwaged labor as well (Harvey 2003; 2005). Because of its cost, I do not think this type of BI guarantee is either feasible or desirable, but I suggest a less expensive form of the benefit could provide an attractive substitute for means-tested public assistance programs (Harvey 2005, 52–55).

MEASURING PROGRESS IN SECURING THE RIGHT TO WORK

Unless policy discussions of the right to work expressly address each of the four dimensions of the right identified earlier, there is a good chance that important aspects of the right will be neglected or, worse, sacrificed for the sake of securing other aspects of the right. This is a serious danger because some policy regimes may create trade-offs between the different dimensions.

Each of the four dimensions of the right to work I have identified are important, and success in securing one of the dimensions cannot compensate, in my view, for a failure to secure the other dimensions – any more than a nation's success in guaranteeing civil and political rights can compensate for a failure to secure economic, social, and cultural rights (or vice versa). Anyone who believes that tradeoffs among the four dimensions of the right to work are acceptable or unavoidable should be called on to acknowledge and justify those tradeoffs. This also means that data measuring the degree to which the right to work has been secured in a particular society should be multidimensional. It should provide us with information concerning the society's success or progress in securing each aspect of the right to work.

These purposes would be best served by data sets in which aggregate measures were built on individualized data, so we could ascertain how many or what proportion of the members of a particular society either enjoyed or did not enjoy particular aspects of the right to work based on information about the status of each member of the society in that regard. That way we could use the same data set to answer questions about the degree of protection afforded the right to work in a society, to identify those persons in the society whose individual right to work had not been fully secured along one or more of the dimensions identified earlier, and to allow conclusions to be drawn concerning the differential effects of strategies to secure the right to work on different population groups.

The next best thing would be sample data that permitted the same aggregate conclusions to be drawn, while establishing standards for judging in individual cases whether a particular aspect of the right to work was or was not secured for a particular individual. Such data could show what proportion of job-seekers – in both the overall population and subgroups of the population – lacked paid employment entirely and what proportion had paid employment that did not satisfy various standards of decency, while also providing standards that interested parties could use in judging the adequacy of particular jobs and whether the right to work of particular individuals had been secured. Comparative statistics for members of different population groups could show whether the members of those groups likely did or did not enjoy equal employment opportunity, and surveys of persons who worked outside the wage-labor market could establish the degree to which such workers did or did not enjoy the entitlements comprising the right to work.

Finally, in the absence of customized data sets such as these, measures of varying degrees of usefulness can be constructed from data collected for other purposes. Reliance on such data is necessary, but in using it to assess a nation's performance in securing the right to work or in identifying individuals and groups who suffer rights deficits in this area, it is particularly important to keep the different dimensions of the right clearly in mind. Otherwise, differences in the quantity or quality of available data may result in certain aspects of the right being ignored. The amount or quality of data available for measuring different aspects of the right to work bears no necessary relationship to the relative importance of the different aspects of the right being measured.

Measuring the Quality of Work: Of the four dimensions of the right to work identified earlier, the qualitative dimension is inherently the most difficult to measure.

Because the terms and conditions of employment that fall under this heading are so varied, the task of defining minimum standards of acceptability and measuring the degree to which those standards are met is particularly challenging. It requires a variety of statistical measures and, for summary purposes, the development of indexes involving combinations of disparate measures – always a difficult undertaking. The ILO's efforts to define and measure the characteristics of decent work are extremely useful in this regard (International Labour Organization 2003).

Measuring the Distribution of Employment Opportunities: Measuring national performance in securing the distributional aspects of the right to work is conceptually easier because the policy goal is clear – ensuring equal access to employment opportunities for all persons. Also, a great deal of research has been undertaken in various countries measuring differences in labor market outcomes for the members of disadvantaged population groups. This means that substantial amounts of data already exist addressing this aspect of the right to work, and the methodological problems associated with collecting and interpreting such data have been extensively discussed in the scholarly literature.

Measuring Efforts to Secure the Right to Work for Nonwaged Labor: Most policy debates concerning the applicability of the right to work to nonwaged labor is conceptual at first. To what extent are the entitlements embodied in the right to work applicable to nonwage workers? To the extent these entitlements extend to particular categories of nonwage workers, policies are needed to secure the entitlements in question. Often these policies will be different from those adopted to secure various aspects of the right to work for wage laborers (Harvey 2003, 23–27). To properly assess the success of policy initiatives in this area, as well as the need for them in the first place, data is needed concerning the number of persons engaged in particular forms of nonwaged work, the conditions under which they labor, the degree to which they are constrained from seeking and accepting other forms of work, the benefits they and society derive from their work, what, if any, indirect compensation they receive for their work, and so forth.

Measuring the Availability of Work: Assessing a society's performance in ensuring the adequate availability of paid employment is also conceptually straightforward. Are there enough suitable jobs in the economy to provide paid employment for everyone who wants it,[12] and is the economy free of structural barriers that might prevent certain categories of job-seekers from filling available jobs? Unfortunately, the data available for addressing these questions is not well suited to the task. Countries count both the employed and the unemployed in exquisite detail. Accordingly, we know a great deal about the level and rate of unemployment in different countries, their labor force participation rate, and their employment to population ratio. We also have similar data for different population groups within particular countries. But none of those figures tells us whether there are enough jobs available in a nation's economy for everyone who wants paid employment. To answer that question, we need to develop new statistical measures that are better suited to the

[12] Prohibitions against child labor are consistent with this goal, provided they are adopted and enforced for the purpose of protecting the rights of children as set forth in documents like the United Nations Convention on the Rights of the Child (1577 U.N.T.S. 3), which entered into force 2 September 1990.

task, and because little research has been devoted to this requirement, the need for further work in this area is particularly pronounced.

Composite Indexes: Where a desired goal consists of multiple subgoals that lack a common measure, it is both tempting and useful to try to construct composite indexes for measuring progress in achieving the overall goal by assigning weights to whatever measures exist for gauging progress in achieving the sub goals. The problem with such indexes, though, is that they necessarily suggest that trade-offs between goals are acceptable when they may not be. For example, suppose we wanted to create an overall "health index" comprised of all the measurements of system function upon which doctors rely. We might include measurements of heart function, lung function, kidney function, and so forth. Now consider two people. One has middling health across the board. The other has excellent health in all respects except one – their heart doesn't work at all. The second person might have an overall health index that is higher than the first, yet live a short, miserable life compared to the first.

The same problem necessarily arises in efforts to measure a society's overall success in securing the right to work. A failure to secure particular components of the right may have devastating effects on those who suffer the deficit, notwithstanding the fact that the society's overall performance in securing the right may appear strong based on its success in securing other aspects of the right.

I do not think this problem argues against the creation of composite indexes for measuring either overall health or overall success in securing the right to work, but it means they must be interpreted with care. It also means that efforts to define minimum performance levels for securing each of the different elements of a composite entitlement may be just as important, or even more important, than creating a composite index for measuring overall performance levels in securing the entitlement as a whole.

When assessing alternative policies for securing the right to work it is particularly important that we not regard success in securing some of the right's constitutive elements as compensating for a failure to secure other elements. Neither a secure right to a substandard job, nor the provision of decent work for employed workers while other job-seekers are denied employment, is acceptable. The success of policies to secure the right to work cannot be properly assessed without considering all aspects of the right, because they all are important.

DEFINING AND MEASURING FULL EMPLOYMENT IN A MANNER CONSISTENT WITH THE RIGHT TO WORK

As noted earlier, our capacity to measure national performance in securing the qualitative and distributional aspects of the right to work has advanced substantially in recent decades, but we are still relying on substantially the same measures of success in securing the quantitative dimension of the right to work that were available in the 1940s – that is, the economy's unemployment rate. To be sure, unemployment statistics themselves have been steadily refined over the years – and much more data has become available concerning the unemployed – but for purposes of judging whether or not there are enough jobs available to achieve full employment, we know little more than we did in the 1940s.

In the balance of this chapter, I will suggest a means of monitoring labor market conditions that focuses on the question of whether there are enough jobs available to achieve full employment, and, if not, how many more jobs are needed. First, though, we need to explore the relationship between job vacancies, structural barriers to the achievement of full employment, and unemployment.

Achieving full employment does not require that the unemployment rate in an economy be reduced to zero. Indeed, based on standard definitions of unemployment, it is impossible for unemployment to be totally eliminated. The reason is that jobless individuals will be classified as unemployed when they first enter the labor force looking for work, as well as when they have left one job and are looking for another, even if they face a surfeit of employment opportunities. It takes time for job-seekers and employers with job vacancies to find one another and complete a hiring even when there is no shortage of jobs, and during that period job-seekers who are not currently employed will be counted as unemployed. For this reason, a "frictional unemployment floor" exists in all market economies, below which unemployment rates cannot fall even if full employment is achieved and the right to work is secured.

Historical experience suggests that the frictional unemployment floor in developed market economies probably lies in the 1% to 2% range, as that is the minimum level to which unemployment rates appear to fall in such economies. Assuming jobs are genuinely plentiful at such times and that virtually all job-seekers are able to find suitable work with little difficulty, the level of unemployment that remains can be presumed to result from frictional factors alone. The actual frictional unemployment floor in an economy could be higher or lower than this, depending on the efficiency of its job matching institutions and its labor turnover rate,[13] but the 1% to 2% range probably constitutes a reasonable baseline estimate.

Unemployment in excess of this frictional floor may be attributable either to a shortage of jobs in the economy or to the existence of "structural" impediments to the job search and hiring process that prevent vacant jobs from being filled. The role of job shortages as a potential cause of unemployment is straightforward. If there are not enough jobs to go around, the unavoidable result is that a certain number of job-seekers will suffer unemployment as a result of the economy's job shortage. The role of "structural" barriers in causing unemployment is a bit trickier, because they can prevent individual workers from being hired (thus "causing" their individual unemployment) without affecting the aggregate level of unemployment (something that would occur only if the structural barriers also prevented job vacancies from being filled). Understanding this distinction is important in my view.

Without attempting a precise definition of the term, I shall use the "structural" designation to refer to any and all barriers to employment that prevent certain

---

[13] The labor turnover rate will have an important effect on an economy's frictional unemployment floor, even if it does not result in any net change in the total number of jobs in an economy. All other things remaining equal, the higher the labor turnover rate, the greater the number of workers who will be between jobs looking for work at any moment in time and the greater the number of job vacancies they will encounter. For the sake of simplicity, I shall ignore this factor in the balance of my analysis, noting only that it needs to be taken into consideration when estimating the actual frictional unemployment floor in a particular economy.

categories of job-seekers from being hired to fill available jobs. These barriers include mismatches between the skills employers are demanding and the skills job-seekers offer, geographic mismatches between the location of available jobs and available pools of unemployed job-seekers, employment discrimination based on characteristics such race or gender, and the unavailability of services – such as child care – that particular categories of job-seekers may need in order to accept available jobs. These factors are familiar because they have been the target of significant programmatic efforts to combat unemployment in developed market economies in recent decades.

The point I think needs to be emphasized is that structural factors will not increase the level of unemployment in an economy unless, in addition to interfering with the ability of particular job-seekers to find work, they also prevent employers from filling job vacancies as quickly as they otherwise would. If structural barriers do not interfere with the ability of employers to fill job vacancies, the structural factors will affect the distribution of unemployment (who is unemployed) but not its level (how many people are unemployed). This distinction is illustrated by the following "parable," which also underscores the importance of the distinction for policy planning and assessment purposes (Harvey 2000a, 683):

Dog Island

There once was an island with a population of 100 dogs. Every day a plane flew overhead and dropped 95 bones onto the island. It was a dog paradise, except for the fact that every day five dogs went hungry. Hearing about the problem, a group of social scientists was sent to assess the situation and recommend remedies.

The social scientists ran a series of regressions and determined that bonelessness in the dog population was associated with lower levels of bone-seeking effort and that boneless dogs also lacked important skills in fighting for bones. As a remedy for the problem, some of the social scientists proposed that boneless dogs needed a good kick in the side to get them moving, while others proposed that boneless dogs be provided special training in bone-fighting skills.

A bitter controversy ensued over which of these two strategies ought to be pursued. Over time, both strategies were tried, and both reported limited success in helping individual dogs overcome their bonelessness – but despite this success, the bonelessness problem on the island never lessened in the aggregate. Every day, there were still five dogs who went hungry.

Structural factors always affect the distribution of unemployment. They constitute an ever-present disadvantage for those individuals and groups that suffer from them, but they are unlikely to affect the level of unemployment in an economy as long as the economy also suffers from a sizable job gap. The reason is that the existence of surplus labor supplies makes it easy for employers to fill their job vacancies, even if significant numbers of workers are prevented by structural factors from competing for those vacancies. In contrast, if there is no job shortage, structural barriers that prevent unemployed job-seekers from being hired also will cause jobs to go unfilled, affecting both the level and the distribution of unemployment.[14]

---

[14] The question of whether structural factors were causing aggregate unemployment rates to rise, in addition to causing increased unemployment among economically isolated population groups, was the subject of a vigorous debate among economists in the late 1950s. Keynesian economists disputed

Unemployment rates alone do not tell us whether the unemployment being measured is attributable to frictional factors, structural factors, or a job shortage. When unemployment rates remain above the frictional unemployment floor in an economy, we know that one or both of the latter two factors must be responsible, but we can't tell which one. We can learn more by comparing unemployment data and job vacancy data. If there are fewer job vacancies than there are unemployed job-seekers, we know the economy is suffering from a job shortage. Moreover, the larger the job shortage, the less likely it will be that structural factors are also causing additional unemployment (as opposed to merely influencing its distribution among population groups).

In addition, the relationship between changes in the unemployment rate and the job vacancy rate can tell us whether the fluctuations are being caused by structural factors or a change in the size of the economy's job gap. This is because additional unemployment caused by a job shortage tends to depress the job vacancy rate (because it increases the number of job-seekers competing for available jobs, thereby making it easier for employers to fill job vacancies), whereas additional unemployment caused by structural factors would tend to cause the job vacancy rate to rise (because the additional unemployment would be attributable to a lengthening in the amount of time it took employers to fill their job vacancies). The former (inverse) relationship between the unemployment and job vacancy rate is the basis of the so-called Beveridge curve, which shows the tendency for unemployment rates and job vacancy rates to move in opposite directions. The latter relationship would be shown by an upward rather than a downward sloping Beveridge curve.

An understanding of these relationships makes it possible to draw reasonably robust conclusions from unemployment and job vacancy data concerning the adequacy of an economy's performance in securing the quantitative dimension of the right to work. The most important question to be answered in this regard is whether there are enough jobs available in the economy to achieve full employment if structural barriers affecting the employability of disadvantaged population groups were removed. That question can be answered by comparing the number of job vacancies in the economy to the number of unemployed job-seekers, a relationship that can be expressed as follows:

$$G = U - V \qquad \text{(The Economy's Job Gap) (1)},$$

where

G = the economys aggregate job gap,
U = the aggregate level of unemployment in the economy, and
V = the aggregate number of job vacancies in the economy

The simplicity of Equation (1) abstracts from a series of classification problems with respect to the measurement of both unemployment (U) and job vacancies (V). For example, both U and V ideally should be converted to full-time equivalent

the claim that increases in the aggregate level of unemployment were being caused by structuralist factors as opposed to changed macroeconomic conditions, and their view became the prevailing one in the 1960s (Mucciaroni 1990, 32–42; Sundquist 1968, 57–110).

figures, as the ratio of part- to full-time job vacancies may not equal the ratio of part- to full-time job-seekers. Also, the equation glosses over the problem of properly classifying involuntary part-time workers (persons who are employed in part-time jobs but who want full-time jobs) and discouraged workers (persons who say they want a job now but are not actively seeking one). With respect to the value of V, the equation glosses over such questions as whether to count vacancies announced in anticipation of future separations that do not yet exist (Farm 2005). Nevertheless, Equation (1) shows how an economy's job gap can be measured using unemployment and job vacancy data.

If an economy's job gap (G) is positive, we know that the economy has not achieved full employment and that its failure to do so is caused, at least in part, by its failure to provide enough jobs to employ everyone who wants to work. Moreover, the larger the value of G, the less likely it is that structural barriers are causing any of that unemployment, however important they may be in determining who suffers its burdens.

In the United States, job vacancy data suitable for the purposes I am describing has been collected only intermittently. Nevertheless, the surveys that have been conducted paint a consistent portrait of U.S. labor markets, showing that in periods of relative prosperity as well as during recessions, the number of job-seekers generally exceeds – and usually by a wide margin – the number of job vacancies employers are seeking to fill.[15]

Figure 6.1 shows job vacancy and unemployment data for the United States from December 2000 through November 2005. The bottom line of the figure shows the number of job vacancies in the economy as reported by the United States Bureau of Labor Statistics (BLS) based on the Agency's new Job Openings and Labor Turnover Survey (JOLTS).[16] The other three lines in the figure show how many officially unemployed individuals, involuntary part-time workers, and discouraged workers there were in the United States at the same time.[17]

---

[15] See Abraham (1983, 722) (noting that if the surveys actually conducted mirrored conditions in the economy as a whole "there were roughly 2.5 unemployed persons for every vacant job during the middle 1960s, an average of close to 4.0 unemployed persons per vacant job during the early 1970s, and an average of 5.0 or more unemployed persons for every vacant job during the latter part of the 1970s"); Holzer (1989, 48, Table 3.8) (reporting that in a study of twenty-eight southern and Midwestern cities, there were 4.7 officially unemployed individuals for every available job in 1980, and 8.4 officially unemployed individuals for every available job in 1982); Holzer (1996, 10, 143–44) (reporting that in a survey conducted between 1992 and 1994 in four large cities, job vacancy rates averaged 2.7 percent while unemployment rates ranged between about 5 percent and 11 percent in different cities at different times during the survey period); Employment and Training Institute (1993–present) (reporting biannual job vacancy rates and estimates of the number of persons seeking work and/or expected to work in the Milwaukee metropolitan area).

[16] For a description of the survey, see Clark and Hyson (2001).

[17] Involuntary part-time workers are persons who are working part time not by choice, but because their hours have been cut due to economic conditions or because they could not find full-time jobs. Discouraged workers are persons who report themselves as wanting a job now but are not actively seeking one for a variety of reasons, including illness, disability, family responsibilities, school enrollment, the belief that there are no jobs available, or that employers will not hire them because of their age, race, or other factors. All of these individuals can be described as "discouraged workers" in the sense that circumstances have discouraged them from seeking the paid employment they say they want. This broad definition of "discouragement" is more consistent with the goal of securing the right to work than more narrow definitions that limit the "discouraged worker" category

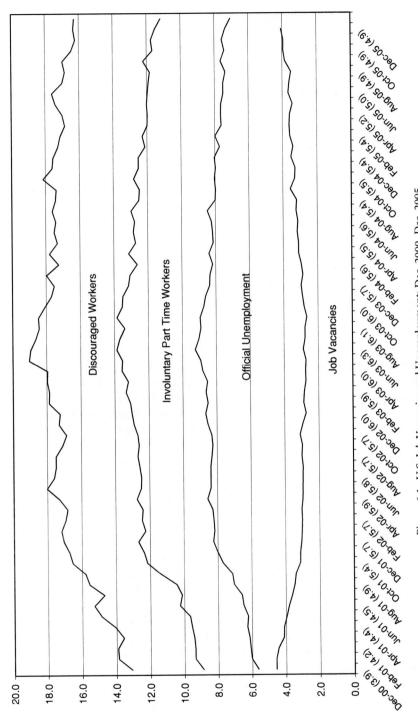

Figure 6.1. U.S. Job Vacancies and Unemployment: Dec. 2000–Dec. 2005
Source: Author's Calculations from BLS Data

The size of the economy's job gap (G) is shown by the distance between the bottom line in Figure 6.1 (job vacancies) and whichever of the upper three lines one considers the better measure of unemployment. Figure 6.2 shows the United States job gap based on each of these three measures of unemployment.

In December 2000, for example, when the economy's unemployment rate was 3.9% and even many progressive economists thought the economy was "at or near full employment" (Bernstein and Baker 2003), there were only 4.6 million job vacancies in the economy compared to 5.6 million officially unemployed workers, 3.2 million involuntary part-time workers, and 4.2 million "discouraged" workers. Using the narrowest of these measures of unemployment, the U.S. economy had a job gap of 1.1 million jobs. Using the broadest measure of unemployment, the economy was short 8.5 million jobs. By May 2003, when the official unemployment rate stood at 6.1% (still close to what many conservative economists define as full employment), the job gap had grown to 6.2 million jobs based on the narrowest measure of unemployment and 16.3 million jobs if we include involuntary part-time and discouraged workers as also needing jobs.

The size and persistency of the job gap shown in this data calls into question the widely held assumption that the neoliberal policy regime adopted by the United States has at least succeeded in providing adequate numbers of jobs for its labor force, even if those jobs are not always adequately paid. The data also calls into question the widely held assumption that when unemployment rates fall to the 4% to 6% range, employment policy should concentrate on overcoming structural barriers to equal employment opportunity rather than trying to drive the unemployment rate lower. Given the size of the economy's job gap, these structuralist measures may simply cause increased churning in the low-wage sector of the labor market as job-seekers who benefit from the policies replace otherwise similarly situated workers in available jobs. However important these measures may be in promoting equal employment opportunity, it seems unlikely that policies designed to overcome the structural barriers that beset disadvantaged population groups in the United States have any effect on the overall level of unemployment.

To the extent that job vacancy data is available in other countries, economic and social human rights advocates should be able to measure the size of those countries' job gaps as well. If that monitoring activity were undertaken, I believe it would show that job shortages are endemic in market economies even at the top of the business cycle, and irrespective of whether their labor markets are "flexible" or heavily regulated. Although hardly good news, facing that fact would be extremely helpful in directing the attention of economists and policy makers throughout the world to the inherent shortcomings of policies to combat unemployment (both neoliberal and social democratic), which focus on eliminating structural barriers to equal employment opportunity while tolerating persistently high job shortages. As in the United States, these policies may be important in securing the distributional aspect of the right to work, but they are no substitute for policies designed to secure the quantitative dimension of the right.

---

to persons who are not seeking work because they think no jobs are available or that employers will not hire them. It does not mean, of course, that all of these persons actually would elect to go to work if suitable jobs were available for them.

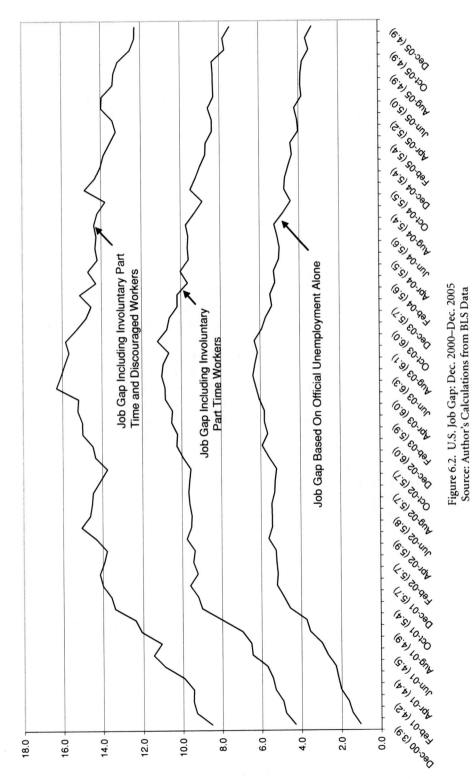

Figure 6.2. U.S. Job Gap: Dec. 2000–Dec. 2005
Source: Author's Calculations from BLS Data

The role of structural factors in causing unemployment also can be monitored by comparing movements in the economy's unemployment and job vacancy rates. As explained earlier, if structural factors are causing changes in the level of unemployment, the unemployment and job vacancy rates will tend to move in the same direction. If the unemployment and job vacancy rates move in the opposite direction, it suggests that changes in the level of unemployment are being caused by changes in the size of the economy's job gap, with structural factors affecting only the distribution of that unemployment.

The job vacancy rate (v) is the proportion of all jobs in the economy (vacant and occupied) that are vacant. This relationship can be expressed as follows:

$$v = V/(V + E) \qquad \text{(The job vacancy rate) (2)}$$

where E = the level of employment in an economy.

Figure 6.3 shows changes in the unemployment rate and job vacancy rate in the United States from December 2000 through November 2005. The fact that these two rates moved in opposite directions over this period suggests that changes in the level of joblessness were being caused by changes in job availability rather than changes in the severity of structural barriers to the achievement of full employment.

Only if the value of G in Equation (1) was negative and the value of v in Equation (2) was moving in the same direction as the economy's unemployment rate would it make sense for efforts to reduce the level of unemployment in an economy to concentrate on the elimination of structural barriers to equal employment opportunity as a strategy for reducing the level of unemployment in society. When the value of G is large relative to the level of unemployment, and job vacancy rates are moving in the opposite direction from unemployment rates, the most that can be expected from a structuralist strategy for combating unemployment is greater equality in its distribution.

Let me again emphasize that this does not mean structuralist measures are either unnecessary or a waste of time.[18] To the contrary, they are essential to secure the distributional aspect of the right to work; but they should not be viewed as a strategy to secure the quantitative dimension of the right in the absence of clear evidence that structural barriers are affecting the level as well as the distribution of unemployment in the economy.

For full employment to be achieved in a strictly quantitative sense, it is necessary to eliminate both an economy's job gap and any structural barriers that are causing job vacancies to remain unfilled. This means that the number of job vacancies must be greater than the number of unemployed job-seekers in the economy, and that all remaining unemployment must be attributable to unavoidable frictional factors. These conditions can be expressed as follows:

$$U = U_f < V \qquad \text{(full employment) (3)}$$

where

U_f = Unemployment attributable to unavoidable frictional factors.

---

[18] I have noted elsewhere, though, that the existence of a large job gap in an economy tends to undermine the effectiveness of efforts to eliminate structural barriers to equal employment opportunity. The effectiveness of such efforts is likely to increase as unemployment rates decline, that is, as the economy's job gap shrinks (2000a, 750–58; 2002, 438–45).

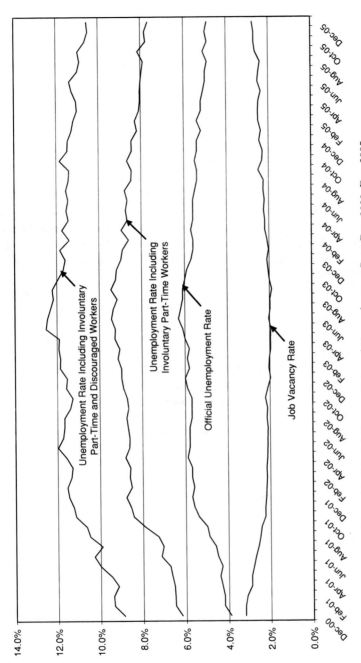

Figure 6.3. U.S. Job Vacancy Rate and Unemployment Rate: Dec. 2000–Dec. 2005
Source: Author's Calculations from BLS Data

This relationship also can be expressed in terms of the unemployment and job vacancy rate as follows:

$$u = u_f < v \quad \text{(full employment) (4)}$$

where

   u = the economy's unemployment rate, and
   u_f = the economy's unavoidable frictional unemployment rate

Accordingly, either Equation (3) or Equation (4) can be used to define full employment in the quantitative sense.

Notice that U cannot equal U_f unless there are more job vacancies (V) than job-seekers (U) in the economy. Similarly, u cannot equal u_f unless the vacancy rate exceeds the unemployment rate. Tracking job vacancies accordingly may seem superfluous to the task of measuring an economy's performance in achieving full employment. All we need to know is the economy's unemployment rate (u) and its frictional unemployment floor (u_f).

There are two reasons, though, why I believe the collection of job vacancy data is necessary as a practical matter. First, although a comparison of the actual unemployment rate in an economy (u) to the economy's presumed frictional unemployment floor (u_f) can tell us whether the economy has achieved full employment, we have to know the economy's frictional unemployment floor for that test to be useful. I have argued that u_f falls in the 1% to 2% range, but other economists may argue that an economy's frictional unemployment floor is substantially higher than that, and if they are right, an unemployment rate of 4% may indeed be full employment.

Comparing job vacancy rates in an economy to the economy's unemployment rate (as in Figure 6.2) or the level of job vacancies to the level of unemployment (as in Figure 6.1) provides a less easily disputed test (if not a completely dispositive one) of whether an economy really has achieved full employment. If such a comparison shows that there still are substantially more unemployed individuals than job vacancies in the economy, we can confidently conclude that full employment has not been achieved. Moreover, this method of measuring an economy's performance in securing the quantitative dimension of the right to work is both easily explained to, and comprehended by, the public. It doesn't take expertise in economics to understand that full employment has not been achieved when there are too few jobs to go around.

The second reason I believe the collection of job vacancy data is important is because the job vacancy data also can help us evaluate claims that the only unemployment which remains in an economy is structural. When steps are taken to "slow down" an economy when unemployment has fallen to the 4% to 5% level, few voices are raised in protest on the grounds that this will prevent the quantitative dimension of the right to work from being secured. The assumption that any unemployment that remains at that level must be either frictional or structural is too readily accepted. Comparing job vacancy and unemployment data provides the best test of this important assumption.

It may be uncomfortable for central bankers and other economic policy makers to admit that the policies they advocate and pursue rely on the involuntary unemployment of millions of people to control inflation; but if the data supports that conclusion, human rights advocates have no reason to let them off easy. Governments should be challenged to justify the economic policies they pursue in this regard with as much persistence and force as they are challenged to justify violations of civil and political rights committed for the purpose of enhancing national security.

CONCLUSION

Of the four dimensions of the right to work identified in this chapter, it should be easiest to monitor the quantitative aspect, as the data needed to do so is relatively easy to collect compared to the data needed to monitor the other three dimensions. If that monitoring activity were undertaken, I believe it would confirm that job shortages are endemic in market economies even at the top of the business cycle, and that efforts to eliminate structural barriers to equal employment opportunity have little, if any, effect on the size of those job shortages. Although hardly good news, facing that fact would be extremely helpful in directing the attention of economists and policy makers to the inherent shortcomings of existing policies for combating unemployment.

It is past due time for progressive policy analysts and progressive policy makers to take up the challenge they have largely abandoned since the mid-1970s, and devote their energies to the task of devising a strategy for securing the right to work that once again includes a commitment to ending job shortages in market economies.

Securing the right to work in all its dimensions is too important to the economic and social human rights enterprise to permit the discouragement that accompanied the collapse of progressive full employment policies in the 1970s to continue to cause human rights advocates to soft-peddle the importance of the full employment goal. Given the practical importance of full employment for the achievement of economic and social human rights in general, the development of policies capable of achieving full employment or its functional equivalent should be among the highest priorities of the human rights movement today. But that will not happen unless the importance of the quantitative dimension of the right to work is once again accorded the emphasis it deserves in discussions of economic and social human rights generally, and the right to work in particular. To that end, any effort to monitor the performance of an economy in securing the right to work that does not accord prominent attention to the quantitative aspect of the right should be viewed as seriously deficient.

To encourage improved monitoring activities related to this task, I have attempted to show how job vacancy data can be combined with unemployment data to provide a reasonably straightforward means of evaluating national efforts to achieve full employment. It is my hope that economic and social human rights advocates will come to see the importance of statistical series like the ones I describe, and that the commitment to and belief in full employment that animated progressive reform efforts in the immediate post–World War II era will once again assume their proper role in the advocacy of economic and social human rights.

REFERENCES

Abraham, Katharine G. 1983. Structural/Frictional vs. Deficient Demand Unemployment: Some New Evidence. *American Economic Review* 73: 708–24.

American Law Institute. 1945. Statement of Essential Human Rights. Reprinted in Louis B. Sohn. 1995. How American International Lawyers Prepared for the San Francisco Bill of Rights, *American Journal of International Law* 89 (3): 540–53.

Bernstein, Jared, and Dean Baker. 2003. *The Benefits of Full Employment: When Markets Work for People*. Washington, DC: Economic Policy Institute.

Beveridge, William. 1944. *Full Employment in a Free Society*. London: G. Allen & Unwin.

Clark, Maurice. 1949. *National and International Measures for Full Employment*. Lake Success, NY: United Nations.

Committee on Economic Security. 1935. Report of the Committee on Economic Security, 15 January 1935. Reprinted in National Conference on Social Welfare. 1985. *The Report of the Committee on Economic Security of 1935 and Other Basic Documents Relating to the Development of the Social Security Act*.

Commons, John R. 1923. Hobson's "Economics of Unemployment." *American Economic Review* 13: 638–47.

Employment & Training Institute. 1993–present. Survey of Job Openings in the Milwaukee Metropolitan Area. Milwaukee: University of Wisconsin-Milwaukee (biannual).

Farm, Ante. 2003. *Defining and Measuring Unmet Labour Demand*. Swedish Institute for Social Research: Stockholm University and Statistics Sweden.

Forbath, William. 1999. Caste, Class and Equal Citizenship. *Michigan Law Review* 98 (1): 1–91.

Glendon, Mary Ann. 2001. *A World Made New: Eleanor Roosevelt and the Universal Declaration of Human Rights*. New York: Random House.

Harvey, Philip. 1989. *Securing the Right to Employment: Social Welfare Policy and the Unemployed in the United States*. Princeton, NJ: Princeton University Press.

Harvey, Philip. 1995a. Paying for Full Employment: A Hard-Nosed Look at Finances. *Social Policy* 25: 21–30.

Harvey, Philip. 1995b. Fashioning A Work-Based Strategy for Welfare Reform Based on International Human Rights Doctrine. *Journal of Public Health Policy* 16: 269–85.

Harvey, Philip. 1999. Liberal Strategies for Combating Joblessness in the Twentieth Century. *Journal of Economic Issues* 33: 497–503.

Harvey, Philip. 2000a. Combating Joblessness: An Analysis of the Principal Strategies that Have Influenced the Development of American Employment and Social Welfare Law during the 20th Century. *Berkeley Journal of Employment and Labor Law* 21: 677–758.

Harvey, Philip. 2000b. Direct Job Creation. In *Commitment to Full Employment: Macroeconomics and Social Policy in Memory of William Vickrey*, ed. Aaron Warner et al., 35–54. Armonk, NY: M. E. Sharpe.

Harvey, Philip. 2002. Human Rights and Economic Policy Discourse: Taking Economic and Social Human Rights Seriously. *Columbia Human Rights Law Review* 33: 363–471.

Harvey, Philip. 2003. The Right to Work and Basic Income Guarantees: A Comparative Assessment, Paper presented at the Second Congress of the U.S. Basic Income Guarantee Network, New York City, Feb. 21–23, 2003. USBIG Discussion Paper No. 57. Available at: http://www.usbig.net.

Harvey, Philip. 2005. Basic Income and the Right to Work: Competing or Complementary Goals. *Rutgers Journal of Law and Urban Policy* 2: 2–59.

Hobson, John A. 1922. *The Economics of Unemployment.* New York: Macmillan.

Holzer, Harry J. 1989. *Unemployment Vacancies and Local Labor Markets.* Kalamazoo, MI: Upjohn Institute for Employment Research.

Holzer, Harry J. 1996. *What Employers Want: Job Prospects for Less-educated Workers.* New York: Russell Sage Foundation.

International Labour Organization. 1964. Employment Policy Convention (Convention 122).

International Labour Organization. 2002. *Global Employment Agenda.* Geneva: International Labour Office. Available at: http://www.ilo.org/public/english/employment/empframe/practice/download/gea.pdf.

International Labour Organization. 2003. Special Issue: Measuring Decent Work. *International Labour Review* 142: 109–271.

Morsink, Johannes. 1999. *The Universal Declaration of Human Rights: Origins, Drafting, and Intent.* Philadelphia: University of Pennsylvania Press.

Mucciaroni, Gary. 1990. *The Political Failure of Employment Policy: 1945–1982.* Pittsburgh: University of Pittsburgh Press.

National Resources Planning Board. 1943. *National Resources Development Report for 1943,* H.R. Doc. No. 78–128, pt. 3, Security, Work and Relief Policies.

Noguera, Jose A., and Daniel Raventos. 2002. Basic Income, Social Polarization and the Right to Work. In *Promoting Income Security as a Right: Europe and North America,* ed. Guy Standing, 269–84. London: Anthem Press.

Rees, Albert. 1957. The Meaning and Measurement of Full Employment. In *The Measurement and Behavior of Unemployment,* 13–49. Cambridge, MA: National Bureau of Economic Research.

Rey, José Luis. 2004. El Derecho Al Trabajo, ¿Forma De Exclusión Social? Las Rentas Mínimas De Integración Y La Propuesta Del Ingreso Básico. *Revista Icade* 62: 239–69.

Roosevelt, Franklin D. 1944. Message to Congress on the State of the Union, 11 January 1944. Reprinted in *The Public Papers & Addresses of Franklin D. Roosevelt,* ed. Samuel Rosenman, 13: 32–42. New York: Harper and Brothers, 1950.

Somavia, Juan. 2000. *Decent Work for All in a Global Economy.* Address to the staff of the World Bank, 2 March 2000. Available at: http://www.ilo.org/public/english/bureau/dgo/speeches/somavia/2000/worldbk.htm.

Standing, Guy. 2002. *Beyond the New Paternalism: Basic Security as Equality.* London: Verso.

Sundquist, James L. 1968. *Politics and Policy: The Eisenhower, Kennedy and Johnson Years.* Washington, DC: The Brookings Institution.

van Parijs, Philippe. 1995. *Real Freedom for All.* New York: Oxford University Press.

7 The Status of Efforts to Monitor Economic, Social, and Cultural Rights

AUDREY R. CHAPMAN

INTRODUCTION

The requirements of article 2 of the International Covenant on Economic, Social and Cultural Rights (hitherto referred to as the ICESCR or the Covenant) have long complicated efforts to conceptualize and monitor economic, social, and cultural rights. Article 2(1) sets a standard of the gradual achievement of the enumerated rights in the Covenant within the framework of the resources available to do so. In other words, although the goal is the full implementation of the rights enumerated in the Covenant, states parties – the countries that have ratified the instrument – are not required to do so immediately. Instead, states parties are instructed as follows:

> Each State Party to the present Covenant undertakes to take steps, individually and through international assistance and cooperation, especially economic and technical, to the maximum of its available resources, with a view to achieving progressively the full realization of the rights recognized in the present Covenant by all appropriate means, including particularly the adoption of legislative measures.

The standard specified by the ICESCR is often spoken of in a shorthand manner as "progressive realization." The concept of progressive realization has been described as the "linchpin of the whole Covenant" (Alston & Quinn 1987, 172).

In contrast, the International Covenant on Civil and Political Rights (ICCPR) imposes an immediate obligation for states parties to respect and ensure all of its enumerated rights. The parallel umbrella article of the ICCPR (article 2(1)) directs states parties "to respect and ensure to all individuals within its territory and subject to its jurisdiction the rights recognized in the present Covenant."

"Progressive realization" constitutes a far more difficult standard to implement and monitor than immediate and full implementation of rights (Chapman 1996, 29–36). In theory, to monitor civil and political rights requires only to ascertain whether or not a country has met the standards enumerated in the right. It suggests that there are only two alternatives – full implementation or failure to do so resulting in violations. In reality, however, the situation is far more complicated, and many civil and political rights require investments of resources and legal and policy inputs that are also only gradually realized.

The primary United Nations treaty monitoring body vested with oversight of the ICESCR, the Committee on Economic, Social, and Cultural Rights (hitherto the Committee or CESCR), has sought to balance the flexibility, gradualness, and variability inherent in the formulation of article 2(1) with meaningful goal setting and accountability measures. The dilemma is how to provide guidelines and to monitor whether states parties are moving expeditiously and effectively toward the goal of the full realization of the rights. In the process of attempting to do so, the Committee has had to wrestle with how to "operationalize" what it means to take steps "to the maximum of its available resources" and "achieving progressively the full realization of the rights." Evaluating compliance also has required clarifying what the phrase "maximum of its available resources" entails in specific circumstances. Difficulties in interpreting and applying these provisions have affected the conceptualization of the scope of state party obligations, the implementation of the rights enumerated in the ICESCR, the development of accountability mechanisms, and the ability to monitor systematically state party performance.

This chapter has two main sections. The first will assess the progress that has been made in interpreting article 2(1) and understanding its four major components for delineating the obligations of states parties. The second section will deal with the implications of article 2(1) for monitoring and accountability. It will consider four methodological approaches consistent with the requirements of article 2(1): focusing on core obligations, identifying violations, utilizing budget analysis, and delineating indicators.

INTERPRETING ARTICLE 2(1)

A. Progressive Realization

According to the Committee on Economic, Social, and Cultural Rights third General Comment, the concept of progressive realization constitutes a recognition that full realization of all economic, social and cultural rights will generally not be able to be achieved in a short period of time (CESCR 1990, ¶ 9). Although the language of "progressive realization" introduces the element of gradual achievement, reflecting the difficulties of any country achieving the immediate and full realization of these rights, the Committee has made clear that it is not meant to eliminate states parties' obligations or to deprive rights of meaningful content. General Comment No. 3 states that "the phrase must be read in the light of the overall objective, indeed the *raison d'etre*, of the Covenant which is to establish clear obligations for States parties with respect to the full realization of the rights in question" (CESCR 1990, ¶ 2). It should be noted, however, that the Covenant itself and the work of the Committee have not made clear what would constitute full realization of specific rights.

Far from "progressive realization" granting governments an excuse to delay indefinitely its efforts to realize these rights, states parties are instructed to move as expeditiously and effectively as possible toward the goal of full implementation. This instruction, which first appears in General Comment No. 3, is also repeated in subsequent general comments dealing with specific rights, for example, the right to the highest attainable level of physical and mental health (CESCR 2000, ¶ 31). The third General Comment makes clear that while the full realization of rights may be achieved progressively, steps toward that goal must be taken within a reasonably short time after the Covenant's entry into force (CESCR 1990, ¶ 2). However, with the exception of its General Comment outlining the requirements of article 14, which directs states parties to adopt a detailed plan of action to achieve free and compulsory primary education for all within two years of ratifying the Covenant, the Committee has not specified the initial steps a state party must undertake (CESCR 1999). Nor has the Committee defined what "moving expeditiously and effectively entails.

According to the Committee's interpretation, deliberately retrogressive measures with regard to economic, social, and cultural rights are problematic. Justification for any such deliberately retrogressive measure would fall on the state party in question. It would need to be fully justified by reference to the totality of the rights provided for in the Covenant and in the context of the full use of the maximum available resources (CESCR 1990, ¶ 9). General Comment No. 14 reiterates the Committee's presumption that retrogressive measures are not permissible (CESCR 2000, ¶ 32).

It can be assumed from the above that the Committee's interpretation of article 2(1) requires a state party to undertake initiatives resulting in continuous improvement in its realization of the rights enumerated in the Covenant. That said, however, the Committee has not defined whether this standard applies to every component of each right. Although the Committee urges states parties to provide data whereby it can assess the situation of numerous groups within the population – particularly those who are disadvantaged, vulnerable, and impoverished – it is also not clear whether "progressive realization" pertains strictly here as well. If so, a state party would need to show that it succeeded in promoting the enjoyment of each significant component of all of the rights recognized in the Covenant for these groups. No state party reports have attempted to do so. Nor has the Committee's dialogue with representatives of states parties, or concluding observations in reference to particular states, suggested that the Committee expects to receive these data or to be able to monitor the human rights situation in particular states on so disaggregated a level. But, again, it is unclear whether this reflects the Committee's interpretation of the requirements of "progressive realization," or whether it is merely a realistic acceptance of the limited capabilities of the states parties and its own monitoring procedures.

It also should be noted that the Committee rarely uses "progressive realization" as a standard in reviewing states parties' reports. Instead, its reviews tend to focus on the status of enjoyment of particular rights with regard to specific groups at that time. Less frequently, the Committee considers whether there has been a change, but it does not do so in a systematic manner.

B. To Take Steps

As noted earlier, article 2(1) instructs states parties "*to take steps*, individually and through international assistance and cooperation, especially economic and technical, to the maximum of its available resources . . . *by all appropriate means, including particularly the adoption of legislative measures.*" This language implies that all states, including the most developed ones, are not expected to implement fully the rights enumerated in the Covenant, but instead to take steps toward that goal. Conversely, the requirement to take steps, and apparently appropriate and meaningful steps, applies to all states, even those with very limited resources. Specifying what these steps entail is therefore key to making article 2(1) a meaningful standard.

In General Comment No. 3 on the Nature of State Obligations, the Committee emphasizes the need for states parties to take meaningful steps within a reasonably short time after the Covenant's entry into force. According to the Committee, "the steps should be deliberate, concrete and targeted as clearly as possible toward meeting the obligations recognized in the Covenant" (CESCR 1990, ¶ 2). In this General Comment, and then again in General Comment No. 9 on the domestic application of the Covenant, the Committee interprets article 2(1) as permitting a broad and flexible approach that enables the particularities of the legal and administrative systems of each state, as well as other relevant considerations, to be taken into account, but at the same time requiring each state party to use all the means at its disposal to give effect to the rights recognized in the Covenant (CESCR 1998).

In terms of specifying what kinds of steps are envisioned, the third General Comment, like the wording of article 2(1) itself, highlights the importance of legislative measures. But the Committee also recognizes the importance of going beyond legislation to other types of initiatives: "It wishes to emphasize, however, that the adoption of legislative measures, as specifically foreseen by the Covenant, is by no means exhaustive of the obligations of States parties. Rather, the phrase 'by all appropriate means' must be given its full and natural meaning" (CESCR 1998, ¶ 4). General Comment No. 3 cites judicial remedies in accordance with the national legal system as being of particular importance (CESCR 1998, ¶ 5). In its ninth General Comment, the Committee returns to the importance of judicial remedies focusing on the need to provide status to the provisions of the Covenant in the national legal order, and to assure there are judicial or administrative remedies available when needed (CESCR 1998).

In addition to legal provisions and to judicial remedies, the third General Comment also identifies other measures that constitute appropriate steps for the purposes of article 2(1). These include, but are not limited to, administrative, financial, educational, and social measures (CESCR 1990, ¶ 7). Over time, the Committee has viewed these initiatives as being of increasing importance. Its later General Comments focus more on required policies and patterns of investments required to respect, protect, and fulfill specific rights than just on legal changes or judicial remedies. For example, General Comment 14 notes: "the right to health must be understood as a right to the enjoyment of a variety of facilities, goods, services and conditions necessary for the realization of the highest attainable standard of health" (CESCR 2000, ¶ 9).

To encourage progressive achievement and accountability, the Committee has begun recommending the adoption and implementation of plans with goals and timetables. One of the core obligations identified in the general comment on the right to health, for example, is to adopt and implement a national public health strategy and plan of action based on epidemiological evidence, addressing the health concerns of the whole population. The plan of action is to be devised and periodically reviewed on the basis of a participatory and transparent process, including such methods as right to health indicators and benchmarks by which to monitor progress (CESCR 2000, ¶ 43(f)).

C. Through International Assistance and Cooperation

Article 2(1) mandates that each state party "take steps, individually and *through international assistance and cooperation, especially economic and technical,* to the maximum of available resources." This formulation underscores the importance of international financial aid and technical assistance to the total pool of resources available to specific states for implementing the rights in the Covenant. It also implies that the human rights responsibilities of states, particularly those with greater financial and technical resources, extend beyond their borders.

Time and again, the Committee has emphasized that the "maximum resources available" to a state party to realize economic, social, and cultural rights includes international aid and technical assistance. The third General Comment reiterates that the phrase "to the maximum of its available resources" was intended by the drafters of the Covenant to refer to both the resources existing within a state and those available from the international community through international cooperation and assistance (CESCR 1990, ¶ 11).

To that end, the Committee has determined that there is an obligation for states that are in a position to do so to provide aid to assist others in realizing economic, social and cultural rights. According to General Comment No. 3:

> It is particularly incumbent upon those States that are in a position to assist others in this regard . . . in the absence of an active programme of international assistance and cooperation on the part of all those States that are in a position to undertake one, the full realization of economic, social and cultural rights will remain an unfilled aspiration in many countries. (CESCR 1990, ¶ 14)

The importance the Committee assigns to the more affluent states contributing development assistance is clear in its review of states parties' reports. Its dialogue with representatives of these states parties and its concluding observations frequently mention the levels of aid being provided, often critically,[1] but occasionally in a more complementary manner.[2] But the Committee has not defined the nature of the obligations of states, at varying levels of development, to provide international assistance and cooperation. Most often, it mentions this obligation in the context of encouraging more affluent states to meet the internationally agreed on

---

[1] Examples from the Committee on Economic, Social, and Cultural Rights' 2002b sessions, outlined in the "Report on the twenty-fifth, twenty-sixth and twenty-seventh sessions," include the Concluding Observations on Japan (¶ 591), Germany (¶ 657), and France (¶¶ 863, 873).

[2] An example is in the Committee's Concluding Observations on Sweden from its 2002b "Report on the twenty-fifth, twenty-sixth and twenty-seventh sessions" (¶ 714).

international development target of 0.7% of GNP.[3] The Committee is not specific, however, how this assistance is to be given – through bilateral or multilateral channels – or the specific purposes for which it is to be provided. Nor does it provide guidelines on how to determine priorities.

The Committee frequently reminds states parties of their responsibilities as members of international organizations, and particularly international financial institutions, to pay greater attention to the protection of human rights. The Committee's Concluding Observations often encourage donor countries to do all they can to ensure that the policies and decisions of those organizations are in conformity with the obligations of states parties to the Covenant. Examples are their Concluding Observations on Japan in 2001 (CESCR 2002b, ¶ 616) and the United Kingdom in 2002 (Skogly 2003, 413). But the Committee also stresses the importance of middle-income recipient countries, such as Korea, taking their Covenant obligations into account when negotiating with international financial institutions to overcome financial crises and restructure their economies (CESCR 2002b, ¶222). And the Committee offers similar advice to poor countries which are the recipients of aid, underscoring the importance of integrating human rights, including economic, social, and cultural rights, in the formulation of the Poverty Reduction Strategy Papers being prepared.[4]

D. To the Maximum of Available Resources

Article 2(1) of the ICESCR specifies that each state party must take steps individually and through international assistance and cooperation to *"the maximum of its available resources"* to achieve progressively the full realization of rights in the Covenant. This language recognizes that the total resource pool states can devote to realizing its rights obligations will vary. It also links compliance with the provision of resources from two sources – the budgets of the state and from international assistance to implement that right.

The dilemma is that, like other phrases in article 2(1), this formulation is vague and imprecise. It leaves open the key issue of how to compute the maximum of the available resources. Although the Committee has dealt with resource issues in many contexts, it has not sought to illuminate this central issue. Nor does the Covenant provide guidance as to what constitutes the appropriate level of investment from the totality of available resources in the rights enumerated in the Covenant. And neither the ICESCR nor the Committee have addressed the even more complex question of how the pool of resources should be allocated among the various rights.

---

[3] Examples are Concluding Observations of CESCR on France, Doc. E/C.12/1/Add.72, November 30, 2001a,b ¶ 24; and Concluding Observations of CESCR on Germany, Doc. E/C.12/1Add.68, September 24, 2001a,b ¶ 15. These examples, as well as the point they underscore, are drawn from Bueno de Mesquita (2003: 9).

[4] Examples in the Committee's "Report on the twenty-fifth, twenty-sixth and twenty-seventh sessions" include Senegal (¶ 376) and Nepal (¶ 554). The Committee has given similar advice to other countries in its Concluding Observations/Comments, including Georgia, Doc. E. C.12/1Add.83, Art. 29 (2002b); Georgia, Doc. E/C.12/1Add.83, Art. 39 (2002b); Solomon Islands, Doc. E/C.12/1/Add.84 (2002b), and Azerbaijan, Doc. E/C.12/1/Add.104, Art. 53 (2004).

An article written by Robert E. Robertson (1994) provides a helpful overview of several problems associated with this formulation. Commenting that the resources issue is so complicated that universal agreement on standards seems unattainable, he characterizes the phrase as two warring adjectives describing an undefined noun: "'Maximum' stands for idealism; 'available' stands for reality. 'Maximum' is the sword of human rights rhetoric; 'available' is the wiggle room for the state" (Robertson 1994, 694). Robertson also points out the difficulties of defining the term "resources" and compiling a truly definitive list of the types of resources that can be marshaled by a state (ibid., 695). In addition to money or financial resources, informational resources; natural resources such as land, seeds, water, and animals; human resources; and technological resources play an important role in achieving ICESCR rights (ibid., 696–97). He raises the issue as to whether the ICESCR requires state direction of all of these resources, to their maximum extent, toward the goal of promoting economic, social, and cultural well-being (ibid., 697).

Beyond identifying the resources that are relevant to the realization of economic, social, and cultural rights is the even more complicated question of what resources are potentially available to a specific state at a particular point in time. Total government expenditures represent one potential source of available resources. It would be possible in principle to assess the distribution of the budget and its investment in economic, social, and cultural rights, as well as trends within the budget over time. The reporting requirements for both the Committee on Economic, Social and Cultural Rights and the Committee on the Rights of the Child ask for the percentage of the GNP, as well as the annual national and/or regional budgets invested in some, but not all, of the enumerated rights, and how these figures compare with five and ten years ago. Very few governments, however, provide these data.

But those who have considered this issue have generally considered the available resources to be a broader category than the governmental budgetary appropriations. Here it should be remembered that article 2(1) of ICESCR specifies that states parties "take steps, *individually and through international* assistance and cooperation, especially economic and technical, to the maximum of *its available resources.*" The Committee has considered international assistance and cooperation to be an essential component of the available resources, and has justified its interpretation that all states parties are obligated to realize the core obligations associated with specific rights, even those states that are resource poor, on these grounds. Its reporting guidelines specify that states parties provide data both for investments drawn from its own resources and from international assistance. The Committee on the Rights of the Child has similar reporting guidelines and even requests disaggregated data on the contributions from international assistance to programs for the realization of specific children's rights (United Nations 2004, ch. VII, ¶ 7).[5]

There are two other sources of potential resources. The first is private sector funding. In recent years, corporate investment and private-public partnerships have figured prominently in development investment strategies, but not explicitly within the framework of realizing economic, social, and cultural rights. The second

---

[5] The guidelines of all the treaty monitoring bodies are compiled into this single document, each constituting a separate chapter. Those of the Committee on the Rights of the Child are contained in chapter VII.

is state strategies for appropriating private sector resources, such as by imposing wealth taxes or directing land reform, for purposes of achieving rights objectives. It is, of course, very difficult to assess the potential resources that can be made available from these sources.

One significant implication of using the framework of "the maximum of its available resources" is that valid expectations and concomitant obligations of states parties under the Covenant are not uniform or universal, but are instead relative to levels of development and available resources. On one level, this makes a great deal of sense, especially within the framework of "progressive realization." However, it is also very problematic, because it necessitates the development of a multiplicity of performance standards for each right in relationship to the varied social, developmental, and resource contexts of specific countries. However, the ICESCR does not offer any specifics on how to make these complex determinations. Nor has the Committee on Economic, Social, and Cultural Rights addressed this central issue.

Even in the absence of clarity on the points mentioned above, the Committee on Economic, Social, and Cultural Rights has criticized specific countries, usually the more affluent or middle income countries, for inadequate expenditures in realizing specific rights. For example, during its consideration of Canadian compliance with the ICESCR in 1993, the Committee noted an unacceptable level of homelessness and inadequate living conditions, and criticized Canada for spending only 1.3% of government expenditures on social housing (Robertson 1994, 703). In 2001, the Committee was disturbed by the portion of the government budget allocated to health spending in the Republic of Korea, which was under 1% and declining (CESCR 2003, ¶ 236). It also criticized the government for the low level of budgetary expenditures for primary schooling and for the failure to make post-primary education free and compulsory despite the state's relatively high level of economic development (ibid., ¶¶ 237, 239).

The Committee has also raised issues of inadequate and inappropriate spending by poor and middle-income countries. Using data made available by the UNDP and not the state party, the Committee expressed concern with the decrease in Algeria's public for health and education in the 1990s (ibid., ¶ 249). In 2001, it expressed concern that the funds allocated by Senegal for basic social services fell short of the minimum social expenditures required, and regret that more money was being spent on the military and debt servicing than on basic social services (2002b, ¶ 249). It recommended that Panama increase the resources available to fight illiteracy (ibid., ¶ 279), that Algeria allot a greater share of its budget to the struggle against poverty (ibid., ¶ 837), and that Colombia allocate a higher percentage of its GDP for the health sector (ibid., ¶ 796).

It is notable that the Committee is raising issues of spending on rights by poor countries despite its awareness of the deleterious impact of poverty, debt-servicing, structural adjustment programs, and austerity measures imposed by international financial institutions. As the Committee has itself observed, the prioritization of funds to meet critical human rights targets for vulnerable sectors of the population is perhaps even more important in poor countries. Many poor countries have particularly glaring problems of misallocation of the limited funds available, as, for example, investing its health budget disproportionately in a few hospitals serving the population in urban centers at the expense of making available resources for primary health centers in rural areas. However, the Committee's review of expenditure patterns has been hampered by the difficulty in gaining access to relevant data.

But even when critical of the inadequate investment, the Committee has not sought to set levels of appropriate investment that specific states should be devoting to particular targets. Instead, it settles for recommending the allocation of more funds for specific purposes, such as, for example, fighting illiteracy. Often, the Committee requests increasing expenditure for comprehensive categories, such as all social expenditures.

IMPLICATIONS OF ARTICLE 2(1) FOR MONITORING AND ACCOUNTABILITY

Monitoring the major international human rights instruments is central to the development of a meaningful international human rights system. Otherwise, countries that ratify or accede to specific human rights instruments cannot assess their own performance in promoting effective realization of the enumerated rights. Furthermore, without effective monitoring, states cannot be held accountable for implementation of, or be made liable for violation of, these rights.

To assist states parties in fulfilling their obligations and to enable international monitors to evaluate a country's performance, each of the major international human rights covenants requires the regular submission of reports for review by the relevant UN committee of experts. Each of the UN treaty monitoring bodies has established reporting guidelines and set reporting schedules, usually requiring states parties to submit an initial report within two years of ratification and additional reports every five years. According to the Committee on Economic, Social and Cultural Rights, these reporting obligations serve a variety of purposes. They encourage states parties to regularly monitor the actual situation with respect to each of the enumerated rights in order to assess the extent to which the various rights are being enjoyed by all individuals within the country. The preparation of the reports and interaction with the Committee enables states parties to develop a better understanding of problems and shortcomings impeding the realization of economic, social, and cultural rights. By doing so, the reviews provide a basis for government elaboration of carefully targeted policies to implement the Covenant. The process also facilitates public scrutiny of government policies with regard to the Covenant's implementation, while encouraging the involvement of a multiplicity of sectors of society in the formulation, implementation, and review of relevant policies (CESCR 1989).

However, these reporting requirements do not necessarily ensure that effective monitoring will take place. Monitoring state compliance with international human rights standards is an exacting process with numerous political and methodological requirements, and the monitoring of economic, social and cultural rights is particularly complex. Systematic monitoring of these rights has five methodological preconditions:

(1) conceptualization of the specific components of each enumerated right and the concomitant obligation of states parties;
(2) delineation of performance standards related to each of these components in the form of indicators and benchmarks, making possible the identification of problems and potential major violations;

(3) collection of relevant, reliable, and valid data – appropriately disaggregated by sex and a variety of other variables – in a consistent format over time, making it possible to evaluate trends;

(4) development of an information management system for these data to facilitate analysis of trends over time and comparisons of the status of groups within a country;

(5) the ability to analyze these data in order to determine patterns and trends.

Up to the present, the UN human rights system, or national governments for that matter, has not been able to meet these requirements. Nevertheless, there has been progress in developing methodologies to deal with some of the dilemmas noted in this paper. This section reviews several of these approaches and tools.

CORE OBLIGATIONS APPROACH

The evolving jurisprudence on economic, social, and cultural rights recognizes that elements of these rights create an immediate duty on the part of the state, and therefore are not subject to the progressive realization standard. Just as under civil and political rights, states parties have the immediate obligation to ensure nondiscrimination and the equal enjoyment of a right. Article 2(2) of the ICE-SCR specifies that states parties undertake to guarantee that the rights enumerated in the Covenant will be exercised without discrimination of any kind as to race, color, sex, language, religion, political or other opinion, national or social origin, property, birth, or other status. The Committee has been clear that the principle of nondiscrimination is not subject to "progressive realization" or "rationally justified" exceptions (CESCR 2002b, ¶ 591).

Article 3 of the ICESCR enunciates a corollary obligation to ensure the equal right of men and women to the enjoyment of the rights set forth in the Covenant. The most recent General Comment of the Committee interprets article 3 in a comprehensive manner as requiring both *de facto* and *de jure* equality (CESCR 2005, ¶ 7). It also is quite explicit that article 3 sets a nonderogable standard for compliance with the obligations to ensure the equal right of men and women in articles 6 through 15 of the ICESCR (CESCR 2005, ¶ 17).

Additionally, the Committee has established that there is a "minimum core content" with regard to each economic, social, and cultural right that all states parties are obligated to fulfill. In its third General Comment, the Committee declares itself to be "of the view that a minimum core obligation to ensure the satisfaction of, at the very least, minimum essential levels of each of the rights is incumbent upon every state party" (CESCR 1990, ¶ 10). According to the Committee, "a State party in which any significant number of individuals is deprived of essential foodstuffs, of essential primary health care, of basic shelter and housing, or of the most basic forms of education is, *prima facie*, failing to discharge its obligations under the Covenant" (ibid.). It goes on to state that "the obligations to monitor the extent of the realization, or more especially of the nonrealization of economic, social, and cultural rights, and to devise strategies and programmes for their promotion, are not in any way eliminated as a result of resource constraints" (Ibid., ¶ 11). The Committee has consistently underscored that, even in times of severe resource constraints, the vulnerable members of society "can and indeed must be protected by the adoption of relatively low-cost targeted programs" (ibid., ¶ 12).

More recently, the Committee has begun to identify these core obligations arising from the "minimum essential levels" of the rights to food, education, and health. In some cases, such as its General Comment on the right to health, these obligations are quite extensive. General Comment No. 14 confirms that states parties have a core obligation to ensure the satisfaction of, at the very least, minimum essential levels of the right to health. In the Committee's view, this core includes the following:

(1) to ensure the right of access to health facilities, goods and services on a nondiscriminatory basis, especially for vulnerable or marginalised groups;

(2) to ensure for everyone access to the minimum essential food which is sufficient, nutritionally adequate and safe, to ensure their freedom from hunger;

(3) to ensure access to basic shelter, housing, and sanitation, and an adequate supply of safe and potable water;

(4) to provide essential drugs, as from time to time defined by the World Health Organization's (WHO) Action Programme on Essential Drugs;

(5) to ensure equitable distribution of all health facilities, goods, and services;

(6) to adopt and implement a national public health strategy and plan of action, on the basis of epidemiological evidence, addressing the health concerns of the whole population; the strategy and plan of action shall be devised, and periodically reviewed, on the basis of a participatory and transparent process; they shall include mechanisms, such as right to health indicators and benchmarks, by which progress can be closely monitored; the process by which the strategy and plan of action are devised, as well as their content, shall give particular attention to all vulnerable or marginalised groups. (CESCR 2000, ¶ 43)

In the next paragraph, the Committee goes on to confirm that obligations of comparable priority also include the following:

(1) to ensure reproductive, maternal (prenatal and postnatal) and child health care;

(2) to provide immunization against the community's major infectious diseases;

(3) to take measures to prevent, treat and control epidemic and endemic diseases;

(4) to provide education and access to information concerning the main health problems in the community, including methods of preventing and controlling them;

(5) to provide appropriate training for health personnel, including education on health and human rights. (CESCR 2000, ¶ 44)

According to the Committee, core obligations are nonderogable, and they therefore continue to exist in situations of conflict, emergency, and natural disaster. Moreover, because poverty and vulnerability are global phenomena, core obligations have relevance for even the richest states. The Committee also has made clear that after a state party has achieved the core obligations related to economic, social, and cultural rights, it continues to have an obligation to move as expeditiously and effectively as possible toward the full realization of all the rights in the Covenant (CESCR 2002a, ¶ 18).

In theory, the core obligations approach offers a more feasible standard to monitor than progressive realization, but it has proven to have problems of its own. One issue is the confusion between the minimum core content or core elements of a right and minimum state obligations. The minimum core content can be defined as the nature or essence of a right; that is, the essential element or elements without which it loses its substantive significance as a human right. In contrast, minimum state obligations refer to the essential requirements of a state party to be considered to be in compliance with its international obligation. It has been described as a "floor" below which conditions should not be permitted to fall. The latter, which is the approach the Committee favors, provides a more precise and often a more limited standard to monitor.

The dilemma is that many human rights specialists are reluctant to give up a broad conception of the essential components of a particular right when conceptualizing the obligations of a state party. Some advocates also fear that a focus on core obligations will mean that states will assume that they are obligated to do that minimum and nothing else. In the process, the "floor" will then become a "ceiling." This hesitance was visible at a 2000 conference in South Africa on exploring the core content of socioeconomic rights organized jointly by the Socio-economic Rights Project of the Centre for Human Rights, University of Pretoria, and the Science and Human Rights Program of American Association for the Advancement of Science (Brand & Russell 2002). It led to the ironic situation whereby representatives of government agencies at the conference were often more favorably inclined to endorsing a core obligations approach than the members of the South African human rights community, even the co-organizers of the event.

Given the strong commitment of most human rights specialists to the right or rights on which they work, there is a tendency for them to translate an expansive notion of core elements of a right into an equally comprehensive view of core obligations. This can be seen in the inclusive manner that many of the various contributors to a volume on core obligations conceptualized the core elements and the related core state obligations (Chapman & Russell 2002). And as the core obligations in the right to health noted earlier indicate, the conceptualization of core obligations in the Committee's General Comments also tends to be quite comprehensive.

It is worth noting, though, that if states actually *did* fulfill their core obligations, it would in most cases represent significant progress. The purpose of the minimum state obligations approach is not to give states an escape hatch for avoiding their responsibilities under the Covenant. It is in fact the opposite: a way to accommodate the reality that many economic, social, and cultural rights (and often civil and political rights as well) require resources that are simply not available in poor countries. The minimum state obligations approach affirms that even in highly strained circumstances, a state has irreducible obligations that it is assumed to be able to meet. If it cannot, the burden of proof shifts to the state to justify its claim of the need to cut back. By definition, minimum core obligations apply irrespective of the availability of resources or any other factors and difficulties.

A central question therefore is whether it is possible to identify such a set of centrally important and universally applicable obligations related to specific rights? In my own writings on the right to health, my answer is both "yes" and "no." I answer yes because carefully targeted policies with modest costs can often make significant contributions toward realizing the right to health. Improved performance on achieving the right to health often depends more on appropriate policy priorities and a better allocation of existing resources than on increasing total expenditures. By contrast, the real life constraints under which many states operate is staggering. Many of the poorest countries with the worst health outcomes have severe resource constraints and limited infrastructure and capabilities. In an era of increasing globalization, the gross and grotesque disparities in resource allocations within and between countries is increasing, and states that can afford to be generous in providing international aid and assistance frequently do not do so. Although it is theoretically possible to define minimum core obligations – related to implementing the right to health and other rights that apply to all states parties, regardless of their economic development or social and political context – defining such a standard requires "thinking small" and setting priorities, and human rights specialists generally have been adverse to doing so (Chapman 2002, 195–97).

VIOLATIONS APPROACH

In a 1996 article in which I reviewed the problems that the standard of "progressive realization" entails for monitoring economic, social, and cultural rights, I proposed a "violations approach" as a more feasible and effective alternative (Chapman 1996). The "violations approach" advocated there focused on identifying three types of violations: (1) violations resulting from actions and policies on the part of governments, (2) violations related to patterns of discrimination, and (3) violations taking place because of a state's failure to fulfill the minimum core obligations contained in the Covenant.

The proposal to develop a "violations approach" was then taken up by a group of international human rights experts (including this author) who met in Maastricht in 1997 to develop guidelines regarding the nature and scope of violations of economic, social and cultural rights and to identify appropriate responses and remedies. The Maastricht Guidelines affirm that "[a]s in the case of civil and political rights, the failure by a State Party to comply with a treaty obligation concerning economic, social and cultural rights is, under international law, a violation of that treaty" (ICJ 1997, ¶ 5).[6] The Maastricht Guidelines define violations of economic, social, and cultural rights in relationship to the three types of obligations on states: the obligations to respect, to protect, and to fulfill enumerated rights. According to the Guidelines, the failure to realize any or all of these three obligations constitutes a violation of these rights. To determine whether an action or omission amounts to

---

[6] The Maastricht Guidelines on Violations of Economic, Social, and Cultural Rights (hereinafter Maastricht Guidelines) were formulated in Maastricht from 22–26 January 1997 by a group of more than thirty experts convened by the International Commission of Jurists (Geneva, Switzerland), the Urban Morgan Institute of Human Rights (Cincinnati, Ohio), and the Centre for Human Rights of the Faculty of Law of Maastricht University (the Netherlands).

a violation of a right, the Maastricht Guidelines distinguish between the inability and unwillingness of a state to comply with its treaty obligations. The Guidelines place on the state party the burden of proving that it is unable to carry out its obligations (International Commission on Jurists 1997, ¶ 13).

The "violation approach" has been used by nongovernmental organizations monitoring economic, social, and cultural rights in many parts of the world. Beginning with its general comment on the right to health, the Committee has determined which actions or omissions amount to a violation of the right (CESCR 2000, 46–52). It provides a detailed and explicit list of the most frequent and serious violations related to the obligations to respect, protect, and implement the right. When reviewing the performance of specific states parties, the Committee still prefers the language of "concerns" to "violations," but it has been willing to label serious problems as violations.

The "violations approach" has generated a vigorous debate among advocates of economic, social, and cultural rights, and this debate has served as an important stimulus to the intellectual refinement and development of economic, social, and cultural rights. One claim is that adoption of a violations approach would weaken the call for eventual full implementation of economic and social rights by concentrating on the most flagrant abuses. A related objection focuses on the concern that calling governments to account for violations might be a risky strategy for nongovernmental organizations in some countries; on the other hand, in working toward progressive realization, nongovernmental organizations are more likely to be seen as taking a more constructive approach. A third complication stems from the difficulty of defining what constitutes a violation. Although major violations tend to be relatively easy to identify, others are more subtle. To claim that a particular deprivation rises to the level of human rights violation may in some cases require an understanding of circumstances, an assessment of degree or magnitude, or an evaluation of intent (Chapman & Russell 2002, 7–8).

Here it is important to note that my motivation in proposing a "violations approach" was to overcome some of the limitations of the progressive realization formula and to deal more meaningfully with the most flagrant abuses of these rights. The "violations approach" was intended as a supplementary and not a sole strategy for monitoring economic, social, and cultural rights. I also had hoped that the "violations approach" might provide a path to understanding the content of these rights more clearly, but I did not assume that it would be the sole methodology to doing so. It is obviously important to go beyond a "violations approach" so as to provide a positive guideline on how best to implement the rights in question, and to assess whether particular states parties are making reasonable progress in improving their human rights implementation.

BUDGET ANALYSIS

The question of resources and how to evaluate the sufficiency of investment is central to implementing and monitoring the realization of economic, social, and cultural rights. One of the several reasons that assessing the standard of "the maximum available resources" has been so difficult is that it requires an ability to analyze budget flows, which is a skill that very few human rights specialists or treaty monitoring bodies have. One critical task, therefore, is to establish a set of concrete and systematic standards and methodologies to assess the extent to which a state is complying with "progressive realization" in the context of available resources. Robertson reviewed several approaches that, used in combination with one another, would offer at least a promising start to the task.

One approach that Robertson evaluated was using a minimum financial threshold in order to assess whether a state was meeting the requirement. He specifically considered the standard of 5% of GNP – the level suggested in the 1991 UNDP *Human Development Report* as an appropriate human expenditure ratio (Robertson 1994, 710). He rightly rejected the figure as too low, but did not offer an alternative (ibid.). He also concluded that it might not be possible to arrive at any one indicator for a minimum level of investment in economic, social, and cultural rights applicable to all countries. Instead, he suggested that it might be preferable to use comparisons between certain countries and between expenditures on ICESCR rights and other items, like military expenditures, to illustrate the trade-offs countries have made (ibid., 711).

It may, however, be feasible to set minimum targets in relationship to specific rights. For example, the World Health Organization has set a global target of a minimum of 5% of GNP for health expenditures. This investment is intended to cover funding for hospitals, maternity and dental centers, clinics with a major medical component, national health and medical insurance schemes, preventive care, and family planning (World Bank 1993, 312).

Recently, there has been progress in developing tools for budgetary analysis for human rights purposes. *Dignity Counts*, a guide on budget analysis to help assess a government's compliance with its economic, social, and cultural rights obligations (Fundar et al. 2004), was prepared by partnership of three groups: Fundar – Centro de Análisis e Investigación (a human rights group based in Mexico City), the International Budget Project, (part of the Washington, DC, Center on Budget and Policy Priorities), and the International Human Rights Internship Program of the Institute of International Education. It is built around a case study of expenditures in the Mexican national budget related to the right to health. This publication shows the promise of budgetary analysis to assess the sufficiency of government investment, the efficiency with which the government resources are being spent, and the equity of patterns of expenditure. It also underscores the importance of combining budget analysis with a knowledge of human rights requirements and the institutional, policy, economic, and social context in which the expenditures are being made.

ROLE OF INDICATORS AND BENCHMARKS

As noted earlier, monitoring progressive realization requires operationalizing each component of article 2(1), specifically determining how to assess compliance and then obtaining the requisite data. Doing so has been very difficult, especially because the progressive realization benchmark assumes that valid expectations and concomitant obligations of states parties under the ICESCR are not uniform or universal but, instead, relative to levels of development and available resources. This necessitates the development of a multiplicity of performance standards for each enumerated right in relationship to the varied social, developmental, and resource contexts of specific countries.

This difficulty is further compounded by the need to disaggregate the analysis, which comes from the recognition that national averages reveal little about the status of specific groups and communities within a country. There are likely to be major disparities in the enjoyment of human rights among different communities, between the sexes, in urban and rural areas, among income/socioeconomic groups, and in various geographic regions. For example, it would be possible for countries to move toward meeting the Millennium Development Goals on a national level without improving equity and overcoming these disparities. To assess inequalities and inequities, as well as the types of changes over time, requires identifying appropriate indicators sensitive to these differentials and applying them over time.

Furthermore, a human rights approach has a particular focus on the status of poor, disadvantaged, and marginalized individuals and communities. This concern is reflected in the reporting guidelines of the Committee on Economic, Social, and Cultural Rights and of the Committee on the Rights of the Child, the manner in which they assess the performance of states parties, and in the orientation of many of their General Comments. Their approach implies that the two Committees believe that it is desirable to evaluate the "progressive realization" of specific rights for each of these specific groups. Up to the present, however, it has not been feasible to do so.

The reporting guidelines of both Committees stipulate that data provided to assess performance on many of the enumerated rights be disaggregated by sex, race, region, socioeconomic group, linguistic group, and urban/rural divisions. In some cases, the Committees identify the groups for which they are seeking specific information. For example, with regard to the right to food, the Committee on Economic, Social, and Cultural Rights' reporting guidelines specify that the statistical data be broken down by geographical areas and also be provided for landless peasants, marginalized peasants, rural workers, rural unemployed, urban unemployed, urban poor, migrant workers, indigenous peoples, children, elderly people, and other especially affected groups (United Nations, 2004, ch. II, ¶ 43). In others, the Committees place the onus on the state party to identify the relevant group. The guidelines of the Committee on Economic, Social, and Cultural Rights dealing with the right to health, for instance, ask the state party whether there are groups in the country whose health situation is significantly worse than that of the majority of the population, and asks them to provide relevant details as well as to specify various policy measures taken to improve the physical and mental health of such vulnerable and disadvantaged groups (ibid., ¶ 51).

Given that this approach is very vague and imprecise, it is not surprising that few, if any, states parties comply and provide the level of disaggregation requested in their reporting. In many cases, the quality statistical data that is necessary to analyze "progressive realization" on a disaggregated basis may not even be available for some of the Covenant-recognized rights in countries with a weak statistical system. And, if the data exist, countries may be reluctant to take the time to compile the reports, or to share them with human rights treaty monitoring bodies or nongovernmental organizations, because the data would reveal significant problems and inadequacies in their implementation of rights.

Moreover, were the data to exist and were it to be made available, efforts to use them to evaluate a country's performance in realizing a particular right would likely overwhelm the two UN committees tasked with monitoring "progressive realization." It would require sophisticated computerized information systems and a level of statistical expertise, which members of the Committee and the Office of the High Commissioner for Human Rights' staff generally lack, to evaluate this large volume of data.

The UN human rights system has therefore long acknowledged that the development of indicators and benchmarks is central both to developing the capacity for monitoring the "progressive realization" of economic, social, and cultural rights and to building accountability. However, the acceptance of the need for indicators has not been matched by their development.

There are, of course, many indicators being used for development purposes, but there is generally an agreement in the literature that human rights and development indicators differ in several key ways. In brief, development indicators measure progress toward development, not the extent to which a government is complying with its obligations under human rights law. The *Human Development Report 2000* identifies three contrasts in the approach of human development and human rights indicators:

(1) Conceptual foundation: Human development indicators assess the status of people's capabilities. Human rights indicators evaluate whether people are living with dignity and freedom and the extent to which critical actors, usually states, have fulfilled their obligations to establish and uphold just social arrangements to enable their residents to do so (UNDP 2000, 91). In human rights terminology, what is key is for indicators to provide ways to assess whether states are respecting, protecting, and fulfilling the rights enumerated in the Covenant.

(2) Focus of attention: although both types of indicators focus on human outcomes and inputs, so as to draw attention to unacceptable disparities and suffering, human rights indicators also need to cover the policies and practice of legal and administrative entities and the conduct of public officials (ibid.).

(3) Additional information: a human rights assessment requires a wider range of data than a development analysis and has greater need for the data to be disaggregated by a variety of variables, such as gender, ethnicity, race, religion, nationality, birth, and social origin (ibid.).

In 1988, the Sub-Commission on the Prevention of Discrimination and Protection of Minorities and the Human Rights Commission appointed Danilo Türk as a Special Rapporteur, with a mandate to prepare a study of the problems, policies, and practical strategies relating to the more effective realization of economic, social and cultural rights. In several of his reports, the Special Rapporteur discussed the potential use of economic and social indicators for assessing progress in the realization of these rights. According to Türk, indicators can provide a quantifiable measurement device of direct relevance to the array of economic, social, and cultural rights; a means of measuring the progressive realization of these rights over time; and a method for determining difficulties or problems encountered by states in fulfilling these rights. In addition, he stated that indicators can assist with the development of the "core contents" of this category of rights and offer yardsticks whereby countries can compare their progress with other states (Türk 1990, ¶ 96).

He recommended that the UN convene a seminar for discussion of appropriate indicators to measure achievements in the progressive realization of economic, social, and cultural rights, to offer an opportunity for a broad exchange of views among experts.

In January 1993, the UN Centre for Human Rights (now the Office of the High Commissioner for Human Rights) convened such an expert seminar, for which this author served as the rapporteur. The expert seminar called for the development of new human rights indicators based on the content of each economic, social, and cultural right (U.N. General Assembly 1993, ¶ 172), but it also recognized that it might be premature to do so. The seminar participants concluded that the development of indicators could not be a means to conceptualizing the content and obligations of specific rights, but instead required the ability to do so. Therefore, the seminar report recommended that the human rights community undertake the following: clarifying the content of specific rights and the nature of states parties' obligations, developing plans to promote the progressive realization of each of the rights, improving evaluation and monitoring of progressive realization, identifying and addressing violations, instituting improved cooperation with the UN system, facilitating the participation of nongovernment organizations and affected communities in the tasks outlined above, and applying scientific statistical methodologies (ibid., ¶ 181). To be able to utilize indicators on a scientific basis for purposes of assessing the realization of economic, social, and cultural rights, it also pointed to the need to establish appropriate computerized information systems with the ability to evaluate a complex series of data on a disaggregated and time-series basis (ibid., ¶ 187).

To achieve the various objectives outlined in the report, the seminar recommended that the UN Centre for Human Rights convene a series of expert seminars focused on specific economic, social, and cultural rights that would include representatives of specialized agencies, chairpersons of treaty monitoring bodies, and relevant nongovernmental organizations (ibid., ¶ 202). Taking up this call, the Commission on Human Rights, beginning in 1994, approved a series of resolutions requesting the UN Centre for Human Rights to do so (see, e.g., Commission on Human Rights 1994, ¶¶ 7–9; 1996, ¶¶ 8–10). The Committee on Economic, Social, and Cultural Rights has also been keen to hold these seminars. To date, however, the UN has failed to do so, possibly because of budget limitations.

The Committee has had a long-standing interest in the development of indicators. In its first General Comment adopted in 1989, the Committee recommended the use of national benchmarks in evaluating progress in the implementation of the Covenant (CESCR 1989, ¶ 6), but it was unspecific as to what it meant by that reference. Three of their General Comments focusing on the content of specific rights have called for the use of indicators for purposes of monitoring: General Comment No. 13 on the right to education (CESCR 1999b, ¶ 52), General Comment No. 14 on the right to the highest attainable standard of health (CESCR 2000, ¶¶ 57–58), and General Comment No. 15 on the right to water (CESCR 2003, ¶¶ 53–54). None of these General Comments, however, specifies the indicators to be applied.

In the absence of agreed-on indicators for the right to health, General Comment No. 14 assigns the task to states parties. It proposes that national health strategies should identify appropriate right to health indicators designed to monitor, at the national and international levels, the state party's obligations under article 12 (CESCR 2000, ¶ 57). The General Comment goes on to recommend that having identified appropriate right to health indicators, states parties set appropriate national benchmarks in relation to each indicator. It then envisions that during the periodic reporting procedure, the Committee will engage in a process of scoping with the state party to set the indicators and national benchmarks which will provide the targets to be achieved during the next reporting period. During the next five-year period, the state party will then use the national benchmarks to help monitor its implementation of article 12. In the subsequent reporting process, the state party and the Committee will consider whether or not the benchmarks have been achieved, and will address the reasons for any difficulties encountered (CESCR 2000, ¶ 58).

Although admirable in its conceptualization, this process is problematic for its implementation. The dilemma, of course, is that the states parties are in no better position than the Committee to develop rights-based health indicators. Nor does the Committee have the expertise, let alone the time, to engage in the scoping process envisioned in the General Comment. This is especially true given its current work load, which limits the time set aside for the public component of each state party review to no more than three half day sessions.

One notable development is that the Office of the High Commissioner for Human Rights has recently established an expert working group on indicators, of which this author is a member. The working group has been assigned the task of developing a conceptual framework for indicators appropriate for treaty monitoring bodies and providing sample indicators, in response to a request by the chairpersons of the UN human rights treaty monitoring bodies. In March 2005, a background workshop dealing with indicators took place in Turku, Finland, jointly sponsored by Abo Akademi University and the Office of the High Commissioner for Human Rights (Institute for Human Rights 2005). The first formal meeting of the expert working group was held in August 2005. At the meeting, the members of the working group adopted a conceptual framework for rights-specific indicators based on the proposal of Paul Hunt, discussed later. They also agreed that this approach to human rights indicators was applicable to civil and political rights, as well as economic, social, and cultural rights (Office of the High Commissioner for Human Rights 2005). This approach was refined at a subsequent meeting in March 2006 and a paper setting forth the framework was drafted for the chairs of the human rights treaty monitoring bodies (OHCHR 2006). Members of the working group are proceeding to draft sample sets of indicators for specific rights – both economic and social rights and civil and political rights.

Paul Hunt was appointed as the first Special Rapporteur on the right to the highest attainable standard of physical and mental health by the Commission on Human Rights in 2002, and his mandate was then renewed in 2005. The approach to indicators he has proposed, although specifically developed for the right to health, has, as noted earlier, now been applied to other human rights as well. He distinguishes between three types of indicators: structural indicators, process indicators, and outcome indicators.

Structural indicators address whether or not the requisite infrastructure is in place that is considered necessary for, or conducive to, the realization of a specific right. Specifically, structural indicators evaluate whether a country has established the institutions, constitutional provisions, laws, and policies that are required. Most structural indicators are qualitative in nature and are not based on statistical data, and many can be answered by a simple yes or no (IHR 2005, ¶¶ 18–19).

Process indicators, along with outcome indicators, monitor the variable dimension of human rights that arise from the concept of "progressive realization." Their key feature is that they can be used to assess change over time (ibid., ¶¶ 22–25). Specifically, process indicators assess the degree to which activities necessary to attain specific rights-related objectives are being implemented, as well as the progress of these activities over time. They monitor effort and not outcome. The types and amounts of governmental inputs are one important kind of process indicator. Unlike structural indicators, process indicators require statistical data (ibid., ¶ 26).

In contrast, outcome indicators assess the status of a population's enjoyment of a right. They show the "facts" and measure the results achieved. Many of the Millennium Development Goal indicators, for example, are outcome indicators. Like process indicators, outcome indicators are variable and therefore require statistical data (ibid., ¶ 28).

In his 2004 report to the General Assembly, Hunt applied the methodology to the development of indicators for one dimension of child health – child survival – with a view to exploring how it might work in practice. In doing so, he took a draft set of core child survival indicators drafted by a UN interagency consultative process, identified which of them corresponded with a right to health norm, and supplemented their list with additional indicators essential to the right to health (including those related to national strategy and plan of action, participation, monitoring/accountability, and international assistance and cooperation). In accordance with his classification noted earlier, he groups the proposed indicators as structural, process, or outcome indicators. In addition, he sets out which indicators require disaggregation, as well as the government department likely to have responsibility for collecting the relevant data (Hunt 2004, ¶¶ 59–84).

CONCLUSION

There is progress in understanding the requirements of economic, social, and cultural rights and in developing methodologies to monitoring them. Nevertheless, there remains considerable work to be done. "Progressive realization" still constitutes a problematic standard to conceptualize, with many key issues unresolved. Each of the four approaches outlined in this chapter needs further development. Hopefully, states parties will develop a stronger commitment to implement these rights, and human rights advocates will continue to progressively attain improved capacities to understand and monitor them.

REFERENCES

Alston, Philip, and Gerard Quinn. 1987. Nature and Scope of States Parties' Obligations under the International Covenant on Economic, Social and Cultural Rights. *Human Rights Quarterly* 9 (2): 156–229.

.d, Danie, and Sage Russell, eds. 2002. *Exploring the Core Content of Socio-Economic ¹ights: South African and International Perspectives*. Menlo Park, South Africa: Protea Press.

ueno de Mesquita, Judith R. 2003. International Covenant on Economic, Social, and Cultural Rights: Obligations of International Assistance and Cooperation. N.p., (prepared ⸱r the Committee on Economic, Social and Cultural Rights), Human Rights Centre, ⸱iversity of Essex.

⸱man, Audrey R. 1996. A "Violations Approach" for Monitoring the International ⸱venant on Economic, Social and Cultural Rights. *Human Rights Quarterly* 18 (1): ⸱–66.

⸱man, Audrey R. 2002. Core Obligations Related to the Right to Health. In *Core ⸱ligations: Building a Framework for Economic, Social and Cultural Rights*, ed. Audrey R. ⸱hapman and Sage Russell. Antwerp; Oxford; New York: Intersentia.

⸱apman, Audrey R., and Sage Russell. 2002. Introduction. In *Core Obligations: Building a Framework for Economic, Social and Cultural Rights*, ed. Audrey R. Chapman and Sage Russell. Antwerp; Oxford; New York: Intersentia.

Commission on Human Rights. 1994. Question of the realization in all countries of the economic, social and cultural rights contained in the Universal Declaration of Human Rights and in the International Covenant on Economic, Social and Cultural Rights, and study of special problems which the developing countries face in their efforts to achieve these human rights. U.N. Doc. E/CN.4/RES/1994/20 (Mar. 1).

Commission on Human Rights. 1996. Question of the realization in all countries of the economic, social and cultural rights contained in the Universal Declaration of Human Rights, and study of special problems which the developing countries face in their efforts to achieve these human rights. U.N. Doc. E/CN.4/RES./1996/11 (Apr. 11).

Committee on Economic, Social, and Cultural Rights (CESCR). 1989. General Comment No. 1: Reporting by States Parties. U.N. Doc. HRI/GEN1 (3rd Sess.).

Committee on Economic, Social, and Cultural Rights (CESCR). 1990. General Comment No. 3: The nature of States Parties' obligations (Art. 2, Par.1). U.N. Doc. HRI/GEN/ 1/Rev.1 (5th Sess., Dec. 14).

Committee on Economic, Social, and Cultural Rights (CESCR). 1998. General Comment No 9: The domestic application of the Covenant. U.N. Doc. E/C.12/1998/24 (19th Sess., Dec. 3).

Committee on Economic, Social, and Cultural Rights (CESCR). 1999a. General Comment No. 11: Plan of action for primary education. U.N. Doc. E./C.12/1999/4 (20th Sess., May 10).

Committee on Economic, Social, and Cultural Rights (CESCR). 1999b. General Comment No. 13, Art. 13. U.N. Doc. E/C.12/1999/10 (21st Sess., Dec. 8).

Committee on Economic, Social, and Cultural Rights (CESCR). 2000. General Comment No. 14: The right to the highest attainable standard of health. U.N. Doc. E/C.12/2000/4 (22nd Sess., Aug.).

Committee on Economic, Social, and Cultural Rights (CESCR). 2001a. Concluding Observations on France. U.N. Doc. E/C.12/1/Add/72, November 30.

Committee on Economic, Social, and Cultural Rights (CESCR). 2001b. Concluding Observations on Germany U.N. Doc. E/C.12/1/Add. 63, September 24.

Committee on Economic, Social, and Cultural Rights (CESCR). 2002a. Poverty and the International Covenant on Economic, Social and Cultural Rights: Statement of the Committee on Economic, Social and Cultural Rights to the Third United Nations Conference on the Least Developed Countries. In *Report on the twenty-fifth, twenty-sixth and twenty-seventh sessions*. U.N. Doc. E/2002/22 (SUPP), Annex VII, Supplement 2.

Committee on Economic, Social, and Cultural Rights (CESCR). 2002b. *Report on the twenty-fifth, twenty-sixth, and twenty-seventh sessions*. U.N. Doc. E/2002/22.

Committee on Economic, Social, and Cultural Rights (CESCR). 2003. General Comment No. 15: the right to water (Arts. 11 and 12 of the ICESCR). U.N. Doc. E/C.12/2002/11 (29th Sess., Jan. 20).

Committee on Economic, Social, and Cultural Rights (CESCR). 2004. Concluding Observations on Azerbaijan. U.N. Doc. E/C.12/1/Add. 104, November 26.

Committee on Economic, Social, and Cultural Rights (CESCR). 2005. General Comment No. 16: The equal rights of men and women to the enjoyment of all economic, social and cultural rights, Art. 3. U.N. Doc. E/C.12/2005/3 (34th Sess., May 13).

Fundar, International Human Rights Internship Program, and International Budget Project. 2004. *Dignity Counts: A Guide to Using Budget Analysis to Advance Human Rights*. Washington, DC: International Human Rights Internship Program.

Hunt, Paul. 2004. Report of the Special Rapporteur on the right of everyone to the enjoyment of the highest attainable standard of physical and mental health. U.N. Doc. A/59/422 (59th Sess., Oct. 8).

Institute for Human Rights (IHR), Åbo Akademi University. 2005. Report of Turku Expert Meeting on Human Rights Indicators, Åbo, Finland, March 10–13, 2005. http://www.abo.fi/instut/imr/research/seminars/indicators/Report.doc.

International Commission on Jurists (ICJ). 1997. The Maastricht Guidelines. In *Economic, Social and Cultural Rights: A Compilation of Essential Documents*, 81–91. Geneva: International Commission of Jurists.

International Covenant on Civil and Political Rights (ICCPR), adopted 16 December 1966, 999 U.N.T.S. 171 (entered into force 23 March 1976), G.A. Res. 2200 (XXI), 21 U.N. GAOR Supp. (No.16) at 52, U.N. Doc. A/6316 (1966).

International Covenant on Economic, Social and Cultural Rights (ICESCR), adopted 16 December 1966, 993 U.N.T.S. 3 (entered into force 3 January 1976), G.A. Res. 2200 (XXI), 21 U.N. GAOR Supp. (No. 16) at 49, UN Doc. A/6316 (1966).

Office of the United Nations High Commissioner for Human Rights (OHCHR). 2005. Indicators for Monitoring Compliance with International Human Rights Instruments: Conclusions and Recommendations. Expert Consultation, Geneva, 29 August 2005.

Office of the United Nations High Commissioner for Human Rights (OHCHR). 2006. Indicators for Monitoring Compliance with International Human Rights Instruments: Conclusions and Recommendations. Second Expert Consultation, Geneva, 30–31 March 2006.

Robertson, Robert E. 1994. Measuring State Compliance with the Obligation to Devote the "Maximum Available Resources" to Realizing Economic, Social and Cultural Rights. *Human Rights Quarterly* 16 (4): 693–714.

Skogly, Sirgun. 2003. The obligation of international assistance and co-operation in the International Conventant on Economic, Social and Cultural Rights. In *Human Rights and Criminal Justice for the Downtrodden: Essays in Honour of Asbjørn Eide*, ed. Morten Bergsmo. Leiden: Martinus Nijhoff.

Türk, Danilo. 1990. The New International Economic Order and the Promotion of Human Rights Progress Report: Realization of Economic, Social and Cultural Rights. U.N. Doc. E/CN.4/Sub.2/1990/19 (42nd Sess., July 6).

United Nations. 2004. Compilation of Guidelines on the Form and Content of Reports to be Submitted by States Parties to the International Human Rights Treaties, U.N. Doc. HRI/GEN/2/Rev.2 (7 May).

United Nations Development Program (UNDP). 2000. *Human Development Report 2000*. Oxford and New York: Oxford University Press.

United Nations General Assembly (UNGA). 1993. Report of the Seminar on appropriate indicators to measure achievements in the progressive realization of economic, social and cultural rights. U.N. Doc. A/CONF.157/PC/73 (25–29 Jan.).

World Bank. 1993. *World Development Report 1993*. New York: Oxford University Press.

8 Measuring the Progressive Realization of Economic and Social Rights

CLAIR APODACA[1]

In order to give the principles articulated in the Universal Declaration of Human Rights greater authority and strength, the United Nations drafted a Covenant on Human Rights. The ensuing debates as to whether economic and social rights are of the same character as civil and political rights resulted in two separate and overlapping documents: The International Covenant on Economic, Social, and Cultural Rights (ICESCR), and the International Covenant on Civil and Political Rights (ICCPR). Although civil and political rights have gained widespread recognition as human rights, there is still substantial disagreement among Western scholars and political leaders over whether social and economic rights are "rights" or goals.[2] The division between the two treaties and the primacy given to political rights has "ever since hovered like an albatross over the development of human rights protection" (Scott 1999).

The debate over the authenticity and legitimacy of economic and social rights has slowed the collection of adequate measures of economic and social rights indicators. Adequate measures are critical in obtaining an overall picture of the realization of these rights and in assessing their progress over time. The development, collection, and presentation of economic and social measures can increase the political and legal accountability of states to fulfill their treaty obligations. Furthermore, statistical measures can provide the evidence necessary to substantiate legal claims, thus rendering void the assertion that economic and social rights cannot be adjudicated in a court of law, and consequently are not legitimate rights.[3]

[1] I would like to thank the College of Arts and Sciences at Florida International University for providing summer funding for the research and writing of this chapter.
[2] The debate on whether economic and social rights are authentic human rights or merely national aspirations is virtually nonexistent outside the West. For many Third World leaders, scholars, and human rights activists, economic rights are the most fundamental of rights, whereas political and civil rights are considered noncrucial, "luxury" rights. However, as Jack Donnelly has stated, "this alleged concern for economic and social rights [on the part of Third World governments] is in fact a concern for growth/development irrespective of its distributional/rights consequence" (1999, 74).
[3] The nonrealization of economic and social rights is not the result of an individual's or group's irrational choice or lack of effort but, more often, the outcome of a government's or international institution's policy choices. Therefore, political accountability and judicial enforcement are reasonable remedies to economic and social rights violations.

Yet, on the face of it, economic and social rights appear to be easily and adequately measured. After all, the World Bank, the International Labour Organization (ILO), the International Monetary Fund (IMF), the United Nations Educational Scientific and Cultural Organization (UNESCO), and the United Nations Development Programme (UNDP), among many other international institutions, do collect and publish volumes of data. However, many measures currently collected and analyzed have limited relevance. Economic and social rights are more than the state's economic development, or on the human side, they are greater than simply measuring poverty.[4] This chapter attempts to determine how extensive a list of variables or indicators is required to measure the progressive realization of economic and social rights. By utilizing an information pyramid – developed by Kempf (1998) – governments, international monitoring bodies, the courts, and human rights researchers can monitor and assess state performance given cultural context and resource availability.

THE INTERNATIONAL COVENANT ON ECONOMIC, SOCIAL, AND CULTURAL RIGHTS

The ICESCR is the principal source of legal obligations and provisions protecting economic and social rights. As of October 2005, 151 countries have ratified the ICESCR and accepted the responsibility to protect and provide the economic and social rights of their citizens. Although the ICESCR was not drafted with the precision and clarity of the ICCPR the ICESCR does detail the rights of individuals and the duties of states. A state's duties concerning human rights, according to Asbjorn Eide (1989), entail three forms of obligations: the obligation to respect human rights, the obligation to protect human rights, and the obligation to fulfill human rights. Eide's formulation of state's duties is similar to the three correlative duties described by Shue (1978): the duty to abstain from depriving people of their rights, the duty to protect people from deprivation of their rights, and the duty to aid people in securing their rights. The obligation to respect human rights, in the area of economic and social rights, requires the state to refrain from interfering in the attainment of the rights or from doing anything that violates or infringes on procuring the rights. The obligation to protect compels the state to prevent other individuals or business concerns from violating economic and social human rights. The third level of state obligation is the duty to provide. The state has the obligation to fulfill the basic human needs, rights outlined in the ICESCR, of all those persons within its jurisdiction. The duty to fulfill requires positive state action and can be costly. The legal obligations imposed by the Covenant are obligations of conduct and result.

Philip Alston and Gerard Quinn (1987) have argued that many of the rights specified in the ICESCR depend on the availability of resources. In recognition

---

[4] This chapter does not attempt to redefine the concepts of economic or social rights but instead relies on the common delineation utilized by the International Covenant on Economic, Social, and Cultural Rights. Social rights are provisions of the basic necessities of life and a fair standard of living, such as food, housing, education, and health care. Economic rights, by contrast, include rights to work, to join trade unions, and to receive equal pay for equal work.

of this reality the framers of the ICESCR opted for the inclusion of the phrase "progressive realization." The phrase "achieving progressively the full realization of rights" was included in recognition of the economic reality in many states. Frequently less developed states simply do not have the resources to guarantee the immediate fulfillment of economic and social rights. Economic, social and cultural rights are positive rights in that they often require the provision of goods and services and the expenditure of scarce resources for their realization. The strength of the state's economy is the yardstick with which to measure state compliance with its duty to protect and provide for the well-being of its citizens. However, the concept of progressive realization was not meant as a defense for states whose rights' achievements failed to equal their available resources. Although a poor state cannot be expected to fulfill all the rights detailed in the ICESCR immediately, this state still maintains its obligation to use its meager resources to protect and provide for the greatest number of people in a nondiscriminatory manner. [5] The burden of proof against a charge of noncompliance due to the state's resource inability falls on the state.

Financial ability notwithstanding, states are still obligated "to take steps" to achieve full realization of these recognized rights without discrimination. These steps would include initiating official administrative, organizational, and judicial reforms necessary to protect and provide for the realization of economic and social rights. The Committee which monitors the ICESCR has concluded that to fully comply with the legal requirements of the treaty, state parties must establish "the provision of judicial remedies with respect to rights which may, in accordance with the national legal system, be considered justifiable. "The Committee notes, for example, that the enjoyment of the rights recognized, without discrimination, will often be appropriately promoted, in part, through the provision of judicial or other effective remedies" (CESCR 1990, ¶ 5).

THE ISSUE OF ADJUDICATION OF ECONOMIC AND SOCIAL RIGHTS

The moral claims to economic and social rights are difficult to translate into legal claims. Some politicians and scholars believe that because economic and social rights can not be adjudicated in a court of law, they are not rights. The ambiguous claim to "adequate food" or to "the enjoyment of the highest attainable standard of physical and mental health" cannot easily be interpreted and adjudicated by a court system. E. W. Vierdag (1978) believes that the "rights" granted by the International Covenant on Economic, Social and Cultural Rights are not "real" – that is, legal – and therefore they cannot be authentic human rights. Economic and social "rights" have, in Vierdag's opinion, two flaws making them non-justiciable. First, the Covenant fails to establish specific or *measurable* obligations on states.

---

[5] Article 2(2) of the ICESCR requires states to guarantee equal enjoyment of economic, social and cultural rights to all. Article 2(2) states:

The State Parties to the present Covenant undertake to guarantee that the rights enunciated in the present Covenant will be exercised *without discrimination of any kind* as to race, colour, *sex*, language, religion, political or other opinion, national or social origin, property, birth or other status [emphasis added].

And, second, courts lack the competence to compel governments to remedy violations. Thus they are not legally enforceable. Vierdag writes, "The goals, plans and programs to which economic, social and cultural rights relate are of an economic, social and cultural nature; and to cloak such ideals with terms of law by calling them 'rights' does not turn them into legal rights that can be enforced by courts of law . . . the implementation of [economic, social and cultural rights] is a political matter, not a matter of law, and hence not a matter of rights" (1978).[6] But the Committee on Economic, Social, and Cultural Rights holds the opposite opinion with regard to the adjudication of the rights outlined in the ICESCR. General Comment No. 9, "The Domestic Application of the Covenant" (CESCR 1998), rejects the argument that the courts cannot properly resolve social and economic rights. Paragraph 10 reads:

> In relation to civil and political rights, it is generally taken for granted that judicial remedies for violations are essential. Regrettably, the contrary assumption is too often made in relation to economic, social and cultural rights. This discrepancy is not warranted either by the nature of the rights or by the relevant Covenant provisions. . . . The adoption of a rigid classification of economic, social and cultural rights which puts them, by definition, beyond the reach of the courts would thus be arbitrary and incompatible with the principle that the two sets of human rights are indivisible and interdependent. It would also drastically curtail the capacity of the courts to protect the rights of the most vulnerable and disadvantaged groups in society.

It is apparent that the Committee wished to invalidate claims that economic and social rights are merely noble aspirations based on the mistaken belief that these rights are unenforceable and nonadjudicable.

In General Comment No. 3, the Committee asserts that the ICESCR includes several rights "which would seem to be capable of immediate application by judicial and other organs in many national legal systems. Any suggestion that the provisions indicated are inherently not self-executing would seem to be difficult to sustain" (CESCR 1990, ¶ 5). Among these rights are Article 2 subsection (2), which specifically requires the state to undertake the responsibility to guarantee that the enunciated rights be enjoyed by all without prejudice, and Article 3, which guarantees equality between men and women in the enjoyment of economic rights. States that are party to the International Covenant on Economic, Social, and Cultural Rights have the responsibility to provide – to the maximum of their resources – equal access to education, basic medical assistance, employment, adequate shelter, and food to all. States are immediately required to eliminate discriminatory laws, regulations, and acts of omission, which affect the full enjoyment of the rights recognized in the ICESCR. The collection of disaggregated measures can demonstrate states' discriminatory practices when certain groups enjoy significantly higher levels of rights fulfillment. Without disaggregated measures, progressive realization

---

[6] To assess the legitimacy of human rights in international law based on a test of enforceability or justiciability is inappropriate in the opinion of Fried van Hoof. He contends that "it is the exception rather than the rule that norms of international law can be enforced through courts of law" (1984, 100). A right can exist without the ability to be adjudicated. Human rights are not legal rights granted by a government, although they may be confirmed by legislation.

in the enjoyment of economic and social rights will often hide the persistent disparities between groups. The collection of measures is once again crucial to the ascertainment of equal access.

The question concerning violations of economic, social, and cultural rights, how they should be recognized, and how violations might be remedied is now being investigated and adjudicated within national, regional, and international tribunals. The courts are being used to interpret the provisions of the ICESCR and clarify state obligations. In particular, domestic and regional courts are asked with increasing frequency to adjudicate petitions relating to economic and social rights. The domestic courts in South Africa, India,[7] and the European Court of Human Rights are, perhaps, the premier examples.[8] Statistical documentation is vital in adjudicating claims involving violations of the rights contained in the ICESCR. It is impossible for the UN Committee on Economic, Social, and Cultural Rights (CESCR), human rights advocates, or even domestic courts, to monitor economic rights if there is no measure to determine improvement or regression in the attainment of the right to adequate housing, food, education, and so on.

THE VALUE OF QUANTITATIVE MEASURES

There are several advantages for both the state parties to the Covenant and for human rights researchers in developing high quality, comparable and straightforward economic and social measures. Some of the advantages are as follows:

1. *Human Rights Monitoring*: The use of measures enables researchers and policy makers to monitor results with respect to the progressive realization of economic, social and cultural rights. The development of relevant and precise information on human rights conditions is an essential tool for human rights monitoring. Because there is often a vast difference between rights achievement as claimed by the government and those rights as actually experienced by the citizens, monitoring governmental practices is crucial for the realization of economic rights. Without a doubt, measures are particularly important in documenting nonfulfillment or outright violations of economic and social rights for use in court proceedings. The use of economic and social measures can determine whether a state is complying with its treaty and moral obligations to provide to the maximum of its available

---

[7] Although many courts are reluctant to hear cases concerning economic rights, it has been claimed that economic rights concern issues of social policy under the purview of politicians. In this domain, the South African and Indian courts have been quite active. For example, with regard to South African cases, see *Government of the Republic of South Africa et al. v. Grootboom; Minister of Health and Others v. Treatment Action Campaign and Others; Thiagraj Soobramoney v. Minister of Health (Kwazulu-Natal)*. The Indian courts have decided several cases concerning economic rights. For example, see *C.E.S.C. Limited v. Subbash Chandra Bose; Consumer Education and Research Centre v. Union of India and Others; Mohini Jain v. State of Karnataka and Others; Air India Statutory Corporation etc. v. United Labour Union and Others*.

[8] For example, the European Court of Human Rights has rendered decisions concerning nondiscrimination (*S.W.M. Broeks v. Netherlands; Gaygusuz v. Austria*) and the right to an education (*Keldsen, Busk Madsen, Pedersen v. Denmark; Campbell and Cosans v. UK; or Belgian Linguistics v. Belgium*).

resources the realization of economic and social rights.[9] Without measures, a state's performance cannot be adequately assessed.

2. *Making Economic and Social Rights Adjudicable*: Statistical indicators are particularly important in developing a jurisprudence of human rights claims. Measures can be used in courts to adjudicate rights violations and determine if discriminatory practices exist. Thus the economic and social rights, which are subject to progressive implementation, can be enforced through domestic courts. The ability to adjudicate economic rights can only be guaranteed if information on the status/realization of these rights is provided. Statistical data can more clearly establish the state's omissions resulting in the nonrealization of economic rights.

3. *Assuring Nondiscrimination in Rights Enjoyment*: Carefully documented measures of those rights not subject to the progressive implementation standard, such as nondiscrimination, impose immediate obligations on the state, which can be adjudicated by the courts. The severe or widespread deprivation of food, health care, shelter, or employment, among certain groups or categories of people, are violations of economic and social rights standards and can be remedied through the use of the court system. If economic rights are not fulfilled because of the unavailability of resources, it is important to determine if the suffering and deprivation is disproportionately shouldered by marginalized or at-risk groups.

4. *Fixing Accountability*: Statistical measures can determine whether the duty bearer, typically the state, is fulfilling its treaty obligations while taking into account the capacity and resources of the duty bearer. The *Human Development Report 2000* emphasized the relationship between accountability and economic measures when it announced that "information and statistics are a powerful tool for creating a culture of accountability and for realizing human rights" (UNDP 2000, 10). Indicators can be used to track trends and identify changes in achievement. Without measures, states cannot be held accountable for not fulfilling their duty to protect and provide for economic and social human rights. Likewise, measures can exonerate a state if they reveal that the state was using its meager available resources in a nondiscriminatory manner to fulfill its treaty obligations.

OBSTACLES TO MEASURING ECONOMIC AND SOCIAL RIGHTS

Despite the emerging recognition of the importance of economic and social rights, scholars have yet to develop a systematic, consistent and universal strategy to define, operationalize, and measure these rights. Researchers, human rights advocates, and policy makers are faced with several obstacles when studying and evaluating economic and social rights. These obstacles include (1) limiting the enormous scope of

[9] The clause "to the maximum of its available resources" imposes an obligation on the state to give social welfare priority in resource allocation, but it also realizes that the state has legitimate interests in maintaining internal and external security. The available resources include domestic, as well as international, monies.

economic and social rights, (2) locating adequate data disaggregated by vulnerable groups (e.g., sex, age, ethnic and religious minorities, urban/rural populations, etc.), (3) finding available data covering enough countries to be useful and, (4) ensuring that these measures are comparable, in that they were defined and collected similarly across all countries.

Because the International Covenant on Economic, Social and Cultural Rights catalogs a multiplicity of rights, human rights scholars are faced with the task of reducing a long and complicated list of rights into a manageable set for both collection and research purposes. There is growing consensus that there are a few rights – basic rights for human survival and dignity – that are considered to be of the highest priority. Henry Shue identifies these rights as subsistence rights: the rights to adequate food, clothing, shelter, unpolluted water, and basic health care. These are the rights needed "for a decent chance at a reasonably healthy and active life of more or less normal length, barring tragic interventions." Shue continues, "By a 'right to subsistence' I shall mean a right to subsistence that includes the provision of subsistence at least to those who cannot provide for themselves" (1980, 23–24). David Trubek refers to these core rights as welfare rights, because they evoke "what is most basic and universal. . . . Behind all the specific rights enshrined in international documents and supported by international activity lies a social view of individual welfare" (1984, 206). The United Nations has also classified certain rights as basic, fundamental, or core rights (Türk 1992). Among those rights identified by the UN are the right to health and well-being, the right to a basic education, the right to work and fair remuneration, and the right to an adequate standard of living. The ILO has also defined these core rights as basic needs. Basic needs, according to the ILO (1982, 1), include:

> First, certain minimum requirements of a family for private consumption: adequate food, shelter and clothing, as well as certain household equipment and furniture. Second, they include essential services provided by and for the community at large, such as safe drinking water, sanitation, public transport and health, educational and cultural facilities.

The second obstacle for research on equality in the realization of economic and social rights is locating data disaggregated by group. The problems of measurement and collection are exacerbated when the dimensions of gender and other disenfranchised groups are added. Yet, in order to determine state compliance with the International Covenant on Economic, Social, and Cultural Rights, and to reveal disparities among the members of different populations, it is crucial to advocate for data that is disaggregated.

The Committee on the Elimination of Discrimination Against Women (CEDAW) noted its concern with the relative absence of disaggregated and precise indicators on the situation of women. The CEDAW remarked, "that statistical information is absolutely necessary in order to understand the real situation of women in each of the states parties to the Convention" (1989, 392). Aggregated data mask portentous differences in the realization of economic and social rights between different groups. The use of aggregate data cannot provide a complete assessment of rights attainment. Measures that are state averages hide the inferior and unacceptable economic and social rights violations experienced by marginalized populations.[10] The CEDAW's General Recommendation No. 9 requests states to make every effort to collect and provide appropriate data on the situation of women. Sex differentiated data are extremely useful in assessing compliance with nondiscrimination and equality of treatment clauses found in both the ICESCR and the Convention on the Elimination of all Forms of Discrimination Against Women. And, in recent years, states and World Bank agencies have begun to collect data disaggregated by sex. However, the importance of the need for disaggregated data applies to other vulnerable groups as well. Although much data are gathered and reported at the aggregate level, recently collected data are less likely to treat issues of gender, race and residence (rural/regional) as irrelevant. Obviously, data not disaggregated is worthless for determining whether obligations for nondiscrimination are discharged or if disadvantaged groups enjoy their economic and social rights.

A further obstacle to research is identifying variables that are comparable between countries and are collected worldwide. First, the researcher must establish whether a variable is comprehensive in that a sufficient number of countries, both developed and developing, collect data on the variable. Given the growth of international data collection organizations, for example, the UN Statistical Office or the World Bank, the lack of comprehensive data collection is becoming less of a problem. If the variable meets the comprehensive criterion, the researcher must next determine if the data is comparable; that is, whether the variable is operationally defined the same way, measured the same way, and calculated the same way across countries. For example, the People's Republic of China (PRC) uses a measure of poverty of less than 637 *yuan* per year, which is well below the standard of less than $1 (U.S.) a day established by the World Bank. By changing the definition and measure of poverty the PRC was able to manipulate its poverty data (Human Rights in China 2005).[11] Although economic and social rights indicators are often deficient and fragmentary, governments and international organizations routinely collect and publish substantial amounts of data relevant to economic and social rights, albeit with varying degrees of quality and precision. Human rights advocates and international monitoring bodies must remember that the data collected are often imperfect. Flawed data can be the result of resource limitations, deficient collection mechanisms, or active attempts by the government to hide its discriminatory or depraved behavior.

THE MEASURES

Although Thomas Hammarburg (2000) begins his report at the Statistics, Development and Human Rights Conference by stating that, "Human rights can never

---

[10] General Comment No. 1 obligates state parties to include specifically at-risk groups, disadvantaged subgroups, and worse off regions when conforming to the ICESCR and reporting to the CESCR (see CESCR 1989).

[11] The result of this definitional manipulation was that China claimed that only 4.6% of its population lived below the poverty level, whereas the World Bank's standard definition put China's poverty rate at 16.6%. The differential in poverty measures excluded approximately 156 million Chinese people.

be fully measured in statistics; the qualitative aspects are too essential," he quickly informs his readers that statistical measures are indeed crucial. In fact, human rights measures are vitally important in monitoring governments' respect for and implementation of their treaty obligations. The construction of comprehensive (both geographically and time progressive), reliable and valid measures is required in order to evaluate the progressive realization or nonfulfillment of economic and social rights. Measures are essential to reveal the extent to which economic and social rights are or are not enjoyed in practice. Researchers, scholars, and the human rights community have to be careful in the collection, organization, presentation, and dissemination of data. One of the major constraints for the effective implementation of the ICESCR has been the lack of accurate information on rights achievements within countries. Poor countries' lack of statistical resources hinders development, political accountability and human rights transparency. So the problem today is to construct measures or indicators that are easy to interpret, are comparable, and are, in fact, available.

I believe that a careful selection of core indicators – as determined by Shue and Trubek – is the key to determining the realization of economic and social rights. The World Health Organization (WHO) asserts that "selectivity must be the keynote. More will be gained by selecting a small number of relevant indicators for which a country can obtain the information within its resources than by aiming at comprehensiveness" (WHO 1981, 12). A smaller number of variables that are disaggregated by many groups are of greater value in understanding the human condition than a large amount of state centered data (which is what is normally collected and reported by international agencies). Measures that become too complex, time-consuming, and expensive will not be collected, or at least will not be collected accurately. The caveat, of course, is that researchers and policy makers must understand that measures often only indirectly or partially gauge a very complex situation. However, with careful selection and meticulous evaluation over time, these measures can indicate the achievement or violation of economic and social human rights.

Furthermore, a smaller number of indicators may be more financially feasible for developing countries to gather. Collecting, organizing, and reporting a larger range of data (the number of indicators) places a considerable burden on the state. As an example, the 2000 U.S. census cost over $6.5 billion (Government Accountability Office 2001).[12] Therefore, it is crucial that we determine which indicators or measures are the most useful for and of highest significance in determining compliance with treaty obligations in order to cut down on the burden of reporting. Careful selection of a few measures will allow the researcher to determine the quality of the data; specifically, the comparability and consistency of the measure, along with its validity. In order to monitor and evaluate progressive realization of subsistence economic and social rights, the measures will need to be collected over time. Thus, a smaller number of disaggregated indicators will make the annual collection more

---

[12] Even with this enormous cost, only one out of six households received the detailed long-form. The majority (60%) of the cost was a result of the need for field collection (GAO 2001). In developing countries where literacy is low, postal service is dubious, and trust is limited, field collection will have greater importance in the collection of data.

feasible. Relying on the commonly collected ten-year census for timely information on economic and social rights will leave vast numbers of people unprotected and in jeopardy.

Measuring a complicated and multifaceted phenomenon of state compliance or rights enjoyment requires the use of multiple indicators, each reflecting distinctive aspects of economic and social human rights. These indicators cannot be selected arbitrarily. The choice of indicators must be derived directly from the ICESCR itself. There is a direct connection between the economic and social right found in the International Covenant on Economic, Social, and Cultural Rights and the chosen indicator. As Mokhiber notes, "Determining *what* to measure in particular has rights implications. A rights-perspective requires that indicators be based upon the internationally agreed human rights norms and standards" (2000). Basing economic and social rights indicators on the treaty also provides understanding of the substantive content of each right and offers a framework for determining state capacity and response.

I propose that one way to improve human rights measures is to use a subsistence rights approach that determines state compliance with the obligations established in the International Covenant on Economic, Social, and Cultural Rights.[13] The indicators are chosen because of their direct connection to the enumerated rights. Here, I want to explore measures for the right to work, education, food, health, and shelter. The measures suggested have the added benefit of being simple and straightforward, in that there is a wide consensus on the underlying assumptions.

Unfortunately, at this time, no measures of economic and social rights are disaggregated by at risk and vulnerable groups. However, the purpose of this chapter is to persuade states and the international community of the importance and benefits of collecting a carefully chosen, restricted, yet highly disaggregated number of indicators based on the widely ratified ICESCR. Disaggregating data should go beyond the crucial factors of gender and urban/rural geographical dichotomies to include disparities with regard to vulnerable and marginalized groups based on race, religion, language, disabilities, HIV status, and other categories of human concern. Balancing a researcher's need for valid and reliable measures with feasibility of collection, Table 8.1 provides an aspiration of possible indicators. The first column lists the core subsistence rights identified by preeminent human rights scholars, Shue (1980), Trubek (1984), and Türk (1992). The second column links the core right with the appropriate ICESCR article. Finally, the third column presents a possible measure of the right. The basic measures are all commonly and regularly collected and published by states and international organizations. The only modification in data collection would be to incorporate subcategories of population groups.

The use of a highly restricted set of indicators, rather than of a broad range of measures, will increase the feasibility of collecting relevant disaggregated data while keeping down the costs. The use of basic measures also will allow researchers and policy makers to present data in more easily understood formats, using graphics,

---

[13] This chapter is limited to economic and social rights, and does not concern itself with cultural rights. At this point, there is still a general lack of clarification and definition over the issue of cultural rights. The problems associated with cultural measures lead to an even more meager and inadequate set of reliable and valid measures.

Table 8.1. *Measuring the progressive realization of economic and social rights*

1		
Subsistence Rights	**International Covenant on Economic, Social, and Cultural Rights**	**Basic Measure (disaggregated by marginalized or at risk groups)**
Work	Article 6: the right of everyone to work.	Unemployment rates
Education	Article 13: the right of everyone to education.	Literacy rates; Primary school enrollment rates
Food	Article 11: the right of everyone to an adequate standard of living, which includes adequate food.	Stunting or wasting
Health	Article 12: right of everyone to the highest attainable standard of physical and mental health.	Infant mortality rates; Life expectancy
Shelter	Article 11: the right of everyone to an adequate standard of living, which includes adequate shelter.	Homeless rates

report cards, charts, and so on for wider audience comprehension and public participation.

INFORMATION PYRAMIDS

There are concerns that a true representation of the human rights situation in a country cannot be achieved using quantitative measures alone. Often statistical measures do not reflect the lived reality of economic and social rights for individuals in a meaningful way. Quantitative indicators are useful because, in principle, they are comparable and verifiable. However, quantitative indicators only provide a snapshot of rights attainment. Qualitative indicators are valuable precisely because of the shortcoming of quantitative indicators. Qualitative measures assess the composition and environment of events and processes, as well as explain the complex and multifaceted nature of the phenomena. Qualitative data can be used as a complement to or explanation of quantitative measures. Therefore, utilizing and organizing a data set based on the "information pyramids" proposed by Isabell Kempf may be a solution to the complexity of economic and social rights.[14] Kempf (1998) suggests using "information pyramids" to capture the multifaceted nature of human rights achievement. In this way, the vague and rather ambiguous, requirements of state responsibility to use the maximum of its available resources

---

[14] Kempf developed the methodology of information pyramids for use in measuring health rights. However, this methodology also can be appropriate for the subsistence rights approach to economic and social rights research and monitoring.

for the progressive realization of the rights found in the ICESCR are given a cultural, economic and political framework within which to judge state compliance.

The first tier of the pyramid is the quantitative measure, or what Kempf refers to as "key indicators of status," for use as comparison across countries and for judicial remedy. Tier 1 provides a cursory snapshot of the economic rights condition within the country. The basic measures of Table 8.1 fulfill this requirement. Tier 1 measures coincide with the outcome indicators later proposed by Paul Hunt in that this level of the pyramid illustrates the level of rights achievement (Hunt 2004). The second tier incorporates both quantitative and qualitative features in the measure, and it represents "a carefully chosen expanded set of statistics that would afford a more in-depth understanding of the forces at work behind the key indicator" (Kempf 1998). This is particularly important, given the ICESCR's allowance of progressive realization and available resources. The researcher or advocate could use state expenditure data, military expenditure, or GDP data as control variables, which can also be useful for judicial remedies. The third tier involves more in-depth explanations, governmental policy examinations, and the inclusion of cultural context. The insertion of qualitative data into Tiers 2 and 3 of the information pyramid heeds Hammarberg's recommendation "to combine figures with context and explanations when reporting on human rights" (2001, 132). Or, to use Hunt's subsequent categorization, Tiers 2 and 3 incorporate structural indicators; that is, they take into account whether the state has the governmental policies and budgetary allocations in place that can allow the fulfillment of the right in question.

To illustrate this strategy, consider the indicator of infant mortality rates. Infant mortality rates are perhaps the single best indicator of health available. Furthermore, they can be collected with some accuracy and are easy to understand. Thus, a raw number of infant mortality (commonly measured as the number of deaths by one thousand live births) fulfills the Tier 1 requirement and provides a general overview of the society's health. Disaggregating the indicator of infant mortality rates by marginalized groups will provide instant detection of discrimination of certain groups' right to health. Tier 2 would include data on government expenditure on health services for a more in-depth understanding of the forces at work. Furthermore, the inclusion of data on government expenditures for health would indicate the government's fulfillment or nonfulfillment of its treaty obligations. The inclusion of government expenditure in Tier 2 would help reveal whether the state is using "all available means," including budgetary measures, toward the full realization of rights. Budgetary allocation is a concrete step in meeting the minimum treaty obligation.

Tier 3 would provide the environmental and political background in the explanation of the fluctuation in infant mortality rates. Because infant mortality rates are quite sensitive to sudden changes in health conditions as a result of natural disasters, epidemics, famine, war, and so on, an in-depth examination of governmental health and emergency policies can either exonerate the state or fix state culpability for the violation of the right to health found in the ICESCR. The use of a pyramid of information about economic and social rights could thus serve "as a way of identifying the obstacles to the realization of rights and creates a better understanding of the common problems faced by States and of the measures, including international assistance, which should be taken to overcome them" (Kempf, 1998).

Table 8.2. *Measuring the progressive realization of economic and social rights*

2

Substance Rights	Tier 1 Key Measures	Tier 2 Expanded Indicators Program Evaluation	Tier 3 Social, Political, and Environmental Context
Work	Unemployment rates	Government funding for work programs, training programs, etc.	Case study of world and state economic conditions affecting employment
Education	Literacy rates; Primary school enrollment rates	Government expenditure on education, transportation, lunch programs	Case study of the cultural context, language difficulties in fulfilling rights, description of functional literacy, normal duration of primary school
Food	Stunting or wasting	Government resources and programs for food policies and emergency actions	Environmental issues, drought, deforestation, desertification
Health	Infant mortality rates; Life expectancy	Government expenditures on health	Evaluation of government health policies and emergency actions
Shelter	Homeless rates	Government expenditures for social services	Laws regarding right to tenancy

Of course, the quantitative data of Tier 1 must be disaggregated for reasons of equality and nondiscrimination, as I argue earlier, whereas Tiers 2 and 3 enable the right in question to be appreciated in its cultural, economic, political, and environmental context. In this fashion, the use of the information pyramid can assist in the monitoring of rights and in measuring the effectiveness of government policies and institutions of redress and enforcement. Thus, the information pyramid can assess a government's compliance with the legal obligations imposed by the ICE-SCR, namely: the obligation of conduct, the ability to measure the government's commitment to human rights (such as the amount of resources spent on health), and also the obligation of result (reducing infant mortality rates).

INDEXES

Scholars and advocates can use the first tier of this information pyramid to conduct their statistical research. However, there is yet another question that needs to be considered. When using a statistical method, should researchers use a cluster of single measures or combine these measures into a composite index of economic rights? There are several examples of indexes that capture some aspect of economic and social rights. The primary exemplars are the Human Development Indicators

(HDI), the Physical Quality of Life Index (PQLI), and the Human Poverty Index (HPI), although it must be noted that none of these indexes are disaggregated. An index has the advantage of being a holistic measure of the human rights condition. But even if it is disaggregated, the creation of an index of economic and social rights will tend to conceal variations within the composite measures. For example, combining economic rights (the right to work) with social rights (food and shelter) can hide huge discrepancies between a strong economy and employment and actual human welfare. In Canada, the Ontario Human Rights Commission has indicated that, "there have been reported increases in reliance on food banks and temporary shelters. These trends are occurring despite a strong economy and a time of unprecedented employment rates" (OHRC 2005). This example makes clear that an index combining food needs and employment rates will mask the fact that many employed people, during a period of a strong economy, still lacked adequate food. Perhaps a short series of individual measures would better serve the purpose of clarifying the realization of economic and social rights. The use of a cluster of single indicators is all the more functional since the researcher can determine on which area of human rights a country needs to focus its attention.

VALIDITY AND RELIABILITY

The construction and evaluation of a measure relies on two technical components: validity and reliability. Establishing a link between the grand concept of economic and social rights and its empirical referents (e.g., the right to education and literacy rates) is an important first step in substantiating validity. Validity, in measurement theory, refers to the extent to which the indicator measures what it is intended to measure; that is, the accuracy of the measure. Validity can never be proven, but it is possible to develop convincing support indicating that a measure is valid through the weight of evidence (Babbie 1992; Bollen 1989). Earl Babbie defines validity as "the extent to which a specific measurement provides data that relate to commonly accepted meanings of a particular concept" (1992, 135). Babbie concludes that, if the measure meets its theoretical expectations, "that constitutes evidence of your measure's construct validity" (1992, 133).[15] Equally important is content validity, where the cluster of measuring instruments includes the full range of all the attributes or aspects of the concept. Nothing relevant to subsistence rights (as a subcategory of the complex and multifaceted ICESCR) is left out. By basing the measures on the rights enumerated in the International Covenant on Economic, Social, and Cultural Rights itself, along with the related state obligations, the issue of measurement validity will be strengthened.

Reliability refers to the stability, consistency, and reproducibility of the measure. A reliable index, can, over repeated attempts, generate consistent scores. The reliability of ICESCR measures needs to be consistent over different countries and over time. Sam Kash Kachigan (1986, 218) states: "When we observe the scores of a set of objects on a variable, is this distribution of scores the result of *chance*, or is it

---

[15] "Construct validity" is a type of validity whereby the measure reflects the concept as specified in the theory.

due to some *intrinsic characteristic* of the object, such that on remeasurement each object will retain approximately its same score? If the objects do retain their scores, we say the measurements are reliable." By using established measures that have proven their reliability in previous research, we can further strengthen the claim to reliability. The basic measures listed on Table 8.1 have proven themselves to be dependable, consistent, and reliable over a wide range of research.

CONCLUSION

One of the major constraints for the effective implementation of the ICESCR has been the lack of accurate information on rights achievements within countries. However, the real problem in collecting economic and social data is political, not methodological or even conceptual. States and international agencies do collect and report enormous amounts of data. Endorsing a limited number of generally available data that need only to be disaggregated will reduce the burden on states in terms of time and resources. The basic indicators, such as infant mortality, life expectancy rates, wasting and stunting, literacy and school enrollment, unemployment rates, and homeless rates, are by and large both reliable and available. These data are routinely collected and reported at regular intervals through standard administration record keeping procedures. However, the availability of disaggregated data based on at-risk or marginalized groups is still problematic. Hammarberg maintains that "fact-finding is hostile only for those who want to suppress knowledge about the true situation. Transparency about the established facts is a threat only against those who are afraid of discussion" (2001, 134). When measures are state aggregates, they often hide the substandard conditions experienced by certain groups or populations. To paraphrase Hammarberg, it is not enough to know that a state's average literacy rate is high if there are large regional, gender, or ethnic disparities in literacy achievement. Only by requiring countries to collect and report data that are disaggregated is it possible to determine not only progressive realization but also violations (backward trends in conditions suffered by certain groups or populations). States may resist the call for disaggregated data to conceal their human rights violations, their misuse of national resources, or their misappropriation of international assistance. But state resistance at this level must be overtaken if genuine representative human rights measures are to be obtained.

REFERENCES

Alston, P., and Gerard Quinn. 1987. The Nature and Scope of States Parties' Obligations under the International Covenant on Economic, Social and Cultural Rights. *Human Rights Quarterly* 9 (2): 156–229.

Babbie, Earl R. 1992. *The Practice of Social Research*, 6th ed. Belmont, CA: Wadsworth Publishing Co.

Bollen, Kenneth A. 1989. *Structural Equations with Latent Variables*. New York: Wiley-Interscience Publication.

Committee on Economic, Social, and Cultural Rights (CESCR). 1989. General Comment No. 1: Reporting by State Parties. UN Doc. E/1989/22 (Feb. 24, 1989).

Committee on Economic, Social, and Cultural Rights (CESCR). 1990. General Comment No. 3: The Nature of State Parties Obligations (Art. 2, par. 1). UN Doc. E/C.12/1990/8 (Dec. 12, 1990).

Committee on Economic, Social, and Cultural Rights (CESCR). 1998. General Comment No. 9: The Domestic Application of the Covenant. UN Doc. E/C.12/1998/24 (Dec. 3, 1998).

Committee on the Elimination of Discrimination Against Women (CEDAW). 1989. General Recommendation No. 9. Official Records of the General Assembly, Forty-fourth Session, Supp. No. 38. UN Doc. A/44/38.

Donnelly, Jack. 1999. Human Rights and Asian Values: A Defense of "Western Universalism." In *The East Asian Challenge for Human Rights*, ed. J. Bauer and D. Bell, D. New York: Cambridge University Press.

Eide, Asbjørn. 1989. Realization of Social and Economic Rights: The Minimum Threshold Approach. *International Commission of Jurists Review* 43: 40–52.

General Accounting Office (GAO). 2001. 2000 Census: Significant Increases in Cost Per Housing Unit Compared to 1990 Census. GAO-02-31. Available at: www.gao.govnnew. items/d0231.pdf.

Hammarberg, Thomas. 2000. Searching the Truth: The Need to Monitor Human Rights with Relevant and Reliable Means. Statistics, Development and Human Rights Conference, Montreux, 4–8 September 2000.

Human Rights in China (HRIC). 2005. *Implementation of the ICESCR in the PCR: A Parallel NGO Report by Human Rights in China*. New York: HRIC. Available at: www. hrichina.org/public/contents/22060.

Hunt, Paul. 2004. Report of the Special Rapporteur on the Right of Everyone to the Enjoyment of the Highest Attainable Standard of Physical and Mental Health. UN Doc. A/59/422 (59th Sess., 8 Oct. 2004).

International Labour Organization (ILO). 1982. *Target Setting for Basic Needs*. Geneva: ILO.

Kachigan, Sam Kash. 1986. *Statistical Analysis*. New York: Radius Press.

Kempf, Isabell. 1998. How to Measure the Right to Education: Indicators and Their Potential Use by the Committee on Economic, Social, and Cultural Rights. Committee on Economic, Social and Cultural Rights, nineteenth session, Geneva, 16 November–4 December 1998. UN Doc. E/C.12/1998/22 (13 November 1998).

Mokhiber, Craig G. 2000. Toward a Measure of Dignity: Indicators for Rights-Based Development. Statistics, Development and Human Rights Conference. Montreux, 4–8 September 2000.

Ontario Human Rights Commission (OHRC 2005). Introduction. www.ohrc.on.ca/en_text/ consultations/economic-social-rights-paper_3.shtml.

Scott, Craig M. 1999. Canada's International Human Rights Obligations and Disadvantaged Members of Society: Finally into the Spotlight? *Constitutional Forum* 10 (4): 97–10.

Shue, Henry. 1978. Rights in the Light of Duties. In *Human Rights and U.S. Foreign Policy*, ed. P. Brown and D. MacLean. Lexington, KY: Lexington Books.

Shue, Henry. 1980. *Basic Rights: Subsistence, Affluence, and U.S. Foreign Policy*. Princeton: Princeton University Press.

Trubek, David. 1984. Economic, Social and Cultural Rights in the Third World: Human Rights Law and Human Needs Programs. In *Human Rights in International Law*, ed. T. Meron. Oxford: Clarendon Press.

Türk, Danilo. 1992. The Realization of Economic, Social and Cultural Rights. Final Report to United Nations, Commission on Human Rights, Sub-Commission on Prevention of Discrimination and Protection of Minorities, 44th session. U.N. Doc. E/CN.4/Sub.2/1996/16.

United Nations Development Programme (UNDP). 2000. *Human Development Report 2000*. New York: Oxford University Press.

Van Hoof, Fried. 1984. The Legal Nature of Economic, Social and Cultural Rights: A Rebuttal of Some Traditional Views. In *The Right to Food*, ed. P. Alston and Katarina Tomasevski. The Hague: Martinus Nijhoff.

Vierdag, E. W. 1978. The Legal Nature of the Rights Granted by the International Covenant on Economic, Social and Cultural Rights. *Netherlands Yearbook of International Law* 9: 69–105.

World Health Organization (WHO). 1981. *Development of Indicators for Monitoring Progress towards Health for All by the Year 2000*. Geneva: World Health Organization.

9 Economic Rights, Human Development Effort, and Institutions

MWANGI S. KIMENYI[1]

1. INTRODUCTION

Economists are not "big" on human rights. This is particularly true for "positive rights," which involve prescribing actions by governments, and even more so for economic rights broadly, that are interpreted to mean positive actions that enhance quality of life through redistribution or other collective actions.[2] Economists, particularly those of the classical liberalism tradition, consider such "social justice" rights to be inconsistent with economic growth and, thus, should not be part of a country's constitution. To the extent that economists advocate for economic rights, it is usually to rights to engage in productive activities with minimal interference – or negative economic rights commonly referred to as economic freedom. To the extent that governments should prescribe policy, they should focus on the preconditions for markets to function efficiently; governments should not direct the actions of market participants. According to economists, economic freedom causes economic growth and wealth accumulation, which benefit all members of the society. Ample empirical evidence shows that economic freedom is a primary determinant of economic growth and development (Berggren 2003). Because there is strong link between economic growth and poverty reduction, economists tend to argue that positive economic rights should not be a priority if conditions for economic freedom exist. In fact, positive rights are considered counterproductive to the extent that they may infringe on economic freedom.

There is no doubt that economic growth is necessary for the improvement of the well-being of all members of the society. For low-income countries, sustained reductions in the levels of poverty require high and sustained rates of economic growth and wealth creation. But economic growth is not synonymous with poverty reduction – higher levels of national incomes do not necessarily translate into lower poverty or overall improvement in well-being of the poor. Evidence shows that

---

[1] An earlier version of this chapter, entitled "Institutions of Governance, Power Diffusion and Pro-Poor Growth and Policies," was presented at a Senior Policy Seminar organized by African Economic Research Consortium, Cape Town, South Africa. I am grateful to members of the Economic Rights Reading Group at the University of Connecticut for helpful comments and suggestions and to the Earhart Foundation for supporting my research on Millennium Development Goals and Institutions.
[2] The positive economic rights accepted under internal law cover various forms of protections and social provisions such as food, worker rights, child labor, and so on (see Charter of the United Nations, *The International Bill of Human Rights*, http://www.ohchr.org).

episodes of economic growth are not always associated with significant poverty reduction (Kakwani & Pernia 2000). As such, the relationship between economic growth and poverty can be weak. In fact, there are cases in which economic growth has been associated with increased poverty.[3] Thus, policy makers should be concerned not just about instituting policies for economic growth but, rather, policies to achieve pro-poor growth.

This chapter focuses on institutions and governance aspects of economic rights, broadly defined.[4] In the section that follows, we briefly explore some of the links between economic growth, inequality, and poverty reduction. A number of simulations of the impact of economic growth and inequality on poverty reduction are presented. The analysis shows that economic growth is important but not sufficient for many countries to achieve the Millennium Development Goals (MDGs). It is demonstrated that overall human development requires inequality reducing economic growth. We show that there are countries that have income levels necessary to achieve the MDG human development targets but that are not in fact meeting these targets. We refer to these countries as being characterized by *human development effort deficit*. For comparison purposes, all countries are ranked according to their human development effort. By contrast, many countries have low incomes and, thus, are not able to meet development targets. We refer these countries as having a *human development income deficit*. Section 3 focuses on institutions and economic rights. The basic argument is that to improve the absolute quality of life, there is need for pro-poor policies and that such policies are directly related to the power relations in society. It is demonstrated that pro-poor policies are implemented in societies where power is sufficiently diffused such that members of the society have significant leverage over the type of policies enacted. Leverage permits citizens to hold leaders accountable and also necessitates that different interests bargain with each other in the process of policy formulation. In essence, power diffusion results in societies where groups bargain with each other on matters of policy, often through compromise. Some recent cases in which power diffusion has associated with improvements in economic rights are discussed. Section 4 concludes with some suggestions for institutional reforms to facilitate power diffusion and, consequently, improvements in the realization of economic rights.

2. ECONOMIC GROWTH, POVERTY REDUCTION, AND OVERALL HUMAN DEVELOPMENT

2.1. Importance of Growth for Poverty Reduction

We define pro-poor growth as economic expansion that associates with reductions in relevant measures of poverty. A simple definition of pro-poor growth is growth that associates with a high elasticity of the poverty reduction (Ravallion 2001).[5]

---

[3] This results when economic growth associates with increased inequality as a result of disproportionate gains by the rich and limited gains by the poor.

[4] Although the paper is fairly general, it has a biased emphasis on African countries primarily because of their low human development record.

[5] Growth elasticity of poverty ξ is computed as follows: $\xi = (\Delta H / \Delta U^* U/H)$, where H is the headcount index and U is the mean income.

Table 9.1. *Economic growth and poverty reduction*

Country	Poverty rate 2001	Growth (low)	Growth (high)	Poverty 2015 low growth	Poverty 2015 high growth
Kenya	56	1.5	3.0	32.79	18.80
Nigeria	60	3.0	6.0	20.14	6.16
South Africa	50	3.0	6.0	16.78	5.13
Uganda	35	5.5	11.0	4.41	0.38
Zimbabwe	70	0.1	3	67.42	23.5

A more precise definition defines pro-poor growth to mean that the poor benefit disproportionately from economic growth (White & Anderson 2001; Klasen 2001; Kakwani & Pernia 2000; Kakwani et al. 2004).[6] This essentially means that income growth by the poorest group exceeds the average growth rate. Cross-country evidence reveals that there are large variations in poverty reduction from the same growth rate – growth is more pro-poor in some countries than in others.[7]

To demonstrate the importance of growth to poverty reduction, we start by presenting simple simulations based on coefficients obtained by Ravallion (2001). Ravallion investigates the relationship between growth and poverty and inequality using data from household surveys for forty-seven developing countries for two successive surveys, making it possible to capture changes in poverty and income distribution. Ravallion finds growth elasticity of poverty equal to 2.5 – meaning that a 1% increase in the mean income results in a reduction of the proportion of the population living below $1 day by an average of 2.5%.[8]

We use the estimated growth elasticity of poverty reduction to simulate expected poverty reduction in five African countries – Kenya, Nigeria, South Africa, Uganda, and Zimbabwe.[9] We first assume that the growth rates achieved in 2001 are maintained for the period up to the year 2015. We then simulate how poverty rates would change if the countries doubled the rates of growth over the same period. The results of the simulations are shown in Table 9.1. The growth elasticity of poverty reduction is assumed to be the same for all countries and constant over time.[10] The simulation results show that given the assumed growth elasticity of

[6] White and Anderson (2001) define pro-poor growth as follows: (1) the poor's share of incremental income exceeds their current share, (2) the poor's share of incremental income exceeds their share of population; and (3) the poor's share of incremental income exceeds some international norm.

[7] Pasha and Palanivel (2004) show that different growth episodes in the same country can have different impacts on poverty reduction.

[8] Simply, change in poverty is given by $P = P_t - \gamma(g)$, where $P =$ the poverty rate, γ is the growth elasticity of poverty reduction and g is the growth rate. Note that the coefficients are only appropriate for developing countries and also poverty is based on the international poverty line of $1 (purchasing power parity) per person per day. Thus, the poverty rates are not comparable, say, to the poverty in the United States, where the poverty line is much higher.

[9] These countries are selected purely for illustrative purposes. The countries are in a way representative of countries in sub-Saharan Africa in terms of their income levels, inequality, and growth experiences over the last few years. Furthermore, the structure of the countries in terms of share of agricultural, mineral, and industrial output are representative of many other African countries.

[10] It is conceivable that the growth elasticity to poverty reduction decreases as poverty declines. When poverty is very high, increases in growth absorb the easily employable poor who may have skills, and

Table 9.2. *Distribution adjusted poverty reduction*

Country	Poverty rate 2001	Growth rate	Gini	Poverty 2015 unadjusted for inequality	Poverty 2015 adjusted for inequality
Kenya	56	1.5	44.9	32.79	39.40
Nigeria	60	3.0	50.6	20.14	31.74
South Africa	50	3.0	59.3	16.78	29.65
Uganda	35	5.5	37.5	4.41	7.62
Zimbabwe	70	0.1	50.1	67.58	68.54

poverty reduction, poverty would fall consistently in all the countries. The main message of this discussion is that growth is important for poverty reduction. As such, when we are concerned about absolute well-being of the population, an emphasis on economic growth is crucial.

2.2. The Role of Inequality on Pro-Poor Growth

This discussion assumes that the growth elasticity of poverty reduction is independent of the state of income distribution. Recent empirical evidence shows that that the initial level of inequality does impact the responsiveness of poverty to economic growth (Kakwani et al. 2004; Son 2004).[11] Ravallion has suggested the use of distribution-corrected rate of economic growth on average income to investigate the impact of inequality on poverty reduction. Borrowing coefficients obtained by Ravallion, we simulate the expected changes in poverty for Kenya, Nigeria, South Africa, Uganda, and Zimbabwe using the distribution corrected rate of economic growth.[12] In Table 9.2, we compare the poverty expected in 2015 when inequality is not taken into account (as in previous case) and when adjustments are made for the prevailing inequality. The results from the simulations show that high levels of inequality reduce the responsiveness of poverty reduction to economic growth. In all cases, inequality adjusted poverty rates are higher, implying that inequality in the distribution of income reduces the responsiveness of poverty reduction to growth. Note that the higher the inequality, the lower the reduction in poverty for a given rate of economic growth.[13]

To demonstrate the importance of inequality on poverty reduction, we investigate how poverty rates would change if we assumed that inequality was half of its 2001 levels. In the case of Zimbabwe, we also assume a higher growth rate of 3%

so on. This suggests a high responsiveness of growth to poverty reduction. However, even with growth the remaining poor may find it increasingly more difficult to exploit the labor market meaning that the growth elasticity to poverty reduction declines. For a similar argument, see Kimenyi and Mbaku (1995).

[11] This result could be because large disparities hinder the poor's capacity to exploit opportunities availed by economic growth. This is consistent with Sen (2001), who emphasizes the importance of capabilities of the poor so that they can be able to exploit opportunities.

[12] The distribution-corrected rate of growth in average income is given by $(1\text{-}Gini/\Delta lnY_t)$, where Gini is the measure of inequality and Y is the income.

[13] Note also that this evidence is not consistent with the Kuznets hypothesis (Kuznets 1955) that, at very low levels of income, there is a positive relationship between inequality and economic growth.

Table 9.3. *Distribution adjusted poverty reduction (assuming inequality was half its 2001 levels)*

Country	Poverty rate 2001	Growth rate	Gini (lower inequality)	Poverty 2015 higher inequality	Poverty 2015 lower inequality
Kenya	56	1.5	22.45	39.40	34.04
Nigeria	60	3.0	25.3	31.74	22.73
South Africa	50	3.0	29.6	29.65	19.99
Uganda	35	5.5	18.7	7.62	4.65
Zimbabwe	70	0.1, 3	25.05	68.54	26.31

and also a reduction in inequality.[14] The results (Table 9.3) show that for all countries, poverty decreases more if inequality is lower. In essence, the main story is that growth is good for poverty reduction. However, the effect of growth on poverty reduction is neutralized by high inequality. In other words, growth is a powerful vehicle to lower poverty, but only when associated with decreases in inequality.[15]

2.3. Human Development Income and Effort Deficits

We now focus on an analysis of countries' human development effort. Economic growth results in increased levels of income over time. If, in fact, growth is key to improving the quality of life, then it would be expected that higher levels of income would associate with higher levels of human development. By and large, there seems to be universal acceptance that most developing countries can only achieve the MDGs through accelerated economic growth. Although this is largely true, we demonstrate that the link between income and achievement of MDGs is not straightforward and much depends on a country's human development effort.

We focus on the overall measure of human development – the Human Development Index (HDI), and also key components of human development including adult literacy, life expectancy, primary and secondary school enrollment, infant mortality, and per capita income. The purpose of this simple exercise is to investigate how these measures relate to per capita income. We estimate ordinary least squares regression of the measures of human development against the log per capita income. The results of the estimation are shown in Table 9.4.[16] In all cases, higher levels of income associate with improvements in the measures of human development, and the relevant coefficients are large. This suggests that a policy for raising incomes is definitely important to achieving the MDGs. Nevertheless,

[14] Zimbabwe has had extremely low rates of economic growth over the last few years. This is primarily because of political uncertainty but we do not expect such policies to be sustained for long because of political pressure both within and from the international community. We therefore assume that the country will change course and attain growth rates comparable to previous record.

[15] This is equivalent to growth with equity – signifying the fact that there is economic growth but at the same time reduction in inequality.

[16] We have excluded HDI because the computation of the index incorporates income.

Table 9.4. *Regressions results of measures of human development against log per capita income (PPP)*

Dependent variable	Adult literacy rate	Life expectancy	Primary and secondary school enrollment	Infant mortality
Constant	−23.72	−8.36	−50.67	288.36
	(−2.66)***	(−1.81)*	(−7.39)***	(282.74)***
Log per capita income	12.33	8.67	14.07	−28.93
	(11.90)***	(16.17)***	(17.64)***	(−19.57)***
Adjusted R–Square	0.451	0.602	0.645	0.691

t–statistics are in parentheses below the coefficients. Asterisks (***) denote significance at the 1% level.

the results also show that there is much more than merely raising income levels to achieve human development. First, the adjusted coefficient of determination shows that income alone explains only between 61% and 88% of the variations in the measures of human development. In addition, the intercepts (constants) of the regression are fairly large.

To investigate the importance of pro-poor growth, we examine the relationship between income and human development by plotting the various measures of human development against per capital income. This is shown in Figures 9.1 to 9.4. The plots show that there is a clear positive relationship between per capital income and measures of human development. As such, the idea that growth is necessary to achieve positive gains in human development is fairy obvious and thus supports the claim that growth (meaning rising incomes) is good for the poor. [17] But that is only part of the story.

Looking at Figure 9.1, we note that only very few countries with a per capita income of $2,400[18] or less have an HDI equal or above the mean (0.698).[19] In fact, a number of countries that have per capita incomes between $2,400 and $7,000 have HDI values that are just about equal or below the mean. It is only after a per capita income of about $7,000 that almost all countries score above the mean HDI.[20] In fact, looking at all the measures of human development, this trend holds true. This means that to achieve the school enrollment goals and reduce infant mortality, the poor countries will have to at least double their incomes on average. For some measures of human development, even higher incomes are necessary. Suppose

[17] Data are for year 2002, as reported in the Human Development Report (2004).

[18] The income data are expressed in terms of purchasing power parity (PPP).

[19] These include Vietnam with a per capita income of $2,300 and HDI of 0.691; Georgia with a per capita income of $2,260 and HDI 0.739; Uzbekistan with a per capita income of $1,670 and HDI of 0.709; and Tajikistan with a per capita income of $1,620 and HDI 0.701. Moldova is also very close with an income of $1,470 and HDI equal to 0.69.

[20] Note that some countries with per capita incomes above $7,000 have HDI values that are lower than the mean. These include South Africa, Gabon, Namibia, Swaziland, Egypt, Morocco, and India. Honduras and Nicaragua have HDI values that are just slightly below the mean.

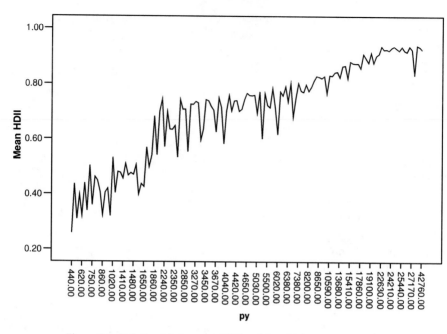

Figure 9.1. Relationship between HDI and Per Capita Income (PPP).

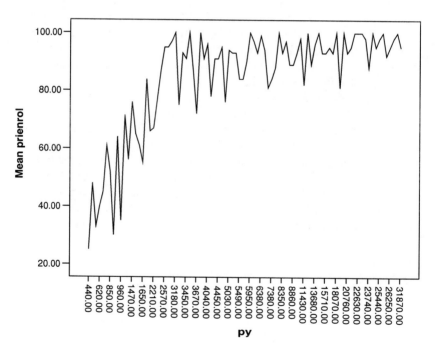

Figure 9.2. Relationship between Primary school Enrollment and Per Capita Income (PPP).

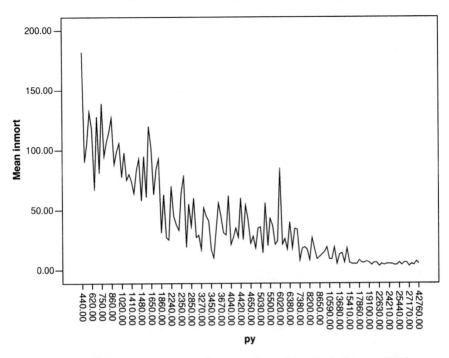

Figure 9.3. Relationship between Infant Mortality and Per Capita Income (PPP).

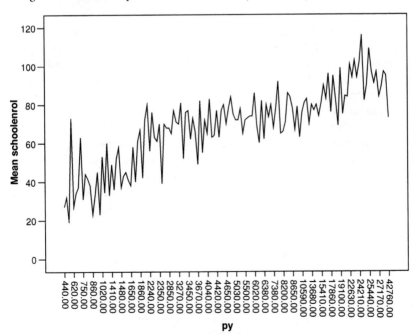

Figure 9.4. Relationship between Combined Primary and Secondary School Enrollment and Per Capita Income.

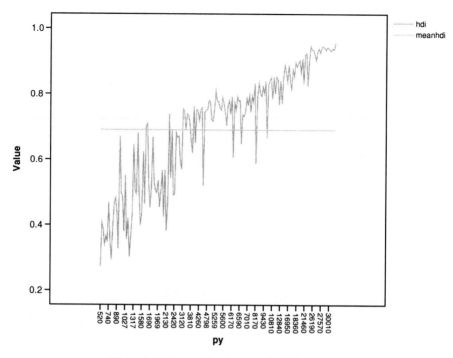

Figure 9.5. Human Development Deficit Income.

we were to target the achievement of the mean HDI by low-income countries. One way to think about this is to consider an HDI of 0.69 as the minimum acceptable quality of life. If income were the primary determinant of HDI, then countries with less than a per capita income of $2,400 would not be able to achieve the desired level of human development. Taking a per capita income of $2,400 as the minimum or threshold income necessary to achieve the target level of Human Development, we can then think of human development *income deficit* as the difference between the threshold income ($2,400) and a country's actual per capita income. Figure 9.5 helps elaborate on the concept of human development income deficit as used in this chapter. The straight line represents the mean HDI = 0.69. The line intersects the HDI line at approximately an income of $2,400, which is the income at which more countries' HDI is above the mean. We refer to countries with incomes below this threshold income as having a *human development income deficit* – measured by the distance between $2,400 and the country's income. The relevant question, then, is if we were to rely on economic growth, how long would it take for poor countries to achieve the minimum acceptable quality of life (HDI = 0.69)?

Table 9.5 lists a number of African countries and their per capita incomes in 2002.[21] If we assume that the countries must have at least $2,400 to meet the human development goals, then we can compute the time it would take for the countries to achieve the human development threshold income. For illustration

[21] We have selected all countries in sub-Saharan Africa whose per capita incomes fell below the threshold income in 2002.

Table 9.5. *Time necessary for countries to meet the human development deficit income (assuming no change in the distribution of income)*

Country	Per capita Income 2002	Number of years to attain $2400 assuming annual growth rate of 1.5%	Years to attain $2400 assuming annual growth rate of 3%	Years to attain $2400 assuming annual growth rate of 4.5%
Ghana	2130	8	4	2.7
Angola	2130	8	4	2.7
Djibouti	1990	12.5	6.3	4.2
Sudan	1820	18.5	9.3	6.2
Gambia	1690	23.5	11.8	7.9
Senegal	1580	28	14.1	9.4
Côte d'Ivoire	1520	30.6	15.4	10.3
Togo	1480	32.4	16.3	10.9
Uganda	1390	36.6	18.4	12.4
Rwanda	1270	42.7	21.5	14.4
Central Africa Rep.	1170	48.2	24.3	16.3
Burkina Faso	1100	52.3	26.3	17.7
Benin	1070	54.2	27.9	18.3
Mozambique	1050	55.5	27.9	18.7
Kenya	1020	57.4	28.9	19.4
Chad	1020	57.4	28.3	19.4
Congo	980	60.1	30.3	20.3
Mali	980	60.1	30.3	20.3
Eriteria	890	66	33.5	22.5
Nigeria	860	68.9	34.7	23.3
Zambia	840	70.5	35.5	23.8
Niger	840	70.5	35.5	23.8
Ethiopia	780	75	38	25.5
Madagascar	740	79.0	39.8	26.7
Guinea–Bissau	710	81	41.2	27.6
Congo Demo. Rep.	650	87.7	44.1	29.6
Burundi	630	89.9	45.2	30.3
Malawi	580	95.3	48	32.2
Sierra Leone	520	102.7	51.7	34.7

purposes, we assume rates of growth of 1.5%, 3%, and 4.5%.[22] It is apparent that majority of African countries are unlikely to meet the Millennium Development Goals unless they were to sustain much higher rates of economic growth than has been the case in the recent past. Even if we assumed a high growth rate of 4.5%, many of the countries would still take over two decades to achieve the mean

[22] The idea is to compute the value of *n* given $Y_n = Y_t(1+g)^n$, where Y_n is the minimum income to meet the human development goals, *n* is the number of years necessary to achieve Y_n, Y_t is the current income, and *g* is the annual income growth rate.

HDI.[23] Given the past record of poor growth, one cannot be optimistic about these countries' ability to achieve higher economic growth rates than in the past unless there are major changes.

It is important to note that although there seems to be a clear income threshold below which most countries do not achieve the mean HDI, there also are cases for which countries have significantly higher incomes and yet their HDI and other measures of human development fall much below the mean. These countries score low HDI but have incomes that are above the average threshold income.[24] In essence, these are countries that otherwise have been able to adopt pro-growth policies but are not achieving human development targets. We could consider these countries as failing to put sufficient effort into achieving human development and thus are characterized by human development *"effort deficit."* Merely looking at the HDI value in relation to the per capita income may not reveal the entire story about the concept of human development *effort deficit*. Even though countries may have an *income deficit* by our definition, it is possible that they are also characterized by human development effort deficit. This would be the case in which a country could achieve higher scores of the measures of human development even with a low income. We have, in fact, noticed that there are some countries that actually have higher HDI scores though their incomes are lower than what we have considered as the threshold income. Thus, some poor countries could be characterized by both *income deficit* and *effort deficit*. Likewise, just because countries have high incomes and values of HDI that are above the mean does not necessary imply that they are not characterized by a human development effort deficit. Simply put, it is possible that these countries could achieve higher levels of human development if they put in more effort. We can therefore classify countries into categories based on human development income and effort deficits. As will be apparent in the next section, the categorization is important in linking institutions and economic rights.

We conduct simple analysis to categorize each country by estimating a simple regression of HDI against the log per capita income. However, we note that because HDI includes an income component, adjustments are necessary to avoid biases. In practice, HDI is an aggregation of one third of each of three components – life expectancy index, education index, and income index in equal weights. We therefore subtract one-third of income index from the HDI to obtain an adjusted income-free HDI, and then regress the log of adjusted HDI against log income.[25] We then look at the predicted values and residuals of the regression.[26] Positive residuals mean that the country's HDI score is higher than predicted values. In

---

[23] Note that we are only looking at achieving a HDI = 0.69. If all countries improve on the levels of human development, then the mean HDI naturally increases and this would mean a much longer time for countries starting poor to achieve the new mean.

[24] This is consistent with Sen (1982), who argues that famines and hunger are not necessarily due to lack of food but due to the inequalities built into mechanisms for distribution. We can refer to such outcomes as due to effort deficit.

[25] The results of the regression are:

Log Adjusted HDI = −0.625 + 0.218 Log Per capita income
(−23.14)*** + (16.48)*** Adj. R-Squared= 0.611, t-statistics in parenthesis.

[26] Cingranelli and Richards (2004) present a similar but more comprehensive analysis focusing primarily on measuring governments' respect for human rights using the Physical Quality of Life Index (PQLI). Although there are some similarities in the results, their analysis focuses mainly on measurement issues, whereas the present chapter emphasizes institutional dimensions of economic rights.

other words, the country is doing better in terms of human development than expected given its level of income. By contrast, negative residuals imply that the country is doing less in terms of human development than expected given its level of income. That is, negative residuals imply *human development deficit*. Of course, the magnitudes of the residuals suggest relative levels of effort. We then rank the countries based on the magnitude of the residuals. Our rankings based on the residuals gives us the Human Development Effort Rankings. Table 9.6 shows the effort rankings compared to the HDI rankings.[27]

Table 9.6 shows that some countries are achieving much better human development outcomes than others when we control for income.[28] For example, Tajikistan has the highest human development effort as shown by the difference between the adjusted HDI and the predicted adjusted HDI. In essence, this country is doing very well given its income. By contrast, virtually all countries in sub-Saharan Africa are ranked lowest in terms of effort. The effort deficit characteristic of these countries implies that they could achieve better human development outcomes even given their low resources if they were to put in more effort.[29] There are also a number of developed countries that are performing poorly in terms of human development effort.[30] The results also show low human development effort rankings for most of the sub-Saharan African countries. Thus, not only are these countries facing an *income deficit*, they also are characterized by human development *effort deficit*.[31]

---

[27] Consistent results are obtained when we regress the HDI rankings against the income index.

[28] A cautionary remark is in order at this juncture. This analysis looks at what levels of human development can possibly be achieved given a country's income. Our human development effort variable is based on deviations from what is achievable given the level of income. There is a major assumption that countries are placing maximum effort in terms of generating income – which may not necessarily be the case. Thus, care is required in interpreting the derived effort variable. In short, a country that has low incomes because it constrains economic freedom may have a reasonably high HDI score but could even do better if it were to improve on negative economic rights.

[29] Based on our analysis and the rankings reported in Table 9.6, some of the worst African performers in terms of human development effort include some of the countries with reasonably good record of economic performance and also strong institutions, such as Botswana and South Africa. Both of these countries score much lower in terms of human development outcomes than would be expected considering their levels of income. In the case of South Africa, the deviation between actual and expected human development outcomes could be a result of the previous history. But the deviation also could be explained by other factors. One possible factor explaining the outcomes in these countries could be the impact of the HIV/AIDS pandemic. More detailed analysis is required to explain the apparent poor performance of these countries in terms of human development effort.

[30] For example, the United States of America ranks number eight in terms of HDI but it is ranked number 147 in terms of human development effort. This would suggest that the United States could do better in improving the well-being of her people given the resources available. For this study, we do not consider countries whose HDI is above the mean as effort deficit though they could achieve higher scores of human development. The reason for this is that as HDI approaches the maximum, it becomes increasingly difficult to make improvements because there are aspects of human development that are beyond the control by standard policy instruments. Likewise, additional effort can be counterproductive after some level, as is the case with regard to the undesirable effects of welfare in advanced countries (see, for example, Kimenyi 1995 on U.S. welfare policy and outcomes). Thus, although we have ranked all countries, our definition of human development effort deficit applies to those with HDI scores below the mean.

[31] Given the fact that many countries are characterized by human development effort deficit, the results provided in Table 9.5 concerning the time necessary for different countries to achieve the Millennium Development Goals should be interpreted with care. Our assumption is that a certain level of income is necessary to achieve the MDGs. However, it is conceivable that the countries can achieve the income level but may not place sufficient emphasis to achieve the MDGs.

Table 9.6. *Human development effort (Pro-Poor) country rankings (based on adjusted HDI = f(log PY)[1]*

Country	PY	HDI	AHDI	LAHDI	PRED	RES	EFFORT
Tajikistan	980	0.671	0.54	−0.61	−1.12610	0.51791	1.00
Uzbekistan	1,670	0.709	0.55	−0.59	−1.01007	0.41646	2.00
Kyrgyzstan	1,620	0.701	0.55	−0.60	−1.01668	0.41460	3.00
Moldova	1,470	0.681	0.53	−0.63	−1.03784	0.40484	4.00
Georgia	2,260	0.739	0.57	−0.57	−0.94421	0.37445	5.00
Sao Tomé	1,317	0.645	0.50	−0.69	−1.06176	0.37194	6.00
Mongolia	1,710	0.668	0.51	−0.67	−1.00491	0.33418	7.00
Armenia	3,120	0.754	0.56	−0.57	−0.87401	0.30130	8.00
Viet Nam	2,300	0.691	0.52	−0.66	−0.94039	0.28196	9.00
Azerbaijan	3,210	0.746	0.55	−0.59	−0.86781	0.27481	10.00
Solomon Is.	1,590	0.624	0.47	−0.75	−1.02075	0.26715	11.00
Myanmar	1,027	0.551	0.42	−0.87	−1.11591	0.25078	12.00
Jamaica	3,980	0.764	0.56	−0.58	−0.82101	0.24238	13.00
Bolivia	2,460	0.681	0.50	−0.68	−0.92575	0.24123	14.00
Cuba	5,259	0.809	0.59	−0.53	−0.76035	0.23102	15.00
Sri Lanka	3,570	0.740	0.54	−0.62	−0.84468	0.22849	16.00
Ecuador	3,580	0.735	0.54	−0.63	−0.84407	0.21858	17.00
Albania	4,830	0.781	0.56	−0.57	−0.77887	0.20676	18.00
Philippines	4,170	0.753	0.55	−0.60	−0.81086	0.20633	19.00
Nicaragua	2,470	0.667	0.49	−0.72	−0.92486	0.20537	20.00
Honduras	2,600	0.672	0.49	−0.71	−0.91370	0.20442	21.00
Lebanon	4,360	0.758	0.55	−0.60	−0.80116	0.19968	22.00
Jordan	4,220	0.750	0.54	−0.61	−0.80826	0.19823	23.00
Ukraine	4,870	0.777	0.56	−0.58	−0.77707	0.19785	24.00
Turkmenistan	4,300	0.752	0.54	−0.61	−0.80417	0.19168	25.00
Belarus	5,520	0.790	0.57	−0.57	−0.74980	0.18182	26.00
Saint Lucia	5,300	0.777	0.56	−0.59	−0.75866	0.17347	27.00
Indonesia	3,230	0.692	0.50	−0.70	−0.86646	0.17065	28.00
Paraguay	4,610	0.751	0.54	−0.62	−0.78902	0.16850	29.00
Syria	3,620	0.710	0.51	−0.67	−0.84165	0.16830	30.00
Venezuela	5,380	0.778	0.55	−0.59	−0.75539	0.16601	31.00
Madagascar	740	0.469	0.36	−1.02	−1.18725	0.16282	32.00
China	4,580	0.745	0.53	−0.63	−0.79044	0.15870	33.00
Maldives	4,798	0.752	0.54	−0.62	−0.78032	0.15545	34.00
Panama	6,170	0.791	0.56	−0.58	−0.72557	0.14753	35.00
Peru	5,010	0.752	0.54	−0.62	−0.77091	0.14604	36.00
Uruguay	7,830	0.833	0.59	−0.53	−0.67370	0.14550	37.00
Bosnia	5,970	0.781	0.55	−0.59	−0.73274	0.14275	38.00
Samoa	5,600	0.769	0.55	−0.61	−0.74667	0.14092	39.00
Yemen	870	0.482	0.36	−1.02	−1.15202	0.13591	40.00
Macedonia	6,470	0.793	0.56	−0.58	−0.71523	0.13482	41.00
Guyana	4,260	0.719	0.51	−0.68	−0.80621	0.13090	42.00
Fiji	5,440	0.758	0.53	−0.63	−0.75298	0.12687	43.00
Congo	980	0.494	0.37	−1.00	−1.12610	0.12462	44.00
Kazakhstan	5,870	0.766	0.54	−0.62	−0.73642	0.11900	45.00
Bulgaria	7,130	0.796	0.56	−0.58	−0.69409	0.11308	46.00

Country	PY	HDI	AHDI	LAHDI	PRED	RES	EFFORT
Saint V. and G.	5,460	0.751	0.53	−0.64	−0.75218	0.11289	47.00
Costa Rica	8,840	0.834	0.58	−0.54	−0.64729	0.10943	48.00
Colombia	6,370	0.773	0.54	−0.61	−0.71862	0.10798	49.00
Suriname	6,590	0.780	0.55	−0.60	−0.71123	0.10732	50.00
Tonga	6,850	0.787	0.55	−0.60	−0.70281	0.10558	51.00
Romania	6,560	0.778	0.54	−0.61	−0.71222	0.10464	52.00
Nigeria	860	0.466	0.35	−1.06	−1.15454	0.09322	53.00
Dominica	5,640	0.743	0.52	−0.65	−0.74512	0.09055	54.00
Libya	7,570	0.794	0.55	−0.59	−0.68105	0.09046	55.00
Kenya	1,020	0.488	0.36	−1.03	−1.11739	0.09017	56.00
El Salvador	4,890	0.720	0.50	−0.69	−0.77618	0.08968	57.00
Chile	9,820	0.839	0.58	−0.54	−0.62440	0.08369	58.00
Latvia	9,210	0.823	0.57	−0.56	−0.63836	0.08149	59.00
Poland	10,560	0.850	0.59	−0.53	−0.60858	0.08095	60.00
Argentina	10,880	0.853	0.59	−0.52	−0.60209	0.07952	61.00
Cape Verde	5,000	0.717	0.50	−0.69	−0.77134	0.07886	62.00
Lithuania	10,320	0.842	0.59	−0.54	−0.61359	0.07802	63.00
Tanzania	580	0.407	0.31	−1.17	−1.24029	0.07018	64.00
Turkey	6,390	0.751	0.52	−0.65	−0.71794	0.06594	65.00
Thailand	7,010	0.768	0.53	−0.63	−0.69778	0.06542	66.00
Russia	8,230	0.795	0.55	−0.60	−0.66285	0.06198	67.00
Croatia	10,240	0.830	0.57	−0.56	−0.61528	0.05899	68.00
Cambodia	2,060	0.568	0.40	−0.91	−0.96438	0.05141	69.00
Mexico	8,970	0.802	0.55	−0.59	−0.64411	0.04990	70.00
Belize	6,080	0.737	0.51	−0.68	−0.72877	0.04952	71.00
Brazil	7,770	0.775	0.53	−0.63	−0.67537	0.04363	72.00
Estonia	12,260	0.853	0.59	−0.53	−0.57609	0.04222	73.00
Ghana	2,130	0.568	0.40	−0.92	−0.95710	0.03580	74.00
Tunisia	6,760	0.745	0.51	−0.67	−0.70569	0.03560	75.00
Egypt	3,810	0.653	0.45	−0.80	−0.83051	0.03126	76.00
Trinidad & T.	9,430	0.801	0.55	−0.60	−0.63322	0.03113	77.00
Barbados	15,290	0.888	0.61	−0.50	−0.52801	0.03043	78.00
Malaysia	9,120	0.793	0.54	−0.61	−0.64050	0.02985	79.00
Laos	1,720	0.534	0.38	−0.97	−1.00364	0.02902	80.00
Dominica	6,640	0.738	0.50	−0.68	−0.70959	0.02573	81.00
Nepal	1,370	0.504	0.36	−1.03	−1.05317	0.02409	82.00
Saint Lucia	12,420	0.844	0.58	−0.55	−0.57327	0.02393	83.00
Comoros	1,690	0.530	0.37	−0.99	−1.00747	0.02219	84.00
India	2,670	0.595	0.41	−0.89	−0.90791	0.02037	85.00
Iran	6,690	0.732	0.50	−0.70	−0.70795	0.01214	86.00
Slovakia	12,840	0.842	0.57	−0.56	−0.56603	0.00741	87.00
Malawi	580	0.388	0.29	−1.23	−1.24029	0.00700	88.00
Grenada	7,280	0.745	0.51	−0.68	−0.68955	0.00636	89.00
Eritrea	890	0.439	0.32	−1.14	−1.14707	0.00451	90.00
Hungary	13,400	0.848	0.57	−0.55	−0.55673	0.00277	91.00
Algeria	5,760	0.704	0.48	−0.74	−0.74054	0.00100	92.00
Guatemala	4,080	0.649	0.44	−0.82	−0.81561	−0.00009	93.00

(*continued*)

Table 9.6 (continued)

Country	PY	HDI	AHDI	LAHDI	PRED	RES	EFFORT
Korea	16,950	0.888	0.60	−0.51	−0.50557	−0.00303	94.00
Greece	18,720	0.902	0.61	−0.49	−0.48395	−0.00707	95.00
Czech	15,780	0.868	0.59	−0.53	−0.52114	−0.00989	96.00
Portugal	18,280	0.897	0.61	−0.50	−0.48913	−0.01010	97.00
Uganda	1,390	0.493	0.35	−1.06	−1.05002	−0.01034	98.00
Israel	19,530	0.908	0.61	−0.49	−0.47473	−0.01195	99.00
Antigua & B.	10,920	0.800	0.54	−0.62	−0.60129	−0.01490	100.00
Slovenia	18,540	0.895	0.61	−0.50	−0.48605	−0.01647	101.00
New Zealand	21,740	0.926	0.63	−0.47	−0.45139	−0.01701	102.00
Spain	21,460	0.922	0.62	−0.47	−0.45421	−0.02060	103.00
Bhutan	1,969	0.536	0.37	−1.00	−0.97421	−0.02184	104.00
Togo	1,480	0.495	0.35	−1.06	−1.03636	−0.02785	105.00
Malta	17,640	0.875	0.59	−0.53	−0.49689	−0.03358	106.00
Cyprus	18,360	0.883	0.59	−0.52	−0.48818	−0.03438	107.00
Bangladesh	1,700	0.509	0.35	−1.04	−1.00619	−0.03699	108.00
Sweden	26,050	0.946	0.64	−0.45	−0.41202	−0.04054	109.00
Mauritius	10,810	0.785	0.53	−0.64	−0.60349	−0.04087	110.00
Morocco	3,810	0.620	0.42	−0.88	−0.83051	−0.04496	111.00
Papua N.G.	2,270	0.542	0.37	−1.00	−0.94324	−0.05462	112.00
UK	26,150	0.936	0.63	−0.47	−0.41118	−0.05722	113.00
Finland	26,190	0.935	0.63	−0.47	−0.41085	−0.05915	114.00
Japan	26,940	0.938	0.63	−0.47	−0.40471	−0.06051	115.00
Australia	28,260	0.946	0.63	−0.46	−0.39429	−0.06352	116.00
Belgium	27,570	0.942	0.63	−0.46	−0.39967	−0.06448	117.00
Vanuatu	2,890	0.570	0.38	−0.96	−0.89068	−0.06817	118.00
France	26,920	0.932	0.62	−0.47	−0.40487	−0.06995	119.00
Sudan	1,820	0.505	0.35	−1.06	−0.99134	−0.07287	120.00
Kuwait	16,240	0.838	0.55	−0.59	−0.51489	−0.07450	121.00
Brunei	19,210	0.867	0.57	−0.56	−0.47833	−0.07738	122.00
Netherlands	29,100	0.942	0.63	−0.47	−0.38792	−0.08156	123.00
Canada	29,480	0.943	0.63	−0.47	−0.38509	−0.08278	124.00
Bahrain	17,170	0.843	0.56	−0.59	−0.50277	−0.08362	125.00
Seychelles	18,232	0.853	0.56	−0.57	−0.48970	−0.08478	126.00
Italy	26,430	0.920	0.61	−0.49	−0.40887	−0.08543	127.00
Iceland	29,750	0.941	0.62	−0.47	−0.38311	−0.08796	128.00
Germany	27,100	0.925	0.61	−0.49	−0.40342	−0.08815	129.00
Singapore	24,040	0.902	0.60	−0.52	−0.42950	−0.08913	130.00
Austria	29,220	0.934	0.62	−0.48	−0.38702	−0.09533	131.00
Switzerland	30,010	0.936	0.62	−0.48	−0.38121	−0.09790	132.00
Denmark	30,940	0.932	0.61	−0.49	−0.37457	−0.11645	133.00
Hong Kong	26,910	0.903	0.59	−0.52	−0.40495	−0.11761	134.00
Pakistan	1,940	0.497	0.33	−1.10	−0.97744	−0.12017	135.00
Cameroon	2,000	0.501	0.33	−1.10	−0.97081	−0.12481	136.00
Congo D.R.	650	0.365	0.26	−1.34	−1.21548	−0.12520	137.00
Saudi Arabia	12,650	0.768	0.50	−0.70	−0.56927	−0.12788	138.00
Norway	36,600	0.956	0.63	−0.47	−0.33800	−0.13041	139.00

Country	PY	HDI	AHDI	LAHDI	PRED	RES	EFFORT
Bahamas	17,280	0.815	0.53	−0.64	−0.50137	−0.13665	140.00
Benin	1,070	0.421	0.29	−1.25	−1.10698	−0.13898	141.00
Oman	13,340	0.770	0.50	−0.70	−0.55771	−0.14213	142.00
Qatar	19,844	0.833	0.54	−0.62	−0.47126	−0.14555	143.00
USA	35,750	0.939	0.61	−0.49	−0.34311	−0.14737	144.00
Zambia	840	0.389	0.27	−1.31	−1.15966	−0.15338	145.00
Haiti	1,610	0.463	0.31	−1.17	−1.01803	−0.15423	146.00
Ireland	36,360	0.936	0.61	−0.50	−0.33943	−0.15596	147.00
Rwanda	1,270	0.431	0.29	−1.23	−1.06967	−0.16476	148.00
Gabon	6,590	0.648	0.41	−0.88	−0.71123	−0.16905	149.00
U. Arab E.	22,420	0.824	0.52	−0.65	−0.44469	−0.20158	150.00
Gambia	1,690	0.452	0.30	−1.22	−1.00747	−0.21218	151.00
Lesotho	2,420	0.493	0.32	−1.15	−0.92931	−0.22164	152.00
Burundi	630	0.339	0.24	−1.45	−1.22229	−0.22305	153.00
Zimbabwe	2,400	0.491	0.31	−1.16	−0.93112	−0.22618	154.00
Ethiopia	780	0.359	0.25	−1.40	−1.17579	−0.22799	155.00
Guinea–Bissau	710	0.350	0.24	−1.43	−1.19626	−0.23085	156.00
Senegal	1,580	0.437	0.28	−1.26	−1.02213	−0.23783	157.00
Namibia	6,210	0.607	0.38	−0.98	−0.72416	−0.25135	158.00
Chad	1,020	0.379	0.25	−1.39	−1.11739	−0.27291	159.00
South Africa	10,070	0.666	0.41	−0.89	−0.61893	−0.27430	160.00
Djibouti	1,990	0.454	0.29	−1.25	−0.97190	−0.27521	161.00
Mauritania	2,220	0.465	0.29	−1.23	−0.94809	−0.28405	162.00
Côte d'Ivoire	1,520	0.399	0.25	−1.39	−1.03055	−0.35975	163.00
Mozambique	1,050	0.354	0.22	−1.50	−1.11108	−0.38503	164.00
Swaziland	4,550	0.519	0.31	−1.19	−0.79187	−0.39339	165.00
Botswana	8,170	0.589	0.35	−1.06	−0.66445	−0.39783	166.00
Guinea	2,100	0.425	0.26	−1.37	−0.96019	−0.40630	167.00
C. African R.	1,170	0.361	0.22	−1.49	−1.08753	−0.40710	168.00
Sierra Leone	520	0.273	0.18	−1.72	−1.26406	−0.45259	169.00
Mali	930	0.326	0.20	−1.60	−1.13750	−0.45869	170.00
Niger	800	0.292	0.18	−1.74	−1.17028	−0.57078	171.00
Angola	2,130	0.381	0.21	−1.56	−0.95710	−0.59880	172.00
Burkina Faso	1,100	0.302	0.17	−1.78	−1.10096	−0.67887	173.00

[1] Some countries in the larger sample were not ranked because of missing variables – hence the blanks that should be ignored in this and the next table.

3. INSTITUTIONS AND ECONOMIC RIGHTS

3.1 Theoretical Underpinnings of Pro-Poor Institutions – The Power Diffusion Principle

The foregoing discussion suggests that failure to raise the absolute quality of life is the result of weak emphasis on economic rights – both negative and positive. The human development income deficit is to a large extent the outcome of low levels of economic freedom – primarily negative rights. By contrast, human development effort deficit is a result of low emphasis on positive economic rights. A country cannot raise the absolute quality of life for all citizens without providing conditions that are conducive to economic growth and wealth accumulation. Likewise, quality of life for the poorest members of society may remain low if there are no concrete efforts to provide social protection. Thus, as far as absolute quality of life is concerned, both positive and negative economic rights are complements rather than substitutes.[32] To the extent that negative economic rights have a positive impact on economic growth, they are pro-poor. Thus, a focus on economic freedom as advocated by classical liberals is not inconsistent with advancement of human rights generally. But, as we have established in the previous section, economic growth is not sufficient for overall human development. There are many cases in which countries have high incomes, but this has not translated into significant reductions in poverty or general improvements in well-being. Thus, significant poverty reduction requires growth that distributes benefits to the poor and enlarges their opportunity set.

Economic growth implies the creation of value from a given set of resources. Standard key ingredients for growth include increases in investment, advances in technology, and improvements in the quality of the labor force through investments in human capital. At the core of achieving and sustaining economic growth is getting the fundamentals right (macroeconomic stability) – inflation, interest rates, openness to trade and reducing the cost of doing business, infrastructure, incentives, and so on. Simply put, creation of value requires some key fundamentals for market actors to enter into gainful transactions. This suggests paying attention to the elements of economic freedom.

Good policies for economic growth may not necessarily result in pro-poor growth. As noted previously, some of the policies implemented by a host of developing countries have not always resulted in pro-poor growth. However, it is has been widely demonstrated that macroeconomic stability is necessary for economic growth. For example, high inflation and large budget deficits undermine economic growth and hurt the poor disproportionately. Likewise, an undervalued exchange rate policy reduces the volume of exports thereby worsening the balance of payment position which hurts the poor. More specific pro-poor growth policies include government spending on human capital investments, policies that target achieving equity in terms of asset ownership, gender and regions, and so on. Klasen (2001) provides a good summary of pro-poor growth policies.[33]

Although good policies are central to the achievement of economic growth, it is now well established that such growth arises from the interactions of good policies and good institutions. North (1990), for example, elaborates on the role of institutions in providing the right economic incentives for capital accumulation. Empirical literature has demonstrated a positive and significant relationship between the quality of institutions and economic growth (de Haan & Siermann

---

[32] See Blume and Voight (2004) for related analysis.

[33] For the purposes of this chapter, we do not go into detailed analysis of the merits of the pro-poor policies but rather focus on institutions that result in the enactment of pro-poor growth policies (see also Timmer 2004). Kimenyi (2006a) outlines what he calls a general theory of pro-poor growth that he summarizes in ten principles.

1995; Rodrik 1998; Nkurunziza & Bates 2003). In fact, evidence shows that some of the resource-rich countries perform dismally in terms of economic growth because of institutional weaknesses. Many scholars even consider institutions to be more important to economic growth than natural resource endowments (North 1990; Keefer 2004; Olson 1993; 1997; Kimenyi & Mbaku 1999; Kaufmann, Kraay & Zoido-Lobaton 1999). Probably the most important institutional factors include improving governance, protection of property rights, and upholding the rule of law. These institutional features are important for growth generally. Our focus is more specifically on the institutions that are necessary for the adoption of pro-poor growth policies. In other words, what type of institutions are necessary for the adoption of pro-poor growth policies?[34]

Based on the previous discussion, there are two key problems related to poverty reduction. The first has to do with the low growth and low incomes, the basis for what we have referred to as human development "*income deficit.*" This income shortfall means that a country does not have the means to deal with poverty. The second problem concerns human development "*effort deficit.*" This is the case in which a country has the necessary resources but policies are not pro-poor. We argue that both of these problems are directly related to institutions, and specifically the degree of leverage that the poor have in society. Pro-poor policies require that those in the bottom of the income distribution scale be in a position to effectively exert leverage on the leadership. We argue that public policy outcomes represent the interplay between various interests in the society and only those groups that are able to exert leverage are favored by the policies. This is consistent with the interest-group theory of government (Stigler 1971; Peltzman 1976). Pro-poor institutions are therefore those whereby the poor have power to influence policy outcomes in their favor. These institutions emerge when the poor are able to constrain the actions of the leaders and also bargain with other groups in society. This is consistent with Sen's (2001) view of development as freedom.

As a basic starting point in our exploration of pro-poor institutions, we view policy makers and bureaucrats as primarily interested in maximizing their own welfare.[35] Absent constraints, those in positions of power will seek to institute policies that best serve their interests. In essence, without institutional constraints, leaders will more often than not act in a predatory manner.[36] Put in another way, the behavior of leaders largely depends on the principal-agent relationships in a society. These relationships, in turn, are largely dependent on the institutional arrangements and the power distribution in society. Thus, adoption of good policies is not the result of "good" people, but primarily because of "good" institutional constraints that limit the predatory nature of leaders. But, of course, this may not

---

[34] A number of studies have focused on links between human rights and institutions. See, for example, Blume and Voight (2004), and Howard and Donnelly (1996).

[35] Viewing individuals as utility maximizers, both in the public and private spheres, is a primary tenet of the theory of public choice. The theory deviates from the traditional analysis of public policy by rejecting bifurcation of human behavior (see Buchanan & Tullock, 1962).

[36] It is important that institutional constraints on the behavior of leaders and members of society come from many sources. For example, at one level, such constraints could be through a formal constitution that limits the actions of leaders. However, constraints could also be more informal, ranging form customs to actions based on reciprocity and trust.

fully explain the two outcomes observed – "human development income deficit" and the "human development effort deficit." We suggest that these outcomes represent institutional failures. Specifically, both outcomes are related to inefficient "banditary."

Leaders who extract rents from producers for their own benefit can be considered bandits. A distinction is made between roving banditry and stationary banditry. Roving bandits are those that move from place to place stealing output from producers. This was the case in China during the 1920s, where bandits moved from village to village ravaging the villagers, killing them and stealing their outputs.[37] For roving bandits, the future output is of no concern since they move on to other villages after destroying the productive assets in one village. Under a roving banditry regime, there is no incentive to encourage higher outputs nor do the bandits invest in key productive activities such as infrastructure. That is, they do not invest in productive public goods. Societies subjected to the rule of roving banditry are likely to be characterized by low growth, limited investment in productivity-enhancing investments and generally low human development. By contrast, stationary bandits are those bandits who actually settle in a particular area, but still extract rents from the population. Stationary bandits do have an interest in the level of output and the future productivity of the community because the welfare of the bandits is directly related to the output of the community. As such, stationary bandits, while not democratic as such, have an interest in promoting production – economic growth so to say. Stationary bandits therefore limit their extractive activities so as not to adversely affect levels of output but also limit redistribution to the poor. Thus, stationary bandits are captured by a few interest groups that benefit from the regime and also constrain the regime from transferring benefits to other members of the society.

The alternative to banditry regimes is the establishment of institutions through participatory governance or by consent. In such institutions, the leaders (bandits) can only establish rule over the polity by seeking consensus involving widespread participation by the members of the relevant society. This implies that decision making powers are not held by the bandits and a few interest groups alone but are widely diffused in the society. In such consensual societies, economic growth and the well-being of all the citizens is directly related to the survival of the regime. Although the leadership in such a society is necessarily influenced more by some interest groups than others, the well-being of all groups is important and must be addressed by such regimes. Because power is sufficiently diffused in the society to different groups (businesses, nonprofit organizations, labor unions, producer groups, poor and wealthy, etc.), economic growth that improves the well-being of all members of the society enters into the leadership's utility function.[38]

Table 9.7, which is an extension of Figure 9.5 and Table 9.6, provides a schema for analyzing human development and institutions by categorizing countries based on the income and level of human development. The middle line represents the mean

---

[37] This analysis follows Olson (1997).

[38] The fact that power is sufficiently diffused implies that none of the groups including the leaders has a monopoly in determining outcomes. As such, policy outcomes require compromise through a process of bargaining.

Table 9.7. *Human development effort and institutions*

A	C	
Low-income (below the threshold income)/high human development countries	*Moderate to high-income (above the threshold income)/high human development*	
	Developed	Developing/Transitional
Uzebekistan	Norway	Armenia
Kyrgyzstan	Sweden	Azerbaijan
Georgia	United Kingdom	Costa Rica
Vietnam	United States	Cuba
	Japan	Jamaica
	Canada	Sri Lanka
	Iceland	Fiji
	Ireland	Albania
Mean HDI	Mean HDI	
B	**D**	
Human development "Income deficit" Countries	*Human development "Effort Deficit" countries (above threshold income but low HDI)*	
Effort deficit *Not Effort Deficit*		
Angola Tajikistan	South Africa	Namibia
Burkina Faso Mongolia	Swaziland	Gabon
Niger Romania	Botswana	Zimbabwe
Mali Moldova	Namibia	
Solomon Islands		

Y*
Per Capita Income (PPP)

HDI, and vertical line Y* is the threshold human development income. Box A represents countries with low incomes but high HDI. Based on the actual data of human development indicators, only a few countries are in this category.[39] Box B represents human development income deficit countries. These low-income countries can be considered as similar to "Roving Bandit" regimes. However, one set of these countries is also characterized by human development effort deficit while others are not. This means that there are differences in the nature of institutions within the roving banditary category.[40] Box D, by contrast, represents Human Development effort deficit countries. These are countries that are able to generate incomes but

[39] Many countries in this category are primarily part of the old Soviet bloc. Thus, how we interpret the results and consequential policy recommendations should take cognizance of the history of these states. Nevertheless, as evidence from Table 9.6 shows, there are many good performers that do not have a history of socialism.

[40] This should not be surprising as countries have different histories. Furthermore, there is ample evidence showing that dictators are not created equal – some are more responsive to human development goals than others.

are not pro-poor. We argue that these countries are similar to "stationary bandits" regimes. These are countries where leadership is captured by producer and business interests. Box C represents countries whose incomes are above the threshold level and also have human development index above the mean – this is the case of consensual governments with sufficient power diffusion. These governments enact policies that result in growth that benefits all groups.[41]

The complementarily of positive and negative rights in raising absolute quality of life is apparent. We have noted that only very few countries with low incomes have HDI values above the mean, and these countries have a unique socialist history. For countries in Box B, regardless of their human development effort, the absolute quality of life is low because of low incomes. These countries may be putting too much emphasis on redistribution (positive rights) and less on production (economic freedom). By contrast, countries in Box C have an emphasis on economic freedom and low effort on positive economic rights.[42]

3.2 Historical and Other Evidence of the Power-Diffusion Principle

Historically, the emergence of institutions with centralized leadership has often started with a high concentration of power amongst a few individuals who comprise a ruling class. In many cases, this ruling class has been royal families or a group of families that monopolize power. In other cases, power has been concentrated amongst landed class and military juntas, or even with religious leadership. For, so long as power is concentrated with a few individuals, public policy outcomes can be expected to favor the group that holds the power. Furthermore, the group that holds power has no interest in enlarging its membership since that would dilute the benefits to each member. In terms of economic growth, it does not matter which group has the power: so long as power is concentrated, the ruling coalition has no interest in broad pro-growth policies that would benefit all members of the society and therefore its members largely act as roving bandits. Absent means by which other groups can share in the power, those outside the ruling coalition continuously seek ways to replace the ruling coalition and establish themselves as rulers and in turn monopolize power. Such change in the ruling coalition is not through bargaining, but rather through use of violence. It is the uncertainty associated with roving banditry regimes that translates into the short-run planning horizon which is not consistent with economic growth.[43] Economic growth is further undermined by the fact that such regimes have necessarily to invest substantial resources to

---

[41] Cuba, Armenia, Azerbaijan, and Albania are not consensual regimes and their human development income and effort rankings reflect the massive resource transfers that characterized Soviet Union to the countries and territories.

[42] Even those who advocate for free markets with minimal intervention agree that economic growth requires public involvement in human capital (education, health, nutrition, etc.). Thus, sustaining high rates of economic growth is unlikely to be sustained in countries that do not invest heavily in human capital. Countries in Box D are unlikely to sustain growth unless they focus more on human capital – meaning emphasis on positive rights.

[43] For a systematic analysis of the behavior of rulers in roving bandit regimes, see Brough and Kimenyi (1986). This is also consistent with the findings of Alesina and Perotti (1996), who find that political instability – by creating uncertainty in the political economy environment – reduces investment (see also Dutt & Mitra 2004).

prevent the formation of strong groups that could otherwise dislodge the regime. At the same time, the regime does not invest in productive public goods whose returns are realized long into the future. This explains the low-income, high-concentration of power characteristic of countries in Box B.

For many other countries, rulers form coalitions with powerful interest groups. These interest groups could be involved in agriculture, extraction of minerals or industrial production, but the groups have an interest in supporting the regime in return for protection. By contrast, the ruling class benefits by selling protection in return for revenue. In essence, such countries do in fact achieve growth and accumulation of wealth but there are no forces to redistribute wealth. In fact, the compact between rulers and producer interest groups is precisely based on implicit or explicit agreement that involves limiting redistribution. This may involve protection of land ownership, unfavorable labor laws, and the erection of barriers to entry that make it difficult for other producers to compete with incumbents. It has been demonstrated that powerful interest groups can be harmful to growth by blocking adoption of new technologies. For example, dominant industry groups can block the introduction of new technology by other firms. If the incumbent firms have captured the rulers, then it is conceivable that entrants will be blocked from entering and thus hindering growth.[44] But rulers only adopt such policies if the increased competition in the market associates with loss of power. Acemoglu and Robinson (2000) propose what they call the "political loser hypothesis" and argue that it is those whose political power, not economic rents, are eroded that block technological progress. Countries in Box D (human development effort deficit) are in this category. A good example includes South Africa, where the state protected members of a producer group but limited the distribution of resources to other groups.[45]

The basic argument advanced in this chapter is that pro-poor growth policies require power diffusion in society. Institutions in which power is sufficiently diffused are characterized by a "balance of power" among the various interest groups (Powelson 1994). This means that each of the groups in society has some degree of "veto power" over public policy outcomes. For groups to be able to influence policy outcomes, they must have leverage – that is, they must be able to block adoption of policies. While individual groups may not necessarily be able to block all policies which do not benefit them, it is acknowledged that it is necessary to bargain with the groups in exchange for supporting other policies. Such bargaining eliminates outcomes that completely ignore the welfare of some groups.

Looking again at Table 9.7, we note that countries in Box B could make a transition either to Box D or Box C. A transition from B to D would mean that the countries achieve growth but policies so adopted are not pro-poor. Of course, this would be a better transition than remaining in B, but such a transition would primarily benefit only some groups. Countries in Box D can also move to C by

---

[44] See, for example, Parente and Prescott (1999); Krusell and Rios-Rull (1996).

[45] Although there is now more power diffusion in South Africa, the effects of the Apartheid regime remain strong and little change has taken place in terms of economic benefits reaching the poor. Although many pro-poor growth policies have been implemented, it will take time to undo the results of the past, particularly when the target is growth with redistribution.

focusing on pro-poor policies. As demonstrated earlier, pro-poor growth policies only emerge when power is diffused.

Lessons from history show that power diffusion takes place over long periods of time and involves increasing the empowerment of groups formerly excluded from decision making in the society. Even for today's advanced nations, power was initially concentrated but eventually diffused even to the peasants who were able to organize and demand better working conditions and wages. Through exerting leverage, those in power slowly but surely were forced to extend the franchise. Powelson (1994, 43–44), for example, writes in the case of Northwestern Europe:

> From the ninth to the nineteenth century, power in Europe not only became more diffuse but also changed its character. At first, it belonged to individuals as a property right. Power positions were inherited, bought and sold, or granted by the monarch. They were based on military force, religion, and wealth. Toward the end of the period, power belonged more to organizations – such as senate, business corporation, or labor union, than to individuals. It was grounded on institutions supported by a balance of tensions among groups.

A significant factor in the power diffusion process is democratization – which typically starts with the extension of voting rights and meaningful participation in the political process. By and large, diffusion of power occurs when groups outside the ruling coalition are well organized and form alliances that pose a threat to the ruling coalition. In analysis of the case of Western Europe, Acemoglu and Robinson (1999, 1) demonstrate that the ruling coalition extended the franchise to avoid social unrest and revolution, and that these political reforms also culminated in what we may call pro-poor policies:

> Britain, for example, was transformed from an "oligarchy" run by an elite to a democracy. The franchise was extended in 1832, then again in 1867 and 1884, transferring voting rights to portions of the society with no previous political representation. The decades after the political reforms witnessed radical social reforms, increased taxation, and extension of education to masses.[46]

This story is consistent with what happened in many of today's developed countries. In all cases, diffusion of power involved the emergence of many interest groups which formed vertical and horizontal alliances to increase their leverage.[47] Important to note is that power diffusion was accompanied with not just growth but also with a focus on the well-being of the poorest members.

For today's poor countries, power diffusion is the primary strategy for achieving pro-poor growth. Evidence from a number of countries has shown that as different

---

[46] See also Acemoglu and Robinson (2002).

[47] The case of the United States in relation to the well-being of blacks is particularly informative. Before the extension of voting rights, the well-being of blacks was not taken seriously by the leadership. Because blacks did not have power to influence outcomes, there was limited focus on key development aspects such as education and health, or even working conditions. This, of course, changed dramatically as blacks became more organized and were able to exert leverage during the 1950s and 1960s, culminating in the civil rights legislation and subsequent transfer and other programs that benefited them substantially. It is also important to note that blacks did not achieve such leverage on their own alone, but by forming alliances with other groups.

groups have become more organized and exerted pressure on the rulers, they have been able to force diffusion of power and consequently adoption of pro-poor growth policies. Power diffusion is not evidenced by mere participation in voting but, rather, by the formation of common-interest groups that have capacity to negotiate with others and collectively these groups exert sufficient leverage (or provide credible threat to a regime). Pernia (2001, 2–3) observes:

> Governments are prone to lobbying by special interest groups. The political feasibility of poverty reduction depends on the distribution of benefits from anti-poverty interventions, which in turn hinges on the prevailing configuration of pressure groups, such as industrialists, landlords, labor unions, peasant movements, consumer associations, and women's groups. The potential for poverty reduction is better where there are strong coalitions of the poor that can pressure governments to act in their favor. Salient examples include the successful land reforms in the Republic of Korea and Taipei, China, on the one hand; and the slow, largely ineffective agrarian reforms in Pakistan and the Philippines, on the other.... By contrast, coalitions of the rural poor and civil society organizations have in recent years managed to bring poverty to the top of the government's agenda in Thailand.

Thus, evidence from both history and contemporary cases confirms the importance of power diffusion on the adoption of pro-poor policies. At the core of the emergence of institutions where power is diffused is the formation of well-organized interest groups. A primary prerequisite for formation of groups is, of course, a political environment that is democratic and allows for freedom of association. To a large extent, the evolution of common interest groups in Africa and other countries has been stunted by autocratic regimes. We can therefore explain the over-representation of human development deficit African countries in Box B of Table 9.7 – which we have called roving bandit regimes – as the result of suppression of political rights. Historical evidence shows that power diffusion was actually occurring – albeit slowly – long before colonialism, but this process was interrupted and distorted by colonial rule. Colonial rule and the postcolonial regimes had the effect of concentrating power. Recent democratization efforts also have been associated with the emergence of numerous interest groups and civil society organizations, and we can predict that these groups force power diffusion – a process already begun.

Power diffusion therefore associates with quality institutions that are consistent with the adoption of pro-growth policies generally, and also pro-poor policies specifically. But the emergence of well-organized interest groups depends on particular societies. Of key importance is the extent of trust amongst members of a group. Trust is necessary for people to form strong cohesive groups that are capable of advancing a common purpose. But even more important is that different groups must trust and cooperate in order to form horizontal and vertical alliances that are necessary to exercise leverage on those who may seek to monopolize power. Trust is one key component of social capital that influences power diffusion. Ethnic divisions are considered a key factor that reduces trust in Africa, and thereby undermines the formation of effective civil society groups.

3.3 Institutions that Facilitate Power Diffusion-Evidence

At least since the late 1990s, there has been concerted emphasis on pro-poor growth. Noteworthy is the almost complete reversal from the exclusive focus on "trickle-down" policies that characterized policy prescriptions during the 1980s and 1990s. There is also an increasing body of empirical literature on the link between institutions and economic growth and poverty reduction. The emerging consensus is that reforms that improve the institutions of governance – characterized by reduced corruption, increased transparency, and enhanced participation of the poor – generally translate into improved economic performance, with the poor benefiting from the growth substantially. For example, as noted by Global Solidarity (2000, 2, Box 3.1):

> An improvement in governance – such as an improvement in the rule of law from the low level in Russia to the high level in Czech Republic, or a reduction in corruption from the high level in Indonesia to that in the Republic of Korea–leads to a two-to-four fold improvement in per capita incomes and in infant mortality rates, and about a 20 percent improvement in adult literacy. These results are not just simple correlations between better governance and better development outcomes. Rather, the causality is from governance to these selected measures of development.[48]

There are a number of indicators of institutional quality, and which are good proxies for empowerment and power diffusion in general. These institutional features include democratization, prevalence of corruption, freedom of press and political stability. These measures of quality of institutions capture the degree to which societies are open, in terms of participation in decision making and the ability of citizens to hold leaders to account. Thus, high levels of corruption suggest that there are weak mechanisms to control the predatory activities of leaders. By contrast, high levels of democratization and press freedom imply that the citizens are able to participate in policy making and have freedom to express their opinions. As noted previously, political instability implies situations in which barriers to political competition exist, often resulting in violence which undermines growth. In addition, the degree of inequality in society is an important institutional variable measuring the concentration of economic power. Kimenyi (2005) investigates the relevance of these institutional measures in explaining the well-being of the poor, and finds that all the measures of institutional quality are statistically significant determinants of HDI.

The evidence suggests some obvious institutional reforms for the achievement of pro-poor growth. First, of course, is the establishment of more open political markets – that is, introduction of political competition. Increased democracy, as we have seen, is at the core of the power diffusion process. Increased democracy can be expected to also reduce political instability and associated violence and civil wars. Second, fighting corruption is pivotal in power diffusion and requires there to be clear mechanisms through which the citizens can hold the leaders to account. Thus, democratization should not just mean opening markets for political competition and extending people's freedoms but also should be associated with institutional

---

[48] See also Rodrik (1998; 1999); Mauro (1995; 1998).

reforms that constrain those in power. This calls for adoption of constitutional rules that limit the powers of rulers, and that strengthen the judiciary and other organs charged with fighting corruption. Finally, our results suggest that inequality in the distribution of income is itself a barrier to the adoption of pro-poor policies. The policy prescription must therefore include institutional arrangements that increase the participation of the poor in all aspects of life. In particular, policies that directly target benefits to the poor – such as public expenditures on education, primary health care and rural infrastructure – expand the opportunity set available to the poor and empower them economically. Therefore, institutions that support economic rights are required.[49]

3.4 Recent Cases of Power Diffusion and Impact on Economic Rights

During the last two decades, power diffusion has accelerated in many developing countries. This has involved a shift away from autocratic rule to semi-autocracy and even consensual governments. Although the changes in the quality of life occur over long periods and thus lag institutional changes, there are in fact some good examples of advancement of economic rights as a result of power diffusion. Although a great deal of focus has been on positive rights, many of these countries have actually made advances in negative economic rights. A number of countries have gone beyond legislating economic rights and have included such rights in their constitutions.

Kenya represents an interesting case of the impact of power diffusion on economic rights. Since independence in 1963, Kenya has been characterized by large inequalities and high concentration of power in the executive and a few members of a ruling coalition. Democratization efforts culminated in the election of a democratic coalition government in December 2002. By January 2003, the new government announced and actually implemented a policy of free and compulsory primary education, among other measures, to provide access to development goods to the majority of the population who had hitherto been marginalized. A proposed constitution that included various provisions on positive economic rights – such as the right to social security, primary education, basic health care, and so on – was subjected to a referendum vote in November 2005 and rejected by the majority of voters.[50]

Uganda is another case study in which dramatic changes in the advancement of economic rights has taken place. Although the current regime is not fully democratic, it represents major improvements in power diffusion from previous regimes. The government of Uganda has undertaken significant steps in social provision,

---

[49] One area that can advance the position of the poor in Africa is in land reform, including both ownership and user rights. Such reform can be expected to empower the poor generally, and specifically rural women who face various forms of marginalization. Appropriate land reform initiatives can also provide incentives for improved productivity. Likewise, access to finance is important in reducing inequalities and empowering the poor. All of these policies improve the capabilities of the poor and directly facilitate power diffusion and pro-poor growth.

[50] The rejection of the proposed draft was primarily because voters considered the proposed draft as concentrating power in the executive – hence not accelerating the diffusion of power (see Kimenyi 2006b).

particularly in areas of education and health. Through decentralization initiatives, the government has been able to improve on human development. Most significant has been adoption of pro-growth and pro-poor policies that have resulted in considerable reductions in poverty.

South Africa is yet another good case of power diffusion. As noted previously, South Africa is a high-income country with a poor record of human development. The Apartheid regime focused on interests of whites, but repressed blacks' economic rights – both positive and negative. Since the end of the Apartheid era, major advances have been made in areas of redistributive justice, particularly in the provision of education, basic health, and housing. Although the quality of life for most black South Africans remains relatively low, there is clear evidence of advances associated with power diffusion. In addition, the post-Apartheid constitution provides for specific rights in pertaining to positive economic rights (Sachs 2004; Porter 1995).

The advancement in economic rights following power diffusion, as discussed earlier, is consistent with our previous analysis suggesting that such diffusion of power results in compromise amongst members of society. As noted by Pieterse and Van Donk (2004, 3):

> The realisation of socio-economic rights is an inherently political process, which needs to involve rights-holders (directly, or through associations and organisations representing their interests) in determining the desired outcomes, objectives, strategies and acceptable trade-offs so that they are enabled to take control of their own destinies. This inevitably implies a political process of negotiation, disagreement, conflict, occasionally consensus, and, at a minimum, forms of mutual accommodation.

Increasingly, countries are including social and economic rights in their constitutions. This appears to be a direct approach to advancing those rights (Napier 2003; Porter 1995). However, this issue is hotly debated to the extent that many such rights are considered unenforceable (Harvey 2004; Sunstein 2003). The American constitution, for example, does not deal with social and economic rights. By contrast, many scholars consider inclusion of such rights in the constitution as paramount:

> Ultimately, a constitution which excludes social and economic rights betrays its own principles. It fails to safeguard the rights of disadvantaged groups and undermines the integrity of the democratic process. As the Indian Supreme Court said on one occasion, social and economic rights, and civil and political rights are like "two wheels of a chariot". Vulnerable minorities are no less in need of protection in the social and economic sphere than in the civil and political realm. An incomplete set of rights, a chariot missing a wheel, cannot help but veer off course. Now, more than ever, we need participatory democracies which hear the voices of their most disadvantaged citizens and address the injustice of social and economic deprivation as issues of fundamental human rights. (Porter 1995, 4)

What is apparent is that recent constitutional reforms in developing countries have tended to include social and economic rights. This is true for the African countries that have recently experienced diffusion of power. Thus, although they may not have made many other institutional reforms, these countries have opted for a more direct route to achieve economic rights.

4. CONCLUSION: INSTITUTIONAL REFORMS

This chapter has highlighted the strong link between institutions and pro-poor growth. It has been demonstrated that, although growth is generally good for all members of the society, it is not sufficient for poverty reduction. It also has been demonstrated that poverty responds to growth but the responsiveness does vary with the inequality. In addition, it has been shown that although increasing incomes is necessary for the overall improvement of human well-being, there are cases when high incomes are associated with low human development, implying that benefits of growth do not always filter down to the poor. The basic argument advanced in the chapter is that institutions supportive of pro-poor growth are those where power is sufficiently diffused in society and where balance of power is maintained through bargaining and compromise amongst interest groups. These institutions require democratic societies, in which many interest groups play a role in the design and implementation of policies.

A particular innovation of this chapter is the introduction of "human development *income deficit*" and "human development *effort deficit*" concepts to categorize countries. This categorization helps us understand some of the constraints to pro-poor growth, as well as transitions that the countries are likely to make depending on their institutional features. The chapter links institutions to human development effort deficit and confirms the importance of institutions in determining countries' propensity to take a pro-poor stance. The chapter also highlights the complementarity between positive and negative economic rights.

The emerging policy recommendations focus on institutional reforms to accelerate power diffusion, including democratization and improvement in transparency. Likewise, well-designed decentralization schemes are key to accelerating the power diffusion process and consequently the adoption of pro-poor policies. Although it is acknowledged that appropriate reforms should depend on a country's unique circumstances, a primary message of the chapter is that pro-poor reforms must entail diffusion of power even to the poorest members of society, so they can participate meaningfully in determining policy outcomes and exercise leverage over leadership.

A recurring theme in the chapter is that large inequalities in the distribution of income are not only anti-poor in general but are also antigrowth. In fact, it has been argued that unless African countries focus on direct approaches to lower inequalities, achievement of the Millennium Development Goals will remain a mirage. Thus, key to achievement of pro-poor growth is a focus on targeting public expenditure on the poor in areas that directly increase their capabilities – for instance, in education, health, land rights, and rural infrastructure. These pro-poor expenditures can be expected to pay handsome dividends in terms of economic growth. However, we note that the adoption of such policies requires that the poor be able to influence outcomes in their favor, thus emphasizing the necessity of reforms that accelerate power diffusion.

This chapter is largely exploratory and more research is required so as to offer concrete reform proposals. More rigorous empirical investigation of the role of African institutions in power diffusion and pro-poor growth is necessary. In particular, there is need to focus on various institutional factors that seem to hinder power diffusion within the African context. A more careful analysis of human development effort deficit in relation to institutional arrangements can help unearth the most important institutional determinants of pro-poor growth and policies. More research is also necessary to evaluate the design of decentralization in Africa. Although in theory decentralization is expected to be pro-poor, there are many cases in which such results have not been realized because of poor design.

As a final remark, it is observed that there has been a tendency for countries to approach the issue of economic rights by including provisions in their constitutions. It is not clear the extent to which such rights have aided in advancing economic rights, and in particular whether that is the most practical way of advancing those rights. Some more analysis of constitutional provisions for economic rights in developing countries, and the degree to which they are enforced, could shed light on the viability and effectiveness of including economic rights provisions in constitutions.

REFERENCES

Acemoglu, Daron, and James A. Robinson. 1999. Why Did the West Extend the Franchise? Democracy, Inequality and Growth in Historical Perspective. *Quarterly Journal of Economics* 115 (4): 1167–99.

Acemoglu, Daron, and James A. Robinson. 2000. Political Losers as a Barrier to Economic Development. Unpublished Paper, Department of Economics, Massachusetts Institute of Technology.

Acemoglu, Daron, and James A. Robinson. 2002. The Political Economy of the Kuznets Curve. *Review of Development Economics* 6 (2): 183–203.

Alesina, A., and R. Perotti. 1996. Income Distribution, Political Instability and Investment. *European Economic Review* 40: 1203–28.

Azfar, Omar, Satu Kahkonen, Anthony Lanyi, Patrick Meagher, and Diana Rutherford. 2004. Decentralization, Governance and Public Services: The Impact of Institutional Arrangements. In *Devolution and Development: Governance Prospects in Decentralizing States*, ed. Mwangi S. Kimenyi and Patrick Meagher, 19–62. Aldershot: Ashgate.

Berggren, Niclas. 2003. The Benefits of Economic Freedom: A Survey. *The Independent Review* 8: 193–211.

Blume, Lorenz, and Stefan Voight. 2004. The Economics Effects of Human Rights. Working Paper, Univ. of Kassel.

Bourguignon, Francois. 2004. The Poverty-Growth-Inequality Triangle. Paper presented at the Indian Council for Research on International Economic Relations, New Delhi, February 2004.

Brough, Wayne T., and Mwangi S. Kimenyi. 1986. On the Inefficient Extraction of Rents by Dictators. *Public Choice* 48: 37–48.

Buchanan, James M., and Gordon Tullock. 1962. *The Calculus of Consent: Logical Foundations of Constitutional Democracy*. Ann Arbor: University of Michigan Press.

Chu, Ke-Young. 2001. Collective Values, Behavioural Normal, and Rules-Building Public Institutions for Economic Growth and Poverty Reduction. Working Paper presented at the

World Institute for Development Economics Research (WIDER) Conference on Growth and Poverty Reduction, Helsinki, May 25–26, 2001.

Cingranelli, David, and David L. Richards, David L. 2004. Measuring Government Respect for Economic Human Rights. Working Paper prepared for the annual meeting of Midwest Political Science Association, Chicago, IL.

Clague, Christopher, ed. 1997. *Institutions and Economic Development: Growth and Government in Less-Developed and Post-Socialist Countries.* Baltimore, MD: Johns Hopkins University Press.

De Haan, Jacob, and C. L. J. Siermann. 1995. New Evidence on the Relationship between Democracy and Economic Growth. *Public Choice* 86: 175–98.

Donnelly, Jack. 1996. "Rethinking Human Rights," *Current History* 95 (November): 387–391.

Dutt, Pushan, and Devashish Mitra. 2004. Inequality and the Instability of Polity and Policy. Working Paper, Dept. of Economics, University of Alberta (Edmonton), Alberta, Canada.

Easterly, William. 2001. The Effect of IMF and World Bank Programmes on Poverty. WIDER Discussion Paper No. 2001/102.

Ferro, Manuela, David Rosenblatt, and Nicholas Stern. 2002. Policies for Pro-Poor Growth in India. Working Paper, Cornell University.

Fischer, Stanley. 1993. The Role of Macroeconomic Factors in Growth. National Bureau of Economic Research (NBER) Working Paper Series No. 4565. Cambridge, MA.

Gaiha, R. 2001. Decentralization and Poverty Alleviation in Developing Asia. Economic and Development Resource Center, Asian Development Bank.

Garofalo, Charles. n.d. Leadership Development and Moral Agency in the Public Service. Dept. of Political Science, Texas State Univ., San Marcos, TX. http://unpan1.un.org/intradoc/groups/public/documents/nispacee/unpan018553.pdf.

Global Solidarity. 2000. Making State Institutions Pro-Poor. www.globasolidarity.org/wdr2000-1/cha3.pdf.

Harvey, Philip. 2004. Aspirational Law. *Buffalo Law Review* 52 (3): 701–26.

Howard, Rhoda E., and Jack Donnelly. 1986. Human Dignity, Human Rights and Political Regimes. *American Political Science Review* 80 (3): 801–17.

Kakwani, Nanak, and Pernia, Ernesto M. (2000), "What is Poor-Poor Growth?," *Asian Development Review*, Vol. 18 (1): 1–16.

Kakwani, Nanak, Shahid Khandker, and Hyun H. Son. 2004. Pro-Poor Growth-Concepts and Measurement with Country Case Studies. Working Paper No. 1, International Poverty Centre, United Nations Development Programme.

Kaufmann, Daniel, Aart Kraay, and Pablo Zoido-Lobaton. 1999. Governance Matters. Washington, DC: World Bank.

Killick, Tony. 1999. Making Adjustments Work for the Poor. ODI Poverty Briefing (May).

Keefer, Philip. 2004. A Review of the Political Economy of Governance: From Property Rights to Voice. World Bank Policy Research Working Paper 3315.

Kimenyi, Mwangi S. 1987. Bureaucratic Rents and Political Institutions. *Journal of Public Finance and Public Choice* 3: 189–99.

Kimenyi, Mwangi S. 1989. Interest Groups, Transfer Seeking and Democratization. *The American Journal of Economics and Sociology* 48: 339–49.

Kimenyi, Mwangi S. 1995. *Economics of Poverty, Discrimination and Public Policy.* Cincinnati, OH: South-Western.

Kimenyi, Mwangi S. 2005. Institutions of Governance, Power Diffusion and Pro-Poor Growth and Policies. African Economic Research Consortium.

Kimenyi, Mwangi S. 2006a. Economic Reforms and Pro-Poor Growth: Lessons for Africa and Other Developing Countries and Economies in Transition. Working Paper, Dept. of Economics, University of Connecticut.

Kimenyi, Mwangi S. 2006b. The Demand for Power Diffusion: A Case Study of the 2005 Constitutional Referendum in Kenya. Working Paper, Dept. of Economics, University of Connecticut.

Kimenyi, Mwangi S., and John Mbaku. 1993. Rent-Seeking and Institutional Stability in Developing Countries. *Public Choice* 77: 385–405.

Kimenyi, Mwangi S., and John Mbaku. 1995. Female Headship, Feminization of Poverty and Welfare. *Southern Economic Journal* 62 (1): 44–52.

Kimenyi, Mwangi S., and John Mbaku. 1999. *Institutions and Collective Choice: Applications of the Theory of Public Choice.* Brookfield, VT: Ashgate.

Kimenyi, Mwangi S., and Patrick Meagher. 2004. *Devolution and Development: Governance Prospects in Decentralizing States.* Aldershot: Ashgate.

Klasen, Stephan. 2001. In Search of the Holy Grail: How to Achieve Pro-Poor Growth. Working Paper commissioned by Deutche Gesellaschaft fur Technische Zusammenarbeit (GTZ) for the "Growth and Equity" Task Team of the Strategic Partnership with Africa (SPA), Dept. of Economics, Univ. of Munich.

Korsun, George, and Patrick Meagher. 2004. Failure by Design? Fiscal Decentralization in West Africa. In *Devolution and Development: Governance Prospects in Decentralizing States,* ed. Mwangi S. Kimenyi and Patrick Meagher, 137–95. Aldershot: Ashgate.

Krussell, Per, and Jose-Victor Rios-Rull. 1996. Vested Interests in a Positive Theory of Stagnation and Growth. *Review of Economic Studies* 63 (2): 301–29.

Kuznets, Simon, Wilbert E. Moore, and Joseph J. Spengler, eds. 1955. *Economic Growth: Brazil, India, Japan.* Durham, N.C., Duke University Press.

Lockie, Scott. 1998. Another Step Towards Indivisibility: Identifying the Key Features of Violations of Economic, Social and Cultural Rights. *Human Rights Quarterly* 20: 81–124.

Lopez, J. Humberto. 2004. Pro-Poor Growth: A Review of What We Know (and of What We Don't). World Bank PREM Poverty Group.

Mauro, Paolo. 1998. Corruption and the Composition of Government Expenditure. *Journal of Public Economics* 69 (2): 263–79.

Mauro, Paolo. 1995. Corruption and Growth. *Quarterly Journal of Economics* 110 (3): 681–712.

Mbaku, John, and Mwangi S. Kimenyi. 1997. Macroeconomic Determinants of Growth: Further Evidence on the Role of Political Freedom. *Journal of Economic Development* 22: 119–32.

Napier, Clive J. 2003. Constitutional Options: Economic Provisions. Paper prepared for the Center of International Cooperation at New York University.

North, Douglass. 1990. *Institutions, Institutional Change and Economic Performance.* Cambridge: Cambridge University Press.

Nkurunziza, Javier D., and Robert H. Bates. 2003. Political Institutions and Economic Growth in Africa. Center for International Development Working Paper No. 98, Harvard University.

Olson, Mancur. 1997. The New Institutional Economics: The Collective Choice Approach to Economic Development. In *Institutions and Economic Development: Growth and Government in Less-Developed and Post-Socialist Countries,* ed. Christopher Clague, 37–64. Baltimore, MD: Johns Hopkins University Press.

Olson, Mancur. 1993. Dictatorship, Democracy and Development. *American Political Science Review* 87: 567–76.

Pasha, A. Hafiz, and T. Palanivel. 2004. Pro-Poor Growth and Policies: The Asian Experience. Asia-Pacific Regional Programme on the Macroeconomics of Poverty Reduction, UNDP.

Parente, Stephen L., and Edward C. Prescott. 1999. Monopoly Rights: A Barrier to Riches. Federal Reserve Bank of Minneapolis, Research Department Staff Report 236/JV.

Peltzman, Sam. 1976. Toward a More General Theory of Regulation. *Journal of Law and Economics* 19: 211–40.

Pernia, Ernesto M. 2001. Is Growth Good Enough for the Poor? Economic and Research Department Policy Briefs Series, Economic Research Department No. 1, Asian Development Bank.

Persson, Torsten, and Guido Tabellini. 2004. Constitutions and Economic Policy. *Journal of Economic Perspectives* 18 (1): 75–98.

Pieterse, Edgar, and Mirjam Van Donk. 2004. The Politics of Socio-Economic Rights in South Africa: Ten Years after Apartheid. *Social Economic Rights Project*, Vol. 5, No. 5, University of Western Cape.

Porter, Bruce. 1995. The Importance of Including Social and Economic Rights in the South African Constitution: A Canadian Perspective. http://www.equalrights.org /cera/docs/ southafrica.html.

Powelson, John P. 1994. *Centuries of Economic Endeavor*. Ann Arbor: University of Michigan Press.

Ravallion, Martin. 2001. Growth, Inequality and Poverty: Looking Beyond Averages. *World Development* 29 (11): 1803–15.

Rodrik, Dani. 1998. Where Did All the Growth Go? External Shocks, Social Conflict and Growth Collapses, NBER Working Paper 6350.

Rodrik, Dani. 1999. Democracies Pay Higher Wages. *Quarterly Journal of Economics* 114 (3): 707–38.

Sachs, Albie. 2004. The Judicial Enforcement of Social Economic Rights: The Grootboom Case. Paper presented at a Conference on Third Party Effects: "What Happens When the State Promotes Rights?," 12th Annual Conference on the Individual versus the State, Central European University, Budapest, June 18–19.

Sen, Amartya. 1982. *Poverty and Famines: An Essay on Entitlements and Deprivation*. Oxford: Claredon Press.

Sen, Amartya. 2001. *Development as Freedom*. Oxford: Oxford University Press.

Son, Hyun Hwa. 2004. A Note on Pro-Poor Growth. *Economic Letters* 82: 307–14.

Stigler, George. 1971. The Theory of Economic Regulation. *Bell Journal of Economics* 2: 3–21.

Sustein, Cass R. 2003. Why Does the American Constitution Lack Social and Economic Guarantees. Working Paper, University of Chicago Law School.

Timmer, Peter C. 2004. The Road to Pro-Poor Growth: The Indonesian Experience in Regional Perspective. Center for Global Development, Working Paper No. 38.

United Nations Development Programme (UNDP). 2004. *Human Development Report 2004*. New York: Oxford University Press.

White, Howard, and Edward Anderson. 2001. Growth versus Distribution: Does the Pattern of Growth Matter? *Development Policy Review* 19 (3): 267–89.

10 Measuring Government Effort to Respect Economic and Social Human Rights: A Peer Benchmark

DAVID L. CINGRANELLI AND DAVID L. RICHARDS

INTRODUCTION

In 2000, the Organization for Economic Co-operation and Development (OECD), International Monetary Fund (IMF), United Nations, and World Bank published a jointly prepared document titled "A Better World for All" (www.paris21.org/ betterworld/home.htm). That document promised substantial progress in reducing world poverty by 2015. The report proposes measuring poverty reduction in seven areas: world poverty (the percentage of people living on the equivalent of one U.S. dollar or less per day), gender gaps in school enrollment, primary school enrollment, infant mortality and maternal mortality, access to health services, and sustainable development. Among other specific goals mentioned in the report, the promises included decreasing rates of infant mortality by two-thirds and maternal mortality by three-fourths, providing access to all that need health service, and ensuring that all children are enrolled in primary school. Taken together, the goals in the report are commonly referred to as the "Millennium Development Goals."

The language of human rights could have been used to frame the Millennium Development Goals Project. A citizen's rights to a government that will try to offer protections against the ravages of disease, hunger, exposure, and illiteracy are protected in international human rights law. Shue (1980) and Pogge (2006) have even argued that these economic and social rights are the most important of all human rights. Still, policy makers are hesitant to treat such things as an adequate education, health care, housing, and decent employment as proper human rights. The general lack of effort by governments around the world to respect economic and social human rights is also mostly ignored by international non-governmental organizations (INGOs) that report on the human rights practices of governments, and by those who conduct scientific research concerning the human rights practices of governments.

In this chapter, we discuss some of the important provisions in international human rights law that make national governments responsible for the protection of the economic and social rights of their citizens. We then discuss some of the reasons why Western policy makers and scholars usually treat economic and social rights

The authors would like to thank Rhonda Callaway and Wesley Milner for sharing their PQLI data and Todd Landman for sharing his treaty ratification data.

as less important than other types of human rights. One important problem, we argue, is that there are no accepted benchmarks for evaluating whether particular governments are providing an adequate level of respect for the economic and social rights of their citizens. In contrast, there are clear standards for determining whether a government is respecting the civil and political rights and personal integrity rights.

Existing benchmarks for economic and social rights, such as the Human Development Index (HDI) or the Physical Quality of Life Index (PQLI), are generally not used to identify well or poorly performing governments, because these measures mainly reflect the extent to which citizens of different countries actually are able to enjoy their economic and social human rights. This enjoyment can be, and often is, affected by nonstate actors. Thus, we are unsure of what actual efforts are made by individual governments. As a result, governments of rich countries are always ranked higher on the PQLI or HDI than the governments of poor countries, given the high correlation of these measures with a country's overall level of wealth. The government of the United States is often criticized for not doing enough to protect the economic and social human rights of its citizens (e.g., Chomsky 1999), but, for at least the next one hundred years, it will have higher PQLI and HDI scores than will Cuba or China. The implication of these measures, then, becomes that governments can significantly improve their economic and social rights performance only by getting richer. Using such measures to compare governments becomes unfair to the extent that these measures say nothing about how much effort a government actually exerts toward improving the level of its citizens' enjoyment of these rights, given what resources that government has at hand.

We assert, therefore, that it is necessary to develop a measure of the economic and social human rights *practices* of governments, which we define as the *efforts* governments actually make to improve those outcomes. These efforts, or lack thereof, should be given attention by policy makers and scholars, because they are more manipulable – at least in the short run. Two governments having the same amount of total resources available often will differ in their use of that wealth to protect the economic and social rights of their citizens (Sen 2001). A government that puts substantially more emphasis on practices to protect those rights will be likely to have better outcomes. Governments that make greater efforts should be praised. Those that do not should be criticized. The international recognition of basic economic and social human rights does not guarantee every human being the full enjoyment of those rights, no matter where he or she lives. However, international law does *legally obligate* all governments to do the best they can, within their resource constraints, to satisfy those rights for their people.

INTERNATIONAL LAW

International law recognizes many human rights that governments representing most of the world's peoples and cultures have formally agreed to respect in practice. The most basic of all international agreements is the United Nations Universal Declaration of Human Rights (UDHR), a nonbinding resolution approved by the General Assembly in 1948. Together with the International Covenant of Economic, Social and Cultural Rights (ICESCR) and the International Covenant on Civil and

Political Rights (ICCPR), both concluded in 1966, these three documents comprise what is commonly referred to as the International Bill of Human Rights. The purpose of the two 1966 covenants is to make legally binding the rights listed in the UDHR.

The UDHR recognizes the right to social security (article 22), to work, to just and favorable conditions of work, to protection against unemployment, to equal pay for equal work, to an existence worthy of human dignity (article 23), to rest and leisure, to reasonable limitation on working hours, to periodic holidays with pay (article 24), to a standard of living adequate to maintain health and well-being, to food, clothing, housing and medical care, to necessary social services, to security in the event of unemployment, sickness, disability, widowhood, old age, or other lack of livelihood in circumstances beyond his or her control (article 25), to free elementary education, and to higher education on the basis of merit (article 26). The ICESCR recognizes the right to work, to equal remuneration for work of equal value, to a decent standard of living, to reasonable working hours (article 7), to social security (article 9), to adequate food, clothing and housing, to continuous improvement of living conditions (article 11), to medical care (article 12), and to education (articles 13 and 14).

Despite the recognition of economic and social rights in international human rights law, until recently most human rights INGOs, including Amnesty International (AI) and Human Rights Watch (HRW), have focused their reports and activities almost exclusively on identifying and remedying government violations of the integrity of the person. Now there is a move toward an "integrated human rights approach" that reflects a belief in the complementarity, universality and indivisibility of all rights. As interpreted by the Deputy Executive Director of Amnesty International USA, an integrated human rights approach:

> means that we recognize and act on the firmly held belief that people have a right to food, to clean water, and to a safe and adequate place to live as much as they are entitled to the right to peacefully express their opinions or exercise their religion; the right of a woman to have access to credit is as much of, and as important a right, as her right to be free from violence in the home; children have a right to education and basic healthcare as much as they have a right not to be sentenced to death; indigenous communities have a right to live and work on their ancestral lands as much as they have the right to be free from extra-judicial slaughter (Goering 2006).

Still, the AI annual human rights report, arguably the most influential annual human rights report produced today, does not evaluate each government's economic and social human rights practices.

In recent years, Human Rights Watch has given more emphasis to reporting on economic and social human rights practices of governments, but it has confined its activities to "naming and shaming" poor performing governments for very specific practices. Kenneth Roth, the Executive Director of HRW, argues that the strength of organizations like HRW is their shaming methodology – their ability to investigate misconduct and expose it to public reproach. That methodology is most effective when an INGO can show persuasively that a particular state of affairs amounts to a violation of human rights standards, that a particular violator is principally or significantly responsible, and that there is a widely accepted remedy for the violation. If any of these three elements is missing, Roth writes, the capacity to shame is greatly diminished. On the basis of this policy, HRW has produced reports exposing such things as the failure of the United States (2000a) and Egyptian (2001a) governments to protect child farmworkers, the failure of the United States government to protect the freedom of workers to form or join trade unions (2000b), and the failure of the Kenyan government to protect children against the ravages of HIV/AIDS (2001b). Unfortunately, reports such as these do not say anything about the relative overall performance of the United States, Egypt, or Kenya relative to each other, or relative to other regimes in the international system in making efforts to protect the economic and social rights of their citizens.

THE LEGITIMACY OF ECONOMIC AND SOCIAL RIGHTS AS HUMAN RIGHTS

The lack of attention given to economic and social rights by human rights INGOs fuels arguments against the legitimacy of economic and social human rights. Some who question the legitimacy of economic and social human rights contend that government respect for other human rights only requires forbearance on the part of the state, while government respect for economic and social rights requires positive action on the part of the state (Cranston 1964). Thus, economic and social rights "belong to a different logical category" (ibid., 54). In other words, they are not really human rights. Shue (1980) and Donnelly (2003) demonstrate that respect for all human rights requires positive action by the state. However, in some cases, government action actually harms realization of economic and social human rights. Cyrus Vance, for a time Secretary of State in the Carter Administration, acknowledged this point in a 1977 speech at the University of Georgia School of Law, when he said that economic and social rights "can be violated by a government's action or inaction – for example through corrupt official processes which divert resources to an elite at the expense of the needy, or through indifference to the plight of the poor" (Laqueur & Rubin 1990, 344).

Others who question the legitimacy of economic and social human rights argue that these rights simply are not as important as other types of human rights. During the administration of Jimmy Carter, the U.S. State Department *Country Reports on Human Rights Practices* included a section on "Government Policies Relating to the Fulfillment of Such Vital Needs as Food, Shelter, Health Care, and Education." However, this section was dropped in the first *Country Reports* issued by the Reagan administration, with the following explanation:

> The urgency and moral seriousness of the need to eliminate starvation and poverty from the world are unquestionable, and continue to motivate large American foreign aid efforts. However, the idea of economic and social rights is easily abused by repressive governments which claim that they promote human rights even though they deny their citizens the basic rights to the integrity of the person, as well as civil and political rights. This justification for repressions has in fact been extensively used. No category of rights should be allowed to become an excuse for the denial of other rights. For this reason, the term economic and social rights is, for the most part, not used in this year's Reports. (United States Department of State Country Reports on Human Rights Practices 1981, introduction)

The best line of reasoning against evaluating the human rights practices of different governments, based on their actual level of protection of the economic and social human rights of their citizens, is Cranston's contention that complete protection of economic and social human rights is utterly impossible to realize in poor countries. Cyrus Vance echoed this point in his aforementioned speech, saying "we recognize that the fulfillment of this right [economic and social rights] will depend, in part, upon the stage of a nation's development" (Laqueur & Rubin 1990, 344).

One claim against the position outlined by Vance is that the empirical relationship between level of economic development and the degree of protection of different types of rights has not been established. That is, some note that it has not been demonstrated that the cost of protecting economic and social rights is higher than the cost of protecting other human rights (Donnelly 2003). However, our data show that Cranston may have been correct. We find a strong correlation (.80, N = 2428) between the log of GDP per capita and PQLI. However, we find only a weak correlation (.29, N = 760) between the log of GDP per capita and the CIRI index of government respect for physical integrity rights (Cingranelli & Richards 2005).

The fact that complete fulfillment of economic and social rights by a poor country depends, in large part, on a country's development has moral significance. If a rich country and a poor country are both evaluated on the basis of whether they are able to protect the same economic and social rights for their citizens – say, the right to good health care – the playing field is unfair. The poor country's government will almost always come out looking worse than the rich country's government in this comparison. It is morally wrong to make comparisons of economic and social human rights performance among countries based on differences in economic and social human rights conditions in those countries without considering the mitigating factor of capability. The arguments of Donnelly (2003) and Shue (1980) notwithstanding, for less-developed countries, a lack of adequate resources prevents the attainment of the highest levels of basic human needs fulfillment even in cases in which all other factors leading to policy success are present. This empirical fact does have moral significance, because to ignore this fact is unfair to the governments of less developed countries, and fairness is a moral issue.

POLICIES, PRACTICES, AND CONDITIONS

It is useful to think of human rights policies and practices as early phases of a process leading to satisfactory human rights conditions. In evaluating government efforts to provide for the economic and social human rights of their citizens, the emphasis should be on human rights practices, not policies or conditions. Human rights policies are statements of intent by governments to change or maintain the degree to which citizens can exercise various types of human rights. Citizens can exercise their human rights if they can use them without fear of reprisal by government officials or with confidence that, if they are interfered with by private actors, government officials will provide an effective remedy. Put simply, human rights policies are what governments say they are going to do to protect the human rights of their citizens. Such policies are contained in national statutes, executive orders, administrative rulings, and judicial decisions. The defining characteristic of human rights policies is that they direct agencies of the state to protect the human rights of citizens. Governments around the world vary in the number of economic and other human rights protected through government policies and the strength of protections promised for various rights.

Human rights practices refer to the efforts of government officials that directly affect the degree to which citizens can exercise various types of human rights. Practices refer to what efforts governments actually make, not what they promised to do. Human rights policies affect practices. A strong policy protecting a human right is a necessary, but not a sufficient, condition for a strong government effort or, in other words, good human rights practices. India, for example, has a strong government policy against the use of bonded child labor, but actual government follow-through in implementing the policy is weak at best (Tucker 1997). Both strong government policies protecting economic and social human rights and significant government efforts to execute the policy are necessary conditions for achieving good human rights conditions. So it is not surprising that bonded child labor remains a significant problem in India today.

By "human rights conditions" we refer to the degree to which citizens actually can exercise various types of human rights. If human rights policies are easiest to change, human rights conditions are the hardest, because many things affect human rights conditions besides what governments say and do. Nongovernmental actors such as terrorists or revolutionaries may violate human rights, and thereby worsen human rights conditions in a country, contrary to government policies and practices. What we know from research in other areas of public policy is that social and economic outcomes result from many things besides the public policies and practices designed to change them. One way to think about the whole field of implementation theory and research is that it is designed to help us understand why policies fail. The most important explanations are the use of an inadequate theory of what factors cause outcomes of interest, lack of commitment by policy makers and implementing officials, and a lack of adequate resources (Mazmanian & Sabatier 1989).

PREVIOUS RESEARCH ON ECONOMIC AND SOCIAL HUMAN RIGHTS PRACTICES

Much of the previous theory building and empirical research concerning government respect for human rights has attempted to explain why some governments respect the human rights of their citizens while others do not. Government abuse of physical integrity rights has, thus far, been the phenomenon of chief theoretical interest in almost all empirical studies of the determinants and consequences of government human rights abuse. Physical integrity rights are the entitlements individuals have in international law to be free from arbitrary physical harm and coercion by their government. Human rights violations in this category include extrajudicial killings, torture, disappearances, and political imprisonment. The leading theoretical perspective guiding this stream of research suggests that governments are rational, utility maximizing actors, and respect these rights of their citizens the least when they are threatened either by domestic or international conflict (Gartner & Regan 1996; Poe & Tate 1994; Poe, Tate, & Camp-Keith 1999). Other studies have broadened the empirical inquiry about variations in government respect for human rights by focusing on government practices leading to the respect or violation of other specific human rights, or on small subsets of rights such as due-process rights (Cingranelli & Wright 1985), the rights of women (Poe, Wendel-Blunt, & Ho 1997), empowerment rights (Richards, Gelleny, & Sacko 2001) or the rights of workers (Adams 1993; Cingranelli 2002).

This research on other types of human rights has focused on government *practices* – not human rights *conditions*. For example, the Political Terror Scale is a measure of government respect for physical integrity rights, and it ranges from one (indicating there are no government violations of physical integrity rights) to five (indicating that a government violates the physical integrity rights of its citizens to the fullest extent possible). The CIRI index of respect for physical integrity rights varies from zero (indicating widespread government violations of those rights) to eight (indicating full government protection of physical integrity rights) (Cingranelli & Richards 2005; Cingranelli & Richards 1999). These two measures are similar, in that although a variety of state and nonstate actors could account for human rights *conditions*, they focus only on the *practices* of governments.

Yet, there exists no similar measure of the economic and social human rights *practices* of governments. That is, because there are both state and nonstate agents that can and do affect the condition of economic and social rights in a country, existing measures of *conditions* alone do not allow us to determine what part a government has in establishing these conditions. However, there is a large and growing literature examining the types of institutional arrangements and government policies that lead to better economic and social human rights *conditions*. That is, the data available are not really valid to answer many questions being asked.

The most widely used measure of the degree to which government policy satisfies basic human needs and basic human rights to unpolluted air, water, food, education, clothing, shelter, and health care is probably the Physical Quality of Life Index (PQLI). Developed by Morris (1979) under the auspices of the Overseas Development Council, the PQLI is a composite of three indicators: infant mortality per thousand live births, life expectancy at age one, and the adult literacy rate. The ranges for the first two indicators are transformed to a 0 to 100 scale, and then the index is computed by taking the unweighted arithmetic mean of all three indicators.

The PQLI is a reasonable measure of the attainment of the desired development outcomes outlined by the "A Better World for All" plan. Some Millennium Development Goals refer to inputs, whereas others refer to outcomes. For example, reducing the percentage of the population who live on less than the equivalent of U.S.$1 per day is not an ultimate objective of development. Achievement of this instrumental or intermediate goal should lead to important ultimate development outcomes such as better health, adequate shelter, and a longer life. However, as Morris (1979) and Sen (2001) point out, societies having the same level of wealth often have widely divergent development outcomes.

There are other composite indices measuring the quality of life of the poor within societies. The Human Development Index, developed by the United Nations Development Programme, is a well-known alternative measure. It includes two components of the PQLI – life expectancy at birth and adult literacy rate. It does not include the infant mortality rate, and it adds the combined gross enrollment ratio for primary, secondary and tertiary schools, and GDP per capita.

Previous research has shown that the average HDI and PQLI scores for developing and economically developed countries have advanced at a modest pace from 1960 to 1990 (Morris 1996), from 1975 to 1994 (Van der Lijn 1994), and from 1976 to 1996 (Callaway & Harrelson-Stephens 2004). Not surprisingly, the average PQLI scores (Callaway & Harrelson-Stephens 2004; Morris 1996; Van der Lijn 1994) and HDI scores were much lower, on average, for developing countries. Regional breakdowns show that HDI and PQLI had improved in all regions, but that countries in Africa had made the least progress in improving their economic and social human rights conditions (Van der Lijn 1994).

It is clear from previous research that wealthier and more democratic societies tend to have higher PQLI scores. The most widely reported and strongest finding is that the greater aggregate wealth of a country (as measured by its GNP or GDP per capita, or the log of GDP per capita) the greater the level of provision for basic human needs (Callaway & Harrelson-Stephens 2004; Milner et al. 2004; Milner 2000; Moon & Dixon 1985; Park 1987; Rosh 1986; Morris 1979). This relationship appears to be nonlinear (Morris 1979). Increases in aggregate wealth produce increases in PQLI up to a point. After that point, there are decreasing marginal returns on investments, so it is exceedingly difficult to reach the best possible outcomes on all three component indicators of PQLI. Although the relationship is somewhat weaker, there also is unanimous support for the idea that, other things being equal, more democratic governments do a better job of providing for the basic human needs of their citizens (Callaway & Harrelson-Stephens 2004; Milner 2000; Milner et al. 2004; Moon 1991; Moon and Dixon 1985; Rosh 1986; Spalding 1986). So, with the rapid democratization of the developing world in the 1990s, one would expect significant improvements in economic and social human rights conditions around the world. Indeed, the world averages for PQLI scores in 1984, 1994, and 2004 were 68.80 (n = 161), 75.76 (n = 186), and 79.24 (n = 185), respectively.[1]

Still, as noted, political scientists and policy makers should be primarily concerned with *government* policies and practices. In the context of economic and social human rights, they should be mainly concerned with policies and practices designed to promote or repress "subsistence rights" or "economic and social rights." What is needed, then, is a measure of *government* efforts to respect economic and social human rights that could be directly compared with measures of *government* practices to respect physical integrity rights or government practices respecting civil liberties. For this task, measures such as PQLI and HDI are not sufficient.

MEASURING EFFORT

"Always look back. You may learn something from your residuals."

−Paul Samuelson, Nobel Laureate in Economics[2]

The effort exerted by a government in respecting economic and social human rights is a function of both its economic ability to provide these rights, and its willingness

---

[1] The differences between these means are statistically significant at the following levels: 1984 and 1994 (p < .01); 1984 and 2004 (p < .00); 1994 and 2004 (p < .03).

[2] Breit and Spencer (1997, 64).

to use available resources to provide these rights. This relationship can be expressed simply as:

$$\text{Effort to Respect Rights} = f\,(\text{Ability} +/- \text{Willingness})$$

As stated previously, wealth is an important factor in determining ability. Both the PQLI and HDI, the dominant measures of economic and social rights conditions, are strongly and nonlinearly related to national wealth. That is, at low levels of national wealth, both PQLI and HDI scores are also low. As national wealth increases, so do both PQLI and HDI. But at the upper end of income, increases in national wealth produce decreasing marginal returns in both PQLI and HDI. This relationship takes the form of a sigmoid or "S" curve. Even the wealthiest countries have some problems with infant mortality, life expectancy and literacy, and totally eradicating these problems would be very expensive despite extremely high levels of national wealth. For many research questions this is problematic, given the previously mentioned linear implication of these measures that the sure path to greater government respect for these rights is for a country to grow richer.

The relationship between wealth and respect for economic and social human rights is so well established that it must be accounted for by any measure of government effort to respect these rights. To do otherwise would be to ignore the generally accepted idea in ethics that "ought" implies "can." We know of no poor country that has achieved as high a score on PQLI or HDI as have the worst-performing rich countries. A fair and objective measure of government effort (and respect, ultimately) must therefore control for differences in national wealth.

Unfortunately, neither PQLI nor HDI takes available resources (i.e., ability) explicitly into account. The HDI does incorporate GDP per capita, but it is used as a proxy indicator for "a decent standard living" for citizens (despite the fact that the United Nations explicitly states that GDP carries no information about the distribution of this wealth in any society). The manner in which wealth is included in the HDI does not explicitly account for, or control for, level of wealth for the purpose of making fair comparisons across many countries.

One possible way to control for differences in national wealth would be to measure governmental economic and social human rights practices as the proportion of the national budget spent on health, education, welfare, and housing. The proportion of resources – not the absolute amount – spent on these policies indicates the priority governments place on improving the economic and social conditions of citizens. The value of this approach is that it refocuses attention on practices rather than conditions. However, we should be skeptical about the use of expenditures as a measure of human rights performance. First, cross-national expenditure data are often not available in developing countries. Second, expenditure categories are not consistent across states. Moreover, some expenditures in categories that otherwise would seem to be positive for enjoyment of economic and social human rights may be expenditures used to finance the violation of other rights. For instance, forced sterilization might be categorized as a health expenditure. Third, both developing and developed countries have been shown to have different spending priorities that are probably related to the different configurations of problems each faces. Thus, it may not be fair to compare expenditure priorities across the full range of national incomes.

THE LOGIC OF THE MEASURE OF EFFORT

The logic behind our measure of government effort to respect economic and social rights is simple: A properly fitted regression of an indicator of how far a country is along the continuum of progressive respect for these rights (e.g., PQLI) on both a government's ability and willingness to provide these rights will provide predicted values. Hereafter, we will use the word "achievement" to denote how far a country is along the continuum of progressive respect for economic and social rights. In this context, the term "achievement" does not indicate that some satisfactory standard of attainment has been met but, rather, how much has or has not been achieved in moving along the continuum of progressive respect for these rights.

The predicted values from the regression of achievement onto ability and willingness say, "given ability and willingness, this is the level of achievement one should expect to see." Very few countries will have an actual level of achievement that is equivalent to the predicted value. Residuals tell how far actual levels of achievement differ from the predicted values. These residuals become our measure of government *effort* to respect economic and social rights. Attributing meaning to residuals is certainly not an innovation of this chapter. Indeed, Nobel Laureate in Economics Robert Solow is known for attributing the residual from his formula of economic growth to technological innovation. This is commonly called the "Solow residual."

The residual for a particular country in a particular year tells us whether a country is overachieving or underachieving, and by how much. More specifically, the residual indicates whether the condition of the poorest people in a country is better or worse than the condition of the poorest people in other countries that are peer benchmarks, because the available wealth per capita is similar. If the residual is positive for a particular country, this indicates that the government of that country raised the standard of living of its poorer citizens more than would be expected given its own available resources and willingness. *This implies a great effort on behalf of that government.* A negative residual indicates worse economic and social human rights performance than would be expected given its available resources and willingness. *This implies a lack of effort on the part of that government.* A residual of zero indicates performance at the expected level expect given the performance of other countries in that year with similar resources and willingness.

In principle, separate residual scores could be developed for men and women in each country. To do so, one would need to collect the three components of the PQLI index for males *and* females in each country, for most countries of the world. Gathering such data would be difficult. Few, if any, governments provide infant mortality statistics for male and female infants. Many governments do not provide information about the adult literacy rates of males and females. Most do provide information about the average life expectancies of men and women. Using this information, separate PQLI scores could be calculated for each country. If adequate information was obtained for almost all countries, each country's male and female PQLI scores could be compared with peer benchmarks, and gender sensitive effort scores could be developed. If information broken down by gender were missing for at least one of the three elements of the PQLI for more than 15% of the cases, the quality of the estimates of effort would be seriously compromised.

DATA AND OPERATIONALIZATION

To measure effort, we must first have indicators of a country's level of achievement in respecting these rights, ability and willingness. When looking for an indicator of *absolute level of achievement*, the question arose, "Should we use PQLI or HDI as the measure of a country's absolute level of achievement in raising the standard of living of the poorest people in its society?" We chose PQLI over HDI for several reasons. First, PQLI is easier to replicate. Also, PQLI does not include a GDP component (this limits the chance of certain empirical confusions). Furthermore, the empirical properties of the PQLI are very similar to those of HDI. For our sample, the correlation between these two measures was .93. Thus, using either indicator would produce similar country scores for governmental economic and social human rights performance.[3]

We conceptualize *ability* as wealth, and this component is simply operationalized as the logarithm of a country's GDP per capita. We use a logarithmic transformation of GDP per capita because of the distribution of the extreme lowest and highest values in these data. These data came from the *World Development Indicators* dataset (World Bank annual).

Operationalizing a government's *willingness* to respect economic rights is a more novel task. Our indicator of *willingness* is whether a country has signed and/or ratified the 1966 ICESCR – the most important legally binding, international norm–guiding government responsibility regarding these rights. Because our examination is at the level of governments, and because governments change over time, one drawback to this approach may be that each government may not have as strong an affinity to respecting these rights as the government(s) that signed/ratified the ICESCR. However, although this may be true, the fact that a particular government in a particular year has not removed its country from this important international norm signifies a formal, important, and continuing *regime-level commitment* to these standards. Our data on willingness come from Todd Landman's (2005a, 2005b) work on human rights treaty commitments of governments. The indicator we use is coded as such:

0 = Country is not a signatory or party to the ICESCR
1 = Country is a signatory to the ICESCR
2 = Country is a party to the ICESCR

One advantage of Landman's indicator is that it allows for us to account for the qualitative distinction, in terms of a country's level of commitment to international norms, between having signed a treaty and having ratified a treaty.

COMPUTING THE MEASURE OF EFFORT

As previously stated, our measure of government effort to respect economic rights is the residual (e) from the regression:

$$\text{Achievement} = a + \text{Ability} + \text{Willingness} + e$$

---

[3] PQLI scores were computed by David Cingranelli and Rodwan Abouharb. Missing scores were interpolated using a linear interpolation technique.

Or, as operationalized:

$$\text{Achievement (PQLI)} = a + \text{Logarithm (GDP per capita)}$$
$$+ \text{ICESCR signatory/party} + e$$

The actual regression assumes the following Gompertz function to provide appropriate nonlinear-based predicted values:

$$Y = b1 * \exp(-b2 * \exp(-b3 * x))$$

Thus, to obtain the residuals, we used three-parameter nonlinear regression on a worldwide sample of 131 countries with observations in the years 1980 through 2000.[4] We ran regressions one year at a time, so that scores would result from countries being compared against one another for the same year. Because PQLI scores trend upward for almost all countries over time, it would be unfair to compare, for example, Senegal in 1980 to Costa Rica in 2000. Pooling the data for purposes of estimation would have done just that.

REPORTING THE SCORES

Table 10.1 lists the highest and lowest ten country scores of the level of government effort to respect economic and social rights in the years 1980, 1990, and 1996. One also can see the range of scores from the lowest negative score, indicating a very low level of effort to respect these rights, to the highest positive score, indicating great effort. Immediately, one sees that those countries exerting the greatest effort are not necessarily the wealthiest countries in the world. Indeed, the correlations between logged GDP per capita and our effort scores for 1980, 1990, and 2000, are -0.0165, -0.0137, and -0.0132, respectively.

Appendix A contains a full listing of country scores for the year 2000, sorted alphabetically. The complete list of scores for all countries and years can be downloaded from http://www.humanrightsdata.org.

EVALUATING THE MEASURE OF EFFORT

There are four key issues relevant to evaluating this measure of government effort to respect economic and social human rights. First, should one engage in the substantive labeling of residuals? Although some may question the labeling of residuals, quality research has used and continues to use this technique. For recent political science examples, aside from the Nobel Prize–winning work of economist Robert Solow, see Gurr and Moore (1997), and Poe, Rost, and Carey (2006).

Second, is GDP per capita alone a sufficient measure of ability? Certainly, many things other than GDP can affect a government's ability to provide for citizens' objective enjoyment of economic and social human rights. Following Richards, Gelleny, and Sacko (2001), we looked at other possible indicators (both positive and negative) of ability, such as foreign direct investment, portfolio investment, official

---

[4] Out of the 195 countries that comprise the CIRI dataset, the 131 included in this analysis were those for which requisite data were available. The countries included are representative of all regime types, geographic regions, and levels of development.

Table 10.1. *The level of government EFFORT to respect economic and social rights in 1980, 1990, and 2000*

1980 Highest 10 scores		1990 Highest 10 scores		2000 Highest 10 scores	
China	36.82	China	23.25	Georgia	22.93
Sri Lanka	30.63	Sri Lanka	22.86	Armenia	22.26
Congo, Republic of	23.94	Tanzania	22.36	Tanzania	18.98
Thailand	19.34	Kenya	18.25	Madagascar	15.50
Kenya	17.92	Lebanon	16.92	Sri Lanka	14.98
Bulgaria	16.91	Malawi	12.65	Mongolia	14.45
Jamaica	16.27	Jamaica	12.29	Jamaica	14.25
Korea, Republic of	15.85	Fiji	12.27	Kenya	13.42
Lesotho	15.48	Panama	11.35	Congo, Republic of	12.28
Chile	13.72	Madagascar	11.31	Ecuador	12.26
1980 Lowest 10 scores		**1990 Lowest 10 scores**		**2000 Lowest 10 scores**	
Mauritania	−17.84	United Arab Emirates	−14.83	Cote d'Ivoire	−13.37
Oman	−19.60	Oman	−15.44	Gambia	−14.11
Sierra Leone	−21.96	Niger	−15.98	Swaziland	−16.43
Haiti	−22.08	Haiti	−16.31	Burkina Faso	−17.19
Niger	−22.58	Saudi Arabia	−17.63	Gabon	−19.19
United Arab Emirates	−23.26	Gabon	−20.08	Guinea	−20.03
Algeria	−23.50	Guinea	−22.23	Namibia	−20.73
Gambia	−24.36	Gambia	−22.42	South Africa	−23.88
Saudi Arabia	−28.09	Sierra Leone	−23.22	Angola	−26.03
Gabon	−30.21	Angola	−29.38	Botswana	−27.66

development assistance, and long-term debt. We also looked at other measures such as tax revenues. However, no matter how many of these indicators of ability, or in what combination, we employed in our analyses, our empirical results remained consistent (rankings were not substantively affected). Thus, for the purposes of introducing the measure/method, we simply kept GDP per capita.

Third, we use ICESCR treaty status to measure willingness, but this does not account for a government that may be a party to this norm – very willing and resource able to respect economic and social human rights – but that engages in failed policies toward the end of respect for these rights. This situation would result in a negative residual, labeled here as a lack of effort given available resources and willingness. Thus, in calling the error term "effort," we are, to some extent, assuming success in policy making and implementation.

Finally, how and in what way will a measure of government effort to protect the economic rights of its citizens be useful? Activists, policy makers, and scholars need a set of measures of the human rights performance of countries around the world that better reflects the range of human rights recognized in the Universal Declaration. Annual reports by AI and HRW that strongly emphasize civil and political rights are not objective in the sense that they are selective. They also are not fair to countries that are weak in this area but have strong points in their efforts to protect other types of human rights. As this analysis has shown, China is a good example of a country that has a poor record of performance of civil and political rights, but an excellent record of protecting economic and social rights. Providing better information about the differences among governments, in their efforts to protect the economic rights of their citizens, would go a long way toward convincing the rest of the world that activists and policy makers who advocate better government respect for human rights are now more sincerely interested in an integrated human rights approach.

Using either the rankings or the actual scores developed here, the UN Committee on Economic, Social and Cultural Rights would be able to compare each country's score over time to help determine whether it was doing a relatively good job of achieving its economic and social human rights goals. Comparing changes in scores over time provides a way to assess whether the country is progressively realizing those goals, or moving in the opposite direction. China's ranking of first in 1980, first in 1990, and fourteenth in 2000 indicates that, between 1980 and 2000, China was doing much better than its benchmark countries in protecting economic and social rights. However, its drop in ranking between 1990 and 2000 signals what may be the start of a troubling decline. In contrast, Saudi Arabia ranked second from the bottom in 1980. It climbed a few places by 1990 but remained among the countries with the ten lowest scores. By 2000, it had moved beyond the bottom ten. Thus, Saudi Arabia is an example of a country that was doing much worse than its benchmark countries, but it is making progress toward better protection of the economic and social rights of its citizens. Using the same information, scholars could develop better explanations of why some governments make a relatively strong effort to protect economic rights, whereas others do not.

REFERENCES

Adams, Roy J. 1993. Regulating Unions and Collective Bargaining: A Global, Historical Analysis of Determinants and Consequences. *Comparative Labor Law Journal* 14: 272–301.

Breit, William and Roger Spencer. 1997. *Lives of the Laureates*, 3rd ed. Cambridge, MA: MIT Press

Callaway, Rhonda L., and Julie Harrelson-Stephens. 2004. The Path from Trade to Human Rights: The Democracy and Development Detour. In *The Systematic Study of Human Rights*, ed. Sabine Carey and Steven C. Poe, 87–109. Hampshire, UK: Ashgate.

Chomsky, Noam. 1999. *The Universal Declaration of Human Rights and the Contradictions of U.S. Policy*. New York: Seven Stories Press.

Cingranelli, David L. 2002. Democratization, Economic Globalization, and Workers' Rights. In *Democratic Institutional Performance: Research and Policy Perspectives*, ed. Edward A. McMahon and Thomas A. P. Sinclair, 139–58. Westport, CT: Praeger Press.

Cingranelli, David L., and Kevin N. Wright. 1985. A Comparison of National Systems of Justice. *Journal of Crime and Justice* 2: 93–114.

Cingranelli, David L., and David L. Richards. 1999. Measuring the Level, Pattern, and Sequence of Government Respect for Physical Integrity Rights. *International Studies Quarterly* 43: 407–17.

Cingranelli, David L., and David L. Richards. 2005. *The CIRI Human Rights Dataset*, version 2005.10.12. http://www.humanrightsdata.org

Cranston, Maurice. 1964. *What are Human Rights?* New York: Basic Books.

Davenport, Christian. 1995. Multi-dimensional Threat Perception and State Repression: An Inquiry into Why States Apply Negative Sanctions. *American Journal of Political Science* 39: 683–713.

Donnelly, Jack. 2003. *Universal Human Rights in Theory and Practice.* Ithaca, NY: Cornell University Press.

Gartner, Scott Sigmund, and Patrick M. Regan. 1996. Threat and Repression: The Non-Linear Relationship between Government and Opposition Violence. *Journal of Peace Research* 33 (3): 273–87.

Goering, Curt. 2006. Amnesty International and Economic, Social and Cultural Rights. In *Ethics in Action: The Ethical Challenges of International Human Rights and Humanitarian Nongovernmental Organizations,* ed. Daniel A. Bell and Jean-Marc Coicaud. Cambridge, UK: Cambridge University Press.

Gross, James A. 1999. A Human Rights Perspective on United States Labor Relations Law: A Violation of the Right of Freedom of Association. Unpublished paper.

Gurr, Ted Robert. 1986. The Political Origins of State Violence and Terror: A Theoretical Analysis. In *Government Violence and Repression: An Agenda for Research,* ed. Michael Stohl and George A. Lopez. Westport, CT: Greenwood Press.

Gurr, Ted Robert, and Will H. Moore. 1997. Ethnopolitical Rebellion: A Cross-Sectional Analysis of the 1980s with Risk Assessments for the 1990s. *American Journal of Political Science* 41 (4): 1079–1103.

Gwartney, James. 1997. *Economic Freedom of the World: 1975–1995.* Vancouver: The Fraser Institute.

Hicks, N., and P. Streeten. 1979. Indicators of Development: The Search for a Basic Needs Yardstick. *World Development* 7: 567–80.

Human Rights Watch. 2000a. *Fingers to the Bone: United States Failure to Protect Child Farmworkers.* New York: Human Rights Watch.

Human Rights Watch. 2000b. *Unfair Advantage.* New York: Human Rights Watch.

Human Rights Watch. 2001a. *Underage and Unprotected: Child Labor in Egypt's Cotton Fields.* New York: Human Rights Watch.

Human Rights Watch. 2001b. *In the Shadow of Death: HIV/AIDS and Children's Rights in Kenya.* New York: Human Rights Watch.

Laqueur, Walter, and Barry Rubin, eds. 1990. *The Human Rights Reader.* New York: Meridian.

Landman, Todd. 2005a. *Protecting Human Rights: A Comparative Study.* Washington, DC: Georgetown University Press.

Landman, Todd. 2005b. *Protecting Human Rights: A Global Comparative Dataset.* Colchester, UK: University of Essex.

Mazmanian, Daniel, and Paul Sabatier. 1989. *Implementation and Public Policy.* Lanham, MA: University Press of America.

Milner, Wesley T. 2000. Economic Freedom, Globalization and Human Rights: Can We Have it All? *Journal of Economic Enterprise* 15 (2): 36–61.

Milner, Wesley T. 2002. Emerging Human Rights Challenges: The Effects of Globalization and Economic Liberalization. In *Globalization and Human Rights: Transnational Problems, Transnational Solutions,* ed. Alison Brysk. Berkeley: University of California Press.

Milner, Wesley T., Steven C. Poe, and David Leblang. 1999. Security Rights, Subsistence Rights, and Liberties: A Theoretical Survey of the Landscape. *Human Rights Quarterly* 21 (2): 403–44.

Milner, Wesley T., Steven C. Poe, and David Leblang. Forthcoming. Providing Subsistence Rights: Do States Make a Difference? In *The Systematic Study of Human Rights*, ed. Sabine Carey and Steven C. Poe, 110–24. Hampshire, UK: Ashgate.

Mitchell, Neil J., and James M. McCormick. 1988. Economic and Political Explanations of Human Rights Violations. *World Politics* 40: 476–98.

Moon, Bruce E. 1991. *The Political Economy of Basic Human Needs*. Ithaca, NY: Cornell University Press.

Moon, Bruce E., and William J. Dixon. 1985. Politics, the State, and Basic Human Needs: A Cross- National Study. *American Journal of Political Science* 29: 661–94.

Morris, David. 1979. *Measuring the Condition of the World's Poor: The Physical Quality of Life Index*. New York: Pergamon.

Park, Han S. 1987. Correlates of Human Rights: Global Tendencies. *Human Rights Quarterly* 9: 405–13.

Poe, Steven C., and C. Neil Tate. 1994. Repression of Personal Integrity in the 1980s: A Global Analysis. *American Political Science Review* 88 (4): 853–72.

Poe, Steven C., Dierdre Wendel-Blunt, and Karl Ho. 1997. Global Patterns in the Achievement of Women's Human Rights to Equality. *Human Rights Quarterly* 19: 813–35.

Poe, Steven C., C. Neil Tate, and Linda Camp Keith. 1999. Repression of the Human Right to Personal Integrity Revisited: A Global Cross-National Study Covering the Years 1976– 1993. *International Studies Quarterly* 43 (2): 291–313.

Poe, Steven C., Nicolas Rost, and Sabine C. Carey. 2006. Assessing Risk and Opportunity in Conflict Studies: A Human Rights Analysis. *Journal of Conflict Resolution* 8 (50): 484–507.

Pogge, Thomas. 2006. Moral Priorities for International Human Rights NGOs. In *Ethics in Action: The Ethical Challenges of International Human Rights and Humanitarian Nongovernmental Organizations*, ed. Daniel A. Bell and Jean-Marc Coicaud. Cambridge, UK: Cambridge University Press.

Richards, David L., Ronald D. Gelleny, and David H. Sacko. 2001. Money with a Mean Streak? Foreign Economic Penetration and Government Respect for Human Rights in Developing Countries. *International Studies Quarterly* 45 (2): 219–39.

Rosh, Robert. 1986. The Impact of Third World Defense Burdens on Basic Human Needs. *Policy Studies Journal* 15: 135–46.

Roth, Kenneth. 2006. Defending Economic, Social and Cultural Rights: Practical Issues Faced by an International Human Rights Organization. In *Ethics in Action: The Ethical Challenges of International Human Rights and Humanitarian Nongovernmental Organizations*, ed. Daniel A. Bell and Jean-Marc Coicaud. Cambridge, UK: Cambridge University Press.

Sen, Amartya. 2001. *Development as Freedom*. New York: Alfred Knopf.

Shue, Henry. 1980. *Basic Rights: Subsistence, Affluence, and U.S. Foreign Policy*. Princeton, NJ: Princeton University Press.

Spalding, Nancy. 1986. Providing for Economic Human Rights: The Case of the Third World. *Policy Studies Journal* 15 (1): 123–35.

Tucker, Lee. 1997. Child Labor in Modern India: The Bonded Labor Problem. *Human Rights Quarterly* 19: 572–629.

United Nations Development Program (2004). *Human Development Report 2004: Cultural Liberty in Today's Diverse World*. New York: UNDP.

World Bank. Annual. *World Development Indicators*. Washington, DC: World Bank.

Van der Lijn. 1994. Measuring Well-Being with Social Indicators, HDI, PQLI, and BWI for 133 Countries for 1975, 1980, 1985, 1988, and 1992. Unpublished paper.

APPENDIX A: COUNTRY SCORES OF THE LEVEL OF GOVERNMENT EFFORT
TO RESPECT ECONOMIC RIGHTS IN 2000

Country	2000 effort score
Albania	11.0021
Algeria	−5.82741
Angola	−26.0254
Argentina	1.245648
Armenia	7.620138
Australia	−0.54697
Austria	0.158509
Azerbaijan	6.477978
Bahrain	−5.67181
Bangladesh	−1.80046
Belgium	0.355726
Benin	0.412295
Bolivia	7.676651
Bosnia Herzegovina	7.446898
Botswana	−27.6646
Brazil	−2.60519
Bulgaria	6.130593
Burkina Faso	−17.1912
Burundi	7.829218
Cambodia	−4.59992
Cameroon	−0.7495
Central African Republic	−10.8096
Chile	5.969201
China	8.801582
Colombia	2.795018
Congo Brazzaville	12.28277
Costa Rica	5.562493
Cote d'Ivoire	−13.3748
Croatia	5.844808
Cyprus	0.444676
Democratic Republic of the Congo	8.12765
Denmark	−1.57169
Dominican Republic	−3.02082
Ecuador	12.263
Egypt	−3.82347
El Salvador	0.723492
Estonia	3.41051
Ethiopia	−3.43971
Fiji	8.034789
Finland	0.537317
France	1.415029
Gabon	−19.1909
Gambia	−14.1147
Georgia	22.93058
Ghana	−3.41306

Country	2000 effort score
Greece	2.533751
Guatemala	−4.80106
Guinea	−20.0292
Guinea–Bissau	−7.86102
Guyana	3.566527
Haiti	−9.46354
Honduras	7.110662
Hungary	1.405771
Iceland	0.466836
India	−4.44683
Indonesia	8.070561
Iran (Islamic Republic of)	−4.51521
Ireland	−2.15409
Israel	0.10382
Italy	0.530799
Jamaica	14.24722
Japan	2.621596
Jordan	11.02183
Kazakhstan	6.857681
Kenya	13.42178
Kuwait	−5.20846
Lao People's Democratic Republic	−2.35588
Latvia	22.25522
Lebanon	6.168276
Lesotho	−10.676
Lithuania	4.142309
Luxembourg	−4.40069
Madagascar	15.49588
Malawi	7.68061
Malaysia	−0.36789
Mali	−10.7371
Mauritania	−12.8818
Mauritius	−2.00982
Mexico	1.147107
Mongolia	14.45303
Morocco	−6.68579
Mozambique	−11.3562
Namibia	−20.7281
Nepal	1.514075
Netherlands	−0.21697
New Zealand	2.680438
Niger	−13.109
Nigeria	9.055957
Norway	−0.00876
Oman	−8.19528
Pakistan	−5.40022
Panama	7.33386

(*Continued*)

Country	2000 effort score
Papua New Guinea	−6.3441
Paraguay	5.577113
Peru	3.622474
Philippines	10.10868
Poland	5.340944
Portugal	−1.01865
Rep. Chad	−7.95285
Republic of Korea	0.042246
Romania	6.151211
Russian Federation	2.677154
Rwanda	−6.51192
Saudi Arabia	−8.36933
Senegal	−5.52152
Sierra Leone	−2.82586
Singapore	−1.09126
Slovakia	3.213453
South Africa	−23.8845
Spain	1.741531
Sri Lanka	14.97741
Sudan	−3.52881
Swaziland	−16.4267
Sweden	2.316411
Switzerland	0.92876
Syrian Arab Republic	7.035074
Tanzania	18.98223
Thailand	3.26623
The Former Yugoslav Republic of Macedonia	7.21983
Togo	−6.69414
Trinidad and Tobago	2.318034
Tunisia	−2.76669
Turkey	−2.02439
Uganda	−6.16861
Ukraine	11.51175
United Kingdom	0.217278
United States of America	−2.52946
Uruguay	5.588206
Venezuela	7.063179
Zambia	7.667354
Zimbabwe	−7.91681

11 Government Respect for Women's Economic Rights: A Cross-National Analysis, 1981–2003

SHAWNA E. SWEENEY

INTRODUCTION

The turn of the twenty-first century has witnessed significant global advances in the achievement of the economic equality of women. In many countries, state policies that prohibit gender discrimination in employment, secure equal pay for equal work, guarantee equality in hiring and promotion practices, and other core economic rights, have been widely adopted. Yet, there continues to be a significant gap between women's *de jure* status and their *de facto* status in many countries. According to the World Bank (2001, 1), systematic indicators show that great disparities exist in women's access to, and control of, resources for economic and social opportunities. These disparities cut across countries and affect women in both developed and developing regions. For example, even in the advanced industrialized nations of France, Japan, and the United Kingdom, women's right to equal pay for equal work is not respected, as women earn as much as 30% to nearly 60% less than their male counterparts (World Bank 2001, 55).

This research seeks to explain the cross-national determinants of government respect for women's economic rights. I focus on government practices toward women's rights because, to a great degree, national governments control the treatment accorded to their citizens.[1] Women's economic rights are defined as internationally recognized rights, including equal pay for equal work, free choice of profession or employment, equality in hiring and promotion practices, nondiscrimination by employers, the right to be free from sexual harassment in the workplace, the right to work in occupations classified as dangerous, and others.[2]

---

[1] Although scholars in recent years have retreated from viewing the nation-state and its institutions as an important determinant of human rights because of global trends that have challenged their sovereignty, this research argues that national governments still exert a significant influence on women's rights attainment. Indeed, the United Nations and other supranational governance institutions have increasingly recognized that national governments possess a wide range of policy instruments to directly impact gender relations and to catalyze social change in the direction of greater gender equality, such as targeted redistribution of state resources, expenditures for education and maternity leave, and equal opportunity legislation.

[2] Refer to the research design section for a more detailed discussion of women's economic rights.

I would like to thank Dr. Todd Landman for the use of his weighted ratification variable to measure the level of national commitment to the Convention on the Eliminatinon of All Forms of Discrimination against Women.

The core argument of this paper is that cross-national variations in government respect for women's economic rights is increasingly being driven by four broad trends. These include (1) rising levels of democracy in many nations, (2) separation of state and religion (i.e., level of political secularism), (3) economic globalization, and (4) the internationalization of human rights norms. These trends have been largely neglected in the comparative cross-national literature on women's human rights. However, documenting how they influence the enjoyment of women's economic rights is timely and relevant because they increasingly influence the course of state affairs in a growing number of countries.[3] This study also incorporates alternative explanations identified in the empirical literature, such as the level of economic development, population size, and conflict.

LITERATURE REVIEW AND THEORETICAL ARGUMENTS

Democracy

In this research, I argue that the trend toward greater gender equality in many countries is intimately linked to the rising levels of democracy in nations across the globe.[4] At the most basic level, democratic rule should advance women's rights because, according to Cingranelli and Tsai (2003, 3), democracies empower the masses and the masses are expected to use that power to improve their social well-being. Democratic political institutions foster increased demands for more genuine political participation among all social groups, thus making it more difficult to exclude disadvantaged groups from the political process (Dahl 1998). Democracy should also promote women's rights because, by its very nature, democracy weakens the power of elites while increasing the ability of nonelites to influence policy making through a system of political participation that equally values individual input into the political process (Bollen 1992). As a result of democracy's equalizing potential, women should become an important political constituency that politicians need to remain accountable to remain in office (Wang 2004).

Democracies also give citizens the tools to exercise their rights to political citizenship, such as freedom of expression and assembly and association. These core democratic rights provide potent institutional mechanisms for disadvantaged

---

[3] For example, since the 1980s, many countries across the globe have abandoned authoritarian rule for democracy as a result of the third wave of democratization. Global governance institutions and national governments have promoted women's rights as a critical strategy in the democratization of countries. Given this fact, it is important to determine, especially from a policy standpoint, whether the growing trend towards democracy across nations actually promotes improvements in women's rights. As another example, the separation of state and religion has important policy implications, especially for the state of women's rights in countries currently undergoing the process of constitution building, such as Afghanistan and Iraq. These countries are confronted with serious questions over whether a mix of democracy and religion is enough to secure women's rights while respecting religious freedom.

[4] It is important to point out that feminist theorists have long debated the merits of democracy for women, especially because most of the well-established democracies, such as the United States, France, and Switzerland, put in place democratic institutions many decades before they extended suffrage to women (Ottawa 2004). Today, however, democracy should promote more genuine equality for women, particularly because there is a growing emphasis on women's rights as a central component in democratization process (Inglehart, Norris & Welzel 2004).

social groups to pressure government to advance their rights and incorporate their interests into government policy (Swank 2001). These rights are especially important for the support of women's interests. In democracies, women legislators should have a more substantial effect on public policy, "since they are in principle free to engage in deliberation within and without their political parties" (Weldon 2002, 22). They may also use their political influence to "raise new issues or insights previously excluded from the legislative arena" (ibid., 22). Conversely, in societies where women lack basic democratic rights and the ability to participate in politics on an equal footing with men, there is no guarantee that anyone will advocate for their interests (Brill 1995).

Significantly, democratic rights are related to greater government respect for workers' rights, which should benefit women's economic rights. Cingranelli and Tsai (2003) found in their cross-national analysis of democracy and government respect for worker's rights that those governments with the highest degree of democratic development provide the greatest protection of workers' rights, such as the right to collective bargaining and the right to strike. Such rights empower women workers to challenge labor policies that may not represent their interests. Without these core democratic rights, women workers cannot advance or negotiate for their economic interests within a democratic framework. As Amartya Sen (2001) argues in his seminal work *Development as Freedom*, political freedoms, such as the freedom to participate in state affairs, are instrumental to securing the enjoyment of a wide array of rights and opportunities, and, importantly, the enjoyment of these rights may actually require the exercise of basic political freedoms. Sen (2001) claims that democracies are more likely to advance citizens' economic rights because countries that allow for effective and open citizen participation tend to better address their needs, as well as pass policies that more closely mirror popular sentiments.[5]

SEPARATION OF STATE AND RELIGION

A long tradition of studies in anthropology, sociology, and theology identify religion as one of the biggest barriers to gender equality and as one of the most important cultural agents of socialization in shaping appropriate roles for women (Inglehart & Norris 2003). As Daniel Maguire (2003, 3) claims, religion is "*a* if not *the* shaper of culture." Cultural values shape women's rights in important ways. Culture determines power relations within society and within the family unit, which, in turn, influences women's access to and control over economic resources and their decision-making authority (Sweetman 1995). Although several studies have identified religion as a primary factor in the oppression of women, they have failed to answer *how* religion negatively influences women's rights attainment. To date, most of the research in the scientific study of human rights has attributed the oppression of women to Islam. This approach does not help advance theoretical

---

[5] Recent large-scale comparative studies also have documented how, in comparison to authoritarian regimes, democracies provide a superior physical quality of life for women and more reproductive freedoms, which should directly influence the enjoyment of their economic rights (see Przeworksi et al. 2003; Zweifel & Navia 2000).

understandings of the causal nexus between religion and state human rights practices. It also treats Islam as being exceptional among other world religions in its
treatment of women, when scholars have documented how both the philosophy
and practice of all major world religions tend to emphasize traditional roles for
women by viewing them as complementary but not equal to men (Htun 2003;
Howland 1999; Maguire 2003; Inglehart & Norris 2003).

The core argument of this research is that it is not the type of religion *per se*
that influences women's rights attainment, but the degree to which religion and
state are separated (i.e., the level of a country's political secularization). I argue
that there can be no meaningful gender equality in countries that lack a formal
separation of church (or mosque) and state, and where religious institutions operate
in conjunction with the constitutional power of the state. In comparison to their
secular counterparts, countries that experience an entanglement between sacred
and secular will allow religion to play a more substantial role in the formulation of
government policies and actual practices. These policies will tend to be inimical to
the acquisition of rights by women, as religious leaders will tend to shape women's
legal status in accordance with patriarchal religious beliefs. This argument does
not deny the fact that governments often take religious factors into account when
they legislate. However, it is a matter of the degree of political secularism that is a
key to how progressively governments interpret women's rights (Reynolds 1999).

In nonsecular countries, restrictive religious doctrines and cultural practices
often prevent women from exercising their economic rights, such as the right to
free choice of employment or profession. In Bangladesh and Sri Lanka, for example,
patriarchal values and cultural practices, such as *purdah* or seclusion, curtail the
educational and employment opportunities of women, although modernization
and education have contributed to the erosion of this practice (Chowdhury 2001,
209). In some Latin American countries that mix religion and politics, such as
Argentina, Bolivia, and Peru, the Catholic Church exerts a strong influence over
state policy in the area of women's familial and reproductive rights. As a result of
Catholic Church influence, women experience some of the most regressive abortion
and divorce laws in the world, with the exception of Catholic Ireland (Htun 2003).
Perhaps a more apt example of the centrality of political secularism to women's
rights is countries such as Turkey and Saudi Arabia. Turkish women enjoy far
more economic rights than women living in Saudi Arabia, even though nearly
equal percentages of citizens in Saudi Arabia (100%) and Turkey (99.8%) adhere
to Islam (CIA World Factbook 2005). The difference is not only due to regime
type, even though Saudi Arabia is a strict authoritarian regime and Turkey is a
democracy. Importantly, these countries differ significantly in the extent to which
religion is institutionalized as part of the state.

ECONOMIC GLOBALIZATION

Two dominant perspectives frame the debate on the impact of the global economy
on human rights: neoliberal and critical perspectives. Neoliberal proponents argue
that, on net, economic globalization should have a beneficial effect on women's economic rights. They rely on the principles of neoclassical economics in arguing that
economic globalization increases developing economies' exposure to competitive

global markets, which, in turn, increases demand for female labor (World Bank 2001).[6] Intense competition in the face of globalization compels companies to use all of the best human resources available, which in turn makes them more receptive to the idea of hiring women (Meyer 2003, 354). Because discrimination is economically costly to employers, in the face of growing competition caused by globalization, employers will find it more difficult to discriminate against women (Forsythe, Korzeniewicz, & Durrant 2000; Behrman & King 2000).

According to neoliberals, the primary advantage of economic globalization for women is that it creates new employment opportunities for them in the formal economy (Gray et al. 2004; Joekes 1995). It does so by breaking down barriers and undermining gender norms that try to keep women in their place through restrictions on their mobility and public presence.[7] According to Meyer (2003, 353), "As nations liberalize their economies and transnational corporations (TNCs) set up operations in developing countries, women (especially young unmarried women) in these nations are increasingly drawn into the manufacturing sector." Additionally, foreign firms often export progressive regulations to foreign subsidiary operations, such as equal pay for equal work and affirmative action. They are also more likely to place women in higher-level management positions than domestic industries (Mears 1995; Meyer 2003). As a result, economic globalization should eliminate discriminatory pay differentials between men and women, diminish the barriers of occupational segregation, and increase the need for female human capital (Meyer 2003; 2001).

Conversely, although their arguments are diverse, the critical viewpoint contends that women's rights deteriorate because globalization contributes to a "race to the bottom" with cheap and exploited female labor driving this race.[8] Feminist theorists argue that women are the most exploited because powerful actors – foreign firms, state elites, and employers – benefit from the gender division of labor through the debasement of their paid work (Mungall 2002). It is argued that globalization encourages this downward trend because the use of ascribed characteristics, contrary to neoclassical theory, helps firms remain competitive through lower labor and production costs (Dunaway 2002). Young female labor is often tapped in export processing zones (EPZs) and free trade areas (FTAs),

---

[6] See Becker (1957) and Friedman (1962) for a more thorough discussion of how increased economic competition heightens the demand for female labor and undermines discriminatory employment practices. For more contemporary viewpoints on this topic, see Meyer (2001; 2003), Black and Brainerd (2002), Forsythe, Korzeniewicz, and Durrant (2000), and Berik, Rodgers, and Zvelich (2003).

[7] As Sen (2001, 115) points out, economic globalization has an important liberating potential for women as their freedom to seek employment outside the family is systematically denied in many cultures.

[8] Feminist development theories of women-in-development (WID), women-and-development (WAD), and gender-and-development (GAD) have made significant contributions to our understandings of the gendered nature of globalization. The primary difference between WID, WAD, and GAD is that the WID approach rests on liberal development theory in its argument that economic development will eventually improve the socioeconomic lot of women through greater integration into the formal economy. WAD and GAD approaches focus more on the structural inequalities in the global economy, but WAD sees class-based inequalities as the root of women's oppression whereas GAD sees unequal gender relations between men and women as the culprit. The nuances of these different theoretical approaches are discussed in greater detail in my doctoral dissertation.

which have mushroomed under contemporary globalization. Although EPZs have undoubtedly opened up new employment opportunities for women, the "working conditions associated with these factories range from bad to horrendous" (Croucher 2004, 161).[9] Furthermore, although trade unionism was associated with a narrowing of the gender wage gap in an earlier period, trade unions today are powerless to demand better working conditions because of the global mobility of capital. Employers can simply relocate or automate their production if workers' press for better working conditions and entitlements (Cingranelli & Tsai 2003, 8).

Critics also charge the International Monetary Fund (IMF) and the World Bank with playing an important role in impoverishing women in developing countries through the imposition of structural adjustment policies (SAPs), which force countries to adhere to neoliberal market principles. The primary policy to cultivate a neoliberal environment is to reduce the size of the state and let markets reign (Peterson 2003; Weiss 2003; Mosley 2003). The neoliberal rollback of the state is more damaging for women in comparison to men because they are more dependent on the state for secure employment and the provision of social services to support family well-being (Peterson 2003, 9; Fall 2001; Buchmann 1996; Elson 1990). During periods of state contraction, female workers are often regarded as more dispensable than male employees, and are often concentrated in industries that are targeted for layoffs (Sullivan 1994; WEDO 1998). Moreover, cutbacks in public child care and other support services for women, as part of the transition from a command to a market economy, have adversely affected women's ability to compete in the job market (Sullivan 1994). As a result of SAPs, the state faces a diminished capacity to promote social welfare and redistributive policies that facilitate the enjoyment of women's economic rights (Catagay, Elson, & Grown 2000, 1147).

Given the conflicting accounts offered by neoliberals and critical scholars as to the human rights effects of economic globalization, it is difficult to determine a priori what type of relationship to expect between globalization and women's rights. For the purposes of generating hypotheses, I adopt the critical argument consistently and hypothesize that, on balance and over time, economic globalization should exert a negative influence on women's rights attainment for a number of reasons. First, case studies by feminist theorists have established that structural inequalities in the global economy have generally had an adverse effect on women's socioeconomic status in developing countries. Second, in recent years, there have been a growing number of criticisms by prominent policy makers regarding the destructive tendencies of globalization (see Stiglitz 2003). Third, as globalization critics aptly point out, the current phase of globalization is dominated by powerful global institutions, such as the IMF and WTO, which facilitate the unregulated spread of global capitalism via free-market laissez-faire policies (Howard-Hassman 2005). Fourth, the contemporary phase of globalization has strengthened the power of

---

[9] Case studies find that foreign firms capitalize on prevailing cultural norms to rationalize the poor working conditions of female workers. Women are viewed as culturally compliant, docile, and dexterous. See Women's Environment and Development Organization (March 1998), Jagger (2001), Croucher (2004), and Ward and Pyle (1995).

transnational corporations, which have been implicated in suppressing workers' rights in developing countries, especially those of women.

INTERNATIONALIZATION OF HUMAN RIGHTS NORMS

Since the end of World War II, there has been an increasing internationalization of human rights norms, culminating in the formation of a global human rights regime (Landman 2005). "By the year 2000, between 95 and 191 countries have become signatories to the main international legal instruments" that govern state human rights practices (Landman 2003, 1). As Landman notes (2003, 1), the international human rights regime "has grown both in *breadth* and *depth* as new categories of human rights have been given express legal protection." In recent years, women's rights have become firmly entrenched in the international human rights regime, in good part due to the growing universal acceptance of human rights (Donnelly 2003; Simmons 2004). This important development has led some commentators to optimistically conclude that women's rights are universal. However, as others are quick to point out, there is often a significant gap between rights in principle (i.e., those protected by international law) and rights in practice (i.e., those rights actually protected by states and enjoyed by citizens) (Landman 2005). As Landman notes (2003, 15), the international human rights regime in general has a low compliance rate among nations because there is no international enforcement mechanism, and there are no penalties that come into play when a state breaches its treaty obligations. More centrally, the universalistic nature of human rights treaties weakens their enforcement powers (von Stein 2004). The prevailing view is that it is better to obtain universality in signature than universality in practice (Mwanza 2003; Apodaca 1996). This is witnessed by the fact that the Convention on the Elimination of All Forms of Discrimination against Women (CEDAW) has more substantive reservations than any other international treaty, and one-third of the ratifying states have issued substantive reservations to parts of CEDAW (Merry 2002, 91).[10]

Although there is often a significant gap in principle and practice, I argue that there should be a positive relationship between international human rights norms embodied in the CEDAW and actual human rights outcomes toward women.[11] However, the mere ratification of the CEDAW is not enough to guarantee women their rights. This becomes evident when we realize that just about every country in the world has signed and ratified the CEDAW, but not every country promotes women's rights. A cursory glance at some of the state signatories to the CEDAW, such as Burma and Saudi Arabia, clearly shows that ratification does not necessarily lead to the advancement of women. Instead, the level of formal commitment expressed by nation-states to the convention is a key to our understanding of how

---

[10] There are other reasons – too numerous to mention here – why nation-states lack an incentive to commit, in practice, to the principle of gender equality.

[11] In my doctoral dissertation, I discuss why the internationalization of human rights norms has a significant potential to transform nation-states' human rights practices through a number of important mechanisms including socialization, growing embeddedness in a global institutional framework, international legitimacy, and others.

human rights norms influence women's rights attainment. Specifically, women's rights should progress the most in countries that have expressed the highest formal commitment to women's rights (i.e., those countries that have issued none or few reservations to the principles of the convention), in comparison to countries that ratify the CEDAW only with significant reservations. It could reasonably be argued that the former countries are expressing a firmer commitment to modify domestic laws and practices to conform to the articles of the convention, whereas the latter countries have less inclination to align their domestic law with the Convention's principles.

CONTROL VARIABLES

This research introduces a number of alternative explanations identified in the empirical literature as important determinants of national human rights practices. They include the level of civil conflict, international conflict, economic development, population size, former colonial experience, Islam, and time. An examination of these factors is important because, though women's rights are conceptually and empirically distinct from other categories of rights, it would allow us to determine whether state abuse of women's rights and other types of human rights share some significant commonalities. Few quantitative studies on women's rights have examined these variables.[12]

Time

A variable that measures time is included in this research to eliminate any explanation that might be linked to natural improvements or declines over time in the level of women's rights. In order to draw firm conclusions about the potential causal impacts of the core independent variables, it is important to determine whether any long-term trends in women's rights are being driven by these factors or by natural improvements that would have occurred irrespective of these factors.

The Level of Conflict (Civil and International)

Studies have found that human rights, particularly the right to physical security and protection from arbitrary treatment by the state, are under threat in times of civil and international conflict (Stohl 1975; Poe et al. 1999; Poe & Tate 1994). Surprisingly, no studies have examined the relationship between conflict and women's rights from a broad cross-national perspective. This gap in the empirical literature is problematic, particularly since recent statistics reveal that the number of conflicts has increased significantly over the last few decades, with women often the specific targets for violations of their human rights by state and nonstate actors (Byrne 1995). Conflict also has been shown to have a particularly disruptive impact on women's daily lives, because conflict and the chaos it creates may lead to the collapse of the state's formal political and economic structures (Newbury & Baldwin 2000). This, in turn, may cause rising inflation, unemployment, a decline in household

---

[12] A notable exception is the pioneering work by Apodaca (1996; 1998).

incomes, and a disruption in state services. External (and internal) conflict also typically heightens the militarization of the state, which, in turn, often leads to more conservative attitudes regarding appropriate gender roles (Byrne 1995).

Economic Development

Economic development is seen as an important precursor of political, cultural, and social changes that benefit women (Apodaca 1998). The United Nations 1994 World Survey on the Role of Women in Development, for instance, states, "Economic development is closely related to the advancement of women. Where women have advanced, economic growth has usually been steady; where women have been restricted, there has been stagnation" (1994, ix). Recent empirical evidence supports this assertion (Poe, Blunt & Ho 1997; Apodaca 1998; Dollar & Gatti 1999; Forsythe, Korzeniewicz & Durrant 2000; World Bank 2001; Young, Fort & Danner 1994).[13]

Former Colonial Experience

Colonial relationships are purported to have been an important agent of socialization and a transmitter of cultural values that played an influential role in shaping women's status in the colonies (Gray et al. 2004). Colonialism, according to some, had beneficial effects because colonial powers brought infrastructure, political and economic institutions, the rule of law, and trade relationships to their colonies (Gray et al. 2004, 13; Poe & Tate 1994; Poe et al. 1999). However, although colonialism can have beneficial effects, a number of case studies and historical analyses by feminist scholars illustrate that colonialism has had an adverse influence on women's economic rights. This is because with colonialism, women generally witnessed a sharp reduction in their status as the structures of colonial rule tended to bolster indigenous male control over the female population (Waylen 1996).[14] In many precolonial societies, women had greater access to and autonomy over vital economic and social resources, such as land and tradable goods (Waylen 1996). Generalizing about the nature of colonialism is exceedingly difficult, because most colonized societies already had in place preexisting gendered social norms and values that accorded less significance to women. However, although precolonial societies were a far cry from genuine gender equality, they were supposedly not as rigidly hierarchical as the social structures put in place by colonial powers (Waylen 1996).

---

[13] The relationship between economic development and women's rights is neither straightforward nor uncontroversial. A large number of case studies in the feminist development literature find that economic development can have negative effects on women. Changes in agriculture, especially the introduction of more advanced technology controlled by men, undermined women's economic roles and channeled them into low-paying, unskilled manufacturing jobs (Clark & Clark 2004). In addition, the traditional roles and status of women, along with kinship support, were often eroded with the advent of industrialization. Although these arguments are certainly valid, a growing body of cross-national studies finds compelling evidence to support the contention that economic development is an ameliorative force for women in the long run.

[14] See Waylen (1996) *Gender in Third World Politics* for a more in-depth discussion of the impact of colonialism on women in developing countries.

Population Size

Research has shown that large populations increase the propensity of governments to repress their citizens' human rights (Poe & Tate 1994; Henderson 1993). Large populations tend to put severe strain on national resources, cause environmental deterioration, and place demands on government for public needs that it may not be able to fulfill (Mitchell & McCormick 1988). As a result, governments may have a harder time meeting their citizens' socioeconomic needs, and may resort to the use of force to restore domestic stability and quell disorder.

Islam

A variable for Islam is included to test the Inglehart and Norris (2003) "religious culture" hypothesis, which states that the predominant religion of a country will leave a distinct and lasting cultural imprint on contemporary beliefs and attitudes toward gender equality via the major channels of cultural transmission and socialization. I specifically examine Islam because it has been associated with the worst outcomes for women compared to other world religions, such as Catholicism, Hinduism, and Protestantism. If Islam really is the main culprit in the oppression of women, then controlling for Islam should weaken the strength of my index of separation of state and religion.

As a result of the foregoing discussion, I suggest that democracy, separation of state and religion (i.e., political secularism), and the internationalization of human rights norms should exert a substantial positive influence on the increasing realization of women's economic rights. I also expect women's economic rights to improve with time and with increases in the level of economic development. Conversely, I expect declines in women's economic rights with economic globalization, civil and international conflict, former colonial experience, population size, and Islam.

RESEARCH DESIGN

This research employs a pooled cross-sectional, annual, time-series design for the period from 1981 to 2003 using ordered logit with robust standard errors. I lag the dependent variable – women's economic rights – by one year, because it is reasonable to assume that the current year's level of women's rights depends upon the previous year's level of women's rights.[15] The country sample includes 160 nations of the world having a population of at least 500,000 in 1981. The unit of analysis is the country year. The actual number of cases is somewhat reduced because of missing data, as information for many countries, particularly developing countries, is not systematically recorded across time and space. Appendix A provides summary statistics of my variables. Appendix B provides a list of countries included in this sample. Figure 11.1 illustrates the relationship postulated between the core independent variables and women's rights.

---

[15] The use of lagged dependent variables in equations of this type is now standard practice to control for problems of temporal dependence in pooled time-series regression analysis (Poe et al. 1999; Poe & Tate 1994).

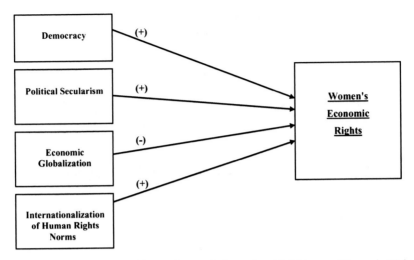

Figure 11.1. Hypothesized Effects of Core Independent Variables on Women's Rights Achievement

THE MODEL

The model employed in this study is a pooled cross-sectional time-series design with a lagged dependent variable. A (+) sign indicates that this variable is expected to increase the level of respect for women's rights, whereas a (−) sign indicates decreasing levels of women's rights attainment.[16] The equation to be estimated is:

Women's Rights = + Women's Rights (t − 1) − FDI − Trade Openness +
Democracy + Political Secularism + Endorsement of CEDAW
+ Time − International Conflict − Civil Conflict − Population
Size + GDP Per Capita − British − Spanish − French −
Portuguese − Dutch − Belgian − Ottoman − Islam

DEPENDENT VARIABLE: WOMEN'S ECONOMIC RIGHTS

The measure for women's economic rights is a four-point standards-based ordinal measure from the *Cingranelli and Richards (CIRI) Human Rights Data Set*, which

---

[16] A second logit model, not reported here, was run to determine whether women's rights varied by region, which include sub-Saharan Africa, the Middle East and North Africa (MENA), East Asia/The Pacific and South Asia, Latin America and the Caribbean, and Central and Eastern Europe. The baseline region is Western Europe and North America. All of the regions exhibited a negative and statistically significant relationship with women's rights in comparison to the baseline region. The results for Eastern and Central Europe are a little surprising considering that many are formerly communist regimes, which have historically been associated with better treatment of women. Interpretation of the findings is problematic because it is difficult to ascertain how each region performs on women's economic rights separately from Western Europe and North America.

captures the extent to which women are able to exercise a number of internationally recognized rights in the economic realm.[17] These include:

- Equal pay for equal work
- Free choice of profession or employment
- The right to gainful employment
- Equality in hiring and promotion practices
- Job security (maternity leave, unemployment benefits, no arbitrary firing or lay-offs, etc.)
- Nondiscrimination by employers
- The right to be free from sexual harassment in the workplace
- The right to work at night
- The right to work in occupations classified as dangerous
- The right to work in the military and the police force

These rights are grounded *historically* in internationally accepted human rights norms of equality and nondiscrimination, which are enunciated in the United Nations Charter, the Universal Declaration of Human Rights (UDHR), and a number of international legal treaties. Specific economic rights of women are also enumerated in several articles of the UDHR, the International Covenant on Economic, Social, and Cultural Rights (ICESCR) and the Convention on the Elimination of All Forms of Discrimination Against Women (CEDAW).[18]

The CIRI measure ranges from situations in which legal barriers prevent women from attaining economic equality (score of 0) to situations in which there is a guarantee of economic equality in law that is fully respected and enforced by the government in practice (score of 3). In countries that receive the lowest score of 0, women have no formal economic rights under law and are denied access to the economic resources and opportunities necessary to attain equality. Countries where women's economic rights are closest to being realized are given the highest score on the scale of 3. See the Data Appendix (Appendix D) for a discussion on the methodology for this measure.

It is important to point out that consumption-related rights, or what are referred to as "subsistence rights," are not included in the CIRI measure because of missing data and quality of the source material that were used to develop the CIRI measure.[19] The U.S. State Department's annual *Country Reports on Human Rights*

---

[17] The CIRI dataset contains standards-based quantitative information on government respect for 13 internationally recognized human rights for 162 countries, annually from 1981 to 2004.

[18] The right to equal pay for equal work is recognized in article 23 of the UDHR, article 7 of the ICESCR, and article 11 of the CEDAW. The rights to gainful employment and to free choice of employment are recognized in article 23 of the UDHR, article 6 of the ICESCR, and article 11 of the CEDAW. The right to job security and just and favorable conditions of work are recognized in article 22 of the UDHR and article 11 of the CEDAW. Article 11 of CEDAW also explicitly recognizes the principle of nondiscrimination and women's right to the same employment opportunities as men in all fields, which, by inference, includes the right to work at night, in occupations classified as dangerous, and in the military and police forces.

[19] A distinction is often made in international human rights law between two different aspects of economic rights: production-related and consumption-related rights (Milner, Poe & Leblang 1999). The former rights relate to legal protections of property, and the use and enjoyment of property and possessions. The latter relate to the fulfillment of basic needs or the necessities required for

Practices, which were used to construct the CIRI indicator, do not include enough information to develop a measure that evaluates government efforts to guarantee female citizens' subsistence rights. Though the information contained in these reports has improved over time, material available to support the construction of such a measure is missing for the earlier years of the report.[20] Furthermore, current international and national statistics are of limited utility because of a lack of coverage and inconsistency in data collection.[21] The lack of data on women's subsistence rights is problematic, especially in light of the growing neoliberal marketization of developing economies. Many countries face a diminished capacity to promote women's subsistence rights, since one of the key objectives of neoliberal free-market policies (i.e., structural adjustment programs) is to roll back the size of the state, which often requires drastic cutbacks in social programs such as health and education. Hence, nation-states have a harder time implementing progressive social welfare and redistributive policies that facilitate the enjoyment of women's subsistence rights.

Finally, the CIRI measure does not capture women's employment experiences in the informal and domestic economies, because most nation-states do not systematically count women's work in these realms as part of their national economic statistics (Apodaca 1996). As Danner et al. (1999, 253) claim, the central problem is that "women remain invisible in national economic accounts because of the failure to consider "women's work" as real or productive labor with an economic contribution to society." Moreover, international statistics on the informal economy are lacking in terms of their breadth and depth of coverage. Until better information is available from centralized data sources, it will be difficult to evaluate women's work experiences outside of the formal economy.

Despite these limitations, there are a number of important advantages to the CIRI economic rights measure. For one, it is far more comprehensive in its coverage of women's rights than existing measures. Using the U.S. State Department reports, it was possible to collect data for a large sample of countries over a respectable period of time. A second advantage is that the CIRI measure focuses on both laws and government practices in contrast to existing measures, which focus primarily on outcomes, such as the female labor force participation rate. Although this measure may capture the quantity of women's work, such a measure says little or nothing

subsistence. The UDHR and the ICESCR recognize that all people have basic subsistence rights (adequate food, clothing, and housing), which are critical to guaranteeing an adequate standard of living for their, and their family's, well-being (Milner, Poe, & Leblang 1999).

[20] In constructing the CIRI measure, the goal was to create an indicator that could be developed from the amount of material available in 1981, when the U.S. State Department reports became widely recognized as an objective source of information about human rights practice around the world.

[21] Although international and national agencies and nongovernmental organizations have recently developed extensive publications and international data on women – such as the United Nations *Women's Indicators and Statistics Database (WISTAT)* and the World Bank's *World Development Indicators* – these data sources provide little statistical information that could be used to develop a reliable measure of women's subsistence rights. Furthermore, comparative indices are often not disaggregated by gender. For example, the most standard indicator of physical well-being, the Physical Quality of Life Index (PQLI) – which includes infant mortality, life expectancy, and literacy – does not disaggregate these factors by gender for most countries of the world. In addition, the PQLI does not capture several important components of subsistence rights, such as caloric intake and access to housing, clean water, and sanitation facilities.

about the actual quality of women's work. Do women work under deplorable conditions in low-paying jobs? Do they receive equal pay for equal work? Does the government intercede on behalf of women to enforce the laws? A measure of female labor force participation cannot get at these issues, whereas the CIRI measure captures these important aspects of women's rights and government practices to enforce these rights.

A third advantage of the CIRI measure is that it facilitates legitimate cross-national comparisons by proposing a "universalistic" measure of women's rights attainment that is nevertheless grounded both *empirically* and *historically* in internationally accepted human rights norms (e.g., the UN Charter, the UDHR, etc.). Although international human rights instruments are substantially rooted in Western philosophical and intellectual traditions, today they have been embraced by virtually every country in the world, in principle, regardless of actual practices (Chinkin 1999, 55). Importantly, my women's rights indicators measure progress toward the attainment of an "ideal" established by international human rights law, so even the most advanced Western countries often fall short of this standard.

INDEPENDENT VARIABLES

Democracy

This research uses the Polity IV democracy indicator developed by Marshall and Jaggers (2003) (http://www.cidcm.umd.edu/inscr/polity/). This indicator measures the level of democracy in a country along an additive continuum that ranges from 0 to 11. A score of 0 represents no democracy in the country and eleven represents a democratic regime. The authors measure democracy based on three criteria: (1) the competitiveness and openness of executive recruitment; (2) the competitiveness of political participation; and (3) constraints on the chief executive.

Political Secularism

My measure of political secularism is an original three-point ordinal indicator that captures the level of institutional secularization (i.e., the degree of formal and actual separation of state and religion). My indicator includes variables for the following: official state religion, freedom of religion, and the institutionalization of religious interests.

Official state religion. The first component examines the legal separation of church and state or whether a country has an official state religion. This variable is coded as:

0. The state has an official religion or the state does not officially endorse a particular religion but one religion serves unofficially as the state religion.
1. The state has no official religion or religions.

The primary source of this measure is the *Cingranelli and Richards (CIRI) Human Rights Dataset*. Information obtained from the *CIA World Factbook* or the *U.S. State*

Department's Annual Report on Religious Freedom was used to fill in any missing information in the CIRI dataset.

Freedom of religion. The second component is a dichotomous measure that taps the extent to which the freedom of citizens to exercise and practice their religious beliefs is subject to actual government restrictions or interference. Does the government prohibit citizens from proselytizing? Does the government force conversions or restrict conversions to minority religions? Does the government place restrictions on access to places of worship? This variable is a good proxy measure of the extent to which the state involves itself in regulating or legislating religion. Instances where the government restricts freedom of religion are coded as 0. The primary source of this measure is the CIRI Dataset.[22]

The institutionalization of religious interests. The third indicator is a measure of the degree to which religion is institutionalized in the governing apparatus. This measure is important because it taps the extent to which religious interests actually control the levers of state power through office holding. A country receives a score of 0 if the chief executive or largest government party represents national religious interests, which includes one or more of the major world religions: Islam, Catholicism, Hinduism, Judaism, Buddhism, or Christianity. The country receives a score of 1 if the chief executive or largest government party does not represent national religious interests. The source of this measure is the World Bank's *Database of Political Institutions* (DPI).

The results of these components – official state religion, freedom of religion, and institutionalization of religious interests – are then totaled to result in an ordinal indicator that ranges from 0 to 3. Countries with a separation of religion and state receive the highest score of 3, whereas countries with no separation receive the lowest score of 0.

Economic Globalization

I use two separate measures of economic globalization: a) net flows of foreign direct investment (FDI); and b) trade openness, which correspond to financial and trade globalization, respectively. Foreign direct investment data are in 1995 U.S. dollars and were drawn from the World Bank's *2002 World Development Indicators CD-ROM*. FDI is measured as the sum of equity capital, reinvestment of earnings, and other long-term capital. The WDI series reports net inflows for a particular country as a proportion of GDP. Trade openness is measured as the sum of the value of imports and exports of goods and services of a country expressed as a percentage of that country's GDP. This variable is logged to minimize problems with skewness, which can bias parameter estimates. Trade data were also drawn from the WDI series.

Trade openness and FDI are analytically and empirically distinct variables that capture different aspects of the economic globalization process. FDI is substantially

---

[22] More detailed coding instructions for this variable can be found at the CIRI Human Rights Data Web Page, available at: http://ciri.binghamton.edu/.

different from trade openness, because it is usually an investment by foreign corporations in productive facilities and fixed capital assets, such as factories, equipment,
and mines, whereas trade openness is a measure that captures the exchange of goods
and services – not fixed assets. Furthermore, countries can have very high levels of
trade openness, but small or inconsequential levels of FDI, and vice versa. Examples
of countries with high levels of exports and fairly small amounts of FDI include
Japan, Germany, Portugal, and Israel. These examples clearly illustrate that FDI and
trade openness measures cannot be used as substitutes for one another in measuring a country's integration into the global economy. Furthermore, though the
bulk of FDI is between Europe, Japan, and the United States, and the major recipients of FDI among developing countries are Brazil and Mexico (and a few other
industrializing countries), my FDI indicator is a valid comparative measure across
countries, because the indicator is measured as a proportion of GDP, meaning that
this measure is adjusted to the relative size of the domestic economy.

Although my measure of trade openness is a commonly used indicator, there is
concern that it is biased toward smaller countries. Because small countries – such
as Singapore or Taiwan – tend to have extensive trading relationships with large
countries – such the United States and Russia – the small country would appear to
be "more open" to trade. However, my study accounts for this bias since it controls
for population size. Furthermore, because my trade openness indicator is measured
as a percentage of GDP, it adjusts for the size of the economy.

Internationalization of Human Rights Norms

I measure the internationalization of human rights norms by the level of nation-
state commitment to the Convention on the Elimination of All Forms of Discrimination against Women (CEDAW). I examine the CEDAW convention because
it is widely viewed as the most important treaty disseminating the global norm
of gender equality (True & Mintrom 2001; Freeman & Fraser 1994). I measure
commitment to CEDAW using a weighted ratification variable developed by Todd
Landman (2005) that ranges from a low of 0 to a high of 8. The variable has four
categories, which are coded as follows:

(4) A country makes no reservations to the CEDAW or any interpretative declarations that modify treaty obligations.
(3) A country makes reservations that could have some but not major impacts
on their obligations. This includes reservations to certain articles of CEDAW
but not nullifying it completely.
(2) A country makes reservations that have a noticeable effect on its obligations
under the convention to a whole article, nullifying or leaving open the
possibility not to abide by a whole article.
(1) A country makes reservations that have significant and severe effects on the
convention's obligations. Reservations that subject the whole convention to
national or religious legislation would receive this score.

A ratifying country's reservation score is then multiplied by two, which is the
original ratification score that all convention signatories receive. Countries that do
not ratify the convention receive a score of 0. Those that sign the convention but

do not ratify it receive a score of 1. Appendix C lists the countries in my study that are signatories to the CEDAW as of 18 March 2005.

THE CONTROL VARIABLES

Time

Time is measured as a count variable, given a score of one in 1981 and continuing in increments of one for each subsequent year.

Conflict (Civil and International)

This variable is a three-point ordinal scale that captures the severity of conflict measured in terms of the number of battle deaths in a given country for a particular year (Strand et al. 2002). The data for this measure were also drawn from the Armed Conflict Dataset.[23] It is coded as:

0 = No war;
1 = Minor conflict, where there have been at least twenty-five battle deaths per year; and
2 = Major conflict, where there have been more than one thousand battle-related deaths per year.

Level of Economic Development

The level of economic development is measured using the logged values of per capita gross domestic product (GDP). These data are drawn from the World Bank's *World Development Indicators*.

Although GDP per capita is a standard measure of economic development, it has some important limitations. The most significant limitation of this indicator is that it does not measure the expansion of substantive freedoms, which is an important constituent component of the development process. In *Development as Freedom*, Amartya Sen advocates an expansive definition of economic development that requires substantially more than growth in gross domestic product. According to Sen, development can be viewed as a process of expanding the elementary freedoms that people enjoy. It requires the removal of major sources of unfreedom that exist in both developed and developing countries – including poverty, tyranny, poor economic opportunities, and various other forms of unfreedoms – that rob people of the ability to shape their own destinies. Growth of gross domestic product can certainly serve as an important enabling condition or as *means* to expanding the elementary freedoms enjoyed by members of society, such as the liberty of political participation, the opportunity to receive basic education, and the freedom from economic deprivation and poverty (Sen 2001, 5). However, substantive freedoms

---

[23] The dataset is available at: http://www.prio.no/cwp/armedconflict/current/codebook_v2_1.pdf). This dataset is a joint project between the Department of Peace and Conflict Studies, Uppsala University, and the Centre for the Study of Civil War at the International Peace Research Institute, Oslo (PRIO).

depend on other important determinants that are not captured by standard indices of development.

Unfortunately, my study does not employ such an expansive conceptualization of development, since it would be difficult to develop a valid indicator for use in a broad cross-national study. Although GDP per capita is a narrower measure of development than Sen's conceptualization of this process, studies have found that per capita GDP does tend to correlate highly with both the UN Human Development Index (HDI) and Morris' Physical Quality of Life Index (PQLI), meaning that they are essentially measuring the same thing – physical and social well-being.

Colonial Experience

A dichotomous variable is used to indicate whether a country had experienced a colonial relationship with the following colonial powers: France, Spain, Britain, Holland, Belgium, Portugal, the Ottoman Empire, and the Soviet Union. The variable for Soviet is treated as the baseline category because communism has historically been associated with better treatment of women. This variable is measured 1 if a country had such a relationship and 0 otherwise (Hensel 1999). In cases in which a country had been colonized by more than one world power, it was coded as a 1 for the power in control at the time of independence. The data for this measure were obtained from Paul Hensel's International Relations Data Site (http://garnet.acns.fsu.edu/p̄hensel/data.html).

Population Size

This measure is of the logged midyear country population of each nation state (U.S. Government Census International Data Base).

Islam

Islam is measured using a dummy variable coded 1 if a country is predominantly Islamic and 0 otherwise.[24] Country classifications for this variable are drawn from *The CIA World Factbook* and a data set collected by Alesina and colleagues, which is derived from the *Encyclopedia Britannica Book of the Year 2001*.[25]

ANALYSES

Table 11.1 reports the results for the cross-sectional time-series model with a lagged dependent variable. Logit coefficients are reported with robust standard errors in parentheses. The asterisks next to the coefficients indicate the levels of statistical significance. Chi-square estimates indicate that the model in Table 11.1 is a significant improvement on its null counterpart (if all slopes were simultaneously zero). The model explains 50% of the cases, which is a reasonably good fit. Not

---

[24] A country is classified as Islamic if the majority of the population identifies with this religion. For example, if 52% of the population of Country X identifies itself as Muslim, the country's predominant religion is recorded as Muslim.

[25] The dataset is available online at: http://www.stanford.edu/~wacziarg/papersum.html.

Table 11.1

Women's Economic Rights	3.21***
(t−1)	(.136)
Democracy	.111***
	(.021)
Political Secularism	.152**
	(.073)
Endorsement of CEDAW	.022
	(.019)
FDI	.001
	(.014)
Log of Trade Openness	.559**
	(.281)
Time	−.267*
	(.011)
International Conflict	−.159
	(.116)
Civil Conflict	−.081
	(.073)
Log of GDP Per Capita	.988***
	(.164)
Log of Population	−.159
	(.104)
British	−.378**
	(.161)
Spanish	−.521***
	(.171)
French	.397**
	(.209)
Portuguese	−.170
	(.323)
Dutch	.818*
	(.493)
Belgian	.167
	(.429)
Ottoman	−.181***
	(.034)
Islam	−.267
	(.169)
Log Likelihood	**−1165**
Prob > chi^2	**0.000**
Number of Cases	**2597**
R^2	**0.50**

surprisingly, the most significant predictor of women's economic rights is the level of women's rights from the previous year.

The results indicate that democracy is a consistently strong predictor of women's economic rights, and is associated with steady increases in government respect for these rights. The sign is statistically significant at better than the .01 level and

Table 11.2

Women's Economic Rights	3.41***
(t−1)	(.128)
Autocracy	−.560***
	(.134)
Political Secularism	.256***
	(.067)
Endorsement of CEDAW	.015
	(.018)
FDI	−.008
	(.013)
Log of Trade Openness	.363
	(.266)
Time	−.023**
	(.010)
International Conflict	−.124
	(.108)
Civil Conflict	−.117*
	(.070)
Log of GDP Per Capita	1.07***
	(.131)
Population	−.127*
	(.096)
Log Likelihood	**−1256**
Prob > chi^2	**0.000**
Number of Cases	**2597**
R^2	**.48**

positive in the correct direction, which confirm my theoretical expectations. An ordered logit analysis was run by political regime type to determine whether women's rights fare the worst in autocratic regimes in comparison to their more democratic counterparts.[26] The variables for regime type were constructed using the Polity IV ten-point measure of democracy. This measure was broken down into three categories: autocracies, semidemocracies, and democracies. A country is classified as an autocracy if it receives a score of between 0 and 3 on the Polity measure. A country is classified as a semidemocracy if it receives a score of between 4 and 5 on the Polity measure. A country is classified as a democracy if it receives a score of between 6 and 10 on the Polity measure. Recent studies have constructed similar measures of political regime type using the Polity IV measure (Fox & Sandler 2003, 474). Table 11.2 reports the ordered logit results, which show that, in comparison to democracies, women enjoy far fewer economic rights under authoritarian regimes.[27] A separate logit analysis was run on semidemocratic regimes. These results are not reported here because they failed to achieve statistical significance at the conventional threshold level. However, the findings indicate that

---

[26] My dissertation more fully addresses the relationship between women's economic rights and political regime type.

[27] Only the core independent variables and necessary control variables are included in this model.

semidemocracies experience higher levels of rights attainment than authoritarian regimes.

The logit results from Table 11.1 confirm my theoretical expectations that political secularism is a strong predictor of women's economic rights attainment.[28] The fact that the secularism indicator maintains its statistical significance while controlling for Islam lends support to my argument that the degree of institutional secularization is a more important determinant of cross-national variations in women's rights attainment than the predominant state religion.[29] Importantly, an examination of the data shows that women's economic rights are lowest in highly authoritarian regimes that experience a fusion of state and religion. For example, whereas the mean level of women's economic rights is 0.82 in nonsecular authoritarian regimes, it is higher in secular authoritarian regimes at 1.10. Not surprisingly, a secular democracy is the best vehicle for women's rights attainment.[30] Countries with the highest democracy scores on the Polity IV indicator (6–10) and the highest score on the separation of state and religion index (3) also exhibit the highest levels of rights attainment. The mean level for women's economic rights is 1.60 (out of 3) in secular democratic regimes.

Next, the results show that the influence of economic globalization on women's rights are partial and inconsistent, which may be a reflection of the multidimensional nature of the globalization process. In Table 11.1, for example, financial globalization appears to have a negligible effect on women's economic rights, whereas trade globalization exerts a statistically significant and positive effect (p <.05). These results should be interpreted with caution because a global sample was used. A global sample may mask important differences in the impact of globalization on developed and developing economies. This could lead to inappropriate policy prescriptions for less developed countries (Richards & Gelleny 2002). Consequently, I decided to run two separate ordered logit analyses to determine where the positive effects of trade globalization were being felt. The first analysis ascertains whether the wealthier countries (middle to upper income) are inflating the actual statistical relationship between trade openness and women's economic rights. First, I included in the ordered logit equation only those countries with an annual GDP per capita of less than $10,000. Then, I ran a separate analysis on only those countries with an annual GDP per capita of greater than $10,000.

The findings reveal that trade openness has a strong positive effect on women's economic rights in the sample of more affluent countries. This may be because there is a growing demand for skilled and well-paid female labor in the service

[28] The fact that political secularism is not associated with women's economic rights at the .01 level is probably a result of some degree of multicollinearity between the variables for former colonial experience and political secularism. When the colonialism variables are dropped from the model, political secularism is associated with women's economic rights at the .01 level or better.

[29] Pearson's correlations between the political secularism indicator and the Islam variable show that there appears to be no serious problems with multicollinearity. Islam shows a fairly significant correlation with political secularism (−.38). However, this correlation does not reach the .60 threshold, whereby multicollinearity would be considered a significant issue.

[30] The question of whether both democracy and political secularism are necessary prerequisites for a fuller advancement of women's economic rights attainment is addressed in greater detail in my dissertation.

and informational sectors of these economies. Many less developed economies still have strong manufacturing and agricultural sectors, where women's wages are often suppressed and there is less demand for a highly educated, skilled female workforce. When the analysis was run on the sample of less-developed countries, the positive effects were significantly weaker and did not obtain statistical significance even at the .10 threshold level. This lends support to the claims made by feminist development scholars that women in industrial economies, especially postindustrial ones, benefit more from globalization than women in developing countries.

There are a number of possible reasons for why financial globalization is not associated with improvements in women's economic rights. For one, the nature of financial globalization has dramatically changed in recent years. In today's global economy the emphasis is on hypermobile capital and quick profit maximization by investors in the form of stocks, bonds, dividends, and other forms of investment. According to Peterson (2003), higher profit expectations erode long-term commitments by foreign firms in favor of short-term strategies that do not contribute to indigenous development and economic growth, both of which are associated with improvements in women's economic rights. Equally important, FDI is also highly selective and is hardly "globalized" as neoliberals claim, because it is concentrated in a few large countries such as China and Brazil. The current distribution of FDI means that more than half of all developing countries are marginalized from credit, infra-structural development, and technology transfer that are historically associated with long-term growth and development (Peterson 2003; Schaeffer 2003).

Surprisingly, the level of national commitment to the CEDAW is not significantly associated with women's economic rights even at the .10 threshold level. This result may be because governments have a harder time advancing women's economic rights when their realization is so sensitive to national economic conditions, such as the level of economic development. In market-based economies, states lack the same level of direct policy instruments for influencing women's rights that they have, for example, in the political sphere.[31] This lack of direct control is more evident, since the onset of economic globalization in the 1990s, where the globalization process has been more or less synonymous with the marketization and privatization of domestic economic relations within countries that are being integrated into the global economic system. Hence, the principles embodied in the CEDAW do not appear to exert a strong normative hold on government practices toward women's economic rights.

The results for alternative explanations were more mixed. Time is an important variable, but the results are not in the hypothesized direction. The negative coefficient signifies a decline in women's economic rights. It is possible that women's economic rights have declined at the micro level as a result of economic globalization, but my measures do not capture these declines. Future research may want to look deeper into the association between globalization and women's rights using a combination of quantitative and qualitative methods. Not surprisingly, the level of economic development of a country is strongly associated with improvements

---

[31] Examples include positive discrimination or affirmative action strategies such as gender quotas, changes to electoral laws and party-systems, passage of antidiscrimination legislation, and the development of institutions and oversight mechanisms to enforce women's political rights.

in women's rights, as the indicator for GDP per capita is significant at the .01 level. These results confirm the findings of the literature that women's economic rights are substantially dependent upon the level of development. International and civil conflict do not appear to be important determinants of women's economic rights attainment, which may signify that conflict is not intense and protracted enough to hinder the state's ability to provide for the socioeconomic needs of its citizens.

The results for former colonial experience are also mixed. Whereas some forms of colonial rule exert a strong negative influence on women's economic rights, other types of colonial rule have negligible effects or strong positive effects. For example, Dutch and French colonial rule are associated with modest to significant gains in women's economic rights. By contrast, British, Spanish, and Ottoman rule are associated with significant declines in women's economic rights. The negative results for Spanish colonial influence make intuitive sense because Spanish colonial rulers probably transmitted the views of traditional Catholicism to their colonies (Gray et al. 2004).[32] Spanish Catholicism, which is associated with traditional views regarding women's appropriate roles, has exerted a strong influence over divorce, abortion, and women's familial rights. Similarly, the negative results for Ottoman colonial rule are not unexpected because former Ottoman nations are predominantly Islamic religious states.[33] Many Islamic regimes accord poor treatment to women because they are highly authoritarian and religious, such as Oman and Saudi Arabia. The positive results for French colonial rule are also not unexpected because France is strongly associated with "liberal" or secularizing tendencies (Gray et al. 2004, 34). The unresolved issue is why British colonial rule would exert a negative influence on women's economic rights. My inconsistent findings give root to many specific questions well suited to small-N case studies. This may be an avenue that researchers may want to explore in the future.

Finally, population size is associated with modest declines in women's economic rights ($p < .10$). These findings are interesting because they infer that a large population may drain the state's ability to redistribute vital economic resources or to allocate state expenditures to programs designed to ameliorate gender inequalities. In countries with scarce economic resources and large populations, women are less likely to have their socioeconomic needs met.

CONCLUDING REMARKS

In this study, I examined the relationship between four major trends – democracy, political secularism, economic globalization, and the internationalization of human rights norms – and government respect for women's economic rights in 160 countries from 1981 to 2003. Taken together, the findings provide significant support for the argument that women's economic rights attainment is increasingly being driven by democracy, political secularism, trade globalization, and economic

---

[32] The Catholic Church enjoyed a deep historical entrenchment in the Spanish government until fairly recently in history. Spain did not begin institutional secularization until the collapse of the Franco regime around 1975.

[33] For this sample, Ottoman nations were those countries that were under the League of Nations mandates between World War I and World War II.

development. Importantly, both democracy and political secularism appear to exert a strong, independent influence on women's rights achievement, controlling for other relevant factors such as Islam. Economic globalization also had important implications for women's rights, but the results are mixed. Trade globalization appears to be most beneficial to women who reside in affluent developed countries, whereas financial globalization exerts a negligible influence on women's economic rights since it is not significantly associated with either gains or declines in these rights. The results also confirm the findings of a wide body of literature that economic development is an essential precondition for the advancement of human rights, including the rights of women. Finally, the size of a nation's population and history of certain types of colonial influence (British, Ottoman, and Spanish) are associated with significant declines in women's economic rights.

REFERENCES

Agosin, Marjorie, ed. 2002. *Women, Gender, and Human Rights A Global Perspective.* London: Rutgers University Press.

Apodaca, Clair. 1996. Progressive Realization for All: State Responsibility Toward the Fulfillment of Women's Economic and Social Rights. Ph.D. Diss., Purdue University.

Apodaca, Clair. 1998. Measuring Women's Economic and Social Rights Achievement. *Human Rights Quarterly* 20: 139–72.

Apodaca, Clair. 2001. Global Economic Patterns and Personal Integrity Rights after the Cold War. *International Studies Quarterly* 45: 587–602.

Bayes, Jane H., and Nayereh Tohidi. 2001. *Globalization, Gender, and Religion.* New York: Palgrave Press.

Becker, Gary S. 1957. *The Economics of Discrimination.* Chicago: University of Chicago Press.

Behrman, Jere R., and Elizabeth M. King. 2000. Competition and Gender Gap in Wages: Evidence from 16 Countries. *Background paper prepared for Engendering Development.* Washington, DC: World Bank.

Berik, Günseli, Yana van der Meulen Rodgers, and Joseph E. Zveglich, Jr. 2003. International Trade and Wage Discrimination: Evidence from East Asia. World Bank Policy Research Working Paper 3111.

Berkovitch, Nitza. 1999. *From Motherhood to Citizenship: Women's Rights and International Organizations.* Baltimore, MD: John Hopkins University Press.

Blanton, Shannon Lindsey, and Robert G. Blanton. 2003. *Human Rights and FDI: A Cross-National Assessment.* Paper presented at the annual meeting of the American Political Science Association, Philadelphia, PA.

Bollen, Kenneth. 1992. Political Rights and Political Liberties in Nations: An Evaluation of Human Rights Measures, 1950–1984. In *Human Rights and Statistics: Getting the Record Straight,* ed. Thomas B. Jabine and Richard P. Claude. Philadelphia: University of Philadelphia Press.

Boserup, Ester. 1970. *Women's Role in Economic Development.* New York: St. Martin's Press.

Brill, Alida. 1995. *A Rising Public Voice Women in Politics Worldwide.* New York: Feminist Press.

Buchmann, Claudia. 1996. The Debt Crisis, Structural Adjustment and Women's Education. *International Journal of Comparative Sociology* 37: 5–29.

Burton-Hafner Emilie. 2002. External Pressures and Human Rights: The State of the Globalization Debate. Paper presented at the annual meeting of the American Political Science Association, Boston, MA.

Byrne, Bridget. 1995. *Gender, Conflict and Development, Volume 1: Overview.* Brighton, UK: BRIDGE: Institute of Development Studies, University of Sussex.

Camp Keith, Linda. 1999. The United Nations International Covenant on Civil and Political Rights: Does It Make A Difference in Human Rights Behavior? *Journal of Peace Research* 36 (1): 95–118.

Camp Keith, Linda. 2002. Constitutional Provisions for Individual Human Rights (1977 – 1996): Are they more than mere "window dressing?" *Political Research Quarterly* 55 (1): 111–44.

Catagay, Nilufer, Diane Elson, and Caren Grown, eds. 2000. Growth, Trade, Finance, and Gender Equality. Special issue, *World Development* 28 (7): 1145–56.

Catagay, Nilufer, and Gunseli Berik. 1991. Transition to Export-Led Growth in Turkey: Is There a Feminization of Employment? *Review of Radical Public Economics 22.*

Chinkin, Christine. 1999. Cultural Relativism and International Law. In *Religious Fundamentalisms and the Human Rights of Women*, ed. Courtney W. Howland. New York: Palgrave Press.

Chowdhury, Najma. 2001. The Politics of Implementing Women's Rights in Bangladesh. In *Globalization, Gender, and Religion*, ed. Jane H. Bayes and Nayereh Tohidi. New York: Palgrave Press.

CIA World Factbook. 2005. http://www.cia.gov/cia/publications/factbook/.

Cingranelli, David L., and Chang-yen Tsai. 2003. *Democracy, Globalization and Workers' Rights: A Comparative Analysis.* Paper presented at the annual meeting of the American Political Science Association, Philadelphia, PA.

Clark, Cal, and Janet Clark. 2004. The Status of Women and the Quality of Life in Developing Societies. Paper presented at the 45th annual convention of the International Studies Association, Montreal, Canada.

Collingsworth, Terry, William Goold, and Pharis Harvey. 1994. Time for a Global New Deal: Labor and Free Trade. *Foreign Affairs* 73: 8–13.

Croucher, Sheila L. 2004. *Globalization and Belonging: The Politics of Identity in a Changing World.* Oxford: Rowman and Littlefield.

Dahl, Robert A. 1998. *On Democracy.* New Haven, CT: Yale University Press.

Danner, Mona, Lucia Fort, and Gay Young. 1999. International Data on Women and Gender: Resources, Issues, Critical Use. *Women's Studies International Forum* 22 (2): 249–59.

Dollar, David, and Roberta Gatti. 1999. Gender Inequality, Income, and Growth: Are Good Times Good for Women? Working Paper Series No. 1. Washington, DC: World Bank Development Research Group.

Donnelly, Jack. 2003. *Universal Human Rights in Theory & Practice.* Ithaca, NY: Cornell University Press.

Dunaway, Wilma A. 2002. Commodity Chains and Gendered Exploitation: Rescuing Women from the Periphery of World-System Thought. In *The Modern/Colonial/Capitalist World-System in the Twentieth Century Global Processes, Antisystemic Movements, and the Geopolitics of Knowledge*, ed. Grosfoguel Ramon and Ana Margarita-Cervantes Rodriguez. Westport, CT: Praeger.

Elson, Diane. 1990. Male Bias in macro-economics: the case of structural adjustment. In *Male Bias in the Development Process*, ed. Diane Elson. Manchester: Manchester University Press.

Fall, Yassine. "Gender and Social Implications of Globalization: An African Perspective," In *Gender, Globalization and Democratization*, eds. Rita Mae Kelly, Jane H. Bayes, Mary E. Hawkesworth, and Brigitte Young. London: Rowman and Littlefield.

Forsythe, Nancy, Roberta P. Korzeniewicz, and Valerie Durrant. 2000. Gender Inequalities and Economic Growth: A Longitudinal Evaluation. *Economic Development and Cultural Change* 48: 573–606.

Fox, Jonathan, and Shmuel Sandler. 2003. Quantifying Religion: Toward Building More Effective Ways of Measuring Religious Influence on State-Level Behavior. *Journal of Church and State* 45 (3): 559–89.

Freeman, Marsha A., and Arvonne S. Fraser. 1994. Women's Human Rights: Making the Theory a Reality. In *Human Rights: An Agenda for the Next Century*, ed. L. Henkin and J. L. Hargrove. Washington, DC: American Society of International Law.

Friedman, Milton. 1962. *Capitalism and Freedom*. Chicago: University of Chicago Press.

Gray, Mark M., Miki Caul Kittilson, and Wayne Sandholtz. 2004. Women and Globalization: A Study of Quality of Life and Status Indicators in 180 nations, 1975–2000. Paper presented at the annual meeting of the American Political Science Association, Chicago, IL.

Haggard, Stephan, and Robert Kaufman. 2002. The Expansion of Welfare Commitments in Latin America and East Asia: 1950–1980. Paper presented at the annual meeting of the American Political Science Association, Boston, MA.

Harrelson-Stephens, Julie, and Rhonda L. Callaway. 2004. Does Trade Openness Promote Security Rights in Developing Countries? Examining the Liberal Perspective. *International Interactions* 29: 143–58.

Hathaway, Oona A. 2002. Do Human Rights Treaties Make a Difference? *Yale Law Journal* 3 (8): 1935–2042.

Henderson, Conway. 1993. Population Pressures and Political Repression. *Social Science Quarterly* 74: 322–33.

Hensel, Paul. International Cooperation and Conflict Data. www.washington.edu/wto/issues/labor.html. Retrieved 15 August 2005.

Howard, Rhoda. 1993. Cultural Absolutism and the Nostalgia for Community. *Human Rights Quarterly* 15 (2): 315–38.

Howard-Hassman, Rhoda E. 2003. The Great Transformation II: Human Rights Leapfrogging in the Era of Globalization. Paper presented at annual meeting of the American Political Science Association, Philadelphia, PA.

Howard-Hassman, Rhoda E. 2005. The Second Great Transformation: Human Rights Leapfrogging in the Era of Globalization. *Human Rights Quarterly* 27 (1): 1–40.

Howland, Courtney W. 1999. *Religious Fundamentalism and the Human Rights of Women*. New York: St. Martin's Press.

Htun, Mala. 2003. *Sex and the State Abortion, Divorce, and the Family Under Latin American Dictatorships and Democracies*. Cambridge: Cambridge University Press.

Inglehart, Ronald, and Pippa Norris. 2003. *Rising Tide Gender Equality and Cultural Change Around the World*. Cambridge: Cambridge University Press.

Inglehart, Ronald, Pippa Norris, and Christian Welzel. 2004. "Gender Equality and Democracy." http://pippanorris.com. Retrieved 15 July 2005.

Jaggers, Keith, and Ted Robert Gurr. 1996. *Polity III: Regime Type and Political Authority 1800–1994*. Ann Arbor, MI: Inter-University Consortium for Social and Political Research.

Joekes, Susan P. 1995. *Trade-Related Employment for Women in Industry and Service in Developing Countries*. Occasional Paper No. 5. Geneva: United Nations Research Institute for Social Development (UNRISD).

Kabeer, Naila. 2000. Globalization, Labour Standards and Women's Rights: Dilemmas of Collective Action in an Interdependent World. Paper Produced for the "Globalization, Production and Poverty: Macro, Meso and Micro Level Studies' Project" funded by the Department for International Development (DFID), UK.

Kaplan, Gisela. 1992. *Contemporary Western European Feminism*. New York: New York University Press.

Kolodner, Eric. 1994. *Transnational Corporations: Impediments or Catalysts of Social Development?* Occasional Paper No. 5. World Summit for Social Development. Geneva: United Nations Research Institute for Social Development (UNRISD).

Landman, Todd. 2003. Norms and Rights: A-Non Recursive Model of Human Rights Protection. Paper presented at the annual meeting of the American Political Science Association, Philadelphia, PA.

Landman, Todd. 2005. *Protecting Human Rights: A Global Comparative Study*. Washington, DC: Georgetown University.

Maguire, Daniel C. 2003. *Sacred Rights: The Case for Contraception and Abortion in World Religions*. New York: Oxford University Press.

Markoff, John. 2003. Margins, Centers, and Democracy: The Paradigmatic History of Women's Suffrage. *Signs* 29 (1): 85–118.

Marshall, Monty G. and Keith Jaggers. 2003. Polity IV: Regime Type and Political Authority 1800–2003. Ann Arbor: Inter-University Consortium for Social and Political Research. http://www.cidcm.umd.edu/inscr/polity/.

Matland, Richard E. 1998. Women's Representation in National Legislatures: Developed and Developing Countries. *Legislative Studies Quarterly* 23 (1): 109–25.

Mayer, Ann Elizabeth. 1995. Cultural Particularism as a Bar to Women's Rights: Reflections on the Middle Eastern Experience. In *Women's Rights Human Rights International Feminist Perspectives*, ed. Julie Peters and Andrea Wolper. New York: Routledge.

Mayer, Ann Elizabeth. 1999. Religious Reservations to the Convention on the Elimination of Discrimination Against Women: What Do They Really Mean? In *Religious Fundamentalisms and the Human Rights of Women*, ed. Courtney W. Howland. New York: Palgrave Press.

Mears, Rona R. 1995. The Impact of Globalization on Women and Work in the Americas. Presented at the Women's Rights Committee Inter-American Bar Association Conference, Quito, Ecuador. Available at: http://www.hayboo.com/briefings/mears1.htm.

Merry, Sally Engle. 2002. Women, Violence, and the Human Rights System. In *Women, Gender, and Human Rights: A Global Perspective*, ed. Marjorie Agosin. New Brunswick, NJ: Rutgers University Press.

Meyer, Lisa B. 2001. International Trade Liberalization and Gender Relations in Labor Markets: A Cross-National Analysis 1970–1998. Ph.D. diss., Emory University.

Meyer, Lisa B. 2003. Economic Globalization and Women's Status in the Labor Market: A Cross-National Investigation of Occupational Sex Segregation and Inequality. *Sociological Quarterly* 44 (3): 351–83.

Meyer, William H. 1996. Human Rights and MNCs: Theory Versus Quantitative Analysis. *Human Rights Quarterly* 18 (2): 368–97.

Milner, Wesley T., Steven C. Poe, and David Leblang. 1999. Security Rights, Subsistence Rights, and Liberties: A Theoretical Survey of the Empirical Landscape. *Human Rights Quarterly* 21 (2): 403–43.

Mitchell, Neil J., and James M. McCormick. 1988. Economic and Political Explanations of Human Rights Violations. *World Politics* 40: 476–98.

Moghadam, Valentine M. 1993. Gender Dynamics of Restructuring in the Semi-Periphery. New York: United Nations University World Institute for Development Economics.

Mosley, Layna. 2003. *Global Capital and National Governments*. Cambridge: Cambridge University Press.

Mosley, Layna, and Saika Uno. 2002. Racing to the Bottom or Climbing to the Top? Foreign Direct Investment and Human Rights. Paper presented at the annual meeting of the American Political Science Association, Boston, MA.

Mungall, Michelle. 2002. Neoliberalism and Globalization Work for Patriarchy: More Challenges to the Women's Movement. http://www.pan-edmonton. 12S.com/educate/articles/neoliberalism.htm.

Mwanza, Iris. 2003. How Nations Misbehave: Compliance with Human Rights Treaties in Commonwealth Africa. Paper presented at the annual meeting of the American Political Science Association, Philadelphia, PA.

Newbury, Catherine, and Hannah Baldwin. 2000. *Aftermath: Women in Postgenocide Rwanda*. Working Paper No. 303. Washington, DC: Center for Development Information and Evaluation, U.S. Agency for International Development.

Norris, Pippa, and Ronald Inglehart. 2004. *Sacred and Secular Religion and Politics World-wide*. Cambridge: Cambridge University Press.

Ottawa, Marina S. 2004. Don't Confuse Women's Rights and Democracy. *International Herald Tribune*. March 30.

Peterson, V. Spike. 2003. *A Critical Rewriting of the Global Political Economy*. London and New York: Routledge.

Poe, Steven C., and C. Neal Tate. 1994. Repression of Rights to Personal Integrity in the 1980s: A Global Analysis. *American Political Science Review* 88: 853–72.

Poe, Steven C., C. Neal Tate, and Linda Camp Keith. 1999. Repression of the Human Right to Personal Integrity Revisited: A Global Cross-National Study Covering the Years 1976–1993. *International Studies Quarterly* 43: 291–313.

Poe, Steven C., Diedre Wendel-Blunt, and Karl Ho. 1997. Global Patterns in the Achievement of Women's Human Rights to Equality. *Human Rights Quarterly* 19: 813–35.

Political Handbook of the World. Annual. New York: McGraw-Hill Book Co.

Przeworkski, Adam, Michael E. Alvarez, Jose Antonio Cheibub, and Fernando Limongi. 2003. *Democracy and Development: Political Institutions and Well-being in the World, 1950–1990*. Cambridge: Cambridge University Press.

Reynolds, Andrew. 1999. Women in the Legislatures and Executives of the World: Knocking at the Highest Glass Ceiling. *World Politics* 51 (4): 547–72.

Richards, David L., and Ronald D. Gelleny. 2002. Is it a Small World after All? Globalization and Government Respect for Human Rights in Developing Countries. In *Coping With Globalization Cross-National Patterns in Domestic Governance and Policy Performance*, ed. Steve Chan and James R. Scarritt. London: Frank Cass.

Richards, David L., Ronald D. Gelleny, and David H. Sacko. 2001. Money with a Mean Streak? Foreign Economic Penetration and Government Respect for Human Rights in Developing Countries. *International Studies Quarterly* 45: 219–39.

Richards, David, Ronald Gelleny, and Shawna Sweeney. 2001. Economic Globalization and Women's Rights: Oppression or Opportunity. Paper presented at the annual meeting of the American Political Science Association, San Francisco, CA.

Roberts, J. Timmons, and Amy Hite, eds. 2000. *From Modernization to Globalization Perspectives on Development and Social Change*. Malden, MA: Blackwell.

Schaeffer, Robert K. 2003. *Understanding Globalization: The Social Consequences of Political, Economic, and Environmental Change*, 2nd ed. New York: Rowman & Littlefield.

Sen, Amartya. 2001. *Development as Freedom*. New York: Alfred Knopf.

Simmons, Beth. 2004. International Law Compliance and Human Rights. Paper presented at the annual meeting of the International Studies Association, Montreal, Canada.

Standing, Guy. 1999. Global Feminization through Flexible Labor: a Theme Revisited. *World Development* 27: 583–602.

Steger, Manfred B. 2003. *Globalization: A Very Short Introduction*. Oxford: Oxford University Press.

Stiglitz, Joseph E. 2003. *Globalization and its Discontents*. New York: W. W. Norton & Co.

Stohl, Michael. 1975. War and Domestic Violence: The Case of the United States, 1890–1970. *Journal of Conflict Resolution* 19: 379–416.

Strand, Havard, Lars Wilhelmsen, and Nils Petter Gleditsch. 2002. *Armed Conflict Dataset Codebook*. Version 1.1. Oslo, Norway: International Peace Research Institute.

Sullivan, Donna. 1994. Women's Human Rights and the 1993 World Conference on Human Rights. *American Journal of International Law* 88: 152–67.

Swank, Duane. 2001. Mobile Capital, Democratic Institutions, and the Public Economy in Advanced Industrial Societies. *Journal of Comparative Policy Analysis: Research and Practice* 3: 133–62.

Sweetman, Caroline 1995. "Women and Culture." Oxfam. http://www.oxfam.org.uk. Retrieved 3 October 2003.

Tavits, Margit. 2004. The Size of Government in Majoritarian and Consensus Democracies. *Comparative Political Studies* 37 (3): 340–59.

True, Jacqui, and Michael Mintrom. 2001. Transnational Networks and Policy Diffusion: The Case of Gender Mainstreaming. *International Studies Quarterly* 45: 27–57.

United Nations. 1995. The Beijing Declaration and The Platform for Action: Fourth World Conference on Women, Beijing, China, 4–15 September 1995. New York: Author.

United Nations. 2000. *The World's Women 2000: Trends and Statistics.* New York: Author.

United Nations. 2005. *Convention on the Elimination of All Forms of Discrimination Against Women: State Parties.* Available at: http://www.un.org/womenwatch/daw/cedaw/states.htm.

U.S. State Department. Annual. Country Reports on Human Rights Practices. Washington, DC: U.S. Government Printing Office.

von Stein, Jana. 2004. Making Promises, Keeping Promises: Ratification and Compliance in International Human Rights Law. Paper presented at the annual meeting of the American Political Science Association, Chicago, IL.

Walsh, Martha. 2000. Aftermath: The Impact of Conflict on Women in Bosnia and Herzegovina. Working Paper No. 302, Center for Development Information and Evaluation, U.S. Agency for International Development, Washington, DC.

Wang, Guang-Zhen. 2004. Reproductive Health in the Context of Economic and Democratic Development. *Comparative Sociology* 3 (2): 135–62.

Ward, Kathryn B., and Jean Larson Pyle. 1995. Gender, Industrialization, Transnational Corporations and Development: An Overview of Trends and Patterns. In *From Modernization to Globalization: Perspectives on Development and Social Change*, ed. J. Timmons Roberts and Amy Hite. Oxford: Blackwell.

Waylen, Georgina. 1996. *Gender in Third World Politics.* Boulder, CO: Lynne Rienner.

Weiss, Linda, ed. 2003. *States in the Global Economy: Bringing Domestic Institutions Back In.* Cambridge: Cambridge University Press.

Weldon, S. Laurel. 2002. *Protest, Policy, and the Problem of Violence Against Women: A Cross-National Comparison.* Pittsburgh, PA: University of Pittsburgh Press.

Women's Environment and Development Organization (WEDO). 1998. *Mapping Progress: Assessing Implementation of the Beijing Platform.* New York: WEDO.

World Bank. World Development Indicators on CD-Rom. Washington, DC.

World Bank. 2001. *Engendering Development through Gender Equality in Rights, Resources, and Voice.* New York: Oxford University Press.

Young, Gay, Lucia Fort, and Mona Danner. 1994. Moving from "the Status of Women" to "Gender Inequality": Conceptualization, Social Indicators, and an Empirical Application. *International Sociology* 9: 55–85.

Zweifel, Thomas D., and Patricio Navia. 2000. Democracy, Dictatorship, and Infant Mortality. *Journal of Democracy* 11 (2): 99–114.

APPENDIX A. DESCRIPTIVE STATISTICS

Variable	N	Mean	Std. Dev.	Min	Max
Women's economic rights	3360	1.277844	.6494083	0	3
FDI	3317	1.922855	4.195284	−82.81054	93.71999
Log of trade openness	3171	1.802768	.2445681	.8	2.63
Democracy	3340	4.373795	4.217466	0	10
Endorsement of CEDAW	3408	4.146714	3.314927	0	8
Political secularism	3387	2.166914	.9256679	0	3
Time	3408	11.60387	6.611781	1	23
Islam	3408	.2901995	.4539209	0	1
International conflict	3318	.0963331	.4873714	0	3
Civil conflict	3310	.4074766	.9147216	0	3
Log of population	3384	38423.03	2234746	5.173763	1.30e+08
Log of GDP	2867	3.558578	.4876361	2.518514	4.730621

APPENDIX B. COUNTRY SAMPLE[a]

Afghanistan	Albania	Algeria	Angola
Argentina	Armenia	Australia	Austria
Azerbaijan	Bahrain	Bangladesh	Belarus
Belgium	Belize	Benin	Bhutan
Bolivia	Bosnia-Herzegovina[b]	Botswana	Brazil
Brunei	Bulgaria	Burkina Faso	Burundi
Cambodia	Canada	Cameroon	Central African Republic
Chad	Chile	China	Colombia
Costa Rica	Cote d'Ivoire	Croatia	Cuba
Cyprus	Czech Republic[c]	Democratic Peoples' Rep. of Korea[d]	Democratic Rep. of Congo[e]
Denmark	Dominican Republic	Ecuador	Egypt
El Salvador	Eritrea	Estonia	Ethiopia
Fiji	Finland	France	Gabon
Gambia	Georgia	Germany	Ghana
Greece	Guatemala	Guinea	Guinea-Bissau
Guyana	Haiti	Honduras	Hungary
Iceland	India	Indonesia	Iran
Iraq	Ireland	Israel	Italy
Jamaica	Japan	Jordan	Kazakhstan
Kenya	Kuwait	Laos	Latvia
Lebanon	Lesotho	Liberia	Libya

Lithuania	Luxembourg	Macedonia	Madagascar
Malawi	Malaysia	Mali	Mauritania
Mauritius	Mexico	Moldova	Mongolia
Morocco	Mozambique	Myanmar ^{f}	Namibia
Nepal	Netherlands	New Zealand	Nicaragua
Niger	Nigeria	Norway	Oman
Pakistan	Panama	Papua New Guinea	Paraguay
Peru	Philippines	Poland	Portugal
Qatar	Republic of Korea ^{g}	Republic of Congo	Romania
Russia	Rwanda	Saudi Arabia	Senegal
Sierra Leone	Singapore	Slovakia	Slovenia
Somalia	South Africa	Spain	Sri Lanka
Sudan	Swaziland	Sweden	Syria
Taiwan	Tajikistan	Tanzania	Thailand
Togo	Trinidad and Tobago	Tunisia	Turkey
Turkmenistan	Uganda	Ukraine	United States
United Arab Emirates	United Kingdom	Uruguay	Uzbekistan
Venezuela	Vietnam	Yemen	Yugoslavia_post ^{h}
Zambia	Zimbabwe		

^{a} Information on some countries in my dataset is not available for all years. For example, Lithuania, Latvia, Ukraine, and other Eastern European countries that were formerly part of the Soviet Union did not come into existence as independent states until 1992. Hence, their time coverage is from 1992 to 2003.

^{b} The 1995 Dayton Accords created the independent state of Bosnia and Herzegovina, which was previously one of the constituent republics of Yugoslavia (http://www.ussd.gov).

^{c} The Czech Republic was formerly part of Czechoslovakia. Its name changed when it became formally independent from the Soviet Union.

^{d} The Democratic People's Republic of Korea is also known as North Korea.

^{e} The Democratic Republic of Congo is formerly known as Zaire.

^{f} Myanmar is also formally known as Burma.

^{g} The Republic of Korea is also known as South Korea.

^{h} Yugoslavia_post is now called Serbia and Montenegro, which is a constitutional republic consisting of the relatively large Republic of Serbia and the much smaller Republic of Montenegro (http://www.state.gov/g/drl/rls/hrrpt/2004/41706.htm).

APPENDIX C. STATE PARTIES TO THE CEDAW

Afghanistan	Albania	Algeria*	Angola	Argentina*
Armenia	Australia*	Austria*	Azerbaijan	Bahrain
Bangladesh*	Belarus	Belgium*	Belize	Benin
Bhutan	Bolivia	Bosnia-Herzegovina	Botswana	Brazil*
Bulgaria	Burkina Faso	Burundi	Cambodia	Cameroon
Canada	CAR	Chad	Chile*	China*
Colombia	Rep. of Congo	Costa Rica	Cote d'Ivoire	Croatia
Cuba*	Cyprus*	Czech Republic	Democratic People's Republic of Korea	Democratic Republic of the Congo
Denmark	Dijbouti	Dominican Republic	Ecuador	Egypt*
El Salvador*	Eritrea	Estonia	Ethiopia*	Fiji*
Finland	France	Gabon	Gambia	Georgia
Germany*	Ghana	Greece	Guatemala	Guinea
Guinea-Bissau	Guyana	Haiti	Honduras	Hungary
Iceland	India*	Indonesia*	Iraq*	Ireland*
Israel*	Italy	Jamaica*	Japan	Jordan*
Kazakhstan	Kenya	Kuwait*	Kyrgyzstan	Laos
Latvia	Lebanon*	Lesotho*	Liberia	Libya*
Lithuania	Luxembourg*	Madagascar	Malawi	Malaysia*
Mali	Mauritania	Mauritius*	Mexico	Mongolia
Morocco*	Mozambique	Myanmar*	Namibia	Nepal
Netherlands*	New Zealand	Nicaragua	Niger	Nigeria
Norway	Pakistan*	Panama	Papua New Guinea	Paraguay
Peru	Philippines	Poland*	Portugal	Republic of Korea
Romania*	Russia	Rwanda	Saudi Arabia*	Senegal
Serbia and Montenegro	Seychelles	Sierra Leone	Singapore*	Slovakia
Slovenia	South Africa	Spain*	Sri Lanka	Swaziland
Sweden	Switzerland*	Syria	Tajikistan	Thailand
The Former Yugoslav Rep. of Macedonia	Togo	Trinidad and Tobago*	Tunisia*	Turkey*
Turkmenistan	Uganda	Ukraine	United Arab Emirates	United Kingdom*
United Republic of Tanzania	United States	Uruguay	Uzbekistan	Venezuela*
Vietnam*	Yemen*	Zambia	Zimbabwe	

Those countries with an asterisk next to their names have current reservations to the Convention. This does not include countries that have issued reservations that were subsequently withdrawn. (http://www.un.org/womenwatch/daw/cedaw/states.htm).

APPENDIX D. DATA APPENDIX

The CIRI economic rights scale measures two things: (1) the extensiveness of laws pertaining to women's rights and (2) actual government practices toward women (i.e., how effectively does government implement or enforce these laws). Coders were instructed to classify the attainment of women's economic rights in four categories using two separate measures, as follows:

(0) There are no economic rights for women under law and systematic discrimination based on sex may be built into the law. The government tolerates a high level of discrimination against women.

(1) There are some economic rights for women under law. However, in practice, the government *does not* enforce the laws effectively or enforcement of laws is weak. The government tolerates a *moderate level* of discrimination against women.

(2) There are some economic rights for women under law. In practice, the government *does* enforce these laws effectively. However, the government still tolerates a *low level* of discrimination against women.

(3) All or nearly all of women's economic rights are guaranteed by law. In practice, the government fully and vigorously enforces these laws. The government tolerates none or almost no discrimination against women.

Multiple coders read and analyzed the information presented in the U.S. State Department reports for each of the years from 1981 to 2003 to ensure reliability and validity of the women's rights measure. Coders then coded the countries as belonging to one of the above four categories based on detailed coding instructions. In some instances, coders had to follow a three-stage coding process for women's economic rights due to occasional lack of comprehensive information in the U.S. State Department reports. During the first stage, coders were asked to base their coding decision upon both laws and government practices or enforcement of these laws. When information on these criteria is missing or is insufficient to make a judgment, coders were instructed to follow a second stage in which they based their coding decision on both laws for women's rights and the level of societal discrimination against women. In rare instances in which there was insufficient information to make a coding judgment following these first two stages, coders were asked to base their decision on the level of societal discrimination against women. Absent other relevant information, the level of societal discrimination should serve as an approximate measure of women's rights situation. Countries where societal discrimination is rampant against women usually make little effort to enforce laws pertaining to their rights. I rechecked a large number of country-years for this measure to ensure integrity of the scores, and also refereed differences not easily resolved by other coders.

Conceptually, my indicator of women's economic rights measures both women's absolute status (i.e., comparisons among women) and their relative status (i.e., comparisons between men and women). Focusing on the former allows us to ask such questions as whether women have the right to free choice of employment or profession and the right to gainful employment. Focusing on the latter allows us to ask important questions such as whether women receive equal pay for equal work vis-à-vis men, whether they have penetrated the highest status occupations, and whether they experience equality in hiring and promotion practices. Focusing on both absolute and relative status is important because absolute improvements offer a good benchmark for comparison of women's rights within countries over time and also between countries over time, and focusing on relative status tells us how far women have to go in terms of achieving gender parity with men in the economic realm.

12 Economic Rights and Extraterritorial Obligations

SIGRUN I. SKOGLY AND MARK GIBNEY

I. INTRODUCTION

One of the great disappointments concerning human rights is the way in which these rights are declared to be "universal," at the same time that the protection of those rights (and even responsibility for the commission of human rights violations) has been severely limited by territorial considerations.[1] In this chapter, we argue that this is an unfortunate misreading of international human rights law. A person's home state is certainly the first place to look to in terms of the protection of economic rights – and all other human rights as well. This point is not being challenged. What *is* being challenged is the refusal to look any further than this, notwithstanding the dictates of international human rights law.

The term "extraterritorial" effect/application/obligation in international law refers to acts that are taken by one actor (state) that have some kind of effect within another country's territory with or without this second country's implicit or explicit agreement. Extraterritoriality within international human rights law,

---

[1] What we are referring to here, in particular, is the attempt by Western states to place territorial limitations on where their human rights obligations begin and end. The most notable example of this is the Bush administration's position that the protection of U.S. domestic law does not reach as far as Guantánamo Bay, Cuba, where "enemy combatants" are being held. In *Rasul v. Bush*, 542 U.S. 466 (2004), the U.S. Supreme Court held that a particular group of enemy combatants being confined at Guantánamo Bay, Cuba did have the right to file a habeas petition in a federal court in the United States. There are, however, several things about the holding and its aftermath that are unsettling. One is that it is not clear if the Court's ruling would apply to any other military base in the world, especially given the kind of "sovereignty" that the United States exercises over Guantánamo Bay, Cuba. Second, there has been some recent discussion in the U.S. Senate that would amend the habeas statute at issue to overturn the Court's decision. Notwithstanding their criticism of the American "black hole" in Guantánamo Bay, the European states have tried to adopt the same position: that the European Convention for the Protection of Human Rights and Fundamental Freedoms does not apply outside of Europe. This issue was directly challenged by a group of Yugoslavian citizens (which is not a Contracting State) alleging that their Convention rights were violated during a NATO bombing mission over Belgrade in 1999. In *Bankovic v. Belgium* (admissibility), App. No. 52207/99 ECHR (2001), the European Court of Human Rights agreed, holding that the claimants were not within the "jurisdiction" of the Convention for purposes of article 1 (Altiparmak 2004; Roxstrom et al. 2005).

then, concerns actions or omissions by one state that have an effect on the human rights of individuals in another state – with or without this other state's agreement.[2] This effect may be positive or negative, in that such actions or omissions by foreign states may contribute positively to the enjoyment of human rights; or alternatively, they may result in a deteriorated human rights situation, and even human rights violations. Recent examples of "extraterritoriality" would include the human rights protection (or lack thereof) for Iraqi civilians under the occupation of Coalition Forces; the effect that support for or rejection of family planning programmes through United Nations agencies by major state donors would have on the right to health of individuals in poor countries; situations in which one state applies economic sanctions against another state, which negatively affects the ability of this other state to feed its population; and, finally, the manner in which funding by foreign states of massive hydroelectric power projects may directly result in the violation of a number of human rights, including the right to housing, to food, to education and so forth.

The acceptance of extraterritorial human rights obligations has been rather controversial from both a legal and a political point of view. There are a number of reasons for this controversy, which include the perception that this is contrary to the equality and sovereignty of states; that it represents extraterritorial jurisdiction beyond what classic international law accepts; and that states find that this may put (undue) constraints on their domestic and foreign policies.

The authors will also add that part of the reason for this controversy is a lack of understanding of the content of extraterritorial human rights obligations, and that through a demystification of these obligations, much may be achieved in terms of further acceptance. The moral – but also legal – basis for these obligations is really very simple: it is a matter of taking responsibility for one's own actions or omissions.

During the course of the past two decades, there has been a growing recognition that many activities in which states are involved may have detrimental human rights effects in other countries, and this is evidenced not least through the attention that these issues have been given by the UN human rights system: the UN Human Rights Commission and Sub-Commission, the High Commissioner for Human Rights, and the various treaty-based committees. Through various studies, reports and statements on such issues as human rights and trade, intellectual property rights, globalization and structural adjustment, there appears to be at least some growing understanding that events taking place beyond the territory and the control of an individual state can have a serious impact on the human rights situation of the people within that state.

Law, however, appears to be a different matter, in that the recognition of extraterritorial obligations has been slow and halting. What is so unusual and unfortunate about this state of affairs – aside from the human suffering that it has engendered – is that many international law instruments (hard and soft law alike) have specific provisions relating to extraterritorial obligations. Although human *rights* are often divided into groups – such as civil, political, economic, social, and cultural – by their very nature the corresponding human rights *obligations* do not vary

---

[2] This is an important qualification, as states cannot justify breaches of extraterritorial human rights obligations by referring to agreements by the territorial state.

depending on which rights are addressed but, rather, the situation or context in which they are applicable. Nevertheless, in this chapter we will discuss extraterritorial obligations as they are relevant to economic rights more explicitly.[3] Part II examines some of the extraterritorial obligations to be found in the language of the United Nations Charter and the Covenant on Economic, Social, and Cultural Rights. Part III extends this by setting forth the argument that *all* of international human rights law is based on the principle of extraterritorial obligations – negative and positive alike – although, to date, this idea has not been commonly accepted by human rights adjudicatory bodies. Finally, Part IV sets forth the extent of states' extraterritorial obligations.

II. SPECIFIC PROVISIONS RELATING TO EXTRATERRITORIAL OBLIGATIONS

The United Nations Charter

International law entered a new era with the adoption of the UN Charter. For the first time, the individual became a subject of international law in terms of having his/her rights directly recognized in an international treaty. With the near-universal ratification of the UN Charter and membership in the UN, this principle is now widely recognized, and according to the Charter and the International Bill of Rights, all individuals are to have their rights and fundamental freedoms protected.

In analyzing the content of the Charter, it is clear that in certain areas (for instance, with regard to the prohibition of the use of force), it establishes rather traditional reciprocal obligations, whereas it also contains provisions that are of a different character – provisions that contribute to a new "public order" (Orakhelashvili 2003, 531). Among these provisions are those guaranteeing respect and protection for human rights.

Furthermore, the International Bill of Human Rights, with the Universal Declaration as its "flagship," confirms this status of human rights as something different from traditional international law. For one thing, it develops the content of human rights, and the covenants further provide the obligations of states in regard to these standards. It has been held that human rights law "comprises more than mere reciprocal engagements between contracting States" (*Ireland v. UK*, ¶ 291), and that the nature of such conventions establishes a "public order," which "are of an objective nature and protect the fundamental rights of individuals than the interests of contracting states" (Orakhelashvili 2003, 531).[4]

---

[3] The division of rights into categories is controversial, and many different kinds of categories have been proposed by various authors. Whether a right is classified as economic, social, or indeed civil or political may vary. Is the right to health a social or an economic right? Is the right to education a civil, political or social right? In principle, we do not find these discussions very helpful. Nevertheless, in this chapter, we will focus on rights such as those included in the International Covenant on Economic, Social and Cultural Rights.

[4] This is clearly implied by the preambular statement in the American Convention on Human Rights, from 1978, where it is stated: "*Recognizing* that the essential rights of man are not derived from one's being a national of a certain state, but are based upon attributes of the human personality, and that they therefore justify international protection in the form of a convention reinforcing or complementing the protection provided by the domestic law of the American states."

Inexplicably enough, however, little attention has been given to the possibility that the UN Charter provides human rights obligations beyond a state's own borders. Commonly, the Charter is criticized for not being specific enough in terms of human rights and the corresponding obligations. In our view, the Charter is quite clear with respect to extraterritorial obligations.

Article 1 of the Charter establishes the purposes of the organization, and as members of the UN each individual state is bound by the Charter and has obligations to assist in fulfilling these obligations. The fundamental principle of universal and international protection of human rights is provided in article 1:

> The Purposes of the United Nations are:...(3) To achieve *international cooperation* in solving international problems of an economic, social, cultural or humanitarian character, and in *promoting and encouraging respect for human rights and for fundamental freedoms for all*... (emphasis added).

The inclusion of the passage that the organization's purpose is *inter alia* to "achieve international cooperation" in relationship to the substantive content of the rest of the paragraph is not insignificant in relation to the question of extraterritorial human rights obligations. If international cooperation is to be achieved, the members of the UN will have an obligation to contribute to this cooperation, which is aimed at addressing problems of economic, social, humanitarian and human rights character. Without Member States' contribution to this international cooperation, it would be impossible to achieve, as the organization can do no more than what the Member States are willing to contribute to. A refusal by Member States to contribute to international cooperation to achieve the purposes of the organization, as provided for in Article 1 of the UN Charter, would constitute a breach of obligations. However, this contribution to cooperation is not only a matter of quantity of cooperation but is equally a question of the quality of any international cooperation taking place. If, however, member states claim that human rights obligations are merely territorial, this would disregard the principle of "international cooperation" in article 1.

Furthermore, articles 55 and 56 provide that the United Nations shall promote "*universal* respect for, and observance of, human rights and fundamental freedoms for all" and that this shall be done through "joint and separate action in co-operation with the Organization." These articles are commonly referred to in UN documents when the international promotion of human rights is discussed. However, there has been little interpretation as to the obligations that stem from these two articles.

In an elaboration of the legislative history and interpretation of article 56, it is explained that the text is a compromise between a wording suggested by Australia and the views of the United States in the drafting process (Simma 1994, 793). Australia had proposed that "all members of the U.N. should pledge to take action, on both national and international levels, for the purpose of securing for all peoples, including their own, such goals as improved labour standards" (ibid.), and thus suggested a formulation in which the pledge would mean that the "members would both co-operate internationally and act within their own countries to pursue the economic and social objectives of the Organization, in their own way and without interference in their domestic affairs by the Organization" (ibid.). This was opposed by the United States, as it claimed that all that could be included in the Charter was to provide for "collective action and thus it could not oblige a nation to take separate action because that would constitute an infringement upon the internal affairs of the member states" (ibid.).

Thus, the interpretation of the article has tended to accept a compromise of the two positions, where the:

rather limited obligatory function of Article 56 is [...] the result of the wording of Article 55, to which it refers. The latter only describes purposes (and not substantive obligations) to be achieved by means of co-operation. To this extent, Article 56 can thus only create substantive obligations (as opposed to procedural obligations) in so far as Article 55 contains a corresponding basis in that respect. (ibid., 794)

However, Simma holds that article 55(c) contains substantive obligations with respect to human rights, and it can thus be held that in terms of human rights articles 55 and 56, in conjunction, establish obligations to take action to promote the respect for human rights. According to this interpretation, there is a firm obligation for states to act individually, as well as collectively, to promote respect for human rights. What is important to note is that the opposition by the United States was not with respect to international obligations but, rather, that the UN Charter could not prescribe what states should do domestically. As domestic human rights obligations have now gained universal acceptance (or close to it), it is rather paradoxical that international (or extraterritorial) obligations have become the source of some controversy.

What remains uncertain, however, is the meaning of "jointly." In Simma's commentary on the UN Charter, the meaning of the term is not substantially discussed. Oddly enough, in this seminal work covering fourteen hundred pages, only three are devoted to article 56. However, jointly could imply action through the United Nations as a way to practically carry out the organization's mandate, in recognition that the organization may not be able to fulfill its purposes without the joint commitment of the membership. However, this understanding would lead to an interpretation of article 56 that would be too narrow. The article provides that this joint action shall take place "in cooperation with the organization." If it was intended to imply a narrow obligation to promote respect for human rights through the work of the United Nations only, one would have expected the wording to reflect this, for instance, by saying "joint and separate action through the United Nations." This, however, is not the wording that was chosen. Rather, a wider formulation is used, and the understanding of "joint" will therefore imply an obligation to act with at least one other state to promote respect for human rights, and also that this implies an obligation to cooperate with the United Nations in this regard (Simma 1994, 948). The larger point is that joint action has a clear extraterritorial element to it: only one of the states acting "jointly" may at any given time address the promotion of the respect for human rights domestically – all the other states involved in the joint action will logically be addressing human rights respect in another state.

Furthermore, article 56 not only calls for joint action but indeed also "separate" action in cooperation with the United Nations. This, seen in conjunction with the provision in article 55(c), which calls for "*universal*" respect of human rights, further strengthens arguments for human rights obligations beyond national borders for individual states. As the article uses the term "universal" rather than "domestic," it is submitted that this has extraterritorial implications, and that it adds to the Charter's nondiscrimination principle in that states shall promote respect for human rights not only to their own population but, indeed, universally as well.

The International Covenant on Economic, Social, and Cultural Rights

The International Covenant on Economic, Social, and Cultural Rights is particularly important to any discussion on extraterritorial human rights obligations (Skogly 2003). Not only does article 2(1) of the Covenant refer specifically to the State Parties' obligations to take steps "individually and through international assistance and cooperation" for the realization of the rights guaranteed, but it also omits the reference to "jurisdiction" or "territory" that is common in other human rights instruments.[5]

Notwithstanding the language in article 2(1), the understanding of the content of the obligations stemming from this provision has not been significantly developed.[6] Still, in recent years, the ESCR Committee has begun to include explicit and implicit references to this provision in their General Comments and in some of the questioning of state delegations that has taken place, and finally, in their concluding observations to states' reports. We examine some of these in Part IV.

The drafting history of article 2(1) is quite instructive. Most noteworthy, although there was some discussion as to the inclusion of the passage "international assistance and cooperation" in the article, the discussions in the Commission on Human Rights and in the General Assembly's Third Committee were not conclusive with respect to the drafting parties' intentions. Yet, what seemed quite clear is that international cooperation and assistance were seen as necessary if the Covenant's rights were to be realized. Indeed, the source of most of the discussion was the nature of this cooperation, and whether the added provision of "especially economic and technical" was too limited (UN 1965; Skogly 2006).

---

[5] See, for example, article 2 in the International Covenant on Civil and Political Rights; article 1 of the European Convention for the Protection of Human Rights and Fundamental Freedoms; article 1 of the American Convention on Human Rights. Note, however, that the African Charter on Human and Peoples' Rights omits any reference to jurisdiction and/or territorial application. Rather, article 1 of that Convention only refers to the obligations of the States Parties to "take legislative and other measures to give effect [to the rights enshrined in the Charter]."

[6] In General Comment No. 3 (1990), the Committee on Economic, Social and Cultural Rights referred to this passage as indicating that "available resources" included those available through international assistance (para. 13). In addition, that read in conjunction with articles 55 and 56 of the UN Charter, "international cooperation for development and thus for the realization of economic, social and cultural rights is an obligation of all States. It is particularly incumbent upon those States which are in a position to assist others in this regard" (para. 14). The Limburg Principles (paras. 29–34) deal with this passage in article 2(1), but use rather general terms, such as "international co-operation and assistance shall give priority to the realization of all human rights . . ."; and that it should contribute to the establishment of a social and international order conducive to human rights, and so on. There is no clear indication as to the content of obligations for states. Additionally, a briefing paper on the content of "international assistance and cooperation" in article 2 was given to the Committee in 2003 (Bueno de Mesquita 2003).

Furthermore, little attention has been given to the difference of this provision from that in article 2(1) of the ICCPR, which reads: "Each State Party ... undertakes to respect and to ensure to all individuals within its territory and subject to its jurisdiction ... " Many have commented on the division of the Covenants into two instruments and argued that this was a result of the different nature of the rights contained in the two covenants: that civil and political rights could be implemented immediately, whereas economic, social, and cultural rights are more of a long-term/programmatic aspiration. Be that as it may (that discussion lies outside the present focus), few, if any, have commented on the fact that the need for international assistance and cooperation was seen as essential for the realization of economic and social rights, and that this was part of the original obligation for economic, social, and cultural rights, even in the draft from 1951 that contained all categories of rights (UN 1951).[7] Consequently, international assistance and cooperation was included as one of the means of realization of the right in the original (and subsequent) general obligation provisions of the Covenant. However, more than fifty years later, this has proven to be one of the more controversial aspects of the document.

III. EXTRATERRITORIAL OBLIGATIONS AS A BASIS FOR *ALL* INTERNATIONAL HUMAN RIGHTS LAW

In the previous section, we examined specific language in the United Nations Charter and in the Covenant on Economic, Social, and Cultural Rights to show that extraterritorial obligations are an essential part of both legal instruments. In this section, we push this further, and argue that international human rights treaty law, by definition, is premised on the notion of extraterritorial obligations. Yet, what we also show is the manner in which territorial considerations continue to limit thinking in this area.

The Meaning and Purpose of Human Rights

Individuals enjoy human rights not because they are members of a particular society, but by simple virtue of their humanity. And, for their part, although states certainly have human rights obligations to their own citizens, their obligations do not suddenly and arbitrarily end at their national borders. The entire premise behind all international human rights instruments is that Swedes are not only concerned with the wellbeing of other Swedes, and Nigerians are not solely concerned with the wellbeing of other Nigerians, and so on. Rather, in becoming a party to an international human rights treaty, the Nigerian government and the Nigerian people are proclaiming (legally and otherwise) that they are also concerned with the wellbeing of Swedes, as well as nationals of all other countries. It is tempting

---

[7] It is also interesting to note that during the drafting of the Convention on the Rights of the Child, the provision in what became article 4 – which provides for international assistance and cooperation in relationship to economic, social, and cultural rights – was not a cause for debate among the drafting parties. Rather, it seems to have been taken for granted that this was a necessary and essential part of the realization of these rights (UN Centre for Human Rights 1995).

to say that it is simply not possible to interpret international human rights law in any other way, yet we know from decades of experience that just the opposite has been true. If human rights protection was something that individual states could (and would) do individually, there would be no need for any international conventions. Stripped to their barest essentials, what each one of these treaties represents is nothing less than this: that everyone has an ethical as well as a legal obligation to protect the human rights of all other people. In that way, extraterritorial obligations are not something that is peripheral to human rights. Rather, extraterritorial obligations are an essential component of human rights. What is deeply troubling, then, is that even the human rights community itself continues to struggle with an idea that goes to the very core of human rights.

The irony in this is that on one level we seem fully aware of our increased interaction and dependence on one another. Few, then, deny the phenomenon of globalization or its meaning. Yet, we continue to live in a world that remains myopically, and tragically, state-centric when it comes to human rights protection. Human rights are declared to be universal and yet, perversely enough, whether the inhabitants of a state receive these "universal" rights appears to be dependent on whether *this* particular state has ratified *this* particular human rights treaty or not. More than this, as we will see in a moment, not only has the protection of human rights remained solidly entrenched behind sovereign walls, but even responsibility for the commission of human rights violations has come to be severely and unduly restricted by territorial considerations. Paradoxically, one of the most fundamental principles of human rights – that of nondiscrimination – is overridden by national borders. The point is that notwithstanding the promise of a world of universal human rights, there continues to be very little that is "international" about international human rights. The most devastating consequence of this approach to human rights is that vast numbers of human beings have been left without human rights protection.

Territory and Negative Obligations

Because we live in a world of nation-states, perhaps it should not be totally surprising that human rights have come to be subsumed into the broader social contract between rulers and citizens within each society. The problem is that human rights are not based on contractarian or communitarian values, but on universal values. Certainly, an individual's state plays a central role in the human rights protection of its citizens; it is not being suggested otherwise. However, when Algeria protects the human rights of its citizens, it does so not because they are Algerian but because they are human beings. Moreover, because it is always lawful for the Algerian government to act within its own territorial borders (and seldom, if ever, lawful to act outside those same borders), it is natural to expect that the Algerian government will serve as the primary source or means of human rights protection for individuals residing within that state. Any other mechanism for human rights protection would not only be grossly inefficient, but it would often find itself beset with international tension as well.

The problem is that rather than serving as facilitators for human rights protection, state borders have served as barriers to that end. In many respects, this is easier to see using Henry Shue's dichotomy between negative and positive duties. Shue writes: "A duty is either negative or positive. It if is negative, it requires us not to do things. If it is positive, it requires us to do or provide things" (Shue 1988, 688).

Let us begin with the former. Negative duties are universal, which is to say that every person (as well as every state) has a duty to every other person not to cause harm. What does not matter, or at least what should not matter, is where this harm takes place. This duty not to cause harm or not to deprive persons of what is due to them would seem to be self evident and uncontroversial. The problem is that international human rights law has struggled mightily with this notion of negative obligations, and the primary reason for this is the continuing domination of territorial considerations and notions of inviolate state sovereignty. What we are left with is a rather bizarre form of human rights protection, in which the duty not to harm has become so restricted by territorial considerations that it ultimately offers very little protection – at least to people in other lands.

Consider the issue of the right to food. Under international law, a state is prohibited from depriving people of food (citizens and noncitizens alike) within its territorial borders. The problem is that, after this, there continues to be enormous uncertainty in the law (Nahapetian 2002). For example, does the prohibition against food deprivation extend so far as prohibit a state from closing its borders for food export, knowing that vulnerable groups in a neighboring state may die of starvation?

Or take another example: the right to health. One state offers to assist another state in the implementation of health policies, and provides finance for hospitals. However, the state that provides the assistance rejects the home state's priorities of creating a number of small, primary care centers in rural areas, and insists on supporting high tech hospitals in the capital city only, where the equipment should be bought from the assisting state. If child mortality rates increase in the countryside, as seems quite likely, is it not disinguous to say that the "assisting" state has not played at least some role in bringing about this end?

The problem is that the law seems to point in the opposite direction. The leading case is the International Court of Justice's (ICJ) holding in *Nicaragua v. United States*. In this case, the Court held the U.S. government responsible for internationally wrongful acts carried out directly by American agents. However, the Court also held that the United States was not responsible for *any* of the violations committed by the Contras – a counterrevolutionary group heavily armed and equipped by the United States – on the rather incredible grounds that the U.S. government had not directed and controlled virtually every aspect of the Contras' actions.[8]

The larger point in all this is that negative obligations – the duty not to harm – would seem to present the easiest and most straightforward examples of extraterritorial state responsibility. Yet, three of the most widely respected judicial bodies in the world – the ICJ, the U.S. Supreme Court and the European Court of Human Rights – have allowed a very sharp distinction to be made between the domestic

---

[8] For example, at one point in its ruling the Court wrote:

> In light of the evidence and material available to it, the Court is not satisfied that *all* the operations launched by the contra force, at *every* stage of the conflict, reflected strategy and tactics *wholly* devised by the United States (ICJ 1986 ¶ 106) (emphasis added).

practices of states, on the one hand, and what these same states are allowed to do when they are operating outside their territorial borders, on the other. The sum of it is that although we proclaim the universality of human rights, we have created a system in which human rights protection has come to be severely limited by territorial considerations. In essence, "universality" is only applied to the enjoyment of rights, not to the corresponding obligations. Rights without obligations are generally considered an illusion. As argued by Shue: "A proclamation of a right is not the fulfillment of a right, any more than an airplane schedule is a flight" (1980, 15).

Territory and Positive Obligations

Just as the notion of territory continues to cause a great deal of confusion (and, ultimately, harm) in the realm of negative obligations, it also has caused enormous problems with our conceptualization of positive obligations – the duty to protect. Although it has repeatedly and convincingly been demonstrated that the dichotomy will not normally hold true, civil and political rights are often associated with negative duties, whereas economic, social and cultural rights are usually associated with positive duties.[9] Although negative duties are invariably simpler than positive duties – reflecting the difference between not doing something and doing something – it is important to note that negative duties are universal, meaning that they are owed to everyone, whereas positive duties are not. Individuals cannot be expected to save the world by themselves, and no state has this duty either. Shue (1988, 690) stresses the importance of recognizing the limitations that need to be placed on positive duties:

> Universal rights . . . entail not universal duties but full coverage. Full coverage can be provided by a division of labor among duty-bearers. All the negative duties fall upon everyone, but the positive duties need to be divided up and assigned among bearers in some reasonable way.

This division of labor will imply that states have a negative duty to refrain from actions that will violate human rights abroad, including economic rights. Furthermore, positive obligations to fulfill human rights abroad are limited by jurisdictional and other practical obstacles, and indeed the nature of influence the foreign

---

[9] Leonard Rubenstein, the Executive Director of Physicians for Human Rights, has written recently this about economic, social and cultural rights: "it is undeniable that the central feature of economic, social and cultural rights is their imposition of an affirmative obligation on states to meet basic needs, and this requires strategies and methods to assure that states do just that." He continues:

> To realize those rights, it is necessary but not sufficient for a state to stop doing something bad, such as engaging in discrimination or acting arbitrarily. The state must also take concerted, rational, well-planned steps forward to finance and build housing, health clinics, and schools; hire teachers, doctors, and nurses; furnish supplies; and much more. Moreover, a human rights approach to meeting human needs is not content merely with more housing, more clinics, and more teachers; it has a lot to say about how they are provided, whom they reach, what their implications are for others, and whether people affected by the decisions participate in making them. (2004, 851–52)

Compare this with works confirming that civil and political rights also require governmental provisions for their fulfillment as expressed *inter alia* through the Maastricht Guidelines on Violations of Economic, Social, and Cultural Rights (adopted in Maastricht in 1997), principle 6 (Eide 1989, 36; Skogly 2001; Nowak 1997, 86).

state has over decisions impacting human rights enjoyment. This will be further addressed later.

This notion of an international division of labor should jibe nicely with the "international cooperation" and "joint and separate action" language in the UN Charter and the "individually and through international assistance and co-operation" language in the Covenant on Economic, Social, and Cultural Rights. Unfortunately, however, this has not been the case. What has happened instead is that states have used the diffuse nature of positive duties as a means of ignoring their duties to protect the economic, social and cultural rights of all people.[10] The point is that while positive duties differ in kind from negative duties, states still have an obligation, and a legal obligation at that. We now turn to what these obligations might entail.

IV. THE EXTENT OF STATES' EXTRATERRITORIAL OBLIGATIONS

Within the framework of the passage on "international assistance and cooperation" in article 2(1), we will devote the final parts of this chapter to consider three key issues for the extraterritorial application of the Covenant on Economic, Social, and Cultural Rights: first, whether the requirements of "international assistance and cooperation" imply the same obligations abroad as at home; second, whether the wording of the Covenant implies that the extraterritorial application of economic, social and cultural rights should be less controversial than such application for civil and political rights; and, third, the positive and negative content of these obligations.

Domestic and International Application

In a perfect world, one might want to advocate that as human rights are universal – there should be no difference in obligations based on the geographic location of an individual. Thus, for instance, France would have equal responsibility for the human rights enjoyment for individuals in Nepal as it does for those residing in Paris. This is obviously not the case. If one is realistic, France will have more human rights obligations toward its own population than people in other countries. This follows both from general principles in international law, and from a utilitarian perspective of what is possible for states. This utilitarian perspective has been reflected in the case law of the Human Rights Committee (*Lópes Burgos v. Uruguay*) and also the European and the Inter-American Courts of Human Rights, in that these bodies have accepted that the territorial limitations for human rights obligations are not absolute but, rather, where states are exercising control over individuals abroad, their human rights obligations follow (Altiparmak 2004). This

---

[10] Certainly, there is nothing "diffuse" about the extraterritorial obligations set forth in the Millennium Declaration:

> We recognize that, in addition to our separate responsibilities to our individual societies, we have a collective responsibility to uphold the principles of human dignity, equality and equity at the global level. As leaders we have a duty therefore to all the world's people, especially the most vulnerable and, in particular, the children of the world, to whom the future belongs. (United Nations 2000, ¶ I(2))

would certainly also be the case for economic, social, and cultural rights – if states have effective control over the enjoyment of these rights extraterritorially, they will also have obligations to protect those rights. Thus, if Norway provides food aid to the Sudan, for example, and the food provided is contaminated and people die as a result of eating this food, Norway will have failed in its obligations. In such a situation, the obligation would be the same as if the Norwegian government had provided contaminated food to a state-run nursing home domestically (Skogly 2006). Thus, the "test" as to whether extraterritorial obligations are triggered will, to a large extent, relate to the level of control or influence that a foreign state has (Happold 2003).

Are the Extraterritorial Obligations with Respect to Economic, Social, and Cultural Rights Less Controversial than They Are in Other Human Rights Treaties?

Most human rights treaties contain provisions with regard to the jurisdictional and/or territorial application of that particular treaty. However, the International Covenant on Economic, Social and Cultural Rights does not contain any such language. Yet, somehow extraterritorial obligations for these rights are as controversial, arguably more controversial, than they are for civil and political rights. This is a paradox in need of an explanation. One reason may be the implementation machinery, which is less individually focused than what is the case for many other human rights treaties. The Committee on Economic, Social, and Cultural Rights is not (yet) able to consider individual complaints, and much of the Committee's attention is put on indicators and benchmarks that are less of an individual nature. Therefore, the Committee has not been "confronted" with specific cases that clearly display the extraterritorial nature of human rights violations.[11]

Are Extraterritorial Obligations both Negative and Positive in Nature?

The wording "international assistance and cooperation" in the Covenant is often associated with positive obligations to provide assistance, and this may have resulted in resentment from governments. However, it is important to recognize that extraterritorial obligations are of a negative as well as a positive nature. In terms of negative obligations, international assistance and cooperation – or, indeed, other extraterritorial activities of states influencing the enjoyment of economic, social, and cultural rights – implies a duty on states to refrain from actions that may adversely affect the enjoyment of these rights. Therefore, extraterritorial obligations do not necessarily call for provisions through international assistance and cooperation, but equally that the international assistance and cooperation that states engage in through their normal foreign policies (be it development assistance,

---

[11] An exception to this is clearly displayed in the Committee's discussions of the report presented to them by Israel. In the latest Concluding Observations (2003), the Committee deals with, and criticizes, Israel's view that the Covenant does not apply to the Occupied Territories. This view of the Committee was accepted and upheld by the International Court of Justice in paragraph 112 of its 9 July 2004 Advisory Opinion on the Legal Consequences of the Construction of a Wall in the Occupied Palestinian Territory.

trade, military cooperation, etc.) should be of a nature and quality that does not adversely affect the enjoyment of economic, social, and cultural rights.

This negative obligation corresponds to the obligation to *respect* human rights, as fully developed by the Economic, Social, and Cultural Rights Committee, and it implicitly builds on articles 55 and 56 of the UN Charter. When the Charter provides that the purposes of the United Nations are to promote and encourage "respect for human rights and for fundamental freedoms," and to this end, to take "joint and separate action to promote universal respect for, and observance of human rights and fundamental freedoms," to understand this as only relating to domestic and not extraterritorial acts (such as international cooperation) is to provide too narrow an interpretation. As held by Simma: "Article 56...does require that Member States co-operate with the UN in a constructive way; obstructive policies are thus precluded" (Simma 2002, 942). This approach indicates a negative obligation to refrain from obstructing, and a positive obligation to cooperate in a constructive way.

The Committee has recognized this obligation to *respect* in extraterritorial activities in several of its General Comments. For instance, in General Comment No. 12 on the Right to Adequate Food (1999, ¶ 37), the Committee holds that states should refrain at all times from food embargoes that endanger the conditions for food production and access to food in other countries. Similarly, in the General Comment No. 14 on the Right to Health (2000, ¶ 41), the Committee has concluded that States "should refrain at all times from imposing embargoes or similar measures restricting the supply of another State with adequate medicines and medical equipment. Restrictions on such goods should never be used as an instrument of political and economic pressure." Even more clearly, the Committee held in General Comment No. 8 (1997, ¶ 7) that in situations of economic sanctions, the target state "and the international community itself [shall] do everything possible to protect at least the core content of the economic, social and cultural rights of the affected peoples of that State."

Second, the obligation to *protect* in an extraterritorial setting would relate to the obligation to regulate the behavior of third (private) parties. These parties may be private individuals or entities, such as NGOs, multilateral corporations, and so on. To illustrate, in 2000 a Norwegian shipowner entered into a contract with a shipbuilding firm in Belfast, Northern Ireland. Part of the contract concerned labor relations, in that it stipulated a three-year wage freeze and a prohibition of the right to strike. From an economic rights perspective, the question would be whether the Norwegian state – a party to the International Covenant on Economic, Social, and Cultural Rights – was under an obligation to regulate the behavior of its own multinational corporations (in this instance the shipping industry) to the effect that they should observe economic rights provided by the Covenant.

This level of extraterritorial obligations also has been recognized by the Committee *inter alia* in the General Comment on the Right to Health (2000, ¶ 39), which held that:

To comply with their international obligations in relation to article 12, States parties have to respect the enjoyment of the right to health in other countries, and to prevent third parties from violating the right in other countries, if they are able to influence these third parties by way of legal or political means, in accordance with the Charter of the United Nations and applicable international law.

The third level of extraterritorial obligations – the obligation to *fulfill* – is the most controversial, and the one that probably has been responsible for most of the hesitation in accepting a responsibility for rights enjoyment abroad. First, this may become a problem in terms of sovereignty. If a state observes that economic, social, and cultural rights are not fulfilled in another state, is it then possible for this first state to intervene and take it on itself to ensure these rights for the individuals in the second state, against the wishes of this state? On one level, this might sound absurd, particularly when viewed against the backdrop of inviolate state sovereignty.

If, however, we look at how some international cooperation is carried out, it no longer seems so far-fetched. For instance, in the 1980s, the Norwegian government decided to put much more emphasis on gender equality in its development assistance. It was decided that all projects should have a gender component. This was partly as a result of Norwegian opinion that the way in which women were treated in other countries represented a violation of their rights – denial of access to credit, land ownership, access to education, and so on – that represented clear discrimination against women. Are such principles of development assistance a right for the Norwegian government – or, indeed, could it be seen to be an obligation for the Norwegian government based on their ratification of the Covenant? If it is a right based on the Covenant for a government to include such principles in its development policies, this would pave the way for better quality development assistance from a human rights perspective. As Norway has ratified the Covenant, and article 2(1) contains the "to take steps . . . through international assistance and cooperation" phrase, it clearly has a right to include such features in its bilateral cooperation. This would be a legitimate policy choice for Norway with regards to the way in which its own bilateral assistance should be spent.

Furthermore, if it is an obligation, this would imply that development assistance that does not contribute to the fulfillment of economic, social, and cultural rights would not be acceptable from a Covenant's perspective, and states receiving assistance may also not consider this as an undue interference in their "internal affairs." Although Norway, as any other state, has the primary responsibility to fulfill economic, social, and cultural rights domestically, its position as a very rich country would also imply an obligation to support fulfillment in other states that are in need of financial assistance to fulfill human rights (UN Commission on Human Rights 2005).

A second reservation against an obligation to *fulfill* economic, social, and cultural rights through "international assistance and cooperation" will, as for domestic implementation, relate to available resources. If there is a general obligation to contribute to the fulfillment of economic, social and cultural rights in other societies, what impact will "available resources" have? Granted, if the domestic state is under an obligation to "take steps . . . to the maximum of available resources," such a qualification would be legitimate for foreign states as well.

But let us assume that resources are indeed "available," as they are in every Western state. Is there a duty to fulfill? We would not only argue that there is, but that to deny such an obligation would constitute a perversion of international human rights law itself. As noted in our earlier discussion of Shue's concept of positive duties, this is not meant to say that each state has an obligation, on its own, to ensure that the economic, social, and cultural rights of all others are met. Rather, what it does mean is that such states have obligations – both moral and legal – to be a part of a coordinated system to fulfill such rights. If they are, their extraterritorial obligations have been met. Such an approach has been recognized by the Special Rapporteur on the right to food, when in his report to the UN Commission on Human Rights in 2005 he emphasized the obligation to "support fulfilment" (¶ 47). The concept of supporting fulfillment recognizes that the "primary obligation to implement the right to food rests with the home Government, so another Government cannot be obliged to guarantee complete implementation of the right to food in other countries, but only to assist." However, if they are not part of such a coordinated system to support fulfillment – and the vast majority of states are not – then these states are violating international law.

CONCLUSION

Human rights limit the freedom of maneuver for states. This has been a hallmark of human rights since its early codification in national legislation. There is no doubt that extraterritorial human rights obligations limit the freedom of maneuver for states as well. This follows from the nature of human rights law, which establishes a public order within which states' actions need to conform. This is generally recognized in Article 28 of the Universal Declaration: "Everyone is entitled to a social and international order in which the rights and freedoms set forth in this Declaration can be fully realized." However, although extraterritorial obligations will set limitations as to permissible behavior, it does not prescribe in detail the way in which states should conduct their international policies or affairs. An essential part of this concept concerns a fundamental principle of nondiscrimination – that it is not acceptable to carry out actions abroad that a state could not do domestically.

Questions of extraterritorial obligations relate directly to a state's duty to take responsibility for its actions. How this is going to be done is still underresearched, and should receive much more explicit attention from the UN human rights system, regional systems, civil society, and academic circles. This is particularly important in terms of the obligation to *fulfill* economic, social, and cultural rights through international assistance and cooperation. What has been shown earlier is that there are many questions, and research is necessary in order to find the answers to those questions. This is necessary to demystify the concept of extraterritorial obligations and to make them understandable and operable.

REFERENCES

Altiparmak, Kerem. 2004. *Bankovic*: An Obstacle to the Application of the European Convention on Human Rights in Iraq? *Journal of Conflict and Security Law* 9: 213–51.
Bankovic v. Belgium, App. No. 52207/99, European Court of Human Rights (2001) (admissibility).
Bueno de Mesquita, Judith. 2003. International Covenant on Economic, Social and Cultural Rights: Obligations of International Assistance and Cooperation. Senior Research Officer, Human Rights Centre, University of Essex (briefing paper).

Committee on Economic, Social and Cultural Rights. 1997. *General Comment No. 8: The Relationship between Economic Sanctions and Respect for Economic, Social and Cultural Rights.* U.N. Doc E/C.12/1997/8 (12 Dec.).

Committee on Economic, Social and Cultural Rights. 1999. General Comment No. 12: The Right to Adequate Food (Art. 11). U.N. Doc E/C.12/1999/5 (12 May).

Committee on Economic, Social and Cultural Rights. 2000. General Comment No. 14: The Right to the Highest Attainable Standard of Health. U.N. Doc E/C.12/2000/4 (11 Aug.).

Committee on Economic, Social and Cultural Rights. 2003. *Concluding Observations.* U.N. Doc E/C.12/1/Add.90 (23 May).

Eide, Asbjørn. 1989. Realization of Social and Economic Rights and the Minimum Threshold Approach. *Human Rights Law Journal* 10: 35–51.

Happold, Matthew. 2003. Bankovic v. Belgium and the Territorial Scope of the European Convention on Human Rights. *Human Rights Law Review* 3: 77–90.

International Court of Justice. Military and Paramilitary Activities (Nicar. v. U.S.), 1986 I.C.J. (June 27).

Ireland v. United Kingdom, App. No. 5310/71, European Court of Human Rights (1978).

Nahapetian, Kate. 2002. Confronting State Complicity in International Law. *UCLA Journal of Law and Foreign Affairs* 7: 99–127.

Nowak, Manfred. 1997. The Covenant on Civil and Political Rights. In An Introduction to the International Protection of Human Rights, ed. Raija Hanski and Markku Suksi. Åbo, Finland: Institute for Human Rights, Åbo Akademi University.

Orakhelashvili, Alexander. 2003. Restrictive Interpretation of Human Rights Treaties in the Recent Jurisprudence of the European Court of Human Rights. *European Journal of International Law* 14: 529–68.

Organization of American States. 1978. American Convention on Human Rights. O.A.S. Treaty Series No. 36, 1144 U.N.T.S. 123.

Rasul v. Bush, 542 U.S. 466 (2004).

Roxstrom, Erik, Mark Gibney, and Terje Einarsen. 2005. The NATO Bombing Case [*Bankovic et al. v. Belgium et al.*] and the Limits of Western Human Rights Protection. *Boston University Journal of International Law* 23: 55–136.

Rubenstein Leonard S. 2004. How International Human Rights Organizations Can Advance Economic, Social, and Cultural Rights: A Response to Kenneth Roth. *Human Rights Quarterly* 26: 845–65 (2004).

Shue, Henry. 1980. *Basic Rights: Subsistence, Affluence and U.S. Foreign Policy.* Princeton: Princeton University Press.

Shue, Henry. 1988. Mediating Duties. *Ethics* 98: 687–704.

Simma, Brunoed, ed. 1994. *The Charter of the United Nations – A Commentary.* Oxford: Oxford University Press

Skogly, Sigrun. 2001. *The Human Rights Obligations of the World Bank and the International Monetary Fund.* London: Cavendish Press.

Skogly, Sigrun. 2003. The Obligation of International Assistance and Co-Operation in the International Covenant on Economic, Social and Cultural Rights. In *Human Rights and Criminal Justice for the Downtrodden,* ed. Morten Bergsmo. Hague: Kluwer Law International.

Skogly, Sigrun. 2006. *Beyond National Borders: Human Rights Obligations of States in International Cooperation.* Antwerp, Belgium: Intersentia.

United Nations. 1951. U.N. Doc. E/CN.4/L.19/Add.6 (May 11).

United Nations. 1965. G.A., 3d Comm., 17th Sess., 1204th mtg., Official Records ¶ 49.

United Nations. 2000. Millennium Declaration. U.N. Doc. A/RES/55/2 (18 Sept.).

UN Centre for Human Rights. *Legislative History of the Convention on the Rights of the Child (1978–1989)*. Article 4 – Implementation of Rights, HR/1995/Ser.1/article.4.

UN Human Rights Committee. 1981. Lopes v. Uruguay, U.N. Doc. A/36/40 (July 29).

UN Commission on Human Rights. 2005. The Right to Food. Report by the Special Rapporteur on the Right to Food, Jean Ziegler, U.N. Doc. E/CN.4/2005/47 (24 January).

13 International Obligations for Economic and Social Rights: The Case of the Millennium Development Goal Eight

SAKIKO FUKUDA-PARR

INTRODUCTION

The idea of human rights as universal – that all human beings, by virtue of the fact that they are human, have certain entitlements to lead a life of freedom and dignity – is one of the most cherished principles of human rights. Yet there is much ambiguity in both law and theory about whether the obligations to respect, promote, and protect these rights stop at the boundaries of a nation state. This question has drawn increasing interest in recent years as the international community has been calling for urgent action to end extreme poverty, especially with the adoption of the Millennium Development Goals (MDGs) as an international consensus. These Goals set quantitative targets for reducing poverty by 2015. They also contain a goal for stronger partnership of the international community to help developing countries achieve these goals. The purpose of this chapter is to examine Goal 8 as an instrument of international human rights obligation to measure progress and hold states accountable.

The chapter is structured as follows: the first section reviews the way in which international obligations of solidarity have been reflected in international human rights instruments and international development cooperation policy. The second section focuses on measurement issues including conceptual approaches and indicators for assessing progress. The third section attempts to identify the content of international obligations for economic and social rights. The final section examines the adequacy of Goal 8 targets and indicators in monitoring those obligations.

INTERNATIONAL OBLIGATIONS OF SOLIDARITY

The idea that human solidarity transcends national boundaries, and that state obligations for achievement of economic and social rights cannot be limited to a country's citizens alone is expressed in key human rights documents from the UN Charter to the Universal Declaration of Human Rights to the International Covenant on Economic, Social and Cultural Rights (ICESCR). And the principle

An earlier version of this chapter was published by *Human Rights Quarterly*, November 2006. The chapter is based on work undertaken for the UN Office of the High Commissioner for Human Rights.

that states have international obligations arising from solidarity is stated in these and several other documents, notably in the Declaration on the Right to Development, and in the 1993 Vienna Declaration and Programme of Action. (These sources are listed in Annex I.)

Yet this cherished idea has not developed beyond a statement of principle, either in concept or international human rights law. Not much work has been done to define these obligations over the last decades. No clear body of norms and standards has emerged. Several UN legal instruments refer to international cooperation but essentially restate the principles set out in the Covenant on Economic, Social, and Cultural Rights. No formal procedures exist to hold states accountable for their international responsibilities. In fact, as the recent review by Dos Santos Alvez (2004) for the UN Sub-Commission on the Promotion and Protection of Human Rights concludes, this concept is a broad area that has not been analyzed adequately.

The principle of international human rights obligations has barely had any influence on formulating international development cooperation policies. Even the most ardent advocates of international solidarity in the fight against global poverty – such as Professor Jeffrey Sachs or British Prime Minister Tony Blair – invoke moral compulsion, not international state obligation, as the reason why rich countries should make greater efforts. And if human rights are invoked in their discourse, it is merely to disparage extreme poverty as a denial of human dignity, stopping short of evoking the correlative duties and responsibilities of states and other actors to do their utmost to help achieve realization of rights. This misses the essential value added of human rights to development policy. At the same time, the growing literature and programmes promoting the "rights-based approach to development" focuses on national policy and has done little to address the international dimension of state obligations. Conceptually, the idea of development cooperation is still rooted in the logic of charity, rather than the logic of shared responsibilities in a global community.

Why has there been so little attention to international obligations for economic and social rights from the time that the UN Charter and the ICESCR were drawn up? In fact, for decades the dominant trend among scholars of international law, philosophy, and international relations has been to reject the idea of international obligations – mostly on pragmatic grounds – or simply not to give it as much attention as obligations focused on the state toward its citizens. Perhaps this was part of the state-centric approach that dominated human rights discourse in general. It also was part of the instrumental arguments that only state policies made any difference to the realization of economic rights.

More recently, important studies have begun to emerge and scholars have developed new arguments for international obligations. Skogly and Gibney, for example, examine international human rights instruments and argue that extraterritorial obligations are in fact "an essential part" of them. They point out in their chapter in this volume that actions of a state have impact on the well being of individuals outside the state territory, and these actions are often taken without consent of the state that is affected (Skogly and Gibney 2007). This goes beyond the initial idea that economic and social rights could only be realized progressively because of domestic resource constraints, and therefore required assistance from the international community.

Pogge takes a similar position (2001). He points out that the moral duty of the rich world is not simply a matter of beneficience, of a positive duty to help the poor of the world. Rather, it is the duty to make serious effort to refrain from doing harm. As he states: "We are not bystanders who find ourselves confronted with foreign deprivations whose origins are wholly unconnected to ourselves" (Pogge 2001, 14). The actions of the rich world are functionally related to the conditions of global poverty in three ways: first, the poverty of poor nations and the affluence and power of rich nations is rooted in a single historical origin; second, the poor and rich worlds use a single natural resource base, with much of the natural resources located in the developing countries; and third, the global economic order (with its institutions and rules) perpetuates or even aggravates global economic inequality.

This focus on the actions of rich states and their role in the global economic order is also reflected in the evolution in the UN instruments. Although the ICESCR emphasizes actions that states can take to provide development assistance for the "progressive" realization of economic, social and cultural rights, the Declaration on the Right to Development of 1986 takes a broader view of what states can do. It goes beyond development cooperation to removing obstacles in general and to development policies, in particular. This reflects an important recognition that it is not just resources but systemic aspects of the global economic order that present obstacles to development and poverty reduction for developing countries, and thus to the full realization of economic and social rights. In fact, the concept of the right to development grows out of the need to deepen the concern with the special obstacles that developing countries face: human rights are more complex than was originally conceptualized, particularly because resources can become an obstacle to the realization of economic and social rights.

In this context, Goal 8 is arguably the most significant development since the ICESCR, because it takes the idea of international state obligations beyond a statement of principle to list specific policy areas of required action – trade, aid, debt relief, and technology transfer. Moreover, Goal 8 is part of an internationally agreed-on mechanism of review and accountability, as I will explain.

Millennium Development Goals and the Eighth Goal

The eight Millennium Development Goals (MDGs) along with their eighteen targets and forty-eight indicators (see annex 2) emanate from the Millennium Declaration adopted at the 2000 UN Millennium Summit.[1] Although it should be acknowledged that there is more to the Right to Development than the MDGs,[2]

---

[1] The Declaration articulates the objectives reflected in the MDGs, whereas the list of goals, targets and indicators is contained in the roadmap document of 2001.

[2] The eight MDGs do not include all relevant priorities of right to development. There are several notable gaps when considering the substantive content of the right to development. First, they omit several important development objectives. For example, only equality in schooling is mentioned as a relevant indicator for gender equality, leaving out all other important areas such as employment and political participation to name just two. Second, the goals do not refer at all to the right to a development process that is transparent, participatory, equitable, and in which rule of law and good governance are practiced. Third, the MDGs miss the equity dimension of right to development. The targets and indicators all refer to national averages, without attention to redressing discrimination that results in exclusion and inequalities (con't.).

these goals are complementary and can take the agenda forward. Moreover, the Millennium Declaration defines a visionary agenda and contains the key human rights principles that are missing from the MDG targets and indicators.

The MDGs provide the strongest instrument ever developed for monitoring international commitment to reduce poverty, because they offer quantifiable targets with a timetable for achievement and indicators to monitor implementation. The MDGs are also unique for their explicit recognition that the goals could not be achieved by national efforts alone, but would require international cooperation. Goals 1 through 7 set benchmarks for assessing progress in addressing income poverty, hunger, primary schooling, gender inequality, child and maternal mortality, HIV/AIDS and other major diseases, and environmental degradation. Goal 8 sets out action to be taken by rich countries, including action on trade, debt, technology transfer, and aid. MDG-8 thus offers a framework for assessing accountability of rich countries. The list of Goals 1 through 7 is attached in annex 2, and Goal 8's targets and indicators are graphically represented in annex 3.

Goal 8 has the potential to be used as a tool of accountability, moving the principle of international solidarity from a conceptual to an operational level. This chapter asks whether the current list of Goal 8 targets and indicators capture the essential elements of international responsibilities for development. To answer this question requires first asking what targets and indicators should measure, what constitutes progress and regression. This in turn requires clarifying the concept of human rights, clarifying what constitutes international obligations, and clarifying the nature of substantive policy priorities. Thus, the chapter addresses these conceptual issues first before going to review the choice of Goal 8 targets and indicators.

MEASUREMENT – A CONCEPTUAL FRAMEWORK AND INDICATORS FOR ASSESSING PROGRESS IN THE REALIZATION OF HUMAN RIGHTS

How should progress in human rights realization be assessed? What are the key elements that define progress? Human rights is a complex concept with multiple dimensions; securing human rights requires progress on multiple fronts. Each of these facets needs to be captured in indicators to assess progress.

Consider the concept of the right to development. The right to development is not the same as development. It is not just about improvement in the economy or in social conditions such as schooling. It is also not the same as "human development" – the expansion of capabilities and freedoms that individuals must experience in order to lead lives they value. The right to development is a much more complex concept; it is about the process of putting in place social arrangements to ensure that people can enjoy their rights and realize their human dignity and freedoms.

---

[2] con't.

However, we should not interpret from this that MDGs have no relevance for human rights. The MDGs are benchmarks of progress and the seven goals do not necessarily claim to represent a comprehensive list of all important development objectives. Moreover, they are indicators of progress and are not intended to be a coherent development strategy nor a new development paradigm.

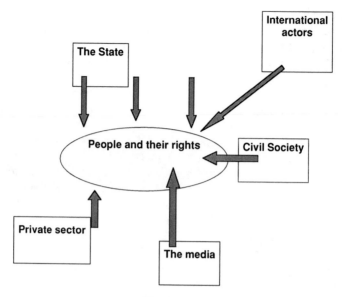

Figure 13.1.

Economists often argue that human rights are incorporated in development policies when these policies promote equitable economic growth and social development. This position misses the essence of the human rights concept, namely that rights carry correlative obligations on individuals and institutions, particularly the state. The concept of human rights is concerned with how these obligations are dispensed to create social arrangements so that people can realize their rights. The concept goes farther and is concerned with obligations of "conduct" as well as "result," and whether conduct that is true to principles of nondiscrimination, participation, adequate progress, and remedy. The value added of human rights to development is therefore the concern with putting in place adequate institutions, norms and processes to ensure these things.

Another way of approaching this concept is to contrast human rights with development aspirations; human rights are claims that are to be enforced, for which other duty-bearers are to be held accountable. To evaluate progress in human rights requires an assessment of the conduct of duty-bearers in putting in place the appropriate social arrangements for the realization of human rights – in particular, economic rights.

Dimensions of Human Rights and Implications for Assessing International Obligations under Goal 8

The realization of human rights needs to progress along multiple dimensions on different fronts. Figure 13.1 illustrates this schematically.

Two areas of outcomes: the condition in people's lives and the social arrangements being put in place. To assess human rights, we are concerned with progress not only in the condition of people's lives but also in the social arrangements that are in place. Much of the work on monitoring human rights focuses on documenting violations of rights by monitoring the condition of people's lives. These make up two quite distinct strands of work on human rights measurement. Lack of consensus in the work on indicators arises from the focus on one or the other priority (Raworth 2001). But progress needs to be assessed in both areas and indicators are needed in both.

The implication for Goal 8 is that indicators should focus on state conduct – on whether adequate public policies are in place – rather than on human outcomes.

Several actors. In addition to the state, any actors in society influence the condition of human lives. The state has the primary responsibility for securing people's rights, but many other actors such as the media, civil society organizations, private companies, other members of the household, and other individuals in society also have a role. In the market economy, the conduct of private companies is a significant factor and that conduct cannot be entirely controlled by the state. In an increasingly globalized world, global actors such as international organizations and global corporations have considerable influence, and are beyond the reach of any individual state to regulate. All these actors are duty-bearers.

The implication for Goal 8 is that international responsibilities reside not only with the state but also with other globally powerful organizations, notably corporations, media, and NGO networks. States also have an obligation to ensure that these other actors do not violate human rights. International cooperation is needed when actors are global such as global corporations.

Several key characteristics of process. It is not only the human condition but social processes in which people participate that are part of human rights. The right to development is conceptualized as a right to a process. The key features of the process include participation, equality, transparency, accountability, nondiscrimination, and access to remedies. To illustrate, what matters in the realization of right to development is not just raising school enrollment rates but also achieving greater equality in schooling, reducing disparities among population groups, and addressing obstacles such as language for marginalized groups. There also must be a process put in place for enhancing accountability and ensuring a remedy in the case of violation.

The implication for Goal 8 is that participation of poor and weak countries in international decision making processes that affect their development is an important concern.

Benchmarking progressive realization. It has long been recognized that the pace of progress in realizing rights depends on the context; obstacles are specific to each country, as is the specific historical conjuncture. Progress cannot be assessed by a uniform standard internationally. What is important is for each country to make the maximum effort; to monitor these efforts requires setting realistic benchmarks.

The implication for Goal 8 is that development partnership targets also should take account of these different needs and be disaggregated, recognizing that some countries face larger obstacles and can be expected to accomplish less than others. Partnership obligations would vary from one group of countries to another.

Structuring Indicators for Assessing State Conduct

Over the last decade, much work has been done on conceptualizing human rights measurement methodologies (Malhotra & Fasel 2005). Some useful approaches have been developed to structure indicators into sets that capture diverse dimensions and objectives. This chapter draws particularly on the framework proposed in the *Human Development Report 2000* (UNDP 2000), which identifies seven aspects of state conduct. This includes identifying the scope of state conduct in three categories of obligations to respect, protect, and fulfill human rights; and identifying four key principles of process, namely, nondiscrimination, participation, adequate progress, and remedy.[3] This framework is consistent with the framework proposed more recently by the Special Rapporteur on the right to health (Hunt 2003), which utilizes three categories of indicators: outcome, process, and structure. Although these frameworks were proposed to develop systems of indicators for accountability at the national level, they are also useful for structuring indicators for accountability at the international level.

Scope of State Conduct: Policies to Respect, Protect, and Fulfill

The "Maastricht principles" have come to be widely used in defining the scope of state responsibility in the national context across three dimensions – to respect, to protect, and to fulfill. The same principles can be usefully applied in conceptualizing the scope of international obligations.[4] This can be illustrated by drawing examples from national state obligations for education, and international obligations stemming from the WTO Agreement on Trade-Related Aspects of Intellectual Property Rights (TRIPS) – specifically, to extend access to patented medicines during a public health emergency.[5] TRIPS and the use of these flexibilities has been a hotly contested issue in trade negotiations that has pitted HIV/AIDS activists against corporations and some governments. Note that in the current situation of potential emergency with the spread of avian flu, governments have been much more proactive in negotiating with the patent holder of Tamiflu, the only known medicine, to ensure that enough supplies can be produced and made accessible to their national populations.

---

[3] The work of Kate Raworth is acknowledged as a main author of chapter 5 of the UNDP *HDR 2000* and as originator of the conceptual framework (see also Raworth 2001).

[4] The intention here is to use these principles to develop a conceptual framework for identifying international obligation, *not* to make a legal argument.

[5] Medicines under patent are expensive in comparison to generics, or in short supply. Although the TRIPS agreement requires WTO member countries to put in place a system of intellectual property rights, it also includes provisions to ensure that patents do not stand in the way of public health and other critical issues of human well being. These provisions include in particular, compulsory licensing – allowing companies to produce without a license – the use of which has been hotly contested in recent years. See the discussion of human rights obligations related to TRIPS in Hunt 2004.

To respect refers to not standing in the way of people's pursuit of their rights. An example in the national context would be to not restrict access to schools by minority populations. In the international context, an example would be refraining from obstructing a country pursuing the use of flexibilities in TRIPS agreement to protect public health. Several years ago, a group of multinationals took the South African government to court over this issue. Their home governments could have refrained from backing these multinational corporations, considering that HIV/AIDS affects over a fifth of the of South Africa's adult population (UNDP 2005).

To protect refers to preventing other actors from violating human rights. An example in the national context would be to intervene when parents refuse to let girls attend school. An example in the international context would be to take measures to encourage multinationals producing HIV/AIDS retrovirals to refrain from standing in the way of using compulsory licensing to allow generic production of the drugs.

To fulfill refers to taking measures that assist in the realization of rights. In the national context an example would be building schools. At the international level, an example would be investing in vaccines for HIV/AIDS that are urgently needed to stem the spread of this pandemic, especially in poor countries.

Key Human Rights Principles as Policy Goals – Nondiscrimination, Participation, Adequate Progress, and Effective Remedy

Cutting through all these outcomes and processes are key human rights principles of nondiscrimination, participation, adequate progress, and remedy.

Nondiscrimination. Equitable treatment of all and equal achievement of all in the realization of human rights is a central policy goal. Disparities in levels of human well being can reveal policy discrimination. In the national context, minority groups may have lower educational achievements reflecting lower spending from public budgets. In the international context, nondiscrimination is an important issue in trade policy. Market access for developing countries may be restricted by higher tariffs or subsidies to domestic production. Policies aimed at achieving greater equality imply greater priority for improvement of the most deprived and excluded.

There are significant implications of this principle for Goal 8. Numerous discriminatory rules exist in the international trading system, in its rules and institutional procedures. It is arguably a matter of human rights obligation on the part of rich countries to dismantle tariffs on developing country exports and subsidies on farm products that compete with developing country exports.

Participation. A key principle of the right to development as a right to a particular kind of process is the ability to participate in making decisions that affect one's life. Participation is secured only when the structures of decision making are democratic, and when institutionalized procedures exist for voices of people to be heard, for transparency of public action, and for embedded accountability.

An important implication for Goal 8 is the human rights obligation of all countries, especially the powerful ones, to ensure that voices of developing countries can
be heard in decision making processes such as in multilateral trade negotiations.

Adequate progress. The realization of rights depends on the context. Progress
has to be assessed in view of the obstacles in the way that are a result of history;
as a result, intermediate targets and benchmarks need to be set. In the national
context, this would imply, for example, achieving a consensus between people
and government as to how much the school enrollment rate should be raised
each year. In the international context, a similar process would be for donors and
government to agree on a framework for implementing enrollment reforms. The
Special Rapporteur on right to development has therefore proposed compacts
between developing countries and partners (Sengupta 2000).

An important implication for Goal 8 is that the MDGs constitute a framework
for benchmarking adequate progress. The MDGs set an ambitious framework;
to achieve them would require significant speeding up of development. Analyses
of trends consistently conclude that at rates achieved over the last decade, only
a handful of countries – mostly in Asia and Latin America – would achieve the
goals by 2015, and most goals would be missed globally and in the majority of
African countries and most of the poorest countries (whether categorized as LDCs,
low-income, or low human development countries).The MDGs are a claim to
international state conduct to do much more.

Remedy. States have the obligation to put in place procedures to remedy violations, and to hold responsible parties accountable. In the national context, procedures exist for legal and administrative recourse, and the effectiveness of these
procedures can be monitored. In the international context, such procedures are
exceptional. The WTO dispute settlement procedure is one of them. Note that
this is an exception; enforcement mechanisms at the international level rely on
peer pressure (i.e., naming and shaming) with no recourse to punitive measures
except for sanctions against states and military intervention, which are rarely
employed.

IDENTIFYING INTERNATIONAL OBLIGATIONS FOR REALISATION
OF ECONOMIC AND SOCIAL RIGHTS

How should international obligations be defined? How has the case been made?
One frequently used argument seeks to explain the existence of mass poverty in poor
countries and persistent inequalities in the world as the result of history and reflective of the huge asymmetries in economic and political power among countries.
However, it is widely agreed among both governments and human rights scholars
that the primary responsibility for human rights and eradication of poverty reside
at the national level, not the international level. This principle is also entrenched
in UN human rights documents. Indeed, most rich country governments insist on
this point and have been reluctant to embrace the notion of international obligations in UN fora and documents because the limits of national responsibility and

international responsibility are ambiguous. So international obligations are not a substitute for national responsibility. International action, however, is indispensable for addressing obstacles that are beyond the capacity of national governments to tackle on their own.

Three Categories of Obstacles Beyond the Reach of National Action

It is often thought that international support for development is essentially about transferring resources – a claim to a handout. The logic of human rights is not that of an entitlement to a handout or charity. The entitlement is to social arrangements that would secure a person's rights. International cooperation is needed because developing countries cannot raise adequate resources on their own, but there are two other obstacles that developing countries cannot address on their own. One is the nature of international policies and the other is systemic asymmetry in global governance.

Resource Constraints

The first obstacle is lack of financial and human resources. There is little argument over the fact that developing countries need additional resources beyond what domestic savings and borrowing can mobilize. There is also wide agreement that achieving the MDGs would require substantial additional resources since at the current pace of development, most of the low income/low human development countries would miss the 2015 targets. Additional resources can come from better national policies for domestic resource mobilization, but they must also come from development aid, debt relief, private investment flows and access to private capital markets.

International policies. The second obstacle concerns constraints that arise from the international policy environment. For example, most developing countries are highly dependent on primary commodities for their foreign exchange earnings, and face wildly fluctuating prices. They also face "tariff escalation" (also dubbed "development tax") – higher taxes imposed by developed countries on processed goods such as tinned tomatoes compared with unprocessed goods such as raw tomatoes. These and other issues have been identified as elements of the "development agenda" of the Doha round of trade negotiations that is actively under negotiation as this chapter is being written. A single country cannot address these problems on its own; international action is needed to create schemes to stabilize resource flows in the face of commodity price fluctuations, or to reform unfavorable trade rules. In fact, it is the need for an "enabling international economic environment" that drove developing countries to advocate for recognizing the right to development in the 1970s and 1980s (Sengupta 2000). In today's context, a host of other critical issues are pressing, such as global warming and other environmental pressures; the need to invest in technology for poor people (such as medicines for "neglected diseases"); low-cost clean energy; higher performing varieties of crops of poorest farmers; human trafficking and other international criminal activity.

Systemic asymmetry in global governance. The third obstacle concerns systemic weaknesses in global institutions and processes. An important issue today relates to the international financial architecture and its ability to monitor and prevent financial crises. Another major issue is the inadequate participation of developing countries in international decision making. This is related to the democratic deficit in global governance, and the lack of transparency, and broad participation in institutional structures and decision-making processes. The most significant concerns have been raised with respect to agreements on norms and standards in trade and finance. For example, developing countries have weak bargaining power in WTO multilateral trade negotiations, which results in trade rules that favor the interests of rich and powerful countries over those of poor ones. Developing country representation is also weak in other institutions such as the World Bank, International Monetary Fund, and the Basel Committee.

Assigning Responsibility for Violation – Imperfect Obligations

State conduct is about state policy and action, whether it is budget allocations, regulation, or institutional procedures. There is intrinsic difficulty in identifying the contents of policies and action that meet state obligations since there is no indisputable consensus on the causal impact of policy on human well-being. There are always policy choice controversies concerning data, methodology, and analysis. For example, human rights activists have often argued that "structural adjustment programmes" have resulted in unemployment, declines in educational enrollment, and other adverse impacts on the realization of right to development. But these policy consequences depend on the specific context, and the causal links are vigorously contested among economists. Many economists argue that these policy packages have had positive effects on employment, education, and other aspects of development.

Moreover, there are multiple factors and actors behind any given outcome that make attributing responsibility for human rights violations extremely difficult. So, for example, if a girl is not in school, is it because the parents oppose girls' education? Is it the community that has not ensured that the school is safe? Is it the Ministry of Education that has mismanaged its budget? Or is it the IMF that insisted that expenditure cuts are necessary to restore macroeconomic balance, and thus encourages the government of the country this girl lives in to adopt school fees? Or is it the Ministry of Finance that controls the national budget?

Although it is clear that it is not possible to ascribe exact responsibility for a human rights failure to an international actor, it does not follow that there are no obligations. There are obstacles that an international actor can address that a national government, a community, or a parent is not able to. As Amartya Sen has argued, obligations for helping realization of a right may not be precisely attributable, but are obligations nonetheless (UNDP 2000) – these should then be considered "imperfect obligations."

These imperfect obligations may be particularly difficult to pin down in a legal framework. But they can be agreed on among stakeholders through a politically negotiated consensus. While there will always be a rich diversity of analyses and disagreements among scholars, there are also areas of agreement and policy makers can draw on a body of social science knowledge on which there is strong consensus.

One of the most important achievements of the international community since the emergence of the Millennium Declaration in 2000, and the MDGs in 2001, has been the agreement on the "Monterrey consensus" in 2002 (UN 2002). Adopted at the 2002 UN Conference on Financing for Development held in Monterrey, Mexico, the consensus identifies key policy priorities and thus provides a framework for "partnership" for development, as well as analyzes the respective roles and commitments of developing countries to put in place effective governance of the development process, and commitment of donors to take new policy actions in areas of trade, debt, technology transfer, financial markets, private sector flows. In the next section, I review whether the Goal 8 indicators and targets reflect the commitments made in the Monterrey consensus.

ASSESSING GOAL 8 TARGETS AND INDICATORS

The text of Goal 8, its seven targets and seventeen indicators are listed in annex 3. Do these targets and indicators address the most serious obstacles to developing countries? Do these targets capture the key human rights dimensions required of state conduct? Do they convey the responsibilities of nonstate actors?

Table 13.1 (see end of chapter) compares Goal 8 targets and indicators with the priorities over which there are broad consensus. These include the priorities that governments have committed to undertake in the Monterrey consensus, and additional commitments that are identified as priority in recent UN commissioned studies. It is outside the scope of this chapter to make an independent assessment of international policy priorities, but we can draw on recent studies commissioned by the UN system that build on the large empirical and analytical literature. In this chapter, I review three of the many UN commissioned reports, because these are global and most comprehensive: the 2005 report of the UN Millennium Project (MP) led by Professor Jeffery Sachs that brought together hundreds of specialists from international academia, civil society, government, and UN agencies (UN 2005); the 2005 World Economic and Social Survey (WESS) published by the UN Department of Social Economic Affairs (UN 2005); and the 2003 and 2005 editions of the Human Development Report commissioned by UNDP.

This comparison shows that Goal 8 indicators and targets set weak standards for accountability and are narrow in their coverage of policy agenda, as well as inadequate in addressing key human rights principles in each of the three areas where international action is required to supplement domestic efforts: lack of resources, improving the international policy environment, and addressing systemic asymmetries in global decision-making processes.

Priority 1: Resources – Aid, Debt, Private Flows

Goal 8 focuses on increasing aid and debt relief, with attention to aid allocation to LDCs and to social services. This is the strongest area of Goal 8 targets and indicators, focusing on official development assistance (ODA) and debt relief. The only quantitative indicator in the Goal 8 framework is included in indicator 32, which specifies a target of 0.7% of GDP for OECD countries and 0.15% of GDP for LDCs. This has already proven to be an important benchmark in driving policy change in the Organisation for Economic Co-operation and Development (OECD) donor countries. Since 2003, aid disbursements have begun to increase, and many donors, especially in the European Union, have committed to increase overall aid budgets.

The Monterrey consensus sets a broader agenda that includes issues of exploring new and innovative sources of financing, exploring innovative mechanisms to address debt problems comprehensively, and measures to encourage private capital flows. These issues are also emphasized in the reports reviewed. The reports address the issue of aid allocation with a slightly different emphasis. Although Goal 8 includes indicators for allocations to LDCs and to the social sectors, the MP report and HDR 2003 argue for aid to be allocated on the basis of a realistic country level analysis of resources required to achieve the MDGs.

Goal 8 Indicators and Targets Raise a Number of Issues

First is aid allocation to the countries in greatest need, in order to achieve the MDGs as well as to fulfill human rights according to principles of equality and nondiscrimination. The 0.7% GDP target is useful for holding donors accountable to their commitment to increase ODA in the aggregate. MDG 8 targets 0.15% of GDP of OECD countries to LDCs out of the aggregate target of 0.7%. The population of LDCs is about 16% of all the developing country population, whereas the 0.15% allocation represents 21% of the aggregate target.

The critical policy issue is ensuring the flow of resources to countries in greatest need, and ensuring that these resources are used effectively. Developing countries can be categorized into two groups. A group of countries are on track to meeting MDGs at current rates of progress. Most of these are middle-income countries or countries such as China that are experiencing rapid growth and development. They do not require additional aid to achieve the targets. Another group of countries are high priority countries that are far behind and progressing slowly, in some cases in development reversal. The 1990s was a decade of unprecedented development success for many countries that managed to integrate into the global economy, realizing its potential benefits and translating these benefits into improvements in the lives of their people. But for others, the 1990s was a decade of human development crisis; about fifty countries have lower per capita GDP in 2000 than they had in 1990. Current aid allocations favor middle-income rather than low-income countries, so there is a need for policy change on the part of donors to reallocate aid.

The UN reports propose that aid allocations should be based on country by country estimates of resources needed to achieve the MDGs. MDG benchmarks are more ambitious for the poorest countries; consider the contrast between Niger and Chile. Achieving universal primary schooling is much more difficult for Niger, which has a current enrollment rate of 30% and a GDP per capita of $890 (PPP), than for Chile, which has an enrollment rate of 89% and a GDP per capita of $9,190 (PPP) (UNDP 2005). MDGs set targets that take no account of this reality; in fact, the reverse is true, as MDGs ask Niger and Chile to achieve universal primary schooling in the same time frame. The countries with the largest backlog of deprivation also tend to have the largest resource constraints and therefore require the strongest support or "partnership." In fact, the Monterrey consensus proposal is to favor countries that have good policies, while working against the poorest countries because many of them have weak policy capacity. A way has to be found for international cooperation to effectively accelerate progress in these countries.

Second, there is a need for new approaches to the debt issue. Goal 8 makes an important commitment to "deal comprehensively with the debt problems." Indicators focus on outcomes such as the proportion of official bilateral Highly Indebted Poor Countries (HIPC) debt cancelled, debt service as a percentage of exports of goods and services, and number of countries reaching HIPC decision and completion points. However, Goal 8 indicators and targets do not reflect policy changes that are needed in the design of debt sustainability initiatives. All UN reports reviewed conclude that the HIPC experience has been important but that progress has been slow, and that deeper relief is required as countries find themselves with unsustainable debt levels not long after benefiting from debt relief.

Third, there is a need to explore new sources of financing. Ideas about innovative sources of financing for development have long been discussed. Proposals have been made by independent researchers for several sources of financing, but have not been vigorously pursued to date. Some ideas, such as the "Tobin tax" on international capital transactions, could raise huge amounts but have support from only a few countries. But the Monterrey consensus has recognized the importance of exploring new sources; in fact, it is widely acknowledged, as reflected in the WESS, that there are serious limitations to ODA as a way of meeting financing requirements for development. Budget constraints and competing priorities, as well as the lack of a political constituency in donor countries, would, for example, make it difficult to double ODA levels; resources required to meet the MDGs are estimated at a ballpark figure of about $50 billion, or the equivalent of doubling current ODA levels. Recently, some policy initiatives have been presented, including the International Financing Facility proposed by the United Kingdom and being launched to finance immunization, the use of Special Drawing Rights, and air transport tax proposed by France.

Priority 2: International Policies

Goal 8 makes an important commitment to working toward greater fairness in trade and finance, with a focus on market access. Goal 8 also refers to access to essential medicines and access to new technologies. The targets and indicators, however, state broad objectives and outcomes without pinpointing concrete policy changes required.

In comparison, the Monterrey consensus not only contains a broader agenda for policy reform in trade, but also extends to issues of financial markets, commodity price fluctuations, intellectual property, and aid effectiveness. The UN reports reviewed also cover these issues.

First, the Monterrey consensus incorporates commitments to address a wider range of issues restricting market access. Such issues include agricultural subsidies and tariffs on labor intensive manufactures, in addition to such measures as sanitary and phytosanitary measures, and the increasingly important issue related to liberalizing movement of persons under the General Agreement on Trade in Services (GATS) mode 4. This would facilitate migration from developing countries.

Second, the Asian financial crisis demonstrated the risk of such crises for emerging economies. The Monterrey consensus commits countries to explore policy reforms toward stable flows. The WESS contains detailed analyses and proposals in this area.

Third, commodity price fluctuations are major obstacles to developing countries, most of which are highly dependent on primary commodity exports as a source of foreign exchange earnings. The Monterrey consensus commits countries to do more to mitigate the effects of these fluctuations through implementation of mechanisms such as the IMF Compensatory Financing Facility, as well as through export diversification.

Fourth, intellectual property rights, access to and development of technology are important issues for developing countries. There is a growing technological inequality in access and capacity. The Monterrey consensus commits countries to proactive positions with respect to access to medicines and traditional knowledge. Intellectual property rights are important for rich and technologically advanced countries with technology based industries. Developing countries also need help with investments in research and development for technologies that can address enduring problems of poverty, such as the need for improved varieties of crops, cures for major diseases, low-cost sources of clean energy, and so on. Developing countries need access to global technology – such as pharmaceuticals – many of which are patented and priced much higher than generics. Goal 8 refers to this problem and states the objective of expanding access to essential medicines, but stops short of identifying concrete action needed, such as increasing investments in pro-poor technology or expanding access to patented medicines through implementation of TRIPS flexibilities such as compulsory licensing.

Goal 8 technology targets focus on information and communications technology (ICT). It is true that developing countries are falling behind in connectivity and the ICT gaps are huge, but Goal 8 ignores some of the other major issues requiring action, including investment in pro-poor technologies and access to pharmaceuticals as mentioned earlier, and measures to recognize rights to indigenous knowledge.

These issues are also addressed in the UN commissioned reports, which in addition propose some quantitative indicators and deadlines – especially for removal of agricultural subsidies and merchandise tariffs.

Fifth, aid effectiveness requires reforms by both recipient and donor. Important progress has been made in the donor community in identifying and addressing key issues, notably to align priorities with recipients' national priorities and to improve harmonization and reduce administrative costs to recipients – both of which contribute to another objective of increasing developing country ownership of the aid process. The March 2005 Paris Declaration – adopted by the Development Assistance Committee (DAC) of the OECD – sets out an important framework for accountability and includes both goals and indicators. Although the Monterrey consensus and UN reports identify these issues, the Goal 8 indicator for aid effectiveness is the proportion of untied aid. This is an important issue but one that was a major policy issue of the 1970s and 1980s, and is less central to the concerns identified today.

Priority 3: Systemic Issues

The Monterrey consensus identifies as a priority the need to address "systemic issues" to enhance the coherence, governance and consistency of international monetary, financial and trading systems. Two types of problems are widely acknowledged. The first is the growing imbalances in the monetary and financial systems that expose the global economy to shocks – such as the Asian financial crisis – to which developing countries are particularly vulnerable. The second is the asymmetry in decision making and norm setting in international trade and finance.

Analysis in WESS and in the HDRs further identify problems. For example, developing countries are not represented at all in the Basel Committees and the Financial Stability forum. The voting structures of the World Bank and the IMF are heavily weighted to developed countries. Although the WTO rules give equal vote to each country, decision making is by consensus, and consensus-making processes are not open and transparent to all.

This issue of developing country voice and participation in decision making is not included in the Goal 8 agenda.

Other Priorities

Corporate responsibility. Although the behavior of private sector actors has always had an important influence on the enjoyment of human rights (such as through impact on working conditions and on the environment), there is no reference in Goal 8 to state responsibilities with respect to corporate conduct. In the age of globalization, with the increase in foreign direct investment and liberalization of the economy, their influence has grown further. An important element of international responsibility of the state is to protect human rights from violations by corporate actors. Goal 8 makes no mention of this role.

CONCLUSIONS

This detailed review of Goal 8 targets and indicators as a potential framework for monitoring international accountability for the right to development – and, with it, economic and social rights – shows that the current formulation of targets and indicators is weak on two accounts. One is that there are no quantitative targets and no timetable for implementation other than the ODA target of 0.7% of GDP. The other is that Goal 8 states general objectives and desired outcomes but stops short of identifying concrete policy changes that can be monitored, even though governments have committed to specific changes in the Monterrey consensus and in subsequent agreements such as the Paris Declaration.

Goal 8 targets and indicators are also narrow; they do not capture the broader and in some sense the more critical policy issues that are included in the Monterrey commitments. The most significant gaps are the commitments to explore new sources of financing, technology issues in TRIPS related to access to medicines and indigenous knowledge, aid effectiveness reforms to enhance ownership by developing countries, and the systemic issues of voice of developing countries in international decision-making processes.

Goal 8 does not take on board key principles and priorities informed by human rights logic. The most glaring omissions concern priority attention to countries in greatest need, protecting human rights against violations by others – notably on the issues of corporate behavior – and addressing the systemic issue of greater transparency and equality by promoting developing country participation in global governance processes. Overall, Goal 8 emphasizes resource transfer through ODA, arguably the mechanism least compatible with the right to development concept that emphasizes empowerment of developing countries. Goal 8 is less concrete on changes in the policy environment, and even less so on systemic issues that other development frameworks develop more fully.

It is beyond the scope of this study to develop a definitive proposal to strengthen Goal 8 targets and indicators. To do so would require an in-depth analysis of each of the policy constraints. Nonetheless, it is possible to identify the key directions for refining Goal 8 targets and indicators as a tool for strengthening accountability for international responsibilities.

Resources (aid, debt). Targets and indicators should focus on aid allocation and reform of donor practices. Some concrete quantitative or action indicators could be considered:

- increase of a specific amount in concessionary financing received by low human development countries;
- agreement before 2015 on new HIPC criteria to provide deeper debt reduction for HIPCs having reached their completion points to ensure sustainability;[6]
- agreement before 2015 on new sources of financing development; and
- agreement before 2015 on reforms in aid practices, to prioritize MDG achievement, to make resource flows more predictable, and to put in place measures to increase ownership by national governments.

Policy environment. Key priorities are removal of agricultural subsidies, removal of tariffs on merchandise exports of developing countries, commodity price fluctuations, TRIPS flexibilities, indigenous knowledge. Some concrete indicators could be considered:

- as proposed by the Millennium Project (MP), set quantitative benchmarks and longer time frame for progressive removal of barriers to merchandize trade, agricultural export subsidies;
- as proposed by the MP, agree to raise public financing of research and development of technologies in agriculture, health, and energy for poverty reduction of $7 billion by 2015.
- as proposed by the World Economic and Social Survey (WESS), compensation facility for commodity price fluctuations;

---

[6] Target proposed in the Human Development Report 2003.

- as proposed by the Human Development Report 2003, agree on introducing protection and remuneration of traditional knowledge in the TRIPS agreement;
- as proposed by Human Development Report 2005, agree on a commitment to avoid "WTO plus" arrangements in regional agreements.

Systemic asymmetry in global governance. Although there has been growing attention to increasing the voice of developing countries, the international community is far from creating significant solutions to this problem. Concrete targets should focus particularly on developing country participation in the WTO decision-making process, where most is at stake.

Globalization, Global Solidarity, and International Obligations

Increasing global interdependence has meant that people's lives are much more influenced by events that take place outside of the country whether it is spread of disease, depletion of fishing stock, or fluctuations in international financial flows. The impact of government policy similarly extends beyond national borders. Developing countries are consequently more dependent on international resources, policy change, and systemic improvement in global governance to accelerate progress in achieving the right to development. The global community needs instruments for making global solidarity work, to strengthen accountability for international responsibilities for global poverty eradication and development.

Goal 8 targets and indicators are operational tools for benchmarking progress in implementing the Millennium Declaration and the international agenda agreed at Monterrey and at the 2005 OECD Summit. These are clearly frameworks for international solidarity and an agenda for promoting the right to development. The Millennium Declaration squarely starts with the statement of values that underpin the entire declaration – freedom, solidarity, equality, shared responsibility.

Targets and indicators are not meant as a substitute for the broader agenda. But the danger is that in policy debates, numbers focus policy makers' attention and risk hijacking the agenda. Thus, raising ODA to 0.7% of GDP dominates much of the reporting and policy advocacy for the MDGs and poverty reduction. Indicators are powerful in driving policy debates. MDG 8 presents an important challenge and an opportunity for effectively using targets and indicators to drive implementation of the right to development. It is therefore urgent for the international community to revisit Goal 8 targets and indicators and realign them with the central policy challenges identified in the Monterrey consensus, and to shift international cooperation from an instrument of charity to an instrument of solidarity.

REFERENCES

Dos Santos Alves, Ruis Baltazar, 2004. Human Rights and International Solidarity. Working paper, submitted to the U.N. Sub-Commission on the Promotion and Protection of Human Rights. U.N. Doc. E/CN.f/Sub.2/2004/4315 (June).

Hunt, Paul. 2003. The Right of Everyone to Enjoy the Highest Attainable Standard of Physical and Mental Health. U.N. Doc. A/58/427 (October).

Hunt, Paul. 2004. Report on the Mission to the WTO by the Special Rapporteur on the Right to Health. U.N. doc. E/CN.4/2004/49/Add.1 (March).

Malhotra, Rajeev, and Nicolas Fasel. 2005. Quantitative Human Rights Indicators: A Survey of Major Initiatives. Working paper for the Oslo Workshop on Developing Justice Indicators, May 15–16, 2006.

Pogge, Thomas. 2001. Priorities of Global Justice. In *Global Justice*, ed. Pogge. Oxford: Blackwell.

Pogge, Thomas. 2002. *World Poverty and Human Rights, Cosmopolitan Responsibilities and Reforms.* Cambridge: Polity Press.

Raworth, Kate. 2001. Measuring Human Rights. *Ethics & International Affairs* 15 (1): 111–31.

Sengupta, Arjun. 2000. The Right to Development: Report of the Independent Expert on the Right to Development. U.N. Commission on Human Rights. U.N. Doc. E/CN.4/2000/WG.18/CRP.1 (September).

Skogly, Sigrun I. and Mark Gibney (2007). Economic Rights and Extraterritorial Obligations. In *Economic Rights: Conceptual, Measurement, and Policy Issues*, eds. Shareen Hertel and Lanse P. Minkler. Cambridge, UK: Cambridge University Press.

United Nations. 2002. Report of the U.N. Conference on Financing for Development. U.N. Doc. A/CONF.198.11.

United Nations. 2005. *Investing in Development: A Practical Plan to Achieve the Millennium Development Goals.* London: Earthscan.

UN Department for Economic and Social Affairs. 2005. *World Economic and Social Survey.* New York: Author.

United Nations Development Programme (UNDP). 2000. *Human Development Report 2000: Human Rights and Human Development.* New York: Oxford University Press.

United Nations Development Programme (UNDP). 2005. *Human Development Report 2005: International Cooperation at a Crossroads.* New York: Oxford University Press.

Table 13.1. *Goal 8 targets and indicators compared with proposals in monterrey consensus and major UN reports*

Category of policy priorities: development constraints requiring international action.	Priorities in Goal 8 targets and indicators	Additional priorities in Monterrey consensus and subsequent agreements	Additional priorities identified in policy research as per Millennium Project Report (MP), World Economic and Social Survey (WESS 2005), Human Development Reports 2003 and 2005[1]
Resources	*ODA* Indictor 32: Raise ODA to 0.7% GNP of OECD countries and 0.15% for LDCs Indictor 33: proportion of ODA to social services. Indictor 34: proportion of ODA that is untied. *Address the special needs of landlocked countries and small island developing States. (target 14)* Indictor 35: proportion of ODA for environment in small island states; Indictor 36: proportion of ODA for transport sector in landlocked countries. *Debt* Target 15 – Deal comprehensively with debt problems of developing countries through national and international measures to achieve debt sustainability – indicators 41–44 on debt cancellation, debt service as% of exports, proportion of ODA provided as debt relief, number of countries reaching HIPC decision and completion points.	*ODA* Make concrete efforts to increase ODA to 0.7% of GNP and 0.15 to 0.2% of GNP to LDCs. *New sources* Explore innovative sources of finance e.g. SDR allocations for development. *Private capital flows* Provide support such as export credit, cofinancing, venture capital, risk guarantees, leveraging aid resources, information on investment opportunities, business development services, business fora, finance feasibility studies. *Debt* Speedy, effective and full implementation of the enhanced HIPC facility. Put in place a set of clear principles for management and resolution of financial crises, ensure debt relief does not detract from ODA resources. Explore innovative mechanisms to comprehensively address debt problems.	*ODA* *Aid allocation* Aid allocations according to requirements for achieving MDGs. (MP) Allocate more ODA to low income countries. (WESS) *New sources* Innovative sources of financing e.g. international finance facility. (WESS)

(Continued)

Table 13.1 (Continued)

Policy environment			
	Trade (Target 12) Develop an open, rule based, predictable, non-discriminatory trading and financial system. Includes a commitment to good governance, development and poverty-reduction – both nationally and internationally. Indicator 37: proportion of exports admitted free of duties and quotas. Indicator 38: average tariffs and quotas on agricultural products, textiles and clothing. Indicator 39: domestic and export agricultural subsidies in OECD countries; Indicator 40: proportion of ODA provided to build trade capacity. *Target 13: Address the special needs of LDCs* including tariffs and quota-free access for least developed countries' exports; enhanced programme for HIPCs and cancellation of official bilateral debt; more generous ODA for countries committed to poverty reduction. *Access to essential drugs (target 17)* Indicator 46: proportion of population with access to affordable essential drugs on a sustainable basis. *Technology (target 18)* Make available benefits of new technologies, especially information and communications. Indicator 47: telephone lines per 1,000 people Indicator 48: Personal computers per 1,000 people.	*Private financial flows:* Measures to sustain sufficient and stable flows – address transparency and information, mitigate excessive volatility. Initiatives to enhance access to financial markets, strengthen capacity for risk assessment. *Trade:* Increase market access. Address trade barriers, trade-distorting subsidies and other trade-distorting measures, especially in sectors of special export interest including agriculture; abuse of anti-dumping measures; technical barriers and sanitary and phytosanitary measures; trade liberalization in labour intensive manufactures; trade in services. Improve supply competitiveness for low-income country exports. *Intellectual property rights.* Implementation and interpretation of TRIPS supportive of public health; protection of traditional knowledge and folklore. *Commodity price fluctuations and dependence on primary commodity exports* – IMF Compensatory Financing Facility. Support export diversification. *Aid effectiveness* Improve aid and effectiveness by addressing following issues: harmonization of procedures, alignment with national priorities, national ownership, untying aid, strengthen recipient capacity to manage aid, ODA as leverage to additional financing and trade, south-south cooperation, and ODA targeting to the poor.	*Trade:* Set longer-term (for example 2025) quantitative targets for the total removal of barriers to merchandise trade, substantial across the board liberalization of trade in services, and universal enforcement of the principle of reciprocity and non-discrimination. (MP) Before 2015 agree and finance, for HIPCs, a compensatory financing facility for external shocks, including collapses in commodity prices. (HDR2003) In the short term, before mid-2005: agriculture – priority effort in agriculture to achieve significant reductions in tariff peaks and escalation, phase out specific duties on low-income country exports. A binding commitment to abolish export subsidies and two-tier price schemes. Nonagricultural merchandise – reduce tariffs to zero by 2015. Services – liberalize mode 4 of GATS – temporary movement of labor to provide services. Special and differential treatment – set up "aid for trade fund" to address adjustment costs associated with implementation of Doha reform agenda. Promote export competitiveness – additional aid, especially for investments in agricultural	

productivity and labor-intensive exports in LDCs. (MP, HDR2003, HDR2004, WESS)

Commitment to avoid "WTO plus" arrangements in regional trade agreements. (HDR2005)

Intellectual property By 2015 introduce protection and remuneration of traditional knowledge in the TRIPS agreement. Agree on what countries without sufficient manufacturing capacity can do to protect public health under TRIPS agreement. (HDR2003)

Regional and global public goods—Aid for overlooked priorities, especially neglected public goods and long-term goals such as scientific capacity, environmental management, regional integration and cross-border infrastructure. (MP)

Public financing of research by $7 billion by 2015 of which $4 billion for public health, $1 billion for agriculture, $1 billion for improved energy, and $1 billion for greater understanding of climate change.

Security – Reduce threats of violent conflict within countries through aid to postconflict states, greater transparency in resource management, and cutting flow of small arms. (HDR2005)

(Continued)

Table 13.1 *(Continued)*

| Systemic (institutional) asymmetry in global governance | Enhance coherence, governance, and consistency of international monetary, financial and trading systems. Including reform of the international financial architecture; strong coordination of macroeconomic policies among leading industrial countries for global stability and reduced exchange rate volatility; national ownership and needs of the poor; effective and equitable participation of developing countries in the formulation of financial standards and codes; stronger IMF surveillance to prevent crises.

 Global governance – broaden the base for decision making and norm setting. IMF and World Bank, WTO, Bank for International Settlements, Base Committees and Financial Stability Forum, and other ad hoc groupings to make efforts to enhance participation of developing and transition countries, and to ensure transparent processes.

 Strengthen the UN system and other multilateral institutions including stronger coordination among UN agencies and funds with the Bretton Woods institutions.

 Strengthen international tax cooperation. Finalize a UN convention against corruption including repatriation of illicitly acquired funds and money laundering. Signature and ratification of the UN Convention against Transnational Organized Crime, and International Convention for the Suppression of the Financing of Terrorism. | Redress global macroeconomic imbalances, and enhance measures to reduce developing country vulnerability to crises such as IMF facilities to compensate for short term shocks. (WESS)

 Enhance voice and participation of developing countries in international financial decision making, especially Basel Committee and Financial Stability Forum which have no developing country representation; (WESS 2005) |

---

[1] Includes points not already in the Monterrey consensus and follow up including the world summit.

ANNEX 1

International solidarity, rights/duties in some sources of international law (from Dos Santos Alves, 2004)

Charter of the United Nations

- Preamble: commitment to "employ international machinery for the promotion of the economic and social advancement of all peoples."
- Article 1, para. 3 defines objectives and principles of the UN: "to achieve international cooperation in solving international problems of an economic, social, cultural or humanitarian character, and in promoting and encouraging respect for human rights and for fundamental freedoms for all . . . "

The Universal Declaration of Human Rights

- Article 22: everyone is "entitled to realization, through national effort and international cooperation and in accordance with the organization and resources of each State, of the economic, social and cultural rights indispensable for his dignity and the free development of his personality."

The International Covenant on Economic, Social and Cultural Rights

- Article 2: States undertake to act "individually and through international assistance and cooperation, especially economic and technical, to the maximum of their available resources," to progressively achieve the rights recognized in the Covenant.

The Declaration on the Right to Development, 1986.

- Article 3: "States have a duty to cooperate with each other in ensuring development and removing obstacles to development."
- Article 4: "States have a duty to take steps, individually and collectively, to formulate international development policies with a view to facilitating the full realization of the right to development."

The Millennium Declaration, 2000

- Para I-2: "We recognize that, in addition to our separate responsibilities to our individual societies, we have a collective responsibility to uphold the principles of human dignity, equality and equity at the global level. As leaders we have a duty therefore to all the world's people, especially the most vulnerable and, in particular, the children of the world, to whom the future belongs."

Millennium Development Goals

Goal and quantitative target

1. Eradicate extreme poverty and hunger: halve between 1990 and 2015, the proportion of people whose income is less than $1 a day and halve between 1990 and 2015, the proportion of people who suffer from hunger.
2. Achieve universal primary education: ensure that by 2015 children will be able to complete a full course of primary schooling.
3. Promote gender equality and empower women: eliminate gender disparity in primary and secondary education, preferably by 2005 and at all levels of education no later than 2015.
4. Reduce child mortality: reduce by two-thirds, between 1990 and 2015, the under-five mortality rate.
5. Improve maternal health: reduce by three-quarters, between 1990 and 2015, the maternal mortality ratio.
6. Combat HIV/AIDS, malaria and other diseases: have halved by 2015 and begun to reverse the spread of HIV/AIDS. Have halved by 2015 and begun to reverse the incidence of malaria and other major diseases.
7. Ensure environmental sustainability: halve by 2015 the proportion of people without sustainable access to safe drinking water and sanitation. Have achieved a significant improvement by 2020 in the lives of at least one hundred million slum dwellers.
8. Devleop a global partnership for development: indicator (not target) net ODA as % of GDP at 0.7% of GDP and 0.15% for LDCs.

ANNEX 3

Goal 8. Develop a global partnership for development[a]

Target 12. Develop further an open, rule-based, predictable, non-discriminatory trading and financial system

Includes a commitment to good governance, development, and poverty reduction — both nationally and internationally

Target 13. Address the special needs of the least developed countries

Includes: tariff and quota free access for least developed countries' exports; enhanced programme of debt relief for HIPCs and cancellation of official bilateral debt; and more generous ODA for countries committed to poverty reduction

Target 14. Address the special needs of landlocked countries and small island developing States

(through the Programme of Action for the Sustainable Development of Small Island Developing States and the outcome of the twenty-second special session of the General Assembly)

Target 15. Deal comprehensively with the debt problems of developing countries through national and international measures in order to make debt sustainable in the long term

Target 16. In cooperation with developing countries, develop and implement strategies for decent and productive work for youth

Target 17. In cooperation with pharmaceutical companies, provide access to affordable essential drugs in developing countries

Target 18. In cooperation with the private sector, make available the benefits of new technologies, especially information and communications

[Some of the indicators listed below will be monitored separately for the least developed countries (LDCs), Africa, landlocked countries and small island developing States]

Official development assistance

32. Net ODA as percentage of OECD/DAC donors' gross national product (targets of 0.7% in total and 0.15% for LDCs)

33. Proportion of ODA to basic social services (basic education, primary health care, nutrition, safe water and sanitation)

34. Proportion of ODA that is untied

35. Proportion of ODA for environment in small island developing States

36. Proportion of ODA for transport sector in landlocked countries

Market access

37. Proportion of exports (by value and excluding arms) admitted free of duties and quotas

38. Average tariffs and quotas on agricultural products and textiles and clothing

39. Domestic and export agricultural subsidies in OECD countries

40. Proportion of ODA provided to help build trade capacity

Debt sustainability

41. Proportion of official bilateral HIPC debt cancelled

42. Debt service as a percentage of exports of goods and services

43. Proportion of ODA provided as debt relief

44. Number of countries reaching HIPC decision and completion points

45. Unemployment rate of 15-to-24-year-olds

46. Proportion of population with access to affordable essential drugs on a sustainable basis

47. Telephone lines per 1,000 people

48. Personal computers per 1,000 people

[Other indicators to be decided]

---

[a] The selection of indicators for goals 7 and 8 is subject to further refinement.

14 The United States and International Economic Rights: Law, Social Reality, and Political Choice

DAVID P. FORSYTHE[1]

It is well known that whereas the international law of human rights recognizes personal and transcendent entitlements to work and adequate food, clothing, shelter, and health care, the United States does not. Naturally I refer primarily to the International Covenant on Economic, Social, and Cultural Rights (ICESCR), and the lack of U.S. ratification (see Felice 2003). It is also well known that although Democratic presidents such as Franklin D. Roosevelt (FDR) and Harry S. Truman were genuinely interested in welfare rights, which comprise a subset of broader economic rights, with time the general subject faded in American public life. Presidents no longer talk about a second bill of rights to expand on civil and political rights, or propose schemes of national health insurance (at least not at the time of writing). Many human rights advocates bemoan this state of affairs. This paper inquires as to whether the situation is as dire as the Cassandras would have us believe.[2]

I first give some historical background, drawing a distinction between fundamental rights and fundamental policies. It is worth recalling that even FDR used the language of "a second bill of rights" as a metaphor for fundamental social policies. He never proposed formal changes to the U.S. Constitution regarding social rights. When he spoke of social or welfare rights, he meant the statutory rights that are embedded in formal policies, not constitutional rights or amendments. (Treaty provisions on social rights did not exist during his era.)

I then argue that the U.S. record on welfare policy is similar in some respects to the other wealthy democracies, even though the latter have seen basic welfare policies as linked to human rights, whereas the United States has not.

The chapter goes on to acknowledge that a human rights approach to subjects such as health care does indeed advance some public goods (along with some public bads). The key point is that a human rights approach to health care does more for the poor and marginalized, even if certain macro-comparisons put the United States more or less on a par with its wealthy democratic siblings.

[1] I thank Kadir Erigin for his research assistance, and Peter R. Baehr and Barbara Ann J. Rieffer for their helpful comments on earlier drafts. Useful comments for revisions were obtained at a conference hosted by the University of Connecticut Human Rights Institute at Storrs during October 2005.
[2] The present author is personally in favor of social human rights. But I want to subject that personal orientation to some "contrarian" arguments, in order to clarify matters.

Ultimately, I suggest that although a human rights approach to welfare policies would logically lead to some improvements, in American society one needs to think carefully about whether there are more effective ways to achieve desirable goals other than the human rights discourse.

In sum, I argue that, consistent with the views of FDR, there are different discourses that can be progressive. The discourse of human rights, anchored in positivistic fundamental law, whatever their possible ultimate grounding in moral philosophy, is one of these. But the simple discourse of wise public policy is another.

The core issue after all is protection of human dignity. The language of human rights, and the notion of legal obligation, is only one means to this end. Whether an emphasis on human rights via fundamental law is clearly the preferred means, and if so, why, is an important question.

In effect, I take David Kennedy's point (2004a) that we should not focus on legal theory and procedure to the exclusion of a focus on what actually happens to individuals in reality, and apply that argument to the human rights domain. I also refer to Oona Hathaway's point (2004) that just because states consent to the UN Convention against Torture, that does not mean that their record on torture is superior to others. So I start by asking whether the social policies of those who have ratified the ICESCR are really superior to those of the United States.

SOME HISTORY: FDR AND SOCIAL RIGHTS

The robust FDR fell victim to polio and the dynamic United States fell victim to the depression. The two together produced in President Roosevelt during the 1930s and 1940s the conviction that "necessitous men are not free men" (Goodwin 1994, 485). Roosevelt, and other prominent international figures to follow like Amartya Sen (2001) and Isaiah Berlin, believed in a broad definition of freedom.[3] To them, freedom, like the concept of security, implied positive duties for governing authority. For them, of what use was a narrow conception of civil and political freedom (and rights) when citizens lacked especially education and health care? To them, talk of equal opportunity was a sham without a foundation in especially adequate education and health. To all of them, in a manner of speaking, socioeconomic rights had their place along with civil and political rights. But "the manner of speaking" merits careful analysis.

Despite FDR's genuine commitment to "freedom from want," he was never as much in favor of radical change as his wife. Eleanor Roosevelt was always pressing FDR to do more for African Americans, for those in substandard housing, for those left behind by either racism or capitalism. Roosevelt, by contrast, was aware of the power in America of conservatives, their power base especially in the South and their control of much of Congress. He needed their deference as the United States moved toward war, and their cooperation when fully engaged in World War II. He was ever aware of what it would take to get reelected. He was sympathetic to capitalism and prided himself on saving American capitalism from its worst features (Goodwin 1994, 53). Eleanor was much more the crusading social democrat

---

[3] David Kennedy (2004b) summarizes the views of the noted British philosopher Isaiah Berlin.

than FDR. FDR was more the calculating politician in a market democracy than Eleanor, more content with incremental change in the face of conservative individualism (Goodwin 1994, passim). It has been said that FDR was a pragmatic idealist (Meacham 2004, 87). If so, the place of pragmatism in this formulation loomed large.

It may be that after FDR's death Eleanor played a key role in keeping the United States supportive of the Universal Declaration of Human Rights, with its references to socioeconomic rights. Just as she had incessantly lobbied her husband in behalf of social democratic values in U.S. domestic policy, so she may have lobbied President Truman to remain committed to the Declaration in late 1948 (Glendon 2001). Although we know that the wording of that part of the Declaration came not from the Soviet Union or its allies but from social democrats in the Western Hemisphere (Morsink 1999; Humphrey 1984), we still do not know exactly why the United States accepted that language despite its variance with the dominant values held by the political elite in the late 1940s. Certainly by 1948, maybe as early as 1940, the New Deal was a spent force, American conservatives already resurgent (Goodwin 1994, 43).

It is now often ignored that FDR never formally proposed an expansion of the U.S. Bill of Rights. His talk about a second bill of rights was entirely genuine but mostly metaphor. In the same way, President George W. Bush talked about a "war on terrorism" as political metaphor rather than formal legal argument. The Bush administration talked about "war" but denied the applicability of the laws of war to most situations supposedly involving terrorism and to most enemy detainees outside of Iraq in 2003–2004. Likewise, FDR talked about a second bill of rights in political rather than constitutional or other foundational legal terms. (Self-executing treaties in the United States are on a legal par with the constitution, as long as they do not contradict it.[4] The ICESCR is surely a non-self-executing treaty.)

In the view of Cass R. Sunstein (2004), FDR saw certain social policies as based on fundamental or constituent principles. These principles were not positivistic constitutional principles, but they were not mere policies either. Constituent principles occupied an intermediate position, short of fundamental rights but superior to routine policies.[5]

Sunstein is persuasive when arguing that access to education has that status in contemporary American society. There was originally no right to education in the U.S. Bill of Rights. Nor have U.S. courts clearly read such a constitutional right into case law. But access to education is a principle firmly entrenched in American society and public policy. In public policy, primary and secondary education is both a right and a duty. It is inconceivable that any level of governing authority in the United States today would officially contradict the importance of basic education or do away with public policies based on it. A U.S. right to education is not as entrenched

---

[4] John F. Murphy (2004, ch. 2) provides a good overview of the status of different forms of international law in the United States.

[5] There is another view, namely, that FDR thought that Congress could establish constitutional provisions as well as the courts and in addition to formal amendment. Given his difficulties with the Supreme Court, as well as the difficulties of formal constitutional amendment, one can understand why he might have held this view. But it is a controversial interpretation of his views, not fully accepted.

as a right to privacy, the latter having been read into the U.S. Constitution by court decisions.[6] Still, a de facto right to education exists via permanent and extensive public policy. It will not be erased. It is based on a constituent principle: access to education is necessary to make equal opportunity a reality.[7]

As I have argued elsewhere, as a matter of principle the United States does not now contest the fundamental importance of education and labor rights for individuals (Forsythe and Heinze 2006). These are not found in the U.S. first ten amendments to the Constitution, but they are based on constituent principles. They are rights provided by public policy, and they are rights that will not be overturned even though they lack constitutional status. Even the Republican Party, the party of big business, does not contest labor rights as reflecting a fundamental principle, even as that Party may strive mightily to restrict their impact on daily life. Indeed, during the cold war Republican Administrations often chided communist countries for violating labor rights. Still further, the Republican Party does not object to U.S. membership in the International Labour Organization, and its principles about the freedom of labor to associate, organize, and bargain. And it was Republicans who led the charge to rename the State Department Bureau of Human Rights and Humanitarian Affairs the Bureau of Human Rights, Democracy, and Labor.

In the United States the real controversy about socioeconomic rights is not about the enduring importance of education and labor rights but about rights to work, and to adequate food, clothing, shelter, and health. It is these latter welfare "rights" that generate more intense debate.[8]

This paper hypothesizes that U.S. welfare policies in their general contours are fundamental and already reflect constituent principles, in the sense that FDR would have understood. Most U.S. welfare policies reflect implicit constituent principles, and thus the basic, general rights found in public policy will not be erased despite their lack of constitutional standing. The United States does not endorse a human right to social security, but, especially given the political strength of senior citizens, it is not going to eliminate altogether some kind of social security policy. The United States does not recognize a human right to health care, but, again because of political factors, it is not going to erase some kind of Medicare program. This situation helps to explain why we should inquire carefully into whether the U.S. national record on most welfare matters is or is not different from most of the other wealthy democracies.

MAURICE CRANSTON REDUX?

Most students of international human rights know that Maurice Cranston argued some time ago that only civil and political rights were really fundamental – really

---

[6] Sunstein argues that U.S. courts were about to interpret the Fourteenth Amendment as supportive of substantive welfare rights when the Burger court and then the Rehnquist court stopped that development in U.S. Supreme Court jurisprudence.

[7] There remains the question of who takes this principle and this right seriously, in the sense of fashioning specific educational policy to reflect genuine equal opportunity through education.

[8] I should emphasize the distinction between arguments of principle and on the other hand practice. Labor rights are widely accepted in principle. As usual, the devil is in the details. And the details of the implementation of this principle show much periodic opposition.

human rights (1964). According to his view, if citizens have civil and political rights, then they can fashion desirable public policies. He and his intellectual followers regarded so-called welfare rights as comprising a wish list of desirable policies that debased the notion of human rights. These so-called positive rights were dependent on the government's ability to pay and thus were not really fundamental rights at all. This libertarian notion of human rights has been ideationally dominant in the United States, especially if one considers property rights, education rights, and labor rights as civil rights.[9] The individualistic American society, believing in a large area of private space, has been reluctant to fully embrace the idea of "big government" presumably required to implement "positive" welfare rights. The societal preference, at least in ideational terms, is for individual rights, responsibilities, and competition. Governmental provision of goods and services is generally suspect, except perhaps in dire emergencies and as a last resort. Socioeconomic rights are not seen as enabling, providing a foundation for the meaningful exercise of civil and political rights. Rather, they are seen as constraining of individual freedom.[10]

Despite all this, since the FDR era the United States has manifested a sizable welfare state. Of course there have been eras of "welfare reform" and efforts to shrink the welfare state in the name of individual responsibility, lower taxes, and other appealing values. The same is true in Sweden and other places; the welfare state expands and contracts in relative terms with changing governments and ideational periods (see Timonen 2003). Nevertheless, the United States is not without its social safety nets and other manifestations of the welfare state.

Has the Cranston or libertarian view of rights been able to protect human dignity in the United States comparable to the experience of other wealthy democracies? In other words, has the American version of liberal democracy done about as well as the social democratic version practiced in most of the rest of the wealthy democratic world with regard to work, food, clothing, shelter, and health? Even with a smaller welfare state, could the United States combine that condition with wealth and private purchasing power to approximate the European social democrats and their like-minded colleagues in places such as Japan?

A macro-comparison shows certain similarities in welfare conditions and policies. Using the UN Human Development Index ("HDI") for 2003, if we look at HDI overall, which is based on life expectancy, adult literacy, gross domestic product per capita, and a few other indicators, the United States is seventh on the HRI rankings, which is in the top half of the twenty-one most wealthy democracies. No doubt the high U.S. gross domestic product (GDP) per capita boosts the position of the United States. Only Luxembourg has a higher GDP/pc figure. Yet Luxembourg ranks only fifteenth on the HDI. So it is possible that the United States, as a nation state, combines wealth and buying power and civil freedom in a way that is socially commendable for most of its citizens – and certainly respectable in comparative terms.

---

[9] Even among students of human rights, there is no agreement on the dividing lines among civil rights, social rights, economic rights, and cultural rights.

[10] I suspect that most Americans, in so far as they think of such things at all, consider access to education to be a civil right, in a category of rights or governmental obligation different from health care or pensions.

The United States does better on these statistical evaluations of social welfare than others like France and Germany manifesting larger welfare states and ratifications of the International Covenant on Economic, Social, and Cultural Rights. The European states have also signed on to the European Social Charter. Although Germany and France appear more virtuous in terms of accepting legal obligations, the U.S. HDI overall ranking is higher. This suggests than on a macro basis, the social dimensions of human dignity fare reasonably well in the United States in comparative perspective, not withstanding Washington's nonratification of the International Covenant on Economic, Social, and Cultural Rights. We should not confuse legal theory with practical social conditions.

As a group, the wealthy democracies accept the idea that there is a human right to work for those that seek it, whereas the United States does not. Yet the 2003 HDI, covering data through 2001, reported that the unemployed in the United States were 4.8% of the workforce. In Australia it was 6.7%, Belgium 6.6%, Canada 7.2%, Finland 9.2%, France 8.7%, Germany 7.3%, Spain 10.5%, Italy 9.6%, Greece 10.4% – just to take the more striking comparisons within this grouping. Particularly here we see that a focus on legal theory alone can be quite misleading as to who really approximates full employment.

On balance, this and other macro-comparative data suggest that citizens in the United States have their social welfare tended to about as well as citizens in most of the other wealthy democracies, despite the fact that the latter acknowledge a human right to welfare protections whereas the United States does not. In the United States, it is not specious to argue that there are constituent principles amounting to the first cousins of constitutional principles (or principles derived from ratification of treaties). Among these constituent principles, there is now a recognition of governmental obligations in the field of social policies. This situation has, so it seems, led to fundamental social policies, not subject to elimination as a practical matter, that are not hugely dissimilar from the other wealthy democracies in their general outlines.

This preliminary comparative judgment, based on some simple quantitative comparisons, is sustained by a brief qualitative analysis of the Dutch situation (Baehr 2006). (Whether this comparison could be duplicated on a larger scale I leave to future studies.)

In the Netherlands, economic, social, and cultural (ESC) rights officially are accepted and placed on a par with civil and political rights. This theoretical position is not altogether matched by practice. There are very few court decisions related to these rights, and the ICESCR is not admissible in Dutch courts. One Dutch philosopher of law argued that although the ESC norms were called rights, they really were not rights in practice. In his view, they were "directive principles of state policy." This is a view similar to Cass Sunstein's view of constituent principles in the United States.[11]

In the Netherlands, despite the discourse on welfare rights as human rights, it appears to be the case that those lacking political power also wind up with difficulties in securing equitable social services. Thus, women, children, the elderly and

---

[11] It is increasingly clear that there can be adjudication of social and economic rights (see Ramcharan 2005).

disabled, illegal aliens, and racial minorities all manifest difficulties in benefiting from available social goods and services provided by public authorities. As we will see, this is also true in the United States.

Now it may be true that in the last analysis the Dutch do a better job than the Americans in protecting the social dimensions of human dignity. The Dutch rank two notches higher on the HDI than the Americans. And it may even be the case that the language of human rights plays some role in this. The government of the Netherlands faces a review of its relevant policies in the UN committee responsible for monitoring the ICESCR. So Dutch ratification of that legal instrument, although not leading to a plethora of court cases, might affect the reality of Dutch social policies. It is possible that this UN review, and comparable review at the regional level under the European Social Charter, might make a difference. Such impact, however, has yet to be clearly documented (see, e.g., Samuel 2002).

In the meantime, it is fair to say that the overall Dutch situation seems to be at first glance not completely dissimilar from the American situation pertaining to social protections of dignity. Both the quantitative and qualitative information would suggest that general conclusion.

Nevertheless, my initial point has been to demonstrate that the difference between the United States and its wealthy democratic siblings with regard to prac-tical social conditions has been overall a matter of degree and not of kind. There are differences, but for the most part they are not the differences of black and white, but rather of shades of gray. There can be stark differences, and the way the United States does public health care policy compared to Canada might be one.[12] In gen-eral, however, the question of whether or not the United States officially ratifies the ICESCR, as the leading test of formally accepting welfare rights as human rights, is a subject that can be blown out of proportion. We should not let legal theory obscure consideration of practical reality. This was precisely David Kennedy's gen-eral point (2004a), although himself a law professor, when addressing the dignity of individuals in international context. What counts is practical protection "on the ground," to which a focus on legal theory does not always contribute in a posi-tive way.

CRANSTON CHALLENGED

One can certainly argue both that the U.S. record on welfare policies is not that dissimilar from its democratic siblings, and that the U.S. record could be improved if it saw welfare rights as human rights – not just technical rights inhering in malleable statutes and subsequent administrative rules. This latter argument has been applied from time to time to the health care field (see, e.g., Chapman 1994), and I will limit myself largely to that policy area in this short essay.

On the one hand, we should note that according to the 2003 HDI the United States spent 5.8% of its GDP on public health in 2000, which is a figure higher than in Ireland, Finland, Luxembourg, Austria, Spain, Portugal, and Greece; and

---

[12] There are perhaps other differences of black and white. The Dutch permit medical assistance in the ending of life, under certain conditions and regulations, whereas it remains illegal under U.S. federal law.

which is approximate to such spending in Australia, Japan, Switzerland, the U.K., and Italy. Moreover, the U.S. federal government pays some 44% of the country's health care costs (Peters 2004, 246).[13] So it is not as if the United States manifested a strongly libertarian approach to health care.

On the other hand, the "Katrina epiphany" pertains to much more than disaster relief – namely, the recognition that those not properly cared for in American society are the poor, and that among the poor it is people of color who make up a disproportionate percentage.[14] As in disaster relief, so in health care, among other welfare policies, we need to look at what happens to the poor.

Disparity of income, which in the United States is a subject interlaced with the history of racial discrimination, is at the core of our subject. The effect of U.S. health care spending is reduced because of relatively or comparatively great disparity of incomes. As a country, the American nation spends more of its wealth on health care than any other country on the planet (Stein 2005). But a relatively large number of Americans simply cannot buy the health care they need (ibid.).

If we look at the HDI regarding life expectancy at birth (presumably a reflection mainly of nutrition and health care, along with reduction of environmental dangers), we find that the United States ranks lower than all the other wealthy democracies save Denmark. The United States comes in at 76.9 years, with the best being Japan at 81.3 years.

Timely social science research on comparative health policy points us in the right direction for further analysis, confirming that disparity of income correlates with less public health care (Ghobarah, Huth, & Russett 2004, 73–94). Those who follow such things know for starters that the United States tolerates greater disparity of income than almost all other wealthy democracies, especially the Nordics and Japan. According to the 2003 HDI, the richest 10% in American society take home 30.5% of the national income. The poorest 10% get just 1.8%. No other wealthy democracy comes close to this disparity, especially the wealth controlled by the top 10%. Germany seems a surprising exception to the democratic pattern, with 28% of national income controlled by the top 10%. But Germany is still adjusting to the integration of the poorer East Germany with the much more affluent West Germany. The German situation is presumably temporary and anomalous, especially given its long history of social policy and, since 1945, social democracy. The U.S. situation, at least since 1980 and the Reagan revolution, which undid the New Deal consensus, is widely considered normal and permanent and not particularly undesirable – certainly by most on the right of the American political spectrum.

Partially because of the disparity of incomes, the United States had the worst record among wealthy democracies on the HDI "Human Poverty Index." Only Ireland came close to the U.S. index score of 15.8, whereas, for comparative purposes, the best two, Sweden and Norway, scored 6.5 and 7.2. So, compared with these, the U.S. poverty score was more than twice as bad. The United Kingdom was similar to the United States, but slightly better, with a score of 14.8. The United States has

---

[13] This figure represents the percentage paid for the year 2001.

[14] The Katrina epiphany refers to the stark awareness, impossible to discount, that those left behind and greatest affected in terms of human dignity by hurricane Katrina in September 2005, especially in and around New Orleans, were the poor, who were mostly black.

more children living in poverty, about 20%, than any other wealthy democracy; U.S. figures for this category approximate Mexico (UNICEF 2005, 28; Klapper 2005).

So, in the United States, the probability at birth of not surviving until age sixty was 12.6%, whereas in Sweden it was 7.3% and in Norway 8.3%. Moreover, all data show that life expectancy for American blacks is lower than for American whites, again suggesting links between poverty and color.

The point here obviously is that despite U.S. democracy, wealth, and relatively peaceful conditions at home, which correlate positively with better public health care, U.S. disparity of income and ethnic heterogeneity show the expected negative correlation with medical well-being (see Ghobarah, Huth, and Russett 2004). There are other factors at work, such as the U.S. tendency to spend more of its public health budget for heroic and end-of-life procedures compared to primary and basic care (see, e.g., Chapman 1994). There also has been some gender bias at work. The bottom line for now is that whereas the United States spends about as much of its GDP on public health as its democratic siblings, and much more in dollar terms, and very much more in combined public and private spending, many do not benefit.

With regard to U.S. health care, whether one speaks of access, cost, or effectiveness, there are major problems (Peters 2004, 250).

A human rights approach to health care would set minimal standards of access and affordable and effective care for all. This is the great difference between American and European (and Canadian and Japanese) approaches to health care. In the United States, there are many who do not obtain access to necessary basic health care, mainly because they cannot afford it. Especially telling is the large number of working poor who cannot afford to purchase the health care they need. So the macro-comparisons cover up this important reality – namely, that the United States tolerates much inadequate health care for the poor, whereas the other wealthy democracies, being social democracies, do not. When it comes to medical care for the poor, the macro-comparisons showing certain socioeconomic similarities among the wealthy democracies comprise either a straw man argument or are irrelevant.

HUMAN RIGHTS DISCOURSE AS REMEDY?

If the United States used the discourse of fundamental human rights, leading to a constitutional right to minimum health care, whether treaty related or not, this might change things for the better by placing a greater emphasis on preventative and primary care for all. It is often enough noted that some forty-five million Americans lack private health insurance (Peters 2004, 246), and thus presumably cannot afford even basic health care. It is often enough noted that the basic Medicare coverage is only for hospital expenses, not for visits to primary care doctors.

The Canadian experience suggests, however, that for the United States, adopting this radical change (for it) of taking a legally based human rights approach to health policy might substitute one set of problems for another. The Canadian health care system – based on a human rights approach – is not free from major problems. I refer particularly to the recent high court ruling pertaining to Quebec that, given the long delays in securing adequate treatment, the government's prohibition on private health insurance was an unconstitutional violation of the right to health (Associated Press 2005). In fact, the United States ranks one spot higher than Canada on the HDI, although Canada has the higher life expectancy (by 2.7 years).

It is likely that with a human rights approach to health in the United States, the poor would be better off and the rich would have fewer elective options at the time of their choice, as more resources were transferred to preventive and basic care. If this is true, namely, that a human rights approach to health care would restrict the options for the wealthier classes while benefiting the poorer classes, it is difficult to see how this sort of major change could be brought about through the contemporary American democratic process – especially because the poor do not vote as much, or have as much influence in Washington, as the wealthier classes. Although the democratic process has produced health care as a human right in the other wealthy democracies, this is not the case so far in the United States. The other democracies evidentially combine a certain type of individualism and competition with a strong communitarian sense of better providing for the poor and marginalized.[15]

Most Americans, including many who are not wealthy, have bought into the ideology of individualism and competition and market approaches to various issues to the exclusion of communitarian concern. For reasons of national security or because of issues such as abortion, they vote Republican. But the Republican Party is not very likely to adopt welfare policies, especially in health care, that benefit them. "The problem with Kansas" is that many voters – in this case poor and middle-class whites – are not rational about socioeconomic rights. They vote Republican for other reasons – patriotism, rugged individualism, family values – when their practical socioeconomic interests lie with the Democratic Party. It is the latter party that is more likely to reflect the orientations of FDR and Truman regarding socioeconomic policies in general and health care in particular (Frank 2005).[16]

Therefore, thus far in the United States, unlike its wealthy siblings, the compassion of the rich has yet to restrict that class so as to benefit the poor. "Compassionate conservatism" is more American campaign rhetoric than policy guideline. Such is the powerful ideology of rugged individualism and "magic of the market."

It is possible that, although there are certainly advocates for a human rights approach to U.S. health care among medical professionals who stress ethical argument (Farmer 2005; Mann et al. 1999), some major changes might come about when and if it were recognized by the middle classes that the U.S. health care system has become too expensive to provide for their needs at affordable cost. They might, therefore, be willing to trade more affordable care on a broad basis for fewer elective options and longer waiting times for certain procedures. But they are likely to be more moved by perception of self interest than by appeals to abstract human rights language. One can say that a human rights approach means a more affordable health care system, but in the United States the reference to socioeconomic policy

---

[15] In 2005, Finland and certain Nordic states were ranked at the very top of certain indexes purporting to measure competitiveness, even while manifesting very large welfare states (see Lopez-Claros, Porter, & Schwab 2005). In 2005–2006, Finland ranked first, Sweden third, Denmark fourth, Norway ninth, the Netherlands eleventh (ibid., 7).

[16] This insight, although expressed by Frank in a captivating way, is not new (see Forsythe 1984, 168) (quoting the novelist John Fowles, who was writing in 1977).

in connection with human rights, especially internationally recognized human rights, carries considerable negative baggage or connotation.

Arguments about fundamental human rights in the social realm, linked to ethics, are not likely to control policy choice – given the dominant culture of conservative individualism. In America, human rights language pertaining to social policy is too easily attacked for being linked to socialism, big government, impersonal bureaucracies, and Canadian-style problems.[17] Language about affordability alone might be more efficacious, especially with the middle class, while arriving at the same end as reference to social human rights. Perhaps affordability could be linked to basic equity or fairness.

Relevant is the view of William Schulz, Executive Director of Amnesty International USA. When he wrote his book on why the United States should be interested in the civil and political rights of others abroad, knowing American society, he pitched his arguments on the basis of self interest, not ethics or legal theory (Schulz 2001). So it is not so clear that reliance on human rights discourse is the preferred approach to change regarding American welfare policies, unless it is tightly tied to self-interest.

In late 2005, a columnist in the *New York Times* detailed the defects of U.S. health care policy, then made arguments about affordability and effectiveness. The concept of human rights, much less reference to international legal instruments, was never mentioned (Krugman 2005). This is probably the advisable path to follow on pragmatic or utilitarian grounds. If one can show that the U.S. status quo on health policy is more bureaucratic, ineffective, and expensive than other options, this is likely to prove more compelling than arguments based on international law and morality.

Even with a human rights approach to health care policy, perhaps linked to affordability, a certain type of politics would remain. This type of politics reflects preferential influence for the wealthier classes. For example, either Congress or the Department of Health and Human Services would need to set the rates at which doctors and hospitals would be paid. Already under Medicare and Medicare, surgeons, hospitals, and others are reimbursed by public authorities for very high charges.[18] Congress could stop this, but Republicans aligned with doctors and pharmaceuticals dominate, and the George W. Bush administration has not exercised progressive

---

[17] For an argument that all welfare states are moving away from guaranteed entitlements and more toward insistence on work and responsibility, see Gilbert 2002.

[18] My own current experience provides a window on basic problems, even though I am dealing with private rather than public services. For a medical problem I first saw my primary care doctor, who referred me to a specialist. A ten-minute visit with the specialist was billed at $250, which my private health insurer paid up to 80%. There was then an MRI, lasting forty minutes, and costing just over $1,000, which my insurer paid up to 80%. There was outpatient surgery, technically elective rather than absolutely essential, of maybe twenty minutes, which resulted in a charge by both the surgeon (over $4,000) and the clinic (over $2,000), which my insurer will pay up to 80%. But first I had to be cleared for even minor surgery via another visit to my primary care doctor, with the usual charges and payments (about $200). There will be follow-up visits to the specialist, even if all goes well in the surgery. So this minor medical procedure, taking about one hour of one day from check in to check out, costs in the neighborhood of $8,000.

High charges could not be sustained if the various insurers would refuse reimbursement. Patients would be unlikely to continue with treatment if they had to pay more than 20%.

The poor, especially those without health insurance, have no hope of getting this kind of expensive medical care. They have to live with the pain that I can choose to have treated.

leadership on the question. Even under a human rights approach, the American Medical Association and other medical lobbies would pressure the relevant public authorities for high payments for medical providers. Drug companies would lobby for preferential treatment for pricing structures of their products. True, on the other side one finds influential lobbies such as the American Association of Retired Persons, reflecting the interests of older consumers of medical goods and services. But today, even the power of AARP has not been able to avoid or correct the high cost of American health care.

Current U.S. welfare policy, especially pertaining to public health care, is clearly defective. Its general effects are roughly similar to the other democracies, but not as beneficial toward the poor. It is also extremely expensive and highly bureaucratic. How best to go about changing it is not as clear. The human rights discourse is one of several that might be put at the service of progressive change in U.S. health care policy. Whether the language of human rights is the best one to secure desired change in social policy in the United States is a question that requires careful judgment.[19]

American culture is very different from the other wealthy democracies. America is indeed exceptional, but not in an entirely positive sense. The American social-democratic tradition is weak; the American suspicion is strong of "socialism," big government, powerful bureaucracy. Perhaps pragmatic argument about affordability and fairness is the way to go, without reference to fundamental rights, much less international legal obligation.

Former State Department Official Harold Koh, a strong supporter of human rights, in the context of a discussion about the U.S. nonratification of the Convention on the Rights of the Child, wrote the following: "But once one weighs in the unfavorable alignment of proratification votes in the Republican-controlled Senate, and considers the amount of political capital that U.S. activists would require to obtain the sixty-seven votes needed for ratification any time soon, one soon concludes that the children's rights advocates are probably better off directing their limited energies not toward ratification, but rather, toward real strategies to reduce the exploitation of child labor" (2003, 1485). A similar argument can be made about the ICESCR and American health care policy.

CONCLUSION

When FDR spoke about a second bill of rights covering social rights, he was really speaking about fundamental social policies, perhaps reflecting what Sunstein has called constituent principles – or in other words, quasi-constitutional principles. In American society today, basic rights to education and to labor protections are widely accepted and thus permanent, even though they originally had no constitutional grounding. They are as permanent, most probably, as in most of the other wealthy democracies. Even in the latter, given severe economic crisis, there would, no doubt, be cutbacks in educational programming. A number of European states have instituted tuition payments for higher education.

---

[19] The American penchant for litigation is also part of the basic problem. Doctors often order expensive tests in order to guard against legal liability.

For those interested in the plight of the poor in the United States and particularly their adequate food, clothing, shelter, and health, one might want to consider taking the same approach. It might be best to use the discourse of progressive policy, based on supposed American principles of fairness and affordability, thus avoiding often contentious debates about fundamental rights, either constitutional or based on international law.

Admittedly, as many Americans fall into the category of "working poor" who cannot afford adequate health care, the discourse about fundamental socioeconomic rights may finally find broad acceptance, as in the other wealthy democracies. But this is by no means certain. It is true that since the 1970s there has been general and passive support for the notion of national health insurance (Peters 2004, 277). But this amorphous sentiment has never been translated into fundamental policy change, and the failure of President Clinton's health care reform package was a manifestation of the same story. Fears about large and impersonal bureaucracy, and the problems in Canada and perhaps elsewhere, loom large.

Moreover, just as the U.S. ratification of the 1949 Geneva Conventions and of the 1984 UN Convention against Torture and Degrading Treatment has not prevented the intentional U.S. mistreatment of certain "enemy prisoners" after September 11, 2001 (Forsythe 2006), so the U.S. ratification of the ICESCR might not make any real difference in U.S. welfare policies.

In any event, one needs to think most importantly about what discourse – that is, what set of arguments – is likely to prove effective in context, rather than just automatically prioritize the human rights discourse as linked to international law. Ironically, this may be a matter of recognizing cultural relativism in the service of universalism. Given the peculiarities and particularities of American culture, to advance policies consistent with universal human rights, it may be necessary to keep quiet about universal human rights – especially socioeconomic ones.

POSTSCRIPT ON SOCIAL RIGHTS AND U.S. FOREIGN POLICY

UNICEF has increasingly presented itself as a human rights agency since the adoption of the 1989 Convention on the Rights of the Child.[20] It increasingly grounds its activities in the discourse about the rights of children and their mothers. Despite U.S. failure to ratify this 1989 legal instrument and its more general opposition to socioeconomic human rights, especially in international form, the United States *increased* both its regular and supplemental financial contributions to UNICEF during the period 1999–2004. U.S. regular contributions to core programming went from $105 million to almost $120 million. Additional contributions for particular projects and emergencies went from just over $98 million to almost $145 million.

We should not let a preoccupation with legal theory and procedures blind us to social reality. The United States clearly sees UNICEF as helpful in a practical way in responding to the needs of women and children abroad, whether that need be defined in terms of compassion, development (and thus indirectly democracy), or the social side of the war against terrorism.

---

[20] All facts in this section are drawn from UNICEF annual reports.

Even when there was some discussion of *reducing* the U.S. contribution to UNICEF in 2005, the key issues stemmed not from a concern with human rights or rights programming, but with the need to find money to support other programs such as the U.S. Millennium Challenge Account, a unilateral program for good government and development in recipient countries.

Relevant trends pertaining to the United States and the World Health Organization (WHO) are similar. The WHO increasingly used the language of human rights in its activities and programming, but the United States did not drastically alter its relevant policies.

U.S. policies toward UNESCO and the WHO were, in general, about as supportive as the other wealthy democracies. Who was more generous toward these social agencies resulted in a debate that compared total dollar amounts (favoring the United States by far), to contributions per capita and/or per capita GDP (favoring most of the other wealthy democracies, especially the Nordics and the Dutch).

We should keep our focus on social and political reality, even when interested in internationally recognized human rights. In all of these matters, international legal logic and legal obligation play a very small role, certainly for the United States. Evaluation of policy efficacy should take pride of place. We should carefully evaluate whether the U.S. rejection of internationally recognized socioeconomic rights makes a real difference at home and abroad, what really is the comparative advantage of the human rights discourse, and what in the American context works best, or might work best.

REFERENCES

Associated Press, "Canada Court Weighs Privatized Health Care: Supreme Court Suspends Its Own Judgment on Private Health Services," *ABC News*, August 4, 2005, http://abcnews.go.com/International/wireStory?id=1010321 (accessed 17 February 2006).

Baehr, Peter R. 2006. The Netherlands: A Walhalla of Economic and Social Rights? In *Economic Rights in Canada and the United States*, eds. Rhoda Howard-Hassmann and Claude Welch, Jr. Philadelphia: University of Pennsylvania Press.

Chapman, Audrey R., ed. 1994. *Health Care Reform: A Human Rights Approach*. Washington: Georgetown University Press.

Cranston, Maurice. 1964. *What Are Human Rights?* New York: Basic Books.

Farmer, Paul. 2005. *Pathologies of Power: Health, Human Rights, and the New War on the Poor*. Berkeley: University of California Press.

Felice, William F. 2003. *The Global New Deal: Economic and Social Human Rights in World Politics*. Lanham: Rowman & Littlefield.

Forsythe, David P. 1984. *Human Rights and World Politics*. Lincoln: University of Nebraska Press.

Forsythe, David P. 2006. U.S. Treatment of Enemy Detainees. *Human Rights Quarterly* 28 (2): 465–91.

Forsythe, David P., and Eric A. Heinze. 2006. On the Margins of the Human Rights Discourse: Foreign Policy and International Welfare Rights. In *Economic Rights in Canada and the United States*, eds. Rhoda Howard-Hassmann and Claude Welch, Jr. Philadelphia: University of Pennsylvania Press.

Frank, Thomas. 2005. *What's The Matter with Kansas?: How the Conservatives Won the Heart of America*. New York: Henry Holt.

Ghobarah, Hazem Adam, Paul Huth, and Bruce Russett. 2004. Comparative Public Health: The Political Economy of Human Misery and Well-Being. *International Studies Quarterly* 48 (1): 73–94.

Gilbert, Neil. 2002. *Transformation of the Welfare State: The Silent Surrender of Public Responsibility.* New York: Oxford University Press.

Glendon, Mary Ann. 2001. *A World Made New: Eleanor Roosevelt and the Universal Declaration of Human Rights.* New York: Random House.

Goodwin, Doris Kearns. 1994. *No Ordinary Time: Franklin and Eleanor Roosevelt: The Home Front in World War II.* New York: Simon and Schuster.

Hathaway, Oona A. 2004. The International Law of Torture. In *Torture: Philosophical, Political, and Legal Perspectives,* ed. Sanford Levinson. Oxford and New York: Oxford University Press.

Humphrey, John P. 1984. *Human Rights and the United Nations: A Great Adventure.* New York: Transnational.

Kennedy, David. 2004a. *The Dark Sides of Virtue: Reassessing International Humanitarianism.* Princeton: Princeton University Press.

Kennedy, David. 2004b. Unfinished Business. *New York Times Book Review,* 19 September 2004, 23.

Klapper, Bradley S. 2005. U.N. Report: Nordics Have Lowest Child Poverty, U.S. Far Behind. Associated Press, 1 March 2005. https://web.lexisnexis.com/universe/.

Koh, Harold Hongju. 2003. On American Exceptionalism. *Stanford Law Review* 55 (5): 1479–1528.

Krugman, Paul. 2005. "Pride, Prejudice, Insurance." *New York Times,* 7 November 2005, late edition, sec. A.

Lopez-Claros, Augusto, Michael E. Porter, and Klaus Schwab, eds. 2005. *The Global Competitiveness Report, 2005–2006.* New York: Palgrave Macmillian.

Mann, Jonathan M., Sofia Gruskin, Michael A. Grodin, and George J. Annas, eds. 1999. *Health and Human Rights: A Reader.* London: Routledge.

Meacham, Jon. 2004. *Franklin and Winston: An Intimate Portrait of an Epic Friendship.* New York: Random House.

Morsink, Johannes. 1999. *The Universal Declaration of Human Rights: Origins, Drafting, & Intent.* Philadelphia: University of Pennsylvania Press.

Murphy, John F. 2004. *The United States and the Rule of Law in International Affairs.* Cambridge: Cambridge University Press.

Peters, B. Guy. 2004. *American Public Policy: Promise and Performance,* 6th ed. Washington, DC: Congressional Quarterly Press.

Ramcharan, B. G., ed. 2005. *Judicial Protection of Economic, Social, and Cultural Rights.* Boston: Brill.

Samuel, Lenia. 2002. *Fundamental Social Rights: Case Law of the European Social Charter,* 2nd ed. Strasbourg: Council of Europe.

Schulz, William F. 2001. *In Our Own Best Interests: How Defending Human Rights Benefits Us All.* Boston: Beacon Press.

Sen, Amartya. 2001. *Development as Freedom.* New York: Anchor Books.

Stein, Rob. 2005. Survey: Health Care in U.S. Lags Behind. *Lincoln Journal Star,* 4 November 2005, 8A.

Sunstein, Cass R. 2004. *The Second Bill of Rights: FDR's Unfinished Revolution and Why We Need It More Than Ever.* New York: Basic Books.

Timonen, Virpi. 2003. *Restructuring the Welfare State: Globalization and Social Policy Reform in Finland and Sweden.* Williston, VT: Edward Elgar Publishing.

United Nations Children's Fund (UNICEF). 2005. *The State of the World's Children 2005: Childhood Under Threat.* New York: UNICEF. http://www.unicef.org/publications/files/-SOWC_2005_(English).pdf

15 Public Policy and Economic Rights in Ghana and Uganda

SUSAN DICKLITCH AND
RHODA E. HOWARD-HASSMANN

GIVING MACROECONOMIC REFORM A CHANCE

This chapter advocates more serious attention by human rights scholars to macroeconomic reform. Macroeconomic reform in some poor countries, including the two on which this chapter focuses, has been necessary during the last twenty-five years for economic growth. In turn, economic growth is necessary, but not sufficient, for economic rights.

Many countries in sub-Saharan Africa have undergone significant macroeconomic reform since the 1980s. Structural adjustment programs (SAPs) advocated by the International Monetary Fund (IMF) and the World Bank (WB) led this reform. Typical characteristics of SAPs in Africa are fiscal austerity, trade liberalization, privatization of state-owned enterprises (SOEs), abolition of state marketing boards, export-led agricultural reform, retrenchment of civil servants, and currency devaluation. There is widespread concern that SAPs have failed Africa (Ibhawoh 1999, 158–67). Aware of this concern, many human rights scholars have concluded that macroeconomic reform and SAPs are always detrimental to economic human rights, as specified in the International Covenant on Economic, Social, and Cultural Rights. In the case of sub-Saharan Africa, the economic rights most commonly referred to in criticism of macroeconomic reform are those to food, health, education, and access to clean water.

We suggest that blanket dismissal of macroeconomic reform as a path to economic human rights may be too hasty. Although macroeconomic reform is not necessarily beneficial to economic rights, it may in some cases contribute to their realization.

Macroeconomic reform can release blocked productive capacities. The release of productive capacities helps citizens to earn their own livelihood. As Sen argues (2001), citizens must be permitted to exercise their own capabilities. In sub-Saharan Africa, citizens' capabilities include the capacity to grow food for subsistence

We are most grateful to Michael Lisetto-Smith for his diligent research assistance, and to James Busumtwi-Sam, Boye Ejobowah, and Richard Sandbrook for their comments on an earlier draft. Rhoda Howard-Hassmann also thanks the Social Sciences and Humanities Research Council of Canada for research funds, and the Canada Research Chairs program for time to conduct research. Any errors of fact or interpretation are our own.

consumption; to engage in local, national, or international market transactions; to engage in industrial production; and to exercise their entrepreneurial agency. Thus, when citizens can rely on their own productive capacities, they can create goods and wealth for their own consumption and use. They can supply some of their own economic rights without reliance on redistributive powers of the state.

Macroeconomic reform can also stimulate economic growth. Economic growth is best stimulated by efficient creation of and participation in a market economy that protects property rights. As Mwangi Kimenyi, another author in this volume, states, "property rights and economic liberties are important determinants of economic growth" (1997, 98). This does not mean that there should be no government regulation of the marketplace. There are no absolutely "free" markets: even the most market-oriented states protect the rule of law and enforce contracts.

Economic growth also may contribute to economic rights, if it results in more equitable distribution of economic goods, and devotion of public resources to the promotion of economic rights such as education or health care. Governments must ensure that those who cannot provide them for themselves enjoy their economic rights. This can occur, however, only if an efficient, welfare-oriented, and redistributive state exists. The emergence of such a state depends on many political and social factors. In agreement with the Ghanaian economist George Ayittey (1998), we maintain that to translate economic growth into policies of economic rights, citizens must enjoy the full range of civil and political rights, especially the rule of law; freedom of speech, press, association and assembly; and political democracy. These rights increase the likelihood that governments will engage in accountable, transparent policy making, and devote resources to the economic human rights of their citizens.

In 1983, Goran Hyden published *No Shortcuts to Progress.* This volume was a wake-up call to scholars of Africa. Hyden argued that the path to African economic growth was a slow one, and that to understand how that path might be taken scholars had to pay attention to orthodox economic theory. He defended a market economy, local capitalist development, and foreign investment (Hyden 1983, 17–28). Before publication of Hyden's work, many scholars of Africa had believed that the continent could achieve economic rights under some variant of "African socialism." Internally, wealth could be redistributed, especially from foreign or minority capitalists to ordinary Africans. Externally, withdrawal from, or avoidance of international capitalism would promote development. This African socialist approach not only ignored but also exacerbated the internal political and economic factors that undermined African economies, hence undermining their capacity to protect economic rights.

Many scholars of human rights are now at the same stage as were scholars of Africa more than twenty years ago. These human rights scholars focus on the external causes of poverty in Africa, paying little attention to internal causes. Some simply dismiss as nefarious the mechanisms of macroeconomic reform, referring for example to "the destructive impact of structural adjustment policies" (Goodhart 2003, 935). There is a tendency to dismiss economic analysis as ideological, attributing a "neoliberal" philosophical agenda to the entire profession (Falk 1999, 1). This "macroeconomic populism" (Sandbrook 2000, 137) cannot but harm the potential for economic growth and, under the right conditions, for economic rights in Africa. Economists who support macroeconomic reform often act on serious analysis of the economies of developing countries, not on ideological motives.

Sometimes SAPs can help release productive forces and promote economic growth as, we argue later, has been the case for Ghana and Uganda. Yet in the human rights literature, one frequently encounters comments such as "[s]tructural adjustment programs and debt payment plans often deepen poverty and worsen social conditions for the poor," without consideration of competing views (Felice 2003, 82). Human rights scholars often refer to the international law of economic human rights, and the obligations of states to protect and implement those rights, as if legal injunctions are sufficient to overcome economic problems (Kent 2005). Yet there are real constraints on resources and on human capacities to organize and administer them (Huntington 1976). The law of economic rights cannot overcome these constraints. Absent a productive economy creating goods that private citizens can use or that governments can redistribute, states cannot guarantee economic rights. Sometimes the alternatives to SAPs are hyperinflation, unemployment, extreme inequality in distribution of resources, or severe malnutrition.

We illustrate the need to give macroeconomic reform a chance by discussing Ghana and Uganda. We investigate macroeconomic reform in only two countries because it is not useful to make generalizations about all of Africa. It is far more instructive to study national cases, asking detailed, nuanced questions about macroeconomic reform. We do not defend all aspects of the SAPs introduced in Ghana and Uganda, nor do we suggest that they were sufficient to introduce or support economic rights. We are no more capable than any other scholars of untangling the effects of SAPs from the effects of regime change, of the end of civil war (in Uganda), and of increased foreign aid as rewards for implementing SAPs. However, macroeconomic reform can sometimes promote economic growth, which in poor countries is necessary for the fulfillment of economic rights. Structural adjustment policies in Ghana and Uganda reversed negative growth figures, and also released productive forces that had been blocked by earlier socialist policies, by coercive theft of national resources by political and military elites, and by civil war.

Severe poverty existed in Ghana and Uganda before the macroeconomic reform of the 1980s and 1990s. Their economies had already been structurally adjusted twice, once during the colonial era and once during the early postindependence decades. The alternative in the 1980s to macroeconomic reform was continuation of a severe downward economic spiral. To promote and protect economic human rights in Ghana and Uganda, in the 1980s and beyond, required both economic growth and the release of their citizens' productive capacities.

GHANA

In 1974, I (Rhoda Howard-Hassmann) spent eight months in Accra, the capital of Ghana, pursuing my doctoral research (see Howard 1978). I recall once joining a line of "market mammies" at a department store to buy soap. The mammies were buying soap at the official control price, to sell later at a higher price in the market. This dual-price system was much more costly to the poor who had to shop in the outdoor market than a single, supply-and-demand driven price would have been. Ghanaian currency in 1974 was overvalued; many foreigners and locals exchanged their hard currency on the black market, removing it from the formal banking system. My landlord suggested I could save money by paying my rent in Canadian dollars to a foreign account, rather than in local currency to an account in Ghana. One of the other flats in my building was occupied by a middle-aged British couple, preparing to leave the country because their timber mill had been nationalized; not many years later, the timber industry in Ghana collapsed. At one point I was obliged to relinquish my passport as part of an "alien registration" exercise, whose purpose was to harass large-scale "foreign" (Lebanese-origin) entrepreneurs, after the expulsion of non-citizen petty entrepreneurs in 1970 (Howard 1986, 104). Food was expensive, and one of the policies ordered by the military dictator was "Operation Feed Yourself," a directive that all citizens should cultivate food, even in urban areas. Yet at the same time, there were so few machetes for farmers' use that they were being personally distributed throughout Ghana by regional commissioners (ibid., 71).

These reminiscences are meant to give the reader a sense of everyday life in a state-controlled economy administered by inefficient, corrupt, self-serving officials. From 1957 until the early 1980s, a series of leaders – starting with Kwame Nkrumah – attempted to impose either "socialist" or military order on the economy. Nkrumah relied on a combination of statism and redistribution to purchase political support (Busumtwi-Sam 1996, 182–3). A series of military and civilian regimes followed Nkrumah's downfall in 1966. Rulers engaged in state-directed "pirate capitalism," to suit their own interests and the interests of those they wished to protect (Schatz 1984, 45–57, cited in Sandbrook 1993, 30). The result was a massive decline in Ghana's economy. "Between 1970 and 1982, income per capita fell by 30 percent and real wages by 80 percent; import volume fell by two-thirds; real export earnings fell by one-half, and the ratio of Ghana's exports to GDP dropped from 21 to 4 percent" (Boafo-Arthur 1999a, 48). This series of regimes culminated in the takeover of power on 31 December 1981, by Flight-Lieutenant Jerry Rawlings, who ruled Ghana until 2001.

In 1983, Rawlings changed his economic policy from antientrepreneurial populism to structural adjustment and a privatized, market-based economy. William Felice, a scholar of economic rights, decries that aspect of neoliberalism that reduces the power of the state (2003, 30). But it was crucial to reduce the Ghanaian state's power. Its policy until 1983 was not to redistribute wealth to the poor. Nkrumah's policy was to exploit Ghana's peasant class. The policies of his various successors were to distribute what little national wealth existed to their kin, their cronies, the military, and whatever sections of the population were perceived to support them. This exploitation of ordinary Ghanaians drastically undermined their economic rights. The infant mortality rate rose from 80 per 1,000 in 1975 to 107 per 1,000 in 1983 (Sandbrook 1993, 10). The average annual growth rate of food production per capita between 1969 and 1971 and 1977 and 1979 was minus 3.1% (Howard 1986, 62). Seventy percent of farmers surveyed in the Ashanti region in 1978 said they did not grow enough food to feed their families (ibid., 71). Without structural adjustment this precipitous downward economic movement would have continued. By contrast, partly in consequence of the Economic Reform Plan introduced by Rawlings in 1982, followed by a SAP in 1983, the economic performance of Ghana from the early 1980s to 2005 was "reasonably strong and stable" (Commission for Africa 2005, 339).

Below we concentrate on four aspects of structural adjustment to which critics often object, but that led to improvements in Ghana's economy after 1983. They are elimination of the state marketing board for cocoa; better protection of private property; reduction in the size of the public service; and privatization of state-owned enterprises.

One of the most devastating of Nkrumah's policies was to underpay cocoa producers. A marketing board purchased cocoa from farmers at a set price, then sold it at the world market price. The difference in the two prices financed the government, and was used to buy the support of the urban classes, who were more likely to challenge Nkrumah's rule than were peasants. By 1984, cocoa farmers were receiving only 10% of the world market price, far below their cost of production (Ayittey 1998, 139). As a result, cocoa production declined drastically; farmers produced 403,000 tons in 1970, but only 179,000 tons in 1983 (Boafo-Arthur 1999a, 47). Much cocoa was smuggled out of the country, to be sold in Ivory Coast or Togo, where farmers received higher prices. After Ghana eliminated the cocoa marketing board, it became worthwhile for farmers to resume producing cocoa and to export it from Ghana.

Structural adjustment often requires more secure private property rights, key both to attraction of foreign investment (Killick 2002, 557), and to encouragement of indigenous enterprise. Insecure property rights in Ghana caused capital flight, speculation, and "political investment," as the middle classes relied for security on political office or influence (Sandbrook 2000, 120). Even after he accepted structural adjustment, Rawlings and his circle were ideologically hostile to private enterprise. In 1982, Rawlings ordered that Makola No. 1, a large Accra market controlled by women traders, be dynamited. Some mammies were beaten or had their heads shaved, while in Kumasi, one mammy was shot to death in the marketplace, her baby first being removed from her back (Robertson 1983, 469). Rawlings denounced big businessmen in his speeches and encouraged his soldiers to harass businessmen (Ayittey 1998, 214–16). Private property was frequently confiscated without cause (Gyimah-Boadi 1994, 77). Well into the 1990s, Rawlings still focused on "economic crime" (ibid., 80).

Property rights must also be extended to land. This is difficult in Ghana, where much land is communally owned. Yet, when small farmers or entrepreneurs are the legal owners of their land, they can safely invest in it and use it as collateral. Without private property in land, farmers in Ghana lack incentive to invest in cocoa trees, which take several years to mature. Farmers also lack security in producing subsistence crops. Women face difficulties when land is privatized: it is usually men who register it, often leaving their wives with less access to land than they previously had (Howard 1986, 190–91). But regularized land registration is still a better option than land theft. Land theft by military officers and senior bureaucrats in the rice-producing areas of northern Ghana contributed to a famine in 1977 (ibid., 51).

SAPs are based, in part, on the assumption that when the state relinquishes control of the economy, private citizens will be more willing to save and invest.

Insecure property rights undermine this likelihood. In 1997, private businesspersons in Ghana still hesitated to reinvest their profits, preferring to invest in real estate. Some were also unsure of their property rights, not knowing if the land they used belonged to them, to some other private owner, to the government, or to a traditional owner (e.g., a clan or extended family). Most upsetting to businesspersons was uncertainty about bureaucratic procedures, and the time and energy required to negotiate multiple rules and offices (Amponsah 2000, 17–28).

One of the most contentious aspects of structural adjustment in Ghana was the reduction of bloated public services, the only route to a secure income for many people (Panford 1997, 84–86). Ghana retrenched 241,400 public servants between 1985 and 1991 (calculated from Appiah-Kubi 2001, 227 n. 34). Of these, about 11,000 were "ghost workers," individuals who collected state salaries but who did not actually work for the government (Sandbrook 1993, 60). The result was a "massive decline in the welfare of former public sector workers" (Appiah-Kubi 2001, 221). That a quarter million individuals suddenly lost their jobs is a great tragedy, but it should also be kept in mind that by 1983 real starting salaries in the state bureaucracy were below subsistence level. Even mid-level officials could not feed their families, and had to neglect their offices to conduct more lucrative private business, or else emigrate (Sandbrook 2000, 91–92).

State-owned enterprises (SOEs) were also a serious drain on the Ghanaian economy. Most were run very inefficiently, operating well below their optimum productivity. Some enterprises were managed by former military officers (Christensen 1998, 286). In 1987, there were about 324 public enterprises in Ghana, including joint ventures (Appiah-Kubi 2001, 201). Output of these enterprises improved after privatization. Manufactures were at only 35% of their efficiency in 1983, whereas production levels of all sectors rose by 300% from 1983 to 1996 (ibid., 214–15). Employment levels in privatized industries increased by 59% by 1999, although this certainly did not compensate for public sector retrenchments (ibid., 217). Tax revenue increased from 4.6% of GDP in 1983 to 20.8% in 2003 (Commission for Africa 2005, 342). The privatization program was not a complete success, however. Although foreign and local investment did increase, assets were often transferred to Rawlings's ministers or supporters (Oelbaum 2002, 310–11), and corruption was still rampant.

Critics who decry SAPs and other policies of international financial institutions (IFIs) often seem to forget that any population is divided into different groups. Observers of SAPs often concentrate on the sectors of the population who lose income: these are often urban, especially employees of the state. Critics do not notice those whose incomes rise, especially when they are in rural areas, as in Ghana. Others who benefited in Ghana were exporters who could sell more when currencies were devalued and export prices no longer inflated, some skilled employees of industrial enterprises, and self-employed individuals (Sandbrook 2000, 77).

The anthropologist George Sefa Dei conducted a micro-study that illuminates how macroeconomic reforms affect the rural population. Dei visited the Ghanaian village of Ayirebi in 1983 and 1990. The people of Ayirebi had been settled subsistence farmers; the men cultivated some cocoa, and the women sometimes sold surplus agricultural produce in local markets. In 1983, they had been reduced to hunting and foraging, partly because of a severe drought, but also because cocoa prices were so low that it was not worth the men's time to cultivate it. Price controls also meant the women farmers did not find it worthwhile to sell in the markets.

By 1990, Ayirebi's economy had improved. Government ministries offered better technologies and extension services to cash crop farmers (although they did not offer analogous goods and services to farmers producing food for local consumption). The cocoa price rose from about $0.40 (U.S.) per 30 kilogram bag in 1979–80, to $13.20 (U.S.) in 1988–89. As a result of the freeing of exchange rates, migrants living in villages outside Ghana now found it worthwhile to remit currency: earlier, the exchange rate had been so low that villagers received far less than the true value of these remittances. The villagers invested these remittances in land, farms and petty trade. At the same time, however, loss of state subsidies for fuel and transport hit Ayirebi hard, as did the loss of school subsidies (Dei 1994; 1992).

Dei's small-scale study shows that although much of Ghana's economic reform encouraged productivity, retrenchment in state expenditure had real costs for ordinary people. Boafo-Arthur argues that gains from higher agricultural prices were offset by other SAP policies, such as "the high cost of utilities, the withdrawal of subsidies on health, education and agricultural inputs, the retrenchment of labor and the consequent high unemployment rate, and chronic low salaries for workers, especially in the public sector" (1999a, 53). One of the short-run consequences of Ghana's SAP was that urban food insecurity rose. Purchasing power in Accra in 1990 was only 49% of what it was in 1970, although this was a significant improvement over 1982, when purchasing power was only 19% of the 1970 level (Maxwell 1999, 1945).

This discussion of Ghana's economic policy since the early 1980s is not meant to be a complete description of its structural reform. It is meant to remind human rights scholars of the necessity to go beyond the laws and principles that they would like to see guide both IFIs and national governments. Economic policy must be followed "on the ground" to ascertain its real consequences. We present here statistics on Ghanaians' access to food, health care, education, and clean water – all basic economic rights. Wherever possible, we compare figures for 1980, before macroeconomic reform, with figures for the early twenty-first century.

The percentage of people who were undernourished declined from 64 in 1980, to 12.5 in 2001 (UNCDB 2005). The infant mortality rate declined from 96 per thousand in 1980 to 59 in 2003, and the under-five mortality rate declined from 157 per thousand in 1980 to 95 in 2003 (ibid.). Life expectancy increased from 51.8 in 1980 to 56.9 in 2000 (ibid.). The adult literacy rate improved from 58.5% in 1990 to 73.8% in 2002 (UNDP 2003, Ghana, Table 11). Although 52% of children were enrolled in primary school in 1990–91, 60% were enrolled in 2001–02 (ibid.). Seventy-nine percent of the population had access to an improved water supply in 2002, as compared to 54% in 1990 (UNCDB 2005). The estimated gross domestic product per capita in constant 2000 international dollars – calculated as purchasing power per person – rose from $1,774 in 1980 to $2,143 in 2004 (World Bank, Ghana-Economic Statistics 2005).

These improvements in Ghanaians' economic rights were not caused by state redistribution of the tiny national pot of stew that had existed in 1980. The improvements were the result in part of changes in organization of the economy to stimulate small enterprises, small farmers, industrial production and exports; that is, to stimulate Ghanaians to exercise their capacities to earn their own livelihoods. The improvements were also not caused by a fortuitous increase in the world price of Ghana's chief export, cocoa. On the contrary, Ghana's terms of trade – the ratio of the prices of its exports to the prices of its imports – declined from a 1980 base of 100 to 53 in 2001 (UNDP 2003, Ghana, Table 15). Nor were the improvements entirely the result of increased foreign aid as a "reward" for following the path suggested by IFIs. There were large increases in foreign aid in the early SAP years, so much so that one analyst argued, "Because of abnormally high levels of assistance from donors there is much difficulty in disentangling the effects of external aid from the effects of adjustment programs on Ghana's development" (Boafo-Arthur 1999a, 52). But official development assistance as a percentage of gross domestic product increased only 1% from 1990 to 2002, from 9.6% to 10.6% (UNDP 2003, Ghana, Table 18).

Ghana did not follow an inevitable, steadily upward economic path from the mid-1980s to 2005, in large part because it was still a dictatorship. In the late 1980s and 1990s, rule of law was still very precarious, and freedom of speech and democracy nonexistent. The early Rawlings regime, from 1982 to 1993, was characterized by severe abuse of power and quite appalling abuse of human rights, unprecedented in Ghana's history (National Reconciliation Commission 2004, vol. 1, 103–19, 123–55; Oquaye 1995). Indeed, it is quite possible that had not Rawlings so violently repressed civil and political rights, it would have been impossible for him to introduce macroeconomic reform, especially in the face of opposition from trade unions, students and professional bodies (Boafo-Arthur 1999b, 5–11). This use of force might suggest that there is a "trade-off" between economic growth and civil and political rights (Donnelly 1989, 184–202). Alternately, one could argue that Rawlings's use of violence delayed that release of productive forces necessary for individuals to realize their own economic rights. State-approved attacks against, and torture of, businesspersons and market traders for allegedly hoarding goods or charging high prices discouraged trade and undermined the market economy.

In the 1990s, Rawlings began to understand that he had to supplement economic reform with a more accountable political system that protected the rule of law. Rawlings reintroduced electoral politics – he was elected president in 1992 and again in 1996. An orderly transfer of power to President John Agyeman Kufuor took place in 2001. One major reason for Rawlings's defeat was the exceptionally poor performance of the economy in 2000, despite the longer term improvements as a consequence of the SAP, which both major political parties intended to continue (van Walraven 2002, 183, 191). After 2000, there was much more freedom of the press and assembly than there had been under Rawlings's rule, civil society organizations were much more active, the rule of law was more entrenched and respected, and Rawlings's highly abusive military and security forces were brought under control (Gyimah-Boadi 2001; Hughes 2003). Kufuor was reelected in 2004. But in 2005, Ghana still scored 65 on Transparency International's index of perceived corruption, with 1 being the least corrupt and 158 the most corrupt (Transparency International 2005, 236). This suggested that state officials were still not adhering to international norms of accountability and good governance.

In 2005, Ghana was still an extremely poor country. From 1990 to 2002, almost 45% of the population lived on less than $1 (U.S.) per day, whereas 78.5% lived on less than $2 (U.S.) (UNDP 2003, Ghana, Table 3). In a survey conducted in 2002, 66% of Ghanaian respondents said they had no regular wage or salary, 35% earned their living from petty trade, and 26% could count only on informal payments-in-kind. Fifty-four percent said they lived from hand to mouth (Gyimah-Boadi and Mensah 2003, v). The population growth rate of 1.25% in 2005 almost completely undermined the GDP per capita growth rate of 1.8% per year from 1990 to 2002 (CIA 2005; UNDP 2003, Ghana, Table 13). And although only 3.1% of the population from age 15 to 49 was estimated to carry HIV/AIDS in 2003 (UNDP 2003, Table 8), this may simply have reflected the relatively late entry of HIV/AIDS into Ghana. Yet despite these problems, 72% of Ghanaians surveyed in 2002 were willing to "endure hardships now," in the hope of future betterment (Gyimah-Boadi and Mensah 2003, xiii).

UGANDA

In 1992–93, I (Susan Dicklitch) spent ten months studying the role that indigenous non-governmental organizations (NGOs) could play in bringing about democratization in Uganda (Dicklitch 1998). At that time, Uganda under President Yoweri Museveni was a heady place, full of international NGOs and foreign ministries directing post-war-torn Ugandan development. Unlike Ghana, Uganda had suffered almost two decades of capricious, murderous rule. In 1986, when Museveni and his guerilla army – the National Resistance Movement (NRM) – took over Uganda, they inherited not an overdeveloped state but a collapsed state and economy. Although there had been too much political control of the economy in Ghana, there was too little in Uganda.

Uganda had not always been violent and anarchic. At independence in 1962, the economy was flourishing. This success, however, was short-lived. The one-time "Pearl of Africa" became Africa's slaughterhouse, synonymous with anarchy, violence, and death, suffering from five violent overturns of power. Politicized ethnicity, combined with regionalism and religious divisions (Protestant versus Catholic), caused disaster in Uganda, with murder rates approaching genocide during both the rule of Idi Amin and Milton Obote's second regime.

Like Nkrumah in Ghana, Milton Obote – the first leader of independent Uganda – decided that the best route for Ugandan development was African socialism. In 1966, Obote abolished the 1962 constitution and made himself President. In his 1969 "Move to the Left," Obote embraced a socialist program. This program called for 60% nationalization of eighty major firms; the abolition of strikes; and unification of pay scales for employees in the state bureaucracy and SOEs (Jorgensen 1981, 234–35; Mamdani 1976, 265–66). But this socialism was largely a façade for corruption and authoritarian rule (Mutibwa 1992, 70).

Obote was overthrown by his general, Idi Amin Dada, in 1971. But the economy did not improve under Amin; rather, Uganda spiraled downward toward disaster. In 1972, Amin expelled all Ugandan citizen and noncitizen ethnic Asians (persons of Indo-Pakistani origin). Over forty-nine thousand Asian merchants, manufacturers, and civil servants fled, resulting in the virtual elimination of the middle class. The Asians, as well as the foreign multinational subsidiaries which were nationalized by Amin in 1972, had provided the foundation for industrial capital in Uganda

(Jorgensen 1981, 249). In their place, Amin promoted his kinsmen and military men, who squandered their newfound wealth and helped to destroy the once productive Ugandan manufacturing and commercial base.

Amin did not reserve his wrath solely for the Asians. "Between 1972–1975 virtually everybody who had been responsible in some way or other for sustaining modern capitalist institutions was forced to leave the country or was killed" (Hyden 1983, 189). Taxes on poor peasants, migrant agricultural laborers and unskilled workers were increased to compensate for the loss of government revenue from taxes that had originally been levied on the Asians (Nabudere 1988, 310). Peasants who produced cash crops – mainly coffee – were the most directly affected by these tax increases. They were obliged to sell their crops to the state marketing boards at artificially low prices, and had to pay export taxes that were increased by 50% to 80% between 1971 and 1978 (Jorgensen 1981, 296). The export-oriented economy suffered as peasants increasingly withdrew from the modern sector, turning to subsistence agriculture and *magendoism* (the parallel economy) (Brett 1994, 62–63).

The return of Obote in 1980 did little to repair the Ugandan economy. By 1985, the Obote II regime was characterized by out of control inflation, widespread human rights abuses and the erosion of popular support and legitimacy (Hansen and Twaddle 1988, 3). The Uganda that the NRM (renamed the Movement in 1995) inherited in 1986 was devastated by years of civil war, chaos, abuse of power, economic stagnation and political and ethnic factionalism. The banking system had virtually collapsed, growth rates went into reverse with real GDP declining by 10% between 1984 and 1985, and the annual inflation rate was 150% (Holmgren et al. 2001, 122). It was clear that the public policies of the previous regimes had led to political and economic chaos. Uganda was ripe for a new political and economic strategy.

The NRM regime has been credited with turning the Ugandan economy around and stabilizing the political arena. Uganda had the sixth fastest-growing economy in sub-Saharan Africa by 1996, and enjoyed an economic growth rate of 7.1% per annum from 1990 to 1998 (UNDP 2000, 205). According to the World Bank, Uganda's economic success can be attributed to several factors. These include strong and single-minded political leadership; capable, committed, and trusted officials in key ministries; and pragmatic external donors prepared to engage with the government at the working level (World Bank 2004). Good public policy was key to successful economic growth and political stability.

In 1986, the NRM instituted its Ten Point Program for economic recovery. The program included state-led development; decentralization of power; and corruption reform and grassroots democracy via a newly implemented five-tier Resistance Council (RC) system, renamed the Local Council (LC) system in 1995. The NRM originally endorsed greater government intervention in the economy, government control over foreign exchange rates, and government control over the prices of essential imports (Harvey and Robinson 1995, 3–4). Yet, although it was initially more statist in orientation than was Ghana after 1983, in 1987 the Movement regime embraced an Economic Recovery Program (ERP) in conjunction with the IMF. This turnabout occurred after disastrous interventionist economic policies resulted in inflation escalating to over 300% by May 1987, and a further deterioration in most economic indicators (ibid.).

Like the Ghanaian structural adjustment program, the Ugandan ERP embraced fiscal austerity, retrenchment and deregulation, privatization and trade liberalization. The ERP took a two-pronged approach, focusing on stabilization and structural change. To stabilize the economy, the Ugandan shilling was devalued and moved to a market-determined exchange rate, while the government deficit was reduced. There were many structural changes. The government liberalized the trade regime by abolishing export and import licenses. It dismantled price controls, repealed the Industrial Licensing Act, developed a new Investment Code, and returned confiscated Asian properties. The government also privatized SOEs, moved to "abolish export and distribution monopolies," overhauled the civil service, restructured the tax system, improved tax administration, and limited social spending to "critical social services" (World Bank 1996, 42).

By July 1990, the government legalized the operation of foreign exchange bureaus, undermining the justification for black market currency trading (Sharer et al. 1995, 5). In addition, Uganda's shilling was devalued by 77% in May 1987, with subsequent devaluation in 1989 of 41.2% (ibid., 3–4). These devaluations caused hardship, especially to those in the import business, but were necessary to create a more realistic exchange rate and encourage export-oriented growth. Farmers benefited from a 182% rise in the price they received for their coffee, once the coffee marketing boards were privatized. Diversification of exports was also encouraged beyond coffee to fish, flowers, and dried fruits. Noncoffee products as a share of total exports increased from 23% in 1994–95 to 75% in 2000–01 (Nkusu 2004, 14; see also Bigsten & Kayizzi-Mugerwa 1999; Brett 1998).

Privatization of SOEs and the return of Asian property confiscated during Amin's rule were important elements in inducing respect for private property, thus stimulating investor confidence in Uganda. By 1990, the NRM government completed an Investment Code to protect foreign investors, especially the returning Asian Ugandans (Van Buren 1994, 935). In 1992, the Ugandan government invited the Asians whom Amin had expelled from the country in 1972 back to Uganda, and established a Departed Asians Property Custodian Board.

The immediate results of the first phase of macro-economic reform were impressive. The annual inflation rate was lowered from 190% to 28% by the end of 1991, and the GDP growth rate rose from negative figures to an average of 6.3% per year from 1988 to 1991 (Holmgren et al. 2001, 121). Ugandan government officials even went on donor-funded study tours to Ghana to learn from its successful structural adjustment reforms (ibid.).

The second phase of macroeconomic reform, from 1992 to 1998, reflected greater government commitment to reform. The government created the Uganda Revenue Authority, and abolished both the Coffee Marketing Board and the export tax on coffee. It also instigated civil service reform. Forty thousand ghost workers were eliminated, and about sixty thousand temporary workers and fourteen thousand civil servants were retrenched. As in Ghana, this caused concern and hardship (World Bank 1996, xii). The government mitigated some of the unpopularity of these retrenchments by offering a substantial voluntary severance package funded by the donor community. Approximately thirty-three thousand soldiers were demobilized and given compensation packages (Sharer et al. 1995, 5); programs funded by donor agencies helped integrate them back into civilian life.

The Ugandan economy benefited from macroeconomic, export-led reform. Inflation rates dropped, growth rates increased, trade as a percentage of GDP increased from 27% in 1990 to 41% in 2004 (World Bank 2005), and the overall economy stabilized. But economic growth is not necessarily sufficient to promote economic human rights. What was the impact of macroeconomic reform on Ugandan society? We present statistics comparable to those presented above for Ghana.

The percentage of people who were undernourished declined from 33 in 1980 to 19.1 in 2001 (UNCDB 2005). The infant mortality rate declined from 107 per thousand live births in 1980 to 81 in 2003 (ibid.), and the under-five mortality rate from 185 per thousand in 1980 to 140 in 2003 (ibid.). The literacy rate improved from 60.1% in 1980 to 70.1% in 1990 (ibid.). In 1997, Uganda introduced Universal Primary Education (UPE). Primary school enrolment figures subsequently increased from 3.4 million in 1996 to 7.3 million in 2002 (UNDP 2005, 20). Fifty-six percent of the population had sustainable access to an improved water source in 2002, as compared to 44% in 1990 (ibid.). The estimated gross domestic product per capita in constant 2000 international dollars, calculated as purchasing power per person, rose from $876 in 1982 to $1440 in 2004. Despite all these improvements, however, life expectancy decreased from 50.4 in 1980 to 42.7 in 2000 (ibid.). That life expectancy had so drastically declined was a consequence of the AIDS epidemic, which had not hit Ghana with the same force.

Overall, Uganda moved up to the category of medium human development, ranking 144 in the 2005 Human Development Index (ibid., 220). By 2005, Uganda, like Ghana, was still very poor, and had a long road to travel to ensure the provision of basic economic rights. Nevertheless, major improvements had been made.

The Movement regime has had mixed results in its attempts to eradicate poverty in Uganda. The Ugandan government recognized that structural adjustment would affect the most vulnerable segment of society – the poor – and developed various programs in an attempt to alleviate some of their suffering. Uganda prepared its first Poverty Eradication Action Plan (PEAP) in 1997, revised in 2000 (Uganda Debt Network 2003, ii). Several different poverty alleviation strategies were implemented by the Movement regime. One of the first was the Rural Farmers Scheme (RFS) launched in 1987 through the Uganda Commercial Bank (UCB). A revolving fund of $6 million (U.S.) was available to rural farmers to assist them in moving from subsistence agriculture to commercial agricultural production (see Muhumuza 2002, n. 17). Another key antipoverty program was the Program for the Alleviation of Poverty and the Social Costs of Adjustment (PAPSCA) (see Republic of Uganda 1993), and the Northern Uganda Reconstruction Program (NURP).[1] PAPSCA was launched in 1989 by the Ugandan government. It aimed to mitigate the "social costs of adjustment" by targeting the most vulnerable segments of society. Because structural adjustment called for a cutting back of government expenditure, social services to the poor were often sacrificed. Programs such as PAPSCA thus provided assistance to communities to construct schools, health centers, and rural roads. It also provided funding for orphans to pay for school fees and credit to widows to engage in productive economic ventures. The NURP was established to help

---

[1] For a critical assessment of the Ugandan poverty alleviation programs, see Muhumuza (2002).

reconstruct war-torn Northern Uganda, focusing on infrastructural development and cotton production.

Fifty-five percent of the population lived below the national poverty line from 1990 to 2002 (UNDP 2005).[2] With 4.1% of the population estimated to carry HIV/AIDS in 2005, and over 1.7 million orphans, Uganda had one of the highest rates of orphanhood in the world (ibid., 29). Although the national poverty rate dropped from 56% in 1992 to 35% in 2001, the rate was increasing, averaging around 38% (Uganda Debt Network 2003, 1). Of most concern was the inequality of poverty. Ninety percent of the poverty was concentrated in rural households and the Northern region was also particularly poor (ibid.). Northern poverty, however, was to a large extent a consequence of insurgency since 1986 by the Lord's Resistance Army (LRA), a fanatical rebel group lead by Joseph Kony and supported by the Sudanese government. Women also tended to be disproportionately affected by poverty, especially because Ugandan culture and law denied most women landownership rights (Goetz and Jenkins 1999). But the women's movement had made inroads under the Movement regime, gaining greater female political representation, and bringing women's issues to the forefront of political and social discourse.[3]

Uganda benefited immensely from foreign donor aid, which was undoubtedly crucial to its reform efforts. Uganda became the first country to qualify for the World Bank and IMF-sponsored Heavily Indebted Poor Country (HIPC) debt-relief initiative in 1998 (original) and 2000 (enhanced). In 2005, loans and grants from foreign donors accounted for 17% and 28% of the Ugandan budget respectively. Thus, 45% of the Ugandan budget was composed of Official Development Assistance (ODA) (Republic of Uganda 2004–5, 5). In June 2005, Uganda (along with Ghana) was granted 100% debt relief by the G8, relieving it of the burden of paying back loans from the IMF, WB, and African Development Bank.[4]

Yet foreign aid alone cannot account for Uganda's economic successes. The political system made economic reforms possible. Strong, visionary political leadership capped popular political participation at the local level. The Movement system created Resistance Councils (renamed Local Council (LC) system in 1995) – a five-tiered hierarchical system that permitted direct participatory democracy at the LCI (Village) level.[5] The Movement's broad-based inclusionary "no-party" system permitted political parties to exist but banned political rallies and meetings: the regime justified this by arguing that Ugandans were not ready for multiparty politics. Given Uganda's bloodied past, the regime contended, to open up the political arena to multiparty competition would encourage sectarianism and voting on the basis of ethnicity, religion, and regionalism rather than political platform. Instead, Ugandans were urged to vote on the basis of a candidate's individual merit.

Thus, although the Movement regime did not permit multiparty political competition, it did permit popular participation in decision making (even if only at the

---

[2] Comparable data on population living below $1 per day in Uganda was not available.

[3] For an excellent analysis of the women's movement and women's rights issues in Uganda, see Tripp (2000).

[4] The total debt relief added up to $2 billion (CIA 2005, Uganda).

[5] For more information on the Local Council system, see Dicklitch (1998, 76–79).

local level) – a necessary ingredient for governmental legitimacy. This limited citizen participation permitted the implementation of the sometimes harsh reforms necessary to stabilize the economy and polity.

Museveni himself was a charismatic, dedicated president who demanded discipline from his military and who tackled corruption, albeit not entirely successfully. Uganda had a score of 80 in Transparency International's Corruption Perceptions Index in 2000, and 102 in 2004 (Transparency International 2005). Similarly, Freedom House assessed Uganda as only "partly free" both in 1990–91 and 2003 (2005).

A Constitutional Commission adopted a new constitution for Uganda in 1995, legitimizing the Movement political system. Presidential and parliamentary elections were held in 1996 and 2001. A national referendum in June 2000 reconfirmed the desire for a no-party system, but in a second referendum in July of 2005, a majority of Ugandans voted to open the electoral system to multiparty political competition. The referendum also removed presidential term limits, enabling Museveni to run again for president in the March 2006 elections.

In early 2006, Uganda was still an extremely poor country and still had a long way to go to secure economic rights and establish a full-fledged multiparty democracy. Continued armed insurgency in the North by the LRA created unequal regional development, tarnishing the image of the Movement regime. The Movement system also became less inclusionary and less tolerant of multiparty competition. Donors were hesitant to criticize the politics of reform in Uganda because they were so impressed by the economic reforms that the Museveni regime had implemented. Yet they worried about Uganda's democratic future, given Museveni's success in altering the constitution to allow himself to remain president indefinitely. Of most concern was Museveni's arrest of presidential candidate Dr. Kizza Besigye in October 2005, for alleged treason and rape. Many Ugandan analysts saw this as nothing less than Museveni's attempt to remove Besigye from the presidential race. As of January 2006, Besigye remained in prison, awaiting trial.

The Movement regime made significant progress in stabilizing the political and economic arena. Although macroeconomic reform had been painful, most Ugandans supported the government's economic polices. An Afrobarometer survey found that "although 73% of Ugandans believe the government's economic policies have hurt most people and benefited only a few, 59% are nonetheless willing to tolerate the hardship of reform now in order to gain its long-term benefits" (Logan et al. 2003). However, whether the Movement could sustain that stability and growth depended, in early 2006, on its future political route and on the personal decisions of President Museveni. Museveni could emulate President Rawlings of Ghana, who permitted competitive multiparty elections and peacefully retired from politics. Or, Museveni could follow the example of President Mugabe of Zimbabwe, who refused to leave political office, severely violating his citizen's human rights in his bid to remain in power. In 2006, the road to progress for Uganda was still a rocky one.

LESSONS FROM GHANA AND UGANDA

We have urged scholars of economic human rights to take macroeconomic policy more seriously, and to recognize that in very poor countries, economic growth is necessary, although not sufficient, to promote and protect economic rights. After the introduction of macroeconomic structural reform, the economies of both Ghana and Uganda improved. Both Rawlings and Museveni had inherited economies in shambles. Impoverishment had a long history in these two states. Much of it was internally generated during the first decades of independence.

But to assign blame for past policy errors is not to explain what works in the present. In the 1980s, both Uganda and Ghana recognized that along with macroeconomic reform, state capacity-building was necessary. As Fukuyama argues, although the state in developing countries required cutbacks in some areas through economic liberalization, it needed to be "simultaneously strengthened in others." The dilemma was how to reduce state scope, while increasing state strength (Fukuyama 2004, 20, 26). There were several components to capacity-building in Uganda and Ghana. Both states built political legitimacy, increased accountability by strengthening the rule of law, and invested more in human capital. In Uganda, this process began as soon as Museveni took power. In Ghana, the 1980s and early 1990s were a period of intense political repression, but during the late 1990s, Rawlings moved to more democratic politics and a freer society. The post-2000 Kufuor regime continued this path.

In the early decades of independence, both Ghana and Uganda had had a neopatrimonial system of governance that promoted personal rule over the rule of law. In a patrimonial state, Max Weber argued, administrative and military staff were considered the personal retainers of the head of state (Leonard & Straus 2003, 2). The private interests of the monarch, tribal chief, or sultan took precedence over the public interest. In postindependence Ghana and Uganda, political leaders acted like Weber's monarchs. The two states were "suspended in mid-air" with no structural roots in society, "unable to function without an indiscriminate and wasteful consumption of scarce societal resources" (Hyden 1983, 19). Neopatrimonialism put national wealth into the hands of a small clique connected to the political ruler, completely undermining public accountability. Citizens of both countries endured capricious rule until the political system stabilized and macroeconomic reforms were introduced. Macroeconomic reforms attacked neopatrimonialism by removing politicians' ability to use state resources to buy political support.

SAPs encouraged the development of a rational-legal state. SOEs were privatized, and an economic class independent of the political class developed. Falk acknowledges that "neo-liberal ideology informing global market forces disseminates constructive ideas about freedom and the rule of law, as well as destructive ideas about greed and materialism" (1999, 69). An alternative perspective is that the turn to a market society in both Ghana and Uganda promoted not "greed and materialism," but reasonable rewards for productive enterprises. Fairer distribution of these rewards might have occurred earlier, had there been political freedom and rule of law. Smoothly functioning legal institutions help promote economic efficiency and long term development (de Soto 1989, 134). Economic improvements and capacity building gave the Ghanaian and Ugandan regimes more credibility among their citizenry.

In the long run, however, whether macroeconomic reforms support economic rights will depend on both domestic and international politics. Surveys in the early twenty-first century showed that both Ghanaians and Ugandans were willing to accept hardships associated with economic reform, as we noted earlier. However, citizens also wanted a political voice, and assurances that corruption would not whittle away economic growth. But whereas Ghana in 2005 was in the process of consolidating multiparty democracy, thus allowing citizens a political voice, Uganda's political future was still uncertain. Museveni had agreed to multiparty competition for the March 2006 elections, but the arrest of the main presidential contender put a fair election into question.

The Ghanaian and Ugandan leadership also needed to maintain the confidence of the international community. International donors had shown their trust in Ghana and Uganda by promising 100% debt relief as a reward for successful completion of the Highly Indebted Poor Countries Initiative – a WB and IMF policy for very poor countries that implemented both economic reform and poverty reduction programs (World Bank, 2004). Presumably, changes to economic policies not approved by these IFIs might reduce Ghana's and Uganda's eligibility for assistance, even if such changes were to improve the economic human rights of their citizens.

Economic rights in Africa also depend on relations with the larger world economy. The economic reforms that both Ghana and Uganda instituted were not enough to lift the majority of Ghanaians and Ugandans out of poverty. There is much that the world community could do to help protect Ghanaians' and Ugandans' economic rights, other than merely advising economic and political reform. Debt relief, better targeted aid, fairer international trade, and a focus on the health and education of Ghanaians and Ugandans are also necessary. So is support for democracy and the rule of law, and for civil society and human rights activists.

But economic rights do require appropriate internal economic policy. This chapter suggests that some aspects of macroeconomic reform helped lift Ghana and Uganda out of economic crisis. This does not mean that all aspects of such reform were necessary or useful, nor that the reform was the only cause of the economic progress enjoyed by Ghana and Uganda. Both countries were rewarded with massive foreign aid for following the prescriptions of the IFIs. It is possible that Ghana and Uganda are not models for other African countries; by contrast, many other African countries were changing from "African socialist" to market economies in the 1980s and 1990s – as was Ghana – and others were emerging from civil war – as was Uganda.

The ambiguities noted in this chapter suggest an urgent need for more dialogue between human rights scholars and economists. It is not useful to unambiguously denounce macroeconomic reform, or other aspects of market-oriented economic reforms suggested by IFIs or indeed by some African economists. Nor is it useful to ignore economists' analyses on the grounds that they merely reflect a neoliberal ideology. Market economies are the path to economic growth for all societies, whether in Western Europe and North America two centuries ago, Southeast Asia a half-century ago, or China and India at present. Neither citizens of very poor societies relying on their own economic capacities, nor redistributive states, can provide for economic rights unless there is economic growth. Human rights scholars should work more closely with economists to try to find the best path to economic growth and economic rights for those suffering so cruelly in sub-Saharan Africa.

REFERENCES

Amponsah, Nicholas. 2000. Ghana's Mixed Structural Adjustment Results: Explaining the Poor Private Sector Response. *Africa Today* 47 (2): 8–32.

Appiah-Kubi, Kojo. 2001. State-Owned Enterprises and Privatisation in Ghana. *Journal of Modern African Studies* 39 (2): 197–229.

Ayittey, George B. N. 1998. *Africa in Chaos.* New York: St. Martin's Griffin.

Bigsten, Arne, and Steve Kayizzi-Mugerwa. 1999. *Crisis Adjustment and Growth in Uganda: A Study of Adaptation in an African Economy.* New York: St. Martin's Press.

Boafo-Arthur, Kwame. 1999a. Ghana: Structural Adjustment, Democratization, and the Politics of Continuity. *African Studies Review* 42 (2): 41–72.

Boafo-Arthur, Kwame. 1999b. Structural Adjustment Programs (SAPs) in Ghana: Interrogating PNDC's Implementation. *West Africa Review* 1 (1). http://www.westafricareview. com/vol1.1/boafohtml.

Brett, E. A. 1994. Rebuilding Organisational Capacity in Uganda under the National Resistance Movement. *Journal of Modern African Studies* 32 (1): 53–80.

Brett, E. A. 1998. Responding to Poverty in Uganda: Structures, Policies and Prospects. *Journal of International Affairs* 52 (1): 314–37.

Busumtwi-Sam, James. 1996. Models of Economic Development in Africa: Lessons from the Experience of Ghana, 1957–95. *Journal of Commonwealth and Comparative Politics* 34 (3): 174–98.

Central Intelligence Agency (CIA). The World Factbook: Ghana. http://www.cia.gov/cia/ publications/factbook/geos/gh.html (accessed 2 May 2005).

Central Intelligence Agency (CIA). The World Fact Book: Uganda. http://www.cia.gov/ cia/publications/factbook/print/ug.html (accessed 5 January 2005).

Christensen, Peter F. 1998. Performance and Divestment of State-Owned Enterprises in Ghana. *Public Administration and Development* 18 (3): 281–93.

Commission for Africa. 2005. *Our Common Interest: Report of the Commission for Africa.* http://www.commissionforafrica.org/English/report/introduction.html.

de Soto, Hernando. 1989. *The Other Path: The Invisible Revolution in the Third World.* New York: Harper and Row.

Dei, George J. Sefa. 1992. The Renewal of a Ghanaian Rural Economy. *Canadian Journal of African Studies* 26 (1): 24–53.

Dei, George J. Sefa. 1994. The Women of a Ghanaian Village: A Study of Social Change. *African Studies Review* 37 (2): 121–45.

Dicklitch, Susan. 1998. *The Elusive Promise of NGOs in Africa: Lessons from Uganda.* New York and London: Macmillan/St. Martin's Press.

Donnelly, Jack. 1989. *Universal Human Rights in Theory and Practice.* Ithaca, NY: Cornell University Press.

Falk, Richard. 1999. *Predatory Globalization: A Critique.* Malden, MA: Polity Press.

Felice, William F. 2003. *The Global New Deal: Economic and Social Human Rights in World Politics.* New York: Rowman and Littlefield.

Freedom House. 2005. Freedom in the World – Uganda (2005). http://www.freedomhouse. org/inc/content/pubs/fiw/inc_country_detail.cfm?country=6854pf (accessed January 5, 2005).

Fukuyama, Francis. 2004. The Imperative of State-Building. *Journal of Democracy* 15 (2), 17–31.

Goetz, Anne Marie, and Rob Jenkins. 1999. Creating a Framework for Reducing Poverty: Institutional and Process Issues in National Poverty Policy, Uganda Country Report, Commissioned by United Kingdom Department for International Development (DFID) and Swedish International Development Cooperation Agency (SIDA).

Goodhart, Michael. 2003. Origins and Universality in the Human Rights Debate: Cultural Essentialism and the Challenge of Globalization. *Human Rights Quarterly* 25 (4): 935–64.

Gyimah-Boadi, E. 1994. Ghana's Uncertain Political Opening. *Journal of Democracy* 5 (2): 75–86.

Gyimah-Boadi, E. 2001. A Peaceful Turnover in Ghana. *Journal of Democracy* 12 (2): 103–17.

Gyimah-Boadi, E., and Kwabena Amoah Awuah Mensah. 2003. The Growth of Democracy in Ghana Despite Economic Dissatisfaction: A Power Alternation Bonus? Accra: Afrobarometer Paper No. 28, Ghana Centre for Democratic Development. Available at: http://www.afrobarometer.org/papers/AfropaperNo28.pdf.

Hansen, Holgert B., and Michael Twaddle. 1988. Introduction. In *Uganda Now: Between Decay and Development*, ed. Holger B. Hansen and Michael Twaddle. London: James Currey Ltd.

Harvey, Charles, and Mark Robinson. 1995. Economic Reform and Political Liberalization in Uganda. *IDS Research Report No. 20*. Brighton, UK: Institute of Development Studies.

Holmgren, Torgny, Louis Kasekende, Michael Atingi-Ego, and Daniel Ddamulira. 2001. Uganda. In *Aid and Reform in Africa: Lessons from Ten Case Studies*, ed. S. Devarajan, D. Dollar, and T. Holmgren. Washington, DC: The World Bank.

Howard, Rhoda E. 1978. *Colonialism and Underdevelopment in Ghana*. London: Croom Helm.

Howard, Rhoda E. 1986. *Human Rights in Commonwealth Africa*. Totowa, NJ: Rowman and Littlefield.

Hughes, Tim. 2003. Ghana: Tarnished Past, Golden Future. In *South African Yearbook of International Affairs 2002/03*, 323–31. Johannesburg: Jan Smuts House.

Huntington, Samuel P. 1976. *No Easy Choice: Political Participation in Developing Countries*. Cambridge, MA: Harvard University Press.

Hyden, Goran. 1983. *No Shortcuts to Progress: African Development Management in Perspective*. Berkeley: University of California Press.

Ibhawoh, Bonny. 1999. Structural Adjustment, Authoritarianism and Human Rights in Africa. *Comparative Studies of South Asia, Africa and the Middle East* XIX (1): 158–67.

Jorgensen. Jan J. 1981. *Uganda: A Modern History*. London: Croom Helm Ltd.

Kent, George. 2005. *Freedom from Want: The Human Right to Adequate Food*. Washington, DC: Georgetown University Press.

Killick, Tony. 2002. Helleiner on Africa in the Global Economy. *Canadian Journal of African Studies* 36 (3): 551–64.

Kimenyi, Mwangi S. 1997. *Ethnic Diversity, Liberty and the State: The African Dilemma*. Cheltenham, UK: Edward Elgar.

Leonard, David K., and Scott Straus. 2003. *Africa's Stalled Development: International Causes and Cures*. Boulder, CO, and London: Lynne Rienner.

Logan, Carolyn J., Nansozi Muwanga, Robert Sentamu, and Michael Bratton. 2003. *Insiders and Outsiders: Varying Perceptions of Democracy and Governance in Uganda*. Afrobarometer Paper No. 27. Available at: http://www.afrobarometer.org/papers/AfropaperNo27.pdf.

Mamdani, Mahmood. 1976. *Politics and Class Formation in Uganda*. New York and London: Monthly Review Press.

Maxwell, Daniel. 1999. The Political Economy of Urban Food Security in Sub-Saharan Africa. *World Development* 27 (11): 1939–53.

Muhumuza, William. 2002. The Paradox of Pursuing Anti-Poverty Strategies under Structural Adjustment Reforms in Uganda. *The Journal of Social, Political and Economic Studies* 27 (3): 271–306.

Mutibwa, Phares. 1992. *Uganda since Independence: A Story of Unfulfilled Hopes.* Kampala and London: Fountain Publishers Ltd., and C. Hurst and Co., Publishers Ltd.

Nabudere, Dani Wadada. 1988. Eternal and Internal Factors in Uganda's Continuing Crisis. In *Uganda Now: Between Decay and Development,* ed. Holger B. Hansen and Michael Twaddle. London: James Currey Ltd.

National Reconciliation Commission (Ghana). 2004. *Report*, vol. 1, chap. 5. Available at: http://www.ghana.gov.gh/NRC.

Nkusu, Mwanza. 2004. Financing Uganda's Poverty Reduction Strategy: Is Aid Causing More Pain than Gain? IMF Working Paper (WP/04/170). Washington, DC: International Monetary Fund.

Oelbaum, Jay. 2002. Populist Reform Coalitions in Sub-Saharan Africa: Ghana's Triple Alliance. *Canadian Journal of African Studies* 36 (2): 281–328.

Oquaye, Mike. 1995. Human Rights and the Transition to Democracy under the PNDC in Ghana. *Human Rights Quarterly* 17 (3): 556–73.

Panford, Kwamina. 1997. Ghana: A Decade of IMF/World Bank's Policies of Adjustment (1985–1995). *Scandinavian Journal of Development Alternatives and Area Studies* 16: 81–105.

Republic of Uganda. 1993. Program to Alleviate Poverty and the Social Costs of Adjustment (PAPSCA) Progress Report April 1992–June 1993, PAPSCA Co-ordination and Monitoring Unit. Kampala: Uganda.

Republic of Uganda, Ministry of Finance. *The Ugandan Budget 2004/2005: A Citizen's Guide.* http://www.finance.go.ug/citizensGuide/citzens%20guide.pdf.

Robertson, Claire. 1983. The Death of Makola and Other Tragedies. *Canadian Journal of African Studies* 17 (3): 469–95.

Sandbrook, Richard. 1993. *The Politics of Africa's Economic Recovery,* New York: Cambridge University Press.

Sandbrook, Richard. 2000. *Closing the Circle: Democratization and Development in Africa.* London: Zed Books.

Schatz, Sayre P. 1984. Pirate Capitalism and the Inert Economy of Nigeria. *Journal of Modern African Studies* 22 (1): 45–57.

Sen, Amartya. 2001. *Development as Freedom.* New York: Alfred A. Knopf.

Sharer, Robert L., Hema R. De Zoysa, and Calvin A. McDonald. 1995. Uganda: Adjustment with Growth, 1987–94, IMF Occasional Paper 121. Washington, DC: International Monetary Fund.

Transparency International. 2005. *Corruption Perceptions Index 2005.* Berlin: Transparency International Secretariat. Available at: http://www.transparency.org/publications/gcr/download_gcr/download_gcr_2005#download.

Tripp, Aili Mari. 2000. *Women and Politics in Uganda.* Madison: University of Wisconsin Press.

Uganda Debt Network. 2003. *The Uganda Budget 2003/2004: What Relevance to the Poverty Situation?* Review Report No. 5. Kampala: Uganda Debt Network. Available at: http://www.udn.or.ug/pub/Relevance%20of%20Budget%20to%20Poverty%20Reduction.doc.

United Nations. United Nations Common Database (UNCDB): *Ghana.* http://unstats.un.org/unsd/cdb/cdb_list_countries.asp (accessed December 1, 2005 and December 10, 2005; password needed).

United Nations Development Programme (UNDP). 2000. *Human Development Report 2000.* New York: Oxford University Press.

United Nations Development Programme (UNDP). 2003. *Human Development Report 2003.* New York: Oxford University Press.

United Nations Development Programme (UNDP). 2005. *Human Development Report 2005.* New York: Oxford University Press.

Van Buren, Linda. 1994. Uganda: Economy. In *Africa South of the Sahara, 1994*, 21st ed. London: Europea Publications Ltd.

van Walraven, Klaas. 2002. The End of an Era: The Ghanaian Elections of December 2000. *Journal of Contemporary African Studies* 20 (2): 183–202.

World Bank. *World Development Indicators Database*. http://web.worldbank.org/WBSITE/ EXTERNAL/DATASTATISTICS/0,,contentMDK:20535285~menuPK:232599~pagePK: 64133150~piPK:64133175~theSitePK:239419,00.html (accessed December 12, 2005).

World Bank. 1996. *Uganda: The Challenge of Growth and Poverty Reduction*. Washington, DC: World Bank.

World Bank. 2004. Uganda: From Conflict to Sustained Growth and Deep Reductions in Poverty. In *Reducing Poverty Sustaining Growth: Scaling Up Poverty Reduction*, 32–36. Case Study Summaries from a Global Learning Process and Conference in Shanghai, 25–27 May 2004. Washington, DC: World Bank. Available at: http://info.worldbank.org/ etools/reducingpoverty/docs/Scaling-Up-Poverty-%20Reduction.pdf.

World Bank Group. *The HIPC Debt Initiative*. http://www.worldbank.org/hipc/about/hipcbr/ hipcbr.htm (accessed April 20, 2004).

16 Human Rights as Instruments of Emancipation and Economic Development

KAUSHIK BASU

1. PRECEPT AND PRACTICE

On 10 December 1948, the General Assembly of the United Nations proclaimed the Universal Declaration of Human Rights, which was a call to a certain universalist commitment to promoting some basic rights that all individuals possessed simply by virtue of being human, and irrespective of their religion, race, gender, and nationality. This was the first time that such a proclamation had been made at a global level and endorsed by virtually every country in the world.[1]

There is of course a long history of individual activism and philosophical pamphleteering for some basic rights for *all* human beings. Jefferson, Kant, Locke, Gandhi, the poetry of sufi saints and the writings of spiritual leaders, and even many nonbelievers, such as India's first prime minister, Jawaharlal Nehru, and the philosophers Bertrand Russell, David Hume, and John Stuart Mill easily spring to mind. There also had been initiatives undertaken by individual countries to recognize some basic rights of individuals within their national boundaries. The UN Declaration has special significance, because it was the first effort to bring the whole world under a common recognition of rights and to give this a semi-legal status.[2] In today's rapidly globalizing world we cannot ask for anything less. The Declaration has had huge ramifications, because many global agreements and initiatives – concerning the rights of the workers, the rights of the children, the treatment of prisoners, the protection of the environment, and economic objectives

---

[1] One reason for such widespread acceptance is – ironically – because, unlike the UN Charter of 1945, the Declaration did not place any legal obligations on nations that accepted it. With time, though, some of its clauses have begun to acquire a more obligatory character.

[2] This harks back to the Kantian dream that "if a single universal, rational, and supreme code of international practice could be established throughout the world, then perpetual peace was possible" (Chatterjee 2004, 98).

I am grateful to the Human Rights Institute, University of Connecticut, for organizing this important conference, and to the conference organizers for having given me the opportunity to address the gathering. This chapter is a revised version of the lecture I gave on that occasion and I am grateful to my audience for the lively discussion, and to Sabina Alkire, Marty Chen, Shareen Hertel, Hyejin Ku and Lanse Minkler for many helpful comments and criticisms at the time of writing up the paper. I presented a part of the paper at the conference on 'Equality and the New Global Order' at Harvard University, on 12 May 2006, and would like to record my thanks to the several commentators for the many valuable suggestions.

like the Millennium Development Goals – are outgrowths of that initial proclamation.[3]

Taking advantage of the fact that the readership of this volume will include
researchers and students, I want to move away from these general, universal declarations – with which we all would easily agree – to some more conceptual and
contentious matters, and focus on economic rights in the context of globalization.

Globalization can confer huge benefits on humankind, but it also can marginalize
and impoverish large sections of the population in both poor and rich countries,
unless it is complemented with intelligently designed policies meant explicitly to
combat these inequities. At least in this context, the need for intelligent design must
be considered above controversy.

Concern for the poor and the risk of their getting further marginalized during
the process of globalization is, I believe, a matter of intrinsic moral significance (see
Pogge 2005). But even if we do not consider it to be so, we must realize that when
large segments of people get marginalized, this can cause political instability, strife
and turmoil; and so it may well be in our self-interest to address these fall-outs.

In an earlier world, these problems were addressed at the level of each nation
state separately, and that may have been, for most purposes, the right strategy. But
in today's world, as the economies of different nations move closer to one another,
it becomes difficult to solve or even begin to address one nation's problem without
some policy coordination with other nations. The right policy to counter poverty or
large inequality in one country may require us to know what is happening in other
nations, because a unilateral move can cause the flight of capital or the diversion
of trade flows.

It follows from this that it may no longer be possible to address the issue of labor
rights in one country without doing so in another. So if we think of some basic
rights – such as a worker's right to a living wage and to certain basic freedoms, a
child's right to basic education, a poor farmer's right to clean air, and even certain
human rights such as the right to bodily integrity – then some global coordination
of policies is crucial.[4] But this is by no means an easy problem. Various economies
of the world are at vastly different levels of development, and cultures and belief
systems across nations can be not just different but contradictory and even con-
frontational. Agreeing even in outline to a common minimal standard for such a
diverse world is unlikely to be easy.

I do not choose my subject because of the academic's love of disputation and
arguments – though I cannot deny finding these innately pleasurable – but because
proclamations that have universal appeal, although extremely important, are of
limited reach and can even harm us if they are not backed up by close reasoning
and scrutiny. The World Bank has enshrined as a virtual logo its aim: "Our dream
is of a world free of poverty." At the International Labour Organization, people
wear T-shirts and badges that declare: "Say No to Child Labor." Individual rights

---

[3] See Brysk (2002) for discussion of many of these rights.
[4] Another interesting link between globalization and rights occurs via the nature of democracy.
Although for small groups democracy may be predicated on common aims and objectives, as the
group becomes larger (for instance, when we go from the nation to a collectivity of nations), interests
become adversarial. This does not mean an abandonment of democracy but, rather, a structuring
of it that recognizes the adversarial interests of its constituents. Equality of rights would then have
to be the basic building block of such a democracy (Mansbridge 1984).

are routinely upheld in public discussions in the United States. If despite this the world is awash in poverty, 186 million children toil as laborers, and fellow human beings are humiliated and tortured not just in remote totalitarian states but in Abu Ghraib and Guantánamo Bay, evidently we are not succeeding in translating our proclamations into action.

These are huge moral lapses, but they are also intellectual failures. They suggest that our charters and laws may not be right, and even when they are, the details of how we translate them into actual actions may be faulty. I hope to persuade the reader that some of these problems are intellectually hard and need a lot of effort and analytical skill to solve them; and abstruse though such an exercise may seem, it is crucial that we do not forsake it if we are to translate our precepts into practice.

I shall be concerned in this chapter with rights that are enforced, if not fully, then in large measure, and if not immediately, then in some foreseeable future. This bears on the long-standing debate on whether a right that is not enforced is even meaningful, with the legal positivist school taking the view that it is not, and the natural rights school arguing that what constitutes a basic human right arises from our idea of what it means to be human and remains valid whether or not it is enforced (Dworkin 1978). This is not the occasion for me to join this debate, though my inclination would be to reject both these polar positions.

To acknowledge something as a right surely imposes on us an obligation to uphold it or to take measures toward its implementation at least in the future. On the other hand, as Harvey (2004, 702) puts it eloquently, the positivist position cannot be exactly right either, for then we would have to presume that it was "a linguistic mistake to assert that apartheid violated the human rights of non-white South Africans." One way to bridge the gap between the two schools is to recognize that the mere assertion of a law or a right or a rule at times creates pressures that lead to partial enforcement, even though there may be no formal mechanism for enforcement.[5] Just as some prophecies can be self-fulfilling, some laws can be self-enforcing or at least give rise to forces that create pressures for its enforcement.[6] To declare that blacks in South African had a right that was being violated wantonly under apartheid is to build up pressure for restoring that right.

In American restaurant bathrooms, one frequently sees signs on the wall which say, "Employees must wash their hands with soap." One may take the view that this demand is useless unless there is a mechanism for enforcing it, because otherwise this will have no effect on behavior. One way to counter this is to argue that the remark before the "because" in the previous sentence is valid, but what follows is not. This is because human beings, or at least some of them, *are* affected by displayed instructions that sound reasonable.[7] Hence, the very fact of putting up a reasonable instruction has a self-enforcing affect on some onlookers.

---

[5] An extremely cogent evaluation of some of these critiques – of the idea of human rights preceding their incorporation into the law and policy – occurs in Sen (2001, ch. 10). He takes the view that "human rights may also exceed the domain of *potential*, as opposed to *actual* legal rights" (229).

[6] The concept of the expressive function of the law embodies some of this idea (Sunstein 1996; Cooter 1998).

[7] At times, one may need to implore twice, as used to happen on Delhi public buses in the 1980s. Above some seats would be the sign "Ladies Seat," and, on occasions, above these would be another beseeching sign: "Let ladies sit on Ladies Seat."

2. THE FALLACY OF BINARINESS: A PRELIMINARY REMARK

It is useful to begin by introducing one specific problem that I shall be concerned with in this essay – that of labor standards. All – or, at least, most – of us will agree that workers should not be exposed to excessive health and safety hazards, children should not have to do hard labor or regular work, no worker should have to work more than a reasonable number of hours (for instance, ten hours a day), and no one should be forced to work against one's wishes. But converting these slogans into action can have many pitfalls.

First, we must not make what I shall call the "fallacy of binariness." In a Woody Allen story, one Mr. Needleman, while discussing what kind of a funeral he would like, says, "I much prefer cremation to burial in the earth," and then, with no further provocation, goes on to add, "and both to a weekend with Mrs. Needleman."[8]

In this particular case, it is not evident why Mr. Needleman proffers the needless information about where in his scale of preferences a "weekend with Mrs. Needleman" stands in comparison to cremation and burial, but there are many situations in life in which it may be crucial to know the "third option." To know that child schooling is better than child labor does not automatically amount to a case for banning child labor, if there is a real possibility of a third outcome for children – for instance, that of neither school nor work, but of malnutrition or starvation. And so, before imposing a ban, we must make sure that banning child labor will lead a child to schooling and not to malnutrition or starvation. This elementary fallacy can lead to errors in the specification of policy with adverse consequences for the very individuals we intend to help. In the above case, this involves child labor, but this is a general point, and a lot of our labor-market policies are flawed precisely because they are founded on the fallacy of binariness.

In other words, in trying to root out one evil we must not become so single-minded that we do not care if this evil is rooted out by replacing it with a bigger evil. This is not a word of empty caution but a trap that ordinary, considerate human beings face the risk of falling into. This is what leads many protestors to unwittingly become pawns in the hands of the very power lobbies that they may be protesting against. I want this thought to remain as a backdrop. We shall have occasion to return to it after we have discussed the meaning and importance of economic rights and move to an analysis of which ones ought to be upheld and which ones abandoned.

3. EMPOWERMENT AND ECONOMIC PROGRESS

The free market is a powerful machine for coordinating the actions of multitudes of human beings absorbed in their own limited pursuits. Given certain preconditions, the free market mechanism can be efficient and can promote economic growth. But, unfortunately, this powerful machine or "invisible hand," as Adam Smith had called it, is no creator of utopia and no respecter of individual needs, fairness or equity. If a person is kind and humane but physically unable to work, she

---

[8] The quote is from page 3 of "Remembering Needleman," which is part of Woody Allen's collected short stories *Side Effects* (Random House, New York, 1975).

will be doomed to poverty and perhaps starvation. If some individuals come into adulthood without the advantage of inheritance or human capital, they will have to live in deprivation. The fact that the ten richest people in the world earn the same as the entire population of Tanzania – some \$37 billion– does not make this mechanism wince.[9]

Anyone with a modicum of sensitivity will realize that, although the market mechanism has its strengths that need to be used, it also needs controls and corrective interventions. As Harvey (2004, 703–04) put it so eloquently:

> Markets are engines of technological innovation . . . and certain kinds of economic efficiency; but they are not very good at securing the economic and social entitlements proclaimed to be human rights in the Universal Declaration. . . . I therefore came to view economic and social human rights as having a similar relationship to the market mechanism that minority rights have to majority rule.

But intervening for the poor and giving people certain basic rights is more than an end in itself. Granting people rights – and working to ensure that they get to exercise these when the need arises – empowers people and can boost an economy's growth and development.[10] For the poor, the destitute, the marginalized, the discriminated against, and the downtrodden, the largest handicap is a lack of self-confidence. Not only do they suffer because others treat them dismissively, but, as a series of psychological experiments and micro-studies show, the biggest damage is that they lose faith in themselves. The granting of certain basic human rights can create a sense of empowerment and give hope to the hopeless,[11] the long-term benefits of which can far outweigh the costs of instituting such empowerment.

Some recent aptitude tests given to school children in India – administered by Karla Hoff and Priyanka Pandey (2005) – where all children were treated the same and no mention was made of anybody's caste before the tests were conducted, revealed that all caste groups performed at roughly the same level. Of course, there were individual variations in performance; however, when averaged out over all members of each caste, the scores turned out to be pretty close to one another. But when the same kinds of tests were given to the children after they were identified in class by the teacher calling out each child's name *and caste group*, the children from the backward castes began faltering in their aptitude tests, getting lower marks on average. The scars of hundreds of years of discrimination and denial of not just property but also basic human rights seemed to suddenly get activated by the public announcement, reminding them of and disclosing to everybody their disadvantaged status. There can be controversy about what the mechanisms are behind this trigger. Perhaps the children lose faith in themselves or, maybe, as the authors

---

[9] These numbers, based on World Bank data and some numbers published in *Forbes* magazine, were computed in Basu (2006b).

[10] The UN has been promoting the idea of the "right to development" – a term that was coined by the Senegalese jurist, Keba M'Baye. On one level, a right like this can be seen as too all encompassing to be of use. But, if we view this as promoting the idea of individual empowerment and freedom so that people have the *scope* for development, then this can be a valuable rallying idea (for discussion, see Sengupta 2006).

[11] Another way of viewing this is to recognize the familiar need all human beings have for basic security – that is, to keep at bay critical pervasive threats, and then to view human rights as a way of ensuring minimal human security (Alkire 2003).

hypothesize, they no longer believe that they will be judged fairly by the teachers. Once their caste status is announced, they feel automatically disenfranchised of the right to good grades.[12]

This general point receives reinforcement in some data that I collected while visiting an NGO-run teaching institute for slum children in Kolkata (formerly Calcutta). The details of the data and the tests I ran on these are reported in Basu (2006a). What comes out quite starkly is that what is most important for a child's aptitude is not the income or the wealth of the child's household, but whether the parents talk to each other and whether the parents talk to the child.

What is of interest to us in the context of the present paper is the suggestion that the child's *social* conditions matter significantly in how he or she performs in school; and they seem to matter more than the *economic* conditions of the child's household. Children whose parents converse among themselves and with the children clearly make for more congenial living conditions for the children; and this seems to translate into human capital for the child. Another suggestion is that a person's "citizenship status" matters. If a person feels a proper "citizen of the household," it bolsters his or her self-confidence and this again results in intelligence and human capital. If the parents talk to you, it bolsters your status in the household and that citizenship status aids intellectual performance.

To give people a sense of status in society, community, and the household – which in turn entails having some minimal rights – unleashes energies and initiatives that, at first blush, seems unexpected. In addition to the kinds of experimental research mentioned earlier, we now have interesting studies of how empowering women can make them come into their own in household decisions. There are studies in India showing that if a household's total income remains the same but the woman's income increases, the woman begins to exercise greater say in household matters.[13]

There are studies from Bangladesh that show that women who join community groups – such as Grameen Bank borrower's group – begin to exercise greater say in their households, even when the outside interaction does not lead to any new earnings for the household.

India has recently enacted a very controversial law that gives people the right to a certain amount of work. It is, however, a very limited right. In each household, the law guarantees that at least one person will have the right to one hundred days of work. If they do not find it in the market, the state government has the responsibility to provide work – if it fails to do so, individuals have the right to take the government to court. As of now the law applies only to some select districts in rural areas, but the intention is to eventually extend it to all rural areas. The activists and the (very few, I must add) economists who campaigned for this policy argued that its aim is not only to mitigate poverty, but to also give the poor a sense

---

[12] Recent tests done in South Africa by Erica Field and Patrick Nolen (2006) seem to confirm something similar. Make children take aptitude tests with no talk of race and they perform at reasonably comparable levels. But charge the atmosphere by talking about race, and then make them take similar level tests, the black children – in this case, especially the boys – begin to falter.
[13] See Basu (2006) for discussion of some of the results discussed in this and the next two paragraphs.

of right and entitlement. If the rich can call up the local government when the road outside their home is not well maintained, surely the poor should be able to call up the government if what they need most – namely, jobs – are not available.

There has been much debate about the fiscal consequences of this law and the labor market distortions that it can create; and indeed, these are not matters to be ignored.[14] But as an instrument for giving people a sense of basic economic rights and entitlement, this cannot be faulted. As the studies mentioned earlier show, the effect of such a law could go well beyond the immediate benefits of the money earned through such employment; for instance, the jobs may bolster self-confidence and superior performance from the awareness that one has the same rights in society that the rich and powerful have always had.

The connection between rights and economic performance and progress seems to be clear and present. But I want to enter more controversial terrain by discussing what exactly the granting of a right means in the context of an economy; and, when there are several possible meanings of granting a right, which ones should we adopt where. I will also discuss which of the many possible kinds of rights ought to be respected, which ones help, and which ones hurt the carrier of the right. My aim here is not to give full answers by actually classifying rights into different categories but, rather, to lay out some general principles and essential taxonomies that can be used in crafting laws and designing policies.

4. TRADEABLE RIGHTS

One philosophically intricate question that we need to confront is whether, when we grant a person a right, we also should grant the person the right to waive that right (or trade that right away). In our laws and proclamations – and even in academic writing – this is not always made clear, and a lack of clarity on this can lead to great inefficiencies and inequities.

I should clarify that I am not talking here about the distinction between alienable and inalienable rights, following Jefferson's famous words about "the unalienable rights of man" – in particular, the right to "life, liberty and the pursuit of happiness." These were drawn, in turn, from John Locke's idea of the right of human beings to "life, liberty and estate" (meaning property). The term "inalienable" typically refers to the fact that no one can take the right away from the person endowed with such a right. But whether the person endowed with the right cannot *himself or herself* waive the right, sell the right, or gift the right to someone else is not automatically clear. Indeed, because Locke clearly did not think of one's "estate" as something that is immoral to sell – such as many would consider one's life or limb – plainly Locke was not thinking of our basic rights as untradeable or unwaivable. In

---

[14] The right to work has a long history. Arguably, it was in the French constitution of 1793, where it was recognized for the first time as a basic human right. But this is one area where there can be serious contention between the legal positivists and the natural rights school, as some would argue that permanent full employment is impossible for any nation – even if it consists of only Japanese. Hence, some would argue that this right can be no more than a pointer to a certain direction and sets a responsibility on the part of the government to keep unemployment as low as technically possible (see Harvey 2002).

fact, my hunch is that Locke was making a categorical mistake by clubbing together rights, which he himself (on cogitation) would consider to be rights in different senses.

Note, first of all, that when most of us talk of a person having a certain right to a certain property (for instance, the person's car), we mean that no one can take it away from him by force. But, by contrast, he certainly can waive that right or trade it. He can give it away to his niece, if he wishes; he can exchange it for money or other goods.

Economists tend to go further and carry this notion of rights not just to goods and services, but to many other things as well. Typically, when an economist says that some person has the right to something – call it R – she presumes that the person can sell that right. This is indeed the presumption behind Ronald Coase's famous law. Suppose we agree that John has the right to a smoke-free atmosphere. Jill comes into his room and strikes a deal with him. She will pay him a dollar and he will not object to her smoking a cigarette. Would this be considered a violation of his right? I think most economists and many people will consider the answer to be "no."

Now consider the case where a rich landlord tells a very poor serf, whom he dislikes intensely, that he will give the serf's family $100 if he will kill himself. Suppose the serf agrees and the "trade" is carried out. Has the serf's right to life been violated? Many would consider the answer to be "yes."[15] As for what economists would say, I prefer not to speculate.

This shows that when we say that a person has a right to R, there is some ambiguity about what this means, for in some cases we mean he has "full right" to R (including the ability to waive the right), whereas in other cases at least some people believe that this means even he himself cannot waive that right. I shall call the former kind a "tradeable right," and the latter an "untradeable right."

It is possible to categorize these further, and my classification also bears resemblance to others that have been suggested in the literature (for instance, Lyons 1979; Feinberg 1980).[16] As Feinberg (1980, 156–58) points out, right-holders are not always obliged to exercise their rights; in fact, the ability to occasionally forego one's rights often makes for a nicer society. But note that when I speak about a tradeable right, I mean it in a stronger sense than the holder having the meta-right to occasionally forego or sell the right. Certainly he or she can do that, but I mean that, in addition, he or she can waive it off forever. Consider the right not to have to work more than ten hours a day. There is a difference between not exercising that right on a particular day (maybe for an overtime fee) and telling the employer that one is giving up that right forever ("If you give me this job I will henceforth work as many hours as you wish, foregoing in advance the right to object."). By a tradeable

---

[15] It is possible to argue that making an offer like this is to immediately diminish the status of a person. Hence, it is not a simple take it or leave it offer. Once an offer like this has been made, there is no returning to the world before the offer was made.

[16] One advantage of classification is that it permits the use of a larger bundle of rights. Although we may not agree to confer the status of rights to several needs if there was only one kind of right, we may be able to accommodate a wider range of human needs as rights if we can separate these out by the use of different epithets.

right, I mean having both these rights – that of not *exercising* a right and that of waiving the right itself.

The ambiguity about whether a particular right is tradeable or not crops up in many areas, and we need to confront it frontally. From the way some basic principles are stated in economics it seems to be implicitly assumed that all rights, the exercise of which has no negative fall-out on others who are not voluntarily party to the deal, should be tradeable rights. This follows from the Pareto principle or, relatedly, from the principle of free contract, which says that if two adults voluntarily agree to an exchange or trade in a contract having no negative fall-outs on uninvolved third parties, then government has no business stopping such a deal. Indeed, the foundation of modern market economies is predicated on contracts and exchanges of this kind being possible. The possibility of such transactions is often taken as an index of economic freedom. A typical economist would argue that governments that intervene and ban such transactions harm enterprise and progress; accordingly, he or she would oppose all such government interventions.

Consider one example of the application of the free contract principle. In the United States, workers have a right not to be sexually harassed in the workplace. Now suppose that a firm puts up a sign outside its personnel office stating the following: "We offer great salaries, excellent health plans, and plenty of vacations, but we reserve the right to sexually harass our workers. If you agree to these conditions, you are welcome to join our firm." In other words, the firm is offering the workers money and benefits in exchange for having them waive their right not to be sexually harassed. Equally, this can be thought of as a trade. A person can trade her right not to be sexually harassed for money and other benefits. Pursuant to the principle of free contract, it appears that such transactions should be allowed.

Most of us, however, feel uncomfortable with this conclusion. But it is not good enough to disallow such waivers purely for reasons of discomfort. We must found the prevention of such waivers in reason and reasonable ethics. One route is the use of deontic rules. "One must not be allowed to trade one's bodily integrity, irrespective of its consequences." "It is wrong for children to work no matter what the consequences of non-work happens to be." These are deontic rules, because they make no reference to the consequences of such rules, such as the effect on the welfares of the citizens involved. I believe such principles should be used minimally. I want to found my arguments for deciding on whether a particular right should be treated tradeable or not on the welfare consequences of such a decision, and make room for deontic rules only when that does not yield a clear answer. There is more to this than personal predilection. When we craft rules for distant societies – for individuals with whom we have little or no interaction – it is natural to underplay the importance of welfare consequences. Distance may or may not lend enchantment, but it always blurs awareness. Hence, when deciding for distant societies, we have a bias toward the use of deontological principles, often in quite an ad hoc fashion. What I am arguing is that we must resist this penchant.

Before discussing the case of what stand we should take on sexual harassment, consider another problem. Workers in most nations have the right not to expose themselves to large health and safety hazards. But suppose a mining firm refuses to put in expensive safety equipment in their mines and offers instead to pay an extra salary to workers willing to go down those shafts. Suppose this is a very poor region and some workers are therefore willing to accept the deal. Has their right to safety been violated? Should such contracts be allowed?

I do not think that the answer to each of these and other similar *sounding* questions will be the same. I have elsewhere taken the view that the right not to be sexually harassed should be a nontradeable right. No one should be given the option of waiving it in order to get other benefits. The reason is not embedded in the person who waives it. I believe an individual should have such a right if that was all there was to it. But if such rights are granted in general and firms are allowed to freely buy up the rights of workers not to be harassed, it can be shown that any worker who insists on signing a no-harassment contract will get a low wage. In other words, in a legal regime that allows "contractual" harassment (like the firm earlier that makes the terms abundantly clear), those with the strongest aversion to harassment will get punished by the market, because they will get a lower wage than they would in an economy in which contractual harassment is declared illegal. And I would maintain that no one should have to pay a penalty for having a preference not to be harassed. As is discussed in the next section, I call certain preferences "inviolable" and argue that the preference not to be harassed ought to be considered an inviolable preference.

Indeed, in the United States you cannot trade your right not to be sexually harassed, *a priori*. This is even clearer in the case of what is called a "yellow dog contract," whereby an employee relinquishes the right to join a trade union during the term of his or her employment. By the Norris-La Guardia Act or the Anti-Injunction Bill (1932), yellow dog contracts are explicitly illegal in the United States. In other words, a person's right to join a trade union is not a tradeable right.

The decision about which rights should and should not be considered tradeable is often hard. Consider the problem of mine safety in a developing country. Typically, poor people will be willing to take undue health risks in order to earn a subsistence income. Our first response may be that no one should be so poor that he has to take such risks. But the counter response is that if they *are* that poor, then surely we do not have the right to take away their right to survive by saying that they should not take undue health risks. That would amount to committing the fallacy of binariness.

The government, we could argue, should get rid of this kind of poverty. But that still leaves the question: "What if government fails to do so?" Should we not in that case give people the option to fend off extreme poverty by, if need be, taking up risky jobs? But that, in turn, implies that there may not be an obvious case for banning hazardous work in poor nations. If government succeeds in obliterating extreme poverty, then people will choose not to take up such hazardous work, so the law will be of no consequence. And if government fails to obliterate extreme poverty, then it is not clear that such a law – which may cause starvation and chronic hunger – is a good idea.

It is, however, possible that a ban on hazardous work will lead employers to install new technology to make the mines safer. But there is also the risk that they will close down their operations and contribute to greater unemployment and poverty in the region. In the field of human and labor rights, much of what starts out looking obvious has the propensity to spring surprising complexities.

5. MAINTAINABLE AND INVIOLABLE PREFERENCES

In general I take the view, in keeping with the analysis of Coase, that rights should be specified as clearly as possible for as many goods and actions as possible. I would then go further and say that we should typically give greater rights to the disadvantaged and the dispossessed, so as to give them a sense of empowerment and enhance their sense of citizenship. The ambiguity is not about these principles, but about which rights should be treated as tradeable and which not. I sketched a few arguments for some specific examples earlier. For developing a transparent and *generalizable* criterion, we need to have some prior normative rules for ranking preferences the same way that we rank actions – castigating some as bad and praising some as good. We do not typically rank preferences morally, but it is arguable that we can and should.[17] If a person says that she does not like people of a certain race, or that she prefers not to be friends with anybody who is overweight, most of us would consider these to be unacceptable preferences. We may not do anything about this, but we still consider such preferences wrong. Let me now call all preferences that we do not consider morally wrong "maintainable preferences." Here are some preferences that I would consider maintainable, and I expect so would most other people:

"I prefer apples to oranges."
"I prefer not to work four days a week."
"I would rather be unemployed than face sexual harassment at work."
"I consider it my right to be able to join a trade union, and I prefer not to join a company that denies this to me."

Clearly we cannot have *moral* objections to this. You may not wish to marry the person who plans to work three days a week or, for that matter, the one who does not share your passion for oranges; but surely you will not morally castigate these people for having these preferences.

However, among maintainable preferences we need to separate out two kinds of such preferences, and the rules for government intervention depend on this categorization. To understand this, observe that some preferences may be dysfunctional in the sense that they could hurt their carriers. A person with the second preference will clearly be poorer for working so little – she has to pay a price for her preference. Now we, outside observers, may decide to take a stand on this "price for preference." We may consider certain preferences to be so understandable that no one should have to pay a price for having that preference. Many would consider the last two – and especially the third – preferences listed earlier to be of this kind. Not only is the strong aversion to harassment a maintainable preference,[18] but most of us would argue that no one should have to pay a price for having this preference. Many would feel similarly about a worker's right to associate with other workers. Let us call a maintainable preference, which has this property, an "inviolable preference."

Notice that this is typically not the case with the second or the first preference. It would be perfectly reasonable to tell the person with the second preference:

---

[17] These ideas were suggested and developed in Basu (2000; 2003).

[18] That is – just to remind the reader – we do not morally disapprove of this preference the way we disapprove of someone's racism preference.

"Yours is a maintainable preference – I have no moral objections to it, but you do understand that you will be poorer by virtue of having this preference. You surely cannot expect society to compensate you for your high leisure preference."

In other words, although the second person's love of leisure and the third person's strong aversion to workplace harassment are both maintainable preferences, only the latter is an inviolable preference.

Of course, being a normative matter, there is no hard and fast rule about where we should draw the line between these categories. It is also possible to see that what we consider inviolable may change through time and even across space. But in most of our minds, at this point of time we can create the categories of inviolable and noninviolable preferences.

Now we are ready to create an argument for why it may be correct to ban yellow dog contracts and to disallow contractual sexual harassment in the workplace. Suppose we consider the fourth preference above to be inviolable and consider the case of yellow dog contracts. Assume firms are permitted to demand that potential employees relinquish the right to join trade unions. This will give rise to two kinds of firms (for the same kind of work) – some paying a lower wage and making no such demands and others paying a better wage but requiring individuals to give up their right to join unions.[19]

Now workers with strong preference for joining unions – the fourth preference in the list – will be joining the former firms. In other words, they will have to be reconciled to a lower income *by virtue of their preference.* But the inviolability of the preference for joining unions means that this should not happen. The way to ensure this is to have a law, like the Norris-La Guardia Act, that bans yellow dog contracts.

This is the crux of the argument about why certain rights may have to be made nontradeable. Allowing the trading of these rights inflicts a cost on some people who have a strong preference for holding onto these rights. And if this preference is inviolable, then government is required to protect people from having to pay a price for having the preference. One way of doing this is disallowing anybody from trading or waiving this right.

It is worth noting that the overall moral system being used here is neither pure welfarism nor deontological ethics. It is a "miscible moral system," which uses welfarism – and in particular, Paretianism – first to weed out certain options, and then permits the use of nonwelfarist considerations – for instance, dignity, autonomy, and agency – to further eliminate options.

We may be able to carry this argument over to other matters; for instance, sexual harassment in the workplace, hazardous work, and so on. Yes, individual freedom would at first sight seem to require that having given a person a right – such as the right not to be harassed at work – we should give the person the additional right to trade this right. Given individual rationality, this can only benefit the individual. But the exercising of this latter right – that is, the right to waive the basic right – could

---

[19] A standard market arbitrage argument leads to this conclusion. But in reality, one often finds that those workers with the least rights and working in the most hazardous conditions are also the poorest. Hence, the theories of "equalizing wage differentials" may deserve further empirical and theoretical investigation.

mean that others who attach a greater value to the basic right will now have to pay a price for that. If this is unacceptable, then the state needs to step in.

But this is not the end of the matter. There may be other reasons for letting people trade their basic rights that arises with extra vehemence in the context of developing countries.

6. TRADE-OFFS AND A COMMENT ON THE THIRD WORLD

There was a time when each country's rights problem was considered of prime interest to the government and civil society of that nation; however, this has changed with globalization. Through a combination of factors – greater information about what is happening in distant lands,[20] interest, even if vicarious, in the lives of the peoples of those lands, the fact that through channels of trade and capital flows the crushing of rights in another nation may actually change the wages and prices of goods in your locality, and the realization that if another nation punctures a hole in the ozone layer, it could be as bad news to you as to the other nation – we have come to take an interest in human (especially economic and labor) rights in other countries. And, nowadays, through international organizations and global activist movements, it is actually possible to give some effectiveness to one's displeasure or approval of what is happening in other lands.[21]

One cannot, however, deny that the scope of influence runs disproportionately from rich countries to poor countries.[22] And with this arises huge responsibilities about how we dispense with the interventions. There is no doubt that some of the worst violations of basic, everyday rights occur in the Third World, but there is a complication that also occurs with special vigor in poor countries that makes this a difficult and sensitive problem that demands care in handling (Basu 2005). The classic example is child labor. This is a dreadful institution and all reasonable people seek its demise as quickly as possible. Without going into the details of this vast subject,[23] I want to conduct a discussion that bears on the concepts developed earlier.

Economists have argued at length about whether a legislative ban on child labor is desirable. The laissez-faire argument – at the risk of oversimplification – goes

---

[20] This does not refer only to television images and journalistic reporting. There are now excellent statistical studies that collate and rank human rights violations in different countries. See, for instance, Cingranelli and Richards (1999), and for up-to-date downloadable data, see http://ciri.binghamton.edu/.

[21] As Brysk (2002, 5) observes: "[The] literature on human rights has moved beyond the conventional wisdom that situated human rights violations and remediation predominantly within the state, to suggest ways in which globalization creates new opportunities to challenge the state 'from above and below.'" See Fung, O'Rourke and Sabel (2001) on the difficulties of thinking about common standards for our contemporary world of such wide disparities.

[22] For a discussion of the modes and technology of cross-country "human rights" influence and the legitimacy of global action that have national or local influences, see Rosenau (2002), Pogge (2005), Basu (2005), Buchanan and Keohane (2006). It has been argued that when we think of the world as a whole, the equivalent of the state is the "global order" (Risse 2005). Responsibility for the *world's* poor therefore rests with the global order in somewhat the same way that the responsibility for a nation's poor lies with the government.

[23] There is a large literature on the subject, covering empirical studies, economic theory, law, and history. For the recent survey and analysis, see Edmonds and Pavnick (2005), as well as Bhaskar and Gupta (2006).

as follows. Suppose parents are altruistic about their children,[24] so that when they take decisions about their children it is *as if* they are deciding for themselves. It then follows, by the principle of free contract, that for parents to send their children to work is not a matter on which the state should come in.

But this argument can be countered using the tools of analysis developed earlier. It is arguable that a parent's desire not to let her children work is not just a maintainable preference but also an inviolable one. No parent should have to pay a price for having such a preference. Now consider what seems quite realistic – to wit, that different parents will have different degrees of aversion to letting their children work. If, under these circumstances, child labor is treated as legal, then it can be shown that parents who have a strong aversion to sending their children to work will be penalized for their preference. To see this in the simplest possible case, suppose some parents are so extreme in their preferences that they will never send their children to work. If child labor is made legal, lots of children will begin to work (recall that we are considering a poor country). This increase in labor supply will certainly cause wages to fall. This may not matter to households that send their children to work, because even though per hour wage may be lower there will now be more hands at work. But households with the strong aversion will be worse off for sure, as they will not send their children to work even when adult wages fall and children are legally allowed to work. Hence, making child labor legal amounts to extracting a price from those with strong preference against child labor. The inviolability of this preference, however, means that this should not happen; accordingly, child labor must be declared unlawful.

Unfortunately, the argument cannot stop here. To see this, consider a person's preference not to suffer food deprivation. Surely we will agree this is an inviolable preference. Now, in a poor country where lots of people live on the threshold of hunger, it is easy to see that we can have situations in which to ban child labor is to violate this inviolable preference. By contrast, not to ban child labor is to violate another kind of inviolable preference, as we saw earlier.

When a person's right comes into conflict with another person's love of opulence, we may easily agree on the primacy of the rights, but we do not have this luxury when one person's right of one kind comes into conflict with another person's right of that or another kind (Osmani 2005). This problem often arises in developing countries, because everything occurs in the shadow of malnutrition and hunger. If avoiding hunger is a right, or aversion to it an inviolable preference, then in the exercise of all other rights or the upholding of all other inviolable preferences we have to be reconciled that upholding all these fundamental values may not be possible. We are then forced to contend with trade-offs, no matter how painful.[25]

---

[24] There is now mounting evidence on this. I find this somewhat embarrassing, since it is a testimony to the power of economics, that we seek statistical confirmation about the fact that parents love their children.

[25] There is a small but growing literature on the algebra of how multiple and conflicting normative criteria can be combined to create a single order or partial order (see, for instance, Tadenuma 2006; Yoshihara 2006). The general exercise of building rights-consciousness into a welfarist setting – that is, in contexts in which people are interested not just in the outcomes but also processes, and in particular the respect of individual rights –also has been formally attempted (see, for instance, Pattanaik & Suzumura 1996).

This is the reason why we cannot sit back, taking the moral high ground, and simply ban what *seems* wrong in developing countries. We cannot just ban certain abhorrent practices and be unmindful of the fact that that may lead to other kinds of deprivations and sufferings, as the fallacy of binariness warns us. This is not so only for child labor. Consider the controversial move made by some countries asking workers to give up their right to collective bargaining in order to work in an export-processing zone (EPZ). Many countries with unruly labor find that, without such a clause, they cannot run EPZs. Now, whereas for moderately prosperous countries we can argue that such exceptions for EPZs cannot be allowed for the same reason that yellow dog contracts are wrong, the decision is more troublesome for a poor country, like some in sub-Saharan Africa or Bangladesh. When the difference between being able to work in an EPZ is equivalent to the difference between being able to feed one's children properly and not, or the difference between being and not being able to send one's children to school, it is not clear that one can take away an individual's right to waive the right to collective bargaining (see Kabeer 2004). The right to collective bargaining, in such situations, may have to be treated as a tradeable right because, whereas the preference for collective bargaining may be an inviolable preference, we are here faced with a situation in which one inviolable preference is pitted against another.

If we want to have a code of crafting policy – where can child labor be banned outright, where should we allow workers to take on the health hazards they are willing to expose themselves to, and so on – we will need to decide on trade-offs between rights and the inviolability of preferences. We would have to decide that while x and y are both rights, one may be lexicographically prior to the other, or that one may be violated up to a certain extent for the sake of the other and so on.

This is a large exercise and will have to be done gradually, maybe effecting changes as and when we encounter conflicts and are forced to choose, and then using these choices to enshrine general rules. But this discussion should alert us to the fact that to call something a right does not mean that it will have to be upheld in all contexts. For one, this may simply not be possible, as Gibbard (1974), Farrell (1976), Suzumura (1978), and Subramanian (2006) have shown in the context of individual liberty, building on the work of Sen (1970). Moreover, we may decide to recognize certain rights in the sense of attaching moral worth to them and *trying* to uphold them, but being prepared to trade them for other moral imperatives.

It must be stressed, however, that to argue that something should not be enshrined in a code of law (for example, not banning child labor) does not mean going over to the laissez-faire extreme of recommending that we do nothing. There are numerous actions governments and international organizations can take that are nonlegislative. Financial support to eradicate certain phenomena such as poverty and illiteracy; subsidies to encourage certain desirable practices; and advertising and campaigning to change people's preferences and opinion are all interventions that are nonlegislative. When fundamental rights are mutually in conflict, this may be the only way out.

7. CONCLUSION

The world is an unfair place. There are the innately disadvantaged; there are those who come into adulthood with no inheritance of wealth, education or heritage.

It takes immense harshness or a convoluted belief in previous lives and sins to be able to sit back and not try to make some amends for these imperfections. This chapter took the view that the market mechanism can confer great benefits, but it needs to be tempered by a specification of minimal human and economic rights and the design of policy interventions that try to offset some of the extreme disadvantages that some people face.

The specification of basic human rights, and the development of institutions for upholding these basic rights, can go a long way to offset some of the natural inequities of the world left laissez-faire. But the subject of rights is not one of mere campaign and activism. To do so without thought is to risk playing into the hands of powerful lobbies and groups with vested interests that are ever present in the wings. We need to think through which rights should be upheld and which not, and, among the ones we choose to uphold, which rights ought to be treated as tradeable and which ones not.

The aim of this chapter was not to make actual suggestions. Indeed, on a variety of matters I, myself, am full of doubts and hesitations. If, after reading this essay, a reader finds herself in a greater dilemma about child labor and hazardous work, or in a quandary about worker rights in export-processing zones, then that would confirm that her earlier complacency was not well founded and that, in turn, would mean that the chapter has served a purpose. The aim of this chapter was to draw out the complexities of this topic, and to suggest some new instruments of analysis and shed new perspectives on old practical problems. Once analysts and policy makers understand these complexities, they may feel less confident about their decisions, but others will have greater reason for confidence in them.

REFERENCES

Alkire, Sabina. 2003. A Conceptual Framework for Human Security. CRISE Working Paper # 2, Oxford University.

Allen, Woody. 1975. *Side Effects.* New York: Random House.

Basu, Kaushik. 2000. *Prelude to Political Economy: A Study of the Social and Political Foundations of Economics.* Oxford: Oxford University Press.

Basu, Kaushik. 2003. The Economics and Law of Sexual Harassment in the Workplace. *Journal of Economic Perspectives* 17 (3): 141–57.

Basu, Kaushik. 2005. Global Labor Standards and Local Freedoms. In *UNU-WIDER, Wider Perspectives on Global Development.* New York: Palgrave Macmillan.

Basu, Kaushik. 2006. Gender and Say: A Model of Household Behavior with Endogenous Balance of Power. *Economic Journal* 116 (511): 558–80.

Basu, Kaushik. 2006a. Participatory Equity and Economic Development: Policy Implications for a Globalized World. CAE Working Paper # 06-07, Cornell University.

Basu, Kaushik. 2006b. Globalization, Poverty and Inequality: What Is the Relationship? What Can Be Done? *World Development* 34 (8): 1361–1373.

Bhaskar, V., and Bishnupriya Gupta. 2005. Were American Parents Really Selfish?: Re-Examining Child Labor in the 19th Century. University College, London, mimeograph.

Brysk, Alison, ed. 2002. *Globalization and Human Rights.* Berkeley: University of California Press.

Buchanan, Allen, and Robert Keohane. 2006. The Legitimacy of Global Governance Institutions. Memorandum prepared for the Conference on the Normative and Empirical Evaluation of Global Governance, Princeton University, 16–18 February 2006.

Chatterjee, Partha. 2004. *The Politics of the Governed*. New York: Columbia University Press.

Cingranelli, David, and David Richards. 1999. Measuring the Level, Pattern, and Sequence of Government Respect for Physical Integrity Rights. *International Studies Quarterly* 43 (2): 407–17.

Cooter, Robert. 1998. Expressive Law and Economics. *Journal of Legal Studies* 27.

Dworkin, Ronald. 1978. *Taking Rights Seriously*. London: Duckworth.

Edmonds, Eric and Nina Pavcnik. 2005. Child Labor in the Global Economy. *Journal of Economic Perspectives* 19.

Farrell, M. J. 1976. Liberalism in the Theory of Social Choice. *Review of Economic Studies* 43 (1): 3–10.

Feinberg, Joel. 1980. *Rights, Justice, and the Bounds of Liberty*. Princeton: Princeton University Press.

Field, Erica, and Patrick Nolen. 2006. Race and Performance in Post-Apartheid South Africa. Cornell University, mimeograph.

Fung, Archon, Dara O'Rourke, and Charles Sabel. 2001. *Can We Put an End to Sweatshops?* Boston: Beacon Press.

Gibbard, Allan. 1974. A Pareto-Consistent Libertarian Claim. *Journal of Economic Theory* 7 (4): 388–410.

Harvey, Philip. 2002. Human Rights and Economic Policy Discourse: Taking Economic and Social Rights Seriously. *Columbia Human Rights Law Review* 33 (2): 363–472.

Harvey, Philip. 2004. Aspirational Law. *Buffalo Law Review* 52 (3): 701–26.

Hoff, Karla and Priyanka Pandey. 2004. Belief Systems and Durable Inequalities: An Experimental Investigation of Indian Caste. World Bank Policy Research Paper # 0-2875.

Kabeer, Naila. 2004. The Cost of Good Intention: "Solidarity" in Bangladesh. *Open Democracy*, http://www.opendemocracy.net/globalization-trade_economy_justice/article_1977.jsp.

Lyons, David, ed. 1979. *Rights*. Belmont, CA: Wadsworth.

Mansbridge, Jane. 1984. Unitary and Adversary: The Two Forms of Democracy. In *Context: A Quarterly of Humane Sustainable Culture*, http://www.context.org/ICLIB/IC07/Mansbrdg.htm.

Osmani, Siddiqur R. 2005. Globalisation and the Human Rights Approach to Development. Paper presented at the UNU-WIDER Jubilee Conference, Helsinki.

Pattanaik, Prasanta, and Kotaro Suzumura. 1996. Individual Rights and Social Evaluation: A Conceptual Framework. *Oxford Economic Papers* 48 (2): 194–212.

Pogge, Thomas. 2005. World Poverty and Human Rights. *Ethics and International Affairs* 19 (1): 1–7.

Rosenau, James. 2002. The Drama of Human Rights in a Turbulent, Globalized World. In *Globalization and Human Rights*, ed. A. Brysk. Berkeley: University of California Press.

Risse, Mathias. 2005. How Does the Global Order Harm the Poor? *Philosophy and Public Affairs* 33.

Sen, Amartya. 1970. The Impossibility of the Paretian Liberal. *Journal of Political Economy* 78 (1): 152–57.

Sen, Amartya. 2001. *Development as Freedom*. New York: Alfred Knopf.

Sengupta, Arjun. 2006. Human Rights. In *Oxford Companion to Economics in India*, ed. K. Basu. New Delhi: Oxford University Press.

Subramanian, S. 2006. *Rights, Deprivation and Disparity*. New Delhi: Oxford University Press.

Sunstein, Cass. 1996. On the Expressive Function of Law. *University of Pennsylvania Law Review* 144 (5): 2021–55.

Suzumura, Kotaro. 1978. On the Consistency of Libertarian Claims. *Review of Economic Studies* 45 (2): 343–46.

Tadenuma, Koichi. 2006. Rationality of the Lexicographic Composition of Two Criteria. Hitotsubashi University, mimeograph.

Yoshihara, Naoki. 2006. A Resolution of Conflicting Claims in Constructing Social Ordering Functions. Hitotsubashi University, mimeograph.

17 Worker Rights and Economic Development: The Cases of Occupational Safety and Health and Child Labor

PETER DORMAN

I. INTRODUCTION: ARE WORKER RIGHTS UNIVERSAL OR CONTINGENT ON THE LEVEL OF ECONOMIC DEVELOPMENT?

The status of worker rights within the larger family of human rights is unsettled. It is true, as Leary (1982) has pointed out, that the International Labour Organization (ILO) conventions preceded modern human rights treaties by several decades, and in that sense they can be regarded as central to the rights tradition. The right of workers to associate and form independent trade unions is widely viewed as a bellweather of political liberties, and it has played a prominent role in U.S. foreign policy initiatives (Dorman, 1989). Nevertheless, a shadow of suspicion has fallen over other worker rights, such as safe working conditions, employment security, and even the prohibition of child labor. Can these be considered as universal rights when their fulfillment appears to depend greatly on the level of a country's economic development? Is it appropriate to apply pressure on behalf of worker rights in countries where mass poverty is also a primary concern? Is it possible that "premature" adherence to certain worker rights may even retard development and restrict the actual freedoms (capabilities) of its intended beneficiaries?

My target in this chapter is the developmentalist argument I have just briefly hypothesized. Rather than attempt a general argument applicable to all worker rights, I will concentrate on two for which large bodies of evidence exist – child labor and occupational safety and health. For each of these, I will consider developmentalist claims in some detail and indicate why I believe they do not hold, provided that worker rights are framed in an appropriate – non-development-specific – manner.

The plan of the chapter is straightforward. The next section takes up occupational safety and health, the third child labor, and the final section concludes with some brief lessons for worker rights generally.

II. OCCUPATIONAL SAFETY AND HEALTH (OSH)

The right to safe and healthy work is one of the original and most impassioned demands of the labor movement. The great safety and health disasters of modern

The author wishes to thank Lanse Minkler, Shareen Hertel, and Sevinç Rende for their comments on earlier drafts.

history – the Triangle Fire, the Kader fire, mine explosions, radium and asbestos poisonings – are monuments to the cruelty of work when basic human rights are denied. From its inception, the ILO has foregrounded occupational safety and health (OSH), and it continues to develop new conventions to improve working conditions that all too often remain substandard.

Nevertheless, from the first appearance of sweatshops in eighteenth-century Europe to the debates over labor standards in today's global economy, there has been a prominent argument, supported in particular by many economists, holding that conventional abhorrence of unsafe work is misguided. Do not forget, these critics point out, that all such work is voluntarily agreed to. If the workers did not judge that the benefits of accepting these jobs exceeded their costs – including the risks of disease, injury, and death – they would not take them (Atiyah 1979; Viscusi 1983). Indeed, denying workers the opportunity to trade risk for income and other benefits could make them worse off, good intentions notwithstanding. The solicitude for the safety and health risks faced by the poor is a middle class prejudice, it is said: what is an acceptable luxury for the well-to-do – a risk-free environment – is an unacceptable limitation on the freedom of ordinary workers to make do as best they can. At a society-wide level, excessive zeal to make workplaces safe and healthy robs countries of the lowest rungs of development; sweatshops are believed to be stepping stones to a future of more productive, better-paid and ultimately safer work (Kristof and WuDunn 2000).

I have critiqued the argument for a free market in physical harm elsewhere and will not repeat it here (Dorman 1996). Relevant to this discussion, however, are specific observations on the nature of worker rights in OSH, their potential costs, and their significance for workers in different social and economic environments.

The developmentalist perspective holds that the more dangerous working conditions found in poorer countries represent a rational response to a scarcity of resources; rather than being deployed to make work more salubrious, they are devoted to basic human needs and the investments necessary for economic growth. If sustained growth can be achieved, this harsh set of priorities can be relaxed. Eventually, the goal is for workers everywhere to enjoy the conditions that can be found in the wealthiest countries today, but prematurely enforcing rigorous safety standards would only delay this process. By trying to make work too safe, we would succeed only in guaranteeing that it remained dangerous longer than necessary. Such an argument has clearly had an impact in the world of policy: few developing country governments give much attention to workplace hazards, and the issue does not even appear on a search of the World Bank research Web site.

My rebuttal to this view will have these elements: I will argue that the burden of unsafe working conditions is far larger in the developing world than it is in the developed countries, that this burden constitutes an impediment to economic growth, and that it is possible to frame workers' rights to safe and healthy work in a way that applies to a wide variety of economic and social contexts.

1. The Burden of Occupational Injury and Disease

If developed countries can be faulted for undercounting rates of occupational morbidity and mortality, the problem in the developing world is that counting rarely takes place at all (Driscoll et al. 2005). The World Health Organization, in its effort to estimate the global burden of occupational health impairments, uses rough extrapolations from industrialized countries to arrive at totals for the rest (Leigh et al. 1999; Concha-Barrientos et al. 2004; Mathers et al. 2004). In the few instances in which developing countries do produce injury and disease data, they appear to be undercounted to a much greater extent. One South African study, for instance, found that fatal occupational injuries, which ought to be identified more readily than nonfatal injuries or diseases, were 28% too low for Capetown and as much as 85% too low for rural areas (Concha-Barrientos et al. 2004).

Nevertheless, there exists a wealth of employer- and locality-specific evidence that cumulatively indicates that risks in developing regions are comparable to those faced by workers a century or more ago in what are now the industrialized countries. Catastrophic fires occur with regularity in textile plants and other establishments; machines impale and lacerate; hazardous chemical exposures are routine; and preventable mining disasters take the lives of hundreds of workers at a time. Because of its rise to global economic prominence, China in particular has been the subject of many journalistic accounts documenting its human cost (Associated Press 2005; Eckholm 2000; Kahn 2003a; Kahn 2003b; Lev 2000). One particularly revealing, if somewhat dated, study considers fatal and major nonfatal industrial accidents in a sample of 392 town and village enterprises in Shunde City, a rapidly growing Chinese locality. In the most recent year cited – 1993 – the fatality rate and major injury rate per 100,000 workers were 39 and 266, respectively. It should be noted that a major injury was defined as an event resulting in at least 105 lost workdays, and it would indeed be a substantial impairment that would keep workers from their jobs this long in a society without workers compensation or similar disability insurance. One way to interpret this is to combine the two totals and consider the likelihood that any individual worker would experience either death or major disablement on the job over a thirty-year career, assuming that the risks each year are independently determined. This comes to approximately a one-in-twelve chance. In the construction sector in Shunde City, the corresponding career risk is nearly one in three, and for fatalities alone it is about one in twelve (Yu et al. 1999).

2. The Economic Cost of Poor Working Conditions

During the past decade, several studies have been conducted to determine the economic impact of occupational injuries and diseases in developed countries. The consensus figure is in the range of 3% of GDP (for details, see Dorman 2000a). Most of this cost is attributable to medical expenses and lost production; it does not take into account the human toll of pain and reduced functionality in the nonwork aspects of life. As Leigh et al. (1996) point out, OSH factors are responsible for greater economic costs than many other health risks that command more public attention and larger public health research and prevention budgets. The relevant question for us, however, is whether the cost in developing countries is likely to be higher or lower than this 3% benchmark.

Because we have no evidence whatsoever on this topic, we can only speculate. Two arguments might be adduced for a lower cost. First, medical systems in the developed world are much more elaborate and expensive than those in developing countries. Presumably fewer injured workers receive medical care in the South, and those that do probably receive less on average. Second, developing countries tend to have larger surplus labor populations, suggesting that workers who die or are seriously impaired can be more easily replaced. This is a harsh judgment, but from a purely economic standpoint it is an appropriate one.

Neither argument is self-evidently true, however. First, although it is undeniable that formal medical treatment is more common in wealthier countries, workers who have been severely injured or who suffer from debilitating illnesses in developing countries are likely to be attended to by someone. Presumably the burden falls most often on other family members, and this can be expected to have significant economic consequences. Perhaps these caretakers must withdraw from the labor force or reduce their contribution to household production. If the caretakers are children, their education is at risk. Both possibilities have the potential to be as burdensome in a developing country context as elaborate medical care is in developed countries – and in the case of lost education, more so. Moreover, reduced adult labor supply may induce children to enter the labor force prematurely – another source of foregone education – which, as we will see shortly, is a significant impediment to economic growth.

Second, death and disablement of workers during their prime years has negative direct and indirect effects on the supply of human capital. The accumulated skill and experience of workers even in less-qualified fields should not be underestimated; the loss of this valuable commodity plays a role in economic analyses of diseases such as malaria (Gallup and Sachs 2000). Indirectly, greater mortality risk appears to discourage investments in the acquisition of new human capital by reducing their expected return and inducing a general attitude of fatalism (Lorentzen et al. 2005). In recent years, a consensus has emerged among development economists that health – as measured through life expectancy, the prevalence of major diseases and biometric indicators – is a central determinant of economic growth, roughly to the same degree as education (Weil 2005). There is no reason to suppose that the health consequences of dangerous working conditions should play a smaller role than those resulting from other stressors.

There is no preponderance of evidence or logic in support of the claim that high rates of occupational injury and illness, rather than simply resulting from low levels of economic development, actually contribute to them – but this proposition cannot be rejected either. Clearly there is an urgent need for research on the question, but for now it should be noted that the developmentalist position rests on the presumption that OSH is *not* an impediment to growth. Given what appears to be true about working conditions in the developing world and the general importance of health for economic outcomes, there is little reason to give this presumption the benefit of the doubt.

3. Worker Rights in OSH

Even if it is granted that the problem of dangerous work is not less urgent for developing countries, it may be argued that the solutions are less feasible. Worker rights to safe and healthy work would need to be assured in some manner, and the most direct approach, in which specific safety procedures are specified as a matter of mandatory enforcement, can hardly be transferred from rich countries to poor ones. There are two reasons for this. First, many health interventions in the workplace are costly, and it is doubtful that poor countries would want to make the same tradeoffs between economic cost and health benefit that rich ones do. (And rich countries, for cultural and political-economic reasons, make different trade-offs among one another). Demanding the safest possible work process in a developing country may result in an industry failing to establish itself altogether, and the loss of income this might entail could be more deleterious to health than the unsafe work. Second, the "command-and-control" approach to OSH regulation, which depends on government inspection of workplaces, is seldom practicable in developing country settings. Governments do not have the resources to perform these inspections, and even if they did, a regime based on imposing penalties on employers presents an unacceptable risk of corruption in systems without a highly developed justice apparatus. Moreover, a large percentage of employment, and the vast majority of the most dangerous employment, in poor countries is found in the informal sector which, by definition, is outside the scope of external regulation. Thus, government regulation of working conditions is likely to be ineffective at best, and may be disruptive of development to the extent that it actually achieves its objectives.

These arguments strike me as sensible, particularly as they apply to some extent even in the industrialized world. They are not fatal to the case for worker rights in OSH, however, because direct government regulation of working conditions is not the only model of assuring these rights. Even in developed countries, a strong case can be made for the superiority of a different approach based on participatory regulation, supplemented by economic incentives (Dorman 1996; Dorman 1998). With modification, such a system is also feasible for developing countries.

Three rights form the centerpiece of a participatory approach: the right to know about workplace hazards, the right to participate in decisions involving risk, and the right to refuse imminently dangerous work. Briefly:

1. Workers should have the right to be informed of all significant risk exposures on the job. This entails a minimal level of training and an obligation on the part of the employer to disclose the presence of substances or conditions (chemicals, heat, noise, air quality) that could prove harmful. It also includes the obligation to maintain accurate occupational injury and disease logs. But the burden does not fall only on the employer; the government may be required to provide OSH education and to convey what it knows about occupational health hazards. In the context of informal sector employment, such a right may obligate the government to assist undercapitalized employers who would otherwise not be able to afford the information-gathering costs.

2. Workers should have the right to participate in committees and other bodies that make decisions concerning the mitigation of OSH risks. In medium and large enterprises, this would normally take the form of an OSH committee with representation from workers and managers; in the informal sector, it may exist at a sectoral or community level, where assistance to entrepreneurs is the predominant mode of intervention. An excellent model of sectoral decision making in a

developed country context is provided by Danish Action Plans (Karageorgiou et al. 2000).

3. Workers should have the right to refuse work that imposes a direct, substantial risk of unacceptable harm. This assertion is necessarily couched in vague language but can be given operational meaning in specific contexts. Tunneling per se, for example, should not be prohibited by such a right, even though there is always great risk associated with digging tunnels. But workers might refuse to continue working if particular safety activities, such as the use of adequate wooden or metal frames, were not adopted. A right of refusal carries with it a corresponding freedom from retaliation, and the resources of government must be sufficient to safeguard it.

In addition, economic incentives can be employed to increase the likelihood that these OSH rights are actually respected. In developed countries, this is typically achieved by tying financial penalties, such as increased workers compensation premia, to a firm's failure to demonstrate sufficient regard for OSH. In developing countries, it is likely that subsidies will play a greater role. For instance, public health officials may provide assistance in improving working conditions, and financial authorities may make low-interest or partially collateralized loans available subject to a satisfactory level of OSH performance by the enterprise. "Performance" in such cases may mean adoption of participatory procedures, rather than the attainment of particular technical standards.

Could such an approach actually work on the ground? Because it has never been implemented in a developing country, one cannot say for sure, but favorable evidence is provided by the developed world's experience with the construction sector. Construction is largely organized along semiformal lines: small entities with limited lifespans converge on projects and then hibernate or reassemble for new work. Record-keeping among subcontractors is often minimal. Employment relations can be casual, with arrangements such as self-employment and day labor common. Construction is also one of the most hazardous of industries, with high injury rates the norm.

Industrialized countries cannot be said to have "solved" the safety problems endemic to construction, but certainly progress has been made over the decades. Many of the elements sketched earlier have been tested, such as sectoral training programs (including apprenticeships), joint safety committees, and financial incentives. In addition, countries have found it helpful to implement responsibility systems, under which the main contractor is held responsible for the safety performance of subcontractors. More traditional modes of regulation, when they are used, are applied on a "common site" basis: the entire project site, rather than the individual employer, is the unit of observation. If workers' rights to OSH can be advanced in construction, there is reason to believe that they can be upheld in other realms of informal and nonstandard employment.

To summarize this section: we do not have firm proof that workplace hazards weigh more heavily on workers in developing countries than in developed ones, nor that they constitute an impediment to development, nor that they can be addressed effectively in the developing world. But the developmentalist perspective, with even less evidence, makes the opposite claims, and we *are* in a position to say that there is no basis at present for accepting them.

III. CHILD LABOR

As in the example of OSH, the case against action to curtail child labor has a long pedigree; indeed, modern-sounding arguments can be found in rather old documents (Folks 1907). Poor families need the income of their children; that is why they send them to work. Prohibiting this work makes the families worse off, not better. Denied their former work opportunities, children may be diverted to new ones that are more hidden and hazardous. Even the laudable goal of increasing education may be undermined if children can no longer earn the money they need to attend school. As if to underline the resurgence of the doctrine of freedom of contract in the modern era, it has been proposed in the pages of a leading economics journal that this logic applies as well to the worst forms of child labor as to the most benign: prohibiting child prostitution, for instance, would be an assault on the well-being of poor families, including those that have no connection to prostitution at all (Dessy and Pallage 2005). There is somewhat less support for the notion that child labor plays a positive role at the economy-wide level, however, as it is not evident that economies with widespread employment of children suffer from shortages of adult labor.

But this extreme position is not representative of developmentalism overall. A developmentalist would be more likely to argue that most child labor is undesirable, and that some measure of policy response is called for. The worst forms of child labor – specified in ILO Convention 182 as prostitution, combat, contraband, and bonded labor – should be targeted as a matter of priority, as no children should be engaged in them at any level of development. Less onerous work should be gradually diminished through reforms that promote education and expand the opportunities available to low-income families (e.g., micro-credit). This can be interpreted as support for a more restricted, conditional "right" to freedom from child labor – one that recognizes a core of activities that should be universally forbidden, surrounded by concentric rings that would be progressively eliminated over the course of development. This is consistent with a view of Convention 182 as superseding in some sense earlier conventions, such as 138, which target child labor more broadly. (This view is not that of the ILO, which promotes these conventions as a package, but is attributed to them by many analysts; see, for instance, Dessy and Pallage 2005).

To put it differently, a plausible developmentalist position would hold that "ordinary" child labor, which does not take one of the worst forms, should be discouraged, but that the main vehicle for reducing it should be poverty allevi- ation. For the most part, this is a recipe for a general orientation to growth – which is to say, economic development. Nevertheless, the reduction in poverty via economic growth has proved to be a slow and on occasion reversible process; hence, an additional boost could be provided by targeted poverty alleviation at the household level, for instance by income transfer programs tied to a parental commitment to remove children from work and place them in the classroom. Such programs – Bolsa Escola (now Bolsa Familia) in Brazil and Progresa in Mexico – have proven to be effective in achieving these goals (Behrman et al. 2001; Denes 2003; Skoufias 2001). Nevertheless, poverty alleviation – whether through growth or redistribution – is the primary vehicle, and child labor reduction would be one of several favorable outcomes (Gunnarsson et al. 2005; Edmonds and Pavcnik 2005).

An intermediate position might be that of Basu (1999). He developed an influential model in which it is possible for an economy to settle in one of two possible equilibria. The undesirable one has high levels of child labor, low adult wages, low family income, and therefore a tendency for families to supply their children's labor. Alternatively, there could be little child labor leading to higher adult wages, higher family incomes, and, therefore, less supply of child labor. Each is self-reinforcing, and there may be a need for policies to promote the second in place of the first. Indeed, because of the vicious-circle character of the (potential) problem, these policies could be far more aggressive than poverty alleviation alone. Direct prohibition of child labor, in particular occupations, might even be justified if it could be shown that there would be substantial wage benefits for adult workers. This is a large "if," however, because there is no evidence that adult wages have ever been put at risk by child labor, and it is not likely that we will see it in the future: the empirical hurdles are much too great and the data too weak.

To sum up the discussion thus far, the developmentalist position regarding child labor tends to be more nuanced than its counterpart for OSH. It recognizes the linkage between education and future economic growth, unlike the more broadly dismissive stance taken toward occupationally induced health impairments. Although they both regard economic development as the main vehicle for achieving better outcomes for workers in the future, the mainstream position on child labor is not so patient, and it is willing to consider policies that might speed up the process. This difference is reflected in the research and policies of the World Bank, which have provided tempered support for campaigns against child labor.

It could be claimed, then, that mainstream developmentalism has relaxed its opposition to activism on child labor to such an extent that it is no longer hostile to a universal approach to the problem, in the spirit of the ILO conventions and the 1989 Convention on the Rights of the Child. Nevertheless, there is a difference in emphasis between the developmental and rights-based views. The former offers conditional support to campaigns against child labor, but because it regards development as the main deterrent to this practice, it is reluctant to propose any measures that might interfere with economic growth. This cautious, case-by-case approach is evident in official World Bank policy, which has not adopted a general position on the issue, and in the absence of any reference to child labor in the Millennium Development Goals. (Universal primary education by 2015 is one such goal, but, since this level is to be attained by eleven- or twelve-year-olds, considerable scope for child labor remains).

In the rest of this section I will outline the reasons why universalism is justified and feasible. Briefly, this is because poverty is only one of several factors responsible for the occurrence of child labor, the social and economic costs of child labor are enormous, and aggressive programs to combat child labor are well within the means of most countries. Once again, it should be noted that these claims do not contradict the arguments put forward by developmentalists; they represent a shift in emphasis on which a universal commitment (such as a Millennium Development Goal) might rest.

1. Causes of Child Labor

It is certainly the case that poverty plays an important role in the extent and intensity of child labor. This is most apparent in cross-country analysis, although even here an element of caution is warranted. First, nearly all such studies obtain their national child labor rates from the ILO's LABORSTA database (Basu 1999; Gunnarsson et al. 2005; Edmonds and Pavcnik 2005), but this source is based on official labor force surveys and almost certainly underestimates the true prevalence. Even so, there are many outliers, and the persistence of child labor in the developed countries suggests that even high levels of average income may not be sufficient to eradicate the problem (Dorman 2000b). In addition, the evidence is mixed concerning the role of poverty within individual countries. Although some panel data results have recently appeared that support the view that poverty promotes child labor, other studies, including several based on closely observed cases, find that children sometimes work more as family income rises (Edmonds and Pavcnik 2005; Bhalotra and Tzannatos 2003).

Once one looks beyond income to other determinants of child labor, the rights dimension becomes more salient. Cultural biases, particularly as they concern the role of girls in household work, are central in many societies (Rende 2006). Even now, data collection routinely ignores the gender aspect of the problem, since surveys use the restrictive definition of "economic" activity embodied in the System of National Accounts. In large parts of the world, marginalized populations are particularly susceptible to high levels of child labor; this can be seen in the Dalit of South Asia, the Roma of Europe and migrant populations wherever they are found. The overall impression is that child labor is characteristic of groups suffering from social exclusion, and that the loss of education and other opportunities will extend this exclusion across generations.

In addition, research on child labor has focused only on the supply side of the phenomenon – the decision by parents or other household members to put children to work – yet the demand side also merits attention. Despite a concern for the possible economic exploitation of children that has been voiced for nearly two hundred years, little research has been devoted to the role of employers. Current work based on employer surveys demonstrates that in many instances the employment of children increases profitability, because the ratio of child to adult wages is lower than the corresponding productivity ratio (Dorman 2006). This highlights the importance of children's relative lack of agency and autonomy, which disadvantage them in labor market settings, and which was an original impetus for social campaigns against child labor.

2. Consequences of Child Labor

Opponents of child labor have typically assumed that work and education are mutually exclusive alternatives for children, but this is not true. Many children combine both activities, and many others engage in neither (Bhalotra and Tzannatos 2003; Rende 2006). It is true that above a threshold, which varies across countries, age groups, and other strata, more work is associated with less schooling, but the principle effect appears to operate through school performance: child laborers do more poorly on performance measures and are less successful at keeping up with their nonworking cohort (Beegle et al. 2004; Sanchez et al. 2005; Sedlacek et al. 2005). The evidence is stronger in developing countries, but there are indications that a similar relationship holds in developed countries such as the United States (National Research Council 1998).

The health and psychosocial burden has barely been investigated at all. The only systematic examination of the injury risks associated with child labor was performed on U.S. data, and even this research excludes most occupational illness (Fassa 2003). It almost certainly underestimates the physical risk to which working children in low-income countries are exposed. Psychosocial risk remains terra incognita.

Despite the lack of essential information, an effort was made by the ILO to provide a rough estimate of the economic costs and benefits of eliminating child labor throughout the world (Dorman 2003). The benefits consist of the education and health burden removed when child labor is ended. For education, an estimate was generated by extrapolating from the wage differentials associated with additional schooling in various studies performed in developing countries; for health, the U.S. data was employed, along with a range of prior estimates of the impact of comparable health impairments on economic growth. The results can be found in Table 17.1, which also includes the costs of achieving these benefits.

The hypothetical program which this report evaluated had three elements: major investments to upgrade the quantity and quality of education, the implementation in every country of an income transfer program compensating poor parents for sending their children to school in place of work, and community-level interventions targeting children at particular risk, such as those in the worst forms of child labor or who belong to marginalized populations. Each of these was given a price tag by drawing on the cost of existing programs in as many countries as data was available. In addition, the opportunity cost of ending child labor – the productivity of the children had they continued working – was included on the cost side.

Table 17.1, which presents point estimates based on preferred assumptions and a 5% discount rate, clearly demonstrates that, in narrowly economic terms, the benefits of ending child labor far exceed the costs, and, most important, in the current context, the benefits are greater the poorer the region in which they are calculated. Thus, sub-Saharan Africa receives the largest percentage benefit relative to its average income, Asia and the Middle East are next, and relatively prosperous Latin America and the former Soviet Bloc last. Lack of development, rather than being a reason for delaying action on child labor, is a justification for accelerating it.

A different way to look at the results of this study is to consider the annual fiscal costs of the hypothetical child labor elimination program. These costs include all the monies transferred to poor parents (which, as transfers, were excluded from benefit-cost calculations), excludes the opportunity cost born by households, and incorporates the assumption that 20% of increased earnings by children who received additional education will be returned to the public sector in taxes in each year they occur. Figure 17.1 summarizes the twenty-year horizon of the calculation, averaging the fiscal costs over each decade and placing them beside the annual expenditures on other items in 2000. Eliminating child labor is far less expensive than other existing budget allocations and averages less than a tenth of debt service.

Table 17.1. *Economic costs and benefits resulting from the global elimination of child labor (in billions of 2000 $PPP, percentage of aggregate annual gross national income in parentheses)*

	Transitional countries	Asia	Latin America	Sub-Saharan Africa	North Africa and the Middle East	Global
Education supply	8.5	299.1	38.7	107.4	39.6	493.4
Transfer administration	0.7	6.3	1.2	1.5	1.1	10.7
Interventions	0.4	2.4	5.8	0.6	0.2	9.4
Opportunity cost	16.0	151.0	30.9	30.1	18.8	246.8
Total costs	**25.6**	**458.8**	**76.6**	**139.5**	**59.7**	**760.3**
Education	145.8	3307.2	403.4	721.8	500.2	5078.4
Health	4.0	14.0	3.8	2.1	3.9	28.0
Total benefits	**149.8**	**3321.3**	**407.2**	**723.9**	**504.1**	**5106.3**
Net benefits	**124.2**	**2862.4**	**330.6**	**584.4**	**444.4**	**4346.1**
	(5.1)	**(27.0)**	**(9.3)**	**(54.0)**	**(23.2)**	**(22.2)**

Source: Dorman (2003).

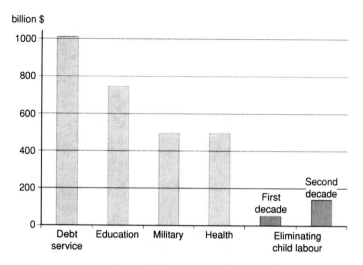

Figure 17.1. The average annual cost of eliminating child labour compared to other expenditures. *Source:* Dorman (2003).

(Recall that all sums are reported in $PPP, which increases U.S. dollar amounts calculated at market exchange rates by an average factor of about 3.) Clearly, if the results of this exercise are even remotely close to real world costs, eliminating child labor is easily within the fiscal resources of nearly every country and could be financed entirely by a very modest degree of debt relief.

The point made at the beginning of this section should be stressed again: the preceding discussion of the economic value of eliminating child labor to developing countries, and the evident sufficiency of resources, is not contradicted by developmentalism. Those who place development first above all other goals are generally willing to view measures to reduce child labor as friendly amendments. The difference is one of emphasis: a universalist approach regards child labor as a problem in its own right and action against it as intrinsically justified. The point to the economic assessment is that rights-based universalism in this domain, as in OSH, is not vulnerable to the argument that rights should be subordinated to differences in development.

IV. CONCLUSION

A brief review of two types of worker rights cannot be sufficient to demonstrate that all worker rights are desirable and feasible in all contexts. There is no reason to presume that other rights, such as the freedom to organize and bargain collectively and the right not to be subject to discriminatory treatment, will survive a developmentalist critique, although I believe that this is very likely to be the case. Nevertheless, these two case studies do point to aspects of the complex relationship between worker rights and economic development that may prove to apply more generally.

1. Rights that protect the interest of workers (and children who should be released from many types of work) are likely to be of greater value in developing country

contexts. As a result of widespread poverty – a surplus labor force and limited social insurance or other public welfare institutions – workers are at greater risk of exploitative or abusive treatment. Market alternatives may be unacceptably punitive. It is in such circumstances that the institutional safeguards embodied in worker rights may make the greatest difference. Moreover, improvement of labor and social standards – in these cases, health and education – is likely to be conducive to economic development as well as to individual well-being.

2. Developmentalist criticisms of worker rights often assume that they will be rigidly codified, with the result that they will be counterproductive in developing country settings. No doubt poorly framed rights can be found in the practice of many governments. But it is also possible to structure worker rights in a flexible manner, taking into account a range of interests and capabilities that spans the many levels of development that can be found within and between countries. This was seen to be particularly important for OSH, where the empowerment of workers to be their own advocates is more suited to informal and other less-developed work settings than the command-and-control approach.

3. In a deep sense, worker rights are inherently developmental. They appear to be consistent with and even promote development in the conventional sense, but they also help recast development as the enhancement of human capabilities, in the sense of Sen (2001). Throughout this chapter, the concept of "development" was treated as unproblematic, but in fact it has been highly contested throughout its history (Rist 2002; Bessis 2003). Skeptics feared that economic growth might be purchased at too high a cost in freedom, equality and community. Without getting into the debate over modernization and development, it is significant that worker rights, at least in the two cases sketched earlier, may belong to that set of measures – valued by Sen – that promotes both economic growth as conventionally measured and the expansion of capabilities. In this way, worker rights can play two roles – selecting a human-centered path of development and facilitating movement down that path.

This brief survey also demonstrates the need for more research on the relevance of particular worker rights in less-developed settings. This was already seen in the case of OSH, but similar gaps can be found for freedom of association and other rights. Enormous resources are expended for research in economic development; it would be unfortunate if developmentalist assumptions discouraged careful study of rights-based approaches to the challenges of global poverty and powerlessness.

REFERENCES

Associated Press. 2005. The Human Cost of China's Economic Boom. 23 September.
Atiyah, P. S. 1979. *The Rise and Fall of Freedom of Contract.* Oxford: Oxford University Press.
Basu, Kausik. 1999. Child Labor: Cause, Consequence, and Cure, with Remarks on International Labor Standards. *Journal of Economic Literature* 37 (3): 1083–1119.
Beegle, Kathleen, Rakeev Dehejia, and Roberta Gatti. 2004. Why Should We Care About Child Labor? The Education, Labor Market, and Health Consequences of Child Labor. National Bureau of Economic Research Working Paper 10980.

Behrman, Jere, Pilyali Sengupta, and Petra Todd. 2001. Progressing Through Progresa: An Impact Assessment of a School Subsidy Experiment. Penn Institute for Economic Research Working Paper 01–033.

Bessis, Sophie. 2003. *Western Supremacy: The Triumph of an Idea?* London: Zed.

Bhalotra, Sonia, and Zafiris Tzannatos. 2003. Child Labor: What Have We Learnt? World Bank Social Protection Discussion Paper No. 317.

Concha-Barrientos, Marisol, Deborah Imel Nelson, Timothy Driscoll, N. Kyle Steenland, Laura Punnett, Marilyn A. Fingerhut, Annette Prüss-Üstün, James Leigh, SangWoo Tak, and Carlos Corvalan. 2004. Selected Occupational Risk Factors. In *Comparative Quantification of Health Risks: Global and Regional Burden of Disease Attributable to Selected Major Risk Factors*, ed. M. Ezzati, A. Lopez, A. Rodgers and C. Murray. Geneva: World Health Organization.

Denes, Christian Andrew. 2003. Bolsa Escola: Redefining Poverty and Development in Brazil. *International Education Journal* 4 (2): 137–47.

Dessy, Sylvain and Stéphan Pallage. 2005. A Theory of the Worst Forms of Child Labor. *The Economic Journal* 115 (1): 68–87.

Dorman, Peter. 1989. *An Analysis of Worker Rights Conditionality under the Generalized System of Preferences*. Washington, DC: U.S. Department of Labor.

Dorman, Peter. 1996. *Markets and Mortality: Economics, Dangerous Work and the Value of Human Life*. Cambridge: Cambridge University Press.

Dorman, Peter. 1998. Cost Internalization in Occupational Safety and Health: Prospects and Limitations. In *Economic and Social Aspects of Occupational and Environmental Health*, ed. Irina Farquhar and Alan Sorkin. Greenwich, CT: JAI Press.

Dorman, Peter. 2000a. *The Economics of Safety, Health, and Well-Being at Work: An Overview*. Geneva: International Labour Organization.

Dorman, Peter. 2000b. *Child Labor in the Developed Countries*. Geneva: International Labour Organization.

Dorman, Peter. 2003. *Investing in Every Child: An Economic Study of the Costs and Benefits of Eliminating Child Labor*. Geneva: International Labour Organization.

Dorman, Peter. 2006. *Wages and Productivity of Child Labor: Demand-Side Factors in Four Countries*. Geneva: International Labour Organization.

Driscoll, Timothy, Jukka Takala, Kyle Steenland, Carlos Corvalan, and Marilyn Fingerhut. 2005. Review of Estimates of the Global Burden of Injury and Illness Due to Occupational Exposures. *American Journal of Industrial Medicine* 48 (6): 491–502.

Eckholm, Erik. 2000. For Want of Safer Glue, Chinese Shoemakers Get Sick. *New York Times*, 6 June, sec. A, p. 12.

Edmonds, Eric and Nina Pavcnik. 2005. Child Labor in the Global Economy. *Journal of Economic Perspectives* 19.

Fassa, Anaclaudia. 2003. *Health Benefits of Eliminating Child Labour*. Geneva: ILO.

Folks, Homer. 1907. Poverty and Parental Dependence as an Obstacle to Child Labor Reform. *Annals of the American Academy of Political and Social Science* 29 (1): 1–8.

Gallup, John L., and Jeffrey D. Sachs. 2000. *The Economic Burden of Malaria*. CID Working Paper 52. Cambridge, MA: Center for International Development, Harvard University.

Gunnarsson, Victoria, Peter F. Orazem and Guilherme Sedlacek. 2005. Changing Patterns of Child Labor around the World since 1950: The Role of Income Growth, Parental Literacy and Agriculture. World Bank Social Protection Discussion Paper No. 0510.

Kahn, Joseph. 2003a. China's Workers Risk Limbs in Export Drive. *New York Times*, 7 April, sec. A, p. 3.

Kahn, Joseph. 2003b. Making Trinkets in China, and a Deadly Dust. *New York Times*, 18 June.

Karageorgiou, Alex, Per Langaa Jensen, David Walters, and Ton Wilthagen. 2000. Risk Assessment in Four Member States of the European Union. In *Systematic Occupational Health and Safety Management: Perspectives on an International Development*, ed. Kaj Frick, Per Langaa Jensen, Michael Quinlan, and Ton Wilthagen. Amsterdam: Pergamon.

Kristof, Nicholas D., and Sheryl WuDunn. 2000. Two Cheers for Sweatshops. *New York Times*, 24 Sept., sec. 6, p. 70.

Leary, Virginia A. 1982. *International Labour Conventions and National Law: The Effectiveness of the Automatic Incorporation of Treaties in National Legal Systems*. The Hague: Martinus Nijhoff.

Leigh, James, Petra Macaskill, Eeva Kuosma and John Mandryk. 1999. Global Burden of Disease and Injury Due to Occupational Factors. *Epidemiology* 10 (5): 626–31.

Leigh, J. Paul, Steven Markowitz, Marianne Fahs, Chonggak Shin, and Philip Landrigan. 1996. Costs of Occupational Injuries and Illnesses. NIOSH Report U60/CCU902886.

Lev, Michael A. 2000. Chinese Die by Thousands in Coal Mines. *Chicago Tribune*, Dec. 18.

Lorentzen, Peter L., John Mcmillan, and Romain T. Wacziarg. 2005. Death and Development. NBER Working Paper No. W11620.

Mathers, Colin D., Christina Bernard, Kim Moesgaard Iburg, Mie Inoue, Doris Ma Fat, Kenji Shibuya, Claudia Stein, Niels Tomijima, and Hongyi Xu. 2004. Global Burden of Disease in 2002: Data Sources, Methods and Results. World Health Organization Global Programme on Evidence for Health Policy Discussion Paper No. 54.

National Research Council, National Academy of Sciences. 1998. *Protecting Youth at Work*. Washington, DC: NAS Press.

Rende, Sevinç. 2006. Children's Work and Opportunities for Education: Consequences of Gender and Household Wealth. Ph.D. Dissertation, University of Massachusetts.

Rist, Gilbert. 2002. *The History of Development: From Western Origins to Global Faith*. London: Zed.

Sanchez, Mario A., Peter F. Orazem and Victoria Gunnarsson. 2005. The Effect of Child Labor on Mathematics and Language Achievement in Latin America. World Bank Social Protection Discussion Paper No. 0516.

Sedlacek, Guilherme, Suzanne Duryea, Nadeem Ilahi and Masaru Sasaki. 2005. Child Labor, Schooling, and Poverty in Latin America, World Bank Social Protection Discussion Paper No. 0511.

Sen, Amartya. 2001. *Development as Freedom*. New York: Alfred Knopf.

Skoufias, E. 2001. *PROGRESA and Its Impacts on the Human Capital and Welfare of Households in Rural Mexico: A Synthesis of the Results of an Evaluation by IFPRI*. Washington, DC: International Food Policy Research Institute.

Viscusi, W. Kip. 1983. *Risk by Choice: Regulating Health and Safety in the Workplace*. Cambridge, MA: Harvard University Press.

Weil, David Nathan. 2005. Accounting for the Effect of Health on Economic Growth. NBER Working Paper No. W11455.

Yu, Tak-Sun Ignatius, Yi Min Liu, Jiong-Liang Zhou, and Tze-Wai Wong. 1999. Occupational Injuries in Shunde City – A County Undergoing Economic Change in Southern China. *Accident Analysis and Prevention* 31: 313–17.

Universal Declaration of Human Rights

Preamble

Whereas recognition of the inherent dignity and of the equal and inalienable rights of all members of the human family is the foundation of freedom, justice and peace in the world,

Whereas disregard and contempt for human rights have resulted in barbarous acts which have outraged the conscience of mankind, and the advent of a world in which human beings shall enjoy freedom of speech and belief and freedom from fear and want has been proclaimed as the highest aspiration of the common people,

Whereas it is essential, if man is not to be compelled to have recourse, as a last resort, to rebellion against tyranny and oppression, that human rights should be protected by the rule of law,

Whereas it is essential to promote the development of friendly relations between nations,

Whereas the peoples of the United Nations have in the Charter reaffirmed their faith in fundamental human rights, in the dignity and worth of the human person and in the equal rights of men and women and have determined to promote social progress and better standards of life in larger freedom,

Whereas Member States have pledged themselves to achieve, in cooperation with the United Nations, the promotion of universal respect for and observance of human rights and fundamental freedoms,

Whereas a common understanding of these rights and freedoms is of the greatest importance for the full realization of this pledge,

Now, therefore,

The General Assembly,

Proclaims this Universal Declaration of Human Rights as a common standard of achievement for all peoples and all nations, to the end that every individual and every organ of society, keeping this Declaration constantly in mind, shall strive by teaching and education to promote respect for these rights and freedoms and by progressive measures, national and international, to secure their universal and effective recognition and observance, both among the peoples of Member States themselves and among the peoples of territories under their jurisdiction.

Article 1

All human beings are born free and equal in dignity and rights. They are endowed with reason and conscience and should act towards one another in a spirit of brotherhood.

Article 2

Everyone is entitled to all the rights and freedoms set forth in this Declaration, without distinction of any kind, such as race, colour, sex, language, religion, political or other opinion, national or social origin, property, birth or other status.

Furthermore, no distinction shall be made on the basis of the political, jurisdictional or international status of the country or territory to which a person belongs, whether it be independent, trust, non-self-governing or under any other limitation of sovereignty.

Article 3

Everyone has the right to life, liberty and security of person.

Article 4

No one shall be held in slavery or servitude; slavery and the slave trade shall be prohibited in all their forms.

Article 5

No one shall be subjected to torture or to cruel, inhuman or degrading treatment or punishment.

Article 6

Everyone has the right to recognition everywhere as a person before the law.

Article 7

All are equal before the law and are entitled without any discrimination to equal protection of the law. All are entitled to equal protection against any discrimination in violation of this Declaration and against any incitement to such discrimination.

Article 8

Everyone has the right to an effective remedy by the competent national tribunals for acts violating the fundamental rights granted him by the constitution or by law.

Article 9

No one shall be subjected to arbitrary arrest, detention or exile.

Article 10

Everyone is entitled in full equality to a fair and public hearing by an independent and impartial tribunal, in the determination of his rights and obligations and of any criminal charge against him.

Article 11

Everyone charged with a penal offence has the right to be presumed innocent until proved guilty according to law in a public trial at which he has had all the guarantees necessary for his defence.

No one shall be held guilty of any penal offence on account of any act or omission which did not constitute a penal offence, under national or international law, at the time when it was committed. Nor shall a heavier penalty be imposed than the one that was applicable at the time the penal offence was committed.

Article 12

No one shall be subjected to arbitrary interference with his privacy, family, home or correspondence, nor to attacks upon his honour and reputation. Everyone has the right to the protection of the law against such interference or attacks.

Article 13

Everyone has the right to freedom of movement and residence within the borders of each State.

Everyone has the right to leave any country, including his own, and to return to his country.

Article 14

Everyone has the right to seek and to enjoy in other countries asylum from persecution. This right may not be invoked in the case of prosecutions genuinely arising from non-political crimes or from acts contrary to the purposes and principles of the United Nations.

Article 15

Everyone has the right to a nationality.

No one shall be arbitrarily deprived of his nationality nor denied the right to change his nationality.

Article 16

Men and women of full age, without any limitation due to race, nationality or religion, have the right to marry and to found a family. They are entitled to equal rights as to marriage, during marriage and at its dissolution.

Marriage shall be entered into only with the free and full consent of the intending spouses.

The family is the natural and fundamental group unit of society and is entitled to protection by society and the State.

Article 17

Everyone has the right to own property alone as well as in association with others.

No one shall be arbitrarily deprived of his property.

Article 18

Everyone has the right to freedom of thought, conscience and religion; this right includes freedom to change his religion or belief, and freedom, either alone or in community with others and in public or private, to manifest his religion or belief in teaching, practice, worship and observance.

Article 19

Everyone has the right to freedom of opinion and expression; this right includes freedom to hold opinions without interference and to seek, receive and impart information and ideas through any media and regardless of frontiers.

Article 20

Everyone has the right to freedom of peaceful assembly and association.

No one may be compelled to belong to an association.

Article 21

Everyone has the right to take part in the government of his country, directly or through freely chosen representatives.

Everyone has the right to equal access to public service in his country.

The will of the people shall be the basis of the authority of government; this will shall be expressed in periodic and genuine elections which shall be by universal and equal suffrage and shall be held by secret vote or by equivalent free voting procedures.

Article 22

Everyone, as a member of society, has the right to social security and is entitled to realization, through national effort and international co-operation and in accordance with the organization and resources of each State, of the economic, social and cultural rights indispensable for his dignity and the free development of his personality.

Article 23

Everyone has the right to work, to free choice of employment, to just and favourable conditions of work and to protection against unemployment.

Everyone, without any discrimination, has the right to equal pay for equal work.

Everyone who works has the right to just and favourable remuneration ensuring for himself and his family an existence worthy of human dignity, and supplemented, if necessary, by other means of social protection.

Everyone has the right to form and to join trade unions for the protection of his interests.

Article 24

Everyone has the right to rest and leisure, including reasonable limitation of working hours and periodic holidays with pay.

Article 25

Everyone has the right to a standard of living adequate for the health and well-being of himself and of his family, including food, clothing, housing and medical care and necessary social services, and the right to security in the event of unemployment, sickness, disability, widowhood, old age or other lack of livelihood in circumstances beyond his control.

Motherhood and childhood are entitled to special care and assistance. All children, whether born in or out of wedlock, shall enjoy the same social protection.

Article 26

Everyone has the right to education. Education shall be free, at least in the elementary and fundamental stages. Elementary education shall be compulsory. Technical and professional education shall be made generally available and higher education shall be equally accessible to all on the basis of merit.

Education shall be directed to the full development of the human personality and to the strengthening of respect for human rights and fundamental freedoms. It shall promote understanding, tolerance and friendship among all nations, racial or religious groups, and shall further the activities of the United Nations for the maintenance of peace.

Parents have a prior right to choose the kind of education that shall be given to their children.

Article 27

Everyone has the right freely to participate in the cultural life of the community, to enjoy the arts and to share in scientific advancement and its benefits.

Everyone has the right to the protection of the moral and material interests resulting from any scientific, literary or artistic production of which he is the author.

Article 28

Everyone is entitled to a social and international order in which the rights and freedoms set forth in this Declaration can be fully realized.

Article 29

Everyone has duties to the community in which alone the free and full development of his personality is possible.

In the exercise of his rights and freedoms, everyone shall be subject only to such limitations as are determined by law solely for the purpose of securing due recognition and respect for the rights and freedoms of others and of meeting the just requirements of morality, public order and the general welfare in a democratic society.

These rights and freedoms may in no case be exercised contrary to the purposes and principles of the United Nations.

Article 30

Nothing in this Declaration may be interpreted as implying for any State, group or person any right to engage in any activity or to perform any act aimed at the destruction of any of the rights and freedoms set forth herein.

International Covenant on Economic, Social and Cultural Rights

Adopted and opened for signature, ratification and accession by General Assembly
resolution 2200A (XXI)
of 16 December 1966
entry into force 3 January 1976, in accordance with article 27

Preamble

The States Parties to the present Covenant,

Considering that, in accordance with the principles proclaimed in the Charter of the United Nations, recognition of the inherent dignity and of the equal and inalienable rights of all members of the human family is the foundation of freedom, justice and peace in the world,

Recognizing that these rights derive from the inherent dignity of the human person, Recognizing that, in accordance with the Universal Declaration of Human Rights, the ideal of free human beings enjoying freedom from fear and want can only be achieved if conditions are created whereby everyone may enjoy his economic, social and cultural rights, as well as his civil and political rights,

Considering the obligation of States under the Charter of the United Nations to promote universal respect for, and observance of, human rights and freedoms, Realizing that the individual, having duties to other individuals and to the community to which he belongs, is under a responsibility to strive for the promotion and observance of the rights recognized in the present Covenant,

Agree upon the following articles:

PART I

Article 1

1. All peoples have the right of self-determination. By virtue of that right they freely determine their political status and freely pursue their economic, social and cultural development.

2. All peoples may, for their own ends, freely dispose of their natural wealth and resources without prejudice to any obligations arising out of international economic co-operation, based upon the principle of mutual benefit, and international law. In no case may a people be deprived of its own means of subsistence.

3. The States Parties to the present Covenant, including those having responsibility for the administration of Non-Self-Governing and Trust Territories, shall promote

the realization of the right of self-determination, and shall respect that right, in conformity with the provisions of the Charter of the United Nations.

PART II

Article 2

1. Each State Party to the present Covenant undertakes to take steps, individually and through international assistance and co-operation, especially economic and technical, to the maximum of its available resources, with a view to achieving progressively the full realization of the rights recognized in the present Covenant by all appropriate means, including particularly the adoption of legislative measures.

2. The States Parties to the present Covenant undertake to guarantee that the rights enunciated in the present Covenant will be exercised without discrimination of any kind as to race, colour, sex, language, religion, political or other opinion, national or social origin, property, birth or other status.

3. Developing countries, with due regard to human rights and their national economy, may determine to what extent they would guarantee the economic rights recognized in the present Covenant to non-nationals.

Article 3

The States Parties to the present Covenant undertake to ensure the equal right of men and women to the enjoyment of all economic, social and cultural rights set forth in the present Covenant.

Article 4

The States Parties to the present Covenant recognize that, in the enjoyment of those rights provided by the State in conformity with the present Covenant, the State may subject such rights only to such limitations as are determined by law only in so far as this may be compatible with the nature of these rights and solely for the purpose of promoting the general welfare in a democratic society.

Article 5

1. Nothing in the present Covenant may be interpreted as implying for any State, group or person any right to engage in any activity or to perform any act aimed at the destruction of any of the rights or freedoms recognized herein, or at their limitation to a greater extent than is provided for in the present Covenant.

2. No restriction upon or derogation from any of the fundamental human rights recognized or existing in any country in virtue of law, conventions, regulations or custom shall be admitted on the pretext that the present Covenant does not recognize such rights or that it recognizes them to a lesser extent.

PART III

Article 6

1. The States Parties to the present Covenant recognize the right to work, which includes the right of everyone to the opportunity to gain his living by work which

he freely chooses or accepts, and will take appropriate steps to safeguard this right.

2. The steps to be taken by a State Party to the present Covenant to achieve the full realization of this right shall include technical and vocational guidance and training programmes, policies and techniques to achieve steady economic, social and cultural development and full and productive employment under conditions safeguarding fundamental political and economic freedoms to the individual.

Article 7

The States Parties to the present Covenant recognize the right of everyone to the enjoyment of just and favourable conditions of work which ensure, in particular:

(a) Remuneration which provides all workers, as a minimum, with:

(i) Fair wages and equal remuneration for work of equal value without distinction of any kind, in particular women being guaranteed conditions of work not inferior to those enjoyed by men, with equal pay for equal work;

(ii) A decent living for themselves and their families in accordance with the provisions of the present Covenant;

(b) Safe and healthy working conditions;

(c) Equal opportunity for everyone to be promoted in his employment to an appropriate higher level, subject to no considerations other than those of seniority and competence;

(d) Rest, leisure and reasonable limitation of working hours and periodic holidays with pay, as well as remuneration for public holidays

Article 8

1. The States Parties to the present Covenant undertake to ensure:

(a) The right of everyone to form trade unions and join the trade union of his choice, subject only to the rules of the organization concerned, for the promotion and protection of his economic and social interests. No restrictions may be placed on the exercise of this right other than those prescribed by law and which are necessary in a democratic society in the interests of national security or public order or for the protection of the rights and freedoms of others;

(b) The right of trade unions to establish national federations or confederations and the right of the latter to form or join international trade-union organizations;

(c) The right of trade unions to function freely subject to no limitations other than those prescribed by law and which are necessary in a democratic society in the interests of national security or public order or for the protection of the rights and freedoms of others;

(d) The right to strike, provided that it is exercised in conformity with the laws of the particular country.

2. This article shall not prevent the imposition of lawful restrictions on the exercise of these rights by members of the armed forces or of the police or of the administration of the State.

3. Nothing in this article shall authorize States Parties to the International Labour Organisation Convention of 1948 concerning Freedom of Association and Protection of the Right to Organize to take legislative measures which would prejudice, or apply the law in such a manner as would prejudice, the guarantees provided for in that Convention.

Article 9

The States Parties to the present Covenant recognize the right of everyone to social security, including social insurance.

Article 10

The States Parties to the present Covenant recognize that:

1. The widest possible protection and assistance should be accorded to the family, which is the natural and fundamental group unit of society, particularly for its establishment and while it is responsible for the care and education of dependent children. Marriage must be entered into with the free consent of the intending spouses.

2. Special protection should be accorded to mothers during a reasonable period before and after childbirth. During such period working mothers should be accorded paid leave or leave with adequate social security benefits.

3. Special measures of protection and assistance should be taken on behalf of all children and young persons without any discrimination for reasons of parentage or other conditions. Children and young persons should be protected from economic and social exploitation. Their employment in work harmful to their morals or health or dangerous to life or likely to hamper their normal development should be punishable by law. States should also set age limits below which the paid employment of child labour should be prohibited and punishable by law.

Article 11

1. The States Parties to the present Covenant recognize the right of everyone to an adequate standard of living for himself and his family, including adequate food, clothing and housing, and to the continuous improvement of living conditions. The States Parties will take appropriate steps to ensure the realization of this right, recognizing to this effect the essential importance of international co-operation based on free consent.

2. The States Parties to the present Covenant, recognizing the fundamental right of everyone to be free from hunger, shall take, individually and through international co-operation, the measures, including specific programmes, which are needed:

(a) To improve methods of production, conservation and distribution of food by making full use of technical and scientific knowledge, by disseminating knowledge of the principles of nutrition and by developing or reforming agrarian systems in such a way as to achieve the most efficient development and utilization of natural resources;

(b) Taking into account the problems of both food-importing and food-exporting countries, to ensure an equitable distribution of world food supplies in relation to need.

Article 12

1. The States Parties to the present Covenant recognize the right of everyone to the enjoyment of the highest attainable standard of physical and mental health.

2. The steps to be taken by the States Parties to the present Covenant to achieve the full realization of this right shall include those necessary for:

(a) The provision for the reduction of the stillbirth-rate and of infant mortality and for the healthy development of the child;

(b) The improvement of all aspects of environmental and industrial hygiene;

(c) The prevention, treatment and control of epidemic, endemic, occupational and other diseases;

(d) The creation of conditions which would assure to all medical service and medical attention in the event of sickness.

Article 13

1. The States Parties to the present Covenant recognize the right of everyone to education. They agree that education shall be directed to the full development of the human personality and the sense of its dignity, and shall strengthen the respect for human rights and fundamental freedoms. They further agree that education shall enable all persons to participate effectively in a free society, promote understanding, tolerance and friendship among all nations and all racial, ethnic or religious groups, and further the activities of the United Nations for the maintenance of peace.

2. The States Parties to the present Covenant recognize that, with a view to achieving the full realization of this right:

(a) Primary education shall be compulsory and available free to all;

(b) Secondary education in its different forms, including technical and vocational secondary education, shall be made generally available and accessible to all by every appropriate means, and in particular by the progressive introduction of free education;

(c) Higher education shall be made equally accessible to all, on the basis of capacity, by every appropriate means, and in particular by the progressive introduction of free education;

(d) Fundamental education shall be encouraged or intensified as far as possible for those persons who have not received or completed the whole period of their primary education;

(e) The development of a system of schools at all levels shall be actively pursued, an adequate fellowship system shall be established, and the material conditions of teaching staff shall be continuously improved.

3. The States Parties to the present Covenant undertake to have respect for the liberty of parents and, when applicable, legal guardians to choose for their children schools, other than those established by the public authorities, which conform to such minimum educational standards as may be laid down or approved by the State and to ensure the religious and moral education of their children in conformity with their own convictions.

4. No part of this article shall be construed so as to interfere with the liberty of individuals and bodies to establish and direct educational institutions, subject always to the observance of the principles set forth in paragraph I of this article and to the requirement that the education given in such institutions shall conform to such minimum standards as may be laid down by the State.

Article 14

Each State Party to the present Covenant which, at the time of becoming a Party, has not been able to secure in its metropolitan territory or other territories under its jurisdiction compulsory primary education, free of charge, undertakes, within two years, to work out and adopt a detailed plan of action for the progressive implementation, within a reasonable number of years, to be fixed in the plan, of the principle of compulsory education free of charge for all.

Article 15

1. The States Parties to the present Covenant recognize the right of everyone:

(a) To take part in cultural life;

(b) To enjoy the benefits of scientific progress and its applications;

(c) To benefit from the protection of the moral and material interests resulting from any scientific, literary or artistic production of which he is the author.

2. The steps to be taken by the States Parties to the present Covenant to achieve the full realization of this right shall include those necessary for the conservation, the development and the diffusion of science and culture.

3. The States Parties to the present Covenant undertake to respect the freedom indispensable for scientific research and creative activity.

4. The States Parties to the present Covenant recognize the benefits to be derived from the encouragement and development of international contacts and co-operation in the scientific and cultural fields.

PART IV

Article 16

1. The States Parties to the present Covenant undertake to submit in conformity with this part of the Covenant reports on the measures which they have

adopted and the progress made in achieving the observance of the rights recognized herein.

2.

(a) All reports shall be submitted to the Secretary-General of the United Nations, who shall transmit copies to the Economic and Social Council for consideration in accordance with the provisions of the present Covenant;

(b) The Secretary-General of the United Nations shall also transmit to the specialized agencies copies of the reports, or any relevant parts therefrom, from States Parties to the present Covenant which are also members of these specialized agencies in so far as these reports, or parts therefrom, relate to any matters which fall within the responsibilities of the said agencies in accordance with their constitutional instruments.

Article 17

1. The States Parties to the present Covenant shall furnish their reports in stages, in accordance with a programme to be established by the Economic and Social Council within one year of the entry into force of the present Covenant after consultation with the States Parties and the specialized agencies concerned.

2. Reports may indicate factors and difficulties affecting the degree of fulfilment of obligations under the present Covenant.

3. Where relevant information has previously been furnished to the United Nations or to any specialized agency by any State Party to the present Covenant, it will not be necessary to reproduce that information, but a precise reference to the information so furnished will suffice.

Article 18

Pursuant to its responsibilities under the Charter of the United Nations in the field of human rights and fundamental freedoms, the Economic and Social Council may make arrangements with the specialized agencies in respect of their reporting to it on the progress made in achieving the observance of the provisions of the present Covenant falling within the scope of their activities. These reports may include particulars of decisions and recommendations on such implementation adopted by their competent organs.

Article 19

The Economic and Social Council may transmit to the Commission on Human Rights for study and general recommendation or, as appropriate, for information the reports concerning human rights submitted by States in accordance with articles 16 and 17, and those concerning human rights submitted by the specialized agencies in accordance with article 18.

Article 20

The States Parties to the present Covenant and the specialized agencies concerned may submit comments to the Economic and Social Council on any general recommendation under article 19 or reference to such general recommendation in any report of the Commission on Human Rights or any documentation referred to therein.

Article 21

The Economic and Social Council may submit from time to time to the General Assembly reports with recommendations of a general nature and a summary of the information received from the States Parties to the present Covenant and the specialized agencies on the measures taken and the progress made in achieving general observance of the rights recognized in the present Covenant.

Article 22

The Economic and Social Council may bring to the attention of other organs of the United Nations, their subsidiary organs and specialized agencies concerned with furnishing technical assistance any matters arising out of the reports referred to in this part of the present Covenant which may assist such bodies in deciding, each within its field of competence, on the advisability of international measures likely to contribute to the effective progressive implementation of the present Covenant.

Article 23

The States Parties to the present Covenant agree that international action for the achievement of the rights recognized in the present Covenant includes such methods as the conclusion of conventions, the adoption of recommendations, the furnishing of technical assistance and the holding of regional meetings and technical meetings for the purpose of consultation and study organized in conjunction with the Governments concerned.

Article 24

Nothing in the present Covenant shall be interpreted as impairing the provisions of the Charter of the United Nations and of the constitutions of the specialized agencies which define the respective responsibilities of the various organs of the United Nations and of the specialized agencies in regard to the matters dealt with in the present Covenant.

Article 25

Nothing in the present Covenant shall be interpreted as impairing the inherent right of all peoples to enjoy and utilize fully and freely their natural wealth and resources.

PART V

Article 26

1. The present Covenant is open for signature by any State Member of the United Nations or member of any of its specialized agencies, by any State Party to the Statute of the International Court of Justice, and by any other State which has been

invited by the General Assembly of the United Nations to become a party to the present Covenant.

2. The present Covenant is subject to ratification. Instruments of ratification shall be deposited with the Secretary-General of the United Nations.

3. The present Covenant shall be open to accession by any State referred to in paragraph 1 of this article.

4. Accession shall be effected by the deposit of an instrument of accession with the Secretary-General of the United Nations.

5. The Secretary-General of the United Nations shall inform all States which have signed the present Covenant or acceded to it of the deposit of each instrument of ratification or accession.

Article 27

1. The present Covenant shall enter into force three months after the date of the deposit with the Secretary-General of the United Nations of the thirty-fifth instrument of ratification or instrument of accession.

2. For each State ratifying the present Covenant or acceding to it after the deposit of the thirty-fifth instrument of ratification or instrument of accession, the present Covenant shall enter into force three months after the date of the deposit of its own instrument of ratification or instrument of accession.

Article 28

The provisions of the present Covenant shall extend to all parts of federal States without any limitations or exceptions.

Article 29

1. Any State Party to the present Covenant may propose an amendment and file it with the Secretary-General of the United Nations. The Secretary-General shall thereupon communicate any proposed amendments to the States Parties to the present Covenant with a request that they notify him whether they favour a conference of States Parties for the purpose of considering and voting upon the proposals. In the event that at least one third of the States Parties favours such a conference, the Secretary-General shall convene the conference under the auspices of the United Nations. Any amendment adopted by a majority of the States Parties present and voting at the conference shall be submitted to the General Assembly of the United Nations for approval.

2. Amendments shall come into force when they have been approved by the General Assembly of the United Nations and accepted by a two-thirds majority of the States Parties to the present Covenant in accordance with their respective constitutional processes.

3. When amendments come into force they shall be binding on those States Parties which have accepted them, other States Parties still being bound by the

provisions of the present Covenant and any earlier amendment which they have accepted.

Article 30

Irrespective of the notifications made under article 26, paragraph 5, the Secretary-General of the United Nations shall inform all States referred to in paragraph I of the same article of the following particulars:

(a) Signatures, ratifications and accessions under article 26;

(b) The date of the entry into force of the present Covenant under article 27 and the date of the entry into force of any amendments under article 29.

Article 31

1. The present Covenant, of which the Chinese, English, French, Russian and Spanish texts are equally authentic, shall be deposited in the archives of the United Nations.

2. The Secretary-General of the United Nations shall transmit certified copies of the present Covenant to all States referred to in article 26.

Index

CPSIA information can be obtained
at www.ICGtesting.com
Printed in the USA
FFOW02n1914190115
10386FF